TRADE
PREFERENCE
EROSION

TRADE PREFERENCE EROSION
MEASUREMENT AND POLICY RESPONSE

Edited by Bernard Hoekman,
Will Martin, and Carlos A. Primo Braga

**A copublication of Palgrave Macmillan
and the World Bank**

©2009 The International Bank for Reconstruction and Development / The World Bank
1818 H Street NW
Washington DC 20433
Telephone: 202-473-1000
Internet: www.worldbank.org
E-mail: feedback@worldbank.org

1 2 3 4 12 11 10 09

A copublication of The World Bank and Palgrave Macmillan.

PALGRAVE MACMILLAN
Palgrave Macmillan in the UK is an imprint of Macmillan Publishers Limited, registered in England, company number 785998, of Houndmills, Basingstoke, Hampshire, RG21 6XS.
    Palgrave Macmillan in the US is a division of St Martin's Press LLC, 175 Fifth Avenue, New York, NY 10010.
    Palgrave Macmillan is the global academic imprint of the above companies and has companies and representatives throughout the world.
    Palgrave® and Macmillan® are registered trademarks in the United States, the United Kingdom, Europe and other countries.

This volume is a product of the staff of the International Bank for Reconstruction and Development / The World Bank. The findings, interpretations, and conclusions expressed in this volume do not necessarily reflect the views of the Executive Directors of The World Bank or the governments they represent.
    The World Bank does not guarantee the accuracy of the data included in this work. The boundaries, colors, denominations, and other information shown on any map in this work do not imply any judgement on the part of The World Bank concerning the legal status of any territory or the endorsement or acceptance of such boundaries.

Rights and Permissions
The material in this publication is copyrighted. Copying and/or transmitting portions or all of this work without permission may be a violation of applicable law. The International Bank for Reconstruction and Development/The World Bank encourages dissemination of its work and will normally grant permission to reproduce portions of the work promptly.
    For permission to photocopy or reprint any part of this work, please send a request with complete information to the Copyright Clearance Center Inc., 222 Rosewood Drive, Danvers, MA 01923, USA; telephone: 978-750-8400; fax: 978-750-4470; Internet: www.copyright.com.
    All other queries on rights and licenses, including subsidiary rights, should be addressed to the Office of the Publisher, The World Bank, 1818 H Street NW, Washington, DC 20433, USA; fax: 202-522-2422; e-mail: pubrights@worldbank.org.

ISBN: 978-0-8213-7707-9 (softcover) and 978-0-8213-7644-7 (hardcover)
eISBN: 978-0-8213-7748-2
DOI: 10.1596/978-0-8213-7707-9

Library of Congress Cataloging-in-Publication Data
Trade preference erosion : measurement and policy response / [edited by Bernard Hoekman, Will Martin, Carlos A. Primo Braga].
    p. cm.
    Includes bibliographical references.
    ISBN 978-0-8213-7707-9 — ISBN 978-0-8213-7748-2 (electronic)
1. Tariff preferences—Congresses. 2. Free trade—Congresses. 3. Commercial policy—Congresses. 4. International trade—Congresses. I. Hoekman, Bernard M., 1959- II. Martin, Will, 1953- III. Braga, Carlos Alberto Primo, 1954-
    HF1703.T735 2009
    382'.7—dc22

2008036218

Cover photos: moodboard/Corbis (ship); Imagemore Co., Ltd./Corbis (bananas).
Printed in the United States.

CONTENTS

Boxes

Figures

Tables

ACKNOWLEDGMENTS

This book is the product of close cooperation between the Economic Research and Statistics Division of the World Trade Organization (WTO), the Trade Directorate of the Organisation for Economic Co-operation and Development (OECD), and the Trade Department of the World Bank. Most of its chapters were originally presented at the International Symposium, "Preference Erosion: Impacts and Policy Responses," held in Geneva, June 13–14, 2005. The symposium was organized by the World Bank in cooperation with the OECD and the WTO, and it had financial support from the Canadian International Development Agency (CIDA) and the U.K. Department for International Development (DfID).

We are indebted to all of the authors for revising and updating their papers, all of which benefited from constructive comments and suggestions from discussants and other participants in the symposium, including Toufiq Ali, Kym Anderson, Bijit Bora, Werner Corrales Leal, Uri Dadush, Simon Evenett, Michael Hadjimichael, Stefano Inama, Joseph K. Ingram, Faizel Ismail, Marcos Jank, Alejando Jara, Sam Laird, Edwin Laurent, Jaime de Melo, Patrick Messerlin, Andrew Mold, Richard Newfarmer, Dominique Njinkeu, Sheila Page, Kipkorir Rana, Rubens Ricupero, Raed Safadi, Sok Siphana, Ransford Smith, and Don Stephenson. We are also very grateful to Kjersti Brokhaug, Ivan Crowley, Emeka Chiedu Osakwe, and Catarina Tully for excellent research assistance and to Rebecca Martin for her help in putting the final manuscript together. Logistical support from the World Bank's Geneva office—in particular from Sophie Bolard, Fabienne Maertens, Patrick G. Reichenmiller, and Isabelle Taylor—is also gratefully acknowledged.

A special note of thanks goes to Uri Dadush (World Bank), Adair Heuchan (CIDA), Patrick Low (WTO), Susan Prowse (DfID), and Raed Safadi (OECD), whose support was critical for the implementation of this project.

We would like to dedicate this book to the memory of Bijit Bora. Bijit was not only a first-rate economist but also a long-standing friend and collaborator on many projects. He was invariably unstinting with his time and willingness to help colleagues. He participated actively in the conference and his insights, as a member of the WTO research team, helped shape our thinking about how best to address the topic of preference erosion. His sudden death in October 2006 was a major loss to all of us.

Bernard Hoekman
Will Martin
Carlos A. Primo Braga

CONTRIBUTORS

Paul Brenton is with the Poverty Reduction and Economic Management Network of the World Bank.

Fabien Candau is with the University of Pau.

Judith M. Dean is with the U.S. International Trade Commission.

Bernard Hoekman is with the World Bank and Centre for Economic Policy Research.

Sébastien Jean is with the Institut National de la Recherche Agronomique and the Centre d'Études Prospectives et d'Informations Internationales.

Norio Komuro is professor of international economic law at Kobe University Law School.

Przemyslaw Kowalski is an economist with the Trade and Agriculture Directorate of the Organisation for Economic Co-operation and Development Secretariat.

Douglas Lippoldt is a senior economist with the Trade and Agriculture Directorate of the Organisation for Economic Co-operation and Development Secretariat.

Patrick Low is chief of the Economic Research and Statistics Division of the World Trade Organization Secretariat.

Will Martin is with the Trade Team in the Development Research Group of the World Bank.

Çağlar Özden is with the Trade Team of the Development Research Group in the World Bank.

Roberta Piermartini is a member of the Economic Research and Statistics Division of the World Trade Organization Secretariat.

Carlos A. Primo Braga is director of economic policy and debt of the Poverty Reduction and Economic Management Network of the World Bank.

Susan Prowse is with the U.K. Department for International Development.

Jürgen Richtering is a member of the Economic Research and Statistics Division of the World Trade Organization Secretariat.

Dominique van der Mensbrugghe is with the Development Prospects Group of the World Bank.

John Wainio is with the U.S. Department of Agriculture.

ABBREVIATIONS

ABS	Australian Bureau of Statistics
ACP	African, Caribbean, and Pacific
AGOA	African Growth and Opportunity Act (United States)
APEC	Asia-Pacific Economic Cooperation
ASEAN	Association of Southeast Asian Nations
ATC	Agreement on Textiles and Clothing (WTO)
ATPA	Andean Trade Preference Act (United States)
AVE	ad valorem equivalent
CAMAD	Common Analytical Market Access Database
CARIBCAN	Caribbean-Canada Trade Agreement
CBERA	Caribbean Basin Economic Recovery Act (United States)
CBI	Caribbean Basin Initiative
CBTPA	Caribbean Basin Trade Partnership Act (United States)
CEPII	Centre d'Études Prospectives et d'Informations Internationales
CGE	computable general equilibrium
CIF	cost, insurance, and freight
DC	developing country
EAFTA	East Asian free trade agreement
EBA	Everything but Arms (program) (European Union)
EC	European Community
EFTA	European Free Trade Association
EU	European Union
FIC	Forum Island Country
FTA	free trade agreement
G-20	Group of 20

GATT	General Agreement on Tariffs and Trade
GPT	General Preferential Tariff (scheme) (Canada)
GSP	Generalized System of Preferences
GSTP	Generalized System of Trade Preferences
GTAP	Global Trade Analysis Project
HS	Harmonized System
HTS	Harmonized Tariff Schedule (United States)
IF	Integrated Framework for Trade-Related Assistance
IMF	International Monetary Fund
LDC	least developed country
LDCT	Least Developed Country Tariff (scheme) (Canada)
LIX	low-income countries excluding India
MAcMap	Market Access Map (database)
Mercosur	Southern Cone Common Market
MFA	Multifiber Arrangement
MFN	most-favored-nation
NAFTA	North American Free Trade Agreement
OECD	Organisation for Economic Co-operation and Development
OPT	outward processing trade for textiles
SDT	special and differential treatment
SRA	Special Rule for Apparel (United States)
SRSE	special rates for specific economies
TIM	Trade Integration Mechanism
UNCTAD	United Nations Conference on Trade and Development
USITC	U.S. International Trade Commission
WTO	World Trade Organization

QUANTIFYING THE VALUE OF PREFERENCES AND POTENTIAL EROSION LOSSES

Bernard Hoekman, Will Martin,
and Carlos A. Primo Braga

The multilateral trade system rests on the principle of nondiscrimination. The most-favored-nation (MFN) clause embodied in article I of the General Agreement on Tariffs and Trade (GATT) was the defining principle for a system that emerged in the post–World War II era, largely in reaction to the folly of protectionism and managed trade that contributed to the global economic depression of the 1930s. From its origins, however, the GATT has allowed for exemptions from the MFN rule in the case of reciprocal preferential trade agreements. It also permits granting unilateral (nonreciprocal) preferences to developing countries.

Unilateral preferences granted by member countries of the Organisation for Economic Co-operation and Development (OECD) create an inevitable tension between "more preferred" developing countries—typically beneficiaries from pre-existing colonial regimes—and other developing countries with respect to the effects of MFN liberalization by preference-granting countries. Concerns about preference erosion have become one of the key points of debate in the negotiations surrounding the Doha Development Agenda. Similar concerns have arisen in the past. In the 1970s, for example, the effect of Tokyo Round–related liberalization on the benefits derived by developing countries from the Generalized System of Preferences (GSP) was extensively debated (see, for example, Ahmad 1977). Although erosion is a long-standing concern for many developing countries, the scope and coverage of unilateral preferential regimes have in the past few years increased

---

The views expressed in this chapter are those of the authors and should not be attributed to the World Bank Group, its executive directors, or the countries they represent.

significantly, especially for the least developed countries (LDCs).[1] In the past, concerns about erosion were not a particularly strong constraint on MFN-based reforms in the GATT—now the World Trade Organization (WTO)—because GSP programs typically gave a *preference* and not duty- or quota-free access. Thus, even if MFN rates were lowered, it was possible to maintain a given preference margin by lowering the preferential tariff or by expanding the coverage of the scheme. But new programs such as the European Union (EU) Everything but Arms (EBA) or the U.S. African Growth and Opportunity Act (AGOA) feature duty- and quota-free access for virtually all products and therefore *any* reductions in MFN tariffs lower the preference margin. It is thus not surprising that preference erosion has attracted a great deal of attention in the current round of WTO multilateral negotiations.

To provide some background for the debate on the potential extent and implications of preference erosion, the chapters in this volume review the value of preferences for beneficiary countries, assess the implications of preference erosion under different global liberalization scenarios, and discuss potential policy responses. One set of chapters focuses on the nonreciprocal preference schemes of individual industrial countries—particularly, Australia, Canada, Japan, the United States, and the member states of the EU. A second set of chapters considers sectoral features of these preference schemes, such as those applying to agricultural and nonagricultural products, and the important arrangements for textiles and clothing. A final set of chapters considers the overall effects of preferences and the options for dealing with preference erosion resulting from nondiscriminatory trade liberalization.

This introductory chapter first briefly discusses the genesis of nonreciprocal preferential trade regimes and describes the mechanics of their operation. It then summarizes the main findings of the contributions to this book and compares and relates those findings to the results of other recent research on preference erosion. It concludes with a discussion of possible policy responses by preference-granting and preference-receiving countries to erosion losses.

Unilateral, Nonreciprocal Trade Preference Regimes

The rationale for grants of preferential market access to developing countries by industrial countries grew out of the arguments favoring special and differential treatment (SDT) for developing countries. The underlying justification for SDT reflected development thinking in the late 1950s and early 1960s—most notably in work by Raúl Prebisch (1950). This approach was premised on the argument that developing countries had to foster industrial capacity, both to reduce import dependence and to diversify away from traditional commodities that were subject to long-term declines in terms of trade (and were also often affected by short-term price volatility). This thinking gave rise to the policy prescription of protecting infant industries—that is, import-substitution industrialization.

At the same time, exports were recognized as important because the domestic market could be too small to enable local industry to achieve economies of scale. The second plank of the SDT agenda, therefore, revolved around calls for a general system of preferences that would give developing countries better than MFN treatment in the major industrial markets of the world. The GSP—the framework for providing such preferences—was established under the auspices of the United Nations Conference on Trade and Development in 1968.[2] The EU and the United States passed legislation establishing their GSP regimes in 1971 and 1974, respectively. Although other OECD countries implemented their own GSP regimes, the EU and the United States have been—and continue to be—the most important markets for the developing countries.[3]

As discussed at greater length in Hoekman and Özden (2006), early evaluations of preferential regimes questioned whether preferences were an efficient way of helping developing countries, noting that producers in beneficiary countries had to be able to compete with domestic producers in the donor country as well as with other exporters (see, for example, Johnson 1967; Patterson 1965). Subject to debate was the extent to which a 5 to 7 percent preference margin would make a significant difference (the GSP involved *preferences*, not duty- and quota-free access of the type now accorded to the LDCs by many OECD countries). Furthermore, analysts pointed out that even in sectors where preferences would make a difference, they might lead to specialization in sectors where the beneficiary country did not have an inherent comparative advantage; this outcome, in turn, would result in socially wasteful investment. Other concerns included the potential political friction between beneficiary and excluded countries, administrative costs such as rules of origin, the danger that preferences might reduce incentives for global MFN liberalization as beneficiaries became concerned about the erosion of preference margins, and—more generally—the politicization of trade policy insofar as donor countries used preferences "to reward and punish the recipients for their behavior and performance" in other noneconomic areas (Johnson 1967: 199).

The GSP conflicted with basic GATT rules. In recognition of this problem, GATT members approved special waivers for the GSP—temporarily in 1971 and permanently in 1979 through the "Enabling Clause" (part of the Tokyo Round set of agreements). This action followed the creation of the Committee on Trade and Development in the mid-1960s and the addition of several articles to the GATT that addressed development issues: Part IV of the GATT, dealing with trade and development.[4] Part IV encompassed the new principle that reciprocity in multilateral negotiating rounds should be limited to whatever was consistent with the development needs of developing countries (article XXXVI). The 1979 Enabling Clause (formally titled "Differential and More Favorable Treatment, Reciprocity, and Fuller Participation of Developing Countries"), which gave permanent legal cover for the GSP, included language on "graduation," thereby indicating that SDT policies were to be phased out as the recipient countries reached a certain level of economic development. However, criteria for SDT eligibility and for graduation remained undefined. A recurring concern expressed by developing countries has been that SDT provisions are best-endeavor commitments and are not enforceable through the dispute-settlement mechanism of the WTO. Eligibility and graduation criteria, as well as product coverage and type of preference, are left to donor countries to determine unilaterally.[5]

Basic Analytics of Preferences and Preference Erosion

The simplest measure of the value of preference programs for an exporter is the difference between the applied tariffs facing a country and the MFN tariffs that would apply to the country's exports without a preferential agreement. This measure can overstate the value of the associated transfers because it ignores the fact that many other countries frequently receive preferences. The "real" preference margins for a given country may need to be adjusted for the preferences that other countries are granted. Moreover, administrative costs must be taken into account. These considerations are discussed later in this chapter. The discussion that follows focuses on the simpler, traditional margin of preference as an upper bound on the value of preferences per unit of exports.

A brief review of the economics of discriminatory application of trade policies may help the reader better understand the effects of preference. Figure 1.1 characterizes the import market for a particular product. In this scenario, a high-income country imports varieties of good X from two suppliers, indicated as S_{LDC} and $S_{non-LDC}$. Initially, the price in the LDC market required to induce any given level of exports is given by the curve $t + S_{LDC}$. The effect of granting tariff preferences to the LDC is represented in panel a of figure 1.1 by a downward shift of the LDC supply curve, with exports by the LDC expanding from $X_{LDC,0}$ to $X_{LDC,1}$. The benefit for the LDC exporter is represented by area A. Because the cost of imports from the LDC supplier is now lower, there is a shift in demand away from the non-preferential supplier. This shift is shown in panel b and results in a loss in this exporter's surplus equal to area B.

Thus, trade preferences involve a mix of benefits for preferred exporters and costs for excluded exporters of identical products or close substitutes. There are potential losses for the importer as well.[6] The magnitude of the costs and benefits for affected exporters depends on the responsiveness (elasticity) of export supply

FIGURE 1.1 The Mechanics of Preferences and Preference Erosion

a. Preference introduction

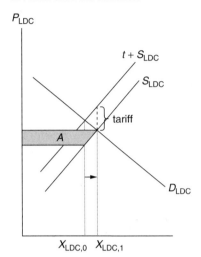

b. Effects of preference introduction

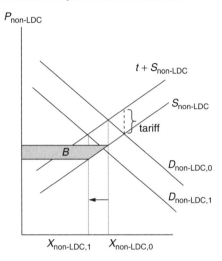

c. Preference erosion

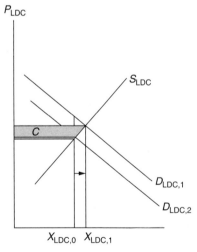

d. Reduction of nonpreferential tariff

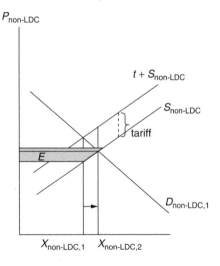

Source: François, Hoekman, and Manchin 2006.

and import demand to price changes, as well as on the degree of substitution between preferential and nonpreferential suppliers. The less close the varieties are as substitutes, the smaller the reduction in demand will be for the non-LDC supplier following the implementation of preferences for the LDC. If either the supply or the demand curve for the products being considered were perfectly elastic, then the simple measure of the gain to the exporting country with preferences would be bigger than that illustrated in figure 1.1: it would equal the area of the rectangle defined by the tariff (or preference margin) times the quantity exported (because the increase in the price received by the exporter would equal the preference margin).

The case of horizontal demand curves seems quite appropriate for situations in which small countries are supplying relatively homogeneous products to much larger economies, as in the case of LDCs supplying raw agricultural products to the EU or United States. In practice, a crude measure of the value of preferences, defined as the product of the preference margin and the quantity exported, provides an upper limit on the potential losses from preference erosion.[7]

Preference erosion involves the reduction or elimination of tariffs on the nonpreferential supplier and is illustrated in panels c and d of figure 1.1. Removing the tariff on other suppliers means that third-country exporters see their exports increase from $X_{\text{non-LDC,1}}$ to $X_{\text{non-LDC,2}}$. In the new equilibrium, there is a gain in their exporter surplus of area E, which may be greater or less than their original loss of exporter surplus resulting from the preferences, area B. The LDC experiences a drop in demand from $D_{\text{LDC,1}}$ to $D_{\text{LDC,2}}$. This drop results in a loss—though generally not a full loss—of the benefits from the original preference scheme. This partial loss is represented by area C, which is shown as being less than area A. The reason the loss is not complete is that preferences generate some trade creation as well as the trade diversion that is the focus of figure 1.1. At the same time, third countries recover some of the costs originally imposed by the preference scheme.

If buyers or intermediaries in the importing country have market power, they, rather than the exporter, may capture—at least in part—the benefits of the preferential tariff reductions.[8] In addition, administrative costs related to the implementation of preferential trade programs, such as rules of origin, will consume some of the benefits. The empirical literature assessing the magnitude of the costs associated with rules of origin and other administrative requirements concludes that on average such costs are on the order of 3 to 4 percent (see for example, Ansón and others 2005; Brenton and Manchin 2003; Cadot and others 2006; François, Hoekman, and Manchin 2006). Although not shown in figure 1.1, this finding implies deadweight losses involving parts of areas A and C. In the case of market power, the result is a redistribution of the benefits of preferences to importers. With administration costs, the share of the gains that is lost is not redistributed but is a deadweight loss. In both cases, the trade effects of preference programs will be less as well.

Trade Preference Programs of Major OECD Countries

Assessing the potential effects of MFN liberalization by preference-granting countries requires a good understanding of the design and incidence of the programs that are in place: which countries are eligible, what criteria are imposed, how extensive is the product coverage, and what is the depth of the preference offered? In addition, it is necessary to estimate the relevant demand, supply, and substitution elasticities previously discussed. Chapters 2 to 6 in this volume describe the preferential trade regimes of five major providers of nonreciprocal preferences for developing countries: Australia, Canada, the EU, Japan, and the United States.

Chapter 2, by Judith M. Dean and John Wainio, provides a detailed assessment of the preferences provided by the United States for both agricultural and nonagricultural imports from developing countries. Dean and Wainio find that more than 140 countries were eligible for preferences, with eligibility rules for preferences more liberal for the LDCs than for other developing countries. The value of the preferences is increased by the fact that U.S. preferences provide duty-free treatment, but the preference margins remain low on average because the MFN tariffs on most goods with preferences are low (except those on textiles and apparel). Access to preferences is, however, reduced by the exclusion of products deemed import sensitive, agricultural products subject to tariff rate quotas, and products that exceed competitive needs limits. Nevertheless, rates of use are generally relatively high, and for 29 countries, the value of tariff preferences was 5 percent or more of their dutiable exports to the United States.

Chapter 3, by Fabien Candau and Sébastien Jean, focuses on EU trade preferences, with an emphasis on their value to countries in Sub-Saharan Africa. The chapter highlights the proliferation of trade agreements involving the EU. Two categories of preferences are provided, depending on whether the good is sensitive or nonsensitive. Nonsensitive products enjoy duty-free market access and account for about 32 percent of all tariff lines. Most sensitive products receive a flat reduction of 3.5 percentage points from the applicable MFN rate. These products account for some 36 percent of tariff lines.[9] Because sensitive products generally carry high MFN rates, the proportional effect of the preference can be rather small.

The EU GSP program is the most inclusive of its preference schemes for developing countries. However, graduation measures are taken when the country becomes more competitive, with all countries classified as high income by the World Bank losing eligibility. Furthermore, the rules of origin tend to be restrictive, with no cumulation among participants. For LDCs, the EBA initiative provides duty- and quota-free access for virtually all products. A key feature of EBA is that, in contrast to the GSP, preferences are not subject to periodic review. The EU has other preference programs. Until 2008, the most notable were those accorded to African, Caribbean, and Pacific (ACP) countries under the Cotonou Convention, which offered preferences that often exceeded those available under the GSP.[10]

Chapter 4, by Norio Komuro, considers the preferential trade regimes of Japan. Komuro finds that GSP coverage is narrow despite expansion of LDC-specific duty-free items. In the agricultural sector, most products remain excluded. Likewise, in the industrial sector, labor-intensive items such as textiles, footwear, and leather-related goods are also excluded. Imports of many industrial goods covered under the GSP are subject to GSP ceiling values or quantities. Komuro also finds that the GSP utilization ratio is frequently low because of the costs of complying with GSP rules of origin and certification. In the future, he believes that GSP preferences will be eroded because of reciprocal trade agreements with current GSP beneficiaries, including Chile, Mexico, and the main member countries of the Association of Southeast Asian Nations. Given these features, he argues that the focus should not be merely on improving the existing GSP by widening its coverage and reforming its rules of origin and certification procedures, but also on lowering MFN tariffs for items of export interest to GSP beneficiaries.

Chapter 5, by Przemyslaw Kowalski, finds that North American Free Trade Agreement (NAFTA) countries are the dominant partners for Canada, supplying 65 percent of its total imports, as against 18.6 percent for developing countries outside of NAFTA. Of imports from these developing countries, 74 percent entered Canada under MFN treatment at an average tariff rate of 5.8 percent, 15 percent under general preferential tariff treatment at an average tariff rate of 2.2 percent, and 0.7 percent under LDC tariff treatment at an average tariff rate of 0 percent. The main beneficiaries of Canadian preferences include more advanced developing economies (such as Brazil; China; Hong Kong, China; India; Israel; Malaysia; Mexico; Republic of Korea) and some LDCs (such as Bangladesh, Cambodia, and Haiti). Expressed as a percentage of each beneficiary's exports to the world, the value of preferences does not typically exceed 1 percent. However, the importance of the Canadian market for LDCs seems to have increased substantially because of the 2003 extension of the LDC scheme to textiles and clothing. A simplified model assessment suggests that the welfare effect of Canadian preferences is very small for most developing countries, largely because of their generally small shares of preferential trade with Canada. For this reason, the chapter concludes that preference erosion does not appear to be a major hurdle to further reduction of Canadian MFN rates.

Chapter 6, by Douglas Lippoldt, concludes that the Australian market for exports from developing countries is very small relative to the four economies that were the focus of chapters 2 through 5 (Canada, the EU, Japan, and the United States, which are together known as the *Quad economies*). Preferences are also relatively unimportant, because Australia's trade regime is relatively open. Australia has an array of preferential schemes for developing countries, including a general scheme for developing countries, an LDC scheme, and arrangements for Papua New Guinea and Pacific countries. Since 2002, the scheme for LDCs has provided duty- and quota-free access with rules of origin that allow inclusion of materials from all developing countries and Australia. The product coverage of preferential programs is relatively high: few products exported by developing countries to Australia are not eligible for some preference. Use of these preferences is relatively low, however, as a consequence of low or zero MFN tariffs. Although the preferential schemes provided additional access opportunities, the share of imports from developing countries that enter under nonpreferential rates rose from around 40 percent to around 60 percent between 1996 and 2004. However, a few of the smaller countries in the region have come to rely relatively heavily on the Australian preferential regime.

Assessing the Magnitude of Potential Preference Erosion

A key difficulty in undertaking empirical analysis of the effects of preferences (and erosion) is identifying the specific impact of preferences as opposed to other factors. The observed growth rate of exports from recipients to the preference-granting countries, for example, is not informative without controlling for other factors. Common approaches have included using simulation methods to estimate trade creation and diversion (which are sensitive to assumptions regarding elasticities) and gravity regressions in which preference status is captured by a dummy variable. To the extent that exceptions in preferential regime are often defined at a highly disaggregated product level, the absence of elasticity estimates at this level of disaggregation—as well as the difficulty of finding the right controls to include in regressions—adds to the controversy surrounding available studies. These data and methodological problems help explain why the policy-oriented literature has tended to rely heavily on descriptive indicators.[11] Four indicators are particularly common:

- *Preference margins*—the difference between MFN tariffs and preferential tariffs for products
- *Potential coverage*—the ratio between products covered by a scheme and the dutiable imports originating in beneficiary countries
- *Utilization*—the ratio between imports that actually receive preferential treatment and those that are in principle covered (a measure of how effectively beneficiaries are able to use preferences)
- *Utility*—the ratio of the value of imports that receive preferences to all dutiable imports from that exporter (the lower this ratio, the less generous the preference scheme)[12]

Focusing on these variables, however, provides at best a partial perspective of the economic value of a preferential regime. To get a more precise estimate of the value of preferences, one has to take into account the extent to which others have preferential access; the costs of compliance in terms of documentation (for example, in proving conformity with rules of origin); the economic costs of sourcing inputs from more expensive sources to comply with origin requirements; the various limitations and constraints embodied in preferential schemes; and the distribution of related rents.

Chapters 7 and 8, by Patrick Low, Roberta Piermartini, and Jürgen Richtering, consider the preferences provided on nonagricultural and agricultural products by the Quad economies (plus Australia in the case of nonagricultural trade covered in chapter 7). Low, Piermartini, and Richtering develop a consistent methodology that takes into account not just the beneficiary's preferences relative to MFN tariffs, but the preferences provided to all other suppliers as well. With this methodology, they evaluate the potential extent to which erosion of preferences might impose costs on individual developing countries. Another key question asked by Low, Piermartini, and Richtering is whether trade solutions to such preference erosion problems might be feasible. They find that developing countries are able to export a much higher fraction of their exports duty free than the LDCs (52 percent versus 20 percent). However, the LDCs benefit from preferential duties on 61 percent of their exports, rather than 16 percent. This benefit makes the LDCs more vulnerable to preference erosion and contributes to a finding that developing countries would gain US$2 billion from liberalization along the lines of a so-called Swiss formula,[13] whereas the LDCs would suffer a net loss of US$170 million. LDCs that would lose from preference erosion include Bangladesh, Cambodia, Haiti, Lesotho, and Madagascar. Much of the preference erosion problem appears to arise from preferences on clothing. Low, Piermartini, and Richtering's analysis suggests that trade solutions to preference erosion, such as improving utilization rates, expanding preferences to other product lines, or expanding the availability of preferences to other markets, have relatively little potential on the basis of current trade flows.

In chapter 8, Low, Piermartini, and Richtering examine agricultural trade with the Quad economies using an approach similar to that of chapter 7. They show that the share of dutiable agricultural exports entering the Quad economies under preferential trade arrangements is much higher for LDCs, where almost 90 percent of dutiable exports are covered, than for other developing countries, where only 37 percent are covered. The estimated benefit to all developing countries is only US$267.0 million, of which just US$10.4 million accrues to the LDCs. However, the risk of preference erosion is much more concentrated in terms of countries and products than it is for nonagricultural products, with bananas, sugar, and beverages and spirits accounting for a large share of the potential losses.

Chapter 9, by Dominique van der Mensbrugghe, builds on the earlier studies and provides a synthesis of the global and national effects of preferences. He concludes that the margin of preference is 3.8 percent on imports into the EU and 0.5 to 0.7 percent on imports into other rich countries. Considering not just the current value of preferences but also increases in trade induced by a global trade reform of the type being negotiated in the Doha Round, he concludes that preferences may account for 0.3 percent of income in the lowest-income countries. However, he finds that these countries as a group would benefit from high-income countries setting all tariffs to zero: the gains from greater market access would outweigh the loss in preferences.

Table 1.1 collects estimates of average nonreciprocal preference margins in the Quad economies and Australia compiled by Low, Piermartini, and Richtering and by van der Mensbrugghe. It also reports estimates from other recent research by Brenton and Ikezuki (2005) and Subramanian (2003). Although there are significant conceptual differences between the measures presented in table 1.1,[14] they provide a consistent message: margins are rather small for most countries. The average margins generally tend to be higher in Europe relative to the other markets. In most studies, average preference margins are lower in Japan than in the EU or the United States, except in the chapters by Low, Piermartini, and Richtering, which are affected by very high preferences on imports of manufactures from Cambodia (more than 150 percent), as well as margins of preference of about 50 percent on imports from Bangladesh and Mauritius.

There are surprisingly small gaps between the preference margins granted to LDCs and to developing countries as a whole under the EU, Japanese, and U.S. preference schemes. In contrast, Australia and Canada appear to give substantially higher margins of preference to the LDCs, with the margin more than twice as high for LDCs as for developing countries as a whole. The gap between the two measures may reflect different coverage of products, with narrower coverage of products from non-LDCs—a difference that will be reflected in the measures of the overall value of preferences.

Although the average rates of export assistance to developing countries suggested by table 1.1 are relatively small, the studies presented in this volume highlight the substantial variation in the preference margins between countries. Candau and Jean (in chapter 3) show that EU preference margins were more than 10 percent of the value of exports in two countries—Dominica and the Seychelles—even after allowing for less than complete use of preferences. For two other countries—Senegal and St. Lucia—preference margins accounted for more than 5 percent. Dean and Wainio (in chapter 2) show an even more divergent pattern in U.S. preferences. Even though

TABLE 1.1 Estimated Nonreciprocal Preference Margins

Beneficiary countries	Margin in export market (percentage points)					
	EU	United States	Japan	Canada	Australia	Quad economies + Australia
LDCs	6.6[a] 4.1[b]	3.2[a] 2.6[b]	2.6[a] 10.9[b]	4.2[b]	3.6[b]	4.6[b]
Sub-Saharan Africa	4.0[c]	1.3[c]	0.1[c]			
African LDCs	2.3[c]	2.1[c]	0.4[c]			
LIX group	3.8[d]	0.5[d]				
All	3.8[a] 3.4[b]	2.6[a] 2.6[b]	2.0[a] 3.4[b]	1.6[b]	1.5[b]	3.4[b]

Sources: Data are from multiple sources, as listed in the notes below.

Note: LDCs refers to the United Nations list of least developed countries. The LIX group refers to the World Bank's low-income countries group, excluding India.
a. Data are from Subramanian (2003: 8).
b. Data are from chapters 7 and 8, by Low, Piermartini, and Richtering.
c. Data are from Brenton and Ikezuki (2005: 27).
d. Data are from chapter 9, by van der Mensbrugghe.

the average value of U.S. preferences is only 0.5 percent of the value of exports, two small countries—Lesotho and Swaziland—had preference margins exceeding 15 percent in 2003, primarily because of apparel preferences.

Table 1.2 presents upper-bound estimates of the value of preferences, calculated on the basis of the simple product of the average preference margin and the value of exports supplied by beneficiary countries. These numbers are based on the Low, Piermartini, and Richtering datasets, which provide precise estimates of the value of imports subject to preferential treatment. It is important to stress that these are maximum estimates; they ignore compliance costs and assume full use of preferential programs. The results reported in table 1.2 reveal that of a total of US$587 million estimated potential value of preferences to LDCs, US$287 million, or almost half, is provided by the EU. The United States is the next largest provider, at US$131 million annually. Japanese preferences amount to about US$49 million a year, while Canada and Australia are much smaller at US$14 million and US$0.4 million a year, respectively. The comparison of the preferences received by LDCs and other developing countries shows that the vast majority of preferences go to non-LDCs. Only one-twentieth of the value of total preferences appears to go to the LDCs, despite the importance of the EU EBA and the U.S. AGOA programs in offering benefits to these countries.[15] For preferences overall, the EU is again the largest contributor by a wide margin, accounting for more than 40 percent of the total.

As already mentioned, commonly used measures of preference margins that involve comparing the preferential tariff to the MFN rate will overestimate the effective preference for a country insofar as other countries also have preferential access. Indeed, other countries may have better access. It is important to take this factor into account when assessing the value of a given preference program for an exporting country. One way to do so is to define the effective preferential margin as the difference between the bilateral trade-weighted preferential tariff imposed by an importer

TABLE 1.2　Upper-Bound Estimates of the Value of Preferences

Beneficiary countries	Value in export market (US$ million)					
	EU	United States	Japan	Canada	Australia	Quad economies + Australia
LDCs	287	131	49	14	0.4	587
Other developing countries	4,945	3,953	743	215	46	11,565

Source: Compiled by the authors on the basis of data from chapters 7 and 8, by Low, Piermartini, and Richtering.

on a beneficiary country and that which confronts other exporters of the same bundle of goods to that country (Hoekman and Nicita 2008). This counterfactual can be constructed by first calculating the tariffs that an importer (say, the United States) imposes on the focus country (say, Mexico) using weights appropriate for its exports.[16] This weighted average can then be compared with the weighted-average tariff imposed on other countries' exports calculated using the same weights.[17]

Calculations of the average effective preferential margins by region show that all regions have positive effective preferential margins for intraregional trade (table 1.3). This finding reflects the prevalence of regional free trade agreements. The regional agreements that are most effective in terms of preferences appear to be in Latin America, where countries enjoy an effective preferential margin of about 3 percent. Latin America both enjoys and provides a substantial preferential margin to Canada and the United States, reflecting trade agreements with those countries, such as NAFTA, and trade agreements within the region, such as Mercosur (the Southern Cone Common Market). Effective preference margins are much smaller for other regions. Sub-Saharan African countries have an average effective preferential margin of only about 0.5 percent in the EU, reflecting competition among themselves and from other countries to which the EU provides preferences. Overall, these data illustrate that, on average, preferential margins are much smaller than are the upper-bound estimates reported in tables 1.1 and 1.2.

One reason for this finding is that much erosion has occurred in recent years. One factor here has been the spread of reciprocal free trade agreements. Another has been the unilateral reform of major preferential programs in the EU—in particular the sugar and bananas regimes, following WTO panel and Appellate Body rulings against the EU. Yet another factor was the implementation of the Agreement on Textiles and Clothing (ATC), under which import quotas and equivalent quantitative export restrictions were abolished in 2005. This agreement has been an important source of erosion losses for many developing countries. In chapter 10, Paul Brenton and Çağlar Özden examine carefully the preference erosion associated with abolition of the binding textile quotas imposed on exports from the most competitive exporters by the Uruguay Round ATC. A key finding is that the prices of exports from these countries had actually begun declining before the abolition of the quotas, thus reducing the need for concern about adjustments to the preference erosion following their abolition.

Estimating the Magnitude of Preference Erosion

Table 1.4 summarizes key results from several of the chapters as well as other recent studies of preference erosion. The findings associated with the nonreciprocal schemes alone generally produce results that are less than the full potential

TABLE 1.3 Effective Preference Margins, 2006

Importers	Margin for exporters (percentage points)						
	East Asia	Eastern Europe and Central Asia	Latin America	Middle East and North Africa	South Asia	Sub-Saharan Africa	High-income countries
East Asia	0.22	−0.06	−0.09	−0.02	−0.03	0.01	−0.03
Eastern Europe and Central Asia	−0.01	0.45	−0.37	0.39	−0.20	0.04	−0.15
Latin America	−2.54	−1.88	2.98	−0.51	−2.13	−1.22	1.69
Middle East and North Africa	−0.29	−0.24	−0.25	0.91	−0.22	0.10	−0.03
South Asia	−0.21	−0.08	−0.04	−0.26	2.03	−0.15	−0.05
Sub-Saharan Africa	−0.10	−0.03	−0.06	−0.02	−0.12	0.30	−0.06
High-income countries	−0.46	0.42	0.71	0.19	−0.46	0.13	0.08
Australia and New Zealand	−0.18	−0.61	−0.28	−0.08	−0.23	0.11	0.10
Canada	−1.00	−0.85	1.75	0.01	1.79	0.02	1.01
European Union	0.05	1.07	0.98	0.64	−0.70	0.51	−0.50
Japan	0.34	0.02	0.07	0.00	0.70	0.08	−0.13
United States	−0.67	−0.03	1.01	−0.08	0.22	0.11	−0.03

Source: Hoekman and Nicita 2008.

TABLE 1.4　Estimates of Losses from Tariff Preference Erosion

Source	Affected countries	Granting economies	Simulated liberalization	Net change (US$ million)		Method used
				Exports	Real income	
Limão and Olarreaga (2006)	LDCs	EU, Japan, and United States	33% cut in MFN tariffs	−624	−88.6	Partial equilibrium method
Subramanian (2003)	LDCs	Quad economies	40% cut in MFN tariffs[a]	−530	−265[b]	Partial equilibrium method
Alexandraki and Lankes (2006)	Middle-income countries	Quad economies	40% cut in preference margins[a]	−914	−457[b]	Partial equilibrium method
Amiti and Romalis (2007)	African LDCs	EU and United States	40% cut in MFN tariffs[c]	−21	n.a.	Partial equilibrium method
Amiti and Romalis (2007)	Non-African LDCs	EU and United States	40% cut in MFN tariffs[c]	683	n.a.	Partial equilibrium method
Amiti and Romalis (2007)	Other developing countries	EU and United States	40% cut in MFN tariffs[c]	18,547	n.a.	Partial equilibrium method
Low, Piermartini, and Richtering (chapter 7)	LDCs	Quad economies and Australia	Swiss formula, coefficient of 10; nonagricultural products	−170	n.a.	Partial equilibrium method
Low, Piermartini, and Richtering (chapter 7)	Other developing countries	Quad economies and Australia	Swiss formula, coefficient of 10; nonagricultural products	2,087	n.a.	Partial equilibrium method

Source						Method
Low, Piermartini, and Richtering (chapter 8)	LDCs	Quad economies	G-20 proposal[d]	10.4	n.a.	Partial equilibrium method
Low, Piermartini, and Richtering (chapter 8)	Other developing countries	Quad economies	G-20 proposal[d]	256	n.a.	Partial equilibrium method
Grynberg and Silva (2004)	Developing countries	Quad economies	Elimination of preferences	n.a.	−570[e]	Partial equilibrium method
François, Hoekman, and Manchin (2006)	African LDCs	EU	Full MFN liberalization	n.a.	−458[f]	General equilibrium method
François, Hoekman, and Manchin (2006)	African LDCs	OECD	Full MFN liberalization	n.a.	−110[f]	General equilibrium method
François, Hoekman, and Manchin (2006)	African and Asian LDCs	OECD	Full MFN liberalization	n.a.	−198[f]	General equilibrium method

Source: Compiled by the authors on the basis of the sources listed.

Note: n.a. = not applicable.

a. Elasticity of export supply equals 1.0.

b. Because the elasticity of supply of exports is 1.0, the real income effect is exactly half the change in the value of exports.

c. Elasticity of substitution is infinite.

d. The G-20 proposal (G-20 2005) for agricultural market access involves placing tariffs in four tiers, rising with the height of the original tariffs and making progressively larger cuts in these tiers. In the industrial countries, the boundaries of the tiers were at 20, 50, and 75 percent, and the cuts were 45, 55, 65, and 75 percent in the four tiers. For developing countries, the boundaries of the tiers were at 30, 80, and 130 percent, and the cuts were 25, 30, 35, and 40 percent.

e. Estimated effects of implementation of the Agreement on Textiles and Clothing are excluded.

f. Effects of rules of origin are not considered. If these effects are included, losses turn into net gains.

value of preference estimates presented in table 1.2. As is true of estimates of the value of preference margins, the reported estimates are not strictly comparable—not only because of the different methodologies (partial equilibrium versus general equilibrium) and focus (welfare or income effects versus trade effects), but also because they tend to operate with distinct liberalization scenarios to estimate the potential for preference erosion.[18] The estimates also tend to overestimate the value of existing preferential regimes because they typically do not take into account the costs of compliance with preferential regimes.

Subramanian (2003) uses a partial equilibrium framework to examine the overall impact on the exports of LDCs of preference erosion arising from trade liberalization by the Quad economies. Assuming a 40 percent cut in protection by the Quad economies and free access by LDCs to these markets, Subramanian concludes that the potential loss at the aggregate level amounts to 1.7 percent of total LDC exports. Individual LDCs, however, may suffer more significant losses from preference erosion because of their concentration on exports in products that enjoy deep preferences. Subramanian (2003) estimates that Cape Verde, Haiti, Malawi, Mauritania, and São Tomé and Príncipe are the most vulnerable to preference erosion. Malawi would experience a loss of 11.5 percent of total exports; Cape Verde, Haiti, Mauritania, and São Tomé and Príncipe between 5 and 10 percent; and another 10 countries between 3 and 5 percent. The total (aggregate) value of lost export revenue would be about US$530 million (of which two-fifths would be accounted for by Bangladesh). Although these numbers are small from a global perspective—less than 1 percent of annual flows of official development assistance—they are significant for some of the countries concerned and may mean substantial adjustment requirements for them.

Also using a partial equilibrium approach, Limão and Olarreaga (2006) estimate that LDCs would lose some US$624 million from a 33 percent reduction in MFN tariffs by the EU, Japan, and the United States). Their estimate is somewhat higher than that found by Subramanian (2003) because of a higher average estimated supply elasticity of five (as opposed to the unitary elasticity assumed by Subramanian) and because of the inclusion of ad valorem equivalents of specific tariffs in the analysis.

Alexandraki and Lankes (2006) analyze potential erosion impacts for middle-income economies. They include the effects of textile quota elimination and the EU banana and sugar programs for ACP countries. Their analysis suggests that the potential erosion problem is heavily concentrated in small island economies that depend on quota-type preferences and the associated rents in these sectors.[19] Their chapter illustrates that the problem is as much commodity specific as it is country specific: losses are concentrated in product areas where OECD protection and thus preference margins are the highest.

In another partial equilibrium study, Amiti and Romalis (2007) provide an integrated treatment of the impacts of preference erosion on both LDCs and other developing countries. They assume an infinite export supply elasticity for developing countries (that is, all countries are treated as price takers). Their methodology improves on those used by Subramanian (2003) and Alexandraki and Lankes (2006) by allowing for substitutability across products. They find that African LDCs would lose slightly as a result of a 40 percent cut in MFN tariffs by the EU and United States, but that other countries would benefit—in particular non-LDC developing countries.[20] LDCs that would stand to lose in terms of exports include Cape Verde (−2.5 percent), Haiti (−4.6 percent), Lesotho (−9.3 percent), and Madagascar (−2.7 percent). Among other developing countries, losers include Belize (−4.4 percent), Cameroon (−4.9 percent), Dominica (−21.8 percent), Jamaica (−3 percent), Jordan (−8 percent), and St. Lucia (−37 percent). These losses are offset by large gains that would accrue to other countries. Barbados; Brunei Darussalam; Cambodia; Fiji; Guyana; Macao, China; Mongolia; Myanmar; Serbia; Uruguay; and Zambia are all estimated to see an export boost exceeding 10 percent. The study concludes—as do chapters 7 and 9 of this book and virtually all of the computable general equilibrium (CGE) analyses of the impacts of further multilateral trade liberalization—that MFN liberalization would benefit non-LDC developing countries as a group.

Of the partial equilibrium, cross-country studies included in this volume, Low, Piermartini, and Richtering estimate in chapters 7 and 8 that the Doha Round liberalization proposals put forward by the Group of 20 (G-20) in 2005 would have a negative impact on LDC nonagricultural exports of US$170 million and would essentially have no net effect on exports of agriculture. As mentioned previously, these estimates take into account the fact that other countries also have preferential access to the major markets, thus reducing the magnitude of the estimated effects of MFN reforms. These studies, like Amiti and Romalis (2007), conclude that preference erosion losses will be substantially smaller than those estimated on the basis of upper-bound methodologies.

From a welfare perspective, estimates of trade effects are not particularly informative. Efforts to assess the real income effects of preference erosion include Grynberg and Silva (2004) and Limão and Olarreaga (2006). The latter estimate that the losses in income transfers for sugar, beef, bananas, and textiles and clothing producers in economies that depend on trade preferences would add up to US$1.72 billion a year. This estimate is heavily influenced by the weight of disappearing quota rents associated with the phaseout of the ATC (which accounts for US$1.1 billion of the loss estimate).

CGE estimates of the value of preference erosion can provide additional insights into the effects of MFN liberalization on preference-receiving countries.

CGE models allow terms-of-trade effects, improved market access opportunities in non-preference-granting countries, and asymmetrical effects of preference erosion in the different markets to be considered. The asymmetrical effects of preference erosion arise because of the different hierarchy of preferences in OECD markets, which span not only nonreciprocal programs but also reciprocal preferences resulting from free trade agreements. One implication of such agreements—already captured in the effective preferential margins reported in table 1.3—is that they lower the value of nonreciprocal preferences and, thus, estimates of the preference erosion effect. François, Hoekman, and Manchin (2006), for example, estimate that full EU liberalization on an MFN basis would translate into real income losses of US$460 million for African LDCs. This figure, however, drops to US$110 million when the experiment is extended to OECD-wide liberalization.

Estimates of the potential impacts should also take into account the administrative costs that may result in underuse of preferences and reduce the *net* value of the programs to developing countries. François, Hoekman, and Manchin (2006) estimate that the ad valorem equivalent of administrative costs averages about 4 percent. If this cost is included in the analysis, they find that MFN liberalization will raise, not lower, the real income of Africa LDCs. If account is taken of the fact that exporters will not capture all of the rents created by preference programs, the magnitude of likely losses will also fall. As noted, Özden and Sharma (2006) estimate that Caribbean exporters capture only two-thirds of the preference margin in the U.S. market, whereas Olarreaga and Özden (2005) conclude that the share of rents captured by exporters under AGOA is even lower.

Notwithstanding differences in approaches, the studies included in this volume and related research therefore come to similar overall conclusions. The chapters on the EU and the United States confirm earlier findings that the value of preferences—measured by the product of the volume of dutiable exports and the preference margin—is significant for a number of countries. Thus, U.S. preferences are equal to 5 percent or more of dutiable exports for 27 countries, while in the EU case, the value of nonreciprocal preferences exceeds 6 percent of dutiable exports for 16 recipient countries. Specific products such as apparel and some agricultural products—especially sugar and bananas in the EU—tend to account for the largest share of the value of preferences. Although trade losses for some countries are large relative to their total dutiable exports to the markets concerned, the overall aggregate value of the preferences—and thus the potential losses—continues to be relatively small and, in the case of the EU, will diminish when reforms in sugar and bananas occur in 2009. Similar findings are reported in chapters 7 and 8 for the Quad group.

Dealing with Preference Erosion: Potential Policy Responses

The basic conclusion emerging from the research on the magnitude of erosion is that it will be very small overall relative to the total potential gains from global MFN liberalization. However, for a limited number of preference-dependent countries, deep global reforms will have significant costs. The precise absolute potential magnitude of erosion remains open to debate, and much depends on what is eventually negotiated in the Doha Round. As important, perhaps, as what happens in the WTO is the spread of reciprocal free trade agreements, which also imply erosion for those developing countries that have preferential access to the markets concerned. Much also depends on the sectoral composition of the potential effects, which is critical in determining the incidence and distribution of adjustment costs within countries.

What could be done to address potential losses? There are two broad options: seek a solution within the trading system (that is, tied to trade and trade policy) or use nontrade instruments. The most obvious trade-based solution is not to liberalize the products that are the most important source of preference rents. The draft modalities in the Doha negotiations adopt an element of this approach by providing for delayed liberalization of products subject to long-standing preferences (WTO 2008a, 2008b). A problem with exclusion or delay in liberalization of these products is the opportunity cost in terms of MFN liberalization forgone. A far more desirable alternative is to frame multilateral trade concessions to address the negotiating priorities of preference-dependent countries in other areas on an MFN basis, in terms of either market access rules or other nontrade assistance. Such a solution has for many years been advocated by several observers (for example, Hudec 1987).

Trade-based options also include enhancing existing preferential programs and improving the rules of the game for access to preferential regimes (for example, adoption of harmonized liberal rules of origin and diminution of compliance costs) by extending coverage of preferential regimes, leveraging utilization rates, and increasing the effectiveness of preferences (Stevens and Kennan 2005). Such enhancements could partially offset the economic impact of preference erosion. Finally, because chapters 7 and 8 show that there is limited scope for expanding preferential schemes to additional product lines in major OECD markets, consideration could be given to implementing a new preferential trade regime by non-OECD importers, as is called for in the 2008 draft proposals for liberalization under the Doha Development Agenda (WTO 2008a).

Some action along these lines could be beneficial. In chapter 10, Paul Brenton and Çağlar Özden find that apparel is an important case in which preferential programs have contributed to export diversification in poor countries. Liberal rules of origin, in particular, appear to have a major influence on success in using preferences.

When rules of origin have been relaxed—as occurred in the case of certain less developed countries under AGOA—exports of apparel have grown rapidly. This growth suggests that a more general relaxation of rules of origin would be of value to recipient countries, allowing greater use of imported inputs and greater harmonization of the specific rules used by different OECD importers.

Trade-based initiatives will not do much to help those developing countries that are not competitive in world markets because of supply constraints and high-cost operating environments. In chapter 11, Bernard Hoekman and Susan Prowse argue in favor of "aid for trade" to help countries deal with the adjustment costs associated with global trade reforms and improve their capacity to exploit trade opportunities and diversify their economies. Hoekman and Prowse note that preferences have not done much to help the poorest countries use trade as a development tool and are unlikely to do so without these countries acting to improve their investment and business environment. Aid for trade can help them do so.

Aid for trade should be seen as a complement, not a substitute, for global trade liberalization (Prowse 2006). One reason is that the overall potential positive net effects of global trade reform are significant and will more than offset preference erosion losses (as shown in chapter 9 by van der Mensbrugghe). That is, losses to preference recipients from OECD liberalization can be offset by gains in other markets—those of other developing countries and those of OECD members that do not already provide full duty-free and quota-free access to their markets.

The limited number and small size of most of the economies concerned with preference erosion suggest that measures to help mitigate the problem should be closely targeted at the countries at risk. Existing instruments, such as the International Monetary Fund's Trade Integration Mechanism (see IMF 2004) for adjustment financing, could be supplemented by bilateral donor funds. A number of proposals have been made to establish new stand-alone, grant-based compensation funds (see, for example, Grynberg and Silva 2004; Page 2005; Page and Kleen 2004). Although such proposals have not found support among the development community, some progress along these lines has been made. The Integrated Framework for Trade-Related Technical Assistance to LDCs has been enhanced with a larger dedicated trust fund—at the time of writing valued at US$200 million—and the donor community has committed itself to providing more resources to help countries improve their trade competitiveness.

Concluding Remarks

The debate about how best to address preference erosion in the context of multilateral negotiations is an important component of the negotiations on the development dimension of the Doha Round. Although one could argue that the jury is still out in terms of the developmental effects of trade preferences, support is growing for the idea of delinking development assistance from trade policy and shifting from "trade as aid" to "aid for trade," as discussed in chapter 11 by Hoekman and Prowse. This growing consensus, however, is challenged by parallel efforts to deepen existing preferential regimes, to introduce new preferential initiatives, or both. Multilateral trade negotiations provide additional ferment to the debate to the extent that they foster alliances between protectionist interests in OECD countries and preference-dependent industries in developing economies.

Recent preferential initiatives have deepened the scope of preferences offered and have simplified administrative procedures, with significant effects in some countries. The EU (reflecting the magnitude of the preference margins offered, the extensive scope of preferences given, and the EU's importance as a destination market for many preference-dependent countries) stands out as the largest provider of preferences and the one where preference erosion is likely to be the most serious problem in the case of MFN liberalization. Although preferences have been instrumental in promoting some developing countries' export diversification into textiles and clothing, the track record of unilateral preferential systems as mechanisms to promote integration of developing economies into the world economy has been mixed at best. In part, this mixed record is because rules of origin and other forms of conditionality remain a major constraint on further expansion in some regimes. More fundamentally, however, it reflects supply capacity constraints in many beneficiary countries.

Arriving at consensus estimates of the degree of preference erosion is difficult because these estimates are a function not only of the methodology adopted, but also of the liberalization scenarios considered. Moreover, the reference point for compensation (for example, whether to focus on reductions in the potential de jure transfer or on the de facto economic value of transfer, taking into account compliance costs and eventual offsetting measures) is an issue open to debate. The limited scope for expanding preferential schemes to additional product lines in major OECD markets as a trade-related solution to preferences and the supply constraints just mentioned suggest that aid-related solutions to preference erosion are preferable to trade solutions that involve continued or additional preferential access to markets.

In sum, preferences are clearly important for some countries in some sectors, insignificant for most, and injurious for others. Preferences are being eroded by liberalization at all levels (national, regional, and multilateral), but the Doha Round is likely to lead to relatively limited preference erosion unless the negotiations become a lot more ambitious (Martin and Mattoo 2008). Independent of the debate on the magnitude and impact of preference erosion, a reorientation of trade policies away from procedures that tend to hollow out the multilateral trade system would clearly enhance welfare at the global level. The aid for trade agenda provides a potential framework for addressing preference erosion concerns.

Notes

1. The LDCs are a group of the poorest countries, as defined by the United Nations, with inclusion based on specific criteria. At the time of writing, the United Nations had classified 50 countries as LDCs.

2. A report written under Prebisch's direction (UNCTAD 1964) outlines the arguments in favor of trade preferences. The primary role of unilateral preferences was to support infant-industry policies, with expansion of exports of manufactured goods being a part of the overall industrialization process.

3. See Onguglo (1999) for a review of schemes in operation at the end of the 1990s.

4. See GATT (1994) for the texts on Part IV of the GATT and the Enabling Clause.

5. Such conditions may include trade and nontrade conditionality, either de jure or de facto. The Enabling Clause applies only to nonreciprocal preference programs covering all developing countries or LDCs. No other tariff discrimination between countries in the application of preferences is formally permitted. Until the early 1990s, this requirement was not enforced. Enforcement began when a report of a GATT panel dealing with the EU banana import policy found the EU regime for banana imports from African, Caribbean, and Pacific countries violated the GATT MFN rule. As a result, the EU was obliged to request waivers for the Lomé Convention in 1994 and its successor, the Cotonou Convention, in 2000.

6. This chapter will not focus on the welfare implications of preferences for the importer, which will be determined by a mix of terms of trade, trade creation, and diversion effects.

7. This crude measure overstates the gain, even in this case, because it ignores the costs involved in increasing exports. In a general equilibrium analysis, second-best considerations also need to be taken into account. Fukase and Martin (2000) note that improved market access may generate second-round welfare gains by allowing the country to increase the volume of imports over its trade barriers.

8. Evidence from the AGOA preference scheme suggests that the pass-through of preference margins is partial. Olarreaga and Özden (2005) find that on average exporters received around one-third of the tariff rent, with poorer and smaller countries tending to obtain lower shares. Özden and Sharma (2006) analyze the U.S. Caribbean Basin Initiative program and find that the program's exporters are able to retain about two-thirds of the preference margin they are granted in the U.S. market.

9. See European Community (EC) Council Regulation 2820/98, December 21, 1998, and EC Council Regulation 2501/01, December 10, 2001, for details of the EU programs.

10. The Cotonou Convention is an international treaty that provides a framework for cooperation between the EU and former colonies of EU member states. The associated commitments are binding and cannot be unilaterally modified by a signatory. The Cotonou Convention superseded two earlier treaties: the Yaoundé Convention (1963–75) and Lomé Convention (1975–99). As of January 2008, market access into the EU for ACP countries is governed by either reciprocal economic partnership agreements or the EBA initiative (for LDCs).

11. Progress has recently been made in improving data—including the development of a comprehensive set of import demand elasticities at the Harmonized System six-digit level (Kee, Nicita, and Olarreaga forthcoming)—that will allow future research and analysis to be undertaken on a more solid analytical foundation.

12. For further discussion of the utility ratio, see chapter 10, by Brenton and Özden, and UNCTAD (2003).

13. The Swiss formula cuts high tariffs more than tariffs that are already low. See chapter 7 for further discussion.

14. The figures calculated by Brenton and Ikezuki (2005) give the margin relative to the overall value of exports from the country to the granting market. In contrast, the results based on the Low,

Piermartini, and Richtering chapters refer to the margin only on those products for which there are exports, a nonzero duty, and a positive apparent preference.

15. These numbers do not imply that preferences have not helped stimulate diversification into manufactured goods for certain developing countries. The case of apparel illustrates that preferences can have this effect, because AGOA has led to substantial increases in imports from a number of Sub-Saharan Africa countries. However, the scope for preferences to facilitate diversification into the apparel sector is limited by the lack of consistency across the different preference schemes. As Brenton and Özden point out in chapter 10, an apparel product from Africa that can enter under one country's preference scheme often will not be able to enter under another because of differences in rules of origin.

16. These weights might be the shares of each product in exports to the United States, or they might, as in Hoekman and Nicita (2008), take into account both the trade shares and the price responsiveness of each export product.

17. See Hoekman and Nicita (2008) for details of the calculation and Kee, Nicita, and Olarreaga (forthcoming) for the methodology used to estimate import demand elasticities. A simpler alternative measure calculated by Low, Piermartini and Richtering (chapters 7 and 8) is to compare the (U.S.) import weighted-average tariff imposed on a country (Mexico) with that imposed on all other countries. A problem is that by using total imports (by the United States) at the Harmonized System six-digit level as weights, this method disregards product composition: if Mexico's export composition to the United States is not representative of the composition of U.S. imports (for example, Mexican exports to the United States are mainly agricultural goods, but the United States imports mainly manufactured goods), using exclusively U.S. imports as weights in the calculation of the counterfactual would likely lead to biased results. This approach also ignores the sensitivity of import demand to prices (tariffs). As shown by Bouët, Fontagné, and Jean (2006), the product composition effect can be very important.

18. Lippoldt and Kowalski (2005) provide further insights on the effects of preference erosion across the globe by adopting a 50 percent cut on all merchandise tariffs in three separate experiments: first, unilateral liberalization by each of the five major preference-granting economies (Australia, Canada, the European Union, Japan, and the United States); second, plurilateral simultaneous liberalization in these economies; and third, multilateral liberalization. In most cases, potential negative effects are mitigated as the liberalization experiment is widened.

19. Preference-dependent or preference-sensitive countries include Cambodia, Cape Verde, the Comoros, Haiti, Malawi, Maldives, Mauritania, Mauritius, São Tomé and Príncipe, and Tanzania. The only large country expected to suffer from preference erosion is Bangladesh, which has benefited significantly from the quota restrictions on textiles and clothing imposed on other large competitive developing countries, such as China. The potential effect of the removal of quotas on non-quota-controlled textile and clothing exporters has been on the agenda since the negotiation to end the Multifiber Arrangement in the Uruguay Round.

20. One reason Amiti and Romalis (2007) find smaller effects is that they assume the tariff reductions by the EU for imports of sugar, bananas, and rice for LDCs have already been implemented.

References

Ahmad, Jaleel. 1977. "Tokyo Rounds of Trade Negotiations and the Generalized System of Preferences." *Economic Journal* 88 (350): 285–95.

Alexandraki, Katerina, and Hans Peter Lankes. 2006. "Estimating the Impact of Preference Erosion on Middle-Income Countries." In *Trade Preferences and Differential Treatment of Developing Countries*, ed. Bernard Hoekman and Çağlar Özden, 397–431. Cheltenham, U.K.: Edward Elgar.

Amiti, Mary, and John Romalis. 2007. "Will the Doha Round Lead to Preference Erosion?" *IMF Staff Papers* 54 (2): 338–84.

Ansón, José, Olivier Cadot, Antoni Estevadeordal, Jaime de Melo, Akiko Suwa-Eisenmann, and Bolormaa Tumurchudur. 2005. "Rules of Origin in North-South Preferential Trading Arrangements with an Application to NAFTA." *Review of International Economics* 13 (3): 501–17.

Bouët, Antoine, Lionel Fontagné, and Sébastien Jean. 2006. "Is Erosion of Tariff Preferences a Serious Concern?" In *Agricultural Trade Reform and the Doha Development Agenda*, ed. Kym Anderson and Will Martin, 161–92. Basingstoke, U.K.: Palgrave Macmillan.

Brenton, Paul, and Takako Ikezuki. 2005. "The Impact of Agricultural Trade Preferences, with Particular Attention to the Least Developed Countries." In *Global Agricultural Trade and Developing Countries*, ed. M. Ataman Aksoy and John C. Beghin, 55–73. Washington, DC: World Bank.

Brenton, Paul, and Miriam Manchin. 2003. "Making EU Trade Agreements Work: The Role of Rules of Origin." *World Economy* 26 (5): 755–69.

Cadot, Olivier, Antoni Estevadeordal, Akiko Suwa-Eisenmann, and Thierry Verdier, eds. 2006. *The Origin of Goods: Rules of Origin in Preferential Trading*. Oxford, U.K.: Oxford University Press.

François, Joseph, Bernard Hoekman, and Miriam Manchin. 2006. "Preference Erosion and Multilateral Trade Liberalization." *World Bank Economic Review* 20 (2): 197–216.

Fukase, Emiko, and Will Martin. 2000. "The Effects of the United States Granting MFN Status to Vietnam." *Weltwirtschaftliches Archiv* 136 (3): 539–59.

G-20 (Group of 20). 2005. "G-20 Proposal on Market Access." World Trade Organization, Geneva.

GATT (General Agreement on Tariffs and Trade). 1994. *The Results of the Uruguay Round of Multilateral Trade Negotiations*. Geneva: GATT.

Grynberg, Roman, and Sacha Silva. 2004. "Preference-Dependent Economies and Multilateral Liberalisation: Impacts and Options." Commonwealth Secretariat, London.

Hoekman, Bernard, and Alessandro Nicita. 2008. "International Regulatory Convergence and Developing Country Trade." World Bank, Washington, DC.

Hoekman, Bernard, and Çağlar Özden. 2006. "Introduction." In *Trade Preferences and Differential Treatment of Developing Countries*, ed. Bernard Hoekman and Çağlar Özden, xi-xli. Cheltenham, U.K.: Edward Elgar.

Hudec, Robert E. 1987. *Developing Countries in the GATT Legal System*. Aldershot, U.K.: Gower.

IMF (International Monetary Fund). 2004. "Fund Support for Trade-Related Balance of Payments Adjustments." IMF, Washington, DC. http://www.imf.org/external/np/pdr/tim/2004/eng/022704.pdf.

Johnson, Harry G. 1967. *Economic Policies toward Less Developed Countries*. Washington, DC: Brookings Institution.

Kee, Hiau Looi, Alessandro Nicita, and Marcelo Olarreaga. Forthcoming. "Import Demand Elasticities and Trade Distortions." *Review of Economics and Statistics*.

Limão, Nuno, and Marcelo Olarreaga. 2006. "Trade Preferences to Small Countries and the Welfare Costs of Lost Multilateral Liberalization." *World Bank Economic Review* 20 (2): 217–40.

Lippoldt, Douglas, and Przemyslaw Kowalski. 2005. "Trade Preference Erosion: Potential Economic Impacts." OECD Trade Policy Working Paper 17, Organisation for Economic Co-operation and Development, Paris.

Martin, Will, and Aaditya Mattoo. 2008. "The Doha Development Agenda: What's on the Table?" Policy Research Working Paper 4672, World Bank, Washington, DC.

Olarreaga, Marcelo, and Çağlar Özden. 2005. "AGOA and Apparel: Who Captures the Tariff Rent in the Presence of Preferential Market Access?" *World Economy* 28 (1): 63–77.

Onguglo, Bonapas Francis. 1999. "Developing Countries and Unilateral Trade Preferences in the New International Trading System." In *Trade Rules in the Making: Challenges in Regional and Multilateral Negotiations*, ed. Miguel Rodríguez Mendoza, Patrick Low, and Barbara Kotschwar, 109–33. Washington, DC: Brookings Institution.

Özden, Çağlar, and Gunjan Sharma. 2006. "Price Effects of Preferential Market Access: The Caribbean Basin Initiative and the Apparel Sector." *World Bank Economic Review* 20 (2): 241–60.

Page, Sheila. 2005. "A Preference Erosion Compensation Fund: A New Proposal to Protect Countries from the Negative Effects of Trade Liberalisation." ODI Opinions 35, Overseas Development Institute, London.

Page, Sheila, and Peter Kleen. 2004. "Special and Differential Treatment of Developing Countries in the World Trade Organization." Report for the Ministry of Foreign Affairs, Stockholm.

Patterson, Gardner. 1965. "Would Tariff Preferences Help Economic Development?" *Lloyds Bank Review* 76 (April): 18–30.

Prebisch, Raúl. 1950. *The Economic Development of Latin America and Its Principal Problems.* Santiago: United Nations.

Prowse, Susan. 2006. "'Aid for Trade': A Proposal for Increasing Support for Trade Adjustment and Integration." In *Economic Development and Multilateral Trade Cooperation*, ed. Simon Evenett and Bernard Hoekman, 229–67. Basingstoke, U.K.: Palgrave Macmillan.

Stevens, Christopher, and Jane Kennan. 2005. "Making Trade Preferences More Effective." Trade Note, Institute of Development Studies, University of Sussex, Brighton, U.K. http://www.ids.ac.uk/ UserFiles/File/globalisation_team/tradepapers/CSJKTradePreferences.pdf.

Subramanian, Arvind. 2003. "Financing of Losses from Preference Erosion: Note on Issues Raised by Developing Countries in the Doha Round." WT/TF/COH/14, International Monetary Fund, Washington, DC.

UNCTAD (United Nations Conference on Trade and Development). 1964. *Towards a New Trade Policy for Development: Report by the Secretary General of United Nations Conference on Trade and Development.* New York: United Nations.

———. 2003. *Trade Preferences for LDCs: An Early Assessment of Benefits and Possible Improvements.* Geneva: UNCTAD.

WTO (World Trade Organization). 2008a. "Draft Modalities for Nonagricultural Market Access." TN/MA/W/103/Rev.2, WTO, Geneva.

———. 2008b. "Revised Draft Modalities for Agriculture." TN/AG/W/4/Rev.3, WTO, Geneva.

2

QUANTIFYING THE VALUE
OF U.S. TARIFF PREFERENCES
FOR DEVELOPING COUNTRIES

Judith M. Dean and John Wainio

There has been much debate over the value of preferential trade programs offered by industrial countries, granting duty-free or reduced-duty access for many exports from developing countries.[1] Some leaders from developing countries and nongovernmental organizations have argued that preference erosion would have serious development consequences and requires compensation (e.g., Oxfam 2005). Other leaders have argued that vulnerability to preference erosion is limited to only a few countries and products, and thus requires more targeted assistance (WTO 2004).

A country that is granted trade preferences would presumably see demand for its exports grow, relative to demand for exports from countries still facing most-favored-nation (MFN) tariffs. If the country receiving preferences is small, its exports would continue to be sold in the importing country at the prevailing tariff-inclusive price, with the exporter earning the difference. Thus, the benefits of such preferences for the exporting country would be increased exports and a transfer of rent from the importing country. But how important are these trade preferences to developing countries? Are the tariff margins large? Do countries fully utilize their preferential access? Is all rent actually earned by the exporting

The authors are grateful to Maya Shivakumar and Nick Grossman for their superb work assembling and analyzing data. They also thank Pat Thomas for her valuable help constructing tables and Peg MacKnight for her help with the U.S. International Trade Commission DataWeb database. The views expressed here are those of the authors only. They do not necessarily reflect the views of the U.S. International Trade Commission, any of its individual commissioners, or the U.S. Department of Agriculture.

countries? If so, how large is this rent relative to a country's overall exports? If it is significant, do trade preferences granted to one developing country come at the expense of another (Panagariya 2002)?

Only recently have studies attempted to answer some of these questions quantitatively. Alexandraki and Lankes (2004) calculate the product-level tariff margins granted by Canada, the European Union, Japan, and the United States and then use these margins to derive an aggregate value of preferences for each beneficiary country. They find that in 18 countries, the value of preferences exceeds 5 percent of the value of their exports. Their results suggest that the problem is heavily concentrated in small island economies that depend on sugar, bananas, and—to a lesser extent—textiles. But as Alexandraki and Lankes note, these values may be overstated because they assume full utilization of preferences, constant world prices, and full rent transfer to the beneficiary countries.

Brenton and Ikezuki (2004) assess the scope and value of U.S. preferences under the African Growth and Opportunity Act (AGOA) for the year 2002. They find that, overall, the least developed countries (LDCs) among the beneficiaries saw little expansion in the list of products eligible for duty-free access under the AGOA because they already had such access under the Generalized System of Preferences (GSP). Thus, countries other than LDCs would be likely to benefit more from the AGOA. But a country's eligibility for apparel preferences significantly affects the rate at which it uses AGOA preferences. Among countries that have such status, the LDCs have the least restrictive rules of origin and are therefore likely to gain more. Brenton and Ikezuki's data show wide variation in AGOA utilization and AGOA tariff preferences that averaged only about 6 percent. In only six AGOA countries did the values of preferences (AGOA plus GSP) exceed 5 percent of that country's total exports to the United States.

This chapter seeks to improve on measures of the size, utilization, and value of all U.S. nonreciprocal trade preference programs in order to shed some light on the debate. Highly disaggregated data are used to quantify the 2003 margins, coverage, and utilization of nonagricultural and agricultural tariff preferences, for all beneficiary countries in U.S. regional preference programs and in the GSP. Estimates of the overall value of preferences are made assuming full utilization and then reestimated to reflect actual utilization. Values for nonagricultural and agricultural preferences are also estimated.

The results show that U.S. regional preference programs are characterized by high coverage of beneficiary countries' exports, high utilization by beneficiary countries, and low tariff preference margins (except on apparel). The GSP has relatively poorer coverage in general and low preference margins. The GSP is little used as an alternative to the regional programs, but is heavily used by countries that have no alternatives. With 2003 actual utilization incorporated, 29 beneficiary countries were found to have U.S. tariff preferences valued at 5 percent or more of their dutiable exports to the United States, and 17 countries had preference values that exceeded 5 percent of their total exports to the United States. In nine countries, U.S. preferences were valued at 15 percent or more of their dutiable exports to the United States. Most of this value was attributable to nonagricultural tariff preferences, especially those for apparel. The remaining value was small and attributable largely to jewelry, chemicals, electrical machinery, petroleum-related products, melons, fresh-cut flowers, frozen orange juice, raw cane sugar, and fresh asparagus. The removal of apparel quantity restrictions in 2005 is likely to have reduced the value of U.S. apparel preferences since 2003. Although further analysis is needed, these results suggest that U.S. preference erosion may be significant for more countries than was previously thought.

U.S. Nonreciprocal Trade Programs in 2003

In 2003, 143 countries and territories were eligible for tariff preferences under the GSP. GSP treatment in the United States is duty free and covers "most dutiable manufactures and semi-manufactures and selected agricultural, fishery, and primary industrial products not otherwise duty-free" (Office of the U.S. Trade Representative 1999). In 1996, nearly 2,000 additional items were designated duty free for LDCs.[2] But relative to other U.S. preferential programs, the GSP covers fewer products. Products deemed import sensitive are excluded by law. Agricultural products that are subject to a tariff rate quota are not eligible for duty-free access on any quantities that exceed the quota. Other ineligible products include most textiles, apparel, watches, footwear, handbags, luggage, work gloves, and other apparel made partly or wholly from leather (U.S. Federal Code 19, chapter 12, subchapter V). The GSP has additional limitations, including periodic expiration, loss of GSP eligibility because of automatic graduation to the World Bank's high-income country category, and loss of GSP eligibility for a specific product once competitive needs limits are exceeded.[3]

AGOA granted duty-free status to more than 6,400 products imported from Sub-Saharan African countries as part of the Trade Act of 2000 (USITC 2004b), a larger set of goods than the GSP covers. In 2003, 38 countries were eligible for preferences under the act (see http://www.agoa.gov). For non-LDC beneficiaries, products are eligible for preferences under AGOA or under the GSP, but not under both. For LDC beneficiaries, however, some products are eligible for both programs. AGOA exempts beneficiary countries from the competitive needs limits. The program also grants duty-free and quota-free access to apparel made in eligible Sub-Saharan African countries from U.S. fabric, yarn, and thread. Apparel imports made with regional fabrics were subject to a cap, which was designed to grow over a period of eight years. In addition, the Special Rule for Apparel (SRA) allowed LDCs to receive duty-free access for apparel made with fabrics originating from third countries until September 2004.[4] AGOA II (part of the Trade Act of 2002) expanded preferential access and increased the cap for apparel made with regional fabric. AGOA III (2004) extended the program until 2015 and the third-country fabric provision until 2007.

The Caribbean Basin Economic Recovery Act (CBERA) is an extension of the Caribbean Basin Initiative (CBI), begun in 1984 (USITC 2005). This program eliminated or reduced tariffs on eligible products imported from designated Caribbean and Central American countries and territories. The Caribbean Basin Trade Partnership Act (CBTPA), the most recent extension of CBERA, was implemented as part of the Trade Act of 2000. In 2003, 24 countries were eligible for CBERA benefits; of those, 14 were eligible for the CBTPA. Under the CBTPA, a number of import-sensitive products became eligible for preferential duty treatment, including apparel, petroleum, and petroleum products. The CBTPA authorizes unlimited duty-free entry for imports of apparel that are assembled in CBERA countries from fabrics made and cut in the United States of U.S. yarns. If the cutting takes place in CBTPA countries, the apparel must be sewn with U.S. thread.[5] The CBTPA also provides some preferential access for apparel made from regional fabric, but unlike AGOA, it has no third-country fabric provision.

The Andean Trade Preference Act (ATPA) granted duty-free access to many imports from Bolivia, Colombia, Ecuador, and Peru beginning in 1991 (USITC 2004a). After expiring in December 2001, ATPA was renewed retroactively as the Andean Trade Promotion and Drug Eradication Act in late 2002.[6] ATPA covers more products than the GSP, and eligibility is not constrained by the GSP competitive needs limits or by the possibility of graduation. In 2002, ATPA preferential treatment was expanded to include previously excluded import-sensitive products such as petroleum and petroleum derivatives, apparel and textiles, footwear, and tuna in foil packages. ATPA allows unlimited duty-free and quota-free treatment for imports of textiles and apparel made in ATPA countries using yarn, fabric, or fabric components wholly formed in the United States. Like the CBTPA, ATPA also provides some preferential access for apparel made from regional fabric, but no third-country fabric provision.

Data Description

For this study, a preference database was constructed using trade and tariff data from the U.S. Harmonized Tariff Schedule (HTS) at the eight-digit level, extracted from the U.S. International Trade Commission (USITC) DataWeb database (http://dataweb.usitc.gov) and the USITC Tariff Database (http://www.usitc.gov/tata/hts/other/dataweb). All 2003 U.S. imports in Harmonized System (HS) chapters 1 through 97 were included.[7] The USITC records U.S. imports from beneficiary countries by customs value in current U.S. dollars.[8] The import data include the preferences claimed, value of total imports, dutiable imports (ex post), duties paid, quantity imported, and preference-eligibility status by country and program. The use of preferences is indicated by the preference claimed when the product entered the United States.[9]

MFN and preferential tariffs, including both ad valorem and specific tariffs, are converted to ad valorem equivalents (AVEs), using the USITC method.[10] Although the USITC Tariff Database includes AVEs of tariff rate quotas, it does not include any AVE estimates of import quotas or other types of quantitative restrictions. The implications of omitting the 2003 U.S. quantitative restrictions on apparel products are discussed later. The tariff data include detailed information on preference eligibility by product and program.

U.S. Tariff Preferences on Nonagricultural Products

Figure 2.1 shows U.S. imports of nonagricultural products in 2003 from beneficiary countries by tariff treatment.[11] The CBERA countries are split into those eligible for CBTPA and those eligible for CBERA only, since the CBTPA includes

FIGURE 2.1 Share of U.S. Nonagricultural Imports by Type of Tariff Regime, 2003

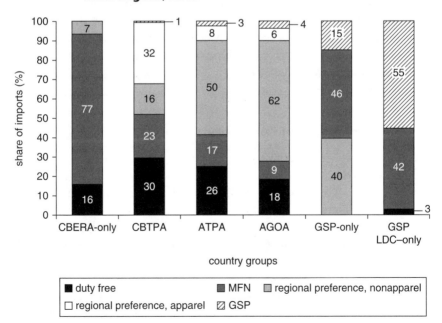

Source: USITC Trade Database and authors' calculations.

apparel preferences and covers other products more broadly. Countries that are exclusively eligible for the GSP are split into two groups: GSP-only and GSP LDC beneficiaries.

The first striking feature of figure 2.1 is the high overall use of the regional preference programs. In 2003, the United States imported about US$19.6 billion of nonagricultural products from CBTPA countries, 50 percent of which was apparel. Nearly half these imports entered the United States under the CBTPA program. Similarly, of the US$9.8 billion imported from ATPA countries (11 percent of which was apparel), nearly 60 percent entered under the ATPA program. AGOA countries accounted for US$19.1 billion of U.S. nonagricultural imports, 8 percent of which was apparel. About 68 percent of these imports entered under the AGOA preference program. In contrast, the CBERA-only beneficiaries made little use of regional preferences. Of the US$1.8 billion in nonagricultural imports from these countries, only 7 percent entered the United States under the CBERA.

The second striking feature of figure 2.1 is the low use of the GSP. Only 1 percent of U.S. imports from the CBPTA countries and from CBERA-only countries came in under this program. U.S. imports from ATPA and AGOA beneficiaries under the GSP were only 3 percent and 4 percent, respectively. Even the non-LDCs that are eligible only for the GSP made little use of the program: only 15 percent of the US$113.8 billion of nonagricultural imports from those beneficiaries entered under the GSP. In contrast, more than half of the US$8.8 billion nonagricultural imports from GSP LDC beneficiaries entered under the GSP program. Although apparel represented 13 percent of U.S. imports from GSP LDC countries, most of it was excluded from the GSP, leaving only 1 percent of apparel imports entering under the program.

Are U.S. Nonagricultural Preferences Comprehensive?

Whether countries underutilize U.S. preferences may depend partly on how extensive the preferences are. The scope of preferences is measured by calculating coverage rates, which are defined as the ratio of eligible U.S. imports to total dutiable U.S. imports, with *dutiable* defined as being subject to duty if no preference program is claimed. Apparel coverage is problematic because, strictly speaking, no apparel product is eligible, ex ante, for preferential tariff treatment. The regional programs all have product eligibility requirements—typically, rules of origin regarding the components of the garments—that may or may not be met. The AGOA program also requires country apparel eligibility and grants nearly all AGOA LDC beneficiaries SRA eligibility. In this study, overall coverage rates for countries in these programs are calculated by assuming that all apparel imports from eligible countries are potentially eligible for duty-free access. This assumption yields apparel coverage rates of 100 percent.[12] For CBERA-only and GSP countries, apparel coverage rates are calculated on the basis of actual product eligibility.

Table 2.1 shows coverage rates for all nonagricultural imports and for apparel and nonapparel imports separately. Data for regional programs are shown on the left, and data for the alternative GSP program on the right. Nearly all U.S. nonagricultural imports from CBTPA and ATPA members were eligible for preferences under these regional programs. Except for El Salvador, coverage rates for nonapparel imports were 90 percent or more under both programs. For CBERA-only countries, the scope of regional preferences was more varied. Of the 10 members, 6 had CBERA coverage rates of 90 percent or more, but the remaining 4 had rates well below 50 percent. Under the alternative GSP program, coverage of nonapparel imports exceeded 90 percent in seven of the CBTPA and ATPA countries, but overall GSP coverage rates were well below 50 percent for most beneficiaries. For CBERA-only countries, GSP coverage was similar to regional program coverage.

There is no overlap between AGOA program coverage and GSP coverage for AGOA non-LDC beneficiaries. Adding up coverage under both programs reveals that virtually all U.S. nonagricultural imports from all AGOA non-LDC beneficiaries (except Eritrea) were eligible for preferences in 2003. The same was true for nonapparel imports (except Botswana and Swaziland). Coverage rates showed more variation among the LDCs. Of the 21 AGOA LDC beneficiaries, 9 had coverage of 90 percent or more; for 9 others, AGOA coverage was negligible. For most other LDCs, low (high) AGOA coverage corresponded to high (low) GSP coverage. Thus, 14 LDCs had complete coverage, and another 4 had 50 to 90 percent coverage under the combined preference programs. AGOA coverage of nonapparel imports was generally low relative to that of the GSP, except for petroleum-related products. In eight of the countries with complete AGOA coverage, exports to the United States consisted almost entirely of petroleum-related products.[13]

Preference coverage was on average much lower and more varied for GSP-only countries (table 2.2). The mean coverage rate for the 60 non-LDCs was just 44 percent, and in nearly half the countries the GSP covered less than 30 percent of their dutiable exports. Of the 15 GSP LDC beneficiaries, half had coverage rates of 90 percent or more, while the other half had coverage rates near or below 25 percent. For countries such as Bangladesh, Cambodia, Nepal, Pakistan, and Sri Lanka, whose exports to the United States are dominated by apparel, GSP coverage rates were extremely low.

(*Text continues on p. 42.*)

TABLE 2.1 U.S. Nonagricultural Imports: Preference Coverage, Utilization, and Average Nominal Tariff Preference, 2003

	CBERA coverage[a] (%)		CBERA utilization[b] (%)			CBERA average tariff preference[c] (%)			GSP coverage[a] (%)		GSP utilization, overall[b] (%)	GSP average tariff preference, overall[c] (%)
	Overall	Nonapparel	Overall	Nonapparel	Apparel	Overall	Nonapparel	Apparel	Overall	Nonapparel		
Antigua and Barbuda	98	98	4	4	n.a.	4.5	4.5	n.a.	27	27	16	3.9
Aruba	(.)	(.)	49	50	0	3.9	3.8	4.6	n.a.	n.a.	n.a.	n.a.
Bahamas, The	29	29	100	100	100	3.4	3.4	4.2	n.a.	n.a.	n.a.	n.a.
British Virgin Islands	44	42	7	8	0	4.3	4.1	10.0	31	34	0	4.0
Dominica	99	100	98	98	n.a.	3.3	3.3	n.a.	99	100	0	3.3
Grenada	100	100	20	20	n.a.	3.8	3.8	n.a.	100	100	0	3.8
Montserrat	91	95	0	0	n.a.	2.1	2.1	n.a.	72	75	0	2.5
Netherlands Antilles	1	1	40	40	n.a.	3.6	3.6	n.a.	n.a.	n.a.	n.a.	n.a.
St. Kitts and Nevis	98	100	96	96	n.a.	2.9	2.9	n.a.	93	95	2	3.1
St. Vincent	100	100	100	100	100	4.3	4.1	4.9	100	100	(.)	4.5

	CBTPA coverage[a] (%)		CBTPA utilization[b] (%)			CBTPA average tariff preference[c] (%)			GSP coverage[a] (%)		GSP utilization, overall[b] (%)	GSP average tariff preference, overall[c] (%)
	Overall[d]	Nonapparel	Overall[d]	Nonapparel	Apparel[d]	Overall[d]	Nonapparel	Apparel[d]	Overall	Nonapparel		
Barbados	100	100	20	20	3	4.8	3.5	15.7	34	35	17	2.9
Belize	100	100	76	4	86	8.8	3.2	14.2	12	98	13	4.2
Costa Rica	99	98	73	79	70	7.4	4.9	16.8	32	92	12	3.7
Dominican Republic	99	97	76	65	82	8.2	4.3	15.8	30	86	7	3.8
El Salvador	98	60	65	77	64	11.2	5.0	15.4	2	38	32	4.0
Guatemala	99	96	42	94	34	10.0	3.2	15.6	5	34	11	4.6
Guyana	96	91	83	81	85	12.1	4.8	18.5	40	91	21	4.3
Haiti	100	100	66	34	67	12.6	3.7	17.3	5	97	18	4.4
Honduras	100	98	71	20	76	10.5	4.4	16.1	8	96	4	4.1
Jamaica	100	100	86	57	87	9.2	5.2	17.2	3	90	6	3.6
Nicaragua	100	100	31	32	31	13.0	5.8	16.6	n.a.	n.a.	n.a.	n.a.
Panama	99	99	48	51	9	6.9	4.8	14.4	49	53	26	3.7
St. Lucia	100	100	61	89	0	9.4	4.3	18.3	11	16	41	3.5
Trinidad and Tobago	100	100	90	90	11	4.3	5.0	14.4	37	37	0	3.5

	ATPA coverage[a] (%)		ATPA utilization[b] (%)			ATPA average tariff preference[c] (%)			GSP coverage[a] (%)		GSP utilization, overall[b] (%)	GSP average tariff preference, overall[c] (%)
	Overall[d]	Nonapparel	Overall[d]	Nonapparel	Apparel[d]	Overall[d]	Nonapparel	Apparel[d]	Overall	Nonapparel		
Bolivia	100	100	90	89	90	10.1	5.3	14.3	77	98	9	4.5
Colombia	99	99	71	74	53	7.8	4.9	14.5	7	8	45	4.0
Ecuador	99	93	85	89	77	8.2	4.6	15.6	7	6	37	4.3
Peru	94	99	89	85	90	8.2	4.9	14.3	52	82	8	4.2

(Table continues on the following page.)

TABLE 2.1 U.S. Nonagricultural Imports: Preference Coverage, Utilization, and Average Nominal Tariff Preference, 2003 (Continued)

	AGOA coverage[a] (%)		AGOA utilization[b] (%)			AGOA average tariff preference[c] (%)			GSP coverage[a] (%)		GSP utilization, overall[b] (%)	GSP average tariff preference, overall[c] (%)
	Overall[d]	Nonapparel	Overall[d]	Nonapparel	Apparel[d]	Overall[d]	Nonapparel	Apparel[d]	Overall	Nonapparel		
Botswana[e,f]	99	0	89	n.a.	89	17.6	n.a.	17.6	1	49	0	2.5
Cameroon[e,f]	99	99	100	100	0	9.7	9.6	9.9	1	1	16	4.0
Congo, Rep. of	100	100	90	90	n.a.	3.8	3.8	n.a.	(.)	(.)	64	4.8
Côte d'Ivoire[e,f]	97	98	80	80	0	7.7	5.7	9.4	2	2	41	3.6
Eritrea	5	11	0	0	n.a.	8.0	8.0	n.a.	40	89	0	3.5
Gabon	100	100	62	62	n.a.	2.0	2.0	n.a.	(.)	(.)	25	3.5
Ghana[e,f]	83	80	89	88	96	11.7	4.3	13.1	17	19	99	5.0
Kenya[e,f]	98	22	93	5	94	15.7	10.2	16.8	2	72	76	4.8
Mauritius[e]	97	1	50	0	50	13.9	7.7	14.1	3	98	82	4.5
Namibia[e,f]	74	(.)	77	84	77	16.5	6.0	17.3	26	100	99	4.0
Nigeria	100	100	96	96	n.a.	6.5	6.5	n.a.	(.)	(.)	73	4.0
Senegal[e,f]	4	2	17	42	0	10.5	11.4	9.9	90	93	83	3.1
Seychelles	98	100	0	0	n.a.	1.5	1.5	n.a.	(.)	(.)	15	3.2
South Africa[e]	56	49	86	95	54	11.5	6.3	15.5	40	46	93	3.8
Swaziland[e]	96	6	90	19	90	17.2	8.8	18.4	1	15	23	3.6
AGOA LDC												
Benin	0	0	n.a.	n.a.	n.a.	n.a.	n.a.	n.a.	0	0	n.a.	n.a.
Cape Verde[e,f]	99	83	83	60	83	20.7	22.1	20.4	2	74	18	17.2
Central African Republic	0	0	n.a.	n.a.	n.a.	n.a.	n.a.	n.a.	99	99	44	3.4

Country												
Chad	100	100	81	81	n.a.	3.0	3.0	n.a.	100	100	(.)	2.0
Congo, Dem. Rep. of[f]	100	100	0	0	n.a.	2.1	2.1	n.a.	100	100	93	5.1
Ethiopia[e,f]	89	2	99	0	99	17.8	4.1	18.3	11	99	97	3.8
Gambia, The	0	0	n.a.	n.a.	n.a.	n.a.	n.a.	n.a.	73	82	29	2.5
Guinea	5	5	0	0	n.a.	7.5	7.5	n.a.	97	99	21	3.6
Lesotho[e,f]	100	0	95	0	95	18.4	n.a.	18.4	(.)	100	30	4.7
Madagascar[e,f]	99	20	95	81	95	15.6	8.3	15.9	1	75	71	4.9
Malawi[e,f]	100	10	97	100	97	18.6	5.3	19.1	(.)	90	100	3.2
Mali[e,f,h]	25	13	0	1	0	11.0	7.2	13.4	68	79	61	5.0
Mauritania	0	0	n.a.	n.a.	n.a.	n.a.	n.a.	n.a.	4	100	93	2.2
Mozambique[e,f]	98	0	100	0	100	20.2	n.a.	20.2	2	78	39	3.0
Niger[e,f,h]	4	2	7	16	0	8.2	8.6	6.7	79	81	12	4.0
Rwanda[e,f]	0	0	n.a.	n.a.	n.a.	n.a.	n.a.	n.a.	98	98	4	4.0
São Tomé and Príncipe	(.)	(.)	0	0	n.a.	n.a.	n.a.	n.a.	99	100	0	2.0
Sierra Leone	13	27	0	0	n.a.	12.3	12.3	n.a.	35	73	9	3.1
Tanzania[e,f]	41	(.)	90	90	91	13.8	5.0	14.7	16	27	90	4.8
Uganda[e,f]	94	0	88	0	88	22.3	n.a.	22.3	6	98	44	3.7
Zambia[e,f]	1	1	0	0	n.a.	3.0	3.0	n.a.	97	97	100	5.1

Source: Authors' estimates.

Note: (.) = less than 1 percent; n.a. = not applicable.

a. Ratio of eligible imports to total dutiable imports.

b. Ratio of imports entering under preference to total eligible imports.

c. Difference between nominal ad valorem tariff equivalent and nominal preferential tariff. Covers all HTS eight-digit lines with eligible U.S. imports in 2003.

d. Apparel is defined as all lines within HS chapters 61 and 62 (including the non-U.S. value of production-sharing, HTS 9802.00.80). For all countries in ATPA, CBTPA, and AGOA (with apparel eligibility), overall calculation assumes all apparel is potentially eligible for apparel benefits. Thus "utilization" is actually the ratio of U.S. imports entering under a preference to total U.S. apparel imports.

e. Country is eligible for apparel benefits.

f. Country is eligible for Special Rule for Apparel for LDC.

g. AGOA benefits delayed until October 31, 2003.

h. AGOA eligibility as of December 2003.

TABLE 2.2   U.S. Nonagricultural Imports: GSP Coverage, Utilization, and Average Tariff Preference, 2003

	Coverage[a] (%)	Utilization[b] (%)	Average tariff preference[c] (%)
Albania	51	69	4.2
Anguilla	94	92	2.8
Argentina	26	78	3.8
Armenia	83	100	4.5
Bahrain	34	99	3.8
Bosnia and Herzegovina	74	86	5.1
British Indian Ocean Territories	39	0	1.7
Brazil	46	64	3.9
Bulgaria	12	85	3.8
Chile	92	32	3.8
Christmas Island	68	0	3.1
Cocos Islands	64	0	4.7
Cook Islands	76	8	5.2
Croatia	76	94	3.7
Czech Republic	79	52	3.9
Egypt, Arab Rep. of	3	82	3.9
Estonia	23	92	4.2
Fiji	2	92	3.6
Georgia	33	96	2.9
Gibraltar	84	0	3.2
Hungary	71	52	3.7
India	50	87	4.0
Indonesia	39	65	4.1
Jordan	15	63	4.0
Kazakhstan	62	100	4.3
Kyrgyz Republic	7	100	5.1
Latvia	4	87	4.1
Lebanon	85	98	3.8
Lithuania	3	80	4.1
Macedonia, FYR	9	85	4.6
Moldova	1	75	2.2
Mongolia	1	12	3.1
Morocco	13	52	4.3
Niue	14	0	4.0
Norfolk Island	8	0	1.9
Oman	16	99	4.7
Pakistan	5	80	4.3
Papua New Guinea	(.)	53	3.1
Paraguay	51	97	4.4

(Table continues on the following page.)

TABLE 2.2   (*Continued*)

	Coverage[a] (%)	Utilization[b] (%)	Average tariff preference[c] (%)
Philippines	39	65	4.0
Pitcairn Island	97	0	2.3
Poland	70	62	3.8
Romania	30	79	4.0
Russian Federation	14	87	4.0
Slovak Republic	13	74	3.7
Solomon Islands	96	0	4.3
Sri Lanka	7	90	4.6
St. Helena	99	0	4.6
Suriname	100	55	2.7
Thailand	56	76	4.0
Tokelau	22	65	4.0
Tonga	95	17	3.1
Tunisia	20	50	4.1
Turkey	31	86	3.9
Turks and Caicos Islands	100	1	2.9
Uruguay	70	93	3.7
Uzbekistan	6	68	4.4
Venezuela, R.B. de	7	96	3.8
West Bank and Gaza	84	74	6.1
Western Sahara	100	0	2.7
Zimbabwe	88	98	4.7
GSP LDC			
Afghanistan	27	0	2.7
Angola	100	94	2.0
Bangladesh	2	89	6.2
Bhutan	22	62	8.0
Burkina Faso	93	61	4.3
Burundi	0	n.a.	n.a.
Cambodia	1	72	5.7
Equatorial Guinea	100	93	1.5
Kiribati	100	0	2.9
Nepal	5	76	4.0
Samoa	8	2	4.1
Somalia	95	0	1.3
Togo	25	100	4.6
Vanuatu	100	100	3.2
Yemen, Rep. of	100	86	1.7

Source: Authors' estimates.

Note: (.) = less than 1 percent; n.a. = not applicable.

a. Ratio of eligible imports to total dutiable imports.

b. Ratio of imports entering under preference to total eligible imports.

c. Difference between nominal ad valorem tariff equivalent and nominal preferential tariff. Covers all HTS eight-digit lines with eligible U.S. imports in 2003.

Are U.S. Nonagricultural Preferences Fully Utilized?

Utilization is defined as the share of eligible imports entering the United States under the preference program. Table 2.1 shows that utilization rates are typically below 100 percent. Some of the evidence suggests that utilization rates may correlate with coverage rates. The ATPA and CBTPA members that have virtually 100 percent coverage of their exports under the regional programs had high average utilization rates: 83 percent and 63 percent, respectively. Rates for nonapparel and apparel were similarly high, although CBTPA countries showed more variable utilization than did ATPA countries. Utilization rates in CBERA-only countries tended to be lower, on average, as were their coverage rates. One might think that some of the underutilization by these beneficiaries could be explained by their use of the GSP program instead. Table 2.1 shows, however, that these countries made little use of GSP preferences.[14] In fact, almost no nonagricultural imports that were eligible both for ATPA, CBERA, or CBTPA preferences and for GSP preferences entered the United States under the GSP.

Among AGOA non-LDC beneficiaries, high combined AGOA and GSP coverage corresponded to high combined utilization. With the exception of Eritrea, Gabon, and Mauritius, each country showed combined utilization rates of 75 percent or more. Average utilization of nonapparel preferences was only 50 percent, although seven countries had rates exceeding 75 percent. For LDCs, AGOA preference coverage was less generous than GSP coverage. Overall, average utilization of each program was about 50 percent. High (low) AGOA coverage tended to correspond to high (low) AGOA utilization. But if AGOA utilization was low, GSP utilization tended to be high. Thus, average utilization of the combined preference programs exceeded 50 percent. Interestingly, the eight AGOA countries that exported exclusively petroleum-related products showed wide variation in utilization, despite complete AGOA coverage.

Of the 20 AGOA apparel-eligible countries, 11 made heavy use of apparel preferences, whereas 5 did not use them at all. Since all the AGOA exporters with high apparel utilization were eligible for the SRA, one might suspect that high utilization was driven by the ability to avoid costly rules of origin. However, of the nine AGOA apparel-eligible countries with low apparel utilization, five were SRA-eligible and two (Mali and Niger) became eligible late in the year. More analysis is therefore needed to determine the role of the SRA in preference usage.

For countries benefiting exclusively from the GSP, preference utilization appears to be quite high, despite the relatively low coverage of GSP preferences (table 2.2). For both non-LDCs and LDCs, average utilization was 60 percent. About half of the non-LDCs and LDCs had utilization rates exceeding 75 percent. Particularly noteworthy are the beneficiaries whose exports include a large share of apparel. Although GSP coverage rates for Pakistan and Sri Lanka were only

7 percent and 5 percent, respectively, their utilization rates were 80 percent and 90 percent. Similarly, for Bangladesh and Nepal, GSP coverage was only 2 percent and 5 percent, respectively, but utilization rates were 89 percent and 76 percent. This finding suggests that countries that lack the alternative of a regional preference program do make heavy use of the GSP but are constrained by the program's limited coverage.

Are U.S. Nonagricultural Preference Margins Large?

High utilization of preferences has occurred despite evidence that preference margins are generally low. The tariff preference margin is calculated as the difference between the nominal MFN tariff AVE and the nominal preferential AVE, at the HTS eight-digit level. Unweighted averages for each country and program are shown in table 2.1. Across member countries and all eligible U.S. nonagricultural imports in 2003, AGOA preference margins averaged the highest (14 percent). CBTPA preference margins ranked second, with a mean of 9 percent, and ATPA preference margins ranked third, with a mean of 8 percent. In all three programs, the range of margins was wide—from less than 1 percent to 59 percent. In contrast, CBERA-only, GSP-only, and GSP LDC programs had low average nominal preferences of 4 percent, 4 percent, and 5 percent, respectively, and much less dispersion. The range of preference margins in CBERA-only countries was narrow—from less than 1 percent to 10 percent. For GSP-only and GSP-LDC-only beneficiaries, preference margins ranged from less than 1 percent to 26 percent and from less than 1 percent to 30 percent, respectively.

Separating margins for nonapparel products from those for apparel (see table 2.1) reveals a different picture. Nonapparel preference margins average 3 to 5 percent for ATPA, CBTPA, and CBERA countries and show little variation across countries within each program. AGOA nonapparel preference margins are much higher—5 to 10 percent for more than half the countries, and 10 to 20 percent for a few (such as Cape Verde, Kenya, Senegal, and Sierra Leone). A major exception was petroleum. Despite the importance of petroleum in U.S.-AGOA trade, average preference margins by country did not exceed 2 percent, and most were well below 1 percent.

Apparel preference margins stand in sharp contrast to margins for nonapparel products. Again if one assumes that all apparel exports from eligible countries are potentially eligible for U.S. tariff preferences, average apparel margins under the AGOA, CBTPA, and ATPA legislation are two or three times as high as those for nonapparel for nearly all member countries. AGOA apparel margins show wide variation, from a high of 22.3 percent for Uganda to a low of 6.7 percent for Niger.

U.S. Tariff Preferences on Agricultural Imports

Figure 2.2 shows U.S. agricultural imports in 2003 from beneficiary countries by tariff treatment.[15] About US$3.9 billion of U.S. agricultural imports entered duty free under nonreciprocal trade preference programs. The largest portion of this preferential trade—about 40 percent, or US$1.5 billion—came in under the GSP. Only a small portion (about US$20.4 million) came in under the GSP LDC program. The CBERA program accounted for 37 percent (US$1.4 billion) of preferential imports, followed by the ATPA program, under which a further 20 percent (US$784 million) was imported. Still relatively new in 2003, the AGOA program accounted for the remainder (US$122 million).

The regional preference programs are particularly important for countries in the Caribbean and Andean regions; almost 50 percent of U.S. agricultural imports from these countries and 40 percent from ATPA countries in 2004 entered the United States under these programs. The GSP program has dwindled in importance for these countries, with only 4 percent of CBERA and 5 percent of ATPA agricultural exports to the United States entering under the GSP. When countries in these regions had a choice between using either the regional preference program or the GSP, they used the regional program in almost 90 percent of cases. The AGOA countries made almost equal use of the two programs, shipping about 11 percent of their agricultural exports to the United States under the GSP and

FIGURE 2.2 Share of U.S. Agricultural Imports by Type of Tariff Regime, 2003

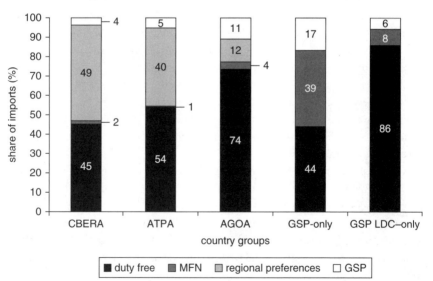

Source: USITC Trade Database and authors' calculations.

12 percent under AGOA. This is because AGOA is an extension of GSP. Thus, product coverage under the two programs does not overlap. Countries that qualified only for the GSP or the GSP LDC programs relied much less on U.S. market preferences. Less than 17 percent of agricultural exports from the GSP beneficiaries came in under preferences, whereas less than 6 percent of exports from GSP LDC beneficiaries entered under the program. Unlike nonagricultural imports, a large percentage of U.S. agricultural imports from these beneficiary countries already had MFN duty-free status.

Are U.S. Agricultural Preferences Comprehensive?

Program coverage varies widely across programs and countries. Table 2.3 shows the share of dutiable agricultural trade that was eligible for preferences in 2003. For participants in the CBERA and ATPA programs, virtually 100 percent of dutiable exports to the United States were covered by regional preferences. None of these beneficiaries shipped much to the United States that was not either duty free under MFN status or eligible for preferences. But duties on the relatively small subset of products not covered by these programs tended to be prohibitively high, averaging about 43 percent.

For some countries and territories, the GSP program alone provided broad coverage for imports. More than 90 percent of the dutiable agricultural exports from 11 of the 26 CBERA and ATPA beneficiaries were eligible for duty-free treatment under the GSP, although that program was seldom used. For the others, however, the regional programs expanded the range of products that were eligible for preferences. In the Bahamas, Costa Rica, Jamaica, Nicaragua, and the Netherlands Antilles, for example, the CBERA program offered much more preferential coverage than the GSP. Aggregating across beneficiaries within each program, one finds that 42 percent of ATPA and 48 percent of CBERA program imports consisted of products not covered under the GSP. Although the remaining products were covered by both the GSP and regional preferences, exporters generally opted for the regional program.

AGOA agricultural coverage was generally quite low for both non-LDCs and LDCs. Only Benin had 100 percent coverage under AGOA. As noted earlier, AGOA does not extend preferences to tariff lines already covered by the GSP for non-LDC beneficiaries. Thus, the sum of coverage rates provided by both programs reflects the overall preferential access provided to their exports in the U.S. market. When the coverage rates of both programs are taken into account, the range of preferences offered to AGOA non-LDC beneficiaries approaches 100 percent. All AGOA LDC beneficiaries already had 100 percent coverage rates under the GSP, with the exception of Tanzania. But the combined coverage of GSP and AGOA also afforded Tanzania full coverage.

TABLE 2.3 U.S. Agricultural Imports: Preference Coverage, Utilization, and Average Nominal Tariff Preference, 2003

	CBERA			GSP		
	Coverage[a] (%)	Utilization[b] (%)	Average tariff preference[c] (%)	GSP coverage[a] (%)	GSP utilization[b] (%)	Average tariff preference[c] (%)
Antigua	100	52	14.8	98	0	0.2
Aruba	n.a.	n.a.	n.a.	n.a.	n.a.	n.a.
Bahamas, The	100	87	4.1	n.a.	n.a.	n.a.
British Virgin Islands	100	100	3.3	100	0	3.3
Dominica	100	61	4.3	71	40	6.4
Grenada	100	0	0.5	100	0	0.5
Montserrat	n.a.	n.a.	n.a.	n.a.	n.a.	n.a.
Netherlands Antilles	100	89	6.4	0	n.a.	n.a.
St. Kitts and Nevis	100	100	0.1	100	0	0.1
St. Vincent	100	71	5.4	99	0	2.0

	CBTPA			GSP		
	Coverage[a] (%)	Utilization[b] (%)	Average tariff preference[c] (%)	Coverage[a] (%)	Utilization[b] (%)	Average tariff preference[c] (%)
Barbados	100	97	8.3	82	0	1.1
Belize	100	98	11.0	60	3	3.2
Costa Rica	100	95	6.4	40	11	6.6
Dominican Republic	100	96	7.1	87	1	4.9
El Salvador	100	70	6.3	83	36	4.9
Guatemala	100	83	6.3	79	17	5.0
Guyana	100	87	4.7	99	11	4.8
Haiti	100	95	6.3	100	4	4.9
Honduras	100	82	7.9	89	20	4.5
Jamaica	100	98	6.6	41	5	4.0
Nicaragua	100	100	8.0	0	n.a.	n.a.
Panama	100	94	7.0	96	5	3.6
St. Lucia	100	76	4.3	100	13	3.6
Trinidad and Tobago	100	93	9.4	91	6	3.5

	ATPA			GSP		
	Coverage[a] (%)	Utilization[b] (%)	Average tariff preference[c] (%)	Coverage[a] (%)	Utilization[b] (%)	Average tariff preference[c] (%)
Bolivia	100	90	2.6	92	7	2.8
Colombia	100	90	6.6	59	16	4.6
Ecuador	100	91	6.0	55	15	4.8
Peru	100	79	5.6	56	34	3.8

(Table continues on the following page.)

TABLE 2.3   U.S. Agricultural Imports: Preference Coverage, Utilization, and Average Nominal Tariff Preference, 2003 (*Continued*)

	AGOA			GSP		
	Coverage[a] (%)	Utilization[b] (%)	Average tariff preference[c] (%)	Coverage[a] (%)	Utilization[b] (%)	Average tariff preference[c] (%)
Botswana	n.a.	n.a.	n.a.	n.a.	n.a.	n.a.
Cameroon	0	n.a.	n.a.	100	92	0.5
Congo, Rep. of	0	n.a.	n.a.	100	100	4.7
Côte d'Ivoire	(.)	100	2.3	100	100	4.8
Djibouti	0	n.a.	n.a.	100	100	1.9
Eritrea	n.a.	n.a.	n.a.	n.a.	n.a.	n.a.
Gabon	n.a.	n.a.	n.a.	99	92	4.9
Ghana	1	42	10.0	13	100	4.3
Kenya	87	60	2.7	97	94	4.9
Mauritius	0	n.a.	n.a.	100	100	3.3
Namibia	0	n.a.	n.a.	99	84	3.3
Nigeria	1	0	7.2	99	84	3.3
Senegal	17	100	8.2	83	100	6.6
Seychelles	n.a.	n.a.	n.a.	n.a.	n.a.	n.a.
South Africa	80	88	9.5	16	96	4.2
Swaziland	10	77	21.9	89	100	3.4
AGOA LDC						
Benin	100	0	1.7	100	0	1.7
Cape Verde	n.a.	n.a.	n.a.	n.a.	n.a.	n.a.
Central African Republic	n.a.	n.a.	n.a.	n.a.	n.a.	n.a.

Chad	n.a.	n.a.	n.a.	n.a.	n.a.	n.a.
Congo, Dem. Rep. of[c,d]	0	n.a.	n.a.	100	100	1.0
Ethiopia	39	6	1.3	100	92	3.1
Gambia, The	n.a.	n.a.	n.a.	n.a.	n.a.	n.a.
Guinea	0	n.a.	n.a.	100	100	6.1
Lesotho	n.a.	n.a.	n.a.	n.a.	n.a.	n.a.
Madagascar	0	30	9.2	100	71	3.7
Malawi	92	n.a.	n.a.	100	49	6.3
Mali[e]	n.a.	n.a.	n.a.	n.a.	n.a.	n.a.
Mauritania	n.a.	n.a.	n.a.	n.a.	n.a.	n.a.
Mozambique	0	0	n.a.	100	100	3.4
Niger[e]	(.)	n.a.	0.1	100	0	3.2
Rwanda	n.a.	n.a.	n.a.	n.a.	n.a.	n.a.
São Tomé and Príncipe	n.a.	n.a.	n.a.	n.a.	n.a.	n.a.
Sierra Leone	60	0	3.1	100	33	11.3
Tanzania	59	94	6.8	41	67	2.8
Uganda	42	68	2.3	100	72	0.7
Zambia	41	0	92.4	100	59	5.8

Source: Authors' estimates.

Note: (.) = less than 1 percent; n.a. = not applicable.

a. Ratio of eligible imports to total dutiable imports.

b. Ratio of eligible imports to total eligible imports.

c. Difference between nominal ad valorem tariff equivalent and nominal preferential tariff. Covers all HTS eight-digit lines with eligible U.S. imports in 2003.

d. AGOA benefits delayed until October 31, 2003.

e. AGOA eligibility as of December 2003.

Table 2.3 shows coverage rates for those countries that qualified for preferences only under the GSP or GSP LDC programs. In general, these coverage rates tended to be low, averaging just 33.5 percent for all 61 countries and territories. In countries that were exclusively GSP LDC eligible, coverage rates were twice as large as in GSP-only countries.

Are U.S. Agricultural Preferences Fully Utilized?

The availability of preferences does not mean that all beneficiaries' products covered by these programs actually enter duty free. Complex and costly program regulations can limit the ability to use these preferences. Rules of origin are most often cited as the primary factor restricting beneficiaries' ability to use tariff preferences (Wainio and others 2005). Table 2.3 shows the utilization rates for each program in 2003. For agricultural exports from CBERA and ATPA countries, those rates were quite high. Except in Peru, ATPA utilization rates were 90 percent or more. Nine of 14 CBTPA countries exhibited utilization rates above 90 percent, whereas the others' rates were between 70 percent and 87 percent. CBERA-only countries showed more variability in using CBERA preferences, but rates were still fairly high. Thus, utilization of regional preferences was quite high but not complete. In contrast, beneficiaries of ATPA, CBERA, and CBTPA made little use of the GSP. In countries that did not completely use a regional program, however, the alternative GSP preferences were utilized. Thus, nearly all beneficiaries' eligible agricultural products entered under one of the preference programs. In sharp contrast, nonagricultural products from ATPA, CBERA, or CBTPA beneficiaries generally had both low coverage and low utilization under the GSP.

The results are more mixed for AGOA countries. Although 14 such countries had overall utilization rates exceeding 90 percent, 2 countries (Benin and Niger) failed to make use of either AGOA or the GSP, even though some of their exports to the United States were eligible for preferences under these programs. Several others failed to use AGOA and made only limited use of the GSP. Still relatively new in 2003, AGOA was used in agriculture by only 10 of the 38 eligible recipients, while 22 AGOA countries used the GSP.

Despite the relatively low coverage rates under the GSP, GSP-only countries recorded high utilization rates (table 2.4). Utilization averaged 89 percent, and nearly three-quarters of the 61 countries that used the GSP and GSP LDC programs did so at rates of 80 percent or more. Countries that were eligible only for the GSP LDC program showed lower average utilization (60 percent), although their coverage rates were far higher than those of GSP non-LDC beneficiaries.

TABLE 2.4   U.S. Agricultural Imports: GSP Coverage, Utilization, and Average Tariff Preference, 2003

GSP	Coverage[a] (%)	Utilization[b] (%)	Average tariff preference[c] (%)
Albania	100	34	1.9
Anguilla	100	100	6.0
Argentina	36	87	4.5
Armenia	57	98	5.5
Bahrain	n.a.	n.a.	n.a.
Bosnia and Herzegovina	90	85	5.8
British Indian Ocean Territories	n.a.	n.a.	n.a.
Brazil	24	95	4.0
Bulgaria	68	97	4.3
Chile	14	83	3.8
Christmas Island	n.a.	n.a.	n.a.
Cocos Islands	n.a.	n.a.	n.a.
Cook Islands	0	n.a.	n.a.
Croatia	87	99	4.6
Czech Republic	88	81	6.2
Egypt, Arab Rep. of	28	98	4.2
Estonia	99	97	3.7
Fiji	98	100	3.9
Georgia	23	82	4.6
Gibraltar	n.a.	n.a.	n.a.
Heard Island and McDonald Island	100	100	7.0
Hungary	71	68	4.2
India	40	95	4.2
Indonesia	37	97	4.4
Jordan	84	76	5.3
Kazakhstan	0	n.a.	n.a.
Kyrgyz Republic	n.a.	n.a.	n.a.
Latvia	6	98	4.2
Lebanon	89	97	4.6
Lithuania	2	83	5.4
Macedonia, FYR	76	97	6.6
Moldova	30	71	6.6
Mongolia	0	n.a.	n.a.
Morocco	49	41	6.8
Niue	n.a.	n.a.	n.a.
Norfolk Island	100	57	2.4
Oman	20	92	1.4
Pakistan	49	99	4.2
Papua New Guinea	100	100	3.4
Paraguay	68	100	3.7

(Table continues on the following page.)

TABLE 2.4   U.S. Agricultural Imports: GSP Coverage, Utilization, and Average Tariff Preference, 2003 (Continued)

GSP	Coverage[a] (%)	Utilization[b] (%)	Average tariff preference[c] (%)
Philippines	41	86	4.9
Pitcairn Island	100	100	5.6
Poland	88	69	5.3
Romania	14	63	4.3
Russian Federation	84	95	3.5
Slovak Republic	24	84	4.5
Solomon Islands			n.a.
Sri Lanka	93	94	3.8
St. Helena	n.a.	n.a.	n.a.
Suriname	100	100	1.8
Thailand	39	96	4.9
Tokelau	100	0	1.7
Tonga	98	100	7.0
Tunisia	94	98	4.2
Turkey	43	97	4.3
Turks and Caicos Islands	n.a.	n.a.	n.a.
Uruguay	11	94	5.3
Uzbekistan	100	100	3.8
Venezuela, R.B. de	95	99	3.7
West Bank and Gaza	100	100	1.3
Western Sahara	n.a.	n.a.	n.a.
Zimbabwe	n.a.	n.a.	n.a.
GSP LDC			
Afghanistan	1	0	3.6
Angola	n.a.	n.a.	n.a.
Bangladesh	100	68	5.9
Bhutan	100	100	3.0
Burkina Faso	100	62	3.7
Burundi	n.a.	n.a.	n.a.
Cambodia	100	88	10.6
Equatorial Guinea	n.a.	n.a.	n.a.
Kiribati	n.a.	n.a.	n.a.
Nepal	100	92	5.0
Samoa	100	23	4.0
Somalia	100	0	0.2
Togo	69	100	8.3
Vanuatu	100	0	9.6
Yemen, Rep. of	n.a.	n.a.	n.a.

Source: Authors' estimates.

Note: (.) = less than 1 percent; n.a. = not applicable.

a. Ratio of eligible imports to total dutiable imports.

b. Ratio of imports entering under preference to total eligible imports.

c. Difference between nominal ad valorem tariff equivalent and nominal preferential tariff. Covers all HTS eight-digit lines with eligible U.S. imports in 2003.

Are U.S. Agricultural Preference Margins Large?

Agricultural products deemed to be import sensitive are excluded from preferential access under U.S. programs. These products tend to have the highest MFN tariffs, whereas products accorded preferential access tend to face low MFN rates. Of the 1,432 agricultural tariff lines facing an MFN rate greater than zero, 1,204 (84 percent) are included in at least one of the nonreciprocal trade preference programs. The MFN tariffs levied on these products in 2003 ranged from less than 1 percent to 79 percent, with the average equal to 6.4 percent. About 55 percent of the products that are granted some preferential access under these programs face MFN tariffs of at least 5 percent. Many of these tariffs are levied as in-quota rates on products facing tariff rate quotas, so they are granted preferential access on only a limited quantity of imports. Clearly, the margin of preference—the extent to which the preferential tariff is below the MFN tariff—on most of these products is somewhat limited.

Tables 2.3 and 2.4 show the simple average nominal tariff preference, or preference margin, that each beneficiary faced on the subset of agricultural products it exported to the United States under these programs. The averages ranged from 0.1 percent for exports from St. Kitts and Nevis under the CBERA to 21.9 percent for exports from Swaziland under AGOA. The overall average across the 101 countries and territories was about 5.4 percent, with the average preference margins under AGOA (9.6 percent) and the CBERA (7 percent) being the highest. Few exported a product mix that faced an average nominal tariff preference greater than the 6.4 percent average tariff across all products eligible for duty-free treatment. One might expect that beneficiaries would tend to export products that face higher MFN rates because preferential exports would have a greater competitive advantage over products from countries paying MFN rates. But many of the agricultural products that beneficiaries tend to export under these programs, particularly those produced in tropical climates, already face low MFN tariffs in the United States.

Quantifying the Value of U.S. Preferences

As noted above, U.S. tariff preferences should raise exports from the beneficiary country to the United States, relative to exports from other countries whose exports face the nonpreferential tariff. The preference will also imply a rent transfer to the exporter, because the beneficiary's exports will face no tariff (or a reduced one) but will sell at the nonpreferential tariff-inclusive price in the U.S. market. The value of the tariff preference would then comprise the rent earned on the level of exports before the preference is applied and the rent earned on the additional exports sold as a result of the preferences.

Following Alexandraki and Lankes (2004), the following simplifying assumptions are made:

A.1. Products are perfect substitutes regardless of their country of origin.
A.2. The exporting country is a price taker in world markets.
A.3. All rents from preferential access accrue to the exporter.
A.4. A change in the U.S. trade policy regime will not lead to a change in world prices.

It is also assumed that in programs with apparel preferences, all apparel is potentially eligible for those preferences. Under these assumptions, the duty savings from preference programs can be approximated by the difference between the duties that would have been collected on existing levels of U.S. imports from a beneficiary in the absence of any program and the actual duties collected given the program. The value of preferences is then the beneficiary's duty savings as a share of its dutiable exports to the United States. Assuming that preferences are fully utilized, their value can be calculated using equation 2.1:

$$Value_j = \sum_i (t_i^{MFN} - t_{ij}^p) \left(\frac{Customs\ Value_{ij}}{Customs\ Value_j} \right) * Eligibility_{ij}, \qquad (2.1)$$

where i is the HTS eight-digit product, j is the exporting country, p is the preference program, and *Customs Value* is the value of dutiable exports to the United States. $Eligibility_{ij}$ equals 1 if the product is eligible for any U.S. preference and 0 if it is not.

Note that calculating equation 2.1 will yield an upper-bound estimate on value for at least two reasons. First, imports from beneficiaries are overstated, since they would be below existing levels in the absence of preferences. Second, the MFN tariff overstates the price increase in the U.S. market attributable to tariffs, because some U.S. trading partners are part of reciprocal preferential trade agreements such as the North American Free Trade Agreement (NAFTA).

The four assumptions listed earlier and the assumptions of complete apparel eligibility and full utilization of preferences all suggest that equation 2.1 would yield upper-bound estimates. Market power and the degree of rent transfer are difficult to quantify. However, the preference utilization rates presented herein reveal that utilization is less than full, often even at the HTS eight-digit level. To incorporate this incomplete utilization, the value of preferences is recalculated using equation 2.2:

$$Value_j = \sum_i (t_i^{MFN} - t_{ij}^p) \left(\frac{Customs\ Value_{ij}}{Customs\ Value_j} \right) * Eligibility_{ij} * Utility_{ij}, \qquad (2.2)$$

where $Utility_{ij}$ is the percentage of imports (again, at the HTS eight-digit level) that entered the United States under any preference program.

Table 2.5 shows the value of all preference programs for all beneficiaries and for all LDC beneficiaries. It then shows the value of preferences for beneficiaries of both regional programs and the GSP and for beneficiaries of GSP alone. For each group, the table shows the value of all preferences for all beneficiaries and for individual countries with duty savings that exceed 5 percent of total dutiable exports to the United States. The first set of columns shows the values assuming full utilization (from equation 2.1) and decomposes these values into the shares attributable to nonagricultural and agricultural preferences. The second set of columns shows the values after incorporating actual utilization (from equation 2.2).

The overall figures in the first set of columns in table 2.5 suggest that the potential duty savings from all U.S. preference programs is a small share of beneficiaries' dutiable exports to the United States. Across beneficiary groups, however, countries in the CBTPA program and in the AGOA LDC program show duty savings that exceed 10 percent of dutiable exports to the United States. Most of this value is attributable to nonagricultural preferences. The most striking feature of table 2.5 is that 35 countries show preference values exceeding 5 percent of dutiable exports to the United States: 3 CBERA-only, 12 CBTPA, 2 ATPA, 15 AGOA, and 3 GSP beneficiaries. Values range from 5.1 percent (Mali) to 22.8 percent (Cape Verde) and tend to be highest for members of the CBTPA and AGOA. For Belize, Botswana, Cape Verde, El Salvador, Ethiopia, Guatemala, Haiti, Honduras, Kenya, Lesotho, Madagascar, Mauritius, Swaziland, and Uganda, the value of U.S. preferences exceeded 15 percent of dutiable exports to the United States in 2003. The second notable feature is that a large proportion of beneficiaries in regional programs make the list, but only three from the GSP-only group do. The third interesting feature is that almost universally the largest proportion of the value of preferences is attributable to nonagricultural preferences.

The second set of columns in table 2.5 shows that the incorporation of actual utilization significantly changes the assessment of the value of preferences for quite a few beneficiaries. The overall values of preferences for those in the CBTPA and AGOA LDC programs fall but remain quite high—at 8.8 percent and 13.6 percent of dutiable exports, respectively. The number of countries with preferences valued above 5 percent of dutiable exports drops to 29. Nearly all those that are members of regional programs remain on the list, but only one of the exclusively GSP-eligible beneficiaries remains. The magnitudes of the values, however, change significantly. The countries for which the value of U.S. preferences exceeds 15 percent of dutiable exports now includes only Belize, Botswana, Cape Verde, Ethiopia, Kenya, Lesotho, Madagascar, Swaziland, and Uganda. The CBTPA beneficiaries show the largest adjustment in value after incorporating utilization, although values for half of them still exceed 10 percent. With a few exceptions, AGOA member countries show virtually no change in the value of preferences.

TABLE 2.5 U.S. Imports: Value of Preferences, 2003

Beneficiaries	Assuming full utilization				Incorporating actual utilization			
	Value (% of total exports to U.S.)	Value (% of dutiable exports to U.S.)	Nonagriculture (% of dutiable exports to U.S.)	Agriculture (% of dutiable exports to U.S.)	Value (% of total exports to U.S.)	Value (% of dutiable exports to U.S.)	Nonagriculture (% of dutiable exports to U.S.)	Agriculture (% of dutiable exports to U.S.)
All preference programs								
All	2.0	3.0	2.8	0.2	1.5	2.3	2.1	0.2
All LDC	2.0	2.2	2.1	0.1	1.8	1.9	1.9	0.0
CBERA-only and GSP								
All	0.4	0.5	0.5	0.0	0.4	0.4	0.4	0.0
Antigua and Barbuda	1.0	5.1	4.4	0.7	0.2	0.8	0.1	0.6
Dominica	3.5	5.3	4.4	1.0	3.4	5.2	4.3	0.9
St. Vincent	4.4	5.3	5.2	0.1	4.3	5.3	5.2	0.1
CBTPA and GSP								
All	8.7	12.7	12.0	0.7	6.0	8.8	8.0	0.7
Barbados	2.6	5.6	1.1	4.5	2.4	5.1	0.6	4.5
Belize	8.2	17.5	4.8	12.7	7.8	16.5	3.8	12.7
Costa Rica	4.2	9.9	7.1	2.9	3.5	8.2	5.4	2.9
Dominican Republic	9.8	12.2	11.8	0.4	7.9	9.9	9.5	0.4
El Salvador	15.3	16.1	16.0	0.1	10.1	10.7	10.5	0.1
Guatemala	12.4	15.6	14.3	1.3	5.1	6.4	5.1	1.3
Guyana	2.5	12.5	11.2	1.4	2.2	11.3	10.0	1.3
Haiti	17.3	18.1	18.0	0.1	12.3	12.9	12.8	0.1
Honduras	14.2	16.1	15.7	0.4	11.2	12.7	12.2	0.4
Jamaica	3.1	9.9	8.3	1.7	4.5	8.8	7.1	1.6
Nicaragua	11.9	14.6	14.2	0.4	4.7	5.7	5.3	0.4
St. Lucia	5.2	6.8	6.7	0.1	1.2	1.6	1.5	0.1

	1	2	3	4	5	6	7	8
ATPA and GSP								
All	2.7	3.8	3.0	0.8	2.2	3.1	2.3	0.8
Bolivia	5.5	7.9	7.8	0.1	5.2	7.5	7.4	0.1
Peru	5.2	6.2	5.3	0.9	4.8	5.7	4.8	0.9
AGOA and GSP								
All	1.4	1.8	1.7	0.1	1.1	1.4	1.3	0.0
Botswana	11.8	21.8	21.8	0.0	10.7	19.9	19.9	0.0
Kenya	14.4	17.4	17.4	0.1	13.4	16.3	16.2	0.1
Mauritius	15.6	16.6	16.6	0.0	8.0	8.6	8.5	0.0
Namibia	6.2	13.1	13.1	0.0	4.8	10.3	10.3	0.0
Swaziland	17.7	18.5	18.3	0.2	15.8	16.5	16.4	0.2
AGOA LDC and GSP								
All	9.7	14.4	13.7	0.7	9.1	13.6	13.0	0.5
Cape Verde	17.3	22.8	22.8	0.0	14.6	19.2	19.2	0.0
Ethiopia	1.6	15.6	14.9	0.7	1.6	15.5	14.8	0.7
Lesotho	18.8	18.8	18.8	0.0	17.9	17.9	17.9	0.0
Madagascar	8.6	16.5	16.5	0.0	8.2	15.8	15.8	0.0
Malawi	13.0	14.5	6.7	7.9	10.9	12.3	6.5	5.8
Mali	1.8	5.1	5.1	0.0	0.8	2.1	2.1	0.0
Mozambique	7.7	8.1	5.8	2.3	7.7	8.1	5.8	2.3
Tanzania	0.9	7.4	6.6	0.8	0.8	6.8	6.0	0.7
Uganda	1.0	18.8	18.8	0.0	0.9	16.9	16.9	0.0
Zambia	0.3	5.7	2.7	3.0	0.2	3.4	2.7	0.7
GSP-only								
All	0.9	1.4	1.3	0.1	0.7	1.1	1.0	0.1
St. Helena	0.6	5.7	5.7	0.0	0.0	0.0	0.0	0.0
Tonga	0.2	6.2	1.1	5.0	0.2	5.1	0.1	5.0
GSP-LDC-only								
All	0.4	0.4	0.4	0.0	0.4	0.4	0.4	0.0
Vanuatu	0.3	6.6	1.5	5.2	0.1	1.5	1.5	0.0

Source: Authors' estimates.

TABLE 2.6   U.S. Nonagricultural Imports: Value of Preferences, 2003

Beneficiaries	Incorporating actual utilization (% of total dutiable nonagricultural exports to the U.S.)		
	Value	Nonapparel	Apparel
CBERA-only and GSP			
St. Vincent	5.5	5.5	0.0
Dominica	5.3	5.3	0.0
CBTPA and GSP			
Guyana	13.6	2.8	10.8
Haiti	13.0	0.2	12.8
Honduras	12.8	0.1	12.7
Jamaica	12.7	0.1	12.6
El Salvador	10.9	0.1	10.8
Dominican Republic	10.6	1.1	9.5
Belize	9.9	0.1	9.8
Costa Rica	8.2	1.2	7.0
Nicaragua	6.1	0.1	6.0
Guatemala	5.8	0.2	5.6
ATPA and GSP			
Bolivia	7.6	4.1	3.5
Peru	5.2	1.0	4.2
AGOA and GSP			
Botswana	19.9	0.0	19.9
Swaziland	17.2	0.0	17.2
Kenya	16.9	0.0	16.9
Namibia	10.3	0.4	9.9
Mauritius	8.6	0.1	8.5
AGOA LDC and GSP			
Ethiopia	22.0	0.3	21.7
Malawi	19.9	0.0	19.9
Cape Verde	19.2	0.6	18.6
Lesotho	17.9	0.0	17.9
Mozambique	17.8	0.0	17.8
Uganda	17.1	0.1	17.0
Madagascar	15.9	0.1	15.8
Tanzania	7.3	0.6	6.7

Source: Authors' estimates.

Once again, the largest proportion of value for all countries comes from nonagricultural trade preferences.

Although the value of preferences may be low for some countries when measured against total dutiable exports, it may represent a large share of the value of their nonagricultural or agricultural exports. Table 2.6 lists countries whose nonagricultural preferences exceed 5 percent of dutiable nonagricultural exports to the United States, after incorporating utilization. This list is nearly the same as the list in table 2.5. For 17 of these 29 countries, preference values exceeded 10 percent. With a few exceptions, most of this value is attributable to apparel preferences. Other significant products include petroleum-related products, chemicals, jewelry, and electrical machinery.[16]

Table 2.7 lists 23 countries and territories whose agricultural preference values exceeded 5 percent of dutiable agricultural exports to the United States, after incorporating actual utilization. Most do not appear in table 2.5. Five of these beneficiaries had preference values exceeding 10 percent. Half of the total preference value of all agricultural products in 2003 was accounted for by five products: melons, fresh-cut flowers, frozen orange juice, raw cane sugar, and fresh asparagus.

There are at least three reasons why apparel accounts for such a large share of the value of preferences for many countries. First, apparel often accounts for a large share of exports; second, apparel exporters had high apparel utilization rates; and third, apparel exports had relatively high preference margins. But the removal of quantitative restrictions on apparel in January 2005 (with the completion of the Agreement on Textiles and Clothing) reduced the relative prices of apparel imports from China, South Asia, and the member countries of the Association of Southeast Asian Nations, for which quantitative restrictions had been high. Thus, U.S. apparel imports from the CBTPA, ATPA, and AGOA beneficiaries were likely to fall relative to their 2003 levels. Even if tariff preference margins in 2005 remained similar to those in 2003, these margins would be applied to a smaller value of apparel imports, thus reducing the value of the preferences below those shown in tables 2.5 and 2.6.

Data from the U.S. Department of Commerce suggest that between 2003 and 2005 U.S. apparel imports from Sub-Saharan Africa dropped by 3.1 percent and imports from members of the CBI dropped by 0.2 percent; in contrast, apparel imports from ATPA countries rose by 35.9 percent (ITA OTEXA 2006). These aggregate figures do not suggest a radical drop in the value of apparel preferences. But changes in imports varied greatly within these regions.[17]

The results in table 2.5 suggest that more countries may be affected by the removal of U.S. preferences than previously thought. To facilitate a comparison, table 2.5 includes the value of preferences calculated with respect to total exports to the United States. Using an approach similar to this study, Brenton and Ikezuki

TABLE 2.7   U.S. Agricultural Imports: Value of Preferences, 2003

Beneficiaries	Incorporating actual utilization (% of total dutiable agricultural exports to the U.S.)			
	Value	Fresh and processed fruits and vegetables	Sugar	Other
CBERA-only and GSP				
Netherlands Antilles	5.7	0.0	0.0	5.7
CBTPA and GSP				
Barbados	22.5	0.0	0.0	22.5
Belize	20.6	19.2	1.3	0.0
Guatemala	11.0	8.7	1.3	1.0
Honduras	9.2	7.3	0.4	1.5
Costa Rica	8.3	7.3	0.1	0.8
Trinidad and Tobago	5.4	0.0	0.0	5.4
ATPA and GSP				
Peru	11.0	10.2	0.3	0.5
Colombia	6.7	0.3	0.6	5.8
Ecuador	6.1	2.2	0.2	3.8
AGOA and GSP				
Senegal	6.8	2.8	0.0	4.0
AGOA LDC and GSP				
Malawi	8.6	0.0	0.3	8.3
Guinea	5.6	2.5	0.0	3.1
GSP-only				
Tonga	7.5	7.5	0.0	0.0
Lebanon	6.8	5.3	0.4	1.1
Heard Island and McDonald Island	6.4	0.0	0.0	6.4
Paraguay	6.4	0.0	6.3	0.1
Anguilla	6.0	0.0	0.0	6.0
Pitcairn Island	5.6	0.0	0.0	5.6
Bosnia and Herzegovina	5.5	0.0	0.0	5.5
GSP-LDC-only				
Cambodia	9.9	9.9	0.0	0.0
Bangladesh	6.9	0.4	0.0	6.5
Togo	5.7	0.0	0.0	5.7

Source: Authors' estimates.

(2004) find six AGOA countries whose preference values in 2002 exceeded 5 percent of total exports to the United States after incorporating preference utilization: Lesotho, Madagascar, Malawi, Mauritius, Kenya, and Swaziland. In the present study, the results for 2003 include these six (with similar value estimates), plus Botswana, Cape Verde, and Mozambique, with much higher value estimates. Both studies find that most of this value is attributable to preferential access for apparel. Using more aggregated data and assuming full utilization, Alexandraki and Lankes (2004) identify 18 countries for which the value of all preferences from Canada, the European Union, Japan, and the United States combined, exceeded 5 percent of total exports. Table 2.5 shows 19 countries—half of Alexandraki and Lankes' list and 10 additional countries—for which the value of U.S. preferences alone exceeds 5 percent of total exports, if full utilization is assumed. After actual utilization is incorporated, 17 have values that exceed this threshold.

Concluding Remarks

Close examination of U.S. import data reveals that members of ATPA, the CBTPA, and the CBERA tended to have very high utilization of regional preferences but lower utilization of the GSP. CBERA utilization was on average lower and more varied than utilization under the other regional programs. AGOA non-LDC beneficiaries showed high combined utilization of AGOA and GSP preferences. In many cases, they fully used both preference programs. AGOA LDC beneficiaries—for which AGOA coverage was less generous than GSP coverage (particularly for nonagricultural, nonapparel products)—showed somewhat lower combined utilization rates, making more use of the GSP than the AGOA. In general, utilization of preferences was strongly related to preference coverage—except for the GSP program. Beneficiaries eligible for GSP only exhibited high GSP utilization rates, despite relatively low coverage rates. This finding was particularly true for beneficiaries whose exports were dominated by apparel.

Although utilization rates are high, average tariff preference margins in the regional programs for nonapparel exports were relatively low for most beneficiaries. The AGOA countries generally had higher nonagricultural preference margins than did other beneficiaries. For all apparel-eligible countries, preference margins on apparel were about three times those of other nonagricultural products. For nonagricultural products, these low margins are mainly the result of low U.S. MFN tariffs. In contrast, for agricultural products, low preference margins are largely attributable to the exclusion of products that face high tariffs. Overall, average GSP preference margins are lower than those offered by regional preference programs, largely because of less extensive product coverage and the lack of apparel preferences.

Although the erosion of U.S. tariff preferences may not have large impacts on development, it may be more significant for a larger number of countries and products than previously thought. After actual utilization was incorporated, the values of U.S. 2003 tariff preferences in 29 countries exceeded 5 percent of dutiable exports to the United States. In 17 countries preference values exceeded 5 percent of total exports to the United States. For nine of these countries, U.S. preferences were valued at 15 percent or more of dutiable exports. The largest proportion of this value was attributable to nonagricultural preferences, particularly preferences on apparel. The removal of U.S. quantitative restrictions on apparel trade reduced apparel imports from CBI and AGOA countries, raised apparel imports from ATPA countries, and led to a wide variation in increases and decreases in imports across beneficiaries in 2005. Thus, more research is needed to clarify the effect of the completion of the Agreement on Textiles and Clothing on the value of U.S. nonreciprocal preferences.

Several other caveats bear noting. This study assumed that the difference between the MFN tariff and the preferential tariff accurately represented the rent transfer on each dollar of exports from the beneficiaries. But the existence of NAFTA and other regional agreements would tend to reduce the prevailing tariff-inclusive U.S. price below the MFN tariff-inclusive price, lowering the rent a beneficiary could earn. In addition, to the extent that this rent is actually shared by the exporters, the intermediaries, or the United States itself, the value of U.S. preferences for beneficiaries would fall. Finally, this analysis has assumed that world prices are unaffected by the introduction of tariff preferences. Yet some beneficiaries are large enough to affect the prevailing price in the U.S. market, thus lowering the value of their preferences. These limitations suggest that further research is needed to assess the importance of preference erosion for beneficiaries.

Notes

1. In this chapter, the term *developing countries* includes territories that are possessions of industrial countries or administer themselves through the governments of such countries (for example, the Netherlands Antilles, the British Virgin Islands, Australia's Christmas Island, New Zealand's Cook Islands, and disputed territories such as Western Sahara and the West Bank).

2. In 2003, 41 countries were eligible for expanded benefits under the U.S. GSP LDC program.

3. Competitive needs limits are ceilings set for each product and each country. They are intended to prevent the extension of preferential treatment to countries that are considered competitive in the production of an item. Barring certain qualifications, a country automatically loses its eligibility for a given product in the year following that in which the ceiling is exceeded.

4. Although Botswana and Namibia are not LDCs, they were given third-country fabric provision eligibility in 2003.

5. For additional eligibility criteria, see USITC (2005: 1–10).

6. Hereafter, ATPA refers to both ATPA and the Andean Trade Promotion and Drug Eradication Act.

7. Note that HS chapters 61 and 62 include the value of apparel entering the United States under the production-sharing program (HTS 9802.00.80), although that value is not broken out separately.

8. Customs value is equivalent to free-on-board value.

9. In some cases, the claim is later denied, but these cases represent a tiny proportion.

10. U.S. AVE tariffs for HTS eight-digit items with specific or compound rates are estimated by the following steps.

 a. If there is U.S. MFN import trade for an HTS item, the AVE is estimated by dividing duties by dutiable U.S. imports. Trade entering under special tariff preference programs is not included.

 b. If there is no U.S. MFN import trade for an item, the quantity and customs value of all U.S. imports under that item are used, and the MFN-specific and compound rates are applied to calculate the tariffs that "would have been collected" had the trade entered as MFN trade rather than under a special program. The duties thus calculated are divided by the customs value to estimate the AVE.

 c. If there is no U.S. import trade for an item in a given year, the quantity and customs value of imports (MFN trade if available, all trade if not) of that item from the previous full year are used, and the MFN-specific and compound rates for the current year are used to calculate the tariffs that "would have been collected" had the trade entered as MFN trade in the current year. The duties thus calculated are divided by the customs value to estimate the AVE.

 d. If there is no U.S. import trade for the given year or the previous year, the Office of Tariff Affairs and Trade Agreements of the USITC is asked to provide an estimated AVE.

11. *Nonagricultural products* are defined as all those not specified in annex 1 of the WTO Agreement on Agriculture. Detailed data are available from the authors on request. All values are based on imports in HS chapters 1 through 97.

12. The alternate extreme would be to assume that the apparel trade that qualified for preferences in 2003 is the maximum that could have qualified that year. This assumption would imply that utilization rates were always 100 percent.

13. The eight countries were Cameroon, Chad, the Republic of Congo, the Democratic Republic of Congo, Côte d'Ivoire, Gabon, Nigeria, and the Seychelles.

14. Colombia and Ecuador have higher GSP utilization rates but very low GSP coverage rates.

15. *Agricultural products* are here defined as those specified in annex 1 of the WTO Agreement on Agriculture. Detailed data are available from the authors on request.

16. Although the value of preferences for some AGOA countries derives exclusively from petroleum-related exports, none of these countries showed values exceeding 1 percent of dutiable exports to the United States.

17. For example, within Sub-Saharan Africa, apparel imports from Swaziland grew by 14.4 percent while imports from Mauritius fell by 38.1 percent. Within the CBI, imports from Nicaragua grew by 47.9 percent, while those from the Dominican Republic fell by 12.9 percent.

References

Alexandraki, Katerina, and Hans Peter Lankes. 2004. "The Impact of Preference Erosion on Middle-Income Developing Countries." IMF Working Paper 04/169, International Monetary Fund, Washington, DC.

Brenton, Paul, and Takako Ikezuki. 2004. "The Initial and Potential Impact of Preferential Access to the U.S. Market under the African Growth and Opportunity Act." Policy Research Working Paper 3262, World Bank, Washington, DC.

ITA OTEXA (International Trade Administration, Office of Textiles and Apparel). 2006. "Major Shippers Report." ITA, Washington, DC. http://www.otexa.ita.doc.gov/msr/cat1.htm.

Office of the U.S. Trade Representative. 1999. *U.S. Generalized System of Preferences Guidebook.* Washington, DC: Office of the U.S. Trade Representative. http://www.ustr.gov/assets/Trade _Development/Preference_Programs.

Oxfam. 2005. "Scaling Up Aid for Trade." Oxfam Briefing Note (November). http://www.uneca.org/atpc/documents/May/oxfam%20on%20aid_trade.pdf.

Panagariya, Arvind. 2002. "EU Preferential Trade Arrangements and Developing Countries." *World Economy* 25 (10): 1415–32.

USITC (U.S. International Trade Commission). 2004a. *The Impact of the Andean Trade Preference Act.* 10th report. USITC Publication 3725. Washington, DC: USITC.

———. 2004b. *U.S. Trade and Investment with Sub-Saharan Africa.* 5th annual report. USITC Publication 3741. Washington, DC: USITC.

———. 2005. *The Impact of the Caribbean Basin Economic Recovery Act.* 17th report. USITC Publication 3804. Washington, DC: USITC.

Wainio, John, Shahia Shapouri, Michael Trueblood, and Paul Gibson. 2005. "Agricultural Trade Preferences and the Developing Countries." USDA-ERS Economic Research Report 6, U.S. Department of Agriculture, Economic Research Service, Washington, DC. http://www.ers.usda.gov/Publications/ERR6.

WTO (World Trade Organization). 2004. "Statement by the IMF Managing Director," WTO News, October. http://www.wto.org/english/news_e/news04_e/gc_stat_imf_22oct04_e.htm.

3

WHAT ARE EUROPEAN UNION TRADE PREFERENCES WORTH FOR SUB-SAHARAN AFRICAN AND OTHER DEVELOPING COUNTRIES?

Fabien Candau and Sébastien Jean

As European Union (EU) Trade Commissioner Pascal Lamy put it, "In the days before we had a Common Foreign and Security Policy, . . . the principal instrument of EU foreign policy was trade preferences" (Lamy 2002: 1403). This fact has led to a situation in which "the [European Commission] maintains preferential trade arrangements with virtually all countries" (Sapir 1998: 717), the only exceptions being the Democratic People's Republic of Korea and a handful of non-European developed countries. The EU is by far the largest market for developing countries' agricultural exports in general and is especially important for most former colonies. The EU's trade preferences are thus important from the perspective of development. This situation is undoubtedly what the ministers of trade of the member states of the African Union had in mind when they recognized, in the Grand-Baie Declaration of June 20, 2003, "the vital importance of long-standing preferences for African countries," and subsequently expressed on three occasions

The study described here benefited from partial financial support by the World Bank. It also received partial financial support under the Agricultural Trade Agreements project funded by the European Commission (Specific Targeted Research Project, contract 513666). The authors thankfully acknowledge Lionel Fontagné's contribution to an earlier stage of this work. They are grateful to the European Commission services for access to the customs data. Special thanks go to Reinhard Binder, Jacques Gallezot, David Laborde, and Xavier Pichot for their help and comments; Louise Curran and Stefano Inama for useful suggestions; and Will Martin for guidance.

their concerns about the erosion of preferences. These concerns are echoed by specific provisions in the draft modalities for market access liberalization in the Doha Round (WTO 2008a, 2008b).

In fact, preferential trade arrangements, whether reciprocal or not, play a central role in shaping trade opportunities for numerous developing countries, notably the poorest ones. They are especially important for Sub-Saharan African countries, owing to the nonreciprocal preferences they are granted, in particular through the Cotonou Partnership Agreement. The prospect of multilateral liberalization thus raises serious concerns about the erosion of these preferences and the possible consequences of such erosion (Bouët, Fontagné, and Jean 2006).

This chapter studies how effective the EU's preferential agreements are in granting developing countries improved market access.[1] To what extent are preferences indeed used by exporters when entering the EU market? What is their value for receiving countries? The EU case raises several methodological issues owing to the complexity of European trade policy, which entails numerous, frequently overlapping preferential arrangements. The analysis here focuses on nonreciprocal preferences granted to developing countries—particularly Sub-Saharan African countries.[2] Still, this chapter covers all agreements and all partners, in order to give a complete picture and because of the difficulty of analyzing some schemes separately from others.

Analysts typically assess the consequences of these trade preferences on the basis of statutory protection—that is, in terms of the preferential access for which exporters are eligible. This access, however, does not necessarily reflect the protection level faced in practice. Indeed, benefiting from a preferential scheme requires complying with several requirements, whether technical, administrative, or related to rules of origin. Given the cost and sometimes the complexity of these constraints, the benefit of preferential agreements cannot be considered automatic, costless, or unconditional. On the contrary, recent studies suggest that exporters systematically underuse EU preferences (Brenton 2003; Brenton and Manchin 2003) with an especially thin utilization of the Everything but Arms (EBA) initiative. This finding is not uncontroversial, however. Inama (2003: 36) shows that utilization of preferences for less developed countries (LDCs) in the African, Caribbean, and Pacific (ACP) states has been "above 70 percent on average for the whole period from 1998 to 2002" and emphasizes that utilization depends on a number of factors, such as the extent of the preference, supply capacity, and implications of the rules of origin. Gallezot (2003) finds that a large proportion of the EU's agricultural imports use a preferential rate.

These results might seem contradictory at first glance. However, they do not deal with exactly the same problem. For instance, Brenton focuses on the utilization of the

EBA initiative (including the year in which it was first implemented, 2001), whereas Gallezot takes a broader measure by studying the utilization of any of the preferential agreements the exporter is eligible for. Indeed, EU trade policy is fairly complex, and numerous trade partners benefit from various preferential agreements, as is the case for Sub-Saharan Africa LDCs with the EBA initiative and the Cotonou Agreement. The analysis of preference utilization must therefore be adapted to this specific context, in which, in addition to the administrative requirements, the rules of origin vary from one agreement to another. The utilization of a given preferential scheme cannot be properly studied without taking into account whether an alternative preferential scheme is offered to the exporter. This is an important premise of the analysis in this chapter, which will take a broad view of all preferential agreements offered by the EU, whether reciprocal or not.

This analysis also argues that the level of the preferential margin—that is, the difference between the preferential and the most-favored-nation (MFN) applied duty—should be accounted for. The economic significance of a given scheme (and of its possible underutilization) is obviously higher, the higher the preferential margin is. Hence, the analysis also uses detailed data about EU statutory protection in association with customs declarations.

Although this analysis covers all trade partners, it devotes special attention to Sub-Saharan African countries for two reasons. The trade relationship between these countries and the EU is particularly relevant, and the erosion of preferences for these countries resulting from future multilateral liberalization has generated the most concern. This study uses data from 2001, the most recent year for which complete statutory and customs data are available at the tariff-line level. More recent anecdotal evidence suggests that the situation has not dramatically changed since then.

European Trade Policy: The Scope and Depth of Preferential Agreements

The EU is by far the largest contributor to the proliferation of trade agreements worldwide, with more than 50 regional trade agreements notified to the World Trade Organization (WTO) up to 2003. As illustrated by figure 3.1, even a simplified overview of the EU's trade policy remains quite intricate. The roots in the political economy of this proliferation of agreements lie in three factors: the heterogeneity of the EU; the specific role played by its trade policy (long the community's only competence in terms of foreign policy); and the strong demand from trading partners, as described in Sapir (1998; see also Lamy 2002 and Panagariya 2002).

Figure 3.1 EU Trade Policy in 2001

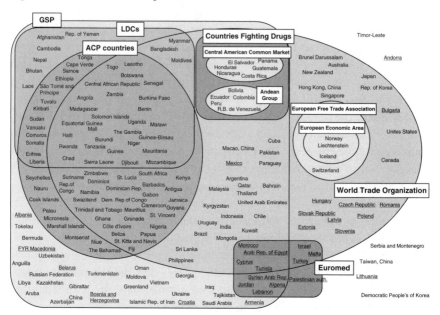

Source: Authors' adaptation, based on Bouët and others (2001).

Note: An underlined country name signals a bilateral agreement with the EU. This figure is a simplified representation of EU trade agreements in 2001. It is not exhaustive, and it does not show the variation across countries of the product coverage of agreements.

Two kinds of schemes must be distinguished from the outset: free trade agreements and nonreciprocal schemes. Free trade agreements are bilaterally agreed-upon, reciprocal commitments between the parties, whereas nonreciprocal schemes are unilaterally granted by the EU to developing countries. Free trade agreements are intended to be a tool of regional economic integration, with legal basis in the multilateral arena under article XXIV of the General Agreement on Tariffs and Trade (GATT). The nonreciprocal agreements grant developing countries more favorable treatment (under the enabling clause or through specific waivers from the WTO). The noncontractual nature of several nonreciprocal schemes—the Generalized System of Preferences (GSP), in particular—also involves uncertainty as to their future (except for the EBA initiative, discussed later) because they can be unilaterally changed.

These numerous agreements can be classified into a few categories. A first set includes close, neighborhood, reciprocal agreements within Europe, including the agreement with the European Free Trade Association, bilateral free trade agreements with Central and Eastern European countries, and a few additional bilateral agreements. Some of these agreements are now defunct, but the categorization is relevant for 2001.

The other agreements concern developing countries. The most inclusive is the GSP, which grants a nonreciprocal, preferential access for a large scope of products, although with a limited preferential margin for so-called sensitive products. The GSP is also temporary and subject to periodic revisions. Graduation measures (that is, exclusion of some or all products from the scheme) are taken when "beneficiary countries may have reached, in certain sectors, a level of competitiveness which ensures further growth even without preferential access to the EU market" (European Commission 2004: 15). The GSP is associated with relatively stringent rules of origin. No diagonal cumulation is allowed among beneficiaries, except under a handful of regional agreements (among them the Association of South East Asian Nations and the South Asian Association for Regional Cooperation).[3] A special and more beneficial regime has been granted in the past to countries fighting drugs. In 2001, this regime concerned only Central American and Andean Pact countries.[4] The latest GSP revised this approach and provides very generous preferences to countries that demonstrate a commitment to sustainable development by ratifying key international treaties and conventions.

In addition, starting in March 2001, the EBA initiative granted duty-free, quota-free access to LDCs for all products but arms, with delayed implementation for sugar, rice, and bananas. Although embedded in the GSP scheme and thus associated with the same general rules, the EBA is not restricted by any limitation on duration, coverage, or protection measure.

The last set of agreements includes a number of bilateral and regional agreements (like those with Chile, South Africa, and the Mediterranean countries) that offer deeper preferences than those to which countries would have been entitled under the GSP. The Cotonou Partnership Agreement between the EU and ACP countries, following up on the former Lomé conventions, is especially noteworthy: this nonreciprocal agreement grants most ACP products duty-free access to the EU market (as well as important preferential tariff quotas) and is particularly relevant to benefiting countries.[5] The Cotonou Agreement allows full cumulation, whereby all operations carried out in the participating countries are taken into account in establishing origin. This provision is far more liberal than the GSP rules of origin, which allow only for bilateral or (in specific cases already mentioned) diagonal cumulation.[6] In addition, the "general tolerance rule," which permits manufacturers to use nonoriginating materials up to a specific percentage value of the ex works price, is higher under the Cotonou Agreement than under the GSP (15 instead of 10 percent; see Brenton 2003 for more details).

Compared with the other "Quad" markets (Canada, Japan, and the United States), the EU appears to offer a relatively high preferential margin to developing countries (table 3.1). This benefit is especially clear for LDCs, which face ad valorem equivalent (AVE) protection of close to zero as a result of the EBA initiative. For non-LDCs, the average preferential margin in the EU market is small (0.8 percentage point) but still

TABLE 3.1 Protection Faced in Quad Markets in 2001, by Partner and Sector

a. Average AVE protection by sector and by partner

Importer	By sector			By partner			
	Agriculture	Manufacturing	Textiles	Rich	DCs	LDCs	Total
Canada	14.9	2.1	10.8	5.7	5.3	4.9	3.4
EU-15	17.9	2.0	5.7	3.5	2.7	0.8	3.1
Japan	35.3	0.9	6.8	3.9	3.9	1.6	3.9
United States	5.0	1.7	9.4	2.3	2.4	5.1	2.3

b. Average AVE protection by sector, for each partner

Importer	Partner								
	Developed countries			Non-LDC developing countries			LDCs		
	Agriculture	Manufacturing	Textiles	Agriculture	Manufacturing	Textiles	Agriculture	Manufacturing	Textiles
Canada	18.1	2.0	11.5	5.8	0.7	13.4	0.4	0.0	16.2
EU-15	18.5	2.5	6.6	14.7	0.8	6.5	2.8	0.0	1.0
Japan	33.0	0.7	10.2	18.1	0.4	10.1	11.6	0.2	0.1
United States	5.8	1.6	9.7	3.7	0.8	10.9	5.2	0.1	13.0

Source: Bouët and others 2008, based on MAcMap.

Note: Agriculture refers to agriculture and agrofood. *Textiles* refers to textile, clothing, leather, and leather products. *EU-15* refers to Austria, Belgium, Denmark, Finland, France, Germany, Greece, Ireland, Italy, Luxembourg, the Netherlands, Portugal, Spain, Sweden, and the United Kingdom.

better than what is available in other Quad markets. In manufacturing, protection is low, but for developing countries it is virtually zero for products other than textiles and clothing. In those cases, non-LDCs do not benefit from any significant preferential margin. In agriculture, the margin is 3.3 percentage points for non-LDCs and as much as 14.3 percentage points for LDCs. Note, however, that the average preferential margin offered to all developing countries (LDC or not) for agricultural products is higher in Canada and in Japan, while it remains low in the United States.[7]

It is also worth emphasizing the particular importance of the European market for developing countries. The case of agricultural products is especially relevant, given both the high level of trade barriers in this sector and the overwhelming importance of these products in developing countries' exports. As illustrated by table 3.2, the EU-25 imports of agricultural products from developing countries were significantly higher in 2001 than the sum of Japanese and U.S. imports of those products.[8] Among providers, developing countries (especially LDCs) accounted for a far larger share of agricultural imports in the EU than they did in Japan or the United States. These figures emphasize the potential importance of EU trade preferences to developing countries. It is therefore worth assessing what their use is in practice.

The Use of EU Preferences: Prima Facie Evidence

Because conditions are attached to benefit-of-trade preferences, their value is not only a question of statutory advantages but also of benefits reaped in practice. This section reconsiders the evidence about the utilization of EU preferential

TABLE 3.2   Agricultural Imports in Three of the Quad Markets by Group of Exporters, 2001

Countries	EU-25 Value (US$ million)	EU-25 Share (%)	United States Value (US$ million)	United States Share (%)	Japan Value (US$ million)	Japan Share (%)
Industrial	15,918	30.5	24,532	56.5	20,982	69.3
Developing, except G-90	27,708	53.1	17,409	40.1	8,750	28.9
G-90	8,566	16.4	1,444	3.3	542	1.8
Total	52,192		43,384		30,273	

Source: Authors' calculations based on Centre d'Études Prospectives et d'Informations Internationales's BACI database.

Note: The G-90 (Group of 90) is composed of all LDCs and of all members of the African Union (which itself includes virtually all African countries).

schemes on the basis of detailed customs declarations. Because competing preferences exist for several partners, this section considers the most beneficial scheme available to each exporter, as well as whether at least one preferential scheme is used.

Related Literature

Benefiting from a preferential scheme requires complying with several requirements: purely administrative issues, technical requirements, other specific conditions, and—in particular—rules of origin. Given the cost and sometimes the complexity of these constraints, the benefit of preferential agreements cannot be considered automatic, costless, or unconditional. Hence, there is a need to assess the extent to which exporters use EU trade preferences and the value of those preferences.

Rules of origin specify the criteria that must be met for commodities to be considered to originate in the country and therefore to be eligible for preferential treatment. Local content requirements (usually expressed as a minimum share of local value added) and sufficient transformation (as witnessed, for instance, by a change in classification heading) are the most common criteria used in practice. Rules of origin are justified by the need to avoid trade deflection—that is, reexport through the preference-receiving country of goods essentially produced in a third country. Rules of origin prevent the misuse of preference schemes, arguably reinforcing the benefit of the scheme for the preference-receiving country, to the extent that they create an incentive to invest in that country to benefit from preferential market access.

However, direct costs are associated with meeting rules of origin. Required administrative paperwork can be cumbersome and costly if it requires operating a parallel accounting system that differs in definition and scope from the system required by domestic laws (see, for example, Inama 2003). Rules of origin also constrain the sourcing of intermediate inputs. These costs have been the subject of close scrutiny because of the widespread suspicion that requirements associated with preferential agreements—and especially rules of origin—are used as protective measures that undermine the benefit of preferential access (Falvey and Reed 1998; Krishna and Krueger 1995; Krueger 1997). Falvey and Reed (2002) show that rules of origin allow the importing country's terms of trade to be improved in both final and intermediate goods, and they can be a complementary tool to the optimal tariff. It has also been argued that rules of origin are used in some instances as export subsidies, insofar as restrictive rules can create an incentive for the preference-receiving country to source its inputs in the preference-granting country (Cadot, Estevadeordal, and Suwa-Eisenmann 2004). The effect of rules of origin depends, however, on their nature, on the time period of the analysis (short run versus long run), and on market structure (see Krishna and Krueger 1995, propositions 1 and 2). Moreover, the effect is not necessarily a monotonic function of the rule's restrictiveness.[9]

The magnitude of these costs is difficult to assess. On the basis of indirect evidence, several studies estimate the administrative compliance costs of preferential schemes to be between 1 and 5 percent of the value of exports (see Ansón and others 2005; Herin 1986), depending on the precise nature of the requirements and on the technical capacity of exporters to comply with them. Nonadministrative costs, linked in particular to the constraint on sourcing imposed by rules of origin, vary even more across products and countries. They depend in particular on the possibility of splitting the value added chain for the product and on the status of competitive input providers with regard to the agreements. In addition, different types of rules of origin are used (see, for example, Estevadeordal and Suominen 2003), the restrictiveness of which differs widely.

On the basis of the detailed work undertaken by Estevadeordal (2000), several studies have focused on the North American Free Trade Agreement and found that rules of origin hamper Mexican exports to the United States, in particular in the automotive and textile-clothing sector (Ansón and others 2005; Cadot and others 2002). Their cost varies with the nature of the rule, but the overall cost seems to be close to the preferential margin itself, suggesting that the value of the agreement would be very low for Mexican exporters. Studying free trade agreements between the EU and the Central and East European countries, Brenton and Manchin (2003) also conclude that the rules associated with the agreement preclude exporters from reaping any substantial benefit, as evidenced by the very poor utilization of these agreements.

Nonreciprocal preferences face the same kinds of issues, but the aforementioned results need not apply because of the differences in rules applied, product specialization, and income levels of exporters. Recent studies suggest that exporters systematically underuse preferences. Brenton and Manchin (2003) found that only 35 percent of exports from the Central and East European countries enter the EU using the lowest tariff for which they are eligible. Reporting that the EBA initiative was very poorly used by LDC exporters to the EU in 2001, Brenton (2003) cast doubt on the actual benefit of this preferential scheme and pointed to the stringency of rules of origin as the main culprit. Mattoo, Roy, and Subramanian (2003) make a similar point as far as the African Growth and Opportunity Act (AGOA) is concerned. They show that rules of origin, in particular, strongly undermine the presumed generosity of this scheme. Using a general equilibrium model, they argue that the benefit of the AGOA would have been five times greater without rules of origin (US$540 million instead of US$140 million).

Gallezot (2003), in contrast, found that a large proportion of the EU's agricultural imports benefited from a preferential rate. Inama (2003) found that 62 percent of imports of Quad economies from all beneficiaries of GSP schemes were actually covered by preferences in 2002. But only 39 percent of the eligible imports were shipped under such schemes. With respect to LDCs only, 64 percent of imports were covered, but preferential treatment was successfully requested for no more than 43 percent of eligible imports. Regarding exports to the EU, the utilization rate in 2001 was 40 percent for LDCs, compared with 30 percent for Japan. Under AGOA, the utilization rate was 67 percent for mineral products (which account for 90 percent of all imports that receive preferential treatment in the United States), with a very tiny preference margin. For textiles and clothing, however, the utilization rate was only 36 percent (for a more specific assessment of U.S. preferences, see chapter 2).

Studying the utilization of various preferential schemes separately may be misleading. When a country is eligible for several preferential schemes (and this is the case with numerous developing countries, as far as access to the EU or the U.S. markets is concerned), underutilization of a given scheme can merely mean that the exporter judges another scheme to be more beneficial. In such cases, underutilization may not be a problem, because the exporter still enjoys the benefit of preferential access—although the preference margin available under the chosen scheme may be lower than under a scheme with more restrictive rules. The very low utilization rate of the EBA initiative among ACP LDCs might well mean that exporters prefer to use the preferential access offered through the Cotonou Agreement, which they have used for a long time and which has less restrictive rules of origin (Inama 2003).[10] Gallezot and Bureau (2005) show that when due account is taken of these competing preference schemes, EU and U.S. nonreciprocal trade preferences are used at a rate of about 90 percent for agricultural products. They also show that the existence of an alternative preferential regime considerably lowers the utilization of a given scheme and that this explains the poor utilization of the EBA initiative by Sub-Saharan African countries. These findings are paralleled by Wainio and Gibson's (2004) analysis of U.S. nonreciprocal preferential regimes for agricultural products, which also found that such regimes are used for more than 90 percent of eligible imports.

In summarizing case studies carried out on exports from Botswana, Kenya, Lesotho, and Mauritius to the EU, Stevens and Kennan (2005) report that very few (1 to 6 percent) do not benefit from any preference (or from zero MFN duty). As Stevens and Kennan (2004: 47) put it, "it is inherently implausible that for the countries and product studied preferences have not been well utilised," given the magnitude of preferential margins and the place they hold in the long-standing structure of these countries' exports. In addition, Stevens and Kennan report that a detailed analysis does not suggest that product coverage significantly limits the benefit of the Cotonou Agreement (except because of quantitative limitations linked to preferential tariff quotas). Indeed, no significant exports were made to the EU or to other Quad markets of products for which preferences were not available (Stevens and Kennan 2004: 8).

The Data

The main source available for studying the utilization of preferences in the EU market is the database of single administration declarations, collected by national customs offices and put together by Eurostat.[11] This database makes it possible to identify, for each tariff line, the value and volume of imports by the preference regime requested. Seasonal tariffs are treated using several lines (one for each time period). Additional information is available about the use of a quota and about tariff suspensions. The analysis carried out here is based on the 2001 data released in the summer of 2003.[12]

It should be emphasized at the outset that the preference regime in the data is the regime requested by the exporter, not the regime used. In other words, no information is available about the determination made by customs officers. This distinction explains why a significant proportion of the declarations are inconsistent. Such inconsistency can occur, for instance, when an exporter requests a regime for which it is not eligible. Obvious inconsistencies need to be corrected during the statistical treatment.

Judging the consistency of customs declarations requires detailed information about the regimes for which exporters are eligible. This information includes the countries covered and the product coverage, given that product coverage can vary from one partner to another because of product exclusions. An important example is the graduation measures under the GSP, for which countries and sectors concerned are determined annually.

In the dataset used, the frequency of inconsistent declarations is about 15 percent. These declarations are excluded from the calculations of the utilization rates of preferences (and of AVE requested duties).

Coverage and Utilization Rates of EU Preferences

The data allow the coverage and utilization of EU trade preferences to be characterized. This characterization is usually made by first calculating the coverage ratio—that is, the ratio of imports eligible for the preference regime to dutiable imports—for the partners and the sectors considered. The utilization ratio of a given preferential regime is calculated as the share of imports eligible for the regime for which exporters request using it. Inama (2003) also calculates the utility ratio of a preference regime, referring to the share of dutiable imports that actually enter under a given preference regime.[13]

This simple arithmetic might be misleading when various preference regimes are available to the exporter. From the comparison of the results obtained by Brenton (2003) and Gallezot (2003), in particular, it follows that although the EBA initiative is very poorly used in Sub-Saharan Africa, the Cotonou Agreement is heavily used. This finding suggests that many African LDCs continue to use the Cotonou regime—even though the EBA initiative would grant them higher preferential margins for some products—notably because 20 years of use has made them familiar with the formalities requested under the Cotonou Agreement, in particular the Form EUR I certificate of origin (Inama 2003). It is useful to understand why this is the case, but it is also necessary to take stock of the fact that these countries still benefit from a preferential regime.

A preferential regime never covers all products, and product coverage varies widely across agreements. However, for products covered, a preferential agreement generally provides a larger preference margin than does the GSP. The only exception is for LDCs: they are eligible for the EBA initiative as a special clause of the GSP scheme, and the EBA regime is the best one available to them in terms of statutory tariff duties—even when they are eligible for another preferential agreement, as is the case with ACP LDCs. The latter case is intricate because the EBA regime is nevertheless associated with tighter rules of origin, so the "best" preferential regime in terms of tariff duty is not necessarily the best one in terms of associated constraints.

This evaluation implies that measuring the utilization rate of a preference regime that is not the most favorable in terms of tariff duties does not always make sense: such a regime ought not be largely used if a better one exists in terms of rules of origin or cumulation. For Sub-Saharan African LDCs, for instance, the utilization rate of the Cotonou regime is, to some extent, inappropriate, as is the utilization rate of the GSP for a non-LDC that also benefits from a preferential agreement, as in the case of Morocco or Tunisia.[14]

Taking into account this hierarchy between preferential schemes, this analysis calculates two kinds of utilization and coverage rates for each type of partner: (a) the rates corresponding to the most favorable preference regime in terms of tariffs (the GSP in the case of LDCs, other preferential agreements for non-LDCs that are also eligible for the GSP) and (b) the rates of coverage and utilization of at least one preference regime (with the corresponding straightforward definitions). By definition, the coverage rate is superior when more than one preference regime is available, but this is not necessarily the case for the utilization rate. The utilization and coverage rates are computed by grouping partners together according to the preference regime for which they are eligible, treating LDCs and Sub-Saharan African countries separately (see annex 3.A).[15]

Overall, 48.9 percent of 2001 imports to the EU were dutiable—that is, they concerned products for which the MFN duty is not zero (table 3.3). Among these dutiable imports, 56.5 percent were eligible for a preferential regime, and the benefit

TABLE 3.3   Average Coverage and Utilization Rates of Preferences in the EU, by Group of Partners, 2001

Partner	Total imports (€ million)	Dutiable imports (€ million)	Share of dutiable imports (%)	Coverage rate (%)			Utilization rate (%)		
				GSP	Preference	At least one	GSP	Preference	At least one
Sub-Saharan African LDCs	8,313	2,046	24.6	95.4	98.7	99.7	1.3	n.a.	92.2
Sub-Saharan African countries other than LDCs	15,583	3,959	25.4	62.5	99.6	99.7	n.a.	92.9	94.2
LDCs outside Sub-Saharan Africa	4,397	4,203	95.6	99.3	0.1	99.4	49.1	n.a.	49.2
Other countries benefiting from the GSP and a preferential agreement	60,739	24,532	40.4	82.2	82.8	89.0	n.a.	72.7	86.4
Countries benefiting only from the GSP	215,459	97,598	45.3	53.1	0.0	53.1	70.3	n.a.	70.3
Countries benefiting from a preferential agreement but not the GSP	238,841	147,726	61.9	0.0	90.7	90.7	n.a.	85.3	85.3
Countries not eligible for any preferential regime	244,657	105,463	43.1	0.0	0.0	0.0	n.a.	n.a.	n.a.
All partners	787,988	385,527	48.9	20.4	41.6	56.5	54.2	83.9	81.3

Source: Authors' calculations based on customs declarations and the TARIC database.

Note: n.a. = not applicable.

of a preferential regime was requested for 81.3 percent of eligible imports. As already emphasized by Sapir (1998), despite the complex web of preferences maintained by the EU, imports actually entering under a preferential duty are thus a small minority of total imports (48.9 percent × 56.5 percent × 81.3 percent = 22.5 percent).

These rates vary substantially across groups of partners. The share of dutiable imports is as low as about 25 percent for Sub-Saharan African countries, largely in raw agricultural exports, while it reaches 95 percent for non-African LDCs, largely in textiles and clothing. The coverage of the GSP itself also varies substantially, from 53 percent for those non-LDCs that do not benefit from any additional agreement (mainly Latin American and East Asian countries) to 99.3 percent for non-African LDCs. This variation occurs because of the specific regime granted to LDCs under the EBA initiative and also because of product specialization and graduation, which predominantly concern fast-growing emerging economies (see Gallezot and Bureau 2005 for a detailed analysis). Preferential agreements other than the GSP have a high coverage rate—particularly the Cotonou Agreement (up to 99.6 percent for Sub-Saharan African non-LDCs).

The utilization rate of the preferential agreement taken alone is rather low (73 percent) for GSP beneficiaries that are party to a preferential agreement, but taking into account both schemes shows a utilization rate of 86 percent for at least one preferential scheme. Although in some cases the regime used is not the most beneficial one, this fact does not reveal any substantial problem of underutilization. The lower utilization (70 percent) of the GSP regime for non-LDCs entitled to access under it is more problematic because it means that almost one-third of eligible imports from those beneficiaries enter under the MFN regime. This situation raises questions about the severity of the constraints associated with the use of the EU's GSP scheme. By contrast, the utilization of the Cotonou scheme by Sub-Saharan African non-LDCs is very high (94 percent). For African countries, the EBA initiative remained virtually unused. As mentioned above, this lack of use is likely because of the alternative these countries have: they can benefit from the Cotonou regime, which is already extremely favorable in terms of both rates and associated constraints, and exporters are accustomed to it. When all preferential agreements offered to Sub-Saharan African LDCs are considered together, the utilization of at least one preferential regime turns out to be high—well above 90 percent. Even for non-African LDCs, for which no alternative preferential agreement exists (except for a few relatively small Caribbean and Pacific states), the utilization rate does not reach 50 percent. The EBA initiative thus stands out as exhibiting an especially low utilization rate. However, it is difficult to judge the meaning of this figure, given that EBA was implemented in March 2001. Not only was the scheme in force over part of the year only, but learning the specific requirements associated with a scheme can take time, especially in poor countries, where information dissemination may be far from perfect.

Although this analysis focuses on 2001, it could investigate the utilization of the EBA initiative in 2002. For Sub-Saharan African LDCs, that utilization increased from 1.3 percent to 2.8 percent; this very small figure is due to the aforementioned preference of exporters for the Cotonou Agreement. For other LDCs, the utilization rate rose from 49.1 percent to 54.8 percent. Although at a slow pace, this increase suggests that exporters are adapting and could draw further benefit from EBA. More time is needed to draw any firm conclusion, but these figures confirm that analyzing the initial year of enforcement tends to understate the potential use of the EBA initiative.

The analysis of the coverage and utilization of preferences for groups of products sheds more light on some underlying issues (tables 3.4 and 3.5). For other LDCs, underutilization is actually limited to textile and clothing products, which account for the bulk of their exports. It is striking that the utilization rate is twice as high in other sectors as in this one. Given the well-known importance of rules of origin in textile and clothing exports (see, for example, Inama 2003), this rate would appear to make intuitive sense.

For non-LDCs that are eligible only for the GSP, the underutilization of preferences is more important in the textile-clothing sector (65 percent utilization), but it is also significant in other manufacturing products (70 percent). Tariff duties on manufacturing products are lower, but they cover a far wider range of products—hence the importance of this result. This lower-than-average utilization of preferences in the "other manufacturing" sector suggests that rules of origin are not a problem that is confined to the textiles and clothing sector. They may also be limiting significantly, although to a lesser extent, the benefit drawn from preferences in other manufacturing sectors (for instance, electronic equipment or transport equipment), in which the international division of labor is now a common practice.

Preference Margins, Utilization, and Value of Preferences

The economic significance of the underutilization of preferences is difficult to gauge without additional information about the corresponding level of protection under alternative import regimes at stake. This information is evaluated here through different approaches, thus paving the way for an assessment of the value of these preferences.

Utilization by Level of Preference Margin

It should not come as a surprise that exporters do not find it profitable to comply with administrative requirements when the preference margin that a regime would provide them is tiny. In contrast, low utilization of a preference regime that

TABLE 3.4 EU Imports Covered by a Preferential Agreement, by Group of Partners and Group of Products, 2001

Partner	Product group (€ million)					
	Raw agricultural products	Food products	Other primary products	Textiles and clothing	Other manufacturing products	All products
Sub-Saharan African LDCs	399	842	17	252	528	2,039
Sub-Saharan African countries other than LDCs	1,075	1,445	75	701	651	3,946
LDCs outside Sub-Saharan Africa	11	235	3	3,884	45	4,178
Other countries benefiting from the GSP and a preferential agreement	1,856	2,269	999	7,139	9,571	21,835
Countries benefiting only from the GSP	759	2,890	123	13,374	34,641	51,787
Countries benefiting from a preferential agreement but not the GSP	1,505	4,334	891	22,118	105,146	133,994
All partners	5,605	12,016	2,107	47,468	150,582	217,778

Source: Authors' calculations based on customs declarations.

TABLE 3.5 Utilization Rate of Preferences, by Group of Partners and Group of Products, 2001

Partner	Product group (%)					
	Raw agricultural products	Food products	Other primary products	Textiles and clothing	Other manufacturing products	All products
Sub-Saharan African LDCs	94.2	91.8	98.6	95.4	89.6	92.2
Sub-Saharan African countries other than LDCs	95.1	97.0	88.7	92.5	88.9	94.2
LDCs outside Sub-Saharan Africa	93.0	90.2	94.5	46.1	89.3	49.2
Other countries benefiting from the GSP and a preferential agreement	84.8	93.6	96.2	94.1	78.3	86.4
Countries benefiting only from the GSP	77.3	88.6	76.5	65.3	70.5	70.3
Countries benefiting from a preferential agreement but not the GSP	77.1	86.7	92.1	89.7	84.3	85.3
All partners	84.3	90.1	93.1	80.0	80.8	81.3

Source: Authors' calculations based on customs declarations.

grants a large preferential margin is a clear sign that significant obstacles prevent exporters from taking advantage of the preference.

To take the utilization of preferences into account, one must match statutory protection with custom duties. Indeed, customs declarations do not provide any information about the level of duties, but only about the preference regime used. This information is thus taken from official information about the EU's statutory protection, as given in the TARIC database (an online customs tariff database of the EC Taxation and Customs Union). The data used are broken down at the EU's tariff-line level, at the 10-digit level TARIC classification (plus two additional codes). Computing the preference margin requires calculating AVEs of specific tariffs, done here using the unit value of imports by partner at the tariff-line level.[16]

These AVE duties allow the AVE preferential margin to be computed for each product and each preferential regime. In table 3.6, the utilization rate of preferences is broadly related to the preferential margin, calculated for the most favorable regime. The table also displays the corresponding share in dutiable exports of each partner, which illustrates the particular importance of trade preferences for LDCs and Sub-Saharan African countries: more than 95 percent of dutiable exports of these partners into the EU are products for which their preferential margin is higher than 3 percentage points. For non-African LDCs, almost 96 percent of exports correspond to products for which their preferential margin is higher than 9 percentage points (overwhelmingly, textile and apparel products).

The utilization rate of preferences may be linked to the magnitude of the preferential margin in two kinds of situations. First, the existence of a significant compliance cost for a given preferential regime should lead exporters not to request that regime, as long as the preferential margin is lower than the compliance cost. Such a situation should be reflected in low utilization for low preferential margins, because compliance costs are generally assumed to be on the order of a few percentage points of the total cost. Second, preferential access may be associated with restrictive rules of origin. When these rules are indeed a binding constraint for exporters, they should lead to a lower utilization of preferences. There is no reason to assume a priori that this underutilization should be restricted to low preferential margins: if the local content requirement and the rules of cumulation associated with a regime prevent exporters from sourcing intermediate inputs from the best providers, they might well entail substantial extra cost, thereby possibly leading to underutilization of significant preference margins.

Low utilization of preferences, when the margin is less than 3 percentage points, is indeed observed for LDCs but is not very significant given the low amounts concerned. More significant is probably the relatively weak utilization of the GSP by non-LDCs when the preferential margin is less than 6 percentage points, even though the GSP is the only scheme open to non-LDCs. This weak rate is consistent

Table 3.6 Coverage and Utilization Rates of Preferences in the EU, by Group of Partners and by Magnitude of Preferential Margin, 2001

Group of partners	Share in dutiable imports (%)					Utilization rate (%)			
		Level of preference margin:				Level of preference margin:			
	0	[0; 3]	[3; 6]	[6; 9]	> 9	[0; 3]	[3; 6]	[6; 9]	> 9
Sub-Saharan African LDCs	0.3	2.8	35.9	15.5	45.4	54	93	92	94
Sub-Saharan African countries other than LDCs	0.3	4.2	21.0	13.6	61.0	71	95	96	95
LDCs outside Sub-Saharan Africa	0.6	0.0	0.8	2.9	95.7	29	89	58	49
Other countries benefiting from the GSP and a preferential agreement	11.0	22.1	18.4	18.1	30.3	81	81	91	91
Countries benefiting only from the GSP	46.9	25.8	22.1	4.5	0.7	68	69	88	79
Countries benefiting from a preferential agreement but not the GSP	9.3	35.9	20.7	12.9	21.3	82	86	91	87
All preferences	22.2	29.9	20.8	10.3	16.8	78	79	91	85

Source: Authors' calculations based on customs declarations and TARIC.

Note: The preference margin is calculated as the difference between the AVE MFN rate and the best preferential rate available. The calculation is made at the tariff-line level. The AVE of specific tariffs is computed based on worldwide weighted median unit values. Hence, "0.3" in the first cell means that products with a zero preference margin account for 0.3 percent of EU imports from Sub-Saharan African LDCs.

with the idea that administrative requirements and rules of origin are constraining in this case.

When the preferential margin is greater than 6 percentage points, EU trade preferences are well used, with two exceptions: non-African LDCs, for which the rate is as low as 49 percent for products with preferential margins greater than 9 percentage points, and non-LDCs that are eligible only for the GSP, for which the rate is 79 percent for products on which the margin is greater than 9 percentage points. The first case is difficult to interpret, given the introduction of the EBA initiative during the year studied. The second, however, suggests that stringent rules of origin might entail significant cost for one-fifth of eligible imports.

Utilization of Preferences and Actual Average Protection

The link between the level of the preference margin and the degree of underutilization can also be summarized by computing average AVE duties. Every exporter has at least access to the MFN regime, without any additional requirements. This regime can be thought of as an upper bound for the level of protection faced. If the exporter complies with administrative requirements, it can at best use the most favorable preferential regime for which it is eligible. Hereafter, this regime is referred to as the best preferential regime, and it corresponds to the lower bound for the level of protection faced by the product. When the utilization of preferences is imperfect for a given product, some of the exports enter the market using the MFN regime, some use the best preferential regime, and some may use another available preferential regime. It is then possible to compute the average AVE duty actually faced by the exporter—that is, the ratio of tariff receipts to the value of imports. This ratio is hereafter referred to as the *average requested duty*.

Table 3.7 shows this average requested duty, compared with the MFN duty and the best duty, by group of partners and group of products. When aggregating across products and partners, a straightforward calculation provides the import-weighted average. This standard way to proceed preserves the definition of *average requested duty* as the ratio of tariff receipts to the value of imports. Its obvious drawback, however, is that imports are strongly endogenous to protection: the higher the protection level, the lesser the import value, other things being equal. In the presence of trade preferences, products for which the preference margin is large (and relatively costless to use) are also likely to be overrepresented. This situation may bias the assessment of the average preferential margin and the average utilization rate upward.

Because of this potential bias, another average is reported. It is computed using exports to all markets except the EU. This weighting scheme may better reflect the structure of export specialization of each country and its weight as an exporter.

TABLE 3.7 AVE of MFN, Requested and Best Preferential Rates in the EU, by Group of Partners and Group of Products, 2001

Product group	Share in partner's exports to the EU (%) (a)	Share in partner's extra-EU exports (%)		Import-weighted average duty (%)				Extra-EU export-weighted average duty (%)					
		All products (b)	Zero-import products (c)	MFN (d)	Requested (e)	Best (f)	Utilization (g)	Zero-import products MFN (h)	Zero-import products Best (i)	Non-zero import products MFN (j)	Non-zero import products Requested (k)	Non-zero import products Best (l)	Non-zero import products Utilization (m)
Sub-Saharan African LDCs													
Raw agricultural products	13.2	12.3	5.4	2.9	0.2	0.0	94.4	5.1	0.0	2.6	0.4	0.0	86.2
Food products	10.7	5.2	3.3	11.0	1.3	0.5	92.5	23.3	7.3	13.2	3.9	3.6	96.8
Other primary products	55.0	67.9	32.4	0.0	0.0	0.0	99.2	0.0	0.0	0.0	0.0	0.0	93.5
Textiles and clothing	3.1	3.9	2.2	10.3	0.5	0.0	95.4	10.6	0.0	11.6	1.3	0.0	89.0
Other manufacturing products	18.0	10.6	6.6	2.0	0.2	0.0	91.8	2.6	0.0	1.6	0.3	0.0	78.5
All products	100.0	100.0	49.9	2.2	0.2	0.1	93.2	2.9	0.5	1.4	0.3	0.1	89.5
Sub-Saharan African countries other than LDCs													
Raw agricultural products	18.9	8.5	2.4	11.3	5.3	4.9	93.6	4.7	0.9	2.4	0.5	0.2	86.5
Food products	9.7	5.1	3.0	20.4	6.7	6.2	96.8	47.9	39.0	16.6	8.0	6.3	84.1
Other primary products	55.5	70.2	14.8	0.1	0.0	0.0	97.6	0.1	0.0	0.0	0.0	0.0	85.0

(Table continues on the following page.)

TABLE 3.7 AVE of MFN, Requested and Best Preferential Rates in the EU, by Group of Partners and Group of Products, 2001 (Continued)

Product group	Share in partner's exports to the EU (%) (a)	Share in partner's extra-EU exports (%)		Import-weighted average duty (%)				Extra-EU export-weighted average duty (%)					
		All products (b)	Zero-import products (c)	MFN (d)	Requested (e)	Best (f)	Utilization (g)	Zero-import products		Non-zero import products			
								MFN (h)	Best (i)	MFN (j)	Requested (k)	Best (l)	Utilization (m)
Textiles and clothing	4.5	4.0	2.2	11.4	1.0	0.0	91.4	11.1	0.0	11.3	2.0	0.0	82.4
Other manufacturing products	11.3	12.2	7.4	1.9	0.2	0.0	91.5	3.3	0.0	2.5	0.4	0.0	83.9
All products	100.0	100.0	29.9	4.9	1.7	1.5	94.5	6.9	4.0	1.2	0.4	0.2	84.0
LDCs outside Sub-Saharan Africa													
Raw agricultural products	1.3	5.0	2.6	3.4	1.1	0.0	66.6	7.0	2.1	1.8	1.5	1.3	62.9
Food products	5.5	6.0	3.8	13.1	1.9	0.8	90.8	16.1	1.0	12.6	6.6	1.4	54.0
Other primary products	0.8	33.6	19.3	1.8	0.1	0.0	96.2	0.3	0.0	0.1	0.0	0.0	81.7
Textiles and clothing	89.4	48.2	14.7	12.0	6.5	0.0	46.0	10.4	0.3	11.2	7.8	0.1	30.9
Other manufacturing products	3.0	7.2	4.9	4.2	0.6	0.4	93.8	2.7	0.9	2.1	1.0	0.7	79.1
All products	100.0	100.0	45.3	11.7	6.0	0.1	49.2	5.5	0.4	7.6	5.2	0.2	33.0

Other countries benefiting from the GSP and a preferential agreement

Raw agricultural products	9.0	3.6	1.3	38.2	35.1	34.1	76.2	16.0	13.6	18.7	17.3	14.8	34.1
Food products	5.2	5.4	2.8	9.3	4.0	2.4	76.9	28.4	22.3	15.0	11.3	8.2	54.4
Other primary products	41.8	19.9	9.6	0.1	0.0	0.0	95.0	0.2	0.0	0.0	0.0	0.0	76.4
Textiles and clothing	11.8	9.3	3.8	10.8	0.9	0.1	92.6	10.4	1.2	11.0	8.8	1.3	22.8
Other manufacturing products	32.2	61.8	24.6	2.5	0.8	0.3	75.6	4.0	0.9	4.3	3.3	0.9	29.8
All products	100.0	100.0	42.2	6.0	3.8	3.3	84.0	5.7	2.5	5.2	4.1	1.6	30.4

Countries benefiting only from the GSP

Raw agricultural products	4.0	2.4	0.9	5.9	5.6	5.4	61.6	10.4	9.6	6.0	5.5	5.1	59.2
Food products	5.8	7.0	3.1	11.3	10.0	9.8	90.9	23.2	20.8	18.9	17.3	16.6	67.3
Other primary products	26.9	26.1	12.7	0.0	0.0	0.0	85.1	0.1	0.1	0.1	0.1	0.1	50.7
Textiles and clothing	15.2	11.6	1.7	9.9	9.2	8.8	67.1	9.1	7.9	10.0	9.6	9.3	56.9
Other manufacturing products	48.1	53.0	16.0	2.6	1.7	1.4	71.9	2.3	1.3	2.8	2.1	1.6	56.3
All products	100.0	100.0	34.4	3.6	3.0	2.8	72.7	4.0	3.1	4.3	3.8	3.4	58.0

(Table continues on the following page.)

TABLE 3.7 AVE of MFN, Requested and Best Preferential Rates in the EU, by Group of Partners and Group of Products, 2001 (*Continued*)

Product group	Share in partner's exports to the EU (%) (a)	Share in partner's extra-EU exports (%)		Import-weighted average duty (%)				Extra-EU export-weighted average duty (%)					
		All products (b)	Zero-import products (c)	MFN (d)	Requested (e)	Best (f)	Utilization (g)	Zero-import products		Non-zero import products			
								MFN (h)	Best (i)	MFN (j)	Requested (k)	Best (l)	Utilization (m)
Countries benefiting from a preferential agreement but not the GSP													
Raw agricultural products	1.0	1.1	0.5	7.3	4.6	4.0	79.8	13.4	10.8	9.5	7.3	6.3	69.3
Food products	2.6	5.1	2.5	13.2	5.2	3.8	84.5	34.1	15.7	29.8	26.7	23.6	50.5
Other primary products	12.2	3.5	0.6	0.2	0.1	0.1	93.1	1.3	1.0	0.2	0.1	0.1	87.9
Textiles and clothing	10.9	10.3	2.2	10.0	2.4	1.5	89.2	7.8	4.7	9.2	6.5	6.1	87.4
Other manufacturing products	73.4	79.9	19.3	3.2	0.9	0.5	86.0	2.4	1.0	2.4	1.5	1.2	76.3
All products	100.0	100.0	25.1	3.9	1.1	0.7	86.7	6.2	3.0	4.0	2.9	2.5	75.0
Countries not eligible for any preferential regime													
Raw agricultural products	1.9	2.1	0.8	2.8	2.8	2.8	n.a.	18.1	18.1	6.3	6.3	6.3	—

Food products	2.5	5.2	2.3	17.6	17.6	17.6	n.a.	32.8	32.8	28.1	28.1	28.1	—
Other primary products	3.5	4.0	1.7	0.2	0.2	0.2	n.a.	0.6	0.6	0.5	0.5	0.5	—
Textiles and clothing	2.0	3.4	0.7	7.1	7.1	7.1	n.a.	6.7	6.7	8.1	8.1	8.1	—
Other manufacturing products	90.1	85.2	17.4	2.1	2.1	2.1	n.a.	2.7	2.7	3.3	3.3	3.3	—
All products	100.0	100.0	22.9	2.5	2.5	2.5	n.a.	6.3	6.3	4.4	4.4	4.4	—
All partners													
Raw agricultural products	3.2	2.4	0.9	12.9	11.1	10.7	82.4	14.3	13.2	8.2	7.6	7.0	49.4
Food products	3.9	5.8	2.7	13.2	9.5	8.9	86.9	28.8	25.1	23.3	22.0	21.1	60.2
Other primary products	17.0	13.8	6.3	0.1	0.0	0.0	93.8	0.2	0.2	0.1	0.1	0.1	65.5
Textiles and clothing	9.6	7.6	1.6	10.0	5.7	4.8	82.7	8.9	5.0	9.6	8.7	7.6	44.2
Other manufacturing products	66.3	70.4	17.7	2.6	1.5	1.3	82.7	2.8	1.8	3.1	2.8	2.5	49.8
All products	100.0	100.0	29.2	3.6	2.3	2.0	83.2	5.3	4.1	4.4	4.0	3.6	49.9

Source: Authors' calculations based on customs declarations and TARIC.

Note: n.a. = not applicable; — = not available. The preference margin is calculated as the difference between the AVE MFN rate and the best preferential rate available. Calculations are made at the tariff-line level. Columns g and m give the utilization rate of the preferential margin, computed as follows: $g = (d − e) / (d − f)$ and, similarly, $m = (j − k) / (j − l)$.

This alternative weighting scheme provides an average across all products for all partners, including those products not imported by the EU from the partner at hand. Note, however, that for those zero-import products, the requested duty cannot be used here because its definition is based on the regime claimed while importing. This analysis thus reports the average across zero-import products separately—that is, across those product-partner pairs for which no import flow is recorded in the EU.

When relying on import-weighted averages, these calculations show that the average requested duty faced by EU imports is 2.3 percent, close to the best preferential duty of 2.0 percent and substantially lower than the MFN average duty of 3.6 percent. This figure corresponds to an average utilization of the preferential margin of 83 percent, very close to the rate calculated previously. Non-African LDCs exhibit the lowest utilization of the preferential margin (49.2 percent). They face an average requested duty of 6.0 percent, while the best preferential duty they are eligible for is as low as 0.1 percent. They do enjoy an average preferential margin of 5.7 percentage points on their exports to the EU, but this margin is significantly below the 11.6 percentage point margin for which they would be eligible. The preferential margin is also significantly underused by non-LDCs that are eligible only for the GSP, but the margin at stake is rather low in this case (0.8 percentage point).

Calculations based on worldwide exports outside the EU deliver a different picture. First, the assessed preferential margin is lower: 0.8 percentage point for all partners, compared with 1.6 percentage points using import-weighted averages. Although moderating the assessed extent of tariff preferences, this result suggests that trade preferences are successful in enhancing exports to the EU, because products that are granted a relatively high preference margin account for a higher share of partners' exports to the EU than to the rest of the world. In particular, EU preferences appear to effectively enhance Sub-Saharan African countries' agricultural exports to the EU. Their large preferential margin in this sector is fairly well utilized (by 84 to 97 percent), reflected in these products occupying a larger share of exports to the EU than to other markets. Broadly speaking, the relatively good utilization of EU preferences by Sub-Saharan Africa is confirmed.

Using a weighting scheme based on worldwide exports outside the EU also results in a far lower utilization rate of preferences—slightly below 50 percent. The difference is especially striking for developing countries that are eligible for both the GSP and another preferential scheme (30 percent). The "other manufacturing" sector plays a significant role in this last case, and the low utilization of preferences in this sector is associated with a significantly lower share of exports to the EU than to the rest of the world.

Non-African LDCs record an average utilization of the preferential margin of 33 percent in this alternative calculation. Again, textiles and clothing play a significant role. However, the share of textiles and clothing is higher in exports to the EU than to the rest of the world. Despite the imperfect utilization of preferences, non-African LDC exporters of textiles and clothing might thus enjoy easier access to the EU market than to other large markets (Canada and the United States in particular; see chapters 2 and 5, respectively), This result is certainly due at least in part to the preferential access offered by the EU.

Using exports outside the EU as a weighting scheme also paves the way for incorporating products in the analysis that are not exported to the EU. One can then assess whether protection and constraints associated with preferential schemes might impede access to the European market for some products. On the whole, the average MFN duty for zero-import products is slightly above the average for other products (5.3 percent, compared with 4.4 percent), but the difference is not striking, and it is even less in terms of the average best duty available (4.1 percent, compared with 3.6 percent). However, the presence of zero-import products is noteworthy in raw agricultural and food products, where the higher MFN protection is not compensated by preference margins. The share of food products in exports to the EU (3.9 percent) is also significantly lower than in exports to other markets (5.8 percent).

Value of EU Preferences

After Alexandraki and Lankes (2004) and chapter 2, a simple calculation of the value of preferences can be provided. Under simplifying assumptions (perfect substitutability across origins and constant world prices, in particular), the value of the rent arising from preferential tariff duties can be computed as follows, for any partner j:

$$V_j = \sum_i \left(t_i^{MFN} - t_{ij}^{PRE} \right) dutiable_{ij}\, util_{ij}^{PRE}, \qquad (3.1)$$

where i is the tariff line; t^{MFN} and t^{PRE} refer, respectively, to the MFN and the preferential applied tariff duty; $dutiable_{ij}$ refers to EU dutiable imports of product i from partner j; and $util$ is the corresponding utilization rate.

This equation is a crude approximation in many respects, but it allows the magnitude of preferences to be compared across countries. Note, however, that these calculations do not account for the EU's preferential tariff rate quotas, which are an important source of rents—in particular for sugar, bananas, and beef—because of the product protocols under the Cotonou Agreement.[17]

The calculation is first carried out assuming full utilization of tariff preferences and then while taking into account incomplete utilization.[18] As an alternative, the value of preferences is also computed as a share of the country's dutiable exports to the EU, thus showing to what extent the country's trade relationships with the EU rely on preferential access. It is also computed as a share of total exports of goods, to better reflect the economy's dependence with regard to preferences.

If one assumes full utilization, tariff preferences granted by the EU amount to €182 million for African LDCs, €521 million for non-LDCs in Sub-Saharan Africa, and approximately the same amount (€510 million) for other LDCs (tables 3.8 and 3.9). For all country groups except those eligible only for the GSP, this amount represents a significant proportion of the value of dutiable exports to the EU—as much as about 10 percent for Sub-Saharan African countries and LDCs. Underutilization does not change this picture substantially, except for non-African LDCs, where the value of preferences is halved.

Except for non-African LDCs, the figures are significantly lower when expressed as a proportion of countries' total exports in goods to the EU. Still, the value of preferences, even accounting for underutilization, amounts to more than 2 percent of total exports to the EU, except for GSP beneficiaries that not eligible for another preferential scheme, and to about 1 percent of world exports on average for Sub-Saharan African countries and LDCs. Although moderate, this value is not negligible for the EU market alone, given that these exports include a significant proportion of nondutiable products (energy and primary materials, in particular).

At the country level, however, the value of EU preferences is in some cases far higher. For 10 countries, it is in excess of 4 percent of their world exports in goods (all are African or Caribbean, apart from the Lao People's Democratic Republic). EU preferences account for more than 10 percent of global exports for Dominica and the Seychelles and for almost half the dutiable exports to the EU of St. Lucia.[19]

Here again, underutilization does not substantially change the picture, except for South Asian LDCs. The value of EU preferences for Bangladesh, for instance, falls from 12.1 percent to 6.4 percent of dutiable exports to the EU (respectively, 3.4 percent and 1.9 percent of its world exports) because of underutilization.

Conclusion

The EU plays a major role with regard to developing countries' exports, both because of the size of its market and because of its numerous reciprocal and non-reciprocal preferential agreements. This assessment confirms that EU tariff preferences are important for a number of developing countries, in particular in Sub-Saharan Africa. Although even the average figures are significant, the dependence on EU preferences is particularly important for a limited number of African and

TABLE 3.8 Average Value of EU Trade Preferences by Group of Partners

Group of partners	Value (€ million)		Share of country's dutiable exports to the EU (%)		Share of country's total exports to the EU (%)	
	Assuming full utilization	Accounting for underutilization	Assuming full utilization	Accounting for underutilization	Assuming full utilization	Accounting for underutilization
Sub-Saharan African LDCs	182	168	8.9	8.2	2.2	2.0
Sub-Saharan African countries other than LDCs	521	491	13.2	12.4	3.3	3.2
LDCs outside Sub-Saharan Africa	510	251	12.1	6.0	11.6	5.7
Other countries benefiting from the GSP and a preferential agreement	1,646	1,422	6.7	5.8	2.7	2.3
Countries benefiting only from the GSP	1,828	1,285	1.9	1.3	0.8	0.6
Countries benefiting from a preferential agreement but not the GSP	7,747	6,604	5.2	4.5	3.2	2.8
Total	12,434	10,221	4.4	3.6	2.3	1.9

Source: Authors' calculations based on customs declarations and TARIC.

TABLE 3.9 Value of EU Tariff Preferences for Selected Countries

Partner	Group the country belongs to	Value (€ million)		Share of country's dutiable exports to the EU (%)		Share of country's total exports (%)	
		Assuming full utilization	Accounting for underutilization	Assuming full utilization	Accounting for underutilization	Assuming full utilization	Accounting for underutilization
Seychelles	Sub-Saharan African countries other than LDCs	37.6	35.5	23.5	22.2	13.4	12.6
Dominica[a]	Other countries benefiting from the GSP and a preferential agreement	6.5	6.3	28.5	27.6	10.7	10.3
St. Lucia[a]	Other countries benefiting from the GSP and a preferential agreement	12.3	12.2	46.8	46.2	10.0	9.9
Senegal	Sub-Saharan African LDCs	29.9	28.3	11.3	10.7	7.3	6.9
Tunisia	Other countries benefiting from the GSP and a preferential agreement	399.2	374.3	8.9	8.3	6.5	6.1

Morocco	Other countries benefiting from the GSP and a preferential agreement	454.3	432.7	10.0	9.6	5.2	5.0
Mozambique	Sub-Saharan African LDCs	33.4	32.5	7.0	6.8	5.0	4.8
Lao PDR	LDCs outside Sub-Saharan Africa	16.5	10.3	12.3	7.6	7.7	4.8
Mauritius	Sub-Saharan African countries other than LDCs	90.3	82.8	12.3	11.2	4.5	4.2
Cameroon	Sub-Saharan African countries other than LDCs	86.3	82.6	25.9	24.8	4.2	4.0
St. Vincent and the Grenadines[a]	Other countries benefiting from the GSP and a preferential agreement	11.1	6.5	29.5	17.2	6.5	3.8
Belize[a]	Other countries benefiting from the GSP and a preferential agreement	16.4	15.8	38.5	37.0	3.9	3.7
Gambia, The	Sub-Saharan African LDCs	1.1	1.0	12.0	11.0	4.0	3.7

(Table continues on the following page.)

TABLE 3.9 Value of EU Tariff Preferences for Selected Countries (Continued)

Partner	Group the country belongs to	Value (€ million)		Share of country's dutiable exports to the EU (%)		Share of country's total exports (%)	
		Assuming full utilization	Accounting for underutilization	Assuming full utilization	Accounting for underutilization	Assuming full utilization	Accounting for underutilization
Namibia	Sub-Saharan African countries other than LDCs	38.3	37.2	10.8	10.5	3.7	3.5
Bosnia and Herzegovina	Countries benefiting from a preferential agreement but not the GSP	28.1	26.0	7.2	6.6	3.7	3.4
Eritrea	LDCs outside Sub-Saharan Africa	0.2	0.1	13.8	11.9	3.9	3.4
Cape Verde	Sub-Saharan African LDCs	0.6	0.6	7.1	6.6	3.4	3.2
Kenya	Sub-Saharan African countries other than LDCs	54.6	50.3	11.2	10.3	3.4	3.2
Romania	Countries benefiting from a preferential agreement but not the GSP	470.9	429.7	7.7	7.0	3.5	3.2
Madagascar	Sub-Saharan African LDCs	45.2	39.4	11.2	9.8	3.4	3.0

Source: Authors' calculations based on custom declarations and TARIC.

a. Denotes a non-African country eligible for the Cotonou Agreement (here, Caribbean countries).

Note: Countries are ranked by decreasing order of value of preferences accounting for incomplete utilization, expressed as a share of the country's world exports (last column). To save space, only those developing countries for which this value exceeds 3 percent of their world exports are shown.

Caribbean countries. On average, the utilization of these tariff preferences turns out to be strong.

The only case where underutilization appears as a significant loss to receiving countries is the EBA initiative for South Asian LDCs. The newness of the EBA scheme is part of the explanation, as witnessed by the slight but significant increase recorded between 2001 and 2002. However, the constraints imposed by rules of origin on textile and clothing exports (the foremost export specialization of South Asian LDCs) appear to be the main reason for underutilization. Relaxing these rules could be an efficient way to substantially increase the benefit that receiving countries are likely to draw from the scheme, at least as far as the textile-clothing sector is concerned and perhaps also for other manufacturing goods.

For Sub-Saharan African countries, the contractual nonreciprocal preferences granted through the Cotonou Partnership Agreement were of significance. By combining deep preferences, broad coverage, and relatively flexible rules, this agreement has proved instrumental for African exporters. The end of this agreement on January 1, 2008, was thus a milestone in the trade relationship of Sub-Saharan African countries with the EU, and finding an acceptable transition out of this regime is a key challenge. The economic partnership agreements signed or being negotiated with the EU should be the way out for most countries, although their reciprocity (even though less than full and tied to long transition periods) will require in return from these countries widespread liberalization to imports from the EU. For Sub-Saharan African LDCs, the EBA initiative might be an alternative in this context. Given the specialization of those countries in raw agricultural products, most of which are produced using few traded intermediates and thus not inhibited by rules of origin, the results of this analysis suggest that EBA could be of high value. For others, the EU's GSP appears to be a very poor substitute.

Annex 3.A: Partner Classification

Table 3.A.1 shows the classification of partners according to the preference regime for which they are eligible.

Annex 3.A.1   Partner Groups

Group	Countries in group
Sub-Saharan African non-LDCs	Botswana; Cameroon; Republic of Congo; Côte d'Ivoire; Gabon; Ghana; Kenya; Mauritius; Namibia; Nigeria; Seychelles; Swaziland; Zimbabwe
Sub-Saharan African LDCs	Angola; Benin; Burkina Faso; Burundi; Cape Verde; Central African Republic; Chad; Comoros; Democratic Republic of Congo; Djibouti; Equatorial Guinea; Ethiopia; The Gambia; Guinea; Guinea-Bissau; Lesotho; Liberia; Madagascar; Malawi; Mali; Mauritania; Mozambique; Niger; Rwanda; São Tomé and Príncipe; Senegal; Sierra Leone; Somalia; Sudan; Tanzania; Togo; Uganda; Zambia
Other LDCs and territories	Afghanistan; Bangladesh; Bhutan; Cambodia; Eritrea; Haiti; Kiribati; Lao PDR; Maldives; Myanmar; Nepal; Samoa; Solomon Islands; Tuvalu; Vanuatu; Republic of Yemen
Non-LDC, non-Sub-Saharan African countries and territories covered by EU's GSP and by another preferential agreement	Algeria; American Samoa; Anguilla; Antigua and Barbuda; Armenia; Aruba; Azerbaijan; The Bahamas; Barbados; Belarus; Belize; Bolivia; Bouvet Island; British Indian Ocean Territories; British Virgin Islands; Cayman Islands; Colombia; Costa Rica; Cyprus; Dominica; Dominican Republic; Ecuador; Arab Republic of Egypt; El Salvador; Falkland Islands; Fiji; French Polynesia; French Southern Territories; Greenland; Grenada; Guam; Guatemala; Guyana; Honduras; Jamaica; Jordan; Lebanon; Mayotte; Mexico; Montserrat; Morocco; Netherlands Antilles; New Caledonia; Nicaragua; Northern Marianas Islands; Panama; Papua New Guinea; Peru; Pitcairn Island; St. Helena; St. Kitts and Nevis; St. Lucia; St. Pierre and Miquelon; St. Vincent and the Grenadines; South Africa; South Georgia and the South Sandwich Islands; Suriname; Syrian Arab Republic; Tonga; Trinidad and Tobago; Tunisia; Turks and Caicos Islands; R.B. de Venezuela; Wallis and Futuna
Countries covered only by EU's GSP	Argentina; Bahrain; Bermuda; Brazil; Brunei Darussalam; Chile; China; Christmas Island; Cocos Islands; Cook Islands; Cuba; Georgia; Gibraltar; Heard Island and McDonald Island; India; Indonesia; Islamic Republic of Iran; Iraq; Kazakhstan; Kuwait; Kyrgyz Republic; Libya; Macao, China; China; Malaysia; Moldova; Mongolia; Nauru; Norfolk Island; Oman; Pakistan; Palau; Paraguay;

Group	Countries in group
	Philippines; Qatar; Russian Federation; Saudi Arabia; Sri Lanka; Tajikistan; Thailand; Tokelau; Turkmenistan; Ukraine; United Arab Emirates; Uruguay; U.S. Virgin Islands; Uzbekistan; Vietnam
Countries not covered by EU's GSP, but covered by another preferential agreement	Albania; Andorra; Bosnia and Herzegovina; Bulgaria; China; Croatia; Czech Republic; Estonia; Faroe Islands; Hong Kong, China; Hungary; Iceland; Israel; Latvia; Liechtenstein; Lithuania; FYR Macedonia; Malta; Marshall Islands; Micronesia; Montenegro; Niue; Norway; Poland; Romania; San Marino; Serbia; Slovak Republic; Slovenia; Switzerland; Taiwan, China; Turkey
Countries not covered by any preferential agreement	Australia; Canada; Japan; Democratic People's Republic of Korea; Republic of Korea; New Zealand; Singapore; United States

Source: Authors' compilation.

Notes

1. Although trade policy is conducted by the European Commission, for ease of exposition this chapter refers only to the EU.

2. In discussing trade policy alone, it is customary to consider Sub-Saharan African countries together with Caribbean and Pacific countries because of the importance of EU-African, Caribbean, and Pacific preferential agreements. Still, these country groups are far from homogeneous in other respects. In particular, the external trade of Sub-Saharan African countries exhibits a higher dependency on the EU, whereas the United States receives a large part of Caribbean countries' exports, as Australia and New Zealand do for Pacific countries.

3. *Diagonal cumulation* means that intermediate inputs originating from other countries that benefit from the schemes can be considered local in order to fulfill the conditions required to establish the origin of the exported product.

4. Pakistan has subsequently benefited from this regime. Note also that two additional incentive clauses, linked to fundamental social rights and environmental protection, were unused in 2001.

5. The WTO waiver for this agreement was due to expire by the end of 2007, and groups of countries are negotiating reciprocal economic partnership agreements to replace it. Although this perspective is not directly dealt with here, it should of course be an essential element of any prospective outlook.

6. In contrast to full cumulation, diagonal cumulation requires that intermediate inputs be granted originating status.

7. The extent to which this situation is due to the partial enforcement of the African Growth and Opportunity Act in 2001 remains an open question.

8. The EU-25 comprises all EU member states prior to January 1, 2007, when Bulgaria and Romania became members.

9. Ju and Krishna (2002, 2005) demonstrate that if the exporting intermediate sector is more protected than the final sector, then the effect of rules of origin in the two sectors goes in the opposite direction. That is, the intermediate price and final good imports follow a bell curve with the increase in the restrictiveness of the rules of origin, while final good price and intermediate

imports follow a U curve. The top and bottom of these curves are reached when firms prefer to disregard rules of origin, importing inputs and paying the MFN tariff.

10. The EU's nonreciprocal preferences for ACP countries were initiated with the Yaoundé Convention in 1964 and followed up until 2000 by four Lomé conventions.

11. The EU notifications concerning the use of the EU's GSP scheme also allows GSP imports to be disentangled from other preferential imports.

12. Compared with previous releases, the quality of this release has been strongly improved, in terms of both the consistency for countries covered and the inclusion of the Netherlands, which previously was missing. The number of inconsistencies in the database was approximately halved with this release, compared with previous ones.

13. The utility ratio is thus the product of the coverage ratio and the utilization ratio.

14. This statement might seem to contradict the practice, given the high utilization of the Cotonou Agreement. Still, it would be logical, in theory, to use the EBA initiative instead of the Cotonou Agreement on products for which the EBA regime offers additional preferences. In such a case, not using the Cotonou preference should not be interpreted as underutilization of this preference scheme.

15. As outlined previously, it would have been more consistent, from the standpoint of pure trade policy, to treat all ACP countries jointly. Because this analysis focuses on Sub-Saharan African countries, however, they are considered separately. Owing to their small size, it was not necessary to create an additional, separate group for Caribbean and Pacific countries, which are therefore included in the group of countries benefiting from the GSP and a preferential agreement.

16. Note, however, that these unit values suffer from two drawbacks: they lack robustness, and they are likely to present endogeneity, in particular when preference creates a rent, materializing in an above-world-average price (see, for example, Olarraega and Özden 2005).

17. See Bureau and Tangerman (2000) for a detailed analysis of the EU's tariff rate quotas. See Bouët, Fontagné, and Jean (2006: table 6.5) for an assessment of the importance for developing countries of rents from tariff rate quotas.

18. The utilization rate is then assumed to be uniformly equal to 100 percent in equation 3.1.

19. Note that the value of preferences in absolute terms is higher for large developing countries. Among non-European developing countries, the highest values are found in decreasing order for Turkey, China, Morocco, Tunisia, Bangladesh, India, and Israel.

References

Alexandraki, Katerina, and Hans Peter Lankes. 2004. "The Impact of Preference Erosion on Middle-Income Developing Countries." IMF Working Paper 04/169, International Monetary Fund, Washington, DC.

Ansón, José, Olivier Cadot, Antoni Estevadeordal, Jaime de Melo, Akiko Suwa-Eisenmann, and Bolormaa Tumurchudur. 2005. "Rules of Origin in North-South Preferential Trading Arrangements with an Application to NAFTA." *Review of International Economics* 13 (3): 501–17.

Bouët, Antoine, Yvan Decreux, Lionel Fontagné, Sébastien Jean, and David Laborde. 2008. "Assessing Applied Protection across the World." *Review of International Economics* 16 (5): 850–63.

Bouët, Antoine, Lionel Fontagné, and Sébastien Jean. 2006. "Is Erosion of Preferences a Serious Concern?" In *Agricultural Trade Reform and the Doha Development Agenda*, ed. Kym Anderson and Will Martin, 161–92. Basingstoke, U.K.: Palgrave Macmillan.

Bouët, Antoine, Lionel Fontagné, Mondher Mimouni, and Xavier Pichot. 2001. "Market Access Maps: A Bilateral and Disaggregated Measure of Market Access." CEPII Working Paper 2001-18, Centre d'Etudes Prospectives et d'Informations Internationales, Paris.

Brenton, Paul. 2003. "Integrating the Least Developed Countries into the World Trading System: The Current Impact of EU Preferences under Everything but Arms." Policy Research Working Paper 3018, World Bank, Washington, DC.

Brenton, Paul, and Miriam Manchin. 2003. "Making EU Trade Agreements Work: The Role of Rules of Origin." *World Economy* 26 (5): 755–69.

Bureau, Jean-Christophe, and Stefan Tangerman. 2000. "Tariff Rate Quotas in the EU." *Agricultural and Resource Economics Review* 29 (1): 70–80.

Cadot, Olivier, Antoni Estevadeordal, Jaime de Melo, Akiko Suwa-Eisenmann, and Bolormaa Tumurchudur. 2002. "Assessing the Effect of NAFTA's Rules of Origin." Université de Lausanne.

Cadot, Olivier, Antoni Estevadeordal, and Akiko Suwa-Eisenmann. 2004. "Rules of Origin as Export Subsidies." French National Institute for Agricultural Research, Paris.

Estevadeordal, Antoni. 2000. "Negotiating Preferential Market Access: The Case of the North American Free Trade Agreement." *Journal of World Trade* 34 (1): 141–66.

Estevadeordal, Antoni, and Kati Suominen. 2003. "Measuring Rules of Origin in the World Trading System and Proposals for Multilateral Harmonization." Inter-American Development Bank, Washington, DC.

European Commission. 2004. "The European Union's Generalised System of Preferences." European Commission, Directorate-General for Trade, Brussels. http://trade.ec.europa.eu/doclib/docs/2004/march/tradoc_116448.pdf.

Falvey, Rod, and Geoff Reed. 1998. "Economic Effects of Rules of Origin." *Weltwirtschaftliches Archiv* 134 (2): 209–29.

———. 2002. "Rules of Origin as Commercial Policy Instruments." *International Economic Review* 43 (2): 393–407.

Gallezot, Jacques. 2003. "Real Access to the EU's Agricultural Market." French National Institute for Agricultural Research, Paris.

Gallezot, Jacques, and Jean-Christophe Bureau. 2005. *Preferential Trading Arrangements in Agricultural and Food Markets: The Case of the European Union and the United States.* Paris: Organisation for Economic Co-operation and Development.

Herin, Jan. 1986. "Rules of Origin and Differences between Tariff Levels in EFTA and in the EC." EFTA Occasional Paper 13, European Free Trade Association, Geneva.

Inama, Stefano. 2003. "Trade Preferences for LDCs: An Early Assessment of Benefits and Possible Improvements." United Nations Conference on Trade and Development, New York and Geneva.

Ju, Jiandong, and Kala Krishna. 2002. "Regulations, Regime Switches, and Non-monotonicity When Non-compliance Is an Option: An Application to Content Protection and Preference." *Economics Letters* 77 (3): 315–21.

———. 2005. "Firm Behaviour and Market Access in a Free Trade Area with Rules of Origin." *Canadian Journal of Economics* 38 (1): 290–308.

Krishna, Kala, and Anne O. Krueger. 1995. "Implementing Free Trade Areas: Rules of Origin and Hidden Protection." In *New Directions in Trade Theory*, ed. Alan V. Deardorff, James A. Levinsohn, and Robert M. Stern, 149–87. Ann Arbor: University of Michigan Press.

Krueger, Anne O. 1997. "Free Trade Agreements versus Customs Unions." *Journal of Development Economics* 54 (1): 169–87.

Lamy, Pascal. 2002. "Stepping Stones or Stumbling Blocks? The EU's Approach towards the Problem of Multilateralism vs. Regionalism in Trade Policy." *World Economy* 25 (10): 1399–413.

Mattoo, Aaditya, Devesh Roy, and Arvind Subramanian. 2003. "The Africa Growth and Opportunity Act and Its Rules of Origin: Generosity Undermined?" *World Economy* 26 (6): 829–51.

Olarreaga, Marcelo, and Çağlar Özden. 2005. "AGOA and Apparel: Who Captures the Tariff Rent in the Presence of Preferential Market Access?" *World Economy* 28 (1): 63–77.

Panagariya, Arvind. 2002. "EU Preferential Trade Arrangements and Developing Countries." *World Economy* 25 (10): 1415–32.

Sapir, André. 1998. "The Political Economy of EC Regionalism." *European Economic Review* 42 (3–5): 717–32.

Stevens, Christopher, and Jane Kennan. 2004. *Comparative Study of G8 Preferential Access Schemes for Africa.* Brighton, U.K.: Institute of Development Studies, University of Sussex.

————. 2005. "Making Trade Preferences More Effective." Trade Note, Institute of Development Studies, University of Sussex, Brighton, U.K. http://www.ids.ac.uk/UserFiles/File/globalisation_team/tradepapers/CSJKTradePreferences.pdf.

Wainio, John, and Paul Gibson. 2004. "The Significance of U.S. Nonreciprocal Trade Preferences for Developing Countries." In *Agricultural Policy Reform and the WTO: Where Are We Heading?*, ed. Giovanni Anania, Mary E. Bohman, Colin A. Carter, and Alex F. McCalla, 369–89, Cheltenham, U.K., and Northampton, MA: Edward Elgar.

WTO (World Trade Organization). 2008a. "Draft Modalities for Nonagricultural Market Access." TN/MA/W/103/Rev.2, WTO, Geneva.

————. 2008b. "Revised Draft Modalities for Agriculture." TN/AG/W/4/Rev.1, WTO, Geneva.

4

JAPAN'S GENERALIZED SYSTEM OF PREFERENCES

Norio Komuro

Little critical analysis has been done of Japan's Generalized System of Preferences (GSP) regime. Because the GSP reflects Japan's broader trade and foreign policy goals, a holistic viewpoint is crucial to an analytical survey of the GSP. This chapter, therefore, not only examines the GSP scheme and practice but also analyzes GSP erosion and potential solutions to this problem.

General Overview of the GSP Scheme

Japan established its GSP on August 1, 1971, just one month after the European Community introduced its GSP. Four decennial GSP schemes have been established: from August 1971 to March 1981; from April 1981 to March 1991; from April 1991 to March 2001; and from April 2001 to March 2011. The current GSP scheme is provided under the Temporary Tariff Measures Law and the implementing regulations of this law.

The GSP scheme includes a general preferential regime and a special preferential regime. Under the general scheme, preferential tariffs are applied to imports of designated items from GSP beneficiaries. Under the special regime, duty-free treatment is granted to imports of designated items from least developed countries (LDCs).

General Preferential Regime

In principle, GSP preferences are not granted in the agricultural-fishery sector, given the weak competitiveness of Japan's domestic industries. Items that are

The author would like to thank Will Martin, Carlos Primo Braga, Bryan Brown, and Bernard Hoekman for their valuable comments on an earlier draft. Any remaining faults are the sole responsibility of the author.

covered under the GSP are enumerated in a Positive List.[1] Safeguards enable the government to suspend preferential treatment for items on the Positive List under certain conditions (discussed subsequently).

GSP preferences are generally granted in the industrial-mining sector. However, some sensitive items are excluded through an Exceptions List.[2] Of GSP-covered items, some are granted GSP treatment up to ceiling (quota) quantities or values, whereas others qualify for GSP benefits without being subject to a ceiling. However, an increase in imports that not subject to a ceiling may trigger GSP suspension under an escape clause, as described later.

Special Preferential Regime

Imports from LDCs of most items that qualify for the GSP receive duty-free treatment. The 2007 reform expanded the scope of products for LDC-specific duty-free preferences in both the agricultural-fishery and the industrial-mining sectors.

Rules of Origin

To benefit from preferential treatment, an imported item must satisfy GSP rules of origin.[3] These rules are intended to prevent third countries from free-riding on preferences. To enforce these rules, imports must be accompanied by a certificate of origin issued by the exporting country's authorities or designated entities.

GSP Scope

Japan's GSP has 155 beneficiaries: 141 developing countries and 14 territories. Of these, as of December 2007, 105 were general GSP beneficiaries and 50 were LDCs. To obtain GSP treatment, an economy must be developing and have its own tariff and trade system. To obtain LDC treatment, a country must be designated an LDC by the United Nations. A country graduates from the GSP program once its economy is officially classified as a *high-income country* by the World Bank for three consecutive years.[4] Before such total graduation, revocation of benefits for particular products may occur under a partial graduation scheme. This revocation occurs if the following conditions are simultaneously met for one year: (a) imports of the item from a high-income supplying country exceed 25 percent of the total imports of that item to Japan and (b) the value of imports of the item exceeds ¥1 billion.[5]

The broad country coverage of the GSP stands in contrast to its narrow product coverage (table 4.1). This difference remains substantially unchanged despite the 2007 reform.[6]

TABLE 4.1 GSP Product Coverage

	Agricultural-fishery sector	Industrial-mining sector
Items (at HS nine-digit level)	HS chapters 1–24 HS tariff items: 2,023 MFN dutiable items: 1,641	HS chapters 25–97 HS tariff items: 7,012 MFN dutiable items: 4,290
Non-LDC GSP product coverage		
Until fiscal year 2006	GSP exclusion principle: 1,301 GSP coverage Positive List items: 340	GSP-granting principle: 3,216 No-ceiling items: 2,033 Ceiling items: 1,183 GSP exclusion items: 1,074 GSP Exceptions List items: 105 LDC-specific, duty-free items: 969
From fiscal year 2007	GSP exclusion principle: 1,301 GSP coverage Positive List items: 340	GSP-granting principle: 3,216 No-ceiling items: 2,033 Ceiling items: 1,183 GSP exclusion items: 1,074 GSP Exceptions List items: 1,028 LDC Exceptions List items: 46
LDC product coverage		
Until fiscal year 2006	GSP exclusion principle: 1,114 LDC duty-free items: 497 Positive List items: 340 LDC-specific, duty-free items: 157	LDC duty-free principle: 4,185 LDC exclusion LDC Exceptions List items: 105
From fiscal year 2007	LDC duty-free principle: 1,523 LDC exclusion LDC Exceptions List items: 118	LDC duty-free principle: 4,244 LDC exclusion LDC Exceptions List items: 46

Source: Compiled by the author from the Tariff Temporary Measures Law and its annexes 2 to 5.

Japan's tariff schedule includes 9,035 items at the nine-digit level, including 2,023 agricultural-fishery items (Harmonized System [HS] chapters 1–24) and 7,012 industrial-mining items (HS chapters 25–97). Of 2,023 agricultural-fishery items, MFN dutiable items and others (MFN duty-free and nonconcessional items) account for 1,641 and 382 of them, respectively. Of the 7,012 industrial-mining items, 4,290 are MFN dutiable and 2,722 are MFN duty free and nonconcessional.[7]

The scope of GSP-eligible products among the MFN dutiable items is a key issue. GSP product coverage in the agricultural-fishery sector is still limited. Of the 1,641 MFN dutiable agricultural-fishery items, 1,301 items (80 percent) are excluded from the GSP scheme, leaving only 340 (20 percent) items on the Positive List. Examples include maize seed, frozen octopus, burdock, truffles, Matsutake mushrooms, and vegetable juices. Items on the Positive List either are duty free or have tariffs lower than MFN duty rates.[8]

LDC-specific duty-free items in the agricultural-fishery sector before the 2007 reform accounted for 157 items at the HS nine-digit level, including black tea, edible *Brassica*, shallots, lettuce, carrots, turnips, cucumbers, beans, and celery. Imports of such items from non-LDC GSP countries were subject to MFN tariffs.[9] The 2007 reform made all GSP-covered agricultural-fishery items duty free for LDCs. However, the newly introduced LDC Exceptions List applies to imports from any LDC. It includes 118 ultrasensitive items at the HS nine-digit level.[10]

In the industrial-mining sector, of the 4,290 MFN dutiable items at the HS nine-digit level, 3,216 items (74 percent) were covered by the non-LDC GSP scheme before the 2007 reform. The remaining items were broken down into 105 items in the Exceptions List for the non-LDC GSP scheme and 969 items in the LDC-specific duty-free list. The 2007 reform did not affect GSP coverage of non-LDCs. Likewise, the GSP exclusion list remained intact, covering 1,074 items at the HS nine-digit level. These consist of 1,028 GSP Exception List items and 46 LDC Exception List items. Some items were moved between the two lists. In addition to most items in the previous GSP Exceptions List (except salt),[11] the current GSP Exceptions List includes the previous LDC Exceptions List items.[12] In exchange, 46 items in the previous GSP Exceptions List[13] were transferred to the current LDC Exceptions List. Brief, non-LDC GSP coverage underwent no amendment, while LDC-specific duty-free coverage was expanded.[14]

GSP coverage, whether in the agricultural-fishery or the industrial-mining sector, may be circumscribed by safeguards. If imports of a GSP-covered item increase because of preferential treatment and cause—or threaten to cause—injury to a domestic industry producing a like or directly competitive item, preferential treatment may be suspended and an MFN tariff applied. No safeguard applications have been reported.

Ceiling Regime

Of GSP-eligible industrial-mining items, sensitive goods are subject to a ceiling regime.[15] Under the regime, GSP treatment is accorded to these goods up to certain ceiling quantities or values, but imports in excess of the ceiling are subject to MFN tariffs.[16] GSP in-ceiling duty rates vary from item to item, from duty free to 20, 40, 60, or 80 percent of the MFN tariff.[17] Two kinds of ceiling regime can be applied: per country and per item. Under the per country ceiling, if imports of an item from one GSP beneficiary exceed 20 percent of the permitted annual ceiling, then GSP treatment is suspended for that item for that beneficiary. Under the per item ceiling, if imports of an item exceed the annual total ceiling value or quantity, then GSP treatment is suspended for the item for all GSP beneficiaries. The ceiling regime is administered on a first-come, first-served basis by the Japanese Customs Authority.

In principle, imports from LDCs are generally not subject to ceilings; however, under the current 10-year GSP scheme (2001–11), the special law introduced ceilings for imports of refined copper from the Democratic Republic of Congo and Zambia (both of which are classified as LDCs). These ceilings applied from 2001 to 2005.

The number of GSP-covered items not subject to ceilings reaches 2,033 at the HS nine-digit level. These items are potentially subject to safeguards, however.

Country-Specific Competitiveness-Focused GSP Exclusion

Imports under the GSP from specific GSP beneficiaries may be excluded from GSP treatment under the country-specific, competitiveness-focused GSP exclusion that has been in effect since fiscal year 2003. This mechanism does not apply to LDCs. Japan has used this exclusion several times since 2003 for a range of products, including canned tuna from Thailand, ethylene glycol from Saudi Arabia, mats and screens of vegetable materials from China, and certain kitchenware and tableware from China.

Two yardsticks are used to determine the effect of a highly competitive item on the domestic industry. One is whether import values of a particular item from a GSP beneficiary to Japan exceed 50 percent of the total value of imports to Japan in two consecutive fiscal years. The other is whether the import values of the item amount to ¥1 billion in two consecutive fiscal years. The yardsticks are not absolute, however; GSP exclusion is ultimately left to the discretion of the government. If, in its view, there is no need for GSP exclusion in light of the amount of domestic output and the effect on a domestic industry, the item in question may remain covered by the GSP scheme despite exceeding the two yardsticks.

Fishing-Specific and Free Trade Agreement–Specific GSP Exclusion

Two additional GSP exclusion regimes were recently introduced. First, if a GSP beneficiary (other than an LDC) infringes on measures that regional maritime organizations have adopted to preserve fishery resources and the environment, imports of the fish from the infringing GSP beneficiary can lose GSP treatment, starting in fiscal year 2007.[18] Second, with the entry into force of free trade agreements (FTAs) with GSP beneficiaries such as Chile, Malaysia, Mexico, and

Thailand, a series of items that are covered by both but for which the FTA prefer-ential duty is lower than the GSP duty were excluded from GSP treatment. Gradual duty reduction on items within FTAs inevitably leads to GSP exclusion of those items for beneficiaries of the FTA, reducing the benefit for them of the GSP.

GSP Rules of Origin and Supplementary Regime

The GSP criteria for rules of origin consist of the *wholly produced goods criterion* and the *substantial transformation criterion*. For preference eligibility, Japanese inputs are included with materials that are produced in a preference-receiving country when local content is considered.[19] For a finished product that is produced using both local materials and third-country inputs, the country of origin is deter-mined according to the substantial transformation principle, as discussed later.

The principle of cumulative origin applies to goods produced within five member countries of the Association of Southeast Asian Nations (ASEAN): Indonesia, Malaysia, the Philippines, Thailand, and Vietnam. These goods may be wholly produced in these ASEAN countries or may be substantially transformed in them—that is, goods made of materials wholly produced in these countries and other materials that have undergone substantial transformation in those coun-tries. The substantial transformation criterion is a key component of GSP rules of origin. When more than two countries are involved in the manufacturing process for particular goods, the finished goods are considered as originating in the preference-receiving country, provided that the inputs have been substantially transformed in that country.

The substantial transformation criterion may be satisfied by one or more of four tests: (a) a change of tariff classification, (b) double processing, (c) a value added test, or (d) a mixed test. A change of tariff heading between the nonorig-inating materials and a finished product is sufficient to confer origin on the preference-receiving country. This test applies to many agricultural products and to some industrial products, such as inorganic chemicals. Double-processing operations are required for some nonmachinery products. For fabrics from staple fibers, for example, the double-processing test requires the manufacture of yarn from staple fibers and the production of fabrics from the yarn. For clothing accessories such as handkerchiefs, the double-processing test may be satisfied by weaving the fabric and producing the goods.

In the machinery sector (HS chapters 84–91) most goods are bound duty free in the General Agreement on Tariffs and Trade (GATT), now the World Trade Organization (WTO). Only a few four-digit goods—insulated wire, carbon elec-trodes, armored fighting vehicles, spectacles and frames, and watchstraps—are dutiable. GSP rules of origin for these product groups are based on value added criteria. Two tests are used: a 55 percent value added test for products assembled of parts that are included within the same tariff heading, and a 60 percent value added test for products assembled of parts from different tariff headings.

Finally, a mixed test of processing operations combined with a value added test is used for a number of products. This test appears in three forms. For certain food preparations, the test requires manufacture of materials from different tariff headings and use of less than 40 percent import content (that is, more than 60 percent value added). For medicaments, odoriferous substances, preparations for use in dentistry, specified chemical products, umbrellas, brushes, buttons, and certain toys and models, the test requires manufacture of materials from different tariff headings and use of less than 50 percent import content. For cutwork containers and glassware, the test requires manufacture from the same tariff heading materials and use of less than 50 percent import content.

GSP Origin Certification and Verification

GSP-covered imports must be accompanied by a certificate of origin issued by one of the following certifying bodies: the exporting country's customs agency, another authoritative government agency, or the chamber of commerce or another similar body, if recognized as adequate by the Japan customs. Names and seals of certifying bodies must be notified to Japan. A certificate of origin without notified seals, with a falsified certificate, or a copy of the certificate will be rejected. In addition, GSP rules require that additional certifications be attached to a certificate of origin where relevant: hand-dyeing (or printing) certification for batik fabrics, donor country content certification, and cumulation certification.[20]

In case of doubts as to the authenticity or the accuracy of the certificate of origin, customs employees can carry out verification under relevant administrative notices. To this end, they may request the beneficiary's authorities to submit additional evidence and certification electronically. However, as seen in the frozen octopus case, customs can also conduct de facto on-the-spot verification to establish the falsification of certificates of origins.[21]

Direct Transportation Requirement

Goods that originate in a preference-receiving country should be consigned directly to Japan without passing through a third country. However, goods are regarded as directly consigned to Japan if they pass through the territory of a third country for transshipment, temporary storage, or exhibitions that are carried out in a bonded area and under customs control of the third country. In the case of transshipment, however, relevant evidence must be submitted to the Japanese Customs Authority.[22]

Sanctions

Sanctions, coupled with origin certification and verification, are stipulated in order to induce compliance with GSP rules of origin. A false declaration of origin is subject to imprisonment for up to five years, a penalty of up to ¥5 million, or both. The same applies to tax evasion through abuse of preferential treatment. In addition, customs may increase the penalty up to 10 times if tax evasion is involved. However, customs does not do enough to pursue criminal prosecution. Rather, it seeks to have the penalties compounded—that is, it requests a financial payment as an out-of-court settlement.

GSP Utilization

About half of Japan's imports (47.1 percent in fiscal year 2005) were exported from GSP beneficiaries. Total imports from GSP beneficiaries doubled from ¥9 trillion in fiscal year 1975 to ¥19 trillion in 1980, increased only marginally during the period of yen appreciation, and then increased from about ¥20 trillion in 2003 to ¥28 trillion in 2005 (table 4.2). Imports from LDCs remained very small compared with total imports from the world and from GSP beneficiaries as a whole, despite LDCs' potential entitlement to duty-free treatment.

Imports from GSP beneficiaries consist of MFN duty-free items and MFN dutiable items. The ratio of MFN dutiable imports from GSP beneficiaries to total imports from GSP beneficiaries decreased from 83.5 percent in 1975 to about 50.0 percent in 2000 and 2001, reflecting trade liberalization under the GATT/WTO. Japan lowered the MFN tariff for a number of goods to zero or low rates, in particular during (and following) the Uruguay Round negotiation.

GSP-covered goods accounted for 52.2 percent of MFN dutiable imports in 2001. However, GSP-covered imports did not necessarily enjoy preferential treatment, for various reasons. On the contrary, the statistics show a poor utilization ratio of GSP treatment. The GSP utilization ratio in the 1980s was about 60 percent. However, the ratio declined to between 32 and 34 percent from 2000 to 2005 (see table 4.2).[23]

The low GSP utilization reflects trade liberalization under GATT/WTO and Japan's legal regime. With the promotion of trade liberalization following the Uruguay Round, the preference margins gradually decreased; hence, the benefits arising from preference margins faded compared to the costs incurred in qualifying for preferences. Major exporting GSP beneficiaries, including Japanese-owned subsidiaries, incurred significant costs in meeting GSP rules of origin and keeping necessary evidence to obtain certificates of origin; moreover, small local industries in GSP beneficiaries frequently lack the financial and human resources to comply with onerous rules of origin.

TABLE 4.2 GSP Utilization Ratio in All Sectors, Fiscal Years 1975–2005

	1975	1980	1985	1990	1995	2000	2001	2002	2003	2004	2005
Imports from the world (¥ billion) (a)	17,266	31,138	28,686	33,746	32,548	41,754	40,781	42,275	44,134	49,564[a]	59,468
Imports from GSP beneficiaries (¥ billion) (b)	9,232	19,270	15,892	16,311	16,789	16,654	17,106	18,590	19,995	23,234	28,523
Ratio of a to b (%)	53.5	61.9	55.4	48.3	51.6	39.9	41.9	44.0	45.3	46.9	48.0
LDC share (%)	0.2	0.2	0.2	0.2	0.4	0.3	0.3	0.5	0.4	1.0	0.8
MFN dutiable imports from GSP beneficiaries (¥ billion) (c)	7,711	15,650	11,939	10,984	9,383	8,597	8,708	9,387	9,580	10,890	13,881
Ratio of b to c (%)	83.5	81.2	75.1	67.3	55.9	51.6	50.9	50.5	47.9	46.9	48.7
LDC share (%)	0.1	0.0	0.2	0.3	0.5	0.5	0.6	1.0	0.6	1.0	1.6
GSP-covered imports (¥ billion) (d)	749	1,864	2,212	3,260	4,062	4,180	4,543	4,634	5,238	5,696	6,338
Ratio of d to c (%)	9.7	11.9	18.5	29.7	43.3	48.6	52.2	49.4	54.7	52.3	45.7
LDC share (%)	0.0	0.0	0.0	0.2	0.2	0.3	0.4	0.4	0.5	0.5	0.4
GSP-receiving imports (¥ billion) (e)	386	1,104	1,334	1,574	1,671	1,432	1,458	1,572	1,749	1,899	2,100
GSP utilization ratio (ratio of e to d) (%)	51.5	59.2	60.3	48.3	41.1	34.3	32.1	33.9	33.4	33.3	33.1
LDC share (%)	0.1	0.1	0.2	0.7	0.5	0.6	0.7	0.7	0.9	0.9	0.9

Source: Compiled by the author from Ministry of Finance statistics on each fiscal year's trade data (from April to March).

a. Main exporting countries are broken down as follows: China, 20.8 percent; GSP beneficiaries, 26.2 percent; LDCs, 0.8 percent; United States, 12.2 percent; European Union, 11.0 percent; other countries, 28.9 percent. Imports from GSP beneficiaries and LDCs include non-GSP-receiving goods.

The protectionist orientation of the GSP partly explains its poor performance. The narrow coverage of products in the agricultural-fishery and industrial-mining sectors, for instance, is further limited by the competitiveness-focused GSP exclusion clause. In the industrial-mining sector, the ceiling regime disadvantages minor GSP beneficiaries relative to Asian Tigers such as Hong Kong, China; the Republic of Korea; Singapore; and Taiwan, China.[24] In addition to the narrow GSP product coverage, access to preferential treatment by GSP beneficiaries and LDCs is restricted by strict and costly requirements under the GSP rules of origin and certification.

GSP Utilization Ratio in the Agricultural-Fishery Sector

In the agricultural-fishery sector, although Japan restricts competitive imports by quota and tariff peaks, it relies on imports from the world to meet domestic demand. The degree of dependence on imports (among others, from China and ASEAN countries) is high with regard to vegetables, fruits, and certain fish, all of which are subject to low MFN duties. The ratio of MFN dutiable imports to total imports of agricultural-fishery products from GSP beneficiaries has reached roughly 80 percent over the past three decades, indicating tariff peaks to protect uncompetitive domestic sectors. GSP-covered imports increased 10 times in nominal terms, from ¥82 billion in fiscal year 1975 to ¥983 billion in fiscal year 2005. However, of GSP-covered imports, the GSP-receiving imports did not significantly increase, declining from ¥430 billion in fiscal year 1995 to ¥338 billion in fiscal year 2005. Hence, the GSP utilization ratio fell from 91 percent in fiscal year 1995 to 34 to 39 percent in fiscal years 2003 to 2005 (table 4.3). The low GSP utilization ratio reflects Japan's protectionism in the agricultural-fishery sector. The principal cause derives from the aforementioned de jure GSP exclusion of non-LDCs' key export items and de facto hindrances to receiving GSP benefits.

GSP Utilization Ratio in the Industrial-Mining Sector

In the industrial-mining sector, imports from GSP beneficiaries totaled about ¥14 billion from 1985 to 2001 (table 4.4). The ratio of imports of industrial-mining goods from GSP beneficiaries to those from the world, however, decreased from 57.6 percent in 1985 to 42.8 percent in 2001. The graduation of former beneficiaries (for example, Hong Kong, China; the Republic of Korea; Singapore; and Taiwan, China) led to a decrease in imports from developing countries.

Approximately half (or less) of imports from developing countries were MFN dutiable in this period (51.5 percent in 1995, 46.7 percent in 2001, 45.8 percent in 2005). The ratio of GSP-covered imports to MFN dutiable imports increased from 11.3 percent in 1980 to about 45 to 57 percent in fiscal years 2001 to 2005.

TABLE 4.3 GSP Utilization Ratio in the Agricultural-Fishery Sector, Fiscal Years 1975–2005

	1975	1980	1985	1990	1995	2000	2001	2002	2003	2004	2005
Imports of agricultural-fishery products from the world (¥ billion) (a)	3,076	3,958	4,290	5,137	5,372	5,485	5,785	5,772	5,691	5,926	6,247
Imports from GSP beneficiaries (¥ billion) (b)	1,107	1,363	1,836	2,058	2,293	1,941	2,111	2,079	2,059	2,215	2,417
Ratio of a to b (%)	36.0	34.5	42.8	40.1	42.7	35.4	36.5	36.3	36.2	37.4	38.7
LDC share (%)	0.8	0.8	0.9	1.1	1.2	1.0	0.8	0.9	0.9	0.9	0.9
MFN dutiable imports from GSP beneficiaries (¥ billion) (c)	934	1,011	1,393	1,686	1,922	1,584	1,704	1,701	1,647	1,779	1,936
Ratio of c to b (%)	84.3	74.1	75.9	81.9	83.8	81.6	80.7	81.8	80.0	80.3	80.1
LDC share (%)	0.4	0.6	1.0	1.8	1.9	1.6	1.4	1.5	1.5	1.6	1.4
GSP-covered imports (¥ billion) (d)	82	214	295	377	472	481	524	553	855	934	983
Ratio of d to c (%)	8.8	21.1	21.2	22.3	24.6	30.4	30.8	32.5	51.9	52.5	50.7
LDC share (%)	0.0	0.0	0.0	1.0	0.9	0.5	0.4	0.5	1.4	1.6	1.4
GSP-receiving imports (¥ billion) (e)	77	197	279	342	430	371	333	342	341	368	338
LDC share (%)	—	—	—	—	—	—	1.3	1.5	2.3	2.8	2.5
Utilization ratio (ratio of e to d) (%)	93.2	92.3	94.5	90.7	91.0	77.0	63.5	61.9	39.9	39.4	34.4
LDC share (%)	0.3	0.2	0.1	4.6	3.7	1.7	1.3	1.5	2.3	2.8	2.5

Source: Fiscal year data compiled by the author from Ministry of Finance statistics.

Note: — = not available.

TABLE 4.4 GSP Utilization Ratio of Industrial-Mining Products, Fiscal Years 1975–2005

	1975	1980	1985	1990	1995	2000	2001	2002	2003	2004	2005
Imports from the world (¥ billion) (a)	14,190	27,180	24,396	28,608	27,176	36,269	34,996	36,553	38,443	43,638	53,220
Imports from GSP beneficiaries (¥ billion) (b)	8,124	17,907	14,056	14,253	14,497	14,713	14,994	16,512	17,936	21,020	26,106
Ratio of b to a (%)	57.3	65.9	57.6	49.8	53.3	40.6	42.8	45.2	46.7	48.2	49.1
LDC share (%)	0.1	0.1	0.1	0.1	0.2	0.2	0.3	0.5	0.3	0.5	0.8
MFN dutiable imports from GSP beneficiaries (¥ billion) (c)	6,777	14,639	10,546	9,298	7,462	7,013	7,004	7,686	7,933	9,111	11,945
Ratio of c to b (%)	83.4	81.7	75.0	65.2	51.5	47.7	46.7	46.5	44.2	43.3	45.8
LDC share (%)	0.1	0.0	0.1	0.1	0.3	0.4	0.5	0.9	0.5	0.9	1.6
GSP-covered imports (¥ billion) (d)	667	1,651	1,917	2,884	3,590	3,699	4,020	4,082	4,383	4,762	5,355
Ratio of d to c (%)	9.8	11.3	18.2	31.0	48.1	52.8	57.4	53.1	55.2	52.3	44.8
LDC share (%)	0.0	0.0	0.0	0.0	0.1	0.3	0.4	0.4	0.4	0.3	0.3
GSP-receiving imports (¥ billion) (e)	309	907	1,055	1,232	1,241	1,061	1,125	1,229	1,408	1,532	1,762
GSP utilization ratio (ratio of e to d) (%)	46.3	54.9	55.0	42.7	34.6	28.7	28.0	30.1	32.1	32.2	32.9
LDC share (%)	0.1	0.1	0.2	0.1	0.1	0.5	0.6	0.6	0.6	0.6	0.6

Source: Compiled by the author from Ministry of Finance statistics.

114

However, the GSP utilization ratio progressively decreased from 54.9 percent in 1980 to 28 to 33 percent in fiscal years 2001 to 2005 (see table 4.4). Thus, industrial-mining goods, although covered by GSP treatment in principle, encountered a number of difficulties in meeting conditions for preferential access.

Reasons for a low utilization ratio are also multiple: strict rules of origin for labor-intensive goods, such as textiles and footwear; high costs incurred in acquiring a certificate of origin;[25] rigid origin verification; inapplicability of the donor content country criterion to sensitive products, such as most apparel;[26] and the ceiling regime for selected items and the competitiveness-focused GSP exclusion.

GSP Ceiling Utilization Ratio under the Ceiling Regime

Under the law, the total ceiling value under the ceiling regime increases by 1.03 percent per year. In reality, however, it has decreased significantly on a number of occasions. The decrease was radical in fiscal years 2000, 2001, and 2003. The ceiling value of ¥1,060 billion in fiscal year 1999 fell to ¥699 billion in fiscal year 2000, ¥269 billion in fiscal year 2001, and ¥275 billion in fiscal year 2003. This fall was a consequence of the graduation of 20 high-income countries from the GSP in fiscal year 2000, a transfer of certain items from the ceiling regime to the safeguards regime in fiscal year 2001, and the removal of two group products (including dolls) from the ceiling regime in fiscal year 2003.

The average ceiling utilization ratio increased from 60.5 percent in fiscal year 1999 to 92.7 percent in fiscal year 2003 (table 4.5).[27] The discrepancy is due to the way the ceiling was used by item and country. Ceiling utilization ratios in fiscal year 2003 differed according to the item and the GSP beneficiary. The lowest

TABLE 4.5 GSP Ceiling Utilization Ratio under the Ceiling Regime, Fiscal Years 1999–2003

	1999	2000	2001	2002	2003
Total imports from GSP beneficiaries (¥ billion)	17,596	14,713	14,994	16,512	17,936
GSP-covered imports from GSP beneficiaries (¥ billion)	3,697	3,699	4,020	4,082	4,383
GSP-receiving imports (¥ billion)	1,232	1,061	1,125	1,229	1,407
GSP ceiling quota (¥ billion) (a)	1,060	699	269	278	275
GSP ceiling utilization value (¥ billion) (b)	641	506	240	247	255
GSP ceiling utilization ratio (ratio of b to a) (%)	60.5	72.4	89.4	88.9	92.7

Source: Compiled by the author from Ministry of Finance statistics.

utilization ratio was 1.7 percent for Paulownia wood. The highest ratio was 9,932 percent for umbrellas. Of GSP beneficiaries, China and some ASEAN countries made use of GSP treatment under the first-come, first-served rule, leaving minor countries with small shares.[28]

Duty-Free Utilization by LDCs

The LDC-specific duty-free scheme was ostensibly an important concession by major developed countries, including Japan. In practice, however, the scheme does not grant substantial benefits to LDCs. Instead of LDCs, MFN countries (such as Australia; the Republic of Korea; Taiwan, China; and the United States) and general GSP beneficiaries (among others, China and ASEAN GSP countries) were the main suppliers of these goods.[29]

Whether the LDC-specific, duty-free, ceiling-free scheme (as applied starting in fiscal year 2007) will raise the GSP utilization ratio for LDCs remains to be seen.[30] The reason is that compliance with origin certification is required for imports from LDCs, and infringement of the certification rule gives rise to severe verification procedures and possible sanction.

GSP-Receiving Countries and Products

The main GSP beneficiaries in the 1980s were China; the Republic of Korea; and Taiwan, China. In 1999, China became the largest beneficiary. With the graduation in 2000 of Korea, Singapore, and Taiwan, China, China and five ASEAN countries became the key beneficiaries. The statistics show that imports from China and those ASEAN countries (Indonesia, Malaysia, the Philippines, Thailand, and Vietnam) account for 55 to 60 percent and 29 to 32 percent, respectively, of imports that enjoy GSP treatment. Imports from China and the five ASEAN countries contributed a total of 86 to 88 percent (table 4.6).

The top 10 LDCs that benefit from preferences have been Asian and African countries. According to statistics for 2001, the ratio of preference-receiving imports from LDCs to total imports from them was 65.8 percent for Asian LDCs (ASEAN LDCs, Bangladesh, and Nepal); 40.9 percent for three ASEAN LDCs (Cambodia, Lao People's Democratic Republic, and Myanmar); 30.3 percent for imports from African LDCs (Angola, the Democratic Republic of Congo, The Gambia, Malawi, Mauritania, Tanzania, and Zambia); and 1.3 percent for Oceania's LDCs (Solomon Islands) (table 4.7). Preference-receiving items from LDCs in 2005 included frozen shrimp and prawns from Bangladesh, Madagascar, Mozambique, and Myanmar; octopus from Mauritania and Senegal; and refined copper from Zambia.

TABLE 4.6 Top 10 Beneficiaries of the GSP, Fiscal Years 1986–2005

Ranking	Beneficiary (% of imports enjoying GSP treatment)										
	1986	1990	1999	2000	2001	2002	2003	2004	2005		
1	Korea, Rep. of (24.5)	Korea, Rep. of (24.1)	China (40.3)	China (53.6)	China (55.5)	China (56.1)	China (57.6)	China (58.9)	China (59.8)		
2	Taiwan, China (21.2)	Taiwan, China (17.1)	Korea, Rep. of (10.6)	Thailand (10.8)	Thailand (9.2)	Thailand (8.8)	Thailand (7.8)	Thailand (7.9)	Thailand (7.6)		
3	China (8.7)	China (11.3)	Taiwan, China (9.2)	Indonesia (8.2)	Indonesia (8.5)	Indonesia (8.4)	Indonesia (7.8)	Malaysia (7.2)	Malaysia (6.7)		
4	Philippines (6.4)	Brazil (7.8)	Thailand (8.9)	Malaysia (7.1)	Malaysia (6.6)	Malaysia (6.6)	Malaysia (6.7)	Indonesia (6.2)	Indonesia (6.2)		
5	Singapore (4.4)	Philippines (4.3)	Indonesia (6.1)	Philippines (5.2)	Philippines (5.2)	Philippines (5.7)	Philippines (5.5)	Philippines (5.5)	Philippines (5.3)		
6	Brazil (4.4)	Indonesia (4.0)	Malaysia (5.8)	Morocco (2.0)	Vietnam (1.8)	Vietnam (1.9)	Vietnam (1.8)	Vietnam (2.0)	Vietnam (2.0)		
7	Saudi Arabia (2.8)	Thailand (3.4)	Philippines (4.8)	India (1.7)	India (1.6)	India (1.5)	India (1.6)	India (1.6)	South Africa (2.1)		
8	Malaysia (2.4)	Venezuela, R.B. de (3.3)	Morocco (1.4)	Vietnam (1.5)	Brazil (1.3)	Brazil (1.3)	Brazil (1.4)	Brazil (1.4)	India (1.8)		

(Table continues on the following page.)

TABLE 4.6 Top 10 Beneficiaries of the GSP, Fiscal Years 1986–2005 (Continued)

Ranking	1986	1990	1999	2000	2001	2002	2003	2004	2005
				Beneficiary (% of imports enjoying GSP treatment)					
9	Thailand (2.4)	Malaysia (3.0)	Brazil (1.3)	Brazil (1.5)	Chile (1.1)	Chile (1.0)	South Africa (1.1)	South Africa (1.3)	Brazil (1.4)
10	Indonesia (2.3)	Singapore (2.2)	Singapore (1.2)	Chile (1.3)	Morocco (0.8)	Morocco (0.8)	Chile (1.0)	Chile (1.0)	Chile (1.0)
ASEAN 5[a]	—	—	—	32.8	31.3	31.4	29.6	28.8	28
China + ASEAN 5	—	—	—	86.4	86.8	87.5	87.2	87.7	87.8
Total amount[b] (¥ million)	—	—	—	—	1,459,638	1,574,839	1,749,895	1,899,372	2,099,925

Source: Compiled by the author from Ministry of Finance statistics.

Note: — = not available.

a. Ratio of the five preference-receiving ASEAN members (Indonesia, Malaysia, the Philippines, Thailand, and Vietnam) to the total GSP.
b. Total amount of GSP preferences granted to GSP beneficiaries and LDCs.

TABLE 4.7 Preference-Receiving LDCs, Fiscal Years 1999–2005

Ranking	Beneficiary (% of imports enjoying preferences)						
	1999	2000	2001	2003	2004	2005
1	Mauritania (36.9)	Mauritania (28.6)	Cambodia (25.8)	Myanmar (25.6)	Myanmar (27.6)	Myanmar (31.0)
2	Bangladesh (16.4)	Bangladesh (21.6)	Bangladesh (23.1)	Cambodia (20.3)	Mauritania (23.1)	Mauritania (19.6)
3	Myanmar (13.6)	Cambodia (21.1)	Mauritania (19.1)	Bangladesh (16.8)	Cambodia (20.0)	Cambodia (19.0)
4	Cambodia (13.1)	Myanmar (12.8)	Myanmar (15.1)	Mauritania (16.8)	Bangladesh (15.8)	Bangladesh (16.6)
5	Gambia, The (7.8)	Nepal (9.5)	Zambia (7.8)	Zambia (6.1)	Senegal (2.5)	Madagascar (2.5)
6	Solomon Islands (3.1)	Lao PDR (1.7)	Nepal (2.0)	Madagascar (3.1)	Madagascar (2.3)	Mozambique (1.9)
7	Nepal (2.7)	Tanzania (1.2)	Congo, Dem. Rep. of (1.5)	Senegal (2.2)	Mozambique (1.8)	Senegal (1.9)
8	Lao PDR (2.4)	Solomon Islands (1.2)	Solomon Islands (1.3)	Mozambique (2.1)	Zambia (1.3)	Zambia (1.5)

(Table continues on the following page.)

TABLE 4.7 Preference-Receiving LDCs, Fiscal Years 1999–2005 (Continued)

Ranking	Beneficiary (% of imports enjoying preferences)					
	1999	2000	2001	2003	2004	2005
9	Angola (1.4)	Angola (0.7)	Angola (1.0)	Solomon Islands (1.3)	Tanzania (1.2)	Tanzania (1.5)
10	Tanzania (1.0)	The Gambia (0.6)	Malawi (0.9)	Tanzania (1.2)	Nepal (1.0)	Nepal (1.1)
Total imports from Asian LDCs (ASEAN LDCs, Bangladesh, and Nepal)	45.5	66.7	65.8	62.8	64.4	57.7
Total imports from ASEAN LDCs (Cambodia, Lao PDR, and Myanmar)	29.1	35.6	40.9	45.9	47.6	50
Total imports from African LDCs (Angola, Dem. Rep. of Congo, The Gambia, Malawi, Mauritania, Tanzania, and Zambia)	47.1	31.1	30.3	n.a.	n.a.	n.a.
Total imports from Oceania LDCs (Solomon Islands)	3.1	1.2	1.3	n.a.	n.a.	n.a.
Total imports from African LDCs	100	100	100	100	100	n.a.

Source: Compiled by the author from Ministry of Finance statistics.
Note: n.a. = not applicable.

Effect of FTAs on the GSP

Increase in Japan's FTAs. In contrast to its rapid introduction of the GSP, Japan has been reluctant to conclude FTAs that constitute an exception to the MFN principle. Japan changed its policy at the turn of the 21st century. It considers that regionalism, while theoretically discriminating against third countries in favor of intraregional trade, could be harmonized within the WTO's trade-promoting and nondiscriminatory system. Japan considered that an increase in regional and interregional FTAs, if conforming to WTO disciplines, would help the WTO liberalize and expand world trade.

Japan chose Singapore—at the time just graduated from Japan's GSP—as its first partner in 2002.[31] Japan then concluded bilateral agreements with a number of GSP beneficiaries in quick succession. Examples include FTAs with Chile,[32] Indonesia,[33] Malaysia,[34] Mexico,[35] the Philippines,[36] and Thailand[37]. Japan and the ASEAN 10 also reached broad agreement on an FTA in August 2007; the FTA still awaits signature and ratification in 2008. In addition, Japan proposed the future conclusion of an East Asian free trade agreement (EAFTA). If concluded between the ASEAN plus three (China, Japan, and the Republic of Korea) and Australia, India, and New Zealand, it would be the largest FTA in the world, involving half of the world's population and more than half of the world's resources and gross national product. The participation of current major GSP beneficiaries in the EAFTA would cause exclusion or graduation of those beneficiaries from the GSP scheme, thus minimizing the number of such beneficiaries. In addition, the preference margin is diminishing following the lowering of MFN tariffs under the WTO. GSP erosion is thus inevitable in the world trading system.

Coexistence of GSP with FTAs. Under the existing bilateral agreements with GSP beneficiaries, Japan made a tariff concession to lower the MFN tariff immediately, or progressively, for numerous goods originating in partner countries. In addition, Japan allowed many agricultural goods to be included in the agreements' tariff concessions for the first time in its history and made use of the existing GSP scheme in the context of FTAs. A refined scheme was therefore introduced to coordinate the GSP with the agreements. They coexist until the intra-FTA liberalization is accomplished. For items covered by both the GSP and an FTA, the lower of the two tariffs applies. Hence, for these items, those that are subject to an FTA tariff that undercuts the GSP tariff are gradually excluded from GSP coverage in accordance with the FTA-specific GSP exclusion scheme. FTA-concessioned items falling outside the purview of the GSP are entitled to FTA tariffs. GSP items that are not covered by FTA concessions remain subject to the MFN tariff or GSP tariff.

Establishment of FTAs. If FTAs cover all trade, the GSP is redundant. In particular, with the establishment of the EAFTA, most GSP-covered items would be supplied from Asian FTA partner countries' suppliers. Hence, other GSP beneficiaries, including LDCs, would be deprived of a favorable market access opportunity.

GSP Erosion and Solution

GSP erosion derives from various factors: de jure narrow GSP coverage, de facto GSP exclusion based on the ceiling regime and competitiveness-focused clause, GSP rules of origin and certification, and the proliferation of Japan's FTAs. The question of how to compensate developing countries for GSP erosion is becoming more important. Two solutions can be contemplated.

GSP Reform

One potential solution is GSP reform. Although it has broadened LDC-specific, duty-free coverage, the government of Japan hesitates to relax GSP rules of origin and origin certification and verification for fear of tax evasion through falsified certification and free-riding. Here lies a dilemma inherent in the GSP regime. The stricter the rules of origin are, the less the GSP is used. The more relaxed the rules of origin are, the more free-riding occurs. To overcome this dilemma, policy makers could explore tools designed to relax rules of origin in parallel with reductions in the cost of origin certification for GSP users.

Simplifying rules of origin could make them easier for GSP beneficiaries to use. Origin criteria based on tests of a change in tariff classification have major advantages over tests of value added. In particular, they avoid complicated cost calculation, burdensome requirements for record keeping, and vulnerability to daily currency changes, which make a beneficiary's ability to satisfy the rule of origin unpredictable. Tools to increase the flexibility of the rules could be developed. These tools might include a toleration test for change-in-tariff classification, conditional outward processing schemes for GSP beneficiaries depending on offshore processing,[38] adoption of full cumulation for intermediate goods, extension of the regional cumulation rule to promote regional division of labor,[39] and conditional exceptions to the direct transport principle. In addition, lower GSP tariffs could be based on an ad valorem duty, as discussed in reference to MFN reform in the nonpreferential area.

Though inevitable to avoid free-riding and trade deflection, origin certification and verification schemes are not costless. Capacity building is needed to help GSP beneficiaries make the best of GSP certification in a cost-saving manner—for example, free, user-friendly governmental certification using the Internet; self-certification by producers and exporters; and approved exporters' certification under the pan-European rules of origin. One alternative might be to model the scheme on the European Union and U.S. new-generation GSP schemes or on provisions such as the flexible rules of origin for clothing for some suppliers under AGOA.

MFN Reform

Another solution is MFN tariff cuts.[40] The rationale is that most developing countries' export items that have a comparative advantage are subject to MFN tariffs. The problem is that Japan's MFN tariffs for most agricultural-fishery items and some sensitive industrial-mining items are high. This high degree of tariff protection is apparent in the case of MFN tariffs expressed in ad valorem terms. By contrast, the degree of protection is much less obvious for MFN tariffs expressed in non–ad valorem form. Converting a non–ad valorem duty to its ad valorem equivalent (AVE) reveals the rate of protection. This AVE may be calculated by dividing collected duties (the quantity multiplied by a specific duty amount) by the total import value. In other words, the AVE is the ratio of the duty amount to the unit value. Therefore, the more expensive the unit value (the denominator) is, the lower the AVE will be. By contrast, the less expensive the unit value is, the higher the AVE will be. Under the WTO, however, it is up to member states to make a choice between ad valorem and non–ad valorem duties. This choice permits a member state to camouflage the degree of protection for sensitive items by applying non–ad valorem duties.

AVE at a Crossroads

It is still an open question whether the AVE is a consistent criterion for measuring the height of a tariff wall, in particular in the nonpreferential area. The reason is that the AVE varies according to the unit value of a good. The unit value, in turn, changes depending on various factors (for example, technical progress, cost performance, and economic development). The AVE will differ between exporting countries, but this difference is meaningful. Because poor countries typically sell products at lower prices, the AVEs they face are higher. Thus, non–ad valorem duties inflict greater damage on imports from developing countries than on those from developed countries. Hence, if non–ad valorem duties were converted to ad valorem duties at the average rate applying to all countries, the tariff burden on imports from developing countries would be reduced.

AVE Issues in the Doha Round. AVEs are particularly important in the Doha negotiations. Reducing tariffs using a nonlinear methodology, such as the tiered formula being used in the agricultural negotiations or the Swiss formula being discussed in the negotiations on nonagricultural products, requires the conversion of non–ad valorem duties to an AVE.

Given the leeway to choose between ad valorem and non–ad valorem customs duty for any goods, high-income WTO members, including Japan, typically adopted non–ad valorem duties for sensitive agricultural products. Higher AVEs of non–ad valorem duties discouraged access by suppliers selling at lower prices. Hence, whether and how to convert non–ad valorem duties to ad valorem duties and lower these converted duties are crucial issues to be dealt with in the next round.

Not surprisingly, the AVE issue was included in the Doha Round agenda. To add political momentum to the Doha negotiations, the mini-ministerial conference held in Paris on May 3 and 4, 2005, reached an important breakthrough on the issue of agricultural AVEs that had stalled progress in nonagricultural negotiations. This agreement on AVEs was a key step in developing a formula for reducing tariffs, especially for agricultural products. This issue was politically sensitive because higher AVEs lead to deeper tariff cuts on these products. In addition, the deal will apply a weighted average of (a) the import prices reported by the governments to the WTO's Integrated Database (the approach favored by the EU and the Group of 10) and (b) the generally lower international market prices in the United Nations' COMTRADE database, the approach favored by farm exporters (the United States and the Cairns Group). Among the goods that will be subject to the mixed weighting formula are bovine meats and processed foods.

AVEs in the agricultural-fishery sector. Most agricultural and fishery products are subject to MFN tariffs expressed as specific, compound, or selective duties. AVEs of those non–ad valorem duties are frequently extremely high. The tariff for rice took the form of a tariff quota consisting of the in-quota tariff for state trading and the over-quota tariff for private trading.[41] Although the former is zero, the latter is specific: ¥341 per kilogram, which consists of the temporary tariff rate (¥49 per kilogram) and an adjustment levy (¥292 per kilogram).[42] The AVE of the over-quota specific tariff for rice—in particular semimilled or wholly milled rice (HS 1006.30-090)—reached 483 percent for Chinese rice and 626 percent for Thai rice in 2004. Even U.S. rice was subject to a 408 percent AVE in 2004 (table 4.8). The weighted average AVEs for durum wheat and meslin in 2004 were 14.7 percent and 18.5 percent, respectively. Wheat and barley are excluded from the GSP and categorized as a tariff peak. The tariff for GSP-excluded maize (HS 1005.90-099) is selective: 50 percent or ¥12 per kilogram, whichever is greater. The AVE of the selective duty exceeded 50 percent for imports from Argentina, Australia, China, South Africa, Thailand, and the United States. The highest AVE was 75.8 percent for imports from Argentina.

TABLE 4.8 AVE of MFN Specific Duty for Rice (Non-GSP Item), 2004

Item (HS number)	Country		Quantity (thousand kilograms)	Value (¥ thousand)	Unit value (¥/kilogram)	AVE at ¥341/ kilogram (%)
Husked rice (1006.20–090)	Developed countries	None				
	Developing countries	China (GSP)	15	1,253	83.5	408
		Thailand (GSP)	1	330	330	103
		Brazil (GSP)	8	4,167	520.1	65
	Total		24	5,750	240.0	142
Semimilled or wholly milled rice (1006.30–090)	Developed countries	Spain	0	582	—	—
		Italy	10	5,887	588.7	58
		United States	87	7,268	83.5	408
	Developing countries	China (GSP)	8	565	70.6	483
		Vietnam (GSP)	6	716	119.3	286
		Thailand (GSP)	142	7,731	54.4	626
		Brazil (GSP)	1	842	—	40
		Bangladesh (LDC)	4	465	116.3	293
	Total		258	24,056	93.2	366
Broken rice (1006.40–090)	None					

Source: Compiled by the author from Ministry of Finance statistics.

Note: — = not available.

Amorphophallus konjac–related goods are divided into tubers used as ingredients for making a final good and prepared final goods. The tariff quota for tubers is composed of an ad valorem duty for the in-quota imports (MFN, bound at 40 percent) and a specific duty for over-quota imports (¥2,796 per kilogram). The average AVE for the over-quota imports in 2004 exceeded 1,000 percent. The highest AVE was 1,547 percent for imports from Myanmar (an LDC). Likewise, AVEs in 2003 ranged from 1,501 percent for imports from Myanmar to 585 percent for those from China, with an average of 971 percent. By contrast, preparations of *Amorphophallus konjac* were subject to an MFN tariff rate of 21.3 percent.

The AVE of the compound tariff (21.3 percent plus ¥114 per kilogram) for low–fat content dairy products, imported only from China, was 32.7 percent. By contrast, AVEs of the compound tariff (21.3 percent plus ¥1,199 per kilogram) for high–fat content goods, imported from Belgium and the United Kingdom, were 394 percent and 92 percent, respectively. Concentrated or sweetened milk and cream under the tariff quota are protected by an in-quota ad valorem duty in the 25 to 30 percent range and an over-quota compound duty. The AVE of the over-quota compound duty for fatty goods (HS 0402.99-129) is more than double (70.9 percent for goods from Brazil and 60.7 percent for imports from Spain) the in-quota ad valorem tariff (30 percent). The AVEs of the over-quota compound duty for non–buttermilk powder of a specified fat content (HS 0403.90-128) from Belgium in 2004 was 409.6 percent. The tariff regime for butter imported by private parties is controlled by a tariff quota. In contrast to in-quota imports (HS 0405.10-121) that are subject to an MFN, which are bound at a 35 percent ad valorem duty, over-quota imports (HS 0405.10-129) face a compound duty: 29.8 percent plus ¥985 per kilogram. The AVE of the compound tariff for Swedish butter in 2003 reached 309 percent.

AVEs in the industrial-mining sector. In the industrial-mining sector, only a few items are subject to MFN non–ad valorem duties. Cotton poplin goods (unbleached, bleached, dyed, and printed items) are subject to the selective duty: (a) 5.6 percent or (b) 4.4 percent plus ¥1.52 per square meter, whichever is greater. AVEs of the selective duty for China and Malaysia in 2004 were 8.6 percent and 8.8 percent, respectively. Footwear under HS 6403.20 from Sri Lanka, a major GSP exporter, is subject to tariff peaks of 21 percent for in-quota imports and a selective duty (30 percent or ¥4,300 per pair, whichever is greater) for over-quota imports. The AVE of the selective duty was 143 percent for Sri Lanka.

Sportswear under HS 6405.90 is subject to an MFN rate of 24 percent for in-quota imports and a selective duty (30 percent or ¥4,300 per pair, whichever is greater) for over-quota imports. AVEs for the over-quota imports from China in 2004 were 76.26 percent (HS 6405.90-112) and 127 percent (HS 6405.90-122), respectively. AVEs of non–ad valorem duties for some mining goods and ballpoint pens in 2004 did not exceed 10 percent.

Reluctance to use ad valorem duties for sensitive items. The government is reluctant to use ad valorem duties for sensitive products. As in the case of specific duties, selective duties for sensitive items not only hinder the use of preferences but also give rise to discrimination between exporting countries. Under selective duties, tariff burdens on imports from different suppliers differ from country to country, as shown in the different AVEs of the selective duty for relevant goods.

Conclusion

The GSP is sharply at odds with the MFN principle of the WTO. The GSP scheme has been compromised by protectionism in sensitive sectors, which subjects competitive imports from GSP beneficiaries and LDCs to the MFN regime. The rules of origin are frequently justified as contributing to industrial development in poor countries. Japan pursues conflicting policies—trade liberalization in strong sectors and protectionism in weak sectors. Contradictions in trade policy throughout the world, however, are everywhere.

Central to resolving the problem of GSP erosion is improvement of the GSP scheme, on the one hand, and MFN reform, on the other. With the inevitable GSP erosion in mind, policy makers should deal with specific MFN tariff issues: residual non–ad valorem tariffs with an effect equivalent to high ad valorem duties, ad valorem tariff peaks, and 106 WTO-unbound items at the HS nine-digit level. Two issues of priority are the conversion of non–ad valorem duties to AVEs and the lowering of tariff rates, because most exports of great interest to developing countries are excluded from the GSP and face high MFN non–ad valorem tariffs.

Notes

1. Appendix 2 of the law.

2. The list in fiscal year 2004 contained 106 items at the Harmonized System nine-digit level that were subject to MFN tariffs—for example, salt and silk-related, leather-related, and footwear-related goods.

3. The implementing regulation of the law provides for GSP rules of origin.

4. Following the graduation of 19 beneficiaries (including Hong Kong, China; the Republic of Korea; Singapore; and Taiwan, China) in 2000, Bahrain, Slovenia, and French Polynesia graduated in 2003, 2006, and 2007, respectively. Graduation may be revoked. If a country or territory is not classified as a high-income economy for three consecutive years following graduation, the government can revive GSP treatment for that country or territory.

5. The precedence of partial graduation over total graduation is designed to mitigate the impact of graduation on economies of the beneficiary country. In other words, partial graduation targets an anchor product of a major high-income supplier. However, under partial graduation, the government

reviews both the gross national product per capita and the product's imports every year. If one of the aforementioned conditions is not met, partial graduation is suspended so that GSP treatment for the concerned product is revived.

6. Japan proclaimed this initiative before the declaration of the World Trade Organization ministerial conference held in Hong Kong, China, in December 2005. The declaration called for World Trade Organization member states to grant duty-free, quota-free market access to all LDCs on more than 97 percent of tariff-line items. Japan complied with the recommendation, increasing LDC-specific duty-free items from 86 percent up to 98 percent tariff lines at the Harmonized System nine-digit level.

7. The number of tariff lines at the nine-digit level changes year by year. This chapter adopted the number published by the Ministry of Finance in November 2007.

8. Examples are 5 percent for octopus (HS 030751), duty free for burdock (HS 070690), and 7.6 percent for vegetable juices (HS 200980-221). These GSP tariffs are accorded to the Positive List items that meet GSP rules of origin and other relevant requirements.

9. Suppose Japan imports black tea, an important duty-free item for LDCs. If it is imported from an LDC such as Bangladesh or Nepal, it is duty free. In contrast, imports from major GSP suppliers, such as China, India, and Sri Lanka, are subject to the MFN tariff of 12 percent.

10. Examples are some fishes; fish filets; rice; sugar items; rice or wheat preparations; food preparations using rice, wheat, or barley; and centrifugal preparations of sugar.

11. Examples are salt, petroleum crude oil, gelatin and glues, fur skin, leather items, tropical tree plywood, silkworm cocoons, footwear, and watchstraps and parts of leather. Whereas salt and petroleum oils are unbound under the World Trade Organization, other items are bound.

12. Examples are petroleum spirits, ethylene, natural gas, raw skins, plywood, silk fabrics, silkworm cocoons (subject to the over-quota tariff), raw silk, cotton yarn, printed fabrics except batiks, woven pile fabrics, apparel, made-up textile articles, and footwear.

13. Among others, these items included gelatin and glues; apparel of leather or leather composition; fur skins of sheep, goats, or rabbits; footwear and parts; and watchstraps, bands, and bracelets of leather or leather composition. Under the current regime, the former GSP Exceptions List was roughly transformed to the new LDC Exceptions List.

14. According to Ministry of Finance statistics for April to August 2007, the newly introduced LDC-specific, duty-free regime enabled LDCs to increase exports to Japan of former LDC exception items, such as dried kidney beans, frozen beef, and natural honey. These three items were subject to MFN tariffs of 10 percent, 38.5 percent, and 25.5 percent, respectively. However, imports of frozen tuna and frozen cuttlefish decreased, despite the duty-free regime replacing the former MFN tariff of 3.5 percent under the LDC Exceptions List. The same holds true with regard to industrial-mining items from LDCs that were newly covered by the duty-free regime. From a short-term viewpoint, the expansion of LDC duty-free, ceiling-free items did not result in significant increases in imports of those items.

15. The GSP-specific ceiling regime is not exactly equated with a tariff quota, strictly speaking. Administered on a first-come, first-served basis and on a monthly basis, the ceiling regime is a wonderland up for grabs. Hence, should imports of a ceiling item from only one or two GSP beneficiaries exceed the ceiling immediately after the beginning of the fiscal year, GSP treatment would be suspended from the 16th of the following month for the same item from any GSP beneficiary. In addition, importers of that item need not pay MFN tariffs for imports in excess of the ceiling value or quantity. For example, umbrellas—one of the important ceiling items—are imported annually from China, and imports from China reach almost a hundredfold of the annual ceiling by the end of April, in just one month following the beginning of the fiscal year.

16. That is, 1,183 items at the HS nine-digit level as of September 2007.

17. Imports from LDCs enjoy duty-free treatment once GSP conditions are met.

18. Several commissions that work to preserve important fishes, such as tuna, are empowered to adopt measures to preserve fishery resources. In the case of their infringement by a GSP beneficiary, the government of Japan may exclude imports of the fish from the infringing beneficiary, taking into account the injury to the domestic industry on a case-by-case basis. The exclusion does not apply to fish covered by the ceiling regime. Once the measure is suspended by the commission, the GSP revives.

19. This principle is known as the *preference-giving country content principle* or the *donor country content principle.*

20. In a power brake wire case, both a certification of cumulation and a donor country content certification were attached to a certificate of origin for the final good imported to Japan. In this case, the wire (7312) was manufactured in Malaysia using steel wires (7312) and a zinc dye-cast clasp exported from Japan and underwent tension testing in Thailand. The Malaysian authorities issued a certification that the power brake wire and zinc dye-cast clasp exported from Japan acquired Malaysian origin under the donor country content test. The Thailand authorities issued a certification that the manufacturing process in Malaysia and the testing operation in Thailand could be cumulated and considered carried out in the ASEAN. Japan customs accorded preferential treatment to the power brake wire from Thailand accompanied by a certificate of origin issued by the Thai authorities, Malaysia's donor country content certification, and Thailand's cumulation certification.

21. In the latter half of the 1990s, a major Japanese fishery company misused the special preference regime for imports from LDCs by submitting falsified certificates of origin to customs. The frozen octopus (HS 0709.50.100) in reality originated in West African GSP beneficiary countries. Japan's MFN tariff and GSP tariff at that time were about 7 to 8 percent (MFN duty rates were progressively lowered following the Uruguay Round) and 5 percent, respectively. The tariff for imports from LDCs was zero. Accordingly, the firm could have benefited from GSP tariffs. Instead, the firm abused duty-free treatment for LDCs. After purchasing blank certificates of origin prepared by certifying bodies in LDCs (The Gambia and Mauritania), the company had an innocent forwarder import the frozen octopus with falsified certificates of origin, disguising the imports as originating in LDCs. The falsified certificates of origin were used 281 times between June 1986 and December 1999, thus allowing the company to evade tariffs of ¥419 million. Customs discovered the falsified certification through on-the-spot investigations at home and abroad. After customs staff filed a criminal accusation, the District Court of Tokyo sentenced the company to a penalty of ¥120 million and the company's director to a suspended two-year prison term. See Tokyo District Court, Heisei 13, Toku (Wa) No. 2206, Judgment, dated January 16, 2002 (in Japanese).

22. Hence, if Chinese-origin Matsutake mushrooms are transshipped in Hong Kong, China, evidence proving that the products were transshipped must be attached to a formal certificate of origin issued by the Chinese mainland authorities.

23. Likewise, the utility ratio, representing the percentage of GSP-receiving imports to MFN dutiable imports, is quite low: only 16 percent, even in 2001.

24. The reason is multifold: low transportation costs, high investment by Japanese manufacturers in the prospect of Asia-wide regional integration, and other politicoeconomic factors.

25. This cost sometimes exceeded the amount of MFN duties payable, according to traders in Japan.

26. To benefit from the donor content test, exporters of a GSP beneficiary developing country must acquire a certificate of origin issued in Japan for Japanese materials that are incorporated into a final good in the GSP beneficiary. Because certification is costly, the test is difficult to meet. Not surprisingly, similar problems have arisen in Japan's bilateral FTAs with Mexico and Singapore. One of the issues arising from implementation of these FTAs is their low utility ratio. Because it is quite difficult for traders in both Japan and its partner countries to obtain a certificate of origin for materials to be cumulated under FTAs, these preferences are rarely used, according to traders in Japan. Though different in character, the reciprocal FTA cumulation rule and the GSP's donor content test pose similar difficulties with respect to submitting relevant evidence and obtaining a certificate of origin for materials to be incorporated into a final good.

27. See table 4.5 for the definition of the *ceiling utilization ratio.*

28. East Asian countries take the lion's share because of the commercially strong ties between Japanese traders and Asian manufacturers, in addition to cost advantages.

29. From the viewpoint of general GSP beneficiaries, their exports are subject to MFN tariffs, as far as LDC-specific, duty-free items are concerned. The LDC-exclusive, duty-free scheme has an adverse effect on GSP beneficiaries in cases where the LDC scheme led to LDC exports displacing exports from GSP beneficiaries.

30. Before the 2007 reform establishing the wide-scope LDC-specific, duty-free scheme, it was doubtful whether many items of export interest to LDCs were given LDC duty-free treatment. First, MFN duty-free items were included in the LDC-specific, duty-free list. Second, the list included many fishery items for which no imports in fiscal year 2004 were recorded. Third, certain LDC-exclusive, duty-free items had in reality been imported only from non-LDCs. The same applies to the current LDC scheme—in particular, items in the LDC Exceptions List (118 agricultural-fishery items and 46 industrial-mining items).

31. The agreement was signed in January 2002 and entered into force in November 2002.

32. The agreement was signed in March 2007 and entered into force in September 2007.

33. The agreement was signed in November 2006 and entered into force in August 2007.

34. The agreement was signed in December 2005 and entered into force in July 2006.

35. The agreement was signed in September 2004 and entered into force in April 2005.

36. The agreement was signed in September 2006 but has not entered into force as of February 2008.

37. The agreement was signed in April 2007 and entered into force in November 2007.

38. In general, FTAs require application of the territoriality principle, under which goods from an exporting partner must be manufactured without interruption in the concerned area to benefit from preferences from the importing partner. If semifinished goods or intermediate materials are exported for further processing in a third country and reimported for finishing in the exporting country, the final goods lose eligibility for preferences. Under the territoriality principle, outward processing in the midst of producing goods is precluded. Hence, at the request of a partner country relying an offshore processing, outward processing schemes were introduced into some FTAs under strict conditions. Examples include (a) Indonesian islands (Pulau Bintan and Pulau Batam) processing in FTAs concluded by Singapore with Australia, Japan, the Republic of Korea, the United States (the Integrated Sourcing Initiative), and the European Free Trade Association (EFTA) and (b) the Democratic People's Republic of Korea's Koesong Industrial Complex processing in FTAs concluded by the Republic of Korea with EFTA and the ASEAN. No similar examples are found in the GSP scheme.

39. Japan's GSP provides for only one regional cumulation for the five ASEAN countries. If regional cumulation is extended to other regions in Africa, Central and South America, and West Asia, the region-wide division of labor could contribute to economic development in GSP beneficiaries and LDCs.

40. Without improving the GSP regime, MFN tariff cuts would not necessarily address preference erosion on specific product lines for specific beneficiaries. MFN reform would, however, benefit developing countries in the aggregate, as other research has found.

41. Rice was a unique item that was not subject to a tariff under the WTO regime. However, the special treatment option required countries to provide larger minimum market access opportunities than would have been the case under a tariff. In addition, owing to abundant harvests in the latter half of the 1990s in Japan, the domestic stock of rice swelled. This abundance led Japan to set tariffs for rice in 1999.

42. The temporary tariff for over-quota imports of rice (¥49 per kilogram), which is lower than the WTO tariff (¥341 per kilogram), seems to apply. However, the substantial tariff is the sum of the temporary tariff and the adjustment levy (¥292 per kilogram)—that is, the WTO tariff based on the tariff equivalent. The same applies to other agricultural goods subject to the tariff quota regime.

5

THE CANADIAN PREFERENTIAL TARIFF REGIME AND POTENTIAL ECONOMIC IMPACTS OF ITS EROSION

Przemyslaw Kowalski

This chapter seeks to identify Canada's trade partners and products that may be potentially vulnerable to the problems of preference erosion following most-favored-nation (MFN) liberalization under the Doha Development Agenda. It follows a two-track approach. First, a detailed statistical analysis of the structure of Canadian preferences is undertaken using data on actual trade flows under preferential arrangements for Canada in 1998, 2002, and 2003. The statistical analysis includes overviews of the structure of preferential trade flows; associated tariff levels and preferential margins; utilization, utility, and coverage rates; and the value of preferences by scheme and beneficiary, as well as information on key tariff lines on which the value of preferences is concentrated. The second, complementary approach uses the Global Trade Analysis Project (GTAP) model to examine the trade and welfare effects of removing Canada's preferential duties.

The views expressed in this chapter do not necessarily represent those of the Organisation for Economic Co-operation and Development or any of its members. The author would like to thank Simon Evenett and Raed Safadi for their helpful comments, Karinne Logez for her statistical assistance, and Caroline Mirkovic for research assistance. The assistance of Diane Kelloway of Finance Canada in providing the underlying trade data and associated technical explanations was greatly appreciated. All remaining errors are those of the author.

An Overview of Canadian Tariff Preferences

The potential economic effects of Canada's preferential schemes on beneficiary countries and territories need to be considered in relation to the market access conditions that Canada's other trading partners face in the Canadian market. In particular, the trade effects of the General Preferential Tariff (GPT) and Least Developed Country Tariff (LDCT) schemes appear to have been limited by the relatively low protection levels afforded to other trading partners, whether on the MFN basis or through reciprocal trade agreements (free trade areas).

Indeed, judging by the simple average tariffs, Canada's tariffs are relatively moderate. The simple average tariff on MFN tariff lines for imports from developing countries was estimated at about 6.0 percent in 2002 and 5.8 percent in 2003 (table 5.1). However, noticeable differences are reported in the levels of protection of agricultural and nonagricultural products (WTO 2003). For example, the average MFN tariff calculated for agriculture in 2002 was 21.7 percent, compared with an average of 4.2 percent for nonagricultural products, according to the WTO definition (WTO 2003). Within agricultural products, the highest tariffs are imposed on imports of dairy products (237.0 percent), live animals and products thereof (52.7 percent), beverages and spirits (8.3 percent), and fruits and vegetables (4.8 percent). Within nonagricultural products, the average MFN tariff on textiles and clothing was 9.9 percent. Tariff escalation continues to inhibit exports of downstream products to Canada by countries that are exporting under MFN treatment (WTO 2003), particularly in the case of imports of food and beverages, textiles and clothing, wood products, chemicals, and nonmetallic mineral products.

Canada had five reciprocal preferential agreements at the time this chapter was written: the Canada-Chile Free Trade Agreement, the Canada–Costa Rica Free Trade Agreement, the Canada-Israel Free Trade Agreement, the Canada–United States Free Trade Agreement, and the North American Free Trade Agreement (NAFTA). These reciprocal agreements offer significant margins of preference over MFN duties and, to a lesser extent, over GPT and LDCT treatment (see table III.2 in WTO 2003). For example, under NAFTA, 93.8 and 98.8 percent of tariff lines of imports originating from Mexico and the United States, respectively, were duty free in 2002 (WTO 2003). The average import duties for Mexico and the United States under NAFTA were 2.7 percent and 2.6 percent, respectively, while those for the GPT and LDCT were 5.4 percent and 4.1 percent, respectively. The significance of these NAFTA suppliers and their potential impact on the market access of other trading partners is strengthened by their sheer size—in 2004 imports from Mexico and the United States together accounted for about 63 percent of all Canadian imports.

TABLE 5.1 Overview of Preferential Tariffs in Canada, 2002 and 2003

Type	Number of lines[a]		Average tariff[b] (%)		Corresponding average MFN tariff[c] (%)		Minimum tariff (%)		Maximum tariff (%)		Number of ad valorem tariffs	
	2002	2003	2002	2003	2002	2003	2002	2003	2002	2003	2002	2003
MFN	6,931	7,057	6.0	5.8	—	—	0	0	298.5	295.5	6,735	6,875
GPT	4,122	4,250	2.1	2.2	4.4	4.3	0	0	16.5	16.5	4,040	4,192
LDCT	170	489	0.0	0.0	6.9	12.4	0	0	0.0	0.0	169	489
Canada-Israel Tariff	761	776	0.0	0.0	6.7	6.8	0	0	5.0	5.0	757	760
Chile Tariff	174	199	0.6	0.0	5.7	7.9	0	0	19.0	0.0	170	197
Commonwealth-Caribbean Tariff	206	182	0.0	0.0	3.8	3.5	0	0	0.0	0.0	206	182
Costa Rica Tariff	2	51	0.0	1.4	6.3	5.5	0	0	0.0	15.0	2	47
Mexican Tariff	3,166	3,097	0.2	0.0	5.5	5.5	0	0	3.0	0.0	3,149	3,091
Mexican-U.S. Tariff	657	650	0.0	0.0	4.0	3.6	0	0	2.5	0.0	656	649
British Preferential Tariff	133	126	—	—	18.9	18.4	—	—	—	—	0	0
General Tariff	30	39	—	—	5.2	4.1	—	—	—	—	0	0
Informal entries and aggregated records	12	8	—	—	6.7	2.4	—	—	—	—	0	0
U.S. Tariff	1,044	1,090	—	—	6.2	5.5	—	—	—	—	0	0

Source: Author's calculations from Finance Canada data.

Note: — = not available. Data are for imports at the HS eight-digit level in 2002 and 2003 (excluding chapter 99) from 181 beneficiaries and 180 beneficiaries, respectively (the same countries minus Timor-Leste) eligible for Canadian GSP preferences.

a. Number of tariff-line products, by HS eight-digit level, that entered Canada under the treatment indicated.

b. Simple average of lines where there have been imports. Calculations are based on ad valorem tariffs and mixed tariffs.

c. Simple average of MFN tariffs in these lines. Calculations are based on ad valorem tariffs and mixed tariffs.

Nonreciprocal Preferential Schemes

Table 5.2 presents basic information on Canada's nonreciprocal preferential tariff schemes for developing countries. Currently, Canada provides nonreciprocal tariff preferences to developing countries under the GPT, the LDCT, and the Caribbean-Canada Trade Agreement (CARIBCAN). However, certain Canadian imports from developing countries are classified under other preferential (reciprocal and nonreciprocal) schemes (table 5.3 shows the composition of preferential trade flows).

The GPT scheme took effect in 1974 and was renewed and expanded in 1984, 1995, and 2004. The 1995 revision aimed to take into account the effects of the erosion of preferential margins that followed the Uruguay Round negotiations, mainly through the expansion of product coverage and the lowering of GPT duty rates (UNCTAD 2001). The evolution of Canada's tariff preferences in favor of developing countries over the past two decades reflects mainly a number of special measures introduced for least developed countries (LDCs) (see Weston 2003). In 1983, LDCs were granted a zero rate on GPT-covered products with some exceptions, including clothing and footwear. As of 1999, the GPT (and LDCT) product coverage was extended by some 220 product lines, and the GPT tariffs were lowered to two-thirds of the corresponding MFN rates. As pointed out by Weston (2003), in addition to improving market access under the GPT, this reform reduced the margins enjoyed by the LDCs. In 2000, another 570 tariff lines were added to the duty-free list for LDCs, bringing their share of duty-free lines to 90 percent.

Weston (2003) indicates that at the beginning of the 2000s, despite the apparently high tariff-line coverage, the LDC program of Canada was granting very little real market access. Only 15 products were exported to Canada. Only about 30 percent of nonoil, nonarms imports from LDCs were duty free in 2000. Of the Quad markets, Canada had the highest proportion of imports from LDCs that faced tariffs above 5 percent. Indeed, the extension of product coverage in 2000 led to very limited changes because of the exclusion of textiles and clothing, which accounted for 38 percent of total LDC exports to Canada in 2000 (Lippoldt and Kowalski 2005). As will be discussed, however, an unambiguous increase in the utilization rates of the LDCT scheme by some LDC beneficiaries points to the beneficial effects of more flexible rules of origin.

On January 1, 2003, all remaining tariff and quota restrictions on imports from LDCs (except on supply-managed agricultural products and on Myanmar) were removed.[1] The initiative included textiles and clothing and modification of the rules of origin. Before the extension to textiles and clothing, excluded products made up 93 percent of total dutiable LDC imports (Lippoldt and Kowalski 2005). By 2003, the share of excluded products had fallen to almost zero. As argued by Weston (2003), the new LDC initiative was controversial not only because of the potential impact on Canadian producers (mainly in the clothing industry) but

TABLE 5.2 Generalized and Selected Regional Preference Schemes of Canada

Country and preference scheme	Dates	Eligible economies	Scope of tariff and nontariff preferences	Exemptions and restrictions
GPT	Brought into effect January 7, 1974, renewed in 2004, effective until 2014	All developing countries, including LDCs	*Type of preference:* Reductions from the MFN rate or duty-free access *Coverage:* Selected agricultural and industrial products	*Excluded items:* Some agricultural products, refined sugar, most textiles, apparel, and footwear *Rules of origin:* • 60% local content • Cumulation from any other GPT beneficiary country or Canada • Direct shipment required *Safeguard measures*
LDCT granted by Canada	1998	LDCs	*Type of preference:* Duty free or preferential rates access (variable from product to product)	*Excluded items:* Food products (ISIC 311c), animal feeds and other food products (ISIC 312c), textiles and clothing (ISIC 322)

(Table continues on the following page.)

TABLE 5.2 Generalized and Selected Regional Preference Schemes of Canada (*Continued*)

Country and preference scheme	Dates	Eligible economies	Scope of tariff and nontariff preferences	Exemptions and restrictions
			Coverage: • 82% of tariff lines in duty-free access for 48 LDCs. • Average of non-duty-free lines: 29% • Average of ad valorem tariff: 5%	*Excluded country:* Myanmar *Rules of origin:* • 40% local content (only content from LDCs or Canada was considered originating for purposes of the 40% rule) • Cumulation only with other LDCs and Canada (since 2000, cumulation with any other GSP country) • Specific rules for textiles and clothing • Direct shipment required
LDCT	In present form since January 1, 2003	LDCs	*Type of preference:* Duty- and quota-free access for 48 LDCs *Coverage:* Almost all products (see excluded items) since extension on January 1, 2003	*Excluded items:* Supply-managed agricultural products such as dairy products, poultry, and eggs *Excluded country:* Myanmar *Rules of origin:* • 40% local content • Cumulation from any other LDCT or GPT beneficiary country or from Canada

CARIBCAN	Introduced in 1986; renewed in 1996 until 2007	Caribbean countries	*Type of preference:* Duty-free access for qualifying goods for most Commonwealth Caribbean States *Coverage:* Similar to GPT; slightly broader for agricultural goods	• Specific rules of origin for textiles and apparel • Direct shipment required *Safeguard measures* *Excluded items:* Some agricultural products, textiles, apparel, and footwear *Rules of origin:* • 60% local content • Cumulation from any other beneficiary country or from Canada • Direct shipment required
Commonwealth Developing Countries Remission Order	Effective January 1, 1998	Commonwealth countries	*Type of preference:* Duty-free access or referential duty rate *Coverage:* 171 tariff lines, mostly textile products Provides preferences equivalent to the British Preferential Tariff, which was revoked on January 1, 1998	*Rules of origin:* • 50% local content • Cumulation is allowed among Commonwealth countries • Direct shipment required

Source: Lippoldt and Kowalski 2005.

TABLE 5.3 Preferential Trade Flows by Scheme, 1998, 2002, and 2003

Total imports scheme	Share (%) 1998	2002	2003	Dutiable imports scheme	Share (%) 1998	2002	2003
MFN	76.5	72.8	74.1	MFN	62.9	62.4	63.7
GPT	15.0	15.5	15.0	GPT	25.2	31.7	33.4
LDCT	0.0	0.0	0.7	LDCT	0.0	0.0	0.0
British Preferential Tariff	0.2	0.9	0.6	British Preferential Tariff	0.7	3.3	2.3
Chile Tariff	0.2	0.2	0.2	Chile Tariff	0.2	0.1	0.0
Commonwealth Caribbean Tariff	0.1	0.3	0.2	Commonwealth Caribbean Tariff	0.0	0.0	0.0
General Tariff	0.0	0.0	0.1	General Tariff	0.0	0.0	0.0
Informal entries and aggregated records	0.0	0.0	0.0	Informal entries and aggregated records	0.0	0.0	0.0
Mexican Tariff	7.2	8.7	7.5	Mexican Tariff	10.9	2.5	0.5
Mexican-U.S. Tariff	0.7	1.3	1.3	Mexican-U.S. Tariff	0.1	0.0	0.0
U.S. Tariff	0.1	0.1	0.1	U.S. Tariff	0.0	0.0	0.0
Canada-Israel Agreement Tariff	0.0	0.3	0.3	Canada-Israel Agreement Tariff	0.0	0.0	0.0
Costa Rica Tariff	0.0	0.0	0.0	Costa Rica Tariff	0.0	0.0	0.0

Source: Author's calculations from Finance Canada data.

also because of the reduction in this benefit when the Multifiber Arrangement quotas disappeared after 2004.

Rules of Origin

Rules of origin can help ensure that the products imported under the preferences are not merely transshipped from ineligible countries by eligible suppliers with little or no local value being added. Although—under certain circumstances— rules of origin can play a role in ensuring that the intended beneficiaries actually gain, they are also widely seen as the main reason for underutilization of preferences (see, for example, Inama 2003).

In the 1980s, Canada introduced more generous rules of origin for LDCs than for other developing countries, with a minimum requirement of 40 percent of local value added compared with 60 percent required for other GPT beneficiaries. The 2000 reform of the system further relaxed the rules of origin, allowing up to half of the 40 percent minimum value added requirement to originate from other developing countries (Weston 2003). The 2003 LDC initiative included a modification of the rules of origin for textiles and clothing products. To be eligible under the new rules of origin, the cloth must be cut and sewn or the fabric woven from yarn produced in the eligible country or territory. The new system allows cumulation of inputs from all beneficiaries as long as a minimum of 25 percent of value added originates from the exporting LDC.

Other Forms of Compliance Verification

To be eligible for the LDCT or GPT, goods must satisfy requirements for certification and direct shipment in addition to rules of origin. Direct shipment requires that goods be shipped directly from an eligible country or transshipped through an intermediate country under customs transit control and without additional processing (CCRA 2003; UNCTAD 2001). The required documentation consists of a through bill of lading, as well as related shipping documents if the bill does not specify all points of transshipment (CCRA 2003). The system distinguishes between certificates of origin for nontextile and nonapparel goods and for textile and apparel goods. The verification procedure involves an origin questionnaire or letter returned by the exporter to the Canada Customs and Revenue Agency.

The Value of Preferences

A number of approaches to measuring the benefits from preferential arrangements—or alternatively the losses from their erosion—have been used. Among the most popular are simple calculations of the value of benefits on fixed trade values; estimations of trade creation or trade diversion impacts; and general equilibrium evaluations. In the first of these approaches, the benefit to the preference-receiving country is estimated as the difference between the MFN rate and the preferential rate multiplied by the value of imports at world prices. The effect of preference erosion is then calculated as the difference between the value of the preference before and after multilateral liberalization. An example of this approach is Yamazaki's (1996) study of agricultural preferences. A limitation of this methodology is that changes in MFN tariffs are likely to induce changes in the volumes traded under both preferential and nonpreferential schemes, thereby reducing the benefit to preference-receiving countries after MFN liberalization.

A number of studies improve on this approach by modeling the demand and supply schedules in partial equilibrium models (see, for example, Alexandraki and Lankes 2004; Subramanian 2003). This methodology differentiates products by country of origin and controls for trade creation and diversion effects in response to changes in trade protection measures. Under this approach, MFN liberalization typically results in an increased demand for products imported under MFN treatment and decreased demand for imports entering under preferential rates. Advantages of this approach include its relative ease of interpretation and the ability to apply it at the very detailed level of product classification. When a far-reaching reform is under consideration, however (as with multilateral liberalization), this approach can result in unrealistic estimates of the economic value of preferential trading arrangements.

Computable general equilibrium evaluations capture the effects of substitution between imports and domestic production, imports from preferential to nonpreferential sources in the preference-giving country, changes in demand for intermediate inputs, reallocation of productive resources across industrial sectors, and effects on terms of trade and balance of payments. They can therefore better capture some of the costs inherent in preferential trading arrangements such as the preference-driven concentration of resources in relatively uncompetitive activities. With this approach, the economywide implications of reallocating productive resources toward other activities are evaluated. This methodology makes it possible to account for the "package" nature of multilateral trade agreements, so that the potential negative effects associated with a particular sector or preferential scheme can be analyzed in conjunction with other effects. One drawback of computable general equilibrium modeling is a need to work at a relatively high level of aggregation—a feature that may be problematic because attention frequently needs to focus on particular product and country categories.

Structure and Utilization of Preferences

The analysis presented here draws on the tariff preference database developed by the Organisation for Economic Co-operation and Development Secretariat. The raw data on tariff lines for which there were imports from developing countries in 1998, 2002, and 2003 were provided by Finance Canada. In addition to LDCT and GPT treatments, imports from developing countries have been registered under the Commonwealth Caribbean Countries' Tariff, the British Preferential Tariff, the Chile Tariff, the General Tariff, the Mexican Tariff, the Mexican-United States Tariff, the U.S. Tariff, the Canada-Israel Agreement Tariff, and the Costa Rica Tariff. The database distinguishes between total and dutiable imports for each specific tariff line and treatment.[2]

Table 5.1 presents an overview of the 2002 and 2003 data that underlie the calculations in this part. It also indicates the number of tariff lines for which at least one positive import flow between Canada and a developing country occurred under the specific tariff treatment. The corresponding minimum, maximum, and simple average tariffs are also provided. For comparison, an average MFN rate—calculated for the corresponding tariff lines—is also presented. The last column indicates the number of lines with only ad valorem duties.

The source data include descriptions of specific duties. Non–ad valorem tariffs on goods imported from developing countries are mostly mixed rates.[3] The share of non–ad valorem tariffs on MFN lines with imports from developing countries in 2003 was 2.6 percent. For the GPT, this figure was even lower (1.4 percent, corresponding to 0.26 percent of the value of GPT imports) and for the LDCT it was nil. In addition, for only 0.40 percent of the value of imports entering Canada under the GPT scheme in 2003 was the corresponding MFN duty rate specified in non–ad valorem terms. For the LDCT, the corresponding ratio was 0.14 percent. In view of the relatively low incidence of non–ad valorem items only, the ad valorem components of mixed and compound rates are used in calculations referring to these lines.

Composition and Significance of Trade Flows

The 2003 data indicate that about three-quarters of imports from developing countries entered Canada under MFN treatment, 15 percent under the GPT, and 0.7 percent under the LDCT (table 5.3). Corresponding shares computed on the basis of dutiable imports are, respectively, 64 percent, 33 percent, and 0 percent. In 2003, about 72 percent of imports from developing countries entering under MFN treatment were duty free, while the corresponding shares for the GPT and LDCT were 41 percent and 100 percent (table 5.4).

TABLE 5.4 Share of Duty-Free Trade by Scheme, 1998, 2002, and 2003

Scheme	Share (%)		
	1998	2002	2003
Total	62	68	70
By scheme			
MFN	65	70	72
GPT	47	42	41
LDCT	100	100	100
Commonwealth Caribbean Tariff	100	100	100

Source: Author's calculations from Finance Canada data.

To shed more light on the importance of the Canadian market for developing countries' exports, tables 5.5 and 5.6 present exports to Canada under all schemes (including MFN) and under all preferential schemes as a share in beneficiaries' exports to all trading partners.[4] Taking 2003 as a reference year, one notes that the share of total exports was up to 30 percent for some developing countries. By contrast, exports under preferential schemes typically accounted for less than 1 percent of total beneficiary exports. In 2003, this ratio was higher than 1 percent for only nine developing countries (Bangladesh, Barbados, Cambodia, Haiti, the Lao People's Democratic Republic, Lesotho, Maldives, Mexico, and Trinidad and Tobago). It is worth noting that for six of these countries significant export increases took place in 2003, most likely as a result of the new LDC initiative.

The remarkable reliance of some developing countries on nonpreferential access to Canada's market suggests their obvious interest in further liberalization of the MFN regime. However, for a few countries—mainly LDCs—trade under preferential schemes accounts for the bulk of their exports to Canada. This observation suggests that the latter group of countries would have no major interest (apart, of course, from preventing any negative effects of preference erosion) in lowering MFN tariffs. These contrasting situations point to potential divisions in developing countries' positions over the issue of lowering Canadian MFN tariffs.

Imports under the LDCT scheme exhibit a heavy concentration in five HS two-digit textile and clothing chapters (61–65).[5] These chapters accounted for 98 percent of imports entering under this scheme. Exports under the GPT scheme were more diversified. Still, the six top HS chapters accounted for more than half of imports under this treatment. Furniture products (HS chapter 94) accounted for 13 percent of imports under the GPT scheme; electrical machinery and equipment (HS chapter 85), 11 percent; toys, games, and sports requisites (HS chapter 95),

(*Text continues on p. 149.*)

TABLE 5.5 Total Exports to the Canadian Market as a Percentage of Beneficiary's Exports

Beneficiary	Share (%)		
	1998	2002	2003
Guyana	24.04	30.17	28.20
Cuba	15.82	17.16	23.68
Turks and Caicos Islands	5.32	6.48	18.40
São Tomé and Príncipe	0.10	7.81	17.93
Equatorial Guinea	0.03	10.02	12.11
Jamaica	9.12	12.43	11.96
St. Kitts and Nevis	6.05	6.92	9.55
Iraq	1.07	7.90	9.46
Algeria	3.13	6.45	7.66
Mexico	4.47	5.12	5.23
Montserrat	0.60	6.96	4.33
Uruguay	1.32	1.51	3.85
Kyrgyz Republic	0.00	0.03	3.83
Haiti	0.92	2.35	3.54
Guinea	2.10	3.24	3.46
Bangladesh	1.88	1.68	3.24
Chile	1.56	2.46	2.98
Trinidad and Tobago	0.99	3.09	2.87
Cambodia	0.54	0.71	2.66
Maldives	2.56	0.85	2.59
Bahamas, The	2.50	0.95	2.55
Peru	2.08	2.94	2.51
Nicaragua	1.76	3.22	2.42
Grenada	1.65	3.21	2.39
China	1.83	2.28	2.31
Macao	1.84	2.46	2.30
Ghana	0.64	1.84	2.07
Costa Rica	2.35	2.29	2.05
Venezuela, R.B. de	3.20	3.45	2.05
Mongolia	1.15	1.28	2.03
Guatemala	2.47	2.41	2.03
Pakistan	1.97	2.25	2.03
Korea, Rep. of	1.87	2.18	2.01
Comoros	0.31	0.23	2.00
Colombia	1.90	2.17	1.99
Brazil	1.76	2.12	1.91
Djibouti	0.13	4.51	1.83

(*Table continues on the following page.*)

TABLE 5.5 Total Exports to the Canadian Market as Percentage of Beneficiary's Exports (Continued)

Beneficiary	Share (%)		
	1998	2002	2003
India	1.64	1.92	1.74
Thailand	1.53	1.75	1.73
Honduras	1.42	2.04	1.59
Dominican Republic	1.53	1.55	1.55
Côte d'Ivoire	1.62	1.21	1.53
Namibia	2.84	1.65	1.52
Sri Lanka	1.50	1.68	1.52
Barbados	3.78	1.96	1.49
Lesotho	1.63	0.94	1.48
Israel	0.83	1.47	1.47
Philippines	1.98	1.76	1.46
Lao PDR	0.52	1.31	1.44
Nigeria	1.72	0.91	1.41
Ecuador	2.46	1.79	1.40
Malaysia	1.61	1.30	1.34
Netherlands Antilles	1.56	0.13	1.30
Belize	1.87	2.46	1.26
Sierra Leone	1.35	1.09	1.20
Syrian Arab Republic	0.26	0.51	1.18
Vietnam	1.30	1.21	1.17
Madagascar	0.54	0.39	1.15
Egypt, Arab Rep. of	0.46	0.62	1.13
Nepal	0.49	1.93	1.13
Nauru	0.25	0.44	1.10
Hong Kong, China	1.64	1.24	1.07
Ethiopia	1.20	0.95	1.04
South Africa	1.28	1.08	1.00
Indonesia	1.21	1.11	0.99
El Salvador	0.79	1.33	0.98
Pitcairn Island	20.23	2.93	0.93
Niger	0.82	0.99	0.92
Argentina	0.66	0.84	0.90
Guam	0.00	1.11	0.85
French Polynesia	0.31	1.03	0.85
Uganda	1.05	0.12	0.82
Singapore	1.00	0.89	0.81
St. Helena	0.17	0.89	0.81

TABLE 5.5   (Continued)

Beneficiary	Share (%)		
	1998	2002	2003
Lebanon	0.88	0.80	0.79
Turkey	0.68	0.79	0.77
Cocos Islands	0.06	0.01	0.72
Lithuania	0.46	0.32	0.71
Bulgaria	0.76	0.84	0.68
Morocco	0.76	0.66	0.67
Burundi	0.77	1.24	0.66
Turkmenistan	0.00	1.63	0.65
Estonia	0.64	0.84	0.62
Dominica	1.38	1.46	0.62
Bolivia	0.99	0.84	0.61
Cook Islands	1.72	0.59	0.60
Malta	1.15	0.33	0.57
Botswana	0.02	0.03	0.57
Paraguay	0.19	0.56	0.57
Romania	0.92	0.60	0.56
Poland	0.45	0.54	0.54
Fiji	0.37	0.79	0.52
Tonga	0.32	0.07	0.49
Russian Federation	0.68	0.26	0.49
Mauritius	0.82	0.55	0.47
Kenya	0.72	0.52	0.46
Slovak Republic	0.44	0.25	0.45
St. Lucia	1.08	0.46	0.45
American Samoa	0.11	0.07	0.42
Uzbekistan	0.43	0.42	0.42
Zimbabwe	0.75	0.41	0.41
Mali	4.13	1.81	0.38
Togo	14.16	0.30	0.36
Seychelles	0.13	0.05	0.36
Hungary	0.27	0.33	0.34
Swaziland	0.02	0.36	0.33
Bahrain	0.16	0.39	0.32
Croatia	0.30	0.35	0.31
Gambia, The	0.06	0.10	0.30
Slovenia	0.49	0.39	0.30
Georgia	0.31	0.09	0.29

(Table continues on the following page.)

TABLE 5.5 Total Exports to the Canadian Market as Percentage of Beneficiary's Exports (*Continued*)

Beneficiary	Share (%)		
	1998	2002	2003
Ukraine	0.36	0.39	0.29
Tanzania	0.11	0.43	0.28
Moldova	0.12	0.32	0.27
Czech Republic	0.34	0.31	0.26
Bermuda	3.30	1.46	0.26
Armenia	0.27	0.52	0.25
Liberia	0.05	0.17	0.25
British Indian Ocean Territory	0.01	0.18	0.25
Christmas Island	0.10	0.27	0.24
Bosnia and Herzegovina	0.04	0.19	0.24
Panama	1.51	0.40	0.24
Falkland Islands	0.10	0.00	0.24
Norfolk Island	0.23	0.11	0.24
Jordan	0.07	0.23	0.23
Latvia	0.07	0.27	0.23
Malawi	0.52	0.27	0.23
Cameroon	0.48	0.36	0.23
British Virgin Islands	0.29	0.14	0.22
Cayman Islands	0.38	1.06	0.22
Macedonia	0.26	0.35	0.22
French Southern Territory	0.37	0.00	0.22
Afghanistan	0.24	0.51	0.22
Kuwait	0.02	0.12	0.22
Tunisia	0.10	0.17	0.18
Eritrea	0.04	0.55	0.18
Iran, Islamic Rep. of	0.85	0.20	0.18
Somalia	0.05	0.66	0.17
Senegal	0.09	0.15	0.14
Suriname	10.16	6.68	0.13
Antigua and Barbuda	6.36	0.26	0.13
St. Vincent and the Grenadines	0.10	0.26	0.13
Kazakhstan	0.19	0.08	0.13
Cyprus	0.18	0.15	0.13
Gibraltar	1.82	0.01	0.11
Papua New Guinea	0.17	0.04	0.10
Mauritania	0.03	0.07	0.10
Belarus	0.02	0.12	0.09
Vanuatu	0.32	0.07	0.09

TABLE 5.5 (*Continued*)

Beneficiary	Share (%)		
	1998	2002	2003
Anguilla	0.07	0.35	0.08
Brunei Darussalam	0.02	0.12	0.07
Gabon	0.01	0.06	0.05
Niue	67.70	2.21	0.05
New Caledonia	0.06	0.05	0.05
Burkina Faso	0.04	0.02	0.05
United Arab Emirates	0.04	0.07	0.05
Qatar	0.13	0.00	0.04
Rwanda	1.74	1.12	0.04
Congo, Rep. of	0.85	0.04	0.04
Zambia	4.58	0.19	0.03
Central African Republic	0.06	0.13	0.03
Chad	0.03	0.04	0.03
Kiribati	0.01	0.01	0.03
Azerbaijan	0.05	0.03	0.03
Cape Verde	0.00	0.05	0.03
Solomon Islands	0.03	0.05	0.02
Bhutan	0.02	0.12	0.02
Western Samoa	0.01	0.14	0.01
Mozambique	0.38	0.01	0.01
Sudan	0.07	0.01	0.01
Western Sahara	0.05	0.00	0.01
Tajikistan	1.42	0.06	0.01
Congo, Dem. Rep. of		0.00	0.00
Yemen, Rep. of	0.01	0.00	0.00
Benin	0.00	0.00	0.00
Angola	0.29	0.00	0.00
Guinea-Bissau	0.00	0.01	0.00
Antarctica	0.00	0.00	0.00
Bouvet Island	0.00	0.00	0.00
Heard and McDonald Islands		0.00	0.00
Timor-Leste	4.50	0.62	
Mariana Islands	59.85		
Marshall Islands	0.02		
Micronesia	0.18		
Tokelau	35.46		

Source: Author's calculations from Finance Canada data.
Note: Sorted by 2003 values.

TABLE 5.6 Preferential Exports to the Canadian Market as a Percentage of Beneficiary's Exports: All Schemes, 1998, 2002, and 2003

Beneficiary	Share (%)		
	1998	2002	2003
Bangladesh	0.3	1.0	2.9
Mexico	1.7	2.3	2.4
Cambodia	0.0	0.0	2.4
Haiti	0.1	0.6	1.6
Lao PDR	0.0	0.0	1.3
Maldives	0.1	0.1	1.2
Barbados	1.9	1.3	1.2
Trinidad and Tobago	0.3	2.6	1.1
Lesotho	0.0	0.0	1.1
Guyana	0.3	0.5	0.9
Cuba	2.3	1.4	0.9
Jamaica	0.7	0.9	0.8
Nepal	0.2	1.0	0.8
China	0.7	0.8	0.8
Pakistan	0.3	0.9	0.7
Sri Lanka	0.5	0.8	0.7
India	0.4	0.8	0.6
Thailand	0.4	0.5	0.4
Peru	0.6	0.9	0.4
Grenada	0.0	0.0	0.4
Brazil	0.3	0.4	0.4
Israel	0.0	0.4	0.4
Lebanon	0.4	0.4	0.4
Chile	0.4	0.5	0.4
Guatemala	0.8	0.5	0.4
Bahamas, The	0.8	0.4	0.3
Fiji	0.2	0.5	0.3
Uruguay	0.2	0.4	0.3
Vietnam	0.2	0.3	0.3
Botswana	0.0	0.0	0.2
Colombia	0.1	0.1	0.2
Korea, Rep. of	0.3	0.3	0.2
Madagascar	0.0	0.0	0.2
Costa Rica	0.1	0.3	0.2
Indonesia	0.2	0.2	0.2
Sierra Leone	0.5	0.2	0.2

TABLE 5.6 (*Continued*)

Beneficiary	Share (%)		
	1998	2002	2003
Turkey	0.2	0.2	0.2
Poland	0.1	0.1	0.1
Belize	1.5	0.6	0.1
Dominica	0.1	0.1	0.1
Egypt, Arab Rep. of	0.1	0.1	0.1
Macao, China	0.1	0.2	0.1
Hong Kong, China	0.2	0.2	0.1
Malaysia	0.2	0.2	0.1
Zimbabwe	0.1	0.2	0.1
Algeria	0.0	0.0	0.1
El Salvador	0.1	0.0	0.1
Swaziland	0.0	0.0	0.1
Philippines	0.2	0.1	0.1
Bulgaria	0.2	0.2	0.1

Source: Author's calculations from Finance Canada data.
Note: Sorted by 2003 values.

7.5 percent; plastics and articles thereof (HS chapter 39), 7.4 percent; articles of leather (HS chapter 42), 6.2 percent; nuclear reactors, boilers (HS chapter 84), 5.3 percent.

The structure of imports from developing countries under MFN tariffs was also relatively concentrated, with more than 50 percent of imports under MFN treatment in four HS two-digit chapters: electrical machinery and equipment (HS chapter 85), 18.2 percent; nuclear reactors, boilers (HS chapter 84), 16.5 percent; mineral fuels, oils, and products thereof (HS chapter 27), 14.3 percent; and vehicles other than railway or tramway rolling stock (HS chapter 87), 5.7 percent.

Preferential Tariff Rates

Substantial shares of imports from developing countries enter Canada under duty-free or low MFN tariff rates. In 2003, 72 percent of imports from developing countries entering Canada under MFN treatment were free of duty (table 5.4), and the simple average MFN tariff rate on lines with imports from developing countries was 5.8 percent, down from 6 percent in 2002 (table 5.7). On a simple average basis, the LDCT offered a 12 percentage point advantage over MFN rates on LDCT-eligible lines. This advantage was significantly higher than that offered

TABLE 5.7 Average Tariff Rates by Scheme

Scheme	Rate (%)		
	1998	2002	2003
Simple average			
LDCT	0.0	0.0	0.0
GPT	2.4	2.1	2.2
British Preferential Tariff	0.0	0.0	0.0
Canada-Israel Agreement Tariff		0.0	0.0
Chile Tariff	2.3	0.6	0.0
Commonwealth Caribbean Countries Tariff	0.0	0.0	0.0
Costa Rica Tariff		0.0	1.4
General Tariff	0.0	0.0	0.0
Informal entries and aggregated records	0.0	0.0	0.0
Mexican Tariff	1.8	0.2	0.0
Mexican-U.S. Tariff	1.0	0.0	0.0
U.S. Tariff	0.0	0.0	0.0
MFN	6.6	6.0	5.8
Trade-weighted average			
LDCT	0.0	0.0	0.0
GPT	3.2	3.1	3.1
British Preferential Tariff	0.0	0.0	0.0
Canada-Israel Agreement Tariff		0.0	0.0
Chile Tariff	1.2	0.0	0.0
Commonwealth Caribbean Countries Tariff	0.0	0.0	0.0
Costa Rica Tariff		0.0	0.2
General Tariff	0.0	0.0	0.0
Informal entries and aggregated records	0.0	0.0	0.0
Mexican Tariff	1.6	0.1	0.0
Mexican-U.S. Tariff	0.3	0.0	0.0
U.S. Tariff	0.0	0.0	0.0
MFN	4.4	3.5	3.1

Source: Author's calculations from Finance Canada data.
Note: Excludes chapter 99. Trade-weighted average is based on total imports.

by the GPT (2 percentage points), CARIBCAN (3.5 percentage points), or various country-specific tariffs (see columns 5 and 6 of table 5.3). Notably, the GPT rates were available on many more lines than were the other Canadian preferential arrangements.

As far as individual tariff lines were concerned, preferential margins were up to 20 percentage points for LDCT treatment, 18.5 percentage points for GPT, and

FIGURE 5.1 Count of Tariff Lines with Positive Trade Flows under LDCT, GPT, and CARIBCAN Treatments and Associated Preferential Margins

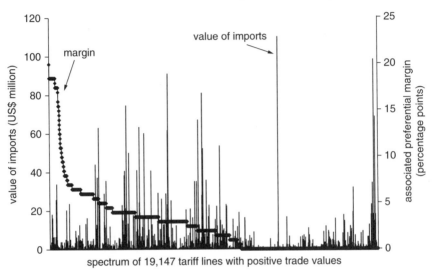

Source: Author's calculations from Finance Canada data.

12.5 percentage points for CARIBCAN. Nevertheless, the bulk of preferential trade associated with these schemes occurred on lines with medium and small preferential margins (see figure 5.1). The simple averages of preferential margins calculated at the HS chapter level for the LDCT, GPT, and CARIBCAN schemes presented in table 5.8 indicate a marked dispersion across products. When the three schemes are assessed together, the highest average margins (up to 13 percentage points) in 2003 were observed in textile and clothing products (HS chapters 61–64)—largely an indication of the margins enjoyed by LDCT beneficiaries (up to 18 percentage points). GPT margins in these chapters were also consistently higher than the average. However, these four chapters accounted for only 6 percent of imports entering under the GPT, LDCT, and CARIBCAN schemes.

One possible solution to preference erosion is a simultaneous lowering of MFN and preferential rates that preserves preferential margins. Figure 5.2 divides the 19,147 lines with positive trade values into a subset for which this option is feasible and one for which it is not (because preferential rates are already zero). In addition, a distinction is made between 7,382 lines for which both preferential and MFN rates are zero and 4,183 lines for which only preferential rates are zero. This distinction is important because the second set of lines would be affected by declining margins under MFN liberalization, but the first set would not. Overall,

(Text continues on p. 157.)

TABLE 5.8   Average Tariff Margins by HS Chapter and Treatment, 2003

HS chapter	Average tariff margin (%)			
	All three	CARIBCAN	GPT	LDCT
01 Live animals	0.0		0.0	
02 Meat and edible meat offal	0.4		0.4	
03 Fish and crustacean, molluscs and other aquatic invertebrates	0.2	1.7	0.0	3.0
04 Dairy produce, birds' eggs, natural honey, edible products of animal origin not elsewhere specified or included	1.8	0.0	1.8	
05 Products of animal origin, not elsewhere specified or included	0.0		0.0	
06 Live tree and other plants; bulbs, roots, and the like; cut flowers; and ornamental foliage	2.1	4.5	2.0	0.0
07 Edible vegetables and certain roots and tubers	0.7	0.0	0.7	5.2
08 Edible fruit and nuts; peel of citrus fruits or melons	0.1	0.3	0.1	0.0
09 Coffee, tea, maté, and spices	1.0	0.8	1.1	0.7
10 Cereals	0.0	0.0	0.0	0.0
11 Products of the milling industry, malt, starches, inulin, and wheat gluten	1.6	1.5	1.6	2.0
12 Oil seeds and oleaginous fruits; miscellaneous grains, seeds, and fruit; industrial or medicinal plants; and straw and fodder	0.2	0.0	0.2	0.0
13 Lac, gums, resins, and other vegetable saps and extracts	0.0		0.0	0.0
14 Vegetable plaiting materials and vegetable products not elsewhere specified or included	0.0	0.0	0.0	
15 Animal or vegetable fats and oils and their cleavage products, prepared edible fats, and animal and vegetable waxes	5.0	7.1	4.8	
16 Preparations of meat, fish or crustaceans, molluscs, or other aquatic invertebrates	1.1	3.7	1.1	
17 Sugars and sugar confectionery	3.6	7.9	3.4	
18 Cocoa and cocoa preparations	2.3	6.0	2.3	
19 Preparations of cereals, flour, starch, or milk; pastrycooks' products	1.4	3.6	1.3	5.0

TABLE 5.8   (Continued)

HS chapter	Average tariff margin (%)			
	All three	CARIBCAN	GPT	LDCT
20 Preparations of vegetables, fruit, nuts, or other plants	1.6	4.8	1.2	4.0
21 Miscellaneous edible preparations	3.5	7.2	3.0	10.5
22 Beverages, spirits, and vinegar	4.7	8.0	4.4	
23 Residues and waste from the food industries; prepared animal fodder	1.2	0.0	1.2	
24 Tobacco and manufactured tobacco substitutes	6.2		6.0	12.5
25 Salt, sulfur, earths and stones, plastering materials, lime, and cement	0.6		0.6	2.5
26 Ores, slag, and ash	0.0		0.0	0.0
27 Mineral fuels, mineral oils, and products of their distillation; bituminous substances; and mineral waxes	3.8		3.8	
28 Inorganic chemicals; organic or inorganic compounds of precious metals, rare earth metals, radioactive elements, or isotopes	1.2		1.2	3.5
29 Organic chemicals	2.4	5.5	2.4	
30 Pharmaceutical products	0.2	0.0	0.2	
31 Fertilizers	0.0		0.0	
32 Tanning or dyeing extracts; tannins and their derivatives; dyes, pigments, and other coloring matter; putty and other mastics; and inks	3.0		3.0	0.0
33 Essential oils and resinoids; perfumery, cosmetic, or toiletry preparations	3.8	3.8	3.8	6.4
34 Soap, organic surface-active agents, washing preparations, lubricating preparations, artificial waxes, prepared waxes, polishing or scouring preparations, candles and similar articles, modeling pastes, "dental waxes," and dental preparations with a basis of plaster	3.8	6.5	3.7	6.5
35 Albuminoidal substances, modified starches, glues, and enzymes	3.2		3.2	

(Table continues on the following page.)

TABLE 5.8 Average Tariff Margins by HS Chapter and Treatment, 2003 (*Continued*)

HS chapter	Average tariff margin (%)			
	All three	CARIBCAN	GPT	LDCT
36 Explosives, pyrotechnic products, matches, pyrophoric alloys, and certain combustible preparations	4.9		4.8	6.5
37 Photographic or cinematographic goods	5.2		5.2	
38 Miscellaneous chemical products	2.5		2.5	
39 Plastics and articles thereof	3.3	7.0	3.2	7.1
40 Rubber and articles thereof	2.2		2.2	
41 Rawhides and skins (other than furskins) and leather	2.4		2.4	2.5
42 Articles of leather; saddlery and harnesses; travel goods, handbags, and similar containers; and articles of animal gut (other than silkworm gut)	3.5		3.1	8.0
43 Furskins, artificial fur, and manufactures thereof	3.0		3.0	
44 Wood, articles of wood, and wood charcoal	3.0	3.0	2.9	6.3
45 Cork and articles of cork	0.0		0.0	
46 Manufactures of straw, esparto, or other plaiting materials; basketware; and wickerwork	3.5		3.2	6.5
47 Pulp of wood or of other fibrous cellulosic material; recovered (waste and scrap) paper or paperboard	0.0		0.0	
48 Paper and paperboard; articles of paper pulp or of paperboard	0.0		0.0	0.0
49 Printed books, newspapers, pictures, and other products of the printing industry; manuscripts; typescripts; and plans	0.2	0.8	0.2	0.0
50 Silk	0.0		0.0	0.0
51 Wool, fine or coarse animal hair, horsehair yarn, and woven fabric	3.3		3.3	
52 Cotton	3.2		1.0	12.0
53 Other vegetable textile fibers; paper yarn and woven fabrics of paper yarn	1.2		1.2	1.5
54 Manmade filaments	1.4		1.4	
55 Manmade staple fibers	1.2		0.6	15.0

TABLE 5.8   (*Continued*)

	Average tariff margin (%)			
HS chapter	All three	CARIBCAN	GPT	LDCT
56 Wadding, felt, and nonwoven; special yarns; twine, cordage, ropes, and cables, and articles thereof	1.3		1.1	7.5
57 Carpets and other textile floor coverings	6.1		5.9	10.9
58 Special woven fabrics, tufted textile fabrics, lace, tapestries, trimmings, and embroidery	3.0		2.4	10.4
59 Impregnated, coated, covered, or laminated textile fabrics; textile articles of a kind suitable for industrial use	3.5		3.4	14.5
60 Knitted or crocheted fabrics	4.3		2.4	15.0
61 Articles of apparel and clothing accessories, knitted or crocheted	12.2		2.1	18.4
62 Articles of apparel and clothing accessories, not knitted or crocheted	13.0		3.9	17.5
63 Other made-up textile articles, sets, worn clothing and worn textile articles, and rags	9.2		5.8	16.8
64 Footwear, gaiters, and the like; parts of such articles	8.4		6.7	17.6
65 Headgear and parts thereof	2.7		1.8	8.7
66 Umbrellas, sun umbrellas, walking sticks, seat sticks, whips, riding crops, and parts thereof	1.6		1.6	
67 Prepared feathers and down and articles made of feathers or down, artificial flowers, and articles of human hair	7.0		7.0	5.0
68 Articles of stone, plaster, cement, asbestos, mica, or similar materials	3.5		3.5	5.0
69 Ceramic products	5.0		4.9	6.8
70 Glass and glassware	0.7		0.6	3.6
71 Natural or cultured pearls, precious or semiprecious stones, precious metals, metals clad with precious metals, and articles thereof; imitation jewelry; and coin	2.6		2.3	7.5

(*Table continues on the following page.*)

TABLE 5.8   Average Tariff Margins by HS Chapter and Treatment, 2003 (*Continued*)

HS chapter	Average tariff margin (%)			
	All three	CARIBCAN	GPT	LDCT
72 Iron and steel	0.5	0.0	0.5	0.0
73 Articles of iron or steel	2.0	6.7	1.9	4.8
74 Copper and articles thereof	2.5		2.5	3.0
75 Nickel and articles thereof	2.3		2.3	
76 Aluminum and articles thereof	2.2	6.5	2.1	6.5
78 Lead and articles thereof	2.8		2.8	78
79 Zinc and articles thereof	0.6		0.6	79
80 Tin and articles thereof	2.6		2.6	80
81 Other base metals, cermets, and articles thereof	1.5		1.5	81
82 Tools, implements, cutlery, spoons, and forks of base metal; parts thereof of base metal	2.7	7.0	2.6	8.9
83 Miscellaneous articles of base metal	2.1		2.1	6.4
84 Nuclear reactors, boilers, machinery, and mechanical appliances and parts thereof	1.5		1.5	
85 Electrical machinery and equipment and parts thereof; sound recorders and reproducers, television image and sound recorders and reproducers, and parts and accessories of such articles	2.0	4.1	1.9	3.8
86 Railway or tramway locomotives, rolling stock and parts thereof; railway or tramway track fixtures or fittings and parts thereof; and mechanical (including electromechanical) traffic signaling equipment of all kinds	3.2		3.2	
87 Vehicles other than railway or tramway rolling stock and parts and accessories thereof	0.6		0.6	
88 Aircraft, spacecraft, and parts thereof	0.6		0.6	
89 Ships, boats, and floating structures	4.0		4.0	

TABLE 5.8   (*Continued*)

HS chapter	Average tariff margin (%)			
	All three	CARIBCAN	GPT	LDCT
90 Optical, photographic, cinematographic, measuring, checking, precision medical or surgical instruments and apparatus; parts and accessories thereof	1.6		1.6	1.5
91 Clocks and watches and parts thereof	2.6		2.6	0.0
92 Musical instruments and parts and accessories of such articles	2.0		2.0	2.0
93 Arms and ammunition and parts and accessories thereof	4.5		4.5	
94 Furniture; bedding, mattresses, mattress supports, cushions, and similar stuffed furnishings; lamps and lighting fittings not elsewhere specified or included; illuminated signs, nameplates, and the like; and prefabricated buildings	2.4	8.3	2.2	8.9
95 Toys, games, and sports requisites and parts and accessories thereof	1.2		1.2	0.0
96 Miscellaneous manufactured articles	2.9	4.5	2.8	7.0
97 Works of art, collectors' pieces, and antiques	1.5		1.5	0.0

Source: Author's calculations from Finance Canada data.

simultaneous reductions of MFN and preferential rates would, in principle, be feasible on up to 7,582 lines, covering 66 percent of total imports entering under the GPT, LDCT, or CARIBCAN schemes.[6] Some 7,382 lines covering 24 percent of preferential trade would not be affected by MFN cuts, because for these lines the MFN and the preferential rates are already zero. Declines in preferential margins would be inevitable on 4,183 lines that cover 20 percent of preferential trade, including all preferential trade with LDCs.

Coverage, Utilization, and Utility of Preferences

The literature considers three indicators of preferential programs: coverage, utilization, and utility.[7] In this assessment, product coverage is calculated as the ratio of imports that are covered by a preferential trade arrangement to total imports

FIGURE 5.2 Count of Tariff Lines with Positive Trade Flows under LDCT, GPT, and CARIBCAN Treatments and Associated Ratio of Preferential to MFN Tariffs

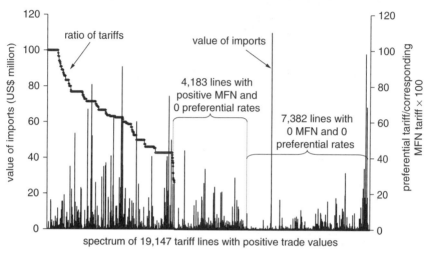

Source: Author's calculations from Finance Canada data.

from beneficiaries. With some exceptions, coverage ratios tend to be high (often close to 100 percent) and consistent across time for CARIBCAN beneficiaries. For the GPT, there is no clear tendency across beneficiaries or time. In fact, 54 percent of GPT beneficiaries recorded a decrease in coverage ratios between 1998 and 2002. This observation is not easily reconciled with the 1999 extension of GPT and LDCT product coverage by some 220 product lines and the lowering of the GPT tariff to two-thirds of the corresponding MFN rates. This finding contrasts with LDC coverage ratios: with the exception of Afghanistan, all beneficiaries moved to a coverage ratio of 100 percent in 2003. Undoubtedly, this trend is a result of the almost complete removal of all remaining tariff and quota restrictions on imports from LDCs in 2003. The expansion of exports under the LDCT scheme, mostly in textile and clothing products that are not covered by the GPT, has also certainly affected the coverage ratios calculated for the GPT scheme.

Utilization rates—computed as ratios of imports actually entering under a preferential scheme to imports covered by the scheme—depend crucially on the stringency and complexity of rules of origin and ancillary requirements (Inama 2003). Utilization rates for the GPT indicate a very uneven uptake. An increase in utilization rates from 1998 to 2002 was observed in only 45 percent of beneficiaries, an increase from 2002 to 2003 in 31 percent of countries, and an increase between 1998 and 2003 in 37 percent. The structure of LDC utilization rates is dichotomous. For 35 LDCs, rates have remained consistently at zero in the three years considered. In most remaining LDC beneficiaries, a positive tendency of increasing utilization rates was observed. In particular, the change of regime in 2003 seems to have had a significant effect on the rates of Bangladesh (89 percent in 2003), Cambodia (89 percent), Lao PDR (89 percent), Madagascar (16 percent), Malawi (16 percent), Maldives (47 percent), and Nepal (51 percent). As is explained in the next section, these substantial increases can be attributed almost entirely to increased trade flows in textiles and apparel.

A key question is why some LDC beneficiaries continue to use both the GPT and LDCT schemes even though the LDCT scheme seems more generous. This situation arises often if the GPT and LDCT rates are the same. Another potential explanation is that access under the GPT scheme may be chosen if the LDCT scheme's compliance procedures constitute more of a hurdle. The 2003 LDC initiative included a modification of the rules of origin for textiles and clothing products to require that cloth be cut and sewn or fabric woven from yarn produced in the country. These new rules of origin are one potential explanation for using both the GPT and the LDCT for shipments of the same products.

The utility rate is the ratio of imports that actually receive preferences to all imports (covered or not). It gives an indication of the importance of preferences in relation to all trade. Similar to utilization rates, utility rates of the LDCT exhibit a dichotomy, with 35 LDCs recording consistent zero utilization rates and other LDCs recording marked increases in 2003. The GPT utility rates are also very dispersed: a significant number of countries display marked reliance on preferences in their trade with Canada; for others, preferences seem unimportant.

Value of Preferences

An initial estimate of the value of Canada's preferences is obtained by calculating the difference between the MFN rate and the corresponding preferential rate and weighting it by the value of imports. Total values of preferences calculated in this way for all preferential schemes and years are presented in table 5.9. Remarkably, the value of preferences granted to Mexico under Mexican and Mexican-U.S. tariffs exceeded the combined value of GPT and LDCT preferences in 2003. Until 2002, the value of GPT preferences was close to 300 times the value of LDCT preferences. In 2003 the value of LDCT preferences increased by a factor of 100 and accounted for one-third of the value of the GPT scheme. The value of CARIBCAN preferences was more than double that of LDCT preferences in 1998 and 2002 but only one-twentieth of that value in 2003.

As far as the individual beneficiaries are concerned, the largest include several more advanced economies, such as Brazil, China, India, Israel, the Republic of

TABLE 5.9   Value of Preferences by Scheme

Scheme	Value of preferences (US$)		
	1998	2002	2003
Canada-Israel Agreement Tariff	n.a.	6,599,067	8,881,239
Chile Tariff	796,849	1,981,289	2,627,091
Commonwealth Caribbean Countries Tariff	977,169	1,297,913	3,022,676
Costa Rica Tariff	n.a.	4,089	87,795
GPT	99,343,661	151,473,214	173,895,632
LDCT	306,747	518,712	53,032,727
Mexican Tariff	79,503,301	189,103,895	212,471,049
Mexican–United States Tariff	8,556,558	26,436,984	34,088,074

Source: Author's calculations from Finance Canada data.
Note: n.a. = not applicable.

Korea, Malaysia, Mexico, and Hong Kong, China, as well as some LDCs, such as Bangladesh and Cambodia. Expressed as a percentage of the beneficiary's total exports, the value of preferences rarely exceeded 1 percent.[8] Some of the LDCs that had relatively high ratios of value of preferences to total exports in 2003 included Bangladesh (0.52 percent), Cambodia (0.43 percent), Haiti (0.28 percent), Lao PDR (0.23 percent), Lesotho (0.20 percent), and Maldives (0.22 percent).

The striking increase in the value of preferences for many LDCs in 2003 reflects an increase both in their utilization and in preferential margins on textile and clothing products that were until then excluded from duty-free treatment. The percentage increases in the value of preferences in 2003 relative to the averages for 1998 and 2002 are very substantial: 4,000 percent for Bangladesh; 5,500 percent for Cambodia; 8,890 percent for Lao PDR; 1.5 million percent for Lesotho; 5,061 percent for Madagascar; and 4,658 percent for Maldives. In Lesotho's case, this increase can be attributed entirely to changes on 11 HS eight-digit tariff lines within textiles and apparel, for which duties fell from 18 or 19 percent to zero.

Value of Preferences by Product

Which products carry the highest value of preferences under the GPT and LDCT schemes? An answer to this question may help to determine whether the exclusion of certain lines from MFN liberalization could alleviate the bulk of negative effects from preference erosion. In addition, and perhaps more important, identifying such lines will be a necessary step in assessing the costs and benefits of such potential exclusion or in designing any prospective compensation schemes. Tables 5.10

TABLE 5.10 LDCT Scheme Tariff Lines Accounting for at Least US$1 Million in Terms of Preference Value, 2003

Tariff item	Beneficiary	Value of preferences (US$)	As share in beneficiary's exports (%)
62046200	Bangladesh	5,915,094	0.08
	Cambodia	2,096,481	0.09
	Lao PDR	3,340	0.00
	Lesotho	115,365	0.03
	Madagascar	114,307	0.01
	Malawi	54,474	0.01
	Maldives	302,259	0.15
	Nepal	43,689	0.01
	Niger	29	0.00
	Total value and average share	8,645,038	0.04
62034200	Bangladesh	4,503,235	0.06
	Cambodia	992,762	0.04
	Lao PDR	366,953	0.12
	Lesotho	179,374	0.04
	Madagascar	28,446	0.00
	Maldives	46,127	0.02
	Nepal	38,815	0.01
	Total value and average share	6,155,712	0.04
61091000	Bangladesh	3,362,902	0.04
	Cambodia	138,571	0.01
	Haiti	552,036	0.15
	Lao PDR	61,916	0.02
	Lesotho	43,314	0.01
	Madagascar	21,308	0.00
	Maldives	17,362	0.01
	Nepal	33,455	0.01
	Niger	21	0.00
	Total value and average share	4,230,885	0.03
61103000	Bangladesh	3,001,476	0.04
	Cambodia	187,092	0.01
	Lao PDR	12,951	0.00
	Lesotho	1,639	0.00
	Madagascar	7,132	0.00
	Nepal	502	0.00
	Total value and average share	3,210,792	0.01

(Table continues on the following page.)

TABLE 5.10 LDCT Scheme Tariff Lines Accounting for at Least US$1 Million in Terms of Preference Value, 2003 (*Continued*)

Tariff item	Beneficiary	Value of preferences (US$)	As share in beneficiary's exports (%)
61102000	Bangladesh	1,903,795	0.02
	Cambodia	803,314	0.04
	Haiti	42,083	0.01
	Lao PDR	29,274	0.01
	Lesotho	228,425	0.05
	Madagascar	95,390	0.01
	Nepal	55,629	0.01
	Total value and average share	3,157,910	0.02
61142000	Bangladesh	1,182,601	0.02
	Cambodia	572,457	0.03
	Lao PDR	23,468	0.01
	Lesotho	69,416	0.02
	Madagascar	18,415	0.00
	Nepal	11,769	0.00
	Total value and average share	1,878,126	0.01
62034300	Bangladesh	1,215,973	0.02
	Cambodia	48,997	0.00
	Nepal	26,386	0.00
	Total value and average share	1,291,356	0.01
63062200	Bangladesh	1,214,958	0.02
	Total value and average share	1,214,958	0.02
61082100	Bangladesh	1,150,011	0.01
	Cambodia	16,703	0.00
	Madagascar	1,343	0.00
	Total value and average share	1,168,057	0.01
62019300	Bangladesh	948,762	0.01
	Cambodia	170,286	0.01
	Total value and average share	1,119,048	0.01
61051000	Bangladesh	721,544	0.01
	Cambodia	161,694	0.01
	Lao PDR	89,300	0.03
	Lesotho	22,749	0.01
	Maldives	29,514	0.01
	Nepal	23,834	0.00
	Total value and average share	1,048,635	0.01

TABLE 5.10 (*Continued*)

Tariff item	Beneficiary	Value of preferences (US$)	As share in beneficiary's exports (%)
62052000	Bangladesh	891,061	0.01
	Cambodia	147,671	0.01
	Madagascar	4,378	0.00
	Nepal	3,592	0.00
	Niger	38	0.00
	Total value and average share	1,046,740	0.00
62045200	Bangladesh	555,095	0.01
	Cambodia	347,958	0.02
	Lao PDR	154	0.00
	Madagascar	2,844	0.00
	Maldives	17,147	0.01
	Nepal	6,452	0.00
	Niger	42	0.00
	Total value and average share	929,692	0.00

Source: Author's calculations from Finance Canada data.

and 5.11 report data on the most important HS eight-digit tariff lines for LDCT and GPT preferences.

As far as the LDCT scheme is concerned, there were altogether 390 eight-digit tariff lines for which positive trade values were recorded in 2003 and 13 lines—all in chapters 61 through 63 (articles of apparel, clothing accessories, and other textiles articles)—on which tariff revenue losses exceeded US$1 million (see table 5.10). These tariff lines accounted for 64 percent of the total value of LDCT preferences in 2003. The associated values of preferences for each of these individual lines did not in any case exceed US$8.6 million and accrued consistently to a small group of beneficiaries: Bangladesh, Cambodia, Haiti, Lao PDR, Lesotho, Madagascar, Malawi, Maldives, Nepal, and Niger.

As far as the GPT scheme is concerned, there were 2,000 eight-digit tariff lines with positive imports in 2003. For 32 such lines, the preferences involved more than US$1 million in forgone tariff revenue. These tariff lines accounted for 38 percent of the total value of GPT preferences in 2003. The noticeable difference is that for each of the identified tariff lines the number of beneficiaries was typically larger than in the LDCT case. However, the highest value of preferences calculated at the tariff-line level was lower than in the LDCT case (about US$5 million), and typically the value of GPT preferences accounted for smaller shares of beneficiaries'

TABLE 5.11 GPT Scheme Tariff Lines Accounting for at Least US$1 Million in Terms of Preference Value, 2003

Tariff item	Value of preferences (US$)	Number of GPT countries with positive value of preferences	China's share in value of preferences (%)	Average share in beneficiary's exports (%)
94036010	5,099,196	42	45	0.000
42031000	4,390,024	18	75	0.000
69089010	3,938,421	22	2	0.000
39269090	3,488,955	39	87	0.000
94032000	3,104,124	34	93	0.000
85281293	3,027,344	6	23	0.000
94016110	2,919,286	32	56	0.000
16041490	2,590,567	12	0	0.001
69120090	2,575,756	39	78	0.000
42032990	2,330,979	16	91	0.000
87120000	2,320,666	9	69	0.000
69111090	2,225,484	30	74	0.000
94017910	2,005,264	18	97	0.000
94035000	1,965,864	37	45	0.000
39241000	1,905,831	28	82	0.000
39249000	1,859,100	30	89	0.000
94051000	1,683,021	24	98	0.000
42029290	1,628,602	28	92	0.000
57011090	1,626,246	15	4	0.001
85091000	1,614,516	5	78	0.000
73269090	1,591,589	32	91	0.000
39231090	1,417,987	26	93	0.000
85281291	1,394,615	4	5	0.000
42022290	1,235,144	24	98	0.000
94054090	1,200,112	20	91	0.000
44111990	1,157,916	6	29	0.000
44219090	1,152,348	40	85	0.000
95069990	1,122,918	17	92	0.000
63014000	1,118,307	14	63	0.000
65059020	1,095,529	31	85	0.000
73239300	1,084,235	25	75	0.000
17049090	1,038,221	44	25	0.000

Source: Author's calculations from Finance Canada data.

exports. A striking feature of the value of GPT preferences transpires from the information in table 5.11: for the majority of the identified tariff lines, most of the value of preferences was associated with imports from China (see the shares in the fourth column of table 5.11). Overall, China accounted for 64 percent of the value of Canadian GPT preferences in 2003.

High tariff-line concentration in the LDCT and GPT schemes suggests that excluding relatively few lines from MFN liberalization could alleviate the bulk of the negative effects of preference erosion in the Canadian market. However, the benefits of such an option would have to be weighed against the costs of unrealized liberalization. For example, the value of LDCT preferences on the HS eight-digit line 62046200 (US$8.6 million; see table 5.10) should be compared with benefits (to Canada and its trading partners) that could be obtained by reducing protection on the US$257 million worth of non-LDC imports on this line.

Economic Value of Preferences in 2001: A General Equilibrium Assessment

This section reports on the results of a model-based assessment of the value of Canadian preferences. The analysis uses the standard GTAP model with the version 6 database.[9] The model-based approach enables a more complete economic assessment of the value of preferences, taking into account the interaction of effects across preference-receiving and other sectors and across supplying countries. Changes in market access conditions for one product category are linked to developments in other sectors through goods and factors markets. Representation of such intersectoral links makes it possible to account for the reality that while some producers in selected preference-receiving sectors may be affected negatively, the resources that are freed from that sector can be used in other sectors that may gain better access to world markets or simply be more productive.

One disadvantage of this approach is a relatively high level of product and country aggregation that may mask some individual effects. The scenario considered here involves an equalization of product-level, bilateral, ad valorem measures of protection (see the next section for an explanation), with the preshock average calculated across all trading partners (a proxy for the MFN rate). This scenario mimics a situation in which, starting from the 2001 base with preferences, all preferential access to Canada is removed.

Preferential Access to Canadian Market in the GTAP Framework

The basic GTAP dataset used for this assessment covered 57 broad economic sectors and 87 countries. For these purposes, it was aggregated to 44 countries and regions and 22 sectors, using trade-weighted tariffs. A key advantage of this dataset is that it fully integrates the information on bilateral ad valorem tariffs (both MFN and preferential), ad valorem equivalents of specific tariffs (MFN and preferential), and tariff rate quotas from the Market Access Maps (or MAcMaps) database from the Centre d'Études Prospectives et d'Informations Internationales and the International Trade Commission.[10] The resulting ad valorem equivalent measures of applied protection are consistent across all bilateral trade flows.

Simulation Results

As indicated previously, the shock considered here is an equalization of product-level bilateral ad valorem measures of protection; the preshock average is calculated across all trading partners (as a proxy for the MFN rate). Welfare results associated with the scenario reported in table 5.12 indicate that the removal of Canadian preferences has a very minor impact on the welfare of developing country partners. For seven developing countries (Chile, Malawi, Mexico, South Africa, Tanzania, Thailand, Uganda) and three composite developing regions (the rest of North America, the rest of the Middle East and North Africa, and the rest of Sub-Saharan Africa), the reported welfare changes are negative. However, the associated proportional welfare changes with respect to the base do not exceed one-tenth of a percent in any of the cases.

At the same time, it is worth bearing in mind that estimates presented here for 2001 are based on a static resource-allocation exercise, in which resources, technology, and institutions are taken as a given. If the trade reform encouraged inflows of technology (as it is expected to do)—for example, through increased imports or exports, foreign direct investment, or licensing—or if it introduced fundamental institutional reform, it could have more pronounced effects on welfare. The magnitude of welfare change estimates obtained would undoubtedly change if some of these components of reality were incorporated into the model structure. Given the nature of this exercise, the results can be interpreted with more confidence in relative terms than in absolute terms.

Table 5.12 compares the effects of a scenario involving a 50 percent lowering of tariff protection in all regions. Such a scenario provides a benchmark for comparing magnitudes with the effects of removing preferences. It may also serve as a comparison with the gains that can be obtained from a worldwide halving of applied tariff rates that would be predicted by this particular computable general equilibrium model and data. Of course, such a scenario embodies elements of both preference erosion in other Quad markets and the effects of liberalization by third countries, including the effects of liberalization by developing countries.

TABLE 5.12 Comparison of Welfare Results of the Removal of Canadian Preferences and Multilateral 50 Percent Reduction of Tariffs

Beneficiary	Per capita utility ratio (%)			Equivalent variation (US$ million)		
	Removal of Canadian preferences	50 percent liberalization by all regions	50 percent liberalization by Canada	Removal of Canadian preferences	50 percent liberalization by all regions	50 percent liberalization by Canada
Asia						
Australia	0.00	0.11	0.00	8.73	336.24	7.62
China	0.01	0.36	0.01	122.47	3,729.30	90.51
Rest of Oceania	0.02	0.81	0.05	9.76	463.9	28.24
North and East Asia	0.02	0.92	0.01	150.49	7,406.60	80.81
Indonesia	0.01	0.31	0.00	6.13	413.19	2.11
Japan	0.01	0.32	0.00	292.27	11,485.46	120.83
Malaysia	0.00	1.64	0.00	1.09	1,273.12	−2.88
Philippines	0.00	0.10	0.00	2.61	62.85	1.31
Singapore	0.01	0.68	0.00	7.41	507.53	1.59
Sri Lanka	0.02	1.26	0.02	2.44	178.76	2.27
Thailand	0.00	1.07	0.00	−2.54	1,063.63	−0.54
Vietnam	0.02	2.64	0.02	6.78	770.67	4.92
Bangladesh	0.02	0.26	0.01	7.72	110.78	6.28
India	0.01	0.44	0.00	27.28	1,915.73	19.45
North America						
Canada	0.05	0.02	0.08	339.81	133.89	484.31
Mexico	−0.01	0.10	−0.01	−25.91	551.23	−31.83
United States	−0.01	−0.01	0.00	−1,173.43	−667.55	−158.69
Rest of North America	−0.06	−6.09	−0.03	−1.70	−165.63	−0.73

(Table continues on the following page.)

TABLE 5.12 Comparison of Welfare Results of the Removal of Canadian Preferences and Multilateral 50 Percent Reduction of Tariffs (*Continued*)

Beneficiary	Per capita utility ratio (%)			Equivalent variation (US$ million)		
	Removal of Canadian preferences	50 percent liberalization by all regions	50 percent liberalization by Canada	Removal of Canadian preferences	50 percent liberalization by all regions	50 percent liberalization by Canada
Central and South America						
Argentina	0.00	0.13	0.00	7.14	319.59	1.74
Brazil	0.01	0.26	0.00	21.29	1,135.55	6.13
Chile	0.00	0.07	0.00	−1.87	41.14	−1.52
Colombia	0.00	−0.2	0.00	0.06	−152.65	−1.26
Peru	0.04	0.06	0.01	18.85	29.62	4.73
Uruguay	0.04	0.26	0.04	6.05	45.80	6.24
Venezuela, R. B. de	0.00	0.10	0.00	1.43	105.57	−1.92
Europe						
EU	0.01	0.12	0.00	477.47	8,992.83	171.17
Rest of Europe	0.00	0.16	0.00	0.95	638.82	2.75
Middle East and North Africa						
Turkey	0.01	0.46	0.00	6.44	610.12	3.70
Rest of Middle East and North Africa	0.00	0.31	0.00	−7.24	2,314.03	−20.95

Africa						
Botswana	0.01	0.58	0.00	0.38	27.11	0.17
Morocco	0.00	0.64	0.00	0.69	196.68	0.75
South Africa	0.00	0.32	0.00	-0.73	311.25	-1.71
Tunisia	0.00	1.50	0.00	0.60	261.27	0.46
Rest of Southern African Customs Union	0.02	1.80	0.01	0.71	80.44	0.49
Malawi	-0.01	1.43	-0.01	-0.08	22.26	-0.08
Mozambique	0.01	-0.22	0.00	0.15	-7.13	0.07
Tanzania	0.00	-0.29	0.00	-0.19	-25.38	-0.13
Zambia	0.01	0.09	0.00	0.17	2.78	0.08
Zimbabwe	0.00	0.65	0.00	0.10	51.67	0.04
Rest of Southern African Development Community	0.00	1.21	0.00	0.04	204.9	-0.74
Madagascar	0.00	-0.14	0.00	0.01	-5.87	-0.03
Uganda	0.00	-0.29	0.00	-0.11	-15.38	-0.07
Rest of Sub-Saharan Africa	-0.01	-0.16	-0.01	-5.72	-199.3	-6.68
Rest of the world	0.00	0.14	0.00	26.89	1,066.37	13.32

Source: Author's calculations based on GTAP model simulations and the GTAP 6 database.

A more detailed discussion of such a scenario in the context of preference erosion is provided in Lippoldt and Kowalski (2005).

Notwithstanding some sign differences, it is clear that the effects of multilateral liberalization are up to two orders of a magnitude higher than those associated with removal of Canadian preferences. Focusing on countries that are affected negatively by the removal of Canadian preferences, one sees that Mexico—which is estimated to lose 0.01 percent of welfare from the removal of Canadian preferences—is estimated to gain 0.10 percent from the worldwide lowering of tariffs. Malawi, which is likewise estimated to lose 0.01 percent from preference erosion, stands to gain 1.42 percent from the worldwide lowering of tariffs. Thailand, which is unaffected by the removal of Canadian preferences, experiences a 1 percent welfare gain from multilateral liberalization. It is worth noting that a number of developing countries—predominantly in Sub-Saharan Africa—that are not affected by the removal of Canadian preferences are affected negatively by worldwide lowering of tariffs, with the negative impacts of the multilateral liberalization scenario reaching up to 0.30 percent of their initial welfare. As discussed in Lippoldt and Kowalski (2005), these negative effects are explained largely by the effects of tariff liberalization in the European Union (EU), which are, in turn, determined by a combination of the high EU shares in the total exports of several beneficiaries and the substantial size of the EU preferential margins in certain sectors.

As already emphasized, this experiment includes tariff cutting by countries other than Canada, so the resulting numbers cannot be used directly to ascertain the effects of MFN tariff reductions on the value of Canadian preferences. Instead, they give a sense of the magnitude of preference erosion. To further facilitate the interpretation of results, table 5.12 includes welfare estimates of a scenario involving a 50 percent lowering of tariff protection by Canada alone. Results from this experiment are very similar to those associated with the removal of Canadian preferences, both qualitatively and quantitatively.

These results need to be treated with considerable caution for a number of reasons. First, the data constraints imply high levels of country and product aggregation, which may mask some effects on smaller developing countries and producers of specific products. Second, as discussed in the first part of the chapter, the 2003 introduction of the new LDC initiative had significant implications for the preferential trade of selected textile- and clothing-producing LDCs with Canada. Nevertheless, even this remarkable change has not had a major effect on total shares of exports to Canada among these countries' exports. For this reason, the small welfare impacts of Canadian schemes estimated with the 2001 data may be not too far from the results that would obtain with 2003 data.

Conclusions

The extent and potential economic impacts on beneficiaries of Canada's preferential schemes need to be considered in relation to market access conditions that Canada's other trading partners face in the Canadian market. In particular, the impact of the GPT and the LDC schemes appears to have been limited by the relatively low protection levels afforded to other trading partners, whether on the MFN basis or through reciprocal trade agreements. The extensive reliance of several developing countries on nonpreferential access to Canada's market suggests their strong interest in further liberalization of the MFN regime. Cases of overreliance on preferential trade with Canada are limited to a few LDCs, for which trade under preferential schemes accounts for the bulk of total exports to Canada and is concentrated in textile and clothing products. A conclusion that could be drawn from the simplified model assessment is that the welfare impact of Canadian preferences is very small for most developing countries analyzed here. Notwithstanding the significant variation in the utilization and value of preferences across beneficiaries, this finding is consistent with the generally small shares of preferential trade with Canada in these countries' total trade. Therefore, erosion of preferential schemes does not appear to be a major hurdle to further reduction of Canadian MFN rates.

Notes

1. The supply-side-managed products referred to here are dairy, poultry, and egg products, the supply of which is regulated in Canada through a system of quotas.

2. *Dutiable imports* refers to the portion of imports that was used for calculating duty paid or payable. The dataset contains some problematic entries; for example, positive values of dutiable imports are recorded for duty-free records. It is important to note that Canada's simplified tariff regime that came into effect on January 1, 1998, was reported to have caused misunderstandings about coding of documents, duty rates, classifications, and so forth. This problem could explain these anomalies for 1998; however, they also occur in other years.

3. Mixed rates take the form of a conditional expression determining either an ad valorem or a specific tariff (for example X cents per kilogram but not less than Y percent or X cents per kilogram but not to exceed Y percent). Other types of specific duties used in the Canadian Customs Tariff schedule include specific, compound (combining both specific and ad valorem components), and technical rates (duty dependent on the input content).

4. Data on total exports of a given developing country were collected from the World Bank Integrated Trade Solution database.

5. See Kowalski (2005) for detailed data for all HS two-digit chapters.

6. The exact number of lines for which this is feasible depends on the ambition of the associated cut to MFN rates.

7. Detailed data by country and preference program on these three variables are reported in Kowalski (2005). Inama (2003) discusses these indicators in greater depth.

8. The Turks and Caicos Islands—an overseas territory of the United Kingdom—represent an exception.

9. The most comprehensive description of the model is in Hertel (1997). Information on more recent developments can be found at http://www.gtap.org.

10. The dataset is documented in detail in Bouët and others (2002).

References

Alexandraki, Katerina, and Hans Peter Lankes. 2004. "The Impact of Preference Erosion on Middle-Income Developing Countries." IMF Working Paper 04/169, International Monetary Fund, Washington, DC.

Bouët, Antoine, Lionel Fontagné, Mondher Mimouni, and Friedrich von Kirchbach. 2002. "Market Access for GTAP: A Bilateral Measure of Merchandise Trade Protection." GTAP Resource 1045, Center for Global Trade Analysis, Purdue University, West Lafayette, IN. http://www.gtap .agecon.purdue.edu/resources/res_display.asp?RecordID=1045.

CCRA (Canada Customs and Revenue Agency). 2003. "An Introductory Guide to the Market Access Initiative for the Least Developed Country and the Least Developed Country Tariff." Canada Customs and Revenue Agency, Ottawa.

Hertel, Thomas W. 1997. *Global Trade Analysis: Modeling and Applications.* Cambridge, U.K.: Cambridge University Press.

Inama, Stefano. 2003. "Trade Preferences and the World Trade Organization Negotiations on Market Access." *Journal of World Trade* 37 (5): 959–76.

Kowalski, Przemyslaw. 2005. "The Canadian Preferential Tariff Regime and Potential Economic Impacts of Its Erosion." Paper prepared for the International Symposium on Preference Erosion: Impacts and Policy Responses, Geneva, June 13–14. http://siteresources.worldbank.org/INTRANETTRADE/Resources/Kowalski_Canada_preferences.pdf.

Lippoldt, Douglas, and Przemyslaw Kowalski. 2005. "Trade Preference Erosion: Potential Economic Impacts." OECD Trade Policy Working Paper 17, Organisation for Economic Co-operation and Development, Paris.

Subramanian, Arvind. 2003. "Financing of Losses from Preference Erosion: Note on Issues Raised by Developing Countries in the Doha Round." WT/TF/COH/14, International Monetary Fund, Washington, DC.

UNCTAD (United Nations Conference on Trade and Development). 2001. *Generalized System of Preferences: Handbook on the Scheme of Canada.* Geneva: UNCTAD.

Weston, Ann. 2003. "Bangladesh's Access to the Canadian Market: Implications of the New Canadian LDC Initiative and Prospects for Export Diversification." North-South Institute, Ottawa.

WTO (World Trade Organization). 2003. "Trade Policy Review: Canada." WT/TPR/S/112, WTO, Geneva.

Yamazaki, Fumiko. 1996. "Potential Erosion of Trade Preferences in Agricultural Products." *Food Policy* 21 (4–5): 409–17.

6

THE AUSTRALIAN PREFERENTIAL TARIFF REGIME

Douglas Lippoldt

In terms of import volumes, Australia is a much smaller player in world trade than the Quad economies (Canada, the European Union, Japan, and the United States). Its monthly average imports of about US$8.6 billion amount to less than 2 percent of the total imports into the Quad economies plus Australia (figure 6.1).[1] Nevertheless, Australia is a major market for some developing countries. Its preferential programs are important regionally, with a total of about US$19 billion in preferential imports claimed in 2004. Consequently, the effects of its preferential arrangements merit a closer look.

This chapter considers Australia's preferential trade according to the standardized approach developed by the World Bank in consultation with the contributors to the World Bank project on preference erosion. It begins by describing the non-reciprocal preferential arrangements available to developing countries exporting into the Australian market. It then provides a detailed statistical review of the usage of these arrangements, citing topics of particular interest for developing countries that may be vulnerable to negative effects from preference erosion. It then presents a simulation of the welfare impacts of preference erosion.

The author gratefully acknowledges the essential contributions of Karinne Logez (statistical assistance) and Caroline Mirkovic (research assistance). The assistance of the Australian Bureau of Statistics in providing the underlying trade data and associated technical explanations made this chapter possible and is greatly appreciated. The opinions expressed do not necessarily reflect those of the Organisation for Economic Co-operation and Development or its member countries.

FIGURE 6.1 Monthly Average Merchandise Imports 2004 (US$ billion)

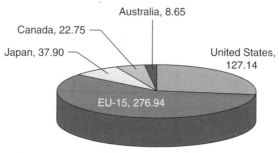

Source: OECD 2005.

Note: EU-15 refers to the 15 member states of the European Union prior to May 1, 2004. The figure for the EU-15 includes intra-European trade. The values for Australia and Canada are free on board. Other values are cost, insurance, and freight.

Description of the Organisation for Economic Co-operation and Development Tariff Preference Database

To analyze Australian preferential trade with developing countries, the Organisation for Economic Co-operation and Development (OECD) Secretariat developed an internal database on preferential trade using data from the Australian Bureau of Statistics (ABS). The building blocks for the database consist of the bilateral import flows by an HS 10-digit product, taking into account country of origin and tariff treatment claimed at the time of import (see annexes). For each year, about 100,000 lines of data were included, with each line representing the aggregate annual imports of an HS 10-digit product from one developing country. The analysis that follows calculated aggregate data and subtotals by summing up individual trade flows. Although the original ABS source data provide at least some information on nearly all Australian imports from developing countries, the present analysis generally excludes products classified as confidential (HS chapter 99).[2] Table 6.1 compares the flows with and without these confidential imports. The exclusion of the confidential trade flows from the analysis was generally necessary owing to the lack of complete information on their nature. In addition, the schedule of most-favored-nation (MFN) tariff rates was not available to the OECD in a database-compatible format.[3] Hence, the MFN rates were inferred as being the maximum applied rate for each product.

The OECD database covers tariff lines for which there were imports from developing countries during 1996, 2002, 2003, and 2004. The selection of years was driven by the evolution of the database over time in the context of the larger OECD trade preference erosion project. The database captures information on a

TABLE 6.1 Australian Imports from Developing Countries by Type of Tariff Treatment, 1996–2004

	Total imports (current US$ million)				Imports excluding HS 99 (confidential) (current US$ million)			
	1996	2002	2003	2004	1996	2002	2003	2004
DC preference (excluding historical)	6,321	10,817	12,714	14,874	6,201	10,581	12,395	14,538
FIC preferences	137	122	156	164	137	96	97	102
SRSE								
Special rate claimed	4,270	4,314	3,007	800	4,135	4,133	2,870	800
Singapore exports receiving DC preference rate	n.a.	n.a.	1,038	3,052	n.a.	n.a.	997	2,943
Singapore free trade agreement, free rate of duty	n.a.	n.a.	33	121	n.a.	n.a.	22	77
Preferences for LDCs and other priority beneficiaries								
LDC preferential rate of duty claimed	n.a.	n.a.	3	9	n.a.	n.a.	3	9
DC preference, historical	17	33	28	23	17	33	28	23
All preferences	10,746	15,285	16,979	19,042	10,490	14,843	16,411	18,491
Nonpreferential treatment								
Special rate that applies has not been claimed and general rate of duty has been used	6,384	11,086	15,353	24,665	6,238	10,652	14,791	24,015
No preferential rate of duty has been claimed	1,172	522	1,495	531	1,110	500	1,475	528
Total	18,303	26,893	33,827	44,238	17,838	25,994	32,677	43,034

Sources: Australian Bureau of Statistics data; OECD Secretariat calculations.

Notes: DC = developing country; FIC = Forum Island Country; SRSE = special rates for specific countries; LDC = least developed country; n.a. = not applicable. Import values are based on customs value.

period of notable change in the Australian preferential tariff schemes: 1996 marks the original implementation of the framework legislation for the current tariff regime; 2003 marks the implementation of expanded duty-free and quota-free access for the least developed countries (LDCs), as well as the entry into force of a free trade agreement with Singapore; and 2002 and 2004 give an impression of the situation before and after the latter developments.

Determining the applied tariff rate at the HS 10-digit product level is a relatively complicated affair in Australia. In the ABS database, imports are classified by product line according to their country of origin and status with respect to each of three classifications: preference (that is, which scheme was claimed); treatment (that is, special considerations such as type of duty concession, the most common of which is "no treatment code"); and nature (that is, normal, concessional, quota, or government).[4] Together these features affect the tariff rate that is applied.

Broadly, the MFN rates are defined as the general rates of duty that apply when no preference has been claimed. These rates are associated with goods entering Australia under one of two specific preference codes (X or Z). Unfortunately, these rates are not always available in the database and must be inferred to assess the importance of preferences.[5] Therefore, two methods were used to determine the MFN rates: *inferred statutory* and *calculated*. Under the inferred statutory approach, MFN rates for each HS 10-digit product were determined by scanning the import lines across all developing countries. The inferred statutory MFN rate for each product is the maximum statutory rate. Specific duties, comparatively rare under the Australian preference regime, were not taken into account under this approach.[6] The calculated MFN rates for each HS 10-digit product were determined on the basis of actual duties collected as a percentage of the customs value of the goods. Here again, the maximum duty rate across the various developing countries is taken to be the MFN rate. Under this approach, specific duties were taken into account. For the purposes of this analysis, both approaches were used so that the results could be compared.

So that the potential biases could be tested, the results for each approach were compared with the general rates of duty with respect to the lines for which both rates were available on an ad valorem basis. For the available tariff lines, the inferred statutory approach yielded an upward bias in the MFN rates of less than one-quarter of 1 percentage point in any year. The calculated MFN approach also yielded an upward bias of less than 1 percentage point in any year. Each of the derived MFN approaches offers much greater product coverage than would otherwise be available from the database. The inferred statutory MFN approach yields estimates closely approximating the actual MFN rates for those lines with ad valorem tariffs. The calculated MFN approach yields approximate estimates but provides information on lines where specific duties apply. This information can be important in some sectors in some years; for example, for dairy products, tobacco, and beverages, spirits and vinegar, 10 percent or more of imports from developing countries entered under specific duties in 2004.

Australian Tariff Preferences: An Overview

In its latest trade policy review of Australia, the World Trade Organization (WTO) concludes that Australia's trade and trade-related policies are transparent (WTO 2007). The customs tariff remains the main trade policy instrument. Australia first extended unilateral trade preferences to developing countries in 1976 under the Australian System of Tariff Preferences (ACS 2004). The primary legislation governing the current Australian tariff regime is the Customs Tariff Act of 1995, as amended, which initially took effect on July 1, 1996. The Australian Customs Tariff Classification is based on the International Convention on the Harmonized Commodity Description and Coding System of 2002. The Australian duty rates refer to the free-on-board value of goods in the exporting port (that is, no duties are levied on the insurance and freight).[7] In Australia, the legislative basis for determining product origin is the Customs Act of 1901 and certain regulations (107A–B).

According to the individual action plan drawn up for Australia by the Asia-Pacific Economic Cooperation (APEC), the general tariff rates for most items were reduced to 5 percent or less by the 1995 Tariff Act (APEC 2004). As of January 2004, nearly 48 percent of tariff lines were duty free, and the average simple applied rate was 4.25 percent. Tariffs remained above 5 percent in several areas, including textiles, clothing, footwear, and passenger motor vehicles. But the government is committed to reducing tariffs in these areas to no more than 5 percent by 2010—except for tariffs on clothing and certain finished textile articles, which will be reduced to that level by 2015. Tariff rates applying to 99 percent of imported products (by value) are bound, including 100 percent of agricultural tariff lines. Except for certain cheese products (0.1 percent of overall tariff lines), agricultural goods are not subject to a tariff quota. Nevertheless, Australia is not a major importer of some of the more sensitive tropical agricultural products (box 6.1).

Nonreciprocal Preferential Tariff Schemes

Australia's nonreciprocal preferential tariff schemes for developing countries are presented in the annexes. These schemes can be grouped into four categories, by the size of the trade flows (figure 6.2): (a) developing country (DC) preferences, (b) special rates for specific economies (SRSE), (c) Forum Island Country (FIC) preferences, and (d) preferences applicable mainly to LDCs. The advantages extended to

Box 6.1   Sugar and Bananas

Sugar and bananas are sensitive tropical products that are often cited as being most affected by preference erosion. In a recent International Monetary Fund working paper, for example, Alexandraki and Lankes (2004) identify middle-income developing countries that are potentially vulnerable to export losses from preference erosion. They use partial equilibrium simulations, by product, to estimate the effects of changes in trade-weighted preference margins between each country in question and the Quad economies. They find that vulnerability to preference erosion among this group of developing countries is particularly concentrated with respect to sugar and banana exports (especially into the European Union and U.S. markets); in many cases, the producers are small island economies that may have major problems in adjusting to preference erosion. They also find vulnerability to preference erosion among middle-income countries with respect to textiles and clothing, but to a far lesser extent than for the other two products. Similarly, a Commonwealth Secretariat (2004) study finds significant value (measured by quota rents) for beneficiaries in preferences for sugar, bananas, and textiles and clothing (as well as beef) and finds that many preference-dependent economies will suffer multiple economic hardships in adjusting to a more liberalized trading environment.

Australia, by contrast, appears to have a competitive domestic industry for both sugar and bananas. It has substantial banana production and is a notable exporter of sugar.[a] Despite having a relatively open trading regime for these products, Australian import volumes for both products remain modest—in terms of both absolute volumes (see accompanying table) and shares of exports for suppliers from developing countries. In the case of bananas, imports are negligible. Most (99 percent) enter under the DC preference, despite the availability of duty-free entry under MFN treatment. In the case of sugar (HS 17), the volumes are somewhat larger and rising in the aggregate. Imports in this sector enter Australia quota free but face a trade-weighted MFN tariff of about 5 percent. In 2004, about 75 percent of imports of HS 17 from developing countries entered under preferential schemes. The effective DC preference margins are modest (less than 1 percentage point, on a trade-weighted basis, in recent years), despite the availability of duty-free treatment for imports from LDCs. Preferences have the effect of reducing the duties collected on sugar imports by less than 10 percent.

Notwithstanding the availability of preferences for imports of these two products, the relative openness of the Australian MFN regime and the small import volumes mean that the potential for negative effects from erosion of Australian preferences in these areas is quite limited.

a. Industry association Web sites provide an overview of these two sectors in Australia: http://www.abgc.org.au/pages/industry/ bananaIndustry.asp and http://www.canegrowers.com.au/ overview.htm. For an overview of Australian exports of sugar, see http://www.fas.usda.gov/htp2/ sugar/1997/ 97-11/nov97cov.htm.

Evolution of Australian Imports of Bananas and Sugar

Economy	Customs value (US$)		
	2002	2003	2004
Fresh or dried bananas, including plantains			
Colombia			19,141
Ecuador		1,343	
India	1,670	1,204	3,680
Indonesia		244	3,371
Israel		934	
Philippines	36,301	28,326	11,735
Sri Lanka		397	
Thailand	2,752	3,517	3,725
Vietnam	14,554	13,834	9,652
Total	55,282	49,800	51,304
Sugars and sugar confectionery			
Argentina	313,318	162,730	236,948
Bangladesh	909	0	253
Brazil	805,864	877,999	1,065,960
Bulgaria	20,483	6,956	0
Chile	307,199	203,123	404,872
China	11,516,776	14,435,358	22,319,595
Colombia	151,694	123,746	211,953
Costa Rica	30,521	13,105	40,088
Croatia	23,339	108,248	122,647
Cyprus	117,131	14,468	34,807
Czech Republic	656,065	837,119	1,357,740
Ecuador	1,240	0	0
Egypt, Arab Rep. of	3,576	13,405	7,640
Fiji	1,506,598	1,463,794	2,177,239
Hong Kong, China	171,986	150,234	294,369
Hungary	121,697	14,968	41,234
India	355,788	491,018	310,544
Indonesia	4,965,858	7,385,264	4,087,510
Iran, Islamic Rep. of	43,289	36,723	96,106
Israel	73,695	114,202	113,583
Jordan	1,848	2,811	2,385
Kenya	0	0	15,476

(Table continues on the following page.)

Box 6.1   Sugar and Bananas (*Continued*)

Evolution of Australian Imports of Bananas and Sugar

Economy	Customs value (US$)		
	2002	2003	2004
Korea, Dem. People's Rep. of	521	0	0
Korea, Rep. of	1,045,504	1,118,292	1,064,673
Lebanon	130,027	231,546	181,059
Macedonia, FYR	414,009	263,385	93,995
Malaysia	1,313,133	2,367,716	2,279,425
Malta	853	0	0
Mauritius	101,761	257,971	126,083
Mexico	332,508	215,590	245,430
Oman	50,334	161,378	260,963
Pakistan	890,680	1,477,529	1,342,391
Paraguay	7,269	7,847	0
Philippines	98,142	205,007	249,041
Poland	156,641	232,037	259,079
Saudi Arabia	46,291	23,415	25,450
Senegal	179	0	0
Singapore	253,106	308,344	549,309
Slovenia	17,837	1,874	15,634
Sri Lanka	53,182	43,039	46,770
Swaziland	23,231	390,249	674,416
Syrian Arab Republic	13,544	53,809	27,754
Taiwan, China	350,263	446,003	475,852
Thailand	821,292	1,624,794	1,314,440
Turkey	191,911	351,855	702,415
United Arab Emirates	156,162	71,683	80,164
Uruguay	1,657	3,355	4,399
Vietnam	194,851	215,440	186,144
Total	27,853,765	36,509,430	43,145,835

Sources: Australian Bureau of Statistics data; OECD Secretariat calculations.
Note: Totals may differ because of rounding.

exporters from developing countries under these tariff schemes are evident from examining some basic parameters presented in the following overview.

Table 6.1 provides a more specific breakdown of Australian preferences, highlighting the relative size of flows under the various tariff schemes and their evolution between 1996 and 2004. As can be deduced from the table, HS 99 confidential imports account for about US$1.2 billion of imports from developing countries,

FIGURE 6.2 Total Imports under the Main Types of Australian Preferential Tariff Rates, 1996–2004

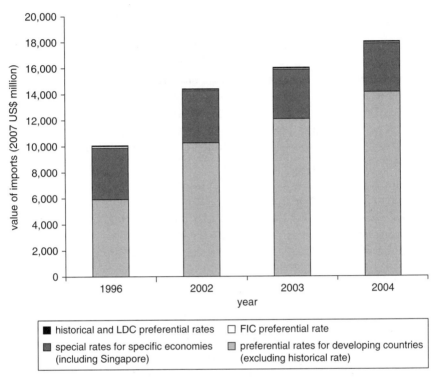

Sources: Australian Bureau of Statistics; OECD Secretariat calculations.

Note: Here and throughout this chapter, ABS data on imports are classified according to the type of tariff treatment claimed for the imports, and imports under HS 99 (confidential) are excluded from the analysis except where otherwise indicated. The Singapore-Australia Free Trade Agreement entered into force on July 28, 2003.

including US$500 million of preferential imports (2.9 percent of total preferential imports). For consistency with the subsequent analysis, the following overview excludes the confidential imports:

- Among Australia's preferential measures, the DC tariff is the broadest preference in terms of the number of eligible economies. It is by far the most heavily used preference, with some US$14.5 billion in imports in 2004, accounting for more than 75 percent of total preferential imports into Australia that year. The volume of imports under this preferential arrangement increased substantially during the period considered in this chapter, more than doubling between 1996 and 2004. As a proportion of overall Australian imports from developing countries, flows under this program ranged between 33 and 40 percent during these years.

- The second-largest Australian preference category consists of SRSE in Asia. This category includes Hong Kong, China; the Republic of Korea; Singapore; and Taiwan, China. In 2002, these beneficiaries exported US$4.1 billion under the SRSE scheme. Singapore was the largest exporter under the scheme. A free trade agreement with Singapore came into effect on July 28, 2003, offering exporters in that country improved or duty-free access to the Australian market.[8] In 2004, excluding imports from Singapore under the free trade agreement, imports under the SRSE category amounted to US$0.8 billion. As a proportion of total Australian imports from developing countries, flows under this scheme fell from 23 percent to 2 percent between 1996 and 2004.

- The third-largest category consists of the preference scheme that targets the FICs. These preferences cover imports from a number of Pacific island economies and were introduced under the South Pacific Regional Trade and Economic Cooperation Agreement, which took effect on June 30, 1982. Papua New Guinea is a special case covered by the Papua New Guinea–Australia Agreement on Trade and Commercial Relations, which became operational on February 1, 1977. Papua New Guinea was subsequently included among FIC beneficiaries.[9] Although the overall trade volumes are relatively modest under these preferences (US$102 million in 2004) and show little growth, they are quite important to some of these economies. Imports under the scheme account for less than 1 percent of total Australian imports from developing countries in each of the selected years from 1996 to 2004 (their share of the total falling from 0.8 percent to 0.2 percent).

- The final category of preferences refers mainly to LDCs. The DC "historical" preference provides preferential access for a limited number of tariff lines for developing countries and a few additional economies, in addition to the benefits available under the DC preferences. Flows under the DC historical scheme amounted to just US$23 million in 2004. In 2003, a new and more generous LDC preference was introduced. Use of this preference has not resulted in a large increase in import volumes from LDCs; indeed, only US$9 million in imports benefited from it in 2004. Goods receiving either the LDC preference or the DC historical preference accounted for about 0.1 percent of exports from developing countries to Australia in each of the selected years.

Nonpreferential Market Access

In 2004, more than half of imports from developing countries entered Australia under nonpreferential tariffs, either because of a failure to claim a preference or because the goods were not eligible for preferences. As can be inferred from table 6.1, the share of imports from developing countries that did not enter under preferential treatment rose over the selected years from 41 percent to 57 percent of the total. Many of these imports entered duty free or under low MFN rates.

Australia operates a schedule of concessional instruments designed to facilitate importation of two types of goods: (a) those with no competing or substitutable Australian products and for which an importer has applied for a tariff concession order and (b) those that are identified under the government's industrial policy as important for reducing business input costs in specific sectors. Certain goods are excluded from this scheme, such as foodstuffs, clothing, and passenger motor vehicles. Concessional duty rates are generally duty free or low (for example, 3 percent), and they are temporary (each month the concessional schedule has about 150 updates).[10] About 17 percent of Australia's imports from developing countries were classified as concessional in 2004, valued at about US$7.3 billion (excluding HS 99); more than two-thirds of them were concentrated in imports of just four HS two-digit categories.[11] In 2004, nearly two-thirds of concessional imports entered under what normally would have been MFN rates, a proportion that had increased since 1996. Interestingly, concessional rates can offer importers better access than preferential programs in some cases. For example, in 2004, about 5.8 percent of imports from developing countries entered under preferential schemes but at concessional duty rates; one-quarter of all concessional imports entered under the DC preferential tariff scheme.

Tariff Summary Statistics

Table 6.2 indicates the scope of the various tariff treatments, highlighting the number of tariff lines with imports in recent years (including those imports classified as "combined confidential" or entering at concessional rates). The nonpreferential treatment and DC preferential had about 6,000 "active" tariff lines (at the HS 10-digit level), whereas other types of tariff treatment had substantially fewer; that is, other preferences were much narrower in the range of active tariff lines concerned. The FIC, SRSE, LDC, and DC historical preferences each covered fewer than 600 HS 10-digit tariff lines with imports in 2004. The change in treatment of imports from Singapore in 2003 is reflected in the shift from reliance on nonreciprocal tariffs toward the new reciprocal free trade agreement between that country and Australia. The shift revealed the comparatively modest range of imports from the other beneficiaries under the SRSE (which include certain advanced Asian developing countries).

Table 6.3 presents key features of the main Australian preferential tariff schemes, focusing on mainstream imports from developing countries. It excludes the comparatively modest flow of imports considered "combined confidential" as well as imports at concessional tariff rates that are available independently of the nonreciprocal preference schemes.

TABLE 6.2   Australian Preferential Trade: Counts of HS 10-Digit Tariff Lines with All Imports from Developing Countries, 2002–04

Type of preference	2002	2003	2004
DC preference (excluding "historical")	6,056	6,100	6,176
FIC preference	608	629	585
SRSE			
Special rate for the specific country claimed	4,944	4,605	577
Singapore exports receiving DC rate	n.a.	3,754	4,555
Singapore free trade agreement free rate of duty	n.a.	423	260
Preferences for LDCs and other priority beneficiaries			
LDC preferential rate of duty claimed	n.a.	158	296
DC preference, historical	536	470	503
Nonpreferential treatment			
Special rate that applies has not been claimed and general rate of duty has been used	5,748	6,028	6,273
No preferential rate of duty has been claimed	1,673	1,337	1,307

Sources: Australian Bureau of Statistics data; OECD Secretariat calculations.
Note: n.a. = not applicable.

As table 6.3 shows, throughout the Australian tariff schedule, the vast majority of tariffs are on lines with imports from developing countries that are taxed on an ad valorem basis (that is, as a percentage of the value). Since 1991, a number of adjustments have been made to the tariff regime. These adjustments have had the effect of liberalizing general access to the Australian market and phasing out access to "full" nonreciprocal preference margins for some developing countries (ACS 2004: 10). This phaseout began with certain advanced Asian developing economies (Hong Kong, China; the Republic of Korea; Singapore; and Taiwan, China) and was subsequently extended to most other developing countries. The most generous provisions for nonreciprocal preferential access are now reserved for two main target groups of developing countries: LDCs and FICs.

In 2004, the Australian tariff scheme for LDCs offered a simple average preference margin of about 13.5 percentage points on the tariff lines with eligible imports. The DC historical preference offered a margin of about 3.4 percentage points to a similar group of countries on a broader set of tariff lines with imports that year. The scheme for the FICs offered a preference margin of about 10.7 percentage points. In comparison, other developing countries tended to have less generous access under the available nonreciprocal preferences, with preference margins ranging from 0.6 percentage point under the DC preference to 4.7 percentage points on a more narrow set of lines under the SRSE scheme.

TABLE 6.3 Overview of Preferential Tariffs, for Product Groups (HS 10-digit) with Imports, 2004

Treatment	Number of lines with imports in 2004[a]	Simple average, applied tariff (statutory rate)[b] (%)	Simple average, inferred statutory "MFN" tariff[c] (%)	Maximum tariff in these lines, under the stated treatment (%)	Count of ad valorem tariffs	Count of non–ad valorem tariffs
DC preference (excluding historical[d])	6,035	6.1	6.7	40	5,962	73
FIC preference	565	0.0	10.7	0	561	4
SRSC	223	1.4	6.1	5	222	1
Special rate for the specific country claimed						
Singapore exports receiving DC rate	4,339	5.3	5.9	25	4,313	26
Singapore free trade agreement duty rate	247	0.0	7.3	0	243	4
Preferences for LDCs and other priority beneficiaries						
LDC preferential rate of duty claimed	289	0.0	13.5	0	289	0
DC preference, historical[d]	483	6.3	9.7	20	476	7

(Table continues on the following page.)

TABLE 6.3 Overview of Preferential Tariffs, for Product Groups (HS 10-digit) with Imports, 2004 (*Continued*)

Treatment	Number of lines with imports in 2004[a]	Simple average, applied tariff (statutory rate)[b] (%)	Simple average, inferred statutory "MFN" tariff[c] (%)	Maximum tariff in these lines, under the stated treatment (%)	Count of ad valorem tariffs	Count of non–ad valorem tariffs
Nonpreferential treatment						
Special rate that applies has not been claimed and general rate of duty has been used	6,105	6.5	6.8	25	6,051	54
No preferential rate of duty has been claimed	1,208	0.0	0.1	5	1,205	3

Sources: Australian Bureau of Statistics data; OECD Secretariat calculations.

Note: Excludes imports classified as "combined confidential" or entering at concessional rates. Australian tariffs are determined on the basis of the HS line, preferential scheme, country of origin, nature of entry, nature of tariff, and treatment code. The original ABS database used in these tables for 2002 lists 156 countries as eligible for the DC preferential rate (17 of 156 countries did not export under this scheme). According to the original ABS database, the following beneficiaries were eligible for the FIC preferential rates: Cook Islands, Fiji, Kiribati, Marshall Islands, Nauru, Niue, Samoa, Solomon Islands, Tonga, Tuvalu, and Vanuatu. According to the original ABS database, the following developing countries were eligible for SRSE: Hong Kong, China; Taiwan, China; the Republic of Korea; Malaysia; Papua New Guinea; and Singapore. Country eligibility for the various tariff preferences as of December 2004 is shown in the annexes.

a. Number of lines at the HS 10-digit level for which there were imports entering in 2004 under the treatment indicated.

b. Simple average of lines for which there have been imports. Calculation based on ad valorem tariffs only.

c. *MFN tariffs* refer to the maximum rate. This column presents the simple averages of MFN tariffs for the lines corresponding to those in the preferential programs with imports. The calculation is based on ad valorem tariffs only.

d. The historical category covers a set of developing countries that tend to be relatively less developed, have been traditionally treated as developing countries under the Australian tariff system, and receive special preferences on a comparatively limited set of tariff lines.

Rules of Origin

Rules of origin are used under preferential tariff schemes in order to require a minimum level of local content in products that are imported from eligible suppliers. They help ensure that the products imported under the preferences are not merely transshipped from ineligible countries through eligible suppliers with little or no local value added. Rules of origin can play an important role in ensuring that the intended beneficiaries actually reap the benefits of preferential programs. Where imports from beneficiaries are indeed stimulated by preferences, origin rules can boost local productive activity. By contrast, as Inama (2003) suggests with respect to the Quad economies, tight rules of origin are often the main reason that preferences are underused.

As do other preference-granting countries, Australia uses provisions about rules of origin to ensure that goods entering at preferential rates are associated with production in the intended beneficiary economies. The Australian origin rules specify that products must be either wholly obtained or substantially transformed in the beneficiary economy (see the annexes). Substantial transformation essentially requires that the last process of manufacture is performed in the country or territory that claims origin and that a minimum level of value added is attained (generally 50 percent of the total factory cost in terms of materials, labor, and overhead) (ACS 2004). The LDC preferential arrangement allows materials from all developing countries, FICs, and Australia to count as local content. But the portion for developing countries that are not LDCs is limited to no more than 25 percent of the total factory cost of the goods.

Australia employs a system of self-assessment for entry clearance that places responsibility for correct clearance of goods through Customs on the importer (ACS 2000). Under the corresponding formalities, the importer provides a certificate of origin from the manufacturer. After clearance of the goods, the Australian Customs Service monitors compliance with the requirements of the various preference schemes.

Composition of Flows

As already noted, more than half of imports from developing countries in 2004 entered Australia without preferential treatment, either because of a failure to claim a preference or because the goods were ineligible. A more concrete indication of why this occurred is that about 75 percent of nonpreferential imports from developing countries had duty-free access to the Australian market. In comparison, only 46 percent of preferential imports benefited from duty-free access. Importers appear to prefer to import under nonpreferential arrangements where the MFN tariff rates are duty free. This approach has the advantage of avoiding rules of origin and other administrative requirements associated with preferential programs. Another peak in the flows occurs at the 5 percent duty rate, at which roughly 25 percent of preferential trade and an additional 13 percent of nonpreferential trade takes place. The next largest flow is at the 25 percent duty rate, with smaller but notable flows at the 3, 4, 10, and 15 percent duty rates. About 80 percent of all imports from developing countries take place duty free or at a 5 percent tariff rate.

Lippoldt (2008) reports data on the reliance on Australian preferences as a share of the total exports of each country that trades with Australia. Australian tariff preference schemes account for a relatively small share of developing countries' global exports. During 1996 to 2004 the overall share was 0.8 percent or less. In 2004, only 14 countries relied on Australian preferential schemes for 1 percent or more of their global exports, Australia being a major market for only Papua New Guinea (34.6 percent in 2004), Fiji (17.9 percent), and Swaziland (7.3 percent). The next two countries on that list are Vietnam (3.9 percent) and the Solomon Islands (3.2 percent). Exporters tended to be fairly consistent in their use of the preferential schemes, with a number of notable exceptions in terms of which countries increased or decreased their reliance on Australian preferences. For example, Samoa reduced its reliance on Australian preferential trade—excluding HS 99—from 31 percent to about 1 percent between 2002 and 2004 (box 6.2). Other notable examples during this period include Papua New Guinea (which more than doubled its preference reliance from 16 percent to 35 percent) and Swaziland (which boosted its preference reliance from 0 to 7 percent).

Two approaches were used by which the MFN-applied tariff rates and preference margins were derived: one based on trade-weighted, average statutory MFN tariffs and one based on collected tariffs by tariff line. This procedure was needed because data on MFN tariffs were not available for tariff lines for which there was no trade (Lippoldt 2008). Generally, the two sets of estimates are not substantially different, except for four sectors with large shares of trade entering under specific duties (HS chapters 4, 22, 24, and 27), where the trade-weighted MFN tariffs are much higher under the calculated approach. This situation is due to the number of lines that potentially face specific duties. For example, about 12 percent of the imports in the mineral fuels, oils, and related products sector face the equivalent of a 90 percent ad valorem tariff; another 12 percent face the equivalent of a 150 percent ad valorem tariff. In practice, however, nearly all the imports of mineral fuels, oils, and products entered Australia duty free or at very low tariff rates (less than 1 percent), owing to the application of concessional tariff rates where the MFN rate would have been quite high.

The preference margins calculated using the two MFN approaches are not strikingly different, except for the four sectors with significant numbers of products that potentially face specific duties. Figure 6.3 highlights changes in the distribution

Box 6.2   A Shift in Samoa's Trade

Samoa, as an FIC and LDC, has enjoyed the full margin of Australian tariff preferences as well as—in some cases—concessional access. Imports from Samoa have profited from this situation, with heavy use of the available tariff advantages. In recent years, however, Samoa's trade situation has become less clear because of a shift in the composition of its exports, with increasing shares of exports under the "combined confidential" (HS 99) classification. Given the exclusion of HS 99 from most of the statistical tables in this chapter, the presentation of Samoa's situation should be viewed with this factor in mind.

The accompanying figure highlights this shift in the composition of exports, presenting exports in two key sectors as a percentage of Samoa's global exports. In 1996, electrical machinery, equipment, and parts (HS 85) constituted two-thirds of Australia's imports from Samoa, virtually all benefiting from concessional rates. For 2002 to 2004, the bulk of Samoa's exports benefited rather from preferential rates under the FIC scheme, including those in both sectors (HS 85 and HS 99). But during these latter years, the composition shifted out of the HS 85 classification and into the confidential sector, and it is not known what sector these confidential imports represent.

Export Concentration in Samoa, 1996–2004

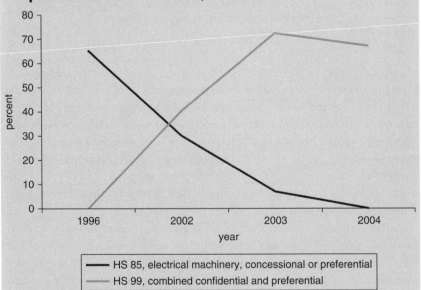

Source: OECD Secretariat calculations based on data from Australian Bureau of Statistics.

Note: The figure presents exports in each sector as a percentage of Samoa's global exports. The global exports are based on mirror data.

FIGURE 6.3 Preference Margins Based on Inferred Statutory MFN Rates, by Sector, 1996 and 2004

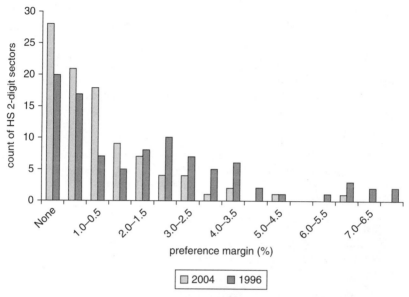

Sources: Australian Bureau of Statistics; OECD Secretariat calculations.

Note: Excludes confidential imports (HS 99) and products facing specific duties.

of preference margins by sector between 1996 and 2004 for the inferred statutory MFN rates. Whereas some change in the average preference margin by sector may reflect changes in the within-sector structure of trade, the consistency of the pattern appears to point to a measure of preference erosion from reductions in MFN rates during the period under consideration here (when Uruguay Round commitments were being implemented).[12] The number of sectors that benefit from preference margins greater than 1.5 percentage points declined notably between the two time periods; conversely, the number of sectors with low or nonexistent preference margins increased substantially.

Rough estimates, by sector, of the tariff revenue forgone because of preferences are calculated individually for each developing country's exports of each HS 10-digit-level product according to each type of preferential treatment received. Each of these flows is then multiplied by the applicable preference margin. The forgone revenue for these flows is then summed across all the detailed product lines for each HS two-digit sector. This calculation is made for both approaches to MFN estimation—inferred statutory rates and calculated MFN rates. Because the "calculated" MFN rates are based on the maximum duty rates paid on tariff lines with import flows, at least some of the product (defined at the

HS 10-digit level) was actually imported at the high calculated MFN duty rate, albeit generally only in small volumes and not necessarily from the same supplier every year. The evolution of the indicators that are calculated is reported by sector and by exporting country in Lippoldt (2008).

Under the inferred statutory MFN approach, the value of forgone duty dropped from US$430 million in 1996 to US$226 million in 2002, and then rose to US$268 million in 2003 and US$366 million in 2004. Under the calculated MFN approach, the value of forgone duty increased substantially between 1996 and 2004, rising from US$1,132 million in 1996 to US$3,203 million in 2004. Much of the increase occurred between 2003 and 2004. Calculations of forgone duties as a percentage of inferred statutory MFN rates suggest that duties in 16 HS chapters were reduced by 50 percent or more as a result of preferential schemes; using calculated MFN rates, 21 HS chapters showed reductions of this magnitude.

The calculation of the value of preferences is complicated by the influence of other tariff measures, apart from preferences on the final duty paid. In particular, the availability of concessional rates can be important for tariff treatment of developing countries.[13] For example, the overall figure for forgone revenue under the calculated MFN approach is much larger than for the inferred statutory approach, owing mainly to the volume of trade in mineral fuels, oils, and related products (HS 27) that potentially faces specific duties. As noted, however, imports in this sector in particular also benefited from concessional access to the Australian market, including imports entering under preferential programs. For example, in 2003 approximately 6 percent of total mineral fuels, oils, and related product imports from developing countries entered at concessional rates, even though they were also classified as imports under a preferential program.[14] Some 28 percent of the total imports of these products entered under preferential schemes but not at concessional rates. In 2004, these percentages dropped sharply to 0.3 percent and 17 percent, respectively. Thus, the value of the forgone duty revenues for a particular product from a given source may not be wholly attributable to preferences in a given year (if concessional tariff treatment was granted and offered even more advantageous access than the preferential rate for the imports of that product from that source).

Table 6.4 breaks down by supplier the estimated value of Australian nonreciprocal tariff preferences in terms of forgone duties. To provide some context for these numbers, the table provides indicators for 2004 relating the forgone duties to each supplier's total exports, potential MFN duty liability on the corresponding exports to Australia, and share in Australia's total duties forgone. Only a few beneficiaries account for most of the value of forgone duties under the inferred statutory approach to MFN. Most are among the larger developing economies: China (38 percent); the Republic of Korea (10 percent); Thailand (8 percent); Malaysia

(Text continues on p. 202.)

TABLE 6.4 The Estimated Value of Australian Tariff Preferences Calculated in Terms of Forgone Duties, by Country, 1996–2004

Economy of origin	Amount of duty forgone on the basis of inferred statutory MFN rates							Amount of duty forgone on the basis of calculated MFN rates						
	Duty forgone (US$ thousand)				2004 duties forgone for each economy			Duty forgone (US$ thousand)				2004 duties forgone for each economy		
	1996	2002	2003	2004	As a % of each economy's total exports	As a % of duty to be paid at inferred statutory MFN rates	As a % of total duties forgone by Australia in 2004 (statutory MFN rates)	1996	2002	2003	2004	As a % of each economy's total exports	As a % of duty to be paid at inferred statutory MFN rates	As a % of total duties forgone by Australia in 2004 (statutory MFN rates)
Afghanistan	0.0	0.0	0.0	2.4	0.00	55.3	0.0	0.0	0.0	0.0	2.4	0.00	55.4	0.0
Albania	1.1	0.0	0.2	0.1	0.00	2.0	0.0	1.1	0.0	0.2	0.1	0.00	2.1	0.0
Algeria	0.0	0.0	0.0	0.6	0.00	46.4	0.0	0.0	0.0	0.0	0.6	0.00	46.6	0.0
American Samoa	0.0	0.2	1.3	1.3		92.3	0.0	0.0	3.5	1.3	1.3		92.3	0.0
Angola	0.0	0.0	1.4	0.1	0.00	36.1	0.0	0.0	0.0	1.4	0.1	0.00	36.1	0.0
Anguilla	0.0	0.0	0.0	0.0				0.0	0.0	0.0	0.0	0.00	0.0	0.0
Antigua and Barbuda	0.0	0.0	0.0	0.0				0.0	0.0	0.0	0.0	0.00	0.3	0.0
Argentina	855.5	1,705.9	1,884.9	2,126.1	0.01	43.5	0.6	955.4	1,732.9	1,907.3	2,158.9	0.01	43.7	0.1
Bahamas, The	0.2	0.0	0.0	2.8	0.00	3.0	0.0	539.3	1,084.6	24.8	5.9	0.00	6.1	0.0
Bahrain	93.8	203.0	266.2	374.3	0.01	19.4	0.1	115.9	209.0	266.1	375.5	0.02	19.5	0.0
Bangladesh	223.7	179.0	353.1	1,280.1	0.02	76.1	0.3	253.9	182.0	353.1	1,280.1	0.02	76.1	0.0

Barbados	22.0	1.4	6.1	0.0	0.00	25.7		952.7	838.2	2,512.5	2,704.9	0.90	76.5	0.1
Belize	0.0	1.8	0.3	0.6			0.0	0.0	1.8	0.3	0.6	0.00	25.8	0.0
Benin	0.0	0.0	0.0	0.0	0.00	55.9	0.0	0.0	0.0	0.0	0.0	0.00	56.4	0.0
Bermuda	0.0	1.7	0.0	0.1	0.01	53.6	0.0	569.5	1.7	0.0	0.1	0.01	53.6	0.0
Bhutan	0.0	0.2	0.0	3.7	0.00	8.5	0.0	0.0	0.2	0.0	3.7	0.00	16.9	0.0
Bolivia	28.4	7.7	17.9	5.9	0.00	40.7	0.0	29.9	7.8	17.9	16.5	0.00	50.2	0.0
Bosnia and Herzegovina	3.3	9.2	9.7	16.4		13.4	0.0	3.3	31.1	9.7	33.6			
Botswana	0.0	0.0	0.1	0.1	0.00	19.2	0.0	0.0	0.0	0.1	0.1	0.00	13.5	0.0
Brazil	6,522.5	2,954.8	3,667.9	5,020.3	0.01	19.2	1.4	32,673.7	3,279.0	4,126.0	8,237.7	0.01	40.7	0.3
British Indian Ocean Territory	0.0	0.0	0.0	0.0				0.0	0.0	0.0	0.0			
British Virgin Islands	0.0	0.1	0.0	0.0	0.00		0.0	0.0	12.7	0.0	0.0	0.00	0.1	0.0
Brunei Darussalam	3.9	3.4	1.5	0.6	0.00	3.0	0.0	4.5	3.7	1.8	0.7	0.00	3.0	0.0
Bulgaria	31.9	45.8	60.4	82.5	0.00	12.6	0.0	1,067.9	4,001.2	2,722.0	5,097.2	0.07	89.9	0.2
Burkina Faso	0.0	0.0	0.8	0.1	0.00	79.1	0.0	0.0	0.0	0.8	1.0	0.00	79.2	0.0
Burundi	0.0	0.0	0.0	0.0				0.0	0.0	0.0				
Cambodia	4.8	52.5	225.7	342.1	0.02	63.0	0.1	9.9	53.1	232.1	485.9	0.02	67.2	0.0
Cameroon	4.2	6.4	10.6	18.5	0.00	98.8	0.0	4.2	6.5	10.6	18.6	0.00	99.2	0.0
Cape Verde	0.0	0.0	0.1	0.0				0.0	0.0	0.1	0.0			
Cayman Islands	0.2	0.0	0.0	0.0				0.8	0.0	0.0	0.0	0.00	2.9	0.0
Central African Republic	0.0	0.0	0.0	0.0				0.0	0.0	0.0	0.0			
Chad	0.0	0.0	0.2	0.0				0.0	0.0	0.2	0.0			

(Table continues on the following page.)

TABLE 6.4 The Estimated Value of Australian Tariff Preferences Calculated in Terms of Forgone Duties, by Country, 1996–2004 (Continued)

| Economy of origin | Amount of duty forgone on the basis of inferred statutory MFN rates | | | | | | | Amount of duty forgone on the basis of calculated MFN rates | | | | | | |
| | Duty forgone (US$ thousand) | | | | 2004 duties forgone for each economy | | | Duty forgone (US$ thousand) | | | | 2004 duties forgone for each economy | | |
	1996	2002	2003	2004	As a % of each economy's total exports	As a % of duty to be paid at inferred statutory MFN rates	As a % of total duties forgone by Australia in 2004 (statutory MFN rates)	1996	2002	2003	2004	As a % of each economy's total exports	As a % of duty to be paid at inferred statutory MFN rates	As a % of total duties forgone by Australia in 2004 (statutory MFN rates)
Chile	284.1	214.3	230.1	233.0	0.00	14.8	0.1	389.3	332.6	259.2	368.4	0.00	21.0	0.0
China	119,985.8	78,703.8	93,964.1	138,015.0	0.02	15.1	37.7	231,685.9	121,605.9	135,004.8	178,824.0	0.03	18.7	5.6
Colombia	128.9	37.1	45.8	81.0	0.00	24.0	0.0	356.5	73.3	93.0	104.5	0.00	28.4	0.0
Comoros	1.6	0.0	0.0	0.0				1.6	0.0	0.0	0.0			
Congo, Dem. Rep. of	0.0	0.0	0.2	0.0			0.0	0.1	0.0	0.2	0.0	0.00	2.6	0.0
Congo, Rep. of	0.3	1.3	0.6	0.1	0.00	100.0	0.0	0.3	1.3	0.6	0.1	0.00	100.0	0.0
Cook Islands	15.2	4.0	1.1	2.3	0.02	87.7	0.0	15.3	4.1	1.1	2.3	0.02	87.7	0.0
Costa Rica	9.0	208.3	176.2	201.0	0.00	57.6	0.1	11.2	211.9	224.9	202.0	0.00	57.4	0.0
Côte d'Ivoire	4.7	0.5	0.8	0.6	0.00	8.9	0.0	5.8	0.5	0.8	0.6	0.00	9.0	0.0
Croatia	98.5	74.7	111.0	302.0	0.01	44.5	0.1	1,079.9	228.0	247.9	619.0	0.01	42.5	0.0
Cuba	3.6	50.8	8.8	3.5	0.00	15.7	0.0	1,539.3	4,645.8	7,049.2	7,330.6	0.66	80.9	0.2
Cyprus	31.3	1.5	1.9	4.0	0.00	8.7	0.0	105.4	326.1	432.7	94.1	0.01	52.9	0.0

Czech Republic	1,216.2	722.6	666.9	1,640.0	0.00	42.3	0.4	1,586.4	1,035.4	1,259.0	3,466.6	0.01	52.3	0.1
Djibouti	0.0	0.0	0.0	0.0	0.00		0.0	0.0	0.0	0.0	0.0	0.00	0.5	0.0
Dominica	0.0	0.0	0.0	0.1	0.00	54.2	0.0	0.1	54.1	411.5	736.2	1.78	59.8	0.0
Dominican Republic	17.4	2.5	10.4	13.0	0.00	13.2	0.0	200.3	1,348.8	1,793.4	2,772.5	0.05	86.7	0.1
Timor-Leste	0.0	0.3	0.1	2.0	0.03	57.5	0.0	0.0	0.3	17.9	86.3	1.65	67.7	0.0
Ecuador	11.4	2.8	0.7	7.5	0.00	20.6	0.0	13.4	38.5	56.3	15.5	0.00	17.3	0.0
Egypt, Arab Rep. of	378.9	32.1	55.4	54.0	0.00	5.6	0.0	414.5	251.0	193.9	13,268.8	0.18	91.8	0.4
El Salvador	2.8	1.1	2.4	2.0	0.00	2.3	0.0	4.0	1.9	2.4	1.6	0.00	2.3	0.0
Equatorial Guinea	0.0	0.0	0.0	0.2	0.00	72.6	0.0	0.0	0.0	0.0	0.2	0.00	73.0	0.0
Eritrea	0.0	0.1	0.0	0.6	0.00	100.0	0.0	0.1	0.1	0.0	0.6	0.00	100.0	0.0
Ethiopia	1.0	0.0	0.1	0.0				1.0	0.0	0.1	17.5	0.00	71.3	0.0
Falkland Islands	0.0	0.0	0.0	0.0		100.0	0.0	0.0	0.0	0.0	0.0			
Fiji	44,758.3	15,179.2	17,741.5	19,434.0	3.48	99.4	5.3	45,817.5	16,695.7	22,202.6	23,734.5	4.25	94.8	0.7
French Polynesia	2.5	7.0	5.2	11.0	0.01	96.1	0.0	3.1	10.9	5.2	24.4	0.01	95.6	0.0
Gabon	0.0	0.8	0.8	6.8	0.00	100.0	0.0	0.0	0.8	0.8	6.8	0.00	100.0	0.0
Gambia, The	0.0	0.0	0.0	0.0				0.0	0.0	0.0	0.3	0.00	0.3	0.0
Ghana	11.1	33.0	18.3	39.7	0.00	43.2	0.0	14.5	33.4	18.3	39.7	0.00	43.2	0.0
Gibraltar	2.1	0.0	1.3	0.0				2.2	0.0	1.3	0.0	0.00	0.0	0.0
Grenada	0.0	0.0	0.0	0.0				0.0	0.0	0.0	0.0	0.00	0.0	0.0
Guam	0.8	0.3	0.5	2.3	0.00	62.9	0.0	1.2	0.3	0.5	2.3	0.00	63.0	0.0
Guatemala	7.9	2.2	2.5	1.9	0.00	9.2	0.0	8.7	2.7	2.5	1.9	0.00	9.3	0.0
Guinea	0.0	0.0	0.0	0.4	0.00	94.2	0.0	0.0	0.0	0.0	0.4	0.00	94.5	0.0
Guyana	0.0	0.0	0.3	5.0	0.00	83.8	0.0	0.0	0.0	0.3	5.0	0.00	83.8	0.0

(Table continues on the following page.)

TABLE 6.4 **The Estimated Value of Australian Tariff Preferences Calculated in Terms of Forgone Duties, by Country, 1996–2004 (Continued)**

Economy of origin	Amount of duty forgone on the basis of inferred statutory MFN rates							Amount of duty forgone on the basis of calculated MFN rates						
	Duty forgone (US$ thousand)				2004 duties forgone for each economy			Duty forgone (US$ thousand)				2004 duties forgone for each economy		
	1996	2002	2003	2004	As a % of each economy's total exports	As a % of duty to be paid at inferred statutory MFN rates	As a % of total duties forgone by Australia in 2004 (statutory MFN rates)	1996	2002	2003	2004	As a % of each economy's total exports	As a % of duty to be paid at inferred statutory MFN rates	As a % of total duties forgone by Australia in 2004 (statutory MFN rates)
Haiti	0.2	0.5	98.0	83.7	0.02	46.6	0.0	0.3	0.6	98.0	83.7	0.02	46.6	0.0
Honduras	0.5	0.1	0.7	0.0	0.00	0.0	0.0	32.2	251.0	430.2	224.4	0.00	26.9	0.0
Hong Kong, China	12,866.6	6,633.3	4,845.0	7,271.6	0.01	17.9	2.0	16,161.3	8,433.5	6,154.2	7,821.7	0.01	18.9	0.2
Hungary	665.6	568.4	924.2	993.7	0.00	24.2	0.3	923.4	1,476.7	1,987.8	1,780.0	0.00	41.7	0.1
India	12,170.4	5,324.1	6,570.6	9,421.3	0.02	21.9	2.6	23,422.3	6,381.8	7,144.9	10,272.2	0.02	23.3	0.3
Indonesia	18,094.4	9,622.5	9,267.8	11,060.9	0.02	21.9	3.0	25,642.9	12,859.0	51,785.0	140,235.9	0.21	77.8	4.4
Iran, Islamic Rep. of	85.8	21.5	30.8	13.2	0.00	3.7	0.0	89.3	25.4	42.8	13.2	0.00	3.7	0.0
Iraq	0.0	0.0	0.0	0.1	0.00	66.7	0.0	0.0	0.0	0.0	0.1	0.00	66.7	0.0
Israel	3,722.2	1,785.5	2,532.5	3,269.3	0.01	34.9	0.9	4,425.3	1,857.7	2,548.8	3,346.5	0.01	35.3	0.1
Jamaica	0.5	10.0	0.1	0.0	0.00		0.0	1,114.7	793.4	4,369.7	6,015.9	0.38	65.0	0.2
Jordan	4.2	1.6	2.8	6.5	0.00	16.6	0.0	4.5	140.2	49.0	42.6	0.00	20.8	0.0
Kenya	15.6	19.4	2.1	1.1	0.00	9.5	0.0	30.6	19.6	2.1	3.9	0.00	25.7	0.0

Country													
Kiribati	0.0	0.0	0.0	0.1	0.00	9.9	0.0	0.0	0.0	0.0	0.1	0.00	10.0	0.0
Korea, Dem. People's Rep.	22.0	25.8	136.4	64.7	0.01	25.8	0.0	26.9	26.1	136.4	77.1	0.01	27.9	0.0
Korea, Rep. of	43,513.8	21,439.2	30,322.0	36,887.3	0.02	22.0	10.1	65,318.2	54,095.0	81,830.7	183,692.6	0.10	64.1	5.7
Kuwait	0.0	0.1	0.5	1.6	0.00	18.0	0.0	4.7	0.1	0.9	2.0	0.00	23.0	0.0
Lao PDR	8.4	3.6	14.6	15.4	0.00	23.9	0.0	9.5	3.9	14.6	15.4	0.01	20.4	0.0
Lebanon	65.5	25.6	38.6	33.5	0.00	11.2	0.0	203.1	58.6	68.6	111.3	0.01	27.6	0.0
Lesotho	0.0	0.0	1.4	3.4	0.00	57.0	0.0	0.0	0.0	1.4	3.4	0.00	57.0	0.0
Liberia	0.0	0.0	0.0	0.1	0.00	69.3	0.0	0.0	0.0	0.0	0.1	0.00	69.7	0.0
Libya	1.3	0.0	0.0	0.0				1.3	0.0	0.0	0.0			
Macao, China	117.4	1.7	20.4	10.4	0.00	1.5	0.0	267.5	8.3	19.2	13.1	0.00	1.9	0.0
Macedonia FYR	29.2	10.1	11.4	11.0	0.00	12.4	0.0	80.9	27.1	14.3	77.3	0.01	28.7	0.0
Madagascar	0.5	1.8	0.1	1.9	0.00	16.6	0.0	1.4	1.8	0.1	1.9	0.00	16.7	0.0
Malawi	0.6	0.1	0.0	1.0	0.00	100.0	0.0	6.7	0.1	0.0	1,088.6	0.23	100.0	0.0
Malaysia	33,340.6	21,781.2	24,687.9	28,543.9	0.02	39.0	7.8	36,493.8	39,931.1	35,960.9	68,521.8	0.06	60.8	2.1
Maldives	0.0	1.0	0.7	0.6	0.00	31.3	0.0	0.0	1.0	0.7	0.6	0.00	31.4	0.0
Mali	3.5	24.1	0.2	2.2	0.00	48.8	0.0	4.1	24.2	0.2	2.2	0.00	48.9	0.0
Malta	61.6	11.8	19.1	45.3	0.00	23.0	0.0	68.7	44.5	46.7	79.3	0.00	40.3	0.0
Marshall Islands	0.0	0.0	0.0	0.0				0.0	0.0	0.0	0.0	0.00	0.0	0.0
Mauritania	0.0	0.0	0.0	0.0	0.00	0.5	0.0	0.0	0.1	0.0	0.1	0.00	25.0	0.0
Mauritius	16.2	1.6	4.8	1.3	0.00	24.3	0.0	201.1	30.7	62.0	68.6	0.00	17.3	0.0
Mexico	3,101.1	2,522.7	4,202.8	5,580.6	0.00	97.7	1.5	28,360.8	38,790.3	41,101.0	77,354.8	0.05	67.5	2.4
Micronesia, Fed. States of	8.3	0.0	0.6	0.8	0.00		0.0	8.4	0.5	7.7	0.8	0.00	97.7	0.0
Midway Island	0.6	0.0	0.0	0.0	0.00			0.8	0.0	0.0	0.0	0.00		
Mongolia	0.0	0.0	0.4	2.0	0.00	70.8	0.0	0.0	0.0	0.4	2.0	0.00	70.9	0.0
Montserrat	0.0	0.0	0.0	0.0	0.00	3.0	0.0	0.0	0.0	0.0	0.0	0.00	3.1	0.0

(Table continues on the following page.)

TABLE 6.4 The Estimated Value of Australian Tariff Preferences Calculated in Terms of Forgone Duties, by Country, 1996–2004 (Continued)

Economy of origin	Inferred statutory MFN rates — Duty forgone (US$ thousand) 1996	2002	2003	2004	Inferred — As a % of each economy's total exports	As a % of duty to be paid at inferred statutory MFN rates	As a % of total duties forgone by Australia in 2004 (statutory MFN rates)	Calculated MFN rates — Duty forgone (US$ thousand) 1996	2002	2003	2004	Calculated — As a % of each economy's total exports	As a % of duty to be paid at inferred statutory MFN rates	As a % of total duties forgone by Australia in 2004 (statutory MFN rates)
Morocco	36.5	7.3	13.6	12.7	0.00	3.2	0.0	42.6	47.6	44.1	13.0	0.00	3.3	0.0
Mozambique	0.1	0.0	0.1	5.1	0.00	98.3	0.0	0.1	0.0	0.1	5.1	0.00	98.3	0.0
Myanmar	4.3	33.3	43.6	48.7	0.00	51.9	0.0	5.0	44.0	43.6	48.8	0.00	51.9	0.0
Namibia	0.2	0.0	0.6	0.0				0.2	11.7	7.9	19.6	0.00	44.3	0.0
Nauru	1.4	1.6	0.5	0.1	0.00	46.4	0.0	1.4	1.6	0.5	0.1	0.00	46.7	0.0
Nepal	104.5	47.1	51.1	61.3	0.01	68.5	0.0	112.8	47.7	52.2	62.2	0.01	68.8	0.0
Netherlands Antilles	0.0	0.5	0.0	0.0				0.0	9.6	0.0	36.0	0.00	10.5	0.0
New Caledonia	21.8	8.0	37.3	11.8	0.00	22.7	0.0	2.5	8.2	37.3	11.8	0.00	22.7	0.0
Nicaragua	0.0	2.7	11.9	19.6	0.00	17.0	0.0	0.0	192.3	28.6	42.4	0.00	29.4	0.0
Niger	0.2	0.0	0.5	0.0				0.2	0.0	3.3	0.0	0.00	0.8	0.0
Nigeria	0.1	0.9	0.6	0.9	0.00	20.4	0.0	0.1	0.9	0.6	0.9	0.00	20.6	0.0
Niue	0.0	0.0	0.0	0.0				0.0	0.0	0.0	0.0	0.00		0.0
Northern Marianas	6.8	3.1	19.3	0.6	0.01	1.0	0.0	9.4	3.1	19.3	0.6	0.01	1.0	0.0

Oman	0.0	33.0	0.00	17.9	27.4	18.7	0.4	0.0	27.8	0.00	14.0	27.4	18.4	0.4
Pakistan	0.1	14.3	0.03	2,648.7	3,262.5	3,225.6	14,658.1	0.7	14.3	0.03	2,649.3	2,941.2	2,973.0	13,234.6
Palau	0.0	14.5	0.00	0.0	0.0	0.0	0.0	0.0	13.3	0.00	0.0	0.0	0.0	0.0
Panama	0.0	11.1	0.00	1.0	3.2	1.0	20.7	0.0	11.1	0.00	1.0	2.8	0.9	20.4
Papua New Guinea	0.5	99.5	0.65	14,542.2	370.1	2,395.7	465.2	0.2	89.6	0.03	639.8	365.3	214.8	176.7
Paraguay	0.0	0.6	0.00	0.1	1.0	0.0	1.2	0.0	0.6	0.00	0.1	1.0	0.0	1.2
Peru	0.0	7.7	0.00	43.8	44.3	41.4	93.8	0.0	7.5	0.00	42.4	40.8	35.5	67.1
Philippines	0.3	46.6	0.02	8,106.2	7,295.0	5,846.6	12,642.5	1.8	42.7	0.01	6,423.5	5,502.4	4,234.1	10,689.0
Pitcairn Island				0.0	0.0	0.0	0.0				0.0	0.0	0.0	0.0
Poland	0.5	78.0	0.03	17,179.1	1,117.4	1,385.9	1,272.0	0.2	5.7	0.00	855.2	837.8	632.4	497.6
Qatar	0.0	26.5	0.00	161.1	0.0	0.3	0.2	0.0	0.1	0.00	0.3	0.0	0.1	0.2
Romania	0.0	17.9	0.00	424.9	465.4	594.5	657.2	0.1	12.7	0.00	283.4	219.5	54.4	265.2
Rwanda				0.0	0.0	0.0	0.0				0.0	0.0	0.0	0.0
Samoa	0.0	51.3	0.02	17.6	308.2	2,898.0	7,153.8	0.0	95.8	0.02	12.7	301.0	2,892.8	6,975.0
São Tomé and Príncipe	0.0	2.2	0.00	0.0	0.0	0.0	0.0				0.0	0.0	0.0	0.0
Saudi Arabia	3.0	99.1	0.12	94,844.0	540.4	316.6	98,116.3	0.4	60.7	0.00	1,363.9	283.7	241.3	140.0
Senegal	0.0	45.6	0.00	0.1	0.4	1.0	0.5	0.0	45.1	0.00	0.1	0.4	0.9	0.2
Seychelles	0.0	0.0	0.00	0.0	0.0	0.0	0.0	0.0			0.0	0.0	0.0	0.0
Sierra Leone	0.0	1.1	0.00	0.2	0.3	0.1	0.0	0.0	1.1	0.00	0.1	0.3	0.1	0.0
Singapore	63.8	98.9	2.24	2,043,314.3	552,121.6	303,211.3	353,709.2	4.6	51.9	0.02	16,852.5	7,111.4	6,549.8	27,441.2
Slovak Republic	0.0	43.4	0.00	474.1	410.8	0.0	86.5	0.1	39.6	0.00	385.1	364.8	0.0	69.7
Slovenia	0.0	49.4	0.01	1,565.3	823.3	611.1	458.5	0.1	24.1	0.00	526.6	606.6	466.6	398.2
Solomon Islands	0.0	99.9	0.05	56.6	37.0	19.1	65.9	0.0	99.9	0.05	56.6	37.0	18.7	65.8
Somalia	0.0	12.9	0.00	0.1	0.0	0.0	0.0	0.0	12.6	0.00	0.1	0.0	0.0	0.0
Sri Lanka	0.0	24.2	0.01	617.4	555.0	477.6	1,175.8	0.2	23.7	0.01	598.7	505.6	439.2	873.2

(*Table continues on the following page.*)

TABLE 6.4 The Estimated Value of Australian Tariff Preferences Calculated in Terms of Forgone Duties, by Country, 1996–2004 (Continued)

Economy of origin	Amount of duty forgone on the basis of inferred statutory MFN rates							Amount of duty forgone on the basis of calculated MFN rates						
	Duty forgone (US$ thousand)				2004 duties forgone for each economy			Duty forgone (US$ thousand)				2004 duties forgone for each economy		
	1996	2002	2003	2004	As a % of each economy's total exports	As a % of duty to be paid at inferred statutory MFN rates	As a % of total duties forgone by Australia in 2004 (statutory MFN rates)	1996	2002	2003	2004	As a % of each economy's total exports	As a % of duty to be paid at inferred statutory MFN rates	As a % of total duties forgone by Australia in 2004 (statutory MFN rates)
St. Helena	0.0	0.0	0.0	0.0				0.0	0.0	0.0	0.0	0.00	0.0	0.0
St. Kitts and Nevis	0.0	0.3	0.0	0.0				0.0	0.3	0.0	0.0			
St. Lucia	0.8	0.0	0.0	0.0				1.0	0.0	0.0	0.0			
St. Pierre and Miquelon	0.0	0.0	0.0	0.0				0.0	0.0	0.0	0.0			
St. Vincent and the Grenadines	0.0	0.0	0.0	0.0	0.00	100.0	0.0	0.0	0.0	0.0	0.0	0.00	0.0	0.0
Sudan	0.0	0.0	0.0	0.0	0.00	0.0	0.0	0.0	0.0	0.0	0.0	0.00	4.3	0.0
Suriname	0.0	0.0	0.0	0.0				0.0	0.0	0.0	0.0	0.00	1.4	0.0
Swaziland	1.6	726.0	1,160.6	1,573.2	0.29	97.6	0.4	2.1	732.2	1,160.3	1,573.2	0.29	97.6	0.0
Syrian Arab Republic	14.5	0.4	2.3	8.4	0.00	10.0	0.0	17.7	0.8	2.5	8.4	0.00	10.1	0.0
Taiwan, China	45,917.8	15,975.3	16,855.0	23,811.3	0.01	29.7	6.5	65,568.4	24,908.4	51,205.3	183,156.5	0.11	76.7	5.7
Tanzania	1.0	6.9	11.9	22.3	0.00	49.3	0.0	1.7	6.9	12.7	23.8	0.00	43.3	0.0

Thailand	17,796.1	15,422.5	22,469.6	30,426.5	0.04	22.5	8.3	26,236.5	33,395.5	64,303.6	73,322.8	0.10	48.9	2.3
Togo	0.0	0.0	0.1	0.4	0.00	59.6	0.0	0.0	0.0	0.1	0.4	0.00	59.9	0.0
Tokelau	0.0	0.5	0.2	0.0				0.0	0.5	0.2	0.0			
Tonga	19.3	0.6	1.4	2.1	0.01	83.1	0.0	26.2	0.6	1.4	2.1	0.01	83.1	0.0
Trinidad and Tobago	0.0	1.5	0.2	1.4	0.00	4.4	0.0	777.1	10.1	741.2	401.7	0.01	88.8	0.0
Tunisia	4.5	7.0	7.4	5.0	0.00	0.9	0.0	5.2	9.7	7.5	5.0	0.00	0.9	0.0
Turkey	1,059.7	1,233.1	1,876.2	2,503.7	0.01	17.7	0.7	1,371.6	1,747.6	2,053.0	2,705.3	0.01	18.6	0.1
Turks and Caicos Islands	0.0	0.0	0.0	0.0				0.0	0.0	0.0	0.0			
Tuvalu	0.0	0.0	0.0	0.0	0.00			0.0	0.0	0.0	0.0	0.00		
Uganda	0.0	0.0	0.0	1.4	0.00	96.6	0.0	0.0	0.0	0.0	1.4	0.00	96.6	0.0
United Arab Emirates	175.0	163.4	297.5	416.0	0.00	18.6	0.1	212.3	748.7	330.8	618.8	0.00	24.5	0.0
Uruguay	51.8	198.1	100.0	116.3	0.00	34.3	0.0	58.1	203.4	99.9	116.3	0.00	34.3	0.0
U.S. Virgin Islands	0.0	0.0	0.0	0.1		4.4	0.0	22,039.1	0.0	0.0	0.1		4.5	0.0
Vanuatu	9.4	9.6	13.3	12.2	0.02	78.4	0.0	12.7	9.7	13.2	12.1	0.02	78.3	0.0
Venezuela, R.B. de	29.0	54.7	84.5	42.3	0.00	39.4	0.0	213.0	446.5	253.3	42.3	0.00	39.4	0.0
Vietnam	1,244.8	2,633.1	2,901.9	3,314.1	0.02	18.9	0.9	2,054.7	3,219.9	3,509.3	3,444.4	0.02	19.5	0.1
Wallis and Futuna Islands	0.0	0.0	0.0	0.3	0.05	100.0	0.0	0.0	0.0	0.0	0.3	0.05	100.0	0.0
Yemen, Rep. of	0.0	0.0	0.0	0.4	0.00	57.7	0.0	0.0	0.0	0.0	0.4	0.00	57.8	0.0
Zambia	0.2	0.1	0.1	0.2	0.00	5.1	0.0	0.3	0.1	0.1	0.2	0.00	5.2	0.0
Zimbabwe	66.1	8.3	8.7	3.0	0.00	7.9	0.0	81.0	9.0	13.4	3.0	0.00	8.0	0.0
Total	430,169.4	225,609.6	268,413.5	365,802.1		100.0	100.0	1,132,775.3	710,495.8	1,106,678.4	3,202,800.9			100.0

Sources: Australian Bureau of Statistics data; OECD Secretariat calculations.

Notes: — = not available. Table excludes HS 99 imports (confidential). For each country, total exports are based on 2003 mirror data.

(8 percent); Taiwan, China (6 percent); Fiji (5 percent); Singapore[15] (5 percent); Indonesia (3 percent); India (3 percent); Hong Kong, China (2 percent); the Philippines (2 percent); and Mexico (2 percent).

A similar situation prevails with the calculated MFN approach, but the distribution is distorted by a large volume of imports from Singapore of mineral fuels, oils, and related products (HS 27), which could be subject to high MFN-specific duties in the absence of preferences and concessional rates. Some of the larger developing countries have experienced sizable reductions—roughly 25 percent or more—in the value of duties forgone during the period covered in the table, even though they still account for a large share of the total duties forgone (for example, Hong Kong, China; India; Pakistan; and the Philippines). Fiji remains a key beneficiary, but it too has seen a decline relative to 1996. The table shows that Samoa has experienced declines as well, but this situation partly reflects a shift of Samoa's trade toward the HS 99 confidential classification (see box 6.2).

In relating the amount of forgone Australian duties on imports from each developing country (on the basis of inferred statutory MFN rates) to each country's global exports, the study finds little evidence of particular preference reliance except in the case of Fiji. Using the calculated MFN rates reveals a few additional cases; for one group of seven beneficiaries, forgone duties equate to 0.5 percent or greater of the developing country's exports.[16] Another group—Jamaica, Malawi, and Swaziland—has seen an increase in forgone duties; the values in 2004 amounted to 0.38 percent, 0.23 percent, and 0.29 percent of their global exports, respectively, based on calculated MFN rates. Among these two groups, nine are small economies, including several islands and two small, landlocked developing countries; Malawi, moreover, is an LDC. The forgone duties generally totaled 60 percent or more of the potential MFN duty for each of these countries under the calculated MFN approach. In other words, in these cases, the preferences appeared to offer a significant reduction in the overall duty liability for the imports concerned.

Coverage, Utilization, and Utility

Table 6.5 presents summary indicators of product coverage, utilization, and utility for the main country groups eligible for Australian preferential tariff schemes: FICs, LDCs (DC historical and DC preferences and, from 2003, the LDC scheme), and other developing countries (DC preferences, excluding FICs and LDCs). The indicators take into account the preferences available to each country group for products imported into Australia in the selected years.

As table 6.5 shows, the product coverage of preferential programs (eligible imports from each country group as a percentage of total imports from the group) is relatively high. Few of the products being exported by developing countries into

TABLE 6.5 Coverage, Utilization, and Utility Rates of Key Australian Tariff Preferences, 1996–2004

Scheme	Indicator	Rate (%)			
		1996	2002	2003	2004
DC preference	DC product coverage	96	97	98	98
(excluding FICs and LDCs)	DC utilization rates	39	44	40	36
	DC utility rates	37	42	39	35
FIC preference	Forum product coverage	18	15	69	67
	Forum utilization rates	62	78	12	11
	Forum utility rates	11	12	9	7
LDCs (DC historical, DC,	LDC product coverage	99	100	95	95
and LDC preferences)	LDC utilization rates	14	28	30	24
	LDC utility rates	14	28	28	23

Sources: Australian Bureau of Statistics data; OECD Secretariat calculations.

Note: Product coverage is defined as eligible imports as a percentage of total imports from the group of eligible countries. The *utilization rate* is defined as imports receiving the preference as a percentage of imports from the group of eligible countries. The *utility rate* is defined as imports receiving the preference as a percentage of total imports from the group. See annexes for country-specific information on coverage, utilization, and utility rates.

Australia are not covered by some preference. But the use of preferences by developing countries for eligible products is limited. Excluding the FICs and LDCs, only about 20 percent of eligible imports from developing countries enter under preferential treatment. For LDCs, the rate is roughly 25 percent, albeit with some yearly fluctuation. Given the high share of imports eligible for preferences, the situation is similar for utility rates (imports from each group receiving preferences as a percentage of total imports from the group). For the FICs, utilization apparently fell as product coverage expanded—partly the result of improvement in access for textiles, clothing, and footwear products, but also because of changes in the treatment of Samoa's exports (see box 6.2).

The main explanation for the fairly modest utility of preferences in Australia would appear to be that a high share of imports without preferential treatment enter Australia on an MFN duty-free basis or at low duty rates. Importers have an incentive to exploit this possibility to avoid the limitations of rules of origin that apply under the preferential schemes, as well as any associated administrative requirements. Moreover, there may be advantages to importing at concessional rates but not under preferential schemes. In 2004, about 11 percent of imports from developing countries entered Australia without preferential treatment but at generally low concessional rates.

Improved LDC Market Access

In recent years, many developed countries have deepened their trade preferences for LDCs. Hoekman, Ng, and Olarreaga (2001) underscore the tension between deepening preferences for LDCs and MFN-based liberalization, whereby the benefit of the first is eroded by the second. Preferential schemes can have significant positive effects on specific beneficiaries, but much depends on their supply-side capacity, their ability to reinvest the rents usefully, and the nature of the administrative requirements (such as rules of origin). Overall, such constraints have limited the actual benefit to many LDCs from preferences, leading Hoekman, Ng, and Olarreaga to suggest that the erosion of current preferences should be of limited concern when it is a result of MFN liberalization. Indeed, they note that one reason it has been possible to expand duty-free access for LDCs is that such countries account for less than 0.5 percent of world trade.

Following a decision announced by Australian Prime Minister John Howard at an APEC summit meeting on October 25, 2002, the Australian government amended the Customs Tariff to provide the LDCs and Timor-Leste with duty-free and quota-free access to the Australian market.[17] As noted previously, the rules of origin for LDCs permit the use of materials from all developing countries, FICs, and Australia to count as local content, except that the portion from developing countries that are not LDCs is limited to no more than 25 percent of the total factory cost of the goods.

The Australian Productivity Commission considered the potential economic effects of this action in a report released that same month (Productivity Commission 2002). The report pointed to the generally limited flow of imports from LDCs and noted that much of this flow was already covered under the DC and FIC preferences. Given the existing pattern of trade and tariffs, the commission concluded that the main effect on LDCs was likely to come from Australian imports of clothing, but that the ability of LDCs to benefit would depend on their capacity to provide an enabling environment for an adequate supply response. In a related paper (Zhang and Verikios 2003), two of the Productivity Commission report's contributors, used the Global Trade Analysis Project (GTAP) model to examine the potential effects of duty-free access for LDCs. They found that LDCs would generally benefit from the new policy, especially major clothing exporters (for example, Bangladesh and Cambodia). The effects on suppliers from developing countries that are not LDCs were estimated to be modest. The model revealed that some countries competing with LDCs (such as China) might not lose, in terms of real gross domestic product, from the change in policy because they could boost their exports of intermediate inputs to the exporting sectors in LDCs.

Table 6.6 sheds light on the situation with respect to Australian imports from LDCs in the years before and after the implementation of duty-free access for

TABLE 6.6 Australian Imports from LDCs and Timor-Leste

Country	Customs value (US$ thousand)				Index value (2002 = 100)			
	1996	2002	2003	2004	1996	2002	2003	2004
Afghanistan	146	98	95	146	150	100	98	150
Angola	0	47	32	3	1	100	67	7
Bangladesh	16,908	24,475	28,049	32,318	69	100	115	132
Benin			0			100		
Bhutan		4	147	139		100	3,505	3,312
Burkina Faso			16	24		100		
Burundi	0	57	48	1	0	100	84	1
Cambodia	623	1,631	2,649	3,121	38	100	162	191
Cape Verde		0	1			100	253	
Central African Republic		5		2		100		
Chad			50	11		100	3	36
Comoros	53	8				100		
Congo, Dem. Rep. of	230	18	27	20	1,308	100	154	116
Djibouti				3		100		
Equatorial Guinea	2		21	4		100		
Eritrea	7	2	1	11	283	100	50	462
Ethiopia	1,063	890	965	1,312	119	100	108	147
Gambia, The	2	11	1	9	23	100	12	81
Guinea	3	6	9	8	57	100	164	138

(Table continues on the following page.)

TABLE 6.6   Australian Imports from LDCs and Timor-Leste (*Continued*)

Country	Customs value (US$ thousand)				Index value (2002 = 100)			
	1996	2002	2003	2004	1996	2002	2003	2004
Haiti	13	20	558	781	64	100	2,842	3,975
Kiribati	256	125	111	191	204	100	88	152
Lao PDR	217	313	324	411	69	100	103	131
Lesotho	17		29	32		100		
Liberia	2		5	3		100		
Madagascar	614	1,009	685	284	61	100	68	28
Malawi	4,014	4,324	2,958	4,386	93	100	68	101
Maldives		33	50	39		100	150	116
Mali	118	669	580	318	18	100	87	48
Mauritania	90	11	35	164	806	100	312	1,481
Mozambique	21	1	17	55	2,146	100	1,761	5,647
Nepal	909	1,431	1,446	1,709	63	100	101	119
Niger	43	152	117	17	28	100	77	11
Rwanda		66	28	0		100	42	1
Samoa	50,210	21,067	6,783	707	238	100	32	3

São Tomé and Príncipe	0			1			
Senegal	336	175	74	20		100	42	11
Sierra Leone	2,435	9	38	184	3,566	100	400	1,955
Solomon Islands	2	726	3,182	3,784	335	100	438	521
Somalia	14	1	3	38	315	100	551	6,539
Sudan	4,403	76	0	47	19	100	0	61
Tanzania		3,730	3,258	2,279	118	100	87	61
Timor-Leste		390	550	6,501		100	141	1,670
Togo		9,638	9,209	8,284		100	96	86
Tuvalu		8	2	2		100	28	26
Uganda	4,383	7,754	7,999	3,975	57	100	103	51
Vanuatu	620	2,542	3,848	2,408	24	100	151	95
Yemen, Rep. of	33	3	12	11,096	929	100	338	317,188
Zambia	607	346	122	837	175	100	35	242
Total	88,394	81,876	74,134	85,685	108	100	91	105

Sources: Australian Bureau of Statistics data; OECD Secretariat calculations.

Note: Not all LDCs supplied imports in each year, as indicated by blank cells in the left panel. It was not possible to calculate the index for countries without 2002 import flows.

LDCs and Timor-Leste. Aggregate imports from LDCs declined in each successive year from 1996 to 2003, before increasing in 2004 to a level approaching that of 1996. Although trade is influenced by many variables, expanded market access has not yet led to imports increasing beyond recent historical levels for these countries. One variable that distorts the situation is the large fall in recorded imports from Samoa (formerly an important supplier of automotive components). Excluding Samoa, Australian imports from LDCs increased from US$38 million in 1996 to US$61 million in 2002—rising somewhat further in 2003 to US$67 million before reaching US$85 million in 2004. Several LDCs managed to boost their exports to Australia by more than US$1 million between 2002 and 2004; they included Bangladesh and Cambodia (especially apparel); Timor-Leste (mineral fuels and oil); Solomon Islands (fish and crustaceans, wood, and other products); and the Republic of Yemen (mineral fuels and oil).[18]

Despite the increases in imports from certain LDC suppliers, imports under the new LDC scheme remain modest (US$9 million in 2004; see table 6.1). Moreover, combined use of the special measures for LDCs (the LDC and the DC historical schemes) has declined in terms of import volumes, from US$33 million in 2002 to US$32 million in 2004. Thus, the experience under the new arrangement has not been inconsistent with the Productivity Commission analysis. The economic effects on suppliers appear to be fairly modest, with some gains for apparel suppliers and also for mineral fuel and oil suppliers.

Sector-Specific Preference Reliance

Table 6.7 presents those sectors in which preferential imports into Australia from any developing economy exceed 0.5 percent of that economy's global exports of all products. The table provides an overview of the concentration of preference reliance on the part of suppliers to the Australian market. Some 25 developing economies exhibited a degree of sector-specific preference reliance in at least one of the years shown. The strongest continued reliance can be seen in relation to (a) apparel imports from Fiji and (b) mineral fuels, oils, and related products and natural and cultured pearls and precious stone from Papua New Guinea. In each year shown, these two countries relied especially on preferences in each of the corresponding sectors. Fiji is represented in the broadest range of sectors among the countries shown in the table. Samoa exhibited strong but temporary preference reliance on one sector (as noted in box 6.2). In recent years, Timor-Leste (coffee, tea, and spices); Swaziland (miscellaneous edible preparations and essential oils and resinoids); and Vietnam (mineral fuels, oils, and related products) each demonstrated notable reliance in at least one sector; that is, they each had preferential imports into Australia in at least one sector that were equal to 2 percent or more of exports in 2003 and 2004.

TABLE 6.7 **Reliance on Australian Preferential Tariff Schemes: Preferential Exports by Sector as a Percentage of Each Beneficiary's Total Exports, 1996–2004**

Beneficiaries	HS 2-digit level	Product name	1996	2002	2003	2004
Albania	84	Nuclear reactors, boilers, machinery, and mechanical appliances and parts thereof		0.71	2.93	
Anguilla	33	Essential oils and resinoids; perfumery, cosmetic, or toiletry preparations				0.58
Bahrain	76	Aluminum and articles thereof		0.98	1.04	1.49
Brunei Darussalam	27	Mineral fuels, mineral oils, and products of their distillation; bituminous substances; and mineral waxes		3.14	2.11	1.80
Cayman Islands	03	Fish and crustacean, molluscs and other aquatic invertebrates	0.56			
Cook Islands	71	Natural or cultured pearls, precious or semiprecious stones, precious metals, metals clad with precious metals, and articles thereof; imitation jewelry; and coin	1.47	1.83	2.10	0.52
Timor-Leste	03	Fish and crustacean, molluscs and other aquatic invertebrates		0.68		
	09	Coffee, tea, maté, and spices			3.29	5.15
Fiji	07	Edible vegetables and certain roots and tubers				0.53
	15	Animal or vegetable fats and oils and their cleavage products, prepared edible fats, and animal and vegetable waxes	0.53			
	19	Preparations of cereals, flour, starch or milk; pastrycooks' products				1.24
	44	Wood, articles of wood, and wood charcoal	0.59		0.53	

(*Table continues on the following page.*)

TABLE 6.7 Reliance on Australian Preferential Tariff Schemes: Preferential Exports by Sector as a Percentage of Each Beneficiary's Total Exports, 1996–2004 (Continued)

Beneficiaries	HS 2-digit level	Product name	1996	2002	2003	2004
	61	Articles of apparel and clothing accessories, knitted or crocheted	3.67	2.31	2.10	2.05
	62	Articles of apparel and clothing accessories, not knitted or crocheted	10.70	8.10	8.39	8.75
	63	Other made-up textile articles, sets, worn clothing and worn textile articles, and rags	2.02			
	64	Footwear, gaiters, and the like; parts of such articles	0.97	1.61	1.39	1.87
	71	Natural or cultured pearls, precious or semiprecious stones, precious metals, metals clad with precious metals, and articles thereof; imitation jewelry; and coin			0.52	
	94	Furniture; bedding, mattresses, mattress supports, cushions, and similar stuffed furnishings; lamps and lighting fittings not elsewhere specified or included; illuminated signs, nameplates, and the like; and prefabricated buildings	0.52			
Indonesia	27	Mineral fuels, mineral oils, and products of their distillation; bituminous substances; and mineral waxes		0.50		
Malawi	24	Tobacco and manufactured tobacco substitutes			0.55	
Nauru	25	Salt, sulfur, earths and stones, plastering materials, lime, and cement		15.35		
Northern Marianas Islands	61	Articles of apparel and clothing accessories, knitted or crocheted	0.88	0.81	0.52	

TABLE 6.7   (*Continued*)

	62	Articles of apparel and clothing accessories, not knitted or crocheted	0.56			
Pakistan	52	Cotton	0.72			
Papua New Guinea	09	Coffee, tea, maté, and spices	0.92			
	27	Mineral fuels, mineral oils, and products of their distillation; bituminous substances; and mineral waxes	9.90	2.19	11.56	14.13
	44	Wood, articles of wood, and wood charcoal				0.50
	71	Natural or cultured pearls, precious or semiprecious stones, precious metals, metals clad with precious metals, and articles thereof; imitation jewelry; and coin	5.51	13.26	16.10	19.07
Samoa	21	Miscellaneous edible preparations	0.91	0.51		
	85	Electrical machinery and equipment and parts thereof; sound recorders and reproducers, television image and sound recorders and reproducers, and parts and accessories of such articles		30.27	6.94	
Samoa (American)	23	Residues and waste from the food industries; prepared animal fodder		0.71		
Saudi Arabia	27	Mineral fuels, mineral oils, and products of their distillation; bituminous substances; and mineral waxes		0.63		
Singapore	27	Mineral fuels, mineral oils, and products of their distillation; bituminous substances; and mineral waxes		0.60		
Solomon Islands	03	Fish and crustacean, molluscs and other aquatic invertebrates			1.23	

(*Table continues on the following page.*)

TABLE 6.7   Reliance on Australian Preferential Tariff Schemes: Preferential Exports by Sector as a Percentage of Each Beneficiary's Total Exports, 1996–2004 (*Continued*)

Beneficiaries	HS 2-digit level	Product name	1996	2002	2003	2004
	44	Wood, articles of wood, and wood charcoal	0.72		1.13	2.39
	71	Natural or cultured pearls, precious or semiprecious stones, precious metals, metals clad with precious metals, and articles thereof; imitation jewelry; and coin				0.52
Swaziland	21	Miscellaneous edible preparations		4.34	5.27	4.42
	33	Essential oils and resinoids; perfumery, cosmetic, or toiletry preparations	•			2.73
Togo	25	Salt, sulfur, earths and stones, plastering materials, lime, and cement		1.37	0.90	0.53
Tonga	08	Edible fruit and nuts; peel of citrus fruits or melons	0.62			
	42	Articles of leather; saddlery and harnesses; travel goods, handbags, and similar containers; and articles of animal gut (other than silkworm gut)	0.96			
Uganda	03	Fish and crustacean, molluscs and other aquatic invertebrates		1.23	0.75	
Vanuatu	15	Animal or vegetable fats and oils and their cleavage products, prepared edible fats, and animal and vegetable waxes		4.46		
	23	Residues and waste from the food industries; prepared animal fodder		0.75	0.61	0.69
	41	Rawhides and skins (other than furskins) and leather	0.71			

TABLE 6.7   (*Continued*)

	90	Optical, photographic, cinematographic, measuring, checking, precision medical or surgical instruments and apparatus; parts and accessories thereof		0.61		
Vietnam	27	Mineral fuels, mineral oils, and products of their distillation; bituminous substances; and mineral waxes	0.58	3.08	2.88	2.53

Sources: Australian Bureau of Statistics data; OECD Secretariat calculations.
Note: This table reflects all sectors in which preferential imports to Australia amount to more than 0.5 percent of an exporter's global exports. Global exports are based on mirror data and held constant for 2004 owing to the limited availability of data for that year.

Assessment of the Possible Economic Implications of Preference Erosion

Lippoldt and Kowalski (2005) use the GTAP computable general equilibrium (CGE) model[19] and the GTAP 6.05 database (which corresponds to the global economy in 2001)[20] to consider the implications of a hypothetical 50 percent reduction in the equivalent measure of protection for Australia—a scenario that would entail considerable preference erosion.[21] The use of a CGE framework permits the assessment of the economic implications in a relatively holistic fashion, taking into account not only the reduced size of preference margins but also the potentially offsetting effects of trade liberalization more generally. Changes in market access conditions for each product category are linked to developments in other sectors through goods and factors markets. Where producers in selected preference-receiving sectors are affected negatively, for example, resources may be freed from that sector and deployed to other sectors that may be better positioned to benefit from improved access to world markets or may simply be more productive.

For each product and trading partner, the GTAP database provides a measure of protection that reflects the degree of protection. By comparing the rates faced by each supplier for a given product with the market average, one can calculate an indication of the preference margin. In figure 6.4, the trade-weighted preference margins based on this approach are presented for imports into Australia by each source region, as of 2001. Where these margins are positive, the source regions enjoyed better than average market access; where they are negative, the suppliers experienced higher than average market restrictiveness. Figure 6.4 reveals fairly consistent treatment of exports from developing countries, with relatively high

FIGURE 6.4 Australia: Average Trade-Weighted Preference Margins by Beneficiary Country, 2001

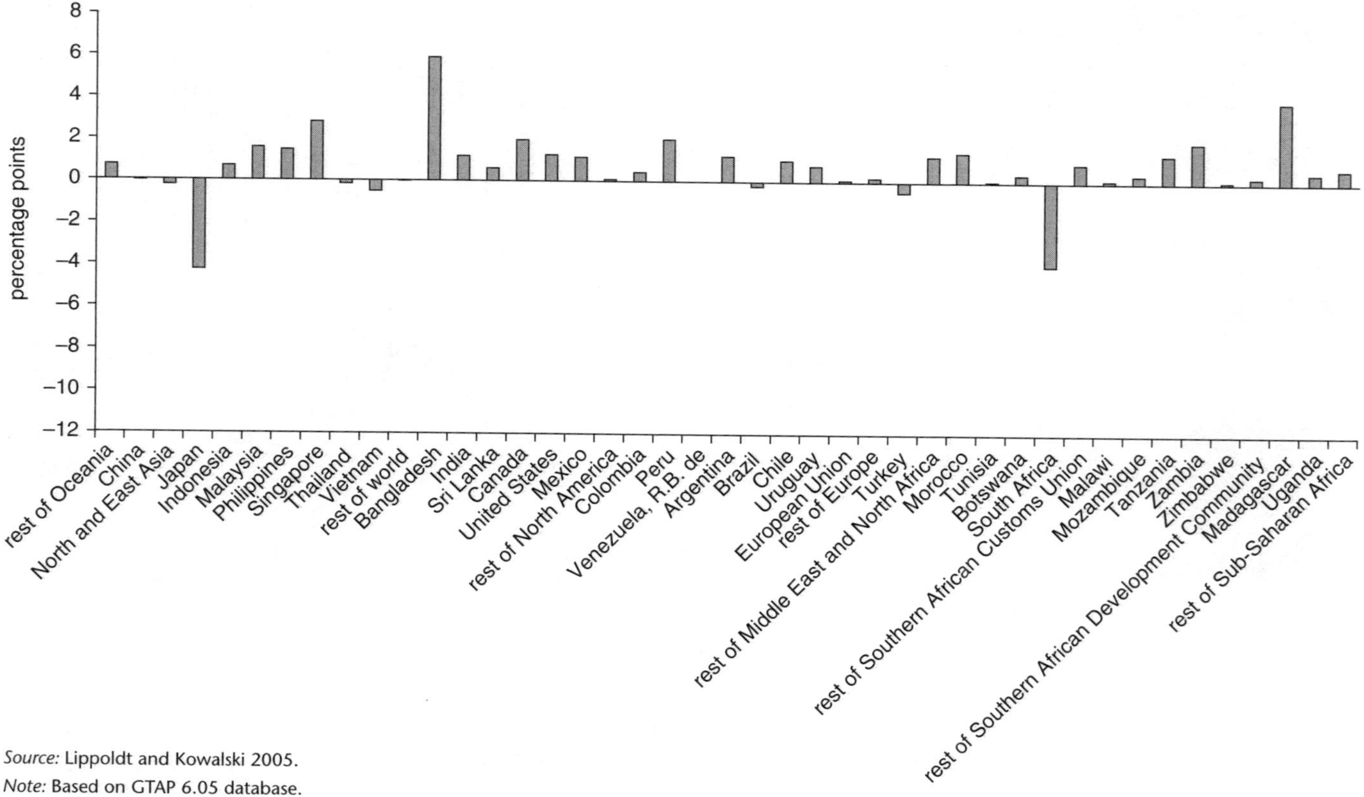

Source: Lippoldt and Kowalski 2005.

Note: Based on GTAP 6.05 database.

preferential margins—reaching up to 6 percentage points—afforded to developing countries in South and East Asia, Latin America, and Africa. A few exceptions include Brazil, South Africa, Thailand, and Vietnam. On average, these countries face barriers higher than those faced by other trading partners, partly because of the composition of their exports to Australia.[22]

Table 6.8 presents the results of the simulated 50 percent tariff liberalization, highlighting those regions that experienced gains or losses in welfare (for regions not shown, the welfare effects were found to be neutral). The measure of change in welfare is expressed as the equivalent variation in income on a per capita basis. In general, the welfare impacts indicated by the model conform to expectations that are based on the statistical review—that is, they are fairly modest. In some cases, such as for the FICs, the gains from improved market access under unilateral liberalization appear to more than offset the losses from preference erosion. Under the simulation, a number of the regions losing out are in Africa—including

TABLE 6.8   Welfare Impacts of a 50 Percent Reduction in the Ad Valorem Equivalent Measure of Protection by Australia: GTAP Simulation

Region	Estimated per capita change in welfare (%)
Regions gaining	
Vietnam	0.5
Rest of Oceania[a]	0.4
Indonesia	0.1
Sri Lanka	0.1
Thailand	0.1
Regions losing	
Singapore	−0.2
Rest of North America[b]	−0.1
Botswana	−0.1
Rest of Southern African Customs Union[c]	−0.1
Malawi	−0.1
Mozambique	−0.1
Zambia	−0.1
Zimbabwe	−0.1

Source: Lippoldt and Kowalski 2005.

a. American Samoa, Cook Islands, Fiji, French Polynesia, Guam, Kiribati, Marshall Islands, Federated States of Micronesia, Nauru, New Caledonia, New Zealand, Niue, Norfolk Island, Northern Marianas Islands, Palau, Papua New Guinea, Samoa, Solomon Islands, Tokelau, Tonga, Tuvalu, Vanuatu, and Wallis and Futuna.

b. Bermuda, Greenland, and St. Pierre and Miquelon.

c. Lesotho, Namibia, and Swaziland.

the rest of the Southern Africa Customs Union (which includes Swaziland) and Malawi. The statistical review presented in the previous section also found some indication that these economies relied on preferences. The GTAP database, however, does not reflect some of the more recent enhancements in market access extended by Australia to LDCs and FICs (including improved access for textile and apparel products). Likewise, the protection data do not yet reflect the recent Singapore-Australia free trade agreement.

Conclusions

Compared with the Quad markets, Australia is a relatively small market for developing countries. At the same time, it is a relatively open market, and some developing countries have come to rely on it as an export market. Given the structure of exports from developing countries, MFN access is often available duty free or at low duty rates and provides an attractive channel for entry. Where access may be constrained by MFN tariffs, concessional rates are sometimes available. Preferential schemes provide an important additional channel for many developing countries exporting goods subject to constraining MFN tariffs. Most of these countries have not come to rely on Australian preferences for a large share of their trade. But a few smaller countries—particularly some in proximity to Australia—have come to rely on the Australian preferential regime for fairly significant shares of their exports. This reliance is associated with a degree of sector-specific concentration in the use of preferences.

Annexes

The annexes to this chapter, as well as additional tables with detailed data on trade and preference utilization by product and country, are available at http://siteresources.worldbank.org/INTRANETTRADE/Resources/Lippoldt_Australia_prefences.pdf.

Notes

1. Australia accounted for about 3 percent of imports from developing countries into the Quad economies plus Australia.

2. The Australian authorities restrict the release of statistics if the imports or exports of an individual or a business are identifiable and that individual or business has requested that the details relating to the movement of these goods be suppressed. For more details, see ABS (1999).

3. The schedule was not available in a Microsoft Excel-compatible electronic format at the HS 10-digit level for many lines.

4. A list of the options under each of these classifications is provided in the annexes.

5. The products that lack available MFN rates (codes X or Z) vary by year. In 1996, of 8,180 HS 10-digit products imported, 1,819 lacked MFN rates in the database. In 2002, of 6,769 types of products

imported, 943 did not have MFN rates available. In 2003, of 6,799 types, 701 did not have MFN rates available. In 2004, of 6,881 types, 565 products did not have MFN rates available.

6. The extent of specific duties in the Australian tariff schedule is limited. With respect to HS 10-digit tariff lines with imports from developing countries, the following data provide an overview:

	1996	2002	2003	2004
HS 10-digit tariff lines with specific duties (as a % of total lines)	0.52	0.76	0.63	0.63
Value of imports facing specific duties (as a % of total imports)	0.30	0.42	0.44	0.56

7. Many countries levy their customs duties on the cost, insurance, and freight value of imported products, which results in a higher effective duty rate than where free-on-board values are used. Examples of countries that use the cost, insurance, and freight valuation include The Bahamas, Chile, and Iceland. More examples can be found from the Trade Information Center of the U.S. Department of Commerce at http://www.ita.doc.gov/td/tic/tariff/country_tariff_info.htm.

8. For comparability, in table 6.1 Singapore's exports under the free trade agreement that received DC or duty-free treatment in 2003 and 2004 were grouped with the SRSE category.

9. Papua New Guinea gained access to preferential rates of duty in 1926 (ACS 2004).

10. For information on the concessional entry of goods into Australia, see the relevant section of the APEC summary on the issue available at http://www.apectariff.org/au/austconc.htm. There is also some discussion of the schemes for concessional imports of goods in WTO (2007).

11. Four product groups accounted for more than two-thirds of concessional imports from developing countries. Together the concessional trade in these four sectors accounted for 12.2 percent of total imports from developing countries into Australia: HS 27, mineral fuels, oils, and related products (5.8 percent); HS 84, nuclear reactors, boilers, and machinery (2.0 percent); HS 85, electrical machinery, equipment and parts thereof (3.2 percent); and HS 95, toys, games, and sports requisites (1.2 percent).

12. The latest trade policy review for Australia also noted that, despite improvements in the Australian preferential tariff schemes, the value of preferential tariffs continued to be eroded as a consequence of MFN tariff reductions (WTO 2007).

13. Additional factors complicating the calculation of the precise value of preferences—even within this rough definition based on preference margins—include the lack of data on confidential trade and the influence of special treatments for particular import cases or uses (for example, government).

14. Also in 2003, about 30 percent of the imports of mineral fuels, oils, and related products benefiting from concessional treatment entered under a preferential program.

15. Imports from Singapore that do not satisfy the rules of origin for the free trade agreement may be imported under the DC preference scheme.

16. The countries satisfying this criterion include Barbados, Cuba, Dominica, Fiji, Papua New Guinea, Singapore, and Timor-Leste.

17. For background, see Bills Digest No. 160 2002-03 at http://www.aph.gov.au/library/pubs/bd/2002-03/03bd160.htm. For the trade minister's press release following enactment of the measure, see http://www.trademinister.gov.au/releases/2003/mvt051_03.html.

18. The importation of mineral fuels and oil from Timor-Leste and the Republic of Yemen was largely on a nonpreferential basis.

19. The GTAP CGE model is a multiregion, multisector model, with perfect competition and constant returns to scale. For more information, see the GTAP Web site: https://www.gtap.agecon.purdue.edu/models/default.asp.

20. The trade protection data in the GTAP 6.05 database integrate information on bilateral ad valorem tariffs (both MFN and preferential), ad valorem equivalents of specific tariffs (MFN and preferential), and tariff rate quotas from the Market Access Maps database. The treatment of tariffs in these databases is documented in detail in Bouët and others (2005).

21. The simulations do not include any change in export credits or nontariff barriers.

22. The main contributors to these preferential margins are such manufacturing categories as textiles, apparel, leather products, and other manufacturing products.

References

ABS (Australian Bureau of Statistics). 1999. "International Merchandise Trade Statistics, Australia: Data Confidentiality." Information Paper 5487.0, ABS, Canberra. http://www.abs.gov.au/Ausstats/abs@.nsf/0/e5adebbd0bf28aeaca256889000db4be?OpenDocument.

ACS (Australian Customs Service). 2000. "Factsheet: Rules of Origin." ACS, Canberra.

———. 2004. *Australian Customs Service Manual: Origin.* Vol. 8B. Canberra: ACS. http://www.customs.gov.au/webdata/resources/files/Volume_8B___Origin1.pdf.

Alexandraki, Katerina, and Hans Peter Lankes. 2004. "The Impact of Preference Erosion on Middle-Income Developing Countries." IMF Working Paper 04/169, International Monetary Fund, Washington, DC.

APEC (Asia-Pacific Economic Cooperation). 2004. "Electronic Individual Action Plan, Report for Australia." APEC, Singapore. http://www.apec-iap.org/document/AUS_2004_IAP.htm.

Bouët, Antoine, Yvan Decreux, Lionel Fontagné, Sébastien Jean, and David Laborde. 2005. "V6 Documentation—Chapter 16.D: Tariff Data." Center for Global Trade Analysis, Purdue University, West Lafayette, IN. http://www.gtap.agecon.purdue.edu/resources/res_display.asp?RecordID=1824.

Commonwealth Secretariat. 2004. "Preference-Dependent Economies and Multilateral Liberalization: Impacts and Options." Commonwealth Secretariat, Canberra.

Hoekman, Bernard, Francis Ng, and Marcelo Olarreaga. 2001. "Eliminating Excessive Tariffs on Exports of Least Developed Countries." Policy Research Working Paper 2604, World Bank, Washington, DC.

Inama, Stefano. 2003. "Trade Preferences and the World Trade Organization Negotiations on Market Access." *Journal of World Trade* 37 (5): 959–76.

Lippoldt, Douglas. 2008. "The Australian Preferential Tariff Regime." Organisation for Economic Co-operation and Development, Paris.

Lippoldt, Douglas, and Przemyslaw Kowalski. 2005. "Trade Preference Erosion: Potential Economic Impacts." OECD Trade Policy Working Paper 17, Organisation for Economic Co-operation and Development, Paris.

OECD (Organisation for Economic Co-operation and Development). 2005. "Main Economic Indicators." OECD, Paris. http://new.sourceoecd.org/rpsv/statistic/s16_about.htm?jnlissn=16081234.

Productivity Commission. 2002. "Removing Tariffs on Goods Originating from Least Developed Countries." Working Paper 1737, Productivity Commission, Government of Australia, Canberra.

WTO (World Trade Organization). 2007. "Trade Policy Review: Australia." WT/TPR/S/104, WTO, Geneva.

Zhang, Xiao-guang, and George Verikios. 2003. "A General Equilibrium Analysis of Australia Providing Duty-Free Access on Goods Imported from Least Developed Countries." Paper prepared for the Sixth Annual Conference on Global Economic Analysis, The Hague, Netherlands, June 12–14.

7

MULTILATERAL SOLUTIONS TO THE EROSION OF NONRECIPROCAL PREFERENCES IN NONAGRICULTURAL MARKET ACCESS

Patrick Low, Roberta Piermartini, and Jürgen Richtering

For nearly 40 years, nonreciprocal preference schemes have sought to promote industrialization, boost exports, and foster growth in developing countries.[1] Many studies have evaluated nonpreferential schemes, showing mixed results.[2] The bulk of the evidence seems to suggest that while certain countries have benefited from nonreciprocal preferences, others have not. One explanation for the mitigated benefits from preferences is the limited supply response capacity in the beneficiary countries and territories. Other explanations are intrinsic to the preference schemes themselves. These schemes include product exclusions where export potential exists, country exclusions on a variety of economic and other grounds, restrictive rules of origin that require higher-than-existing levels of manufacturing activity in preference-receiving countries, and administrative costs incurred in gaining access to the schemes.

These limitations clearly do not undermine current preference schemes to such a degree that beneficiaries are content with the potential erosion of preference

The authors are members of the Economic Research and Statistics Division of the Secretariat of the World Trade Organization. Any views expressed here are those of the authors and should not be attributed to World Trade Organization members or to the World Trade Organization Secretariat. Particular thanks are due to Eric Ng Shing for his untiring efforts in preparing data for the paper. Takako Ikezuki also assisted in preparing utilization data. We are grateful to José Ansón, Marc Bacchetta, Marco Fugazza, and Donald MacLaren for useful comments on an earlier draft.

margins in the Doha negotiations. On the contrary, in the negotiations on both agriculture and nonagricultural market access, a concerted effort is being made to ensure that preference erosion is addressed. Several proposals have been made on nonagricultural market access, mostly by member states of the African, Caribbean, and Pacific (ACP) countries and by least developed countries (LDCs).[3] These suggestions build on a number of texts associated with the negotiations, including the Doha Declaration and various iterations of negotiating mandates or understandings on nonagricultural market access. For example, paragraph 16 of annex B of the General Council Decision of August 1, 2004, refers to the "particular needs that may arise for the members concerned due to the challenges that may be faced by nonreciprocal preference beneficiary members." Broadly speaking, four approaches have been proposed:

- To extend existing preference schemes[4]
- To improve the scope for utilizing existing preferences
- To mitigate the product coverage or pace of most-favored-nation (MFN) liberalization[5]
- To take compensatory action[6]

In agricultural market access, much the same reasoning applies. But paragraph 44 of annex A of the August 1, 2004, decision makes a cross-reference to paragraph 16 of the Harbinson text (TN/AG/W/1/Rev. 1 of March 18, 2003). The Harbinson text proposes an arrangement that would slow the pace of MFN liberalization for "tariff reductions affecting long-standing preferences in respect of products which are of vital export importance for developing country beneficiaries."

Some members harbor strong reservations about tampering with the content or pace of MFN liberalization. But demands for such action to prevent preference erosion are not new, even if the intensity of the debate in the current negotiations is unprecedented. In the Tokyo Round, for example, Brazil tabled a proposal calling for MFN tariff-cutting exemptions to preserve certain preferential margins and for ways to improve and extend the Generalized System of Preferences (GSP).[7] The option of moderating MFN liberalization on the altar of avoiding preference erosion is not popular with countries for which nonreciprocal preferences are limited or nonexistent. But considering the negotiating positions of the ACP states, LDCs, and others, this option is certainly not off the table.

This chapter focuses on trade solutions to mitigate preference erosion other than arresting MFN liberalization, notably improving the content and workings of existing schemes, extending the product coverage of preference schemes, and broadening the geographic spread of such arrangements. It bears noting, however, that any compensatory trade solutions to preference erosion are inevitably temporary, unless existing levels of market access are frozen and trade liberalization is permanently halted.[8] Because this is inconceivable in practical terms—whether because of continuing MFN liberalization or the extension of reciprocal preferences through regional trade agreements—the basic objective in guarding against preference erosion is to smooth the process of adjustment.

Following some preliminary observations about the trade and welfare effects of preferences and preference erosion is a description of the approach used here to measure preference erosion. Baseline estimates of adjusted risk from preference erosion are provided. Next, a nonlinear MFN tariff cut is simulated to provide a sense of what such a scenario of MFN liberalization would mean by way of preference erosion among recipients of nonreciprocal preferences. On the basis of simplified calculations, an indication is provided of which countries and which product categories in those countries are seemingly most vulnerable to preference erosion. Then trade policy actions that could ameliorate preference erosion are considered.

Two caveats should be noted about the limitations of this analysis. First, it does not attempt to simulate the possible effects of changes in relative prices (from MFN liberalization) on supply and demand. Such a simulation could obviously be done with a general equilibrium model or with a partial equilibrium elasticity analysis, but at this stage analysis is limited to a simple comparison of what happens to the estimated value of preferences at the country level when MFN tariff rates are cut, all else staying the same. Second, because the estimates for this chapter are all built on existing trade flows, there is no way of knowing whether a reduction in preference margins may be compensated for by trade in product lines against which zero trade has been recorded in the dataset.

Some Theoretical Considerations

What are the consequences for preference receivers and third parties of a change in a preference margin?[9] And what determines the value of a preference from the point of view of preference receivers and their ability to benefit from preferences? In answering those questions, one must distinguish between the concept of preference erosion and the welfare consequences of a change in a preference margin.

Effects of a Preferential Tariff

When exporters in one country are granted preferential trade treatment, they may export more to the preference-giving country than they could have under MFN tariffs. Trade preferences may improve market access and stimulate diversification toward a broader range of exports. Over the longer term, enhanced market access may foster export-driven economic development.[10] Ideally, the trade opportunities afforded by preferential access would engender trade performance that would be sustainable under fully competitive trade conditions among all suppliers.[11] However, preferences may prove somewhat disadvantageous or more costly than anticipated for beneficiaries. They may encourage an inefficient allocation of resources by fostering specialization in sectors where the preference-receiving country does not have a comparative advantage. Preferences may entail administrative burdens associated with origin requirements. The rules of origin may also require that inputs be sourced from higher-cost suppliers (Krueger 1993; Krishna and Krueger 1995). Moreover, preferences are sometimes linked to the adoption of labor and intellectual property standards that can be costly (Bhagwati 2002). Over the longer term, preferences may create a disincentive for trade liberalization (Özden and Reinhardt 2003).

It is worth considering the basic analytics of tariff preferences. The simplest analytical framework is a partial equilibrium model of three countries and one traded good. One developed country (country A) grants a preference on a given imported product, one developing country (country B) benefits from the preference, and another country or the rest of the world (W) faces the MFN tariff rate. The first instance assumes that regardless of any changes in the demand for imports in country A, the rest of the world supplies the good at a fixed price, while country B supplies more of the good at higher prices.[12]

Suppose W is the most efficient producer of the product in question, while country A is less so. Suppose also that with no preference, country A imports from both country B and W at a fixed price. The introduction of the preference shifts relative prices in favor of the good produced in country B. The demand for imports in country A will shift from W to country B. The preference constitutes a transfer from country A (through tariff revenue losses) and W (through loss of exports) to country B.

The diversion of imports in country A from the globally most efficient producers (W) to imports from country B (less efficient) induces a negative allocative efficiency effect. In country B, the price received by exporters will rise by the preference margin (the difference between the MFN and the preferential rate), and the supply of exports will then increase. The extent to which exports rise will depend on the responsiveness of country B's export supply to the price change (export supply elasticity). The higher this elasticity is, the larger the trade effects and, therefore, the gains will be.

Now consider the impact of a preference for nonbeneficiary countries (W). Because of the preferential treatment of imports from country B, W's exports to country A will become relatively more expensive. Demand for W's production will decrease, and its exports will be replaced by country A's imports from country B. Producers in W will lose.

These effects depend on several assumptions. For example, they assume that the preference-receiving country is not the most efficient producer of the good for which a preference is provided and that the initial MFN rate is not prohibitive. If a preference for a developing country applies to a product that the country can export efficiently once the import barrier is reduced, a new market is thereby opened to trade (for example, where tariff barriers were previously prohibitive) and no trade diversion from the rest of the world would occur.

In sum, on the basis of the simplest analytical framework, preferences result in a transfer from the producers of the preferred good and the government in the preference-granting country to the producers in the preference-receiving country. Preferences may also divert trade from nonbeneficiary countries, thus lowering these countries' welfare. But if preferences open a new market or if the beneficiary is globally efficient, nonbeneficiary countries will not necessarily suffer a welfare loss.

Does Preference Erosion Imply Welfare Losses for Beneficiaries?

The preceding sections have looked at what happens when a country introduces a preference, from the perspective of both the beneficiary country and the other countries supplying the preference-giving country. Using the same simple framework as above, this section considers a situation in which a preference margin is eroded, either through a modification of the preferential conditions of access or as a result of MFN liberalization. The erosion of country B's preference margin will reduce country B's competitive advantage, leading to reduced exports to country A and lower welfare for exporters in country B. At the same time, those countries (W) that did not receive the preference but are more efficient than country B are better off, since they gain market in country A. The trade-diverting effect of country B's preference in country A will be reduced.

On the basis of this simple analysis, it may seem appropriate to associate preference erosion directly with welfare loss. There is a clear relationship between the two: the greater the erosion of preferences is, the larger the welfare losses for exporters in beneficiary countries and territories will be. But this relationship is only one of the possible outcomes of preference erosion. Various alternative outcomes result when preference erosion is analyzed in the context of more complex economic frameworks. An alternative plausible situation is one in which following MFN liberalization, domestic prices in country A fall by less than the reduction of the MFN tariff—implying a smaller loss for country B or even a gain.[13] A possible reason for this outcome is that the increase in the demand for the good in country A is so large that the world price of the good increases.[14] Another possible reason may be that imperfect competition among importing firms in country A may impede the full-price transmission of a fall in the tariff.

Situations may arise in which preference erosion that is attributable to MFN liberalization does not lead to negative welfare consequences for preference-receiving countries, even abstracting from terms-of-trade effects. The simplest case is where exports of a given product from a preference-receiving country to a preference-giving country occur at both the preferential and the MFN rates.

Suppose, for example, that different exporters of the same product face different costs in actually using a preference. Because producers use different technologies, it may be convenient for some to use the preference and satisfy the requirements, while the origin rules may make it less convenient for others.[15] In this situation, a lower MFN rate will benefit those exporters subject to the MFN rate. These benefits may outweigh the losses of those receiving the preference. One can argue that the lower the share of preferential trade is relative to MFN trade in a product, the more likely it is that exporters will gain from MFN liberalization, despite the erosion of their preferences. The trade-off between gains from MFN liberalization and losses from preference erosion will also depend on whether it can be made easier to take advantage of preferences (for example, through modified rules of origin).

In sum, although preference erosion is generally associated with a welfare loss, beneficiary countries may not evince a monotonic relationship between changes in preference margins and welfare effects. The assessment of the welfare implications of MFN liberalization on preference-receiving countries after the erosion of preference margins is not always straightforward, even when one is looking at a single market.[16] For example, preference erosion may not imply welfare losses for the preference-receiving country if the country benefits from large positive terms-of-trade effects or if exporters do not use the preferences to any large extent.

Preference Margin: Which Measure?

This section discusses the limitations of the traditional measures of the value of preferences and then describes the measures of preference erosion used and provides the rationale for them.

Traditional Measures of the Value of a Preference

The simplest framework reveals a direct link between the extent of a preference and the potential gains for a beneficiary. Therefore, as a first approximation, the value of the preference for the preference-receiving country is often measured by the preference margin. At the tariff line, this margin is simply the difference in percentage points between the MFN rate and the preferential tariff rate.

The preference margin has a number of limitations as a measure of the value of a preference. First, it ignores the question of whether the advantage given to the preference-receiving country effectively helps it export to the preference-giving country. For example, if the MFN rate is set prohibitively high, a comparably high preference margin may not be sufficient to allow any trade in that sector. Similarly, preferences given in sectors where the receiving country is highly inefficient may not be sufficient to trigger exports. In addition, tariff rate quotas may circumscribe the actual preference margin, because preferences are limited to a certain quantity of exports, whereas the calculation of the preference margin or preference erosion refers to the beneficiary's overall exports.

One can account for bilateral trade by calculating the trade-weighted value of the preference margin as the value of the preference. This value is defined as the preference margin per unit of imports multiplied by the bilateral import value.

This measure of the value of the preference still neglects two important issues. First, it is based on the assumption that MFN rates are applied to the trade of all other countries supplying the same market. In reality, numerous and overlapping regional trade agreements exist around the world, so the MFN rate does not provide an appropriate basis for calculating the preference margin. Moreover, the value of a preference for one country will ultimately depend on how many other countries are competing in the same market with a preferential margin. For example, Özden and Sharma (2004) show that apparel producers from the Caribbean Basin Initiative countries received less benefit in the U.S. market after the North American Free Trade Agreement (NAFTA) was formed because of competition from Mexico.

Second, the weighted preference margin is also based on the assumption that preferences are used for all exports, whereas, in practice, utilization rates vary across both countries and sectors. Utilization rates, defined as the ratio of imports receiving a preference to imports covered by the preferential agreement, can be substantially less than 100 percent.

Adjusted Measures of the Value of the Preference

This chapter adjusts the value of the preference margin for the de facto erosion of preferences attributable to the existence of other exporters benefiting from the same preferential scheme and other nonreciprocal and reciprocal preferences. An "adjusted" preference margin is calculated as the percentage point difference between the weighted average tariff rate applied to the rest of the world and the preferential rate applied to the beneficiary country, where weights are represented by trade shares in the preference-granting market (hereafter, this measure is referred to as the *competition-adjusted preference margin*). The idea for this adjustment follows from the findings of Anderson and van Wincoop (2004), which emphasize that bilateral imports depend on bilateral barriers to trade relative to the rest of the world. A second measure adjusts the preference margin for the rate of preference utilization (the utilization-adjusted preference margin); that is, the preference margin is weighted by the volume of trade that actually benefits from the preference. Because of data deficiencies, this calculation could be made only for the United States.

The computation of these adjusted measures of the value of the preference requires information about MFN and preferential rates and the volume of trade by type of market access. For example, assume that the tariff profile and trade pattern of country A are those portrayed in table 7.1. Country A provides preferential access to country B but also abides by a number of other preferential agreements with countries in the rest of the world. Country B's preference margin, calculated as the simple difference between the MFN rate and the preferential rate, would be $10 - 5 = 5$. The competition-adjusted preference margin would instead be the (cross-country) trade-weighted average rate applied to the rest of the world and the preferential rate: $7.5 - 5 = 2.5$. Moreover, if country B uses its preference for only half its trade with country A, then the utilization-weighted duty for country B would be 7.5 and the actual preference margin equal to zero.

Despite the adjustment, these estimates remain a rough approximation of the actual value of a preference for the beneficiary country. One reason is that it cannot be safely assumed that the benefits of preferences accrue fully to the exporting country. The scarcity "rent" from preferences is usually shared in some measure by both exporters and importers. The distribution of the rent will depend on the relative bargaining power in the market and on the strategic responses of third parties. The volume of trade and the preference margin do not provide information on

TABLE 7.1   Access Provided by a Hypothetical Country *A*

Trading partner by type of market access	Duty rate (%)	Trade values (US$)	Weighted duty (%)
Country B			5.0
Preferential	5.0	10	
Rest of the world			7.5
MFN	10.0	60	
Preferential	5.0	30	
Free trade agreement	0.0	10	

Source: Authors.

the distribution of rents generated by tariff preferences. Actual gains from preferences enjoyed by exporters may be lessened if monopsonistic distributors are operating in the importing market or if third parties that are not receiving preferences strategically cut their prices.[17] Olarreaga and Özden (2005) find that African exporters of clothing to the United States under the African Growth and Opportunity Act (AGOA) capture only one-third of the available rent. Recent studies have also highlighted how rules of origin can affect the distribution of the rent from preferences. Cadot, Esteovadeordal, and Suwa-Eisenmann (2005) argue, for example, that the preferential tariff is the price to be paid for Mexican assemblers to agree to a rule of origin that forces them to buy U.S. intermediate goods.

Unresolved Issues on the Measure of Preference Erosion

Preference erosion is calculated as the difference in the value of the preference before and after MFN liberalization. In the analysis that follows, preference erosion is calculated on the basis of both the unadjusted and the adjusted measure of preference erosion.

Despite being based on a more realistic measure of the value of the preference, these measures of preference erosion have certain limitations that need to be taken into account in interpreting the results. One relates to the likelihood that a reduced preference margin will also be reflected in reduced export volume. Because the common measure for preference erosion is calculated using a fixed value of exports, the real extent of erosion may be underestimated. Moreover, the analysis should not be limited only to existing suppliers, because new entrants may appear in the market following MFN liberalization and may affect competitive conditions. Ideally, the quantification of potential preference erosion should be undertaken in the context of a general equilibrium model that includes information at the tariff-line level on the responsiveness of demand and supply to price variation (including all cross-product links).

A second limitation relates to preference utilization rates. Even if utilization were taken into account, preference erosion is calculated assuming that utilization rates are unaffected by MFN liberalization. But the erosion of the preference margin may affect an exporter's decision on whether to use a preference. Candau, Fontagné, and Jean (2004) find, for example, that the utilization of preferences in the European Union (EU) is lower when the preference margin is low, which they interpret as evidence of significant compliance costs. This interpretation seems to suggest that a reduction of the preference margin following MFN liberalization may have a negative impact on the utilization rate, thus further increasing the extent of the preference erosion relative to that measured assuming no relationship between preferential margins and utilization.

A third limitation relates to the fact that in adjusting estimates of nonreciprocal preference margins by allowing for other preferential trade arrangements, one may erroneously assume that those other preferences are fully utilized when they are not. Under regional free trade agreements, for example, traders may not take advantage of the right to sell into a partner market duty free because of restrictions on rules of origin or the heavy administrative costs involved in securing free trade agreement treatment relative to the cost of paying the MFN tariff. This is exactly the same utilization issue that applies in the case of nonreciprocal preferential trade, and it should be treated comparably in estimating the true value of preferences and risk from preference erosion.

The Value of Nonreciprocal Preferences: Setting the Scene

This section introduces the basic data used to calculate the value of nonreciprocal preferences, adjusted for non-MFN trade (and in the case of the United States, for less than full preference utilization). These data include information on the relative importance of preferential and nonpreferential trade from the point of view of both the preference giver and the beneficiary. This backdrop makes it possible to consider the scope for additional nonreciprocal preferences later in the chapter. It also makes it possible to gauge how far potential preference erosion poses a threat to beneficiaries, depending on the degree of MFN liberalization that occurs. The next section develops a specific MFN liberalization scenario.

The data presented here refer to selected country examples. Detailed information about all countries that benefit only from nonreciprocal preferences from the Quad economies (Canada, the EU, Japan, and the United States) and Australia is reported in different sets of tabulations included as annexes.[18] Information on data sources, the list of preferential schemes covered in the database, and guides to the annex tables are shown in the annexes.

Preferential Schemes by Providers

The initial focus is on the various nonreciprocal preferential schemes offered by the Quad economies plus Australia. Figures 7.1 and 7.2 show import shares for each of the five preference-giving economies by type of market access under the GSP and the various LDC schemes, respectively.[19] Figure 7.1 shows that a large share (nearly 70 percent) of Quad plus Australia imports from beneficiaries of the GSP enter their markets duty free (under either the MFN or preferential schemes). The percentage of dutiable imports (paying either MFN or preferential duty) under the GSP scheme varies across preference-giving countries, ranging between approximately 50 percent (for Australia and the United States) and about 23 percent (for Japan). The comparison between the LDC schemes and the GSP

FIGURE 7.1 Imports under the GSP Scheme by Type of Market Access

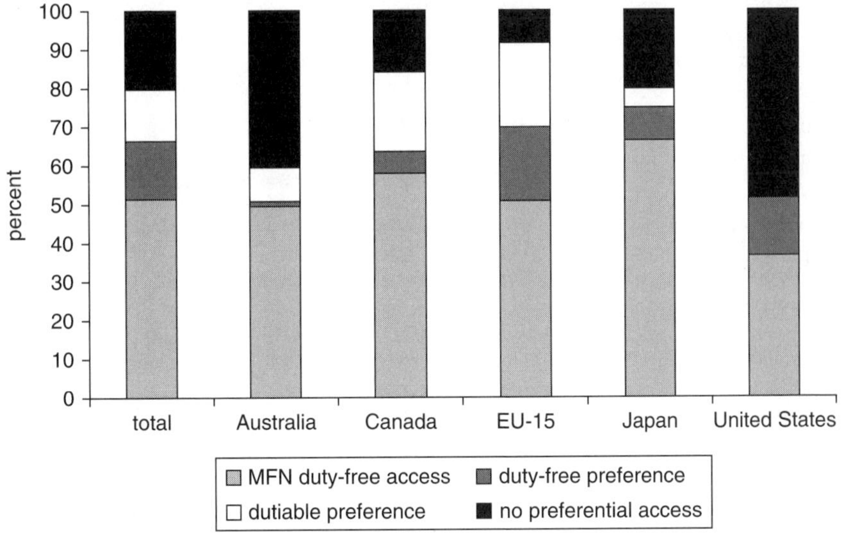

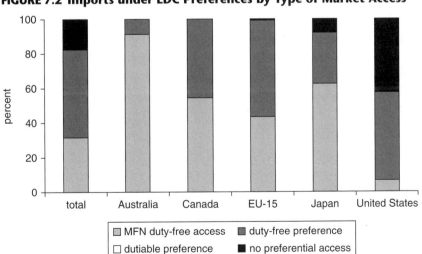

Source: Authors' calculations.

Note: EU-15 refers to the 15 countries that were members of the European Union prior to May 1, 2004: Austria, Belgium, Denmark, Finland, France, Germany, Greece, Ireland, Italy, Luxembourg, Netherlands, Portugal, Spain, Sweden, and the United Kingdom.

FIGURE 7.2 Imports under LDC Preferences by Type of Market Access

Source: Authors' calculations.

TABLE 7.2   Scope to Extend Preferences

Market	GSP (%)		LDC (%)		Other schemes (%)	
	Tariff lines	Imports	Tariff lines	Imports	Tariff lines	Imports
Australia	53.3	50.2	0.0	0.0	—	—
Canada	32.1	37.7	0.0	0.0	—	—
EU-15	32.7	28.1	1.2	0.1	0.9	3.5
United States	31.6	50.4	18.8	44.1	11.0	0.5
Japan	34.2	23.0	5.5	8.6	—	—

Source: Authors' calculations.

Note: — = not available. *Other schemes* are the ACP scheme for the EU and the AGOA scheme for the United States.

schemes shows that a much larger percentage of imports under the LDC schemes enters the preference-giving countries duty free. In the case of Australia, Canada, and the EU, all imports entering under LDC preferences are duty free. In addition, table 7.C.1 shows that nearly all imports entering under AGOA or ACP preferences (for example, for the United States and the EU, respectively) are duty free.

If one looks at the data in terms of possible trade solutions to preference erosion, there is no scope to compensate for the erosion of preferences by either introducing new preferences or reducing the preferential rate. A similar picture arises from tariff-line information. Table 7.2 shows data for each of the five preference-giving economies on the percentage of tariff lines that either attract a positive MFN rate with no preferences or enjoy preferences at a positive rate under both the GSP and the LDC schemes. In addition, for the EU and the United States, the percentage of remaining tariff lines and the corresponding percentage of imports where there may be further scope to introduce preferences are reported for the ACP and the AGOA schemes, respectively. Overall, the data show that the scope for extending preferences to compensate for preference erosion is limited, especially under some schemes.

Importance of Preferences by Beneficiaries

This section looks at preferences from the point of view of beneficiaries. The importance of preferences for preference-receiving countries and territories and their vulnerability to preference erosion will depend on their dependence on preferences and their value.

To provide an overall picture of the importance of preferences for beneficiaries, table 7.3 reports overall percentages for developing countries and LDCs by type of market access to the Quad economies plus Australia and average values of

TABLE 7.3   The Value of Preferences: Nonagricultural Products, 2003

Beneficiary	Exports to the Quad markets + Australia (%)			Preference margin (%)	
	MFN duty free	MFN dutiable	Preferential	Unadjusted	Competition adjusted
Developing countries	52.1	31.8	15.9	0.7	−0.5
LDCs	20.2	18.3	61.2	6.4	1.6

Source: Authors' calculations.

preferences (measured both according to the traditional unadjusted measure of preference margins and the competition-adjusted measure).[20] Although developing countries enjoy a higher share of duty-free trade (52.1 percent) than LDCs do (20.2 percent), a much larger share of LDC trade benefits from preferences (61.2 percent, compared with 15.9 percent for developing countries). The average preference margin for LDCs in the Quad economies plus Australia drops from 6.4 to 1.6 when competition from other countries that benefit from preferences is taken into account. Moreover, the equivalent preference margin for the developing countries that benefit only from nonreciprocal preferences as a whole is negative. Hence, at least some developing countries face market conditions worse than those of their trade competitors.[21] As noted earlier, for data reasons, the figures for the utilization-adjusted preference margins can be provided only for the United States.

The percentage of exports that enjoy preferences in the Quad markets plus Australia (table 7.C.2, columns 2–4) and preference margins (table 7.C.3) differ considerably across individual countries.[22] For some countries—such as Chad, Guatemala, El Salvador, Haiti, Lesotho, Madagascar, Malawi, Mauritius, Mozambique, and Senegal—preferential schemes (including both nonreciprocal and reciprocal preferential schemes) cover more than 90 percent of their total exports. For other developing countries, preferential trade is not a significant share of their trade with the Quad economies and Australia; among these countries are Botswana and the Central African Republic (with a share of preferential trade below 5 percent).[23] Similarly, the estimated figures for the average (unadjusted) preference margin enjoyed by developing countries exporting to the Quad economies plus Australia range between zero for developing countries such as Angola, Botswana, the Democratic People's Republic of Congo, and Nigeria and 19 percentage points for Lesotho and Malawi.

Nine of the 10 countries named above whose preferential trade represents more than 90 percent of total exports (excluding only Chad) also appear among the countries enjoying the highest preference margins from the Quad economies plus Australia, whether adjusted for competition or not (table 7.C.3, columns 7 and 1, respectively). These 10 countries also appear to have narrow export bases (table 7.C.2, columns 5–7), exporting a range of products that cover no more than 3 percent of tariff lines. And some of them (for example, Lesotho, Malawi, and Mozambique) hardly export at all at the MFN rate. The extent of coverage of preferences for the products exported by these countries, the large margin of preference, and the low degree of export diversification (especially for those products not covered by preferences) seem to suggest little scope for a trade solution for these countries.

Estimates of the value of preferences are highly sensitive to the specific measure used for the calculations. For example, figure 7.3 shows the value of preferences for nonagricultural exports to the United States as being estimated using four alternative measures: the simple weighted preference margin, the preference margin adjusted for the rate of preference utilization, the margin adjusted for the preferences that the United States grants to other countries, and an overall measure adjusting for both competition from other preference beneficiaries and the utilization rate.[24] For some

FIGURE 7.3 Value of the Preference for Nonagricultural Product Exports to the United States: Selected Countries, 2003

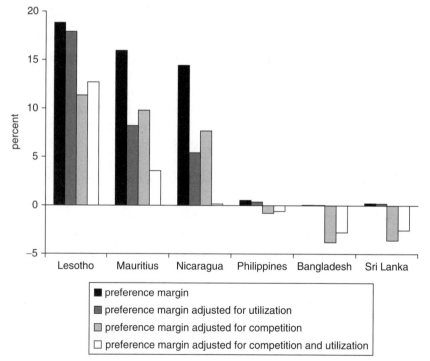

Source: Authors' calculations.

countries—such as Bangladesh, the Philippines, and Sri Lanka—preference margins prove to be negative when adjusted for competition from other preference beneficiaries. Thus, on an overall basis, these countries' exports benefit from less beneficial treatment than other countries competing in the U.S. market.

Simulating an MFN Tariff Cut in Nonagricultural Market Access: What Happens to Preference Margins?

This section simulates an MFN tariff cut on nonagricultural products and estimates the effect of this cut on the value of preferences. Preference erosion is calculated as the change in the value of the preference before and after the MFN cut. The simulations undertaken here include only estimates of preference margins adjusted for competing non-MFN trade, not for utilization rates. The Swiss formula proposed in the modalities for nonagricultural market access (WTO 2008) is used with a coefficient of 10 to calculate the tariff cuts on 2003 MFN applied rates. The base for cutting tariffs in the negotiations would be bound rates rather than applied rates. But the three major reporters (excluding Australia) represent 90 percent of imports, and their bound and applied rates differ only slightly. Therefore, one can confidently assume that the margin of error introduced with this approximation is low.

To illustrate, figure 7.4 shows the impact of MFN liberalization on the value of preferences for LDCs—particularly for Lesotho and Nepal. The comparison between the impact estimated on the basis of the traditional measure of preference erosion and that estimated on the basis of the competition-adjusted measure shows that when one takes into account competition arising from other preference-receiving countries, the estimated losses from preference erosion generally ease. In some countries (for example, Nepal in figure 7.4), the adjustment may even result in a gain from MFN liberalization as opposed to a loss relative to a reduced preference margin.

Examples of this type also exist among developing countries. Table 7.C.4 in the annexes provides the results of the exercise for LDCs and those developing countries that benefit only from nonreciprocal preferences in the Quad markets plus Australia. Malaysia, for example, is estimated to lose US$70 million in terms of preference erosion before the adjustment and then to gain US$47 million after the adjustment. The second figure represents what Malaysia gains as a result of the losses of others from preference erosion. Countries that rely less on preferences or have competitors with better preferential access typically suffer from preference erosion without adjustments and then score gains after the adjustments are made.

Overall, developing countries (excluding LDCs) as a group would gain some US$2 billion after the MFN tariff cut. The gains, however, are concentrated in only about a third of the countries, whereas the losses are more widespread.

FIGURE 7.4 Change in the Value of the Preference, Selected LDCs

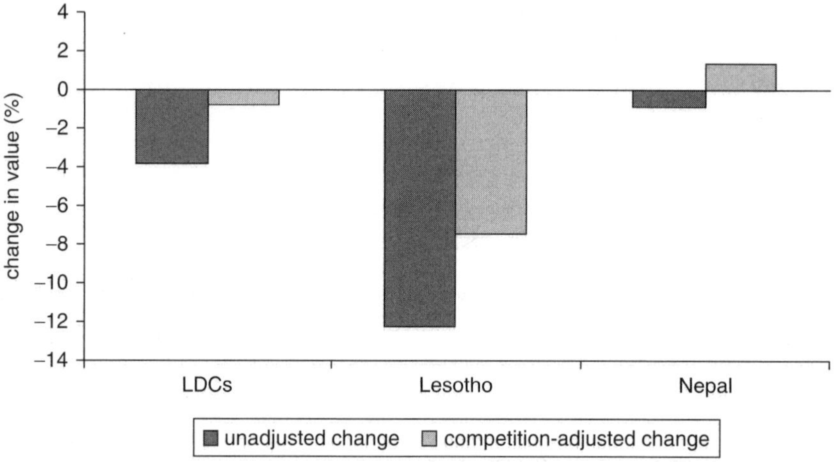

Source: Authors' calculations.

As far as LDCs are concerned, two countries show significant gains from MFN liberalization in terms of an increased preference value: Nepal (US$4 million) and Maldives (US$2 million). Overall, the LDCs experience a loss from preference erosion, equal to about US$170 million after adjusting for competing non-MFN trade (US$841 million before adjusting). The adjusted preference erosion figures for the LDCs reveal some striking differences. The major losers from preference erosion include Bangladesh, Cambodia, Haiti, Lesotho, and Madagascar. By contrast, a significant number of LDCs do not appear to incur any losses from preference erosion following the MFN tariff cut simulated here, largely because these countries rely on preferences to a limited extent. The bulk of their exports into the five reporter economies (the Quad markets plus Australia) are MFN duty free (first three columns of table 7.C.2). Countries in this group include Benin, Burkina Faso, Burundi, the Central African Republic, Chad, the Democratic Republic of the Congo, Djibouti, Guinea, Mali, Niger, Rwanda, Sierra Leone, Solomon Islands, Togo, and Zambia.

To obtain an indication of the relative vulnerability of countries to preference erosion, one must calculate the change in the value of the preference as a percentage of bilateral trade (table 7.C.4, column 4). The estimates suggest that the 10 developing countries most affected by MFN liberalization are likely to be the Dominican Republic, El Salvador, Guatemala, Honduras, Kenya, Mauritius, Namibia, Nicaragua, and Swaziland. The five most affected LDCs are Bangladesh, Cambodia, Haiti, Lesotho, and Madagascar.

The analysis then looked at preference erosion at the product level for these 15 most vulnerable countries. Some broad product categories (MTN categories) were identified, and an "adjusted" preference erosion was calculated for those categories. The results of these calculations for each of the five preference-giving economies are reported in table 7.C.5 in the annexes. The table shows that in the five reporter markets, clothing is by far the largest part of the preference erosion story for the most affected countries. In fact, among nearly all countries reported in the table, the highest variation in the preference margin before and after the MFN cut is recorded for the clothing sector. Some countries also experience significant figures for preference erosion in other sectors—such as textiles; fish and fish products (especially Namibia, but also Madagascar and Mauritius); leather and leather products (especially Cambodia but also Bangladesh); electrical machinery; and wood and wood products.

Trade Solutions to Preference Erosion

Increased Preference Utilization

A number of studies have calculated preference utilization rates to assess the actual coverage of eligible products, the de facto exclusion of some potential beneficiary countries, and the access conditions in the markets of preference-giving countries. Some studies suggest that nonreciprocal preference utilization rates are frequently low. Focusing on the EU's Everything but Arms (EBA) initiative, Brenton (2003) finds very low utilization rates for LDC exports to the EU in 2001. Inama (2003) estimates that less than 40 percent of Quad imports from all beneficiaries eligible for GSP preferences entered under the preferential scheme. For Japan, utilization rates in 2001 are estimated at about 30 percent. Under the AGOA scheme, utilization rates vary between 36 percent for textile and 67 percent for mineral products.

Some have argued, however, that it may be misleading to measure utilization rates for single preferential schemes to assess the importance of preferential access to certain markets. They argue that an exporter may have preferential access to a certain market through various preferential schemes. In the case of preferential access to the EU market, for example, Sub-Saharan African countries benefit from preferential access through the EBA initiative and the Cotonou Agreement.[25] When a broader measure of utilization is used that is based on the utilization rate of at least one preferential agreement, figures on the overall use of preferences are much higher. Candau and Jean (2005) find that when all EU preference schemes are examined together, utilization rates are considerably higher. Bureau and Gallezot (2004) find a rate of utilization across eligible imports for all preferential schemes of some 90 percent for both the United States and the EU in agriculture and food products. Overall, Candau, Fontagné, and Jean (2004) find that utilization rates above 80 percent prevail for textiles, clothing, and other manufactured products in the EU.

The difference in the results for the EU arises primarily because the EBA program is poorly used in Sub-Saharan Africa, whereas the Cotonou regime is strongly used.

These results are reported at a high level of aggregation. Utilization rate data show wide variation across countries and preference schemes. Brenton and Ikezuki (2006) find, for example, that Côte d'Ivoire and Madagascar use 86 percent and 58 percent, respectively, of the value of preferences for which they are eligible in the U.S. market. Exporters from Mali request preferential treatment for 66.8 percent, 49.8 percent, and 87.5 percent, respectively, of the exports under eligible product categories in EU, Japanese, and U.S. markets.

Utilization rates also vary across sectors. A recent World Trade Organization (WTO) study (Ansón and Bacchetta 2005) of the textile and clothing sector finds high variability in the utilization rates calculated at the tariff-line level across all preferential regimes for the Quad economies. This finding is important to bear in mind more generally—namely, that aggregation often hides high variance. High variability also suggests that producers of similar products facing similar preferential margins react differently; some use MFN tariffs while others use preferences.

Why are utilization rates less than 100 percent, and why do they vary across sectors, countries, and preferential regimes? Most studies point to rules of origin in answering these questions. Rules of origin can impose additional production costs on exporters in developing countries, which reduce the attraction of preferences or perhaps simply render them unusable. Exporters may incur additional production costs as a result of an obligation to source inputs from high-cost suppliers or because of the need to design production structures that comply with rules of origin requirements. Such documentation requirements as certificates of origin and complex accounting systems may also add to costs.[26]

Owing to the higher costs, restrictive rules of origin will affect the exporter's decision about whether to use the preference. Clearly, if the cost of compliance[27] with rules of origin exceeds the margin of preference, the producer would not use the preference. The producer would source inputs on the basis of profit considerations and export at the MFN rate. For example, Brenton and Manchin (2003) note that many Eastern European exporters have preferred to continue exporting under OPT (outward processing trade for textiles) arrangements[28] rather than under the free trade agreement, despite the lower tariffs, because of origin constraints. Similarly, some researchers have argued that the strong preference for the Cotonou regime over the EBA regime is attributable to more restrictive rules of origin for the EBA scheme.

Ansón and Bacchetta (2005) demonstrate a clear inverse relationship between the restrictiveness of origin rules and utilization rates by LDCs in the textile and clothing sector. Some of the results of their study are reported in table 7.4. The data for Australia, Canada, Japan, and Switzerland refer to the GSP regime for

TABLE 7.4 Utilization Rates and Rules of Origin Restrictiveness for LDCs in Clothing (HS 61–62), 2004

	Australia (%)	Japan (%)	Switzerland (%)	Canada (%)	United States (%)		EU (%)	
					AGOA	CBTPA	Cotonou	EBA
Utilization rates	37.9	40.3	43.8	71.6	79.8	71.3	76	37.8
Rules of origin								
Local content	25[a]	No mention	60[a]	25[a]	7[b]	7[b]	47.5[a]	47.5[a]
Product-specific rules	No	Yes	Yes	No	No	No	Yes	Yes
Cumulation	Bilateral	No mention	Regional	Bilateral	Global	Regional	Full for ACP	Bilateral, regional

Source: Ansón and Bacchetta 2005.

Note: Regional defines diagonal cumulation of inputs from a set of countries.

a. Highest percentage of value added.

b. Percentage of weight.

LDCs. For the EU and the United States, data are for the Cotonou and EBA regimes and for AGOA and the Caribbean Basin Trade Partnership Act (CBTPA), respectively. Although based on qualitative information on rules of origin, the data suggest that utilization rates tend to be higher when the local content requirement is lower; the rules are less complex (see, for example, the case of Japan); and the cumulation regime is more liberal in terms of both country coverage and type of cumulation.[29]

Canada is a particularly successful example of the effect of reforms in existing preferential regimes on utilization rates. Starting on January 1, 2003, Canada added 903 tariff lines at the Harmonized System (HS) eight-digit level to the list of duty-free tariff items for LDCs. Canada also introduced new requirements for rules of origin for textiles and clothing. For this sector, these reforms implied duty-free access to the Canadian market for all LDC imports, as well as more liberal rules of origin.[30] The effects of this reform have been remarkable. Ansón and Bacchetta (2005) show a substantial rise in preference utilization rates for Bangladesh in textiles and clothing. Not only have utilization rates increased for all four-digit categories previously used, but Bangladesh has substantially diversified its exports. Bangladesh's utilization rates of Canadian preferences were low in 2002, with the highest rate equal to 45.1 percent and with the utilization rate equal to zero for most of the tariff headings for clothing for which exports are recorded (subsectors at the four-digit level). But the situation changed completely only one year after the reform; just 6 of 40 sectors showed a utilization rate of less than 40 percent. Bangladesh's exports have been diversified across 40 tariff headings, and only 2 tariff headings show a zero utilization rate. More generally, the study shows that the reforms of Canada's preferential regime led to a higher value of textile and clothing exports for all LDCs and favored the entry of more countries into the Canadian market. The number of LDCs exporting to Canada increased from 33 in 2002 to 41 in 2004.

A low utilization rate is generally interpreted as a sign that the design of the preferences limits their utility to developing countries. More liberal rules of origin may, in many cases, help compensate for preference erosion following MFN liberalization. But MFN liberalization per se in sectors characterized by a low preference utilization rate may be thought of as compensatory trade policy for preference beneficiaries (and others). The rationale is as follows: a low preference utilization rate with respect to a specific tariff line implies that producers of the same good facing the same rules of origin and preference margin make different decisions about whether to use the preference or the MFN rate to export. They do so because they use different technologies or have different information and, hence, face different costs for switching to different inputs or fulfilling the administrative requirements of rules of origin. Where exports from developing countries to developed countries take place at both the preferential rate and the MFN rate, the reduction of the MFN rate will benefit MFN-rate exporters. This benefit may out-weigh the loss to those who receive a preference. In other words, when the option of liberalizing rules of origin is not available, countries or sectors that have low utilization rates may be better off pursuing a policy aimed at deepening MFN lib-eralization rather than preserving preference margins.

The data on utilization rates are scarce and make it hard to draw a conclusion. Overall, however, available data appear to suggest that while there are undoubtedly areas and countries where low preference utilization occurs at least partly because of limitations in rules of origin, for the most part underutilization of preferences is not a major factor. Therefore, improvements in utilization offer only limited scope for mitigating preference erosion in the face of MFN liberalization.

Scope for Extending Nonreciprocal Preferences in the Quad Markets plus Australia

As noted previously, an obvious trade solution to nonreciprocal preference ero-sion arising from MFN liberalization would be to extend preferential arrange-ments to other product areas where positive MFN rates apply. This chapter does not address the situation with respect to preferences at a detailed product- or tariff-line level. Therefore, it is not possible to give a precise indication of which products in which markets may lend themselves to new preferential arrangements.

Table 7.C.4 in the annexes shows the aggregate value of trade by exporter with respect to which additional preferences could potentially be extended by prefer-ence receivers. Just as all the data in this chapter are essentially static (that is, they take no account of possible supply and demand responses to changes in relative prices), the data are also based exclusively on actual trade performance—that is, the numbers reflect actual rather than potential trade patterns. Thus, the chapter considers the scope for extending preferences only with respect to products actu-ally traded by countries. No doubt some exporters would be able to export other products under different tariff arrangements.

With this important analytical limitation in mind, the scope for additional preferential treatment on aggregate exports from developing countries to the five reporter economies (the Quad markets plus Australia) amounts to nearly US$11 billion (in terms of 2003 trade flows). This amount more than covers the sum of the losses faced by some developing countries. The comparable figure relating to the scope for extending preferential treatment to LDCs is US$217 mil-lion. This amount would also appear to cover the US$170 million preference ero-sion estimate for LDCs.

Although the aggregate picture may suggest that extending preferential treatment to new product lines offers a solution to preference erosion in the five reporter

TABLE 7.5   Scope for Compensation: Total Number of Countries

Beneficiary category	With scope for compensation	Total
Developing countries	9	65
LDCs	4	32
Most affected countries	2	15

Source: Authors' calculations.

economies, this suggestion is severely undermined when the data are disaggregated by country. For example, comparing columns 3 and 5 of table 7.C.4 in the annexes by individual countries reveals scope for compensation in just 13 countries (9 developing countries and 4 LDCs) out of 97 (65 developing countries and 32 LDCs) for which simulations were run (table 7.5).

In particular, of the 15 countries most affected by preference erosion (Bangladesh, Cambodia, the Dominican Republic, El Salvador, Guatemala, Haiti, Honduras, Kenya, Lesotho, Madagascar, Mauritius, Namibia, Nicaragua, St. Lucia, and Swaziland), only two (Bangladesh and Cambodia) have scope for additional preferences in excess of the value of preference erosion incurred as a result of MFN liberalization. The others lack sufficient scope for additional preferences to cover the value of estimated losses from preference erosion. With the caveats already discussed, the evidence suggests that this particular trade solution to preference erosion does not hold much promise in the immediate future.

Scope for Compensating Preference Erosion through Preferences in Other Markets

This chapter has focused only on nonreciprocal preferential exports from developing countries to Australia, Canada, the EU, Japan, and the United States (the five reporter economies). Although these markets represent a large share of the trade of many developing countries, the question arises whether part of a trade solution to preference erosion resulting from MFN liberalization may lie in extending preferential treatment in markets other than the five reporter economies. This question is not systematically addressed in this chapter. All developed countries not covered here, however, already have nonreciprocal preference schemes. These schemes would need to be studied in detail to determine the degree to which their value to developing countries would be lessened through MFN liberalization and the extent to which such losses were amenable to trade solutions.

What about trade between developing countries, which is enjoying a growing share of global trade? The possibility of rejuvenating the Generalized System of Trade Preferences (GSTP) among developing countries has been mooted recently. Many reciprocal preferential trade agreements already exist or are being negotiated among developing countries. Moreover, some 20 developing countries provide some nonreciprocal preferences to LDCs, under either the GSTP or some other agreement.[31]

Finally, table 7.C.4 (column 6) provides a rough indicator of the possible scope for individual developing countries to seek trade solutions to preference erosion in markets other than those of the five reporter markets. Column 6 shows the ratio (in percentage terms) of exports to the five reporter economies to exports to the rest of the world. A low percentage value in column 6 suggests possible scope for recouping losses from preference erosion in the five reporter economies through preferential trading arrangements in other markets. This value is obviously a rough indicator of potential, but once again, by abstracting from possible supply responses to new trade opportunities, it shows that this trade solution is not too promising for the countries most hurt by preference erosion in the five reporter markets. In the case of the 16 countries most affected, for example, the five reporter economies accounted for well over 75 percent of their total exports in 2003. Three outliers were Kenya (49 percent), Namibia (53 percent), and Swaziland (23 percent). But in each case, a significant part of this trade share is already likely to be preferential—East African Community trade in the case of Kenya and South African Customs Union trade in the case of Namibia and Swaziland. Once again, the conclusion is that trade solutions are not too promising for the majority of the countries most seriously at risk from preference erosion stemming from MFN liberalization.

Conclusions

This chapter has taken a fairly detailed look at the likely dimensions of nonreciprocal preference erosion for developing countries arising from MFN trade liberalization. It has estimated the degree of preference erosion affecting all developing countries as a result of an MFN tariff cut on nonagricultural products. (Chapter 8 discusses the effects of a tariff cut on agricultural products.) This chapter has also considered the extent to which "trade" solutions may be found for preference erosion by improving preference utilization rates and extending preferential arrangements to new products, either in the preference-giving countries examined here or in other markets.

The main conclusions, summarized below, are based on a static MFN liberalization scenario that does not take account of possible supply and demand responses to relative price changes. Moreover, the analysis is based on observed trade flows and therefore does not allow the possibility of new trade occurring in new product lines as a result of relative price changes:

- Developing countries would enjoy a net gain of US$2 billion in the value of adjusted preference margins if the Quad economies plus Australia were to reduce

MFN tariffs on nonagricultural products using a Swiss formula with a coefficient of 10. Significant gains and losses underlie the net figure. The 10 largest losers among developing countries (excluding LDCs) from nonreciprocal preference erosion are, in order, the Dominican Republic, Honduras, Kenya, Mauritius, St. Lucia, El Salvador, Guatemala, Namibia, Nicaragua, and Swaziland.

- LDCs would suffer a net loss of US$170 million under the same liberalization scenario, but in this case only two LDCs (Maldives and Nepal) register a gain. The major losers from preference erosion are Bangladesh, Cambodia, Haiti, Lesotho, and Madagascar. Many LDCs would suffer little or no preference erosion, however, because their export structure is such that they enjoy MFN duty-free treatment on a large share of their exports to the five reporter markets. This group includes Benin, Burkina Faso, Burundi, the Central African Republic, Chad, the Democratic Republic of Congo, Djibouti, Guinea, Mali, Niger, Rwanda, Sierra Leone, the Solomon Islands, Togo, and Zambia.

- Much of the preference erosion story in the most affected countries is about clothing, especially for the LDCs (except Madagascar). Other sectors of some interest to certain affected countries in the five reporter markets include textiles, fish and fish products, leather and leather products, electrical machinery, and wood and wood products.

- As to trade solutions to preference erosion, improved utilization levels may or may not have a decisive effect in most of the affected countries. There may, however, be one or two important exceptions. Some preliminary evidence suggests a positive effect from reforms of preferential schemes. More definitive conclusions are not possible because of an acute lack of comprehensive and reliable information. What information there is provides a mixed picture. Although utilization problems seem to emerge in some reciprocal and nonreciprocal preference schemes, most developing countries and LDCs appear to enjoy reasonably high utilization rates (for example, ACP countries into the EU and most countries into the United States). This issue requires additional research based on better information.

- Limited scope exists for expanding preference schemes to other product lines in the five reporter economies to ameliorate the impact of preference erosion on the countries most affected because significant positive tariffs do not fall on nonpreferential trade flows to the reporter markets. Countries that are exceptions to this conclusion are Bangladesh and Cambodia and, to a lesser extent, Myanmar and Nepal.

- Limited scope also exists, at least in the near future, for softening the impact of preference erosion in the most affected countries through exports to markets other than those of the reporter economies because the latter account for a substantial share of the exports of the most affected countries.

Annex 7.A: Data Sources

The data are sourced from CAMAD (Common Analytical Market Access Database), which is maintained by the International Trade Commission, the United Nations Conference on Trade and Development, and the WTO Secretariat. The reference year for both trade and tariff data is 2003; tariff lines outside chapters 01 to 97 of the 2002 Harmonized System have been excluded. Note the following:

- Total imports may not be in line with other international sources because some confidential trade flows are not submitted to the WTO Integrated Data Base.
- Only those bilateral trade flows higher than US$1,000 have been included in the analysis.
- Whenever available, ad valorem equivalents calculated by the International Trade Commission for the Millennium Development Goals have been used.

The analysis has been carried out at the national tariff-line level. Australia, Canada, and the United States use 8-digit tariff numbers, Japan uses 9 digits, and the EU provides import data at the 8-digit level but preferential tariffs are defined at the 10- or 12-digit level. To align EU tariff data with imports, the data are aggregated at 10 digits and then at 8 digits.

The tariff information for the United States does not identify the clothing products that benefit from AGOA and the CBTPA. It has been assumed that all products under chapters 61 and 62 of the 2002 HS are eligible under those two preference schemes.

Countries benefiting from the GSP and LDC programs may vary from one donor country to another.

Annex 7.B: Coverage of Preferential Schemes[32]

This annex lists the preferential schemes in the Quad economies and Australia. Exclusions to preferential schemes have been taken into account.

Australia

- GSP
- LDC initiative
- South Pacific Regional Trade and Economic Cooperation Agreement
- Scheme covering Hong Kong, China; Republic of Korea; and Separate Customs Territory of Taiwan, China; Penghu; Kinmen; and Matsu
- Australia-Malaysia Free Trade Agreement

- Agreements for Norfolk Island, Christmas Island, Cocos Islands, Australian Territories, Heard Island, and McDonald Island
- Papua New Guinea Agreement on Trade and Commercial Relations Agreement
- Canada-Australia Trade Agreement
- Australia-New Zealand Closer Economic Relations Trade Agreement
- Singapore-Australia Free Trade Agreement

Canada

- GSP
- LDC initiative
- Commonwealth Caribbean Countries Tariff
- Australia Tariff
- Canada–Costa Rica Free Trade Agreement
- Canada-Israel Free Trade Agreement
- Chile Tariff under the Canada-Chile Free Trade Agreement
- Mexico Tariff under NAFTA
- Mexico–United States Tariff under NAFTA
- New Zealand Tariff
- United States Tariff under NAFTA

Japan

- GSP
- LDC initiative

United States

- GSP
- Least-developed beneficiary developing countries initiative
- AGOA program
- Andean Trade Preference Act and Andean Trade Promotion and Drug Eradication Act program
- Caribbean Basin Economic Recovery Act initiative
- CBTPA initiative
- Automotive Products Trade Act scheme
- Canada Tariff under NAFTA

- Mexico Tariff under NAFTA
- United States–Israel Free Trade Area
- United States–Jordan Free Trade Area

European Union

- GSP
- LDC initiative
- Preferential tariff for ACP countries
- Preferential tariff for countries fighting drug trafficking
- Preferential tariff for overseas countries and territories
- Preferential tariffs for Albania; Algeria; Andorra; Bosnia and Herzegovina; Bulgaria; Chile; Croatia; Cyprus; Czech Republic; Arab Republic of Egypt; Estonia; Faeroe Islands; Palestinian Authority of the West Bank and Gaza Strip; Hong Kong, China; Hungary; Iceland; Israel; Jordan; Latvia; Lebanon; Liechtenstein; Lithuania; former Yugoslav Republic of Macedonia; Malta; Mexico; Montenegro; Morocco; Myanmar; Norway; Poland; Romania; Serbia; Slovak Republic; Slovenia; South Africa; Switzerland; Syrian Arab Republic; Taiwan, China; Tunisia

Annex 7.C: Guidelines on Annex Tables

The data in these tables are relatively complex. A simple guide follows.

Table 7.C.1: Nonreciprocal Schemes in Selected Markets
for Nonagricultural Markets, 2003

Table 7.C.1 provides information on the GSP and LDC schemes and on other selected individual nonreciprocal schemes for each of the five preference-giving markets. The import value data represent the value of total nonagricultural imports of each reporter economy from all beneficiaries in 2003. The second column shows the number of national tariff lines for products with trade from those beneficiaries. It may be observed, for example, that 49.1 percent of Australia's nonagricultural imports from GSP beneficiaries entered MFN duty free, whereas 9.4 percent of imports were eligible for preferential access, of which 0.7 percent was duty free. The MFN dutiable imports would stand at 41.5 percent (100.0 − 49.1 − 9.4).

TABLE 7.C.1   **Nonreciprocal Schemes in Selected Markets: Nonagricultural Products, 2003**

Type of scheme	Imports		Number of national tariff lines		
	Value (US$ million)	Share (%)	Number	Share (%)	With trade (%)
Australia					
GSP					
All tariff lines	**19,649.5**	**100.0**	**5,330**	**100.0**	**77.9**
MFN duty-free access	9,647.5	49.1	2,332	43.8	31.2
Preferential access	1,855.2	9.4	790	14.8	11.6
Duty-free preference	136.7	0.7	158	3.0	1.8
LDC					
All tariff lines	**110.7**	**100.0**	**5,330**	**100.0**	**7.6**
MFN duty-free access	99.6	90.0	2,332	43.8	2.7
Preferential access	11.1	10.0	2,998	56.2	4.9
Duty-free preference	11.1	10.0	2,998	56.2	4.9
Canada					
GSP					
All tariff lines	**41,656.9**	**100.0**	**7,125**	**100.0**	**81.8**
MFN duty-free access	23,778.7	57.1	3,710	52.1	41.5
Preferential access	11,168.0	26.8	2,484	34.9	28.4
Duty-free preference	2,188.4	5.3	1,131	15.9	12.5
LDC					
All tariff lines	**703.4**	**100.0**	**7,125**	**100.0**	**10.0**
MFN duty-free access	366.1	52.0	3,710	52.1	3.9
Preferential access	337.3	48.0	3,415	47.9	6.1
Duty-free preference	337.3	48.0	3,415	47.9	6.1
Commonwealth Caribbean countries					
All tariff lines	**519.1**	**100.0**	**7,125**	**100.0**	**5.3**
MFN duty-free access	456.2	87.9	3,710	52.1	3.2
Preferential access	56.8	10.9	2,678	37.6	1.6
Duty-free preference	56.7	10.9	2,412	33.9	1.6
EU-15					
GSP					
All tariff lines	**393,955.5**	**100.0**	**8,289**	**100.0**	**94.3**
MFN duty-free access	202,725.2	51.5	1,774	21.4	19.3
Preferential access	165,321.0	42.0	6,179	74.5	71.6
Duty-free preference	80,639.3	20.5	3,804	45.9	43.8

TABLE 7.C.1 (*Continued*)

Type of scheme	Imports Value (US$ million)	Imports Share (%)	Number of national tariff lines Number	Number of national tariff lines Share (%)	Number of national tariff lines With trade (%)
LDC					
All tariff lines	**12,143.8**	**100.0**	**8,289**	**100.0**	**32.9**
MFN duty-free access	5,115.7	42.1	1,774	21.4	7.3
Preferential access	7,017.9	57.8	6,414	77.4	25.6
Duty-free preference	7,017.9	57.8	6,414	77.4	25.6
ACP					
All tariff lines	**22,101.5**	**100.0**	**8,289**	**100.0**	**42.7**
MFN duty-free access	15,803.9	71.5	1,774	21.4	9.4
Preferential access	5,516.8	25.0	6,439	77.7	33.0
Duty-free preference	5,516.8	25.0	6,439	77.7	33.0
Countries fighting drugs					
All tariff lines	**10,815.9**	**100.0**	**8,289**	**100.0**	**41.7**
MFN duty-free access	6,154.5	56.9	1,774	21.4	7.9
Preferential access	4,487.5	41.5	6,307	76.1	33.1
Duty-free preference	4,182.7	38.7	6,291	75.9	33.1
United States					
GSP					
All tariff lines	**160,732.0**	**100.0**	**8,688**	**100.0**	**81.9**
MFN duty-free access	57,070.5	35.5	2,836	32.6	26.7
Preferential access	22,771.2	14.2	3,106	35.8	29.4
Duty-free preference	22,731.1	14.1	3,106	35.8	29.4
LDC					
All tariff lines	**9,691.8**	**100.0**	**8,688**	**100.0**	**13.0**
MFN duty-free access	413.4	4.3	2,836	32.6	3.6
Preferential access	5,006.6	51.7	4,215	48.5	3.6
Duty-free preference	5,006.6	51.7	4,215	48.5	3.6
African Growth and Opportunity Act					
All tariff lines	**18,018.1**	**100.0**	**8,688**	**100.0**	**27.8**
MFN duty-free access	3,470.1	19.3	2,836	32.6	9.7
Preferential access	14,457.1	80.2	4,900	56.4	15.0
Duty-free preference	14,457.1	80.2	4,900	56.4	15.0

(Table continues on the following page.)

**TABLE 7.C.1   Nonreciprocal Schemes in Selected Markets:
Nonagricultural Products, 2003 (*Continued*)**

Type of scheme	Imports		Number of national tariff lines		
	Value (US$ million)	Share (%)	Number	Share (%)	With trade (%)
Andean Trade Preference Act and Andean Trade Promotion and Drug Eradication Act					
All tariff lines	**9,077.8**	**100.0**	**8,688**	**100.0**	**26.3**
MFN duty-free access	2,505.2	27.6	2,836	32.6	8.5
Preferential access	5,347.6	58.9	4,559	52.5	11.8
Duty-free preference	5,347.6	58.9	4,559	52.5	11.8
Caribbean Basin Economic Recovery Act					
All tariff lines	**20,615.4**	**100.0**	**8,688**	**100.0**	**28.7**
MFN duty-free access	6,114.5	29.7	2,836	32.6	10.8
Preferential access	2,587.6	12.6	4,668	53.7	13.0
Duty-free preference	2,549.5	12.4	4,618	53.2	12.6
Japan					
GSP					
All tariff lines	**159,684.1**	**100.0**	**7,438**	**100.0**	**77.6**
MFN duty-free access	109,728.6	68.7	2,888	38.8	32.3
Preferential access	20,513.4	12.9	3,087	41.5	29.3
Duty-free preference	13,274.4	8.3	2,008	27.0	20.5
LDC					
All tariff lines	**1,387.0**	**100.0**	**7,438**	**100.0**	**8.8**
MFN duty-free access	818.4	59.0	2,888	38.8	3.4
Preferential access	449.4	32.4	4,143	55.7	4.7
Duty-free preference	449.4	32.4	4,141	55.7	4.7

Source: Authors' calculations.

*Table 7.C.2: Imports of Nonagricultural Products from
Preference Beneficiaries by Type of Market Access, 2003*

Tables 7.C.2 presents disaggregated data for individual preference-receiving developing countries; it indicates the shares of nonagricultural imports from developing countries that are preference beneficiaries into the five reporter markets by different kinds of tariff treatments. The first columns of the table show the value of imports into the reporter market concerned, the share of total bilateral exports

TABLE 7.C.2 Imports of Nonagricultural Products from Preference Beneficiaries, by Type of Market Access, 2003

		Quad markets + Australia					
		Imports (% of total bilateral imports)			Average share of tariff lines with trade (%)		
Beneficiary	Bilateral imports (US$ million) (1)	MFN duty-free access (2)	MFN dutiable access (3)	Preferential access (4)	MFN duty-free access (5)	MFN dutiable access (6)	Preferential access (7)
Developing							
Albania	184	30	2	68	0.50	0.14	0.86
Antigua and Barbuda	416	81	0	19	0.14	0.00	0.10
Argentina	5,055	30	37	32	3.68	2.18	4.00
Armenia	202	66	6	27	0.29	0.17	0.23
Bahrain	770	20	38	42	0.56	0.36	0.70
Barbados	39	54	0	45	0.42	0.03	0.30
Belize	84	70	7	23	0.23	0.06	0.16
Bolivia	233	49	16	35	0.52	0.43	0.48
Botswana	1,712	98	0	2	0.22	0.03	0.13
Brazil	28,711	52	24	23	8.98	5.61	8.06
Brunei Darussalam	2,579	88	12	0	0.25	0.31	0.13
Cameroon	1,534	79	1	20	0.64	0.11	0.65
China	343,804	46	40	14	24.86	27.40	11.78
Colombia	6,361	40	9	51	2.33	1.54	2.61
Congo, Rep. of	731	47	0	53	0.39	0.00	0.24
Côte d'Ivoire	778	62	0	37	0.58	0.04	0.64

(Table continues on the following page.)

TABLE 7.C.2 Imports of Nonagricultural Products from Preference Beneficiaries, by Type of Market Access, 2003 (Continued)

| Beneficiary | Bilateral imports (US$ million) (1) | Quad markets + Australia | | | | | |
| | | Imports (% of total bilateral imports) | | | Average share of tariff lines with trade (%) | | |
		MFN duty-free access (2)	MFN dutiable access (3)	Preferential access (4)	MFN duty-free access (5)	MFN dutiable access (6)	Preferential access (7)
Cuba	362	77	6	16	0.54	0.07	0.44
Dominica	18	13	22	64	0.13	0.06	0.07
Dominican Republic	4,135	23	1	76	1.64	0.61	1.78
Ecuador	2,496	19	6	75	1.49	0.52	1.16
Egypt, Arab Rep. of	4,189	31	26	43	1.81	1.32	3.05
El Salvador	1,917	3	3	93	0.63	0.54	0.82
Gabon	1,934	27	0	73	0.43	0.00	0.26
Georgia	335	35	51	14	0.54	0.11	0.24
Ghana	647	46	1	54	0.78	0.11	0.62
Grenada	7	50	0	50	0.07	0.09	0.03
Guatemala	2,244	5	2	93	0.81	0.54	1.17
Guyana	294	93	0	7	0.40	0.02	0.18
Honduras	3,136	9	2	89	0.70	0.51	0.77
Hong Kong, China	20,332	46	52	0	11.79	21.17	1.47
India	29,057	31	28	41	12.07	12.36	10.65
Indonesia	37,349	57	22	21	8.68	7.86	7.44
Jamaica	740	44	0	56	0.52	0.06	0.35

Kenya	335	18	2	80	0.79	0.15	0.97
Korea, Rep. of	84,674	53	45	2	16.36	29.67	2.08
Kuwait	8,591	68	25	7	0.64	0.26	0.54
Kyrgyz Republic	49	65	20	16	0.12	0.13	0.09
Macao, China	2,200	2	86	12	0.77	2.69	0.53
Malaysia	54,093	80	13	7	10.02	8.39	5.89
Mauritius	1,125	6	1	92	0.77	0.40	1.53
Moldova	183	5	59	36	0.27	0.35	0.57
Mongolia	209	1	94	5	0.21	0.50	0.17
Namibia	615	39	1	60	0.40	0.05	0.39
Nicaragua	665	18	1	82	0.35	0.16	0.38
Nigeria	17,398	40	4	56	0.79	0.04	0.81
Oman	3,216	82	15	3	0.55	0.41	0.60
Pakistan	5,922	3	45	51	2.20	4.02	3.44
Panama	531	64	21	15	0.93	0.14	0.77
Paraguay	95	65	8	27	0.29	0.12	0.30
Peru	4,753	64	13	24	1.82	1.60	1.98
Philippines	23,065	75	12	13	7.22	4.52	5.12
Qatar	7,242	90	9	1	0.53	0.20	0.53
Sri Lanka	3,286	14	51	35	1.73	2.45	2.26
St. Kitts and Nevis	50	35	1	63	0.22	0.01	0.16
St. Lucia	13	25	0	75	0.15	0.01	0.16
St. Vincent and the Grenadines	47	94	0	6	0.07	0.01	0.04
Suriname	341	71	4	25	0.32	0.01	0.20
Swaziland	173	9	3	88	0.37	0.03	0.29
Taiwan, China	70,460	65	35	0	17.42	32.42	0.31
Thailand	37,574	53	21	26	11.19	9.77	8.86

(Table continues on the following page.)

TABLE 7.C.2 Imports of Nonagricultural Products from Preference Beneficiaries, by Type of Market Access, 2003 (*Continued*)

Beneficiary	Bilateral imports (US$ million) (1)	Quad markets + Australia						
		Imports (% of total bilateral imports)			Average share of tariff lines with trade (%)			
		MFN duty-free access (2)	MFN dutiable access (3)	Preferential access (4)	MFN duty-free access (5)	MFN dutiable access (6)	Preferential access (7)	
Trinidad and Tobago	4,796	58	1	41	0.71	0.04	0.55	
United Arab Emirates	19,673	84	8	8	2.77	2.08	3.34	
Uruguay	511	38	20	42	1.02	0.51	0.91	
Venezuela, R.B. de	16,611	41	53	6	1.79	0.56	1.55	
Zimbabwe	321	28	2	70	0.48	0.21	0.46	
Developing total	**871,202**	**52.1**	**31.8**	**15.9**	**n.a.**	**n.a.**	**n.a.**	
LDC								
Angola	5,361	26	0	74	0.38	0.01	0.27	
Bangladesh	6,460	3	30	67	0.69	0.81	2.15	
Benin	11	34	1	65	0.13	0.01	0.11	
Burkina Faso	16	32	0	67	0.21	0.01	0.18	
Burundi	3	71	0	29	0.05	0.00	0.03	
Cambodia	1,962	0	64	36	0.30	0.49	0.99	
Central African Republic	98	97	0	3	0.10	0.00	0.05	
Chad	22	3	0	97	0.06	0.00	0.06	
Congo, Dem. Rep. of	970	86	0	14	0.30	0.00	0.15	

Djibouti	4	82	0	18	0.07	0.00	0.06
Gambia, The	3	16	1	83	0.10	0.01	0.11
Guinea	474	88	0	12	0.24	0.01	0.18
Guinea-Bissau	8	30	0	70	0.03	0.00	0.03
Haiti	330	2	0	98	0.28	0.01	0.43
Lesotho	406	1	0	99	0.03	0.00	0.19
Madagascar	594	4	0	95	0.51	0.06	1.10
Malawi	25	4	0	96	0.10	0.00	0.09
Maldives	138	1	79	21	0.09	0.12	0.18
Mali	13	44	1	55	0.30	0.03	0.27
Mauritania	406	50	0	49	0.26	0.01	0.32
Mozambique	640	2	0	98	0.20	0.00	0.15
Myanmar	844	14	31	55	0.52	0.78	0.75
Nepal	276	4	57	23	0.49	0.56	1.39
Niger	13	77	1	22	0.28	0.01	0.20
Rwanda	8	88	0	12	0.08	0.00	0.06
Senegal	297	9	1	90	0.55	0.03	0.68
Sierra Leone	121	87	0	13	0.41	0.00	0.58
Solomon Islands	22	39	30	31	0.14	0.02	0.02
Tanzania	656	75	0	25	0.50	0.01	0.33
Togo	39	61	0	39	0.21	0.02	0.19
Uganda	102	24	0	76	0.33	0.00	0.27
Zambia	113	60	0	40	0.26	0.01	0.19
LDC total	**20,436**	**20.2**	**18.3**	**61.2**	**n.a.**	**n.a.**	**n.a.**
Total	**891,638**	**51.4**	**31.5**	**17.0**	**n.a.**	**n.a.**	**n.a.**

Source: Authors' calculations.

Note: n.a. = not applicable.

for each developing country listed that is duty free, the share of MFN dutiable imports that pay duty, and the share of total imports that benefit from preferences (reciprocal and nonreciprocal), whether at zero duty or a positive duty. For example, 52 percent of Brazil's exports of nonagricultural products enter the five reporter markets MFN duty free. A further 24 percent attract a positive MFN duty, and 23 percent enjoy a preference. Table 7.C.2 also provides statistics expressed in terms of tariff lines rather than import values using the same type of breakdowns. This information shows how narrow the export base is for many countries, especially LDCs.

An important difference between tables 7.C.1 and 7.C.2 is that in table 7.C.2 the preference data refer to all non-MFN trade—that is, both nonreciprocal and reciprocal preferential trade—whereas the data in table 7.C.1 relate only to specific nonreciprocal preference schemes.

Table 7.C.3: Weighted Duty Margins, Nonagricultural Products, 2003

Table 7.C.3 presents weighted preference margins for nonagricultural products, detailed by preference-receiving countries and by markets. There is a preference margin if the duty applied to a beneficiary of a preferential scheme is lower than the MFN statutory applied duty. The margin is calculated as the difference between those two duties and then weighted for bilateral trade. Note that, for the sake of simplification, MFN statutory duties have been applied to countries that are not part of WTO; hence, general duties for Japan and the United States have not been used.

Columns 1 to 6 report preference margins for each individual country in the five markets. For example, in the case of Jamaica, the table indicates that the average preference margin, weighted by imports flows of all nonagricultural products, is 5 percent.

In columns 7 to 12, the values for preference margins have been adjusted to take account of all MFN and better-than-MFN exports to the reporter economies that compete in these markets with each of the countries listed in the table. For a particular country and tariff line, the adjusted preference margin has been defined as the difference between the trade-weighted average of the best duties that all other countries would benefit from (calculated on the basis of bilateral imports) and the best duty of the specific country.[33] For example, Jamaica's preferential margin for all exports products expressed in terms of all exports to the five reporter markets has fallen from 5 percentage points before the adjustment to 2 percentage points. Some countries have a

(*Text continues on p. 262.*)

TABLE 7.C.3 Weighted Duty Margins: Nonagricultural Products, 2003

Beneficiary	Weighted preference margins						Adjusted weighted preference margin						Adjusted weighted preference margin, further adjusted for competitors and utilization
	Quad markets + Australia (1)	Australia (2)	Canada (3)	EU (4)	Japan (5)	United States (6)	Quad markets + Australia (7)	Australia (8)	Canada (9)	EU (10)	Japan (11)	United States (12)	United States (13)
Developing													
Albania	5	0	0	5	0	2	1	0	−1	2	0	1	2
Antigua and Barbuda	0		0	0	4	2	0		0	0	3	2	0
Argentina	1	0	0	3	0	0	0	0	0	0	0	0	0
Armenia	1	0	0	1	0	4	0	0	−4	0	0	1	1
Bahrain	1	0	0	3	0	1	−2	0	−3	−1	0	−4	−3
Barbados	1	0	1	2	0	1	1	0	0	1	0	0	0
Belize	3	1	1	1	0	3	2	0	−1	0	0	2	1
Bolivia	2	1	0	1	0	2	0	0	0	0	0	0	0
Botswana	0	3	0	0	0	12	0	3	0	0	0	7	8
Brazil	1	1	1	1	0	1	0	0	−1	0	0	0	0

(Table continues on the following page.)

TABLE 7.C.3 Weighted Duty Margins: Nonagricultural Products, 2003 (Continued)

Beneficiary	Weighted preference margins						Adjusted weighted preference margin						Adjusted weighted preference margin, further adjusted for competitors and utilization
	Quad markets + Australia (1)	Australia (2)	Canada (3)	EU (4)	Japan (5)	United States (6)	Quad markets + Australia (7)	Australia (8)	Canada (9)	EU (10)	Japan (11)	United States (12)	United States (13)
Brunei Darussalam	0	0	0	0	0	0	−1	0	−4	−1	0	−4	−3
Cameroon	1	5	0	1	0	0	0	2	0	0	0	0	0
China	0	0	1	1	1	0	−1	−1	−1	−1	0	−1	−1
Colombia	1	0	0	2	2	1	0	0	−1	0	0	−1	0
Congo, Rep. of	0	5	0	0	0	0	0	1	0	0	0	0	0
Côte d'Ivoire	5	4	0	5	0	0	1	1	0	1	0	0	0
Cuba	1	0	0	4	0	0	0	0	0	−1	0	0	1
Dominica	2	0	3	2	0	4	1	0	−1	1	0	0	2
Dominican Republic	10	0	1	3	2	11	5	0	−2	1	0	6	4
Ecuador	3	0	1	16	0	0	0	0	0	3	0	0	0

Egypt, Arab Rep. of	3	0	0	4	0	0	0	0	−1	1	0	−3	−3
El Salvador	16	0	0	7	0	16	9	0	−5	2	0	9	5
Gabon	1	5	0	2	0	0	0	2	0	0	0	0	0
Georgia	1	0	2	0	2	1	0	0	0	0	1	0	0
Ghana	5	2	0	6	0	2	1	0	0	1	0	1	1
Grenada	4	0	0	7	0	0	1	0	0	−1	0	0	0
Guatemala	15	0	0	8	0	15	10	−1	−4	0	−1	10	2
Guyana	1	0	0	1	0	2	1	0	0	0	0	2	1
Honduras	15	0	0	9	0	15	8	0	−5	2	0	9	7
Hong Kong, China	0	0	0	0	0	0	−2	0	−2	−2	0	−3	−2
India	1	1	0	2	1	1	−1	0	−2	−1	0	0	0
Indonesia	1	1	0	2	0	1	0	0	−1	−1	0	−1	−1
Jamaica	5	0	0	6	0	6	2	0	0	2	0	3	2
Kenya	12	1	0	6	0	17	7	0	−4	1	0	10	11
Korea, Rep. of	0	0	0	0	0	0	−1	0	−2	−2	0	−1	−1
Kuwait	0	0	0	1	0	0	0	0	0	0	0	0	0
Kyrgyz Republic	1	1	0	2	0	0	−1	0	0	−1	−1	−1	−4
Macao, China	0	0	0	1	0	0	−5	−1	−3	−5	−5	−6	−4
Malaysia	0	0	0	1	0	0	0	0	0	0	0	0	0
Mauritius	12	0	0	11	0	16	5	−1	−4	3	5	10	4
Moldova	1	0	0	1	0	0	−2	−8	−2	−1	0	−4	−3
Mongolia	0	0	0	2	0	0	−5	0	−5	−3	0	−5	−4
Namibia	6	0	0	6	0	6	4	0	0	4	0	4	3

(Table continues on the following page.)

TABLE 7.C.3 Weighted Duty Margins: Nonagricultural Products, 2003 (Continued)

Beneficiary	Weighted preference margins						Adjusted weighted preference margin						Adjusted weighted preference margin, further adjusted for competitors and utilization
	Quad markets + Australia (1)	Australia (2)	Canada (3)	EU (4)	Japan (5)	United States (6)	Quad markets + Australia (7)	Australia (8)	Canada (9)	EU (10)	Japan (11)	United States (12)	United States (13)
Nicaragua	14	1	0	6	0	14	7	0	−1	0	0	8	0
Nigeria	0	0	0	0	0	0	0	0	0	0	0	0	0
Oman	0	0	0	3	0	0	0	0	−4	−1	0	−2	−1
Pakistan	5	0	1	9	1	0	0	−1	−5	4	0	−3	−2
Panama	1	0	1	2	0	1	0	−5	−2	0	0	0	0
Paraguay	1	0	0	1	1	1	0	0	0	0	0	−1	0
Peru	1	0	1	1	0	1	0	0	0	0	0	−1	−1
Philippines	0	0	0	1	0	1	0	0	0	0	0	−1	−1
Qatar	0	0	0	1	0	0	0	0	0	0	0	−2	−2
Sri Lanka	1	0	1	2	1	0	−3	0	−3	−3	0	−4	−3
St. Kitts and Nevis	2	0	2	3	0	2	1		1	1		1	1

St. Lucia	6	0	0	3	1	6	4		−1	1	0	4	0
St. Vincent and the Grenadines	0	0	0	0	0	4	0	−2	0	0	0	2	2
Suriname	2	0	0	3	0	0	0	0	0	1	0	0	0
Swaziland	17	0	1	3	0	18	10	0	−1	1	0	11	12
Taiwan, China	0	1	0	0	0	0	−1	0	−2	−1	0	−1	−1
Thailand	1	0	1	1	0	1	0	0	−1	−1	0	0	0
Trinidad and Tobago	1	0	2	4	0	1	0	0	0	1	0	0	0
United Arab Emirates	0	0	1	2	0	0	0	0	−2	0	0	0	
Uruguay	1	0	1	2	0	1	0	−1	0	0	0	0	−1
Venezuela, R.B. de	0	3	0	1	0	0	0	1	0	0	0	0	0
Zimbabwe	3	0	0	3	4	3	1	0	0	0	2	0	0
Developing total	**0.7**	**0.3**	**0.7**	**1.1**	**0.3**	**0.6**	**−0.51**	**−0.40**	**−1.30**	**−0.95**	**0.15**	**−0.46**	
LDC													
Angola	0	1	0	0	0	0	0	0	0	0	0	0	0
Bangladesh	9	3	17	12	46	0	2	3	13	4	10	−4	−3
Benin	5		7	5	0	0	1		0	1	0	0	0
Burkina Faso	2	5	1	2	3	1	0	4	0	0	2	0	0
Burundi	1		11	1	3	0	0		9	0	3	0	0
Cambodia	13	12	18	12	202	0	1	11	14	5	50	−5	−4
Central African Republic	0		1	0	0	0	0		0	0	0	0	0

(Table continues on the following page.)

TABLE 7.C.3 Weighted Duty Margins: Nonagricultural Products, 2003 (Continued)

Beneficiary	Weighted preference margins						Adjusted weighted preference margin						Adjusted weighted preference margin, further adjusted for competitors and utilization
	Quad markets + Australia (1)	Australia (2)	Canada (3)	EU (4)	Japan (5)	United States (6)	Quad markets + Australia (7)	Australia (8)	Canada (9)	EU (10)	Japan (11)	United States (12)	United States (13)
Chad	1	15	0	4		0	0	14	0	2		0	0
Congo, Dem. Rep. of	0	15	5	0	0	0	0	14	0	0	0	0	0
Djibouti	1		0	1	0	0	1	6	0	1	0	0	0
Gambia	10		1	11	0	1	3		0	4	0	1	0
Guinea	1	8	0	1	3	0	0		0	0	2	0	0
Guinea-Bissau	8			10	7	0	2			3	4	0	0
Haiti	18	25	14	8	6	19	10	24	9	2	6	10	7
Lesotho	19	15	18	3	10	19	11	14	13	1	10	11	13
Madagascar	14	0	16	13	1	16	6	0	12	4	1	10	11
Malawi	19		16	1	2	20	12		11	1	1	12	14
Maldives	4	8	17	19	1	0	-2	7	12	6	0	-5	-5

Mali	2	0	1	2	2	2	1	0	0	1	1	1	1
Mauritania	5	1	2	4	7	2	2	1	1	1	5	1	0
Mozambique	6	0	0	7	1	17	3	0	0	3	1	7	8
Myanmar	12	1	0	10	51	0	2	1	−2	4	9	−4	−3
Nepal	2	6	12	8	5	0	−2	5	8	4	3	−5	−3
Niger	1	3	3	1	0	1	0	2	1	0	0	1	0
Rwanda	1		1	1	0	0	0		0	0	0	1	0
Senegal	11	1	1	12	5	0	3	0	1	3	3	0	0
Sierra Leone	1	5	4	1	3	3	0	3	2	0	3	2	0
Solomon Islands	3	1	0	2	3	1	2	0	0	2	2	1	0
Tanzania	2	1	1	3	0	1	0	1	0	0	0	1	1
Togo	3	0	5	4	3	0	1	0	0	2	3	0	0
Uganda	7	0	1	7	3	6		0	0	1	3	3	3
Zambia		2	3	1	2	0	1	2	2	0	0	0	0
LDC total	**6.4**	**2.3**	**14.8**	**7.4**	**41.9**	**2.1**	**1.6**	**2.1**	**11.3**	**2.6**	**10.2**	**−0.7**	
Total	**0.8**	**0.3**	**0.9**	**1.4**	**0.5**	**0.7**	**−0.5**	**−0.4**	**−1.1**	**−0.8**	**0.2**	**−0.5**	

Source: Authors' calculations.

Note: Weighted by bilateral imports.

negative preference margin, because other competitors benefit, on average, from more favorable preferential schemes.

Column 13 provides an indication of the effects on the value of preference margins of factoring in preference utilization rates for the United States.[34] It shows the overall preference margin after adjustments have been made for best-duty treatment of all competitors in the U.S. market. It should be noted at the outset that part of the underutilization of preferences recorded in the table reflects an initial overestimate of the value of preferences. In the case of clothing, it was assumed that all lines (chapters 61 and 62) received duty-free treatment under AGOA and the CBTPA.

Table 7.C.4: Impact of MFN Tariff Reduction for Nonagricultural Market Access on Preference Value and Scope for Future Preferences, 2003

Table 7.C.4 reports the change in the value of the preference of a MFN liberalization scenario.[35] For simulation purposes, a Swiss formula with a coefficient of 10 has been applied: $t_1 = (t_0 \times 10)/(t_0 + 10)$ on 2003 MFN applied rates. Note that the Swiss formula implies that the higher the initial tariff (t_0) is, the higher the cut will be. All new tariffs (t_1) will be lower than 10.

Columns 1 and 2 of table 7.C.4 show what MFN liberalization has done to the value of average preference margins before any adjustment is made for competing non-MFN trade. Columns 3 and 4 show the effects of the MFN cut with adjustments for competing MFN trade in the five reporter markets. Negative numbers are reduced after adjustment; for example, Namibia's US$19.7 million (shown in the first column as the amount by which Namibia would lose overall from preference erosion) is reduced to US$10.7 million. Hence, Namibia suffers preference erosion to the value of some US$10.7 million in the five reporter economies according to the simulations.

Table 7.C.5: Impact of Swiss Formula Cut on Preferences by Selected Countries, 2003

Table 7.C.5 provides details of some broad product categories (MTN categories) in nonagricultural products for selected countries, on the basis of calculations of "adjusted" preference erosion. The imports share in terms of all imported products (agricultural and nonagricultural) is shown first, followed by the adjusted preferential margin before and after the cut, using the same Swiss formula as for table 7.C.4.

(*Text continues on p. 272.*)

TABLE 7.C.4 Effect of Nonagricultural Market Access MFN Tariff Reduction on Preference Value and Scope for Future Preferences, 2003

	Quad markets + Australia					
	Change in the preference value for unadjusted and adjusted preference margin				Scope for additional preferences (US$ million) (5)	Total exports to Quad markets + Australia (%) (6)
	No adjustment		With adjustment			
Beneficiary	US $ million (1)	% of imports (2)	US $ million (3)	% of imports (4)		
Developing						
Albania	−4.0	−1.9	−1.2	−0.6	0	46
Antigua and Barbuda	−0.3	−0.1	0.0	0.0	0	100[a]
Argentina	−40.6	−0.4	0.3	0.0	51	35
Armenia	−1.1	−0.5	0.1	0.0	1	30
Bahrain	−5.0	−0.7	8.3	1.1	20	12
Barbados	−0.2	−0.2	−0.1	−0.1	0	40
Belize	−1.3	−0.7	−0.7	−0.3	0	98
Bolivia	−1.5	−0.5	0.8	0.3	2	19
Botswana	−1.7	−0.1	−0.8	0.0	0	61
Brazil	−100.3	−0.2	7.3	0.0	228	55
Brunei Darussalam	−0.1	0.0	8.5	0.3	14	62
Cameroon	−2.8	−0.1	−1.0	0.0	1	96
China	−810.3	−0.2	1,274.6	0.4	5,930	80
Colombia	−28.7	−0.3	19.5	0.2	36	70

(Table continues on the following page.)

263

TABLE 7.C.4 Effect of Nonagricultural Market Access MFN Tariff Reduction on Preference Value and Scope for Future Preferences, 2003 (Continued)

Beneficiary	Quad markets + Australia					
	Change in the preference value for unadjusted and adjusted preference margin				Scope for additional preferences (US$ million) (5)	Total exports to Quad markets + Australia (%) (6)
	No adjustment		With adjustment			
	US $ million (1)	% of imports (2)	US $ million (3)	% of imports (4)		
Congo, Rep. of	−0.4	0.0	0.0	0.0	0	30
Côte d'Ivoire	−25.3	−0.7	−6.0	−0.2	0	59
Cuba	−3.2	−0.5	−0.4	−0.1	2	39
Dominica	−0.1	−0.3	0.0	−0.1	0	75
Dominican Republic	−262.4	−5.5	−139.2	−2.9	3	88
Ecuador	−43.7	−1.1	−6.8	−0.2	12	68
Egypt, Arab Rep. of	−49.4	−1.1	5.8	0.1	42	75
El Salvador	−193.3	−9.1	−110.5	−5.2	4	67
Gabon	−3.5	−0.2	−0.5	0.0	0	68
Georgia	−0.7	−0.2	−0.1	0.0	5	79
Ghana	−19.9	−1.4	−4.4	−0.3	0	59
Grenada	−0.1	−0.6	0.0	−0.1	0	59
Guatemala	−220.5	−6.5	−141.7	−4.2	4	100[a]
Guyana	−1.6	−0.3	−1.0	−0.2	0	88

Country						
Honduras	−303.2	−8.3	−167.0	−4.6	4	100[a]
Hong Kong, China	−2.4	0.0	264.2	1.3	505	9
India	−226.7	−0.7	94.8	0.3	569	55
Indonesia	−159.1	−0.4	105.9	0.3	527	65
Jamaica	−17.8	−1.7	−6.4	−0.6	0	91
Kenya	−26.4	−2.2	−14.0	−1.2	0	49
Korea, Rep. of	−19.5	0.0	382.3	0.4	1,292	44
Kuwait	−9.7	−0.1	1.4	0.0	54	42
Kyrgyz Republic	−0.2	−0.3	0.4	0.7	1	9
Macao, China	−8.7	−0.4	72.6	3.3	123	85
Malaysia	−70.1	−0.1	46.6	0.1	303	53
Mauritius	−81.9	−5.6	−31.0	−2.1	1	77
Moldova	−1.5	−0.6	1.5	0.6	5	31
Mongolia	−0.2	−0.1	6.9	3.0	12	37
Namibia	−19.7	−2.9	−10.7	−1.6	0	53
Nicaragua	−59.2	−6.7	−31.1	−3.5	1	100[a]
Nigeria	−6.6	0.0	−1.3	0.0	5	90
Oman	−3.3	−0.1	5.7	0.2	12	28
Pakistan	−139.7	−2.2	3.3	0.1	138	52
Panama	−3.9	−0.5	−0.4	−0.1	4	94
Paraguay	−0.3	−0.1	0.1	0.0	0	33
Peru	−14.9	−0.3	17.2	0.3	36	61
Philippines	−46.9	−0.2	66.0	0.3	188	66
Qatar	−2.1	0.0	3.0	0.0	19	55

(Table continues on the following page.)

TABLE 7.C.4 Effect of Nonagricultural Market Access MFN Tariff Reduction on Preference Value and Scope for Future Preferences, 2003 (Continued)

| Beneficiary | Change in the preference value for unadjusted and adjusted preference margin | | | | Quad markets + Australia | |
| | No adjustment | | With adjustment | | | |
	US $ million (1)	% of imports (2)	US $ million (3)	% of imports (4)	Scope for additional preferences (US$ million) (5)	Total exports to Quad markets + Australia (%) (6)
Sri Lanka	−22.3	−0.6	56.7	1.6	137	69
St. Kitts and Nevis	−0.2	−0.4	−0.1	−0.1	0	100[a]
St. Lucia	−0.4	−1.1	−0.3	−0.7	0	95
St. Vincent and the Grenadines	−0.1	−0.1	0.0	0.0	0	100[a]
Suriname	−2.4	−0.7	−0.2	−0.1	0	55
Swaziland	−19.2	−5.8	−11.9	−3.6	0	23
Taiwan, China	−6.0	0.0	245.2	0.3	797	47
Thailand	−182.5	−0.4	69.2	0.2	502	51
Trinidad and Tobago	−15.8	−0.3	−2.8	−0.1	1	94
United Arab Emirates	−21.7	−0.1	13.3	0.1	78	30
Uruguay	−4.1	−0.4	−0.2	0.0	7	46
Venezuela, R.B. de	−22.6	−0.1	−3.7	0.0	33	70
Zimbabwe	−5.5	−0.7	−1.9	−0.3	4	62
Developing total	**−3,348.9**	**−0.4**	**2,087.1**	**0.2**	**11,718.5**	**53.5**

LDC						
Angola	52	0	0.0	−0.3	0.0	−0.9
Bangladesh	93	111	−1.0	−61.6	−5.2	−335.2
Benin	7	0	−0.1	0.0	−0.7	−0.3
Burkina Faso	17	0	0.0	0.0	−0.1	−0.1
Burundi	81	0	0.0	0.0	0.0	0.0
Cambodia	96	74	−1.0	−18.8	−11.0	−215.6
Central African Republic	87	0	0.0	0.0	0.0	0.0
Chad	15	0	0.0	0.0	−0.1	−0.1
Congo, Dem. Rep. of		0	0.0	0.0	0.0	−0.1
Djibouti	6	0	−0.2	0.0	−0.3	0.0
Gambia	80	0	−0.4	0.0	−1.8	−0.2
Guinea	84	0	0.0	−0.2	−0.4	−2.1
Guinea-Bissau	15	0	−0.5	0.0	−3.2	−0.3
Haiti	100[a]	0	−6.1	−21.7	−11.3	−40.3
Lesotho	85	0	−7.4	−30.1	−12.2	−49.6
Madagascar	100[a]	0	−2.0	−19.1	−5.0	−48.7
Malawi	70	0	−0.6	−2.0	−1.0	−3.3
Maldives	91	5	1.1	1.6	−2.5	−3.5
Mali	6	0	−0.1	0.0	−0.1	−0.1
Mauritania	100[a]	0	−0.4	−1.7	−2.3	−9.3
Mozambique	81	0	−0.8	−5.5	−2.5	−17.1
Myanmar	35	15	−1.0	−8.3	−9.1	−79.7
Nepal	43	10	1.3	3.8	−0.9	−2.6
Niger	5	0	−0.1	0.0	−0.2	0.0

(Table continues on the following page.)

TABLE 7.C.4 Effect of Nonagricultural Market Access MFN Tariff Reduction on Preference Value and Scope for Future Preferences, 2003 (Continued)

Beneficiary	Change in the preference value for unadjusted and adjusted preference margin				Quad markets + Australia	
	No adjustment		With adjustment		Scope for additional preferences (US$ million) (5)	Total exports to Quad markets + Australia (%) (6)
	US $ million (1)	% of imports (2)	US $ million (3)	% of imports (4)		
Rwanda	0.0	−0.2	0.0	−0.1	0	39
Senegal	−19.3	−4.9	−3.6	−0.9	0	30
Sierra Leone	−0.6	−0.4	−0.2	−0.2	0	100[a]
Solomon Islands	−0.3	−1.2	−0.1	−0.5	0	32
Tanzania	−7.2	−0.9	−1.2	−0.1	0	67
Togo	−0.6	−0.7	−0.2	−0.2	0	13
Uganda	−3.3	−1.0	−0.7	−0.2	0	57
Zambia	−0.4	−0.2	0.0	0.0	0	21
LDC total	**−840.5**	**−3.8**	**−170.3**	**−0.8**	**216.6**	**61.6**

Source: Authors' calculations.

Note: Swiss formula cut with $a = 10$ applied on 2003 MFN applied rates.

a. Imports from beneficiaries into the Quad markets and Australia are greater than exports to world because of inconsistencies in data reporting.

TABLE 7.C.5 Effect of Swiss Formula Cut on Preference Margins: Selected Countries, 2003

| | Quad markets + Australia | | | | | | | | | | | | | | | |
| | Developing countries | | | | | | | | | | | LDCs | | | | |
MTN	Dominican Republic	Honduras	Kenya	Mauritius	St. Lucia	El Salvador	Fiji	Guatemala	Namibia	Nicaragua	Swaziland	Bangladesh	Cambodia	Haiti	Lesotho	Madagascar
02a: Clothing																
Import share	44.2	72.2	16.1	61.3	7.6	82.9	30.7	52.8	6.2	55.4	42.3	83.8	90.0	85.1	98.6	33.6
Preference margin adjustment	9.3	9.6	10.8	5.5	12.9	9.7	7.0	12.0	10.6	9.8	12.4	1.9	−2.2	10.5	11.4	8.5
Preference margin adjustment after cut	3.2	3.3	3.7	2.4	4.3	3.4	1.7	4.1	3.9	3.4	4.0	1.1	−0.6	3.5	3.9	3.4
02b: Textiles																
Import share	5.0	0.5	0.7	0.9	2.4	2.1	1.0	0.5	0.1	0.1	2.6	6.2	1.2	2.1	0.0	1.2
Preference margin adjustment	1.0	0.1	0.6	1.9	3.2	−0.6	6.1	−0.3	2.0	3.6	2.0	1.5	−0.2	8.0	4.8	2.3
Preference margin adjustment after cut	0.6	0.2	0.4	1.2	2.3	−0.4	3.7	−0.1	1.2	1.7	1.5	0.7	−0.1	3.4	2.8	1.4
03: Leather, rubber, footwear, and travel goods																
Import share	2.2	0.0	0.5	0.1	0.2	0.5	1.5	0.8	1.0	0.2	0.0	2.3	8.0	0.6	0.0	0.1
Preference margin adjustment	9.1	0.7	0.5	3.1	0.5	7.6	13.8	1.9	0.3	0.2	2.1	10.7	32.5	1.0	13.2	2.7

(Table continues on the following page.)

269

TABLE 7.C.5 Effect of Swiss Formula Cut on Preference Margins: Selected Countries, 2003 (Continued)

| | Quad markets + Australia | | | | | | | | | | | | | | | |
| | Developing countries | | | | | | | | | | | LDCs | | | | |
MTN	Dominican Republic	Honduras	Kenya	Mauritius	St. Lucia	El Salvador	Fiji	Guatemala	Namibia	Nicaragua	Swaziland	Bangladesh	Cambodia	Haiti	Lesotho	Madagascar
Preference margin adjustment after cut	3.6	0.2	0.2	1.7	0.2	4.1	5.5	1.4	0.2	0.1	1.5	3.0	3.4	0.6	5.5	1.9
08: Electric machinery																
Import share	9.1	2.8	1.5	1.0	19.7	1.6	0.5	0.1	0.1	4.5	0.6	0.1	0.0	1.6	0.0	0.2
Preference margin adjustment	1.0	0.4	0.1	0.1	1.0	0.1	3.9	0.6	0.3	0.3	0.1	0.5	0.5	0.8	0.0	0.3
Preference margin adjustment after cut	0.7	0.3	0.1	0.1	0.8	0.0	2.5	0.4	0.3	0.2	0.1	0.4	0.4	0.6	0.0	0.3
09: Mineral products, precious stones, and metals																
Import share	6.3	1.9	1.6	3.9	0.1	0.0	9.3	1.3	21.3	4.8	0.0	0.9	0.2	0.2	1.1	1.3
Preference margin adjustment	1.8	0.0	0.5	0.6	2.6	1.8	0.0	1.6	0.0	0.5	9.0	2.9	2.4	17.9	0.0	0.2

Preference margin adjustment after cut	1.1	0.0	0.3	0.4	1.7	1.2	0.0	1.0	0.0	0.3	3.4	1.5	1.6	4.8	0.0	0.1
10: Manufactured articles not elsewhere specified																
Import share	10.6	0.5	0.8	2.4	1.4	0.7	0.2	1.1	0.2	0.0	0.8	0.4	0.1	1.0	0.0	1.3
Preference margin adjustment	0.1	1.9	1.6	1.7	0.1	0.5	1.5	0.6	0.3	0.6	0.8	1.2	0.3	1.3	1.4	0.9
Preference margin adjustment after cut	0.1	1.3	1.1	1.3	0.1	0.3	1.0	0.4	0.2	0.4	0.5	0.8	0.2	0.7	1.1	0.7
11: Fish and fish products																
Import share	0.1	5.0	4.8	5.4	0.2	1.0	15.3	2.0	46.8	9.2	0.1	5.0	0.1	1.0	0.0	22.3
Preference margin adjustment	0.1	0.7	1.6	4.0	0.0	1.9	-0.1	-0.3	6.3	0.0	8.6	2.6	0.2	1.7	9.6	3.5
Preference margin adjustment after cut	0.1	0.2	0.8	1.3	0.0	0.7	-0.1	-0.4	3.9	-0.1	4.2	2.3	0.2	1.2	4.8	2.4
Total imports (US$ million)	**4,806**	**3,656**	**1,184**	**1,462**	**38**	**2,113**	**468**	**3,386**	**684**	**880**	**333**	**6,478**	**1,965**	**357**	**406**	**972**

Source: Authors' calculations.

Notes

1. See Resolution 21(ii) of the 1968 UNCTAD II conference for the rationale of preferences.

2. For instance, Borrman, Borrmann, and Steger (1981); Brown (1987, 1989); Grossman and Sykes (2005); Karsenty and Laird (1986); Murray (1977); OECD (1983, 2003); Özden and Reinhardt (2003); Sapir and Lundberg (1984); UNCTAD (1999); WTO (2004).

3. See, for example, TN/MA/W/21, TN/MA/W/22, TN/MA/W/27, TN/MA/W/30, TN/MA/W/31, TN/MA/W/34, TN/MA/W/38, TN/MA/W/39, TN/MA/W/47, and TN/MA/W/53, all of which are available on the WTO Web site, http://www.wto.org.

4. An example of this approach is the submission by Bangladesh on behalf of the LDCs (TN/MA/W/22 of January 8, 2003). This submission calls for improvements in existing preference schemes to ensure duty-free and quota-free access for all LDC exports. It also proposes that other developing countries develop nonpreferential preference schemes.

5. Mauritius, for example, proposes maintaining MFN tariffs above certain levels on a limited range of products (TN/MA/W/21/Add. 1, July 15, 2003). Papua New Guinea suggests that MFN tariff reductions on goods of "vital importance" be implemented over twice the length of time decided for all other products and that implementation of reductions on the former group of products commence only after three years (TN/MA/W/39, July 2, 2003). A submission by Benin on behalf of the ACP states develops a vulnerability index to determine which products should be treated differently in terms of MFN liberalization. The index captures a country's degree of reliance on preferences, the extent of dependency on a few products and a few markets, and the size of an exporter in relation to world trade. Vulnerability according to the index would then lead to the inclusion of a correction coefficient in the overall tariff reduction formula agreed in the negotiations (TN/MA/W/53, March 11, 2005).

6. A submission by Ghana, Kenya, Nigeria, Tanzania, Uganda, Zambia, and Zimbabwe, for example, calls for "a procedure for establishing measures and mechanisms to deal with erosion of preferences, with the aim of avoiding or offsetting this problem or compensating the affected members" (TN/MA/W/27, February 18, 2003).

7. See Document MTN/W/2, October 26, 1973. The authors are grateful to Roy Santana for pointing this document out.

8. Other mitigating action to compensate for preference erosion, such as financial compensation, is not intrinsically limited in this manner.

9. This chapter does not examine the implications of preferences from the perspective of preference-giving countries.

10. See, for example, the experience of Mauritius in Subramanian and Roy (2002).

11. For a review of relevant literature, see Langhammer and Sapir (1987) and Tangermann (2002).

12. That is, assume infinitely elastic export supply from the rest of the world.

13. Although country B's preference margin falls following MFN liberalization, the price received by exporters in country B may still rise, and exports and welfare may increase. The likelihood of this outcome depends on the original margin of preference and on the responsiveness of export supply and import demand. In particular, the price received by the preferred exporter will be greater as the responsiveness of demand for imports in country A to a variation of domestic prices (import demand elasticity) is higher and the responsiveness of the export supply from the rest of the world to export price variations is lower.

14. This possibility can occur if country A is large. Also, in terms of the analytical framework, the assumption of a perfectly elastic supply curve from the rest of the world needs to be relaxed. Rather than a flat supply curve, the supply curve from the rest of the world would be, in this case, positively sloped.

15. The theoretical model for this case is one with heterogeneous firms, as in Melitz (2003).

16. The assessment of the welfare impact of preference erosion becomes even more complex when other markets are taken into account. For example, preference erosion in one market may prove to be positive for the beneficiary country as a whole if preferences encouraged an inefficient allocation of resources by fostering specialization in sectors where the preference-receiving country does not have a comparative advantage.

17. This scenario requires imperfect market conditions.

18. For the developing countries that benefit from both reciprocal and nonreciprocal preferences, this analysis cannot distinguish between the impact of MFN liberalization on the erosion of reciprocal preferences and its impact on the erosion of nonreciprocal preferences. These excluded countries are Bulgaria, Chile, Costa Rica, Croatia, Fiji, Israel, Jordan, the former Yugoslav Republic of Macedonia, Mexico, Morocco, Papua New Guinea, Romania, Singapore, South Africa, Tunisia, and Turkey.

19. Table 7.C.1 in the annexes provides detailed information on the GSP and LDC schemes and on other selected individual nonreciprocal schemes for each of the five preference-giving markets, in terms of both imports and tariff lines.

20. See the earlier discussion of preference margin measures for the definition of *competition-adjusted preference margin* and a discussion on alternative measures of preference value.

21. Recall that the adjustment for competition is made considering all competitors in the same markets, thus including countries that benefit from reciprocal preferences.

22. Table 7.C.2 in the annexes reports data on the percentage of exports to the Quad markets plus Australia that benefit from preferential access or MFN treatment by exporting developing country (beneficiary of exclusively nonreciprocal preferences) or LDC. In addition, for the same set of countries, it reports data on how diversified exports are (measured by the percentage of tariff lines on which the countries export). The figures for the value of the preferences, including the adjustment for competition, for each country are reported in table 7.C.3. Note that the overall figures for developing countries refer to all developing country members of the World Trade Organization.

23. Individual data can be found in column 4 of table 7.C.2 in the annexes.

24. Data for preference margin, adjusted and unadjusted, are reported in table 7.C.3 in the annexes.

25. The Cotonou Agreement is a treaty between the EU and the group of ACP states. It was signed in June 2000 in Cotonou, Benin, by 79 ACP countries and the 15 countries that then constituted the EU. The agreement is aimed at reducing and eventually eradicating poverty, while contributing to sustainable development and to the gradual integration of ACP countries into the world economy.

26. Recent studies focusing on NAFTA (Ansón and others 2005; Cadot, Estevadeordal, and Suwa-Eisenmann 2005; Estevadeordal 2000) show that rules of origin effectively limit Mexico's duty-free access to Canada and the United States. In particular, Ansón and others (2005) estimate total compliance costs for Mexican exporters at 6 percent of the value of preferential exports, of which about a third is due to administrative costs.

27. Carrère and de Melo (2004) show that compliance costs change across different rules of origin. They are lowest for a change in the tariff classification, somewhat higher for regional value content restrictions, and highest for technical requirements. Focusing on Mexican exports to the United States, they find that in some circumstances preference margins of at least 10 percent would be required to offset the cost-raising effect of a typical regional value content rule.

28. OPT is a trading arrangement that allows manufacturers of clothing garments within the EU to take advantage of cheaper production costs outside the EU when quantitative restrictions (quotas) are in place for that country.

29. Cumulation rules indicate the conditions under which a preference beneficiary may combine inputs originating from other countries while maintaining the preferential status of the final product. Three types of cumulation rules can be distinguished: bilateral, diagonal (or regional), and full cumulation. *Bilateral cumulation* implies that the beneficiary can use only domestic inputs and inputs imported from the preference-giving country. *Diagonal cumulation* implies that materials supplied by a specific set of countries can be used, provided that the input processing requirements have been fulfilled. Under *full cumulation*, any input originating from the defined set of countries can be used, regardless of the processing or transformation undertaken.

30. The relevant WTO notification is WT/COMTD/N/15/Add. 1, February 13, 2003.

31. See annex table 10 of WTO document WT/COMTD/LDC/W/35.

32. Exclusions to preferential schemes have been taken into account.

33. The *best duty* for a tariff line is defined as the lowest duty that a country can benefit from. If no ad valorem equivalent is available, the best duty would exclude the non–ad valorem duty. If there is no preference for a particular tariff line, the MFN statutory applied duty is used.

34. In case of unmatched tariff lines between CAMAD data and the utilization data, it is assumed that the preference utilization is zero.

35. The value of preferences of a beneficiary is defined as the bilateral import value multiplied by the preference margin. Overall preference margins are calculated by dividing the value of preferences by the beneficiary's overall bilateral imports.

References

Anderson, James E., and Eric van Wincoop. 2004. "Trade Costs." *Journal of Economic Literature* 42 (3): 691–751.

Ansón, José, and Marc Bacchetta. 2005. "Non-reciprocal Preferences for LDCs in Textile and Clothing." World Trade Organization, Geneva.

Ansón José, Olivier Cadot, Antoni Estevadeordal, Jaime de Melo, Akiko Suwa-Eisenmann, and Bolormaa Tumurchurdur. 2005. "Rules of Origin in North-South Preferential Trading Arrangements with an Application to NAFTA." *Review of International Economics* 13 (3): 501–17.

Bhagwati, Jagdish. 2002. "The Poor's Best Hope." *Economist* (June 22): 24–26.

Borrmann, Axel, Christine Borrmann, and Manfred Stegger. 1981. *The EC's Generalized System of Preferences.* The Hague: Martinus Nijhof.

Brenton, Paul. 2003. "Integrating the Least Developing Countries into the World Trading System: The Current Impact of EU Preferences under Everything but Arms." Policy Research Working Paper 3018, World Bank, Washington, DC.

Brenton, Paul, and Takako Ikezuki. 2006. "Trade Preferences for Africa and the Impact of Rules of Origin." In *The Origin of Goods: Rules of Origin in Regional Trade Agreements*, ed. Olivier Cadot, Antoni Estevadeordal, Akiko Suwa-Eisenmann, and Thierry Verdier, 295–314. New York: Oxford University Press.

Brenton, Paul, and Miriam Manchin. 2003. "Making EU Trade Agreements Work: The Role of Rules of Origin." *World Economy* 26 (5): 755–69.

Brown, Drusilla K. 1987. "General Equilibrium Effects of the U.S. Generalized System of Preferences." *Southern Economic Journal* 54 (1): 27–47.

———. 1989. "Trade and Welfare Effects of the European Schemes of the Generalized System of Preferences." *Economic Development and Cultural Change* 37 (4): 757–76.

Bureau, Jean-Christophe, and Jacques Gallezot. 2004. "Assessment of Utilisation and Motives for Under-utilisation of Preferences in Selected Least Developed Countries." COM/AGR/TD/ WP(2004)12/REV2, Organisation for Economic Co-operation and Development, Paris.

Cadot, Olivier, Antoni Esteovadeordal, and Akiko Suwa-Eisenmann. 2005. "Rules of Origin as Export Subsidies." CEPR Discussion Paper 4999, Centre for Economic Policy Research, London.

Candau, Fabien, Lionel Fontagné, and Sébastien Jean. 2004. "The Utilization Rate of Preferences in the EU." Preliminary draft, presented at the Seventh Global Economic Analysis Conference, Washington, DC, June 17–19.

Candau, Fabien, and Sébastien Jean. 2005. "Are EU Trade Preferences Under-utilised?" CEPII Working Paper 2005-19, Centre d'Études Prospectives et d'Informations Internationales, Paris.

Carrère, Celine, and Jaime de Melo. 2004. "Are Different Rules of Origin Equally Costly? Estimates from NAFTA." CEPR Discussion Paper 4437, Centre for Economic Policy Research, London.

Estevadeordal, Antoni. 2000. "Negotiating Preferential Market Access: The Case of the North America Free Trade Agreement." *Journal of World Trade* 34 (1): 141–66.

Grossman, Gene M., and Alan O. Sykes. 2005. "A Preference for Development: The Law and Economics of GSP." *World Trade Review* 4 (1): 41–67.

Inama, Stefano. 2003. "Trade Preferences and the World Trade Organization Negotiations on Market Access." *Journal of World Trade* 37 (5): 959–76.

Karsenty, Guy, and Sam Laird. 1986. "The Generalized System of Preferences: A Quantitative Assessment of the Direct Trade Effects and of Policy Options." UNCTAD Discussion Paper 18, United Nations Conference on Trade and Development, Geneva.

Krishna, Kala, and Anne O. Krueger. 1995. "Implementing Free Trade Areas: Rules of Origin and Hidden Protection." In *New Directions in Trade Theory*, ed. Alan V. Deardoff, James A. Levinsohn, and Robert M. Stern, 149–87. Ann Arbor: University of Michigan Press.

Krueger, Anne O. 1993. "Free Trade Agreements as Protectionist Devices: Rules of Origin." NBER Working Paper 4352, National Bureau of Economic Research, Cambridge, MA.

Langhammer, Rolf J., and André Sapir. 1987. *Economic Impact of Generalized Tariff Preferences*. London: Trade Policy Research Centre.

Melitz, Mark J. 2003. "The Impact of Trade on Intra-industry Reallocation and Aggregate Industry Productivity." *Econometrica* 71 (6): 1695–725.

Murray, Tracy. 1977. *Trade Preferences for Developing Countries*. New York: John Wiley & Sons.

OECD (Organisation for Economic Co-operation and Development). 1983. *The Generalized System of Preferences: Review of the First Decade*. Paris: OECD.

———. 2003. "The Economic Impact of the Generalised System of Preferences." OECD Trade Committee, Room Document 1, OECD, Paris.

Olarreaga, Marcelo, and Çağlar Özden. 2005. "AGOA and Apparel: Who Captures the Tariff Rent in the Presence of Preferential Market Access." *World Economy* 28 (1): 63–77.

Özden, Çağlar, and Eric Reinhardt. 2003. "The Perversity of Preferences: GSP and Developing Country Trade Policies, 1976–2000." Policy Research Working Paper 2955, World Bank, Washington, DC.

Özden, Çağlar, and Gunjan Sharma. 2004. "Price Effects of Preferential Market Access: The Caribbean Basin Initiative and the Apparel Sector." Policy Research Working Paper 3244, World Bank, Washington, DC.

Sapir, André, and Lars Lundberg. 1984. "The U.S. Generalized System of Preferences and Its Impacts." In *The Structure and Evolution of Recent U.S. Trade Policy*, ed. Robert E. Baldwin and Anne O. Krueger, 195–231. Chicago: University of Chicago Press.

Subramanian, Arvind, and Devesh Roy. 2002. "Who Can Explain the Mauritian Miracle: Meade, Romer, Sachs, or Rodrik?" In *In Search of Prosperity: Analytical Narratives on Economic Growth*, ed. Dani Rodrik, 205–43. Princeton, NJ: Princeton University Press.

Tangermann, Stefan. 2002. *The Future of Preferential Trade Arrangements for Developing Countries and the Current Round of WTO Negotiations on Agriculture*. Rome: Food and Agriculture Organization.

UNCTAD (United Nations Conference on Trade and Development). 1999. "Quantifying the Benefits Obtained by Developing Countries from the Generalized System of Preferences." UNCTAD, Geneva.

WTO (World Trade Organization). 2004. *World Trade Report 2004: Exploring the Linkages between the Domestic Policy Environment and International Trade*. Geneva: WTO.

———. 2008. "Draft Modalities for Nonagricultural Market Access." TN/MA/W/103, WTO, Geneva.

NONRECIPROCAL PREFERENCE EROSION ARISING FROM MOST-FAVORED-NATION LIBERALIZATION IN AGRICULTURE: WHAT ARE THE RISKS?

Patrick Low, Roberta Piermartini, and Jürgen Richtering

As in previous trade rounds, a significant objective of the Doha negotiating agenda is to reduce trade barriers and open up new market opportunities for members of the World Trade Organization (WTO). Unlike in previous rounds, however, concern about the erosion of nonreciprocal preferences has found clear expression in the negotiating positions of dozens of WTO members and in negotiating texts.[1] Over the years, major trading countries have extended nonreciprocal preferences to developing countries through a range of schemes aimed at promoting export growth in beneficiary countries. The schemes have met with varying success.[2] They have clearly been effective enough, however, to give rise to demands from their beneficiaries for something to be done to mitigate or compensate in some way for the loss of competitive advantage that will result from nondiscriminatory (most-favored-nation, or MFN) trade liberalization. These demands have surfaced in the negotiations on trade in agricultural and nonagricultural products.

The paper represents the opinions of the authors and is the product of professional research. It is not meant to represent the position or opinions of the World Trade Organization or its members, nor the official position of any staff members. Any errors are the fault of the authors.

This chapter applies a very similar methodology to that used in chapter 7 to estimate the dimensions of the risk of preference erosion in agriculture. The estimates pertain only to the preference schemes maintained by the so-called Quad members (Canada, the European Union, Japan, and the United States). The data are for 2003. On the basis of tariff-line-level information, "theoretical maxima" estimates are established of nonreciprocal preference erosion in agriculture. The theoretical maximum is taken to be the trade-weighted difference between MFN duties and preferential duties. This estimate is then subject to an adjustment factor. The adjustment recognizes that from the point of view of a nonreciprocal preference beneficiary, competing trade from other preference receivers—of both nonreciprocal and reciprocal preferences—does not face MFN tariff rates. When this competition from other geographic areas is taken into account, it is apparent that risks from preference erosion are lower than if the relevant comparison is made simply with respect to MFN trade. Another adjustment factor that would have further reduced the estimates of preference erosion relates to utilization rates under the various preferential schemes. Data limitations have prevented the inclusion of this element in the estimates. Where nonreciprocal preferences have not been fully used for one reason or another, an exporter is effectively at less risk from preference erosion as a consequence of MFN liberalization.

To focus on the value of nonreciprocal preferences, the chapter reports estimates for those developing countries that receive only nonreciprocal preferences from at least one of the Quad members. In other words, developing countries involved in reciprocal preferential trading arrangements with the Quad economies in 2003 are excluded.[3]

After baseline estimates of adjusted risk from preference erosion are provided, MFN tariff cuts are simulated on the basis of the Group of 20 (G-20) agriculture proposal, in order to gain a sense of what such a scenario would mean by way of preference erosion among recipients of nonreciprocal preferences. This exercise is strictly illustrative, and the choice of the G-20 proposal as the scenario does not imply any judgment as to the desirability of this outcome over any other in the agriculture negotiations. Moreover, simulation techniques are not applied so as to estimate the possible aggregate trade or welfare outcomes arising from MFN liberalization and the resulting erosion of preferences. The calculations estimate the value of potential preference erosion only in terms of margins lost through MFN liberalization, multiplied by the observed trade flows of the countries concerned. This measure approximately indicates the potential loss of economic rent that exporters face following MFN liberalization—that is, the loss in the extra income from which exporters benefited because of preferences. The results show that in net terms some countries lose overall because of reduced preference margins, but others gain as a result of MFN cuts.

Certain observations about the limitations of the analysis are in order. First, like virtually all simulations, regardless of the chosen methodology, these calculations are based on trade flows that are already influenced by the protection in place. Observed trade flows would be quite different if they were free trade flows. Second, no attempt is made to simulate the possible effects of changes in relative prices (from MFN liberalization) on supply and demand and, therefore, on trade. Such a simulation could have been done with a partial equilibrium elasticity analysis, but the analysis here is limited to a simple comparison of what happens to the estimated value of preferences at the country level when MFN tariff rates are cut, with everything else staying the same.

The use of a partial equilibrium model to analyze the effect of MFN liberalization on preference erosion would have allowed an assessment of the effect that a change in preference margin on one product would have on the exports of a substitutable product and on the redistribution of export shares across countries. In other words, the analysis could have assessed the trade effects of liberalization, rather than just looking at changes in the preference margins. But such estimates of the trade effects arising from eroded preference margins require knowledge of the responsiveness of supply and demand to price changes, as well as the degree of substitution that would occur between preferential and nonpreferential suppliers. These measures of responsiveness to price changes—or elasticities—are subject to broad estimation based on limited information. It is therefore unclear what would be gained by trying to translate the margin erosion estimate into a trade flow consequence.

Partial equilibrium analyses are limited in that they do not capture all the interactive consequences of a policy change on the economy as a whole. Analysts are well aware that policy changes have ripple effects throughout the economy and that a comprehensive picture of the economywide effects of a policy change would require a general equilibrium model. In fact, a general equilibrium model, by taking into account income and resource constraints, would be able to estimate the effects of preference erosion on income as well as on trade flows. Once again, however, such models have formidable data requirements, produce highly aggregated results, and are typically sensitive to relatively small changes in assumptions.[4] Given these limitations and the utility of a high degree of disaggregation among products, exporters, and import markets, it was preferable to limit the examination of the preference erosion issue to the simple analysis of changes in "rents" for exporters losing preference margins.

A third limitation of the analysis is that because the estimates are all built on existing trade flows, there is no way to know whether a reduction in preference margins might be compensated by trade in product lines against which zero trade has been recorded in the dataset. This issue clearly is a concern in agriculture, as will be seen later in the consideration of "sensitive" product exclusions from the tariff cuts. Many of the selected sensitive products have zero trade flows because of the height of existing tariffs. It should be noted that this particular problem may also exist in more sophisticated analyses involving partial or general equilibrium simulations.

Several aspects of this analysis suggest that the estimates of preference erosion arising from the MFN liberalization scenario may be upper-bound estimates. First, the analysis uses applied tariff rates rather than bound rates as the simulation baseline. In the Quad economies, most bound rates are not much higher than applied rates, but to the extent that a binding overhang exists, the assumption here is of deeper MFN cuts than would actually occur, thus leading to higher estimates of preference erosion. Second, it is assumed that all the "economic rent" that accrues from preferences goes to the exporter. In practice, some of the margin is likely to be appropriated by the importing country, which means that the loss occurring from preference erosion is correspondingly less.[5] Third, it is assumed that the full impact of MFN liberalization will be felt immediately following agreement on the tariff reductions. In practice, MFN cuts are likely to be phased in over several years.

Other working assumptions underlying the analysis may go either way in terms of lowering or raising the estimates of preference erosion. First, as already noted, no attempt has been made to calculate preference utilization rates; they are simply assumed to be 100 percent. If utilization rates are less than 100 percent, which is almost certainly the case in many instances, then the initial value of preferences is lower, and the risk from erosion is less. However, since full utilization of all preferences, including reciprocal preferences, is assumed, one cannot be sure whether overall the preference margins are overestimated or underestimated. Second, for lack of data for the European Union (EU), it is assumed that trade on all lines subject to tariff rate quotas pays the MFN out-of-quota tariff rate.[6] Hence, given a certain preferential tariff rate, as long as trade remains within quota, a higher preference margin is estimated than actually exists and, therefore, a greater risk from preference erosion is estimated. However, because on some tariff lines uncertainty exists about whether preferential rates are in- or out-of-quota rates, it is possible that preference erosion is underestimated for these products.

The rest of this chapter is organized into three sections. The first section presents the basic data used to calculate the value of nonreciprocal preferences for each reported beneficiary country, adjusted for actual competition (including non-MFN trade) from all other suppliers to the Quad markets. The second section explains the underlying assumptions of the simulation of an MFN tariff cut and presents the results. The final section concludes. Three short annexes clarify aspects of the analytical approach. Annex 8.A takes four countries for illustrative purposes and explains how nondiscriminatory liberalization will affect preference margins, emphasizing how different the effect can be among countries. Annex 8.B uses a numerical example to describe exactly how calculations are made of adjusted preference margins—that is, how account is taken of the fact that not all the competitors of a preference-receiving country will be paying MFN tariffs on a given product in a particular market. Annex 8.C analyzes the consequences of a key assumption occasioned by a lack of data—namely, that where tariff quotas are used, the out-of-quota tariff rates are applicable for the preference margin calculations.

The Value of Nonreciprocal Preferences in Agriculture

This section first lays out the preference schemes providing assistance to developing countries. It then turns to an assessment of the benefits provided.

Preference Schemes by Providers

The data presented show the relative importance of preferential and nonpreferential trade from the viewpoint of both preference-giving and preference-receiving countries. Figures 8.1 and 8.2 show the import shares in each Quad market by type of access under the Generalized System of Preferences (GSP) and various least developed country (LDC) schemes, respectively. These figures are derived from the data contained in table 8.1. Figure 8.1 shows that the share of trade of beneficiaries of the GSP entering the Quad markets under MFN duty-free rates varies from about 30 percent for Japan to about 70 percent for Canada. The share of trade that receives preferential treatment, but at a positive duty rate, ranges from zero in the United States to about 25 percent in the EU. As for duty-free preferences, shares vary between about 6 percent for the EU and 25 percent for the United States. All the Quad markets deny preferential access on some imports subject to positive MFN duties. This category represents a 14 percent share of Canada's imports, and 22 percent, 50 percent, and 27 percent of imports, respectively, for the EU, Japan, and the United States. For the Quad as a whole, the figure is 27 percent. If the extension of new preferences to beneficiaries that were going to suffer from the erosion of existing preferences were to be considered as a possible compensatory mechanism, these figures suggest that considerable scope exists for such a move.

The picture for LDCs depicted in figure 8.2 is quite different. In Canada, practically all imports from LDCs are MFN duty free. For LDCs, therefore, no risk of preference erosion from MFN tariff cuts exists in the Canadian market. In Japan,

TABLE 8.1 Nonreciprocal Schemes in Selected Markets, Agricultural Products, 2003

Market	Scheme	Category	Imports		Number of national tariff lines		
			Value (US$ million)	Share (%)	Number	Share (%)	With trade (%)
Canada	GSP	All tariff lines	2,848.7	100.0	1,372	100.0	71.7
		MFN duty-free access	2,032.1	71.3	551	40.2	33.7
		Preferential access	482.1	16.9	297	21.6	15.9
		Duty-free preference	296.0	10.4	101	7.4	6.0
		Non–ad valorem duties	0.7	0.0	1	0.1	0.1
	LDCs	All tariff lines	35.6	100.0	1,372	100.0	14.1
		MFN duty-free access	35.2	98.9	551	40.2	9.4
		Preferential access	0.4	1.1	724	52.8	4.7
		Duty-free preference	0.4	1.1	724	52.8	4.7
		Non–ad valorem duties	0.0	0.0	1	0.1	0.1
	Commonwealth Caribbean countries	All tariff lines	38.6	100.0	1,372	100.0	17.1
		MFN duty-free access	14.4	37.4	551	40.2	9.7
		Preferential access	24.1	62.6	667	48.6	7.2
		Duty-free preference	24.1	62.6	667	48.6	7.2
		Non–ad valorem duties	0.0	0.0	1	0.1	0.1
EU-15[a]	GSP	All tariff lines	42,372.2	100.0	2,115	100.0	76.1
		MFN duty-free access	19,041.2	44.9	402	19.0	16.5
		Preferential access	12,936.1	30.5	843	39.9	35.6
		Duty-free preference	2,431.4	5.7	128	6.1	5.5
		Non–ad valorem duties	1,188.5	2.8	43	2.0	1.9

LDCs	All tariff lines	1,560.5	100.0	2,115	100.0	23.9
	MFN duty-free access	870.8	55.8	402	19.0	7.6
	Preferential access	565.3	36.2	1,652	78.1	15.3
	Duty-free preference	565.3	36.2	1,652	78.1	15.3
	Non–ad valorem duties	6.8	0.4	43	2.0	0.7
African, Caribbean, and Pacific countries	All tariff lines	8,519.7	100.0	2,115	100.0	35.7
	MFN duty-free access	4,190.4	49.2	402	19.0	9.5
	Preferential access	3,331.4	39.1	1,018	48.1	20.0
	Duty-free preference	2,643.4	31.0	765	36.2	16.6
	Non–ad valorem duties	39.9	0.5	43	2.0	0.8
Countries fighting drugs	All tariff lines	4,617.4	100.0	2,115	100.0	32.9
	MFN duty-free access	1,236.9	26.8	402	19.0	8.4
	Preferential access	1,525.1	33.0	1,498	70.8	22.3
	Duty-free preference	1,435.0	31.1	1,322	62.5	19.1
	Non–ad valorem duties	66.2	1.4	43	2.0	1.1
Japan GSP	All tariff lines	10,795.1	100.0	1,858	100.0	59.7
	MFN duty-free access	3,308.5	30.7	461	24.8	16.8
	Preferential access	2,035.7	18.9	343	18.5	14.3
	Duty-free preference	1,063.6	9.9	155	8.3	6.7
	Non–ad valorem duties	0.0	0.0	5	0.3	0.0
LDCs	All tariff lines	175.9	100.0	1,858	100.0	6.5
	MFN duty-free access	163.7	93.1	461	24.8	3.4
	Preferential access	6.8	3.9	460	24.8	1.5
	Duty-free preference	6.8	3.9	457	24.6	1.5
	Non–ad valorem duties	0.0	0.0	5	0.3	0.0

(Table continues on the following page.)

TABLE 8.1 Nonreciprocal Schemes in Selected Markets, Agricultural Products, 2003 (*Continued*)

Market	Scheme	Category	Imports		Number of national tariff lines		
			Value (US$ million)	Share (%)	Number	Share (%)	With trade (%)
United States	GSP	All tariff lines	13,073.1	100.0	1,808	100.0	65.4
		MFN duty-free access	6,321.8	48.4	384	21.2	16.8
		Preferential access	3,240.3	24.8	554	30.6	24.7
		Duty-free preference	3,239.2	24.8	554	30.6	24.7
		Non–ad valorem duties	19.3	0.2	1	0.1	0.1
	LDCs	All tariff lines	350.4	100.0	1,808	100.0	10.1
		MFN duty-free access	285.6	81.5	384	21.2	4.4
		Preferential access	64.6	18.4	1,149	63.6	5.5
		Duty-free preference	64.6	18.4	1,149	63.6	5.5
		Non–ad valorem duties	0.0	0.0	1	0.1	0.0
	African Growth Opportunity Act	All tariff lines	1,044.3	100.0	1,808	100.0	17.4
		MFN duty-free access	763.9	73.2	384	21.2	6.1
		Preferential access	274.5	26.3	1,171	64.8	10.8
		Duty-free preference	274.5	26.3	1,171	64.8	10.8
		Non–ad valorem duties	0.0	0.0	1	0.1	0.0
	Andean Trade Preference Act and Andean Trade Promotion and Drug Eradication Act	All tariff lines	1,943.4	100.0	1,808	100.0	26.1
		MFN duty-free access	1,048.3	53.9	384	21.2	6.7
		Preferential access	893.8	46.0	1,191	65.9	18.4
		Duty-free preference	893.8	46.0	1,191	65.9	18.4
		Non–ad valorem duties	0.0	0.0	1	0.1	0.0

Caribbean Basin Economic Recovery Act	All tariff lines	2,907.6	100.0	1,808	100.0	30.3
	MFN duty-free access	1,340.2	46.1	384	21.2	7.8
	Preferential access	1,555.0	53.5	1,193	66.0	21.3
	Duty-free preference	1,555.0	53.5	1,193	66.0	21.3
	Non–ad valorem duties	11.3	0.4	1	0.1	0.1
Quad markets	GSP	All tariff lines	69,089.1	100.0	7,153	100.0	68.3
	MFN duty-free access	30,703.6	44.4	1,798	25.1	20.0
	Preferential access	18,694.2	27.1	2,037	28.5	23.5
	Duty-free preference	7,030.3	10.2	938	13.1	10.8
	Non–ad valorem duties	1,208.5	1.8	50	0.7	0.6
	LDCs	All tariff lines	2,122.4	100.0	7,153	100.0	14.0
	MFN duty-free access	1,355.2	63.9	1,798	25.1	6.0
	Preferential access	637.0	30.0	3,985	55.7	7.2
	Duty-free preference	637.0	30.0	3,982	55.7	7.2
	Non–ad valorem duties	6.8	0.3	50	0.7	0.2

Source: Authors' calculations.

a. *EU-15* refers to the 15 countries that were members of the European Union prior to May 1, 2004: Austria, Belgium, Denmark, Finland, France, Germany, Greece, Ireland, Italy, Luxembourg, Netherlands, Portugal, Spain, Sweden, and the United Kingdom.

FIGURE 8.1 Imports under the GSP Scheme by Type of Market Access, 2003

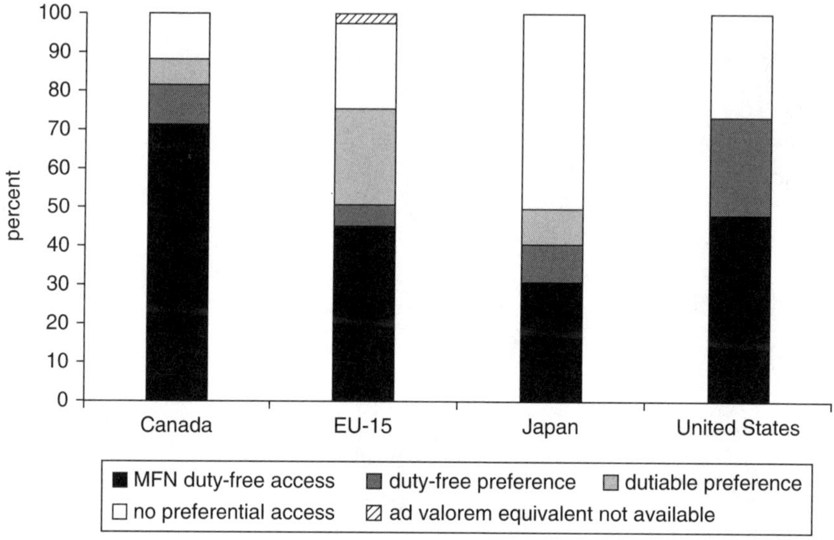

Source: Authors' calculations.

Note: EU-15 refers to the 15 countries that were members of the European Union prior to May 1, 2004: Austria, Belgium, Denmark, Finland, France, Germany, Greece, Ireland, Italy, Luxembourg, Netherlands, Portugal, Spain, Sweden, and the United Kingdom.

the picture is similar, with more than 93 percent of LDC exports entering MFN duty free and the remaining 7 percent divided roughly equally between duty-free preferential access and MFN dutiable trade with no preferences. In the United States, the share of imports from LDCs entering MFN duty free is 81 percent, with the balance having duty-free preferential access. The picture for the EU is a little different, with only 56 percent of LDC exports entering MFN duty free. A further 36 percent of LDC trade enjoys duty-free preferential access and 8 percent is MFN dutiable with no preferential access. For the Quad as a whole, the share of LDC exports subject to risk from preference erosion is 30 percent, which is accounted for primarily by the EU and, to a lesser degree, by the United States.

Table 8.1 provides an interesting indication of the degree of individual commodity dependence of different country groupings. The product concentration of trade flows can be observed from the last column in table 8.1, which shows the number of tariff lines against which trade occurs. In each case, the numbers are much lower for LDCs than for GSP beneficiaries. For the Quad as a whole, GSP

FIGURE 8.2 Imports under the LDC Schemes by Type of Market Access, 2003

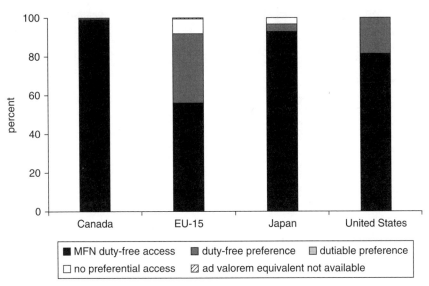

Source: Authors' calculations.
Note: EU-15 refers to the 15 countries that were members of the European Union prior to May 1, 2004: Austria, Belgium, Denmark, Finland, France, Germany, Greece, Ireland, Italy, Luxembourg, Netherlands, Portugal, Spain, Sweden, and the United Kingdom.

beneficiaries record trade on 68 percent of all agriculture tariff lines. The comparable figure for the LDCs is only 14 percent.

Importance of Preferences by Beneficiaries

Annex table 8.A.1 looks at preferences from the point of view of beneficiary countries.[7] The table shows for each beneficiary the share of exports by destination market. The data highlight the overall strong reliance, especially of LDCs, on the EU market. Among LDCs, only Myanmar and Madagascar export the largest share of their exports to other markets (Japan and the United States, respectively). Table 8.2 reports overall percentages for exports of GSP beneficiaries and LDCs by type of market access to the Quad economies. This information is provided at the country level in annex table 8.A.2. In addition, table 8.A.3 reports export shares of preference beneficiaries by type of market access for the EU. Table 8.2 also shows the average value of preferences measured according to both the traditional unadjusted measure of preference margins and the competition-adjusted measure.[8] These data come from annex table 8.A.4.

TABLE 8.2   Export Shares by Tariff Regime: Agricultural Products, 2003

Beneficiary	Exports to Quad markets (%)			Preference margin (%)	
	MFN-duty free	MFN dutiable	Preferential access	Unadjusted	Competition-adjusted
Developing countries	46	29	23	1.3	−0.4
LDCs	59	4	37	2.5	0.1
Total	46	29	24	1.4	−0.4

Source: Authors' calculations.

The LDCs have a higher share of MFN duty-free trade (59 percent) in their total trade than the GSP beneficiaries do (46 percent). LDCs also have a lower share of MFN dutiable trade (4 percent) than the GSP beneficiaries do (29 percent). In addition, the LDCs are relatively more prone to preference erosion than the GSP beneficiaries are, because 37 percent of their exports enjoy preferential access compared with 23 percent for GSP beneficiaries. This observation is borne out by the average preference margin calculations reported in the final two columns of table 8.2. The average preference margin for LDCs in the Quad markets drops from 2.5 to 0.1 when competition from other countries benefiting from preferences is taken into account. In the case of GSP beneficiaries, the unadjusted preference margin is only 1.3 and the adjusted margin is negative (−0.4). Thus, at least some developing countries face market conditions worse than their competitors in Quad markets.[9]

Generating the data in table 8.A.4 and for the simulation of the MFN duty reduction reported in the next section required information on ad valorem equivalent (AVE) tariffs. Many tariffs in agriculture are expressed as specific duties, and the analysis would have been severely limited in terms of product coverage if it had not used AVEs. The calculation of AVEs can be complex, and a number of methodologies are available. For the present purposes, AVE calculations are based on the estimates undertaken by the International Trade Centre for the joint exercise by the International Trade Centre, the United Nations Conference on Trade and Development, and the WTO of reporting to the United Nations on progress toward the attainment of the Millennium Development Goals. The exception is the United States, for which data on AVEs that were submitted to the WTO Secretariat were used.[10] It was not possible to obtain data for a few AVEs, and the associated trade flows have been excluded from the analysis. Columns 5 and 9 of tables 8.A.2 and 8.A.3 show at the country level what shares of imports and of tariff lines are affected by this problem. For the vast majority of countries, the share of imports for which AVEs are not available is lower than 3 percent. The aggregate trade share for the countries featured in table 8.A.2 was only 2 percent.

The percentage of exports that enjoy preferences in the Quad markets (table 8.A.2, column 4) and preference margins (table 8.A.4) are very different across individual countries.[11] For some countries, preferential schemes cover more than 75 percent of total agricultural exports to the Quad. Such countries include Bangladesh, Belize, Botswana, Dominica, the Dominican Republic, Georgia, Guyana, Mauritius, Namibia, St. Kitts and Nevis, St. Lucia, St. Vincent and the Grenadines, Senegal, Swaziland, and Zimbabwe. For other developing countries, preferential trade is not a significant share of trade. Among these countries are Brunei Darussalam, Burundi, the Central African Republic, Chad, Guinea, Guinea-Bissau, the Republic of Korea, Maldives, Mali, Mongolia, Myanmar, Rwanda, and Sierra Leone. For all of them, preferential access into the Quad markets represents less than 5 percent of their agricultural exports. It is worth noting that most of these countries (with the exception of the Dominican Republic, Myanmar, and the Republic of Korea) strongly rely on the EU market for their exports (table 8.A.1) and that it is their type of market access to the EU that determines their dependence on preference (table 8.A.3).

It is also interesting to note that the countries named here whose preferential trade represents more than 75 percent of total exports also tend to appear among the countries enjoying the highest preference margins from the Quad markets, whether adjusted for competition or not (see table 8.A.4, columns 6 and 1, respectively). In addition, the majority of these countries have a very narrow export base (see table 8.A.2, columns 6–8). For many of these countries, bananas or sugar account for the high degree of product concentration in their export composition. As will be seen in the next section, bananas and sugar are among the key commodities for which preference erosion is a significant consequence of MFN liberalization, particularly in the EU market.

Estimates of the value of preferences are quite sensitive to the specific measure used for the calculations. For example, figure 8.3 shows the value of preferences for agricultural exports to the Quad markets, estimated with and without the margin adjusted for the preferences that the Quad markets grant to other countries.[12] For some countries, such as Colombia, Ecuador, and Thailand, preference margins turn out to be negative when adjusted for competition from other preference beneficiaries. Overall, the exports of these countries benefit from less beneficial treatment than those of other countries competing in the Quad markets.

Simulating an MFN Tariff Cut in Agriculture

This section simulates an MFN tariff cut on agricultural products and estimates the effect of this cut on the value of nonreciprocal preferences. Preference erosion is calculated as the change in the value of the preference before and after the MFN cut. It is important to emphasize, once again, that the assumptions that define the

**FIGURE 8.3 Value of the Preference for Agricultural Products
Exports to the Quad Markets: Selected Countries, 2003**

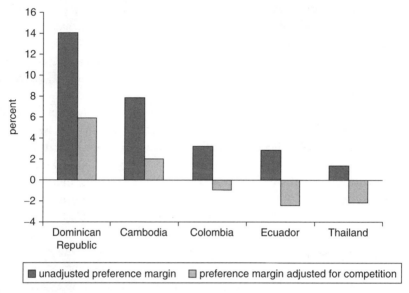

Source: Authors' calculations.

simulated MFN liberalization scenario should not in any way be taken as an opin-
ion about the desirability or likelihood of a particular outcome in the agricultural
negotiations. The scenario simply makes it possible to illustrate the degree of preference erosion risk that would arise for nonreciprocal preference beneficiaries
were a nondiscriminatory liberalization episode of this magnitude to occur.

A simulation in agriculture is more complex than a comparable exercise in
nonagricultural market access because of the multiple parameters used to define
the MFN cut. As noted previously, this analysis simulates the G-20 proposal in
relation to market access. Hence, four parameter assumptions were worked into
the analysis. First, the tariff reductions involve cuts that vary according to the base
rate from which the cut is made. Lower base rates attract lower cuts. Ranges of
base rates from 0 to 20 percent, 20 to 50 percent, 50 to 75 percent, and above
75 percent were cut by 45 percent, 55 percent, 65 percent, and 75 percent, respectively. Second, allowance was made for sensitive products representing 2 percent
and 4 percent of tariff lines in two different simulation exercises.[13] For these tariff
lines, only half the calculated cut was applied. It was assumed that the 2 (or 4) percent of selected sensitive tariff lines were those that attracted the highest applied

duties in each of the Quad markets. Third, a cap of 100 percent was applied on all other tariffs. Fourth, in the absence of data on in-quota and out-of-quota imports for the EU against tariff lines subject to tariff rate quotas and given that only out-of-quota tariffs are available, it was simply assumed that all imports against these lines were outside the quota, except for Japan.[14] A consequence of this assumption is that overall preference margins are underestimated when the in-quota preference margin is larger than the out-of-quota preference margin. However, this assumption will translate into an underestimation of the risk of preference erosion only when the MFN tariff rate, after MFN liberalization, falls below the preferential out-of-quota rate. Another consequence of this assumption is that the analysis does not consider the benefits arising from country-specific quota allocation on an MFN basis. Annex 8.C provides a detailed explanation of the effect of using preferential and MFN out-of-quota rates to estimate the risk of preference erosion.

EU and U.S. tariff rate quotas in the sugar and banana sectors are treated differently. In the case of cane or beet sugar, the EU has in place a tariff quota system that allocates duty-free quotas entirely to India and to eligible producers in the African, Caribbean, and Pacific (ACP) states, according to the Sugar Protocol and Special Preferential Sugar scheme. Because there are no out-of-quota preferences, using out-of-quota rates would not capture preference margins. To take into account the actual preferences given to beneficiaries of this EU quota system, one must assume that all preferential trade occurs in quota and an in-quota duty-free rate is used for sugar preferences. A similar operating assumption was made for the United States, which has in place a preferential duty-free tariff quota system. Box 8.1 provides further information on the trade regimes for sugar in the Quad markets.

In the case of bananas, it was assumed that the MFN ad valorem rate for the EU was 30 percent and that the preferential rate for ACP countries was duty free.[15] This assumption is introduced to reflect the measures relative to the import regime for bananas recently adopted by the Council of the European Union. These measures entered into force on January 1, 2006.[16] Box 8.2 provides further information on the trade regime for bananas in the EU, Canada, United States, and Japan.

The results of the simulation are reported in annex table 8.A.5 for the Quad markets as a whole. Table 8.A.6 presents results for the EU and the United States only, without the assumptions about sensitive product exclusions. Table 8.A.5 shows, for each beneficiary of nonreciprocal preferences, the change in the aggregate value of preference margins before and after adjustment for competition and with and without the exclusion of sensitive products. Columns 3 and 8 of the table show the fully adjusted estimate of preference erosion in the cases, respectively, of

BOX 8.1   The Sugar Regime

The sugar regime greatly differs across the Quad markets. Japan does not grant any preference on sugar. Canada provides MFN duty-free access on raw sugar for use by sugar refineries in the production of refined sugar used in wine. On other raw sugar, Canada applies MFN duties in the range between US$22 and US$31 per metric ton and provides duty-free preferences depending on the preference regime and specific tariff lines. The EU and the U.S. regimes for sugar imports share some common features: both the EU and the United States apply a tariff quota regime on sugar and provide domestic support. As a result, domestic sugar prices are two or three times higher than prevailing world prices. Therefore, valuable quota rents can be captured by exporters that hold quota licenses. Both the United States and the EU operate a three-tariff quota system for sugar with out-of-quota duties that effectively prohibit access outside the quotas.

In the EU, three different systems apply to cane or beet sugar, raw cane sugar for refining, and chemically pure fructose. The tariff quota for cane and beet sugar is reserved entirely for ACP countries and India, and it is in-quota duty free. Mauritius receives the largest share of the quota. The Everything but Arms initiative will provide duty-free and quota-free access to sugar originating in LDCs by July 1, 2009. Until that time, LDCs benefit from duty-free quota access, which increases on an annual basis. Out-of-quota imports for cane or beet sugar are subject to bound duties up to €419 per metric ton. In addition, the EU allocates country-specific quotas to Brazil and Cuba and an MFN quota for raw cane sugar for refining for which the bound in-quota duty is €98 per ton and the out-of-quota duty is €339 per ton. Finally, the tariff quota on chemically pure fructose is administrated on an MFN basis. The price of sugar in the EU is maintained through export refunds. These refunds are intended to cover the difference between the EU domestic market price for sugar and the world price. Refunds are paid for beet sugar or cane harvested in the EU and sugar imported under the ACP Protocol and the agreement with India. The EU sugar system has been challenged under the existing WTO rules by other members.

The United States operates three tariff quota regimes for raw cane sugar, other cane or beet sugars or syrups, and sugar-containing products. In the United States, sugar imports are subject to out-of-quota bound duties up to US$704 per metric ton plus 8.5 percent. In-quota rates are significantly lower. For example, for raw cane sugar, they are between US$9.43 and US$14.61 per metric ton, whereas the out-of-quota rate is bound at US$338.70 per metric ton. Caribbean countries that have quota allocations benefit from duty-free access under the GSP and the Caribbean Basin Initiative.

Box 8.2   The Banana Regime

Among the Quad economies, only the EU maintains a preferential tariff quota for bananas. Canada and the United States grant duty-free MFN treatment to bananas, with the sole exception of a 1.4 percent tariff on dry plantains in the case of the United States. Japan applies an ad valorem MFN rate of 20 percent (from April to September) and 25 percent (from October to March) on fresh bananas, a rate of 3 percent on dried bananas, and duty-free access for LDCs.

The EU import regime for bananas has changed several times. The regime has been challenged by other members of the WTO. For 2005, the EU tariff quota system consisted of a total MFN tariff quota of more than 3 million metric tons (of which 2.2 million metric tons were bound), subject to a bound in-quota duty of €75 per metric ton and a preferential tariff quota of 750,000 metric tons at zero duty. The final bound out-of-quota rate for nonpreferential suppliers was €680 per metric ton, and the out-of-quota preferential duty was €380 per metric ton. The banana import measures adopted by the Council of the European Union on November 29, 2005, provide that from January 1, 2006, the tariff rate for bananas will be €176 per metric ton and that a zero-duty autonomous tariff quota of 775,000 metric tons should be opened to bananas originating from ACP countries.

Belize, Cameroon, Côte d'Ivoire, Dominica, St. Lucia, and St. Vincent and the Grenadines depend significantly on this system, because a large share of their 2003 exports to the Quad markets consisted of bananas (20.9 percent, 9.9 percent, 4.6 percent, 26.5 percent, 62.4 percent, and 24 percent of total exports, respectively). Moreover, the EU absorbs virtually all exports of bananas from most of these countries.

no flexibility and 2 percent flexibility for sensitive products. A separate section in table 8.A.5 shows in aggregate form the difference made to the results by using a sensitive product threshold of 4 percent instead of 2 percent. Varying the flexibility assumption in this manner makes very little difference to the aggregate simulation results.

Column 3 of table 8.A.5 shows that following the MFN tariff reduction, developing countries (excluding LDCs) register a positive margin gain of US$256.2 million under the best scheme available to them in each Quad market. Underlying this net figure are aggregate losses of US$205.1 million and gains of US$461.3 million. In the case of LDCs, the corresponding net gains are US$10.4 million, reflecting aggregate losses of US$3.8 million and gains of US$14.1 million. These results show that if all developing countries and LDCs receiving nonreciprocal preferences are taken together, the net benefit in terms of changes in adjusted preference margins is positive following MFN liberalization. In other words, in terms of this margin analysis, these countries, taken together, stand to gain more from MFN liberalization[17] than they lose from the consequential preference erosion.[18] However, although the degree of preference erosion may be rather modest in the aggregate, some countries are particularly affected, either in terms of the share of lost preference margin in total exports (column 4) or in terms of absolute amounts (column 3).

Columns 5 and 10 indicate the value of trade under tariff lines that continues to attract positive MFN or positive preferential duty rates after the simulated cuts. This information provides an idea of the scope that may exist for additional preferences that could compensate for the erosion of existing ones. Granting additional preferences would be a temporary palliative, because additional preferences today imply an additional threat from preference erosion tomorrow. In any event, several of the countries that would suffer large losses in preference margins, or losses that represent a large share of total trade, do not enjoy much scope for additional preferences in the Quad markets based on the existing commodity composition of trade.

Before exploring these results in a more disaggregated manner, a few points about the simulations are worth mentioning. First, the fact that the numbers in columns 1 to 5 and columns 6 to 10 in table 8.A.5 are virtually the same for nearly all countries (with the exception of Argentina, Brazil, China, Fiji, Guatemala, Malawi, Thailand, and Zimbabwe) means that preference erosion estimates are barely influenced by the exclusion of 2 percent or 4 percent of sensitive products from MFN tariff cuts. The reason is clear. The assumption that Quad economies would choose to exclude the tariff lines attracting the highest applied tariffs under the sensitive products rubric means that these lines are also the ones on which preferential treatment is unlikely to be on offer. Moreover, under a number of the selected tariff lines, no trade occurs at all, on account of the high tariffs. Thus, little or no erosion can occur. This finding does not, of course, mean that the exclusion of sensitive products from MFN reductions has no effect on real market access opportunities; on the contrary, high protection is inhibiting trade. Table 8.3 lists the sensitive products selected under the exclusion criterion in each of the Quad markets, indicating the total trade against these products.

In a recent study, Jean, Laborde, and Martin (2006) claim that allowing 2 percent of tariff lines of sensitive products in developed countries and 4 percent in developing countries dramatically reduces the effectiveness of tariff reduction as a means of increasing market access. Their result appears to contradict the findings of this analysis. A number of important factors explain the differences in the results. First, Jean, Laborde, and Martin assume that countries choose to exclude those products from the MFN formula cut that account for the highest levels of tariff revenues. The analysis in this chapter assumes that countries classify as

TABLE 8.3   Sensitive Agricultural Products Selected under the Exclusion Criterion in Each Quad Market, 2003

Market	Chapters	Description	Number of national tariff lines
Canada	02	Meat and edible meat offal	3
	04	Dairy produce, birds' eggs, natural honey, and edible products of animal origin, not elsewhere specified or included	11
	16	Preparations of meat, of fish, or of crustaceans, molluscs, or other aquatic invertebrates	3
	18	Cocoa and cocoa preparations	2
	19	Preparations of cereals, flour, starch, or milk and pastrycooks' products	4
	21	Miscellaneous edible preparations	2
	22	Beverages, spirits, and vinegar	1
	35	Albuminoidal substances, modified starches, glues, and enzymes	1
		Imports in selected tariff lines as a % of total imports in agriculture: 0.577	
EU	02	Meat and edible meat offal	5
	04	Dairy produce, birds' eggs, natural honey, and edible products of animal origin, not elsewhere specified or included	21
	07	Edible vegetables and certain roots and tubers	2
	15	Animal or vegetable fats and oils and their cleavage products, prepared edible fats, and animal or vegetable waxes	4
	17	Sugars and sugar confectionery	1
	20	Preparations of vegetables, fruit, nuts, or other parts of plants	4
	22	Beverages, spirits, and vinegar	4
	23	Residues and waste from the food industries and prepared animal fodder	1
		Imports in selected tariff lines as a % of total imports in agriculture: 0.782	

(Table continues on the following page.)

TABLE 8.3 **Sensitive Agricultural Products Selected under the Exclusion Criterion in Each Quad Market, 2003 (*Continued*)**

Market	Chapters	Description	Number of national tariff lines
Japan	04	Dairy produce, birds' eggs, natural honey, and edible products of animal origin, not elsewhere specified or included	15
	10	Cereals	10
	17	Sugars and sugar confectionery	2
	19	Preparations of cereals, flour, starch, or milk and pastrycooks' products	5
	21	Miscellaneous edible preparations	4
	50	Silk	1
	Imports in selected tariff lines as a % of total imports in agriculture: 0.780		
United States	04	Dairy produce, birds' eggs, natural honey, and edible products of animal origin, not elsewhere specified or included	15
	12	Oilseeds and oleaginous fruits; miscellaneous grains, seeds, and fruit; industrial or medicinal plants; and straw and fodder	2
	16	Preparations of meat, of fish, or of crustaceans, molluscs, or other aquatic invertebrates	1
	17	Sugars and sugar confectionery	2
	18	Cocoa and cocoa preparations	1
	19	Preparations of cereals, flour, starch, or milk and pastrycooks' products	2
	20	Preparations of vegetables, fruit, nuts, or other parts of plants	3
	21	Miscellaneous edible preparations	3
	24	Tobacco and manufactured tobacco substitutes	7
	Imports in selected tariff lines in percent of total imports in agriculture: 0.954		
Quad economies	Imports in selected tariff lines as a % of total imports in agriculture: 0.814		

Source: Authors' calculations.

sensitive the products with the highest tariff rates—in other words, the products that are already the most protected. Hence, while Jean, Laborde, and Martin's study would exclude highly traded products, this study excludes products with very high duties and mostly little or no trade. In this analysis it was considered more likely that tariff (protection) patterns, not tariff revenue collections, would be more influential in determining the selection of sensitive products.

Second, Jean, Laborde, and Martin (2006) used 2001 tariff data from the Market Access Map (MAcMap) database at Harmonized System (HS) six-digit classification levels, whereas this study uses 2003 data from the Common Analytical Market Access Database (CAMAD) at the tariff-line level. Hence, Jean, Laborde, and Martin are aggregating up the excluded tariff lines, when the modality for sensitive products is in reality expressed at the tariff-line level. Third, Jean, Laborde, and Martin assume that sensitive products tariffs are reduced by 15 percent, whereas this analysis applies the established modality of half of the otherwise applicable cut to sensitive products. Finally, they assume a progressive tariff reduction formula with cuts of 45 percent, 70 percent, and 75 percent in bound rates, with tariff intervals' transition points at 15 percent and 90 percent. This analysis uses the tariff intervals and percentage cuts considered in the G-20 proposal on applied rates.[19] The 2006 study does separately identify the effect of sensitive product flexibilities on changes in the access of developing countries to markets in developed countries following liberalization.

Overall, the conclusion that permitted flexibilities will significantly reduce the gains from a plausible tariff-cutting scenario under the Doha negotiations would appear questionable at best. Nevertheless, it is important to note that results are likely to change, perhaps significantly, for different hypotheses about sensitive products. What would the results have been, for example, if products selected for exclusion had been those on which the risk of preference erosion was most acute rather than those that were currently the most protected?

Another notable feature of the results in this chapter is that the 100 percent cap is not relevant for nonsensitive products. For the cap to operate in this analysis, a tariff would have to exceed 400 percent before it was cut. Under the G-20 proposal, a tariff of 400 percent would attract a 75 percent cut, bringing it down to 100 percent.

Now consider the question of which countries are most susceptible to preference erosion. Column 4 of table 8.A.5 shows the calculated value of preference erosion risk as a share of total agriculture exports for each country. The countries most severely affected in these terms are Belize (8.1 percent), Botswàna (15.5 percent), Cameroon (4.9 percent), Dominica (8.9 percent), Fiji (4.3 percent), Guyana (4.1 percent), Mauritius (7.0 percent), Namibia (9.5 percent), St. Kitts and Nevis (4.7 percent), St. Lucia (12.1 percent), St. Vincent and the Grenadines (11.9 percent), and Swaziland (4.3 percent). Table 8.A.6 indicates that all these countries suffer from preference erosion primarily in the EU market.

Table 8.A.7 examines the commodity composition of preference erosion risk for 13 of the most severely affected countries.[20] Fruit and vegetables (mainly denoting bananas) and sugar represent the highest product shares of exports to the Quad markets for most of these countries and constitute the bulk of the threat of preference erosion. The table shows that the adjustment for competition from other traders in the Quad markets has relatively less effect on the preference margin for bananas than for sugar in most cases, because more than 75 percent of the banana market was already subject to MFN duties in 2003.

The situation with respect to sugar is somewhat different. In columns 1 and 2 of table 8.A.5, many beneficiaries of sugar preferences appear to lose significantly from preference erosion in terms of overall export shares. But after the adjustment for competition from other suppliers, including preferential suppliers, the preference erosion estimate falls dramatically. This drop occurs because, unlike in the case of bananas, where a good deal of competition comes from nonpreferential or less favored sources, competition in the EU sugar market is predominantly among countries that enjoy the same favorable treatment in the importing market. More than 90 percent of EU imports of cane sugar (HS 17011) are from countries that benefit from the EU Sugar Protocol. Adjustment for this competition offers a more realistic view of what is really at stake in the sugar market and demonstrates that preference margins are simply not worth as much to individual countries when many other countries are enjoying the same advantages. The countries for which this is true include Barbados, Fiji, Guyana, Jamaica, Mauritius, St. Kitts and Nevis, Swaziland, and Trinidad and Tobago. An important point to note here is that this analysis of the vulnerability of sugar exporters to preference erosion is based only on what happens to tariffs. It does not include any consideration of what is likely to occur in the EU market when the impending reform of the guaranteed price system for countries under the Sugar Protocol takes effect.

Returning briefly to table 8.A.7, one may note that other products vulnerable to preference erosion in these selected countries include coffee and tea, sugar, alcoholic beverages, and tobacco. For the group of 13 most affected countries, table 8.A.8 reports the three most important export products at the HS six-digit level, their shares of total exports to the Quad markets, and their average adjusted preference margins. For each of these countries except Jamaica, only three quite narrowly defined products account for more than 75 percent of total exports to the Quad markets.

Conclusions

It is worth emphasizing once again the nature of these calculations and the way they should be interpreted. Essentially, what is observed in the calculations of preference erosion is how preference margins are reduced when an MFN tariff reduction is introduced. The estimates of preference erosion for individual countries were made taking into account the fact that competing suppliers into given markets may also enjoy preferential treatment. Thus, it is unrealistic simply to calculate changes in preference margins in terms of differences between MFN and preferential duty rates on bilateral trade flows. The competition must be reckoned with to appreciate what is really at stake. The adjustment of preference margin calculations in this manner makes a major difference for some product lines in certain markets.

But what is calculated here is not the trade consequence of preference erosion. This analysis only computes changes in preference margins and assigns them a monetary value by multiplying estimated erosion margins by the associated trade flow (under the relevant tariff line). This approach gives a magnitude that can be compared with trade flows, but it is not an estimate of changes in trade flows. What happens to trade flows after a policy change will depend on how different suppliers react to changes in the conditions of competition and how consumers react to changes in relative prices. For this reason, the chapter often refers to preference erosion *risk*. The estimates are useful in identifying relative risks among countries, but they should not be taken as indicators of trade effect—and far less as income or welfare consequences of trade liberalization.

A general caveat to this analysis also bears repetition. The trade liberalization process in agriculture is complex. A range of assumptions have had to be made to calculate these estimates. These assumptions have been spelled out. Choosing a single simulation scenario obviously excludes other possible outcomes in which preference erosion risk could assume different dimensions. Perhaps the most sensitive and potentially influential assumption here concerns the sensitive product exclusions, particularly in terms of the choice that importing members will make of which lines to exclude. The simulation assumes that the lines chosen will be those that carry the highest applied tariff rates. But what if the choice included products for which preference erosion risk was most acute? In that case, the preference erosion risk would be greatly mitigated, with the resultant loss of potential trading opportunities for nonpreferential or less preferred suppliers. As it is, in this chapter, sensitive product exclusions turn out to have a small effect on preference erosion risk, precisely because the highly protected products chosen for exclusion from formula cuts are traded relatively little.

Assuming that trade flows subject to tariff rate quotas would occur outside quota values could have understated or overstated the preference erosion risk. It will also have oversimplified stories in such product lines as sugar and bananas, in which the existence of tariff rate quotas renders market outcomes more complex than this analysis has allowed. These oversimplifications have not fundamentally undermined the estimates; rather, they may have simply made them more approximate.

Other notable assumptions that have influenced the estimates are intrinsic to the choice of a particular negotiating proposal. They include the designation of tariff ranges and the MFN cuts to be applied to these ranges, the size of the sensitive product designation, and the value of the cap. Although the magnitude of the preference erosion risk would be affected to a degree by changes in these parameter assumptions, it is less obvious that relative impacts among affected members would change very much.

The main conclusions of this study may be summarized as follows:

- Like nonagricultural market access, the overall estimates of risks from preference erosion constitute small numbers. The aggregate estimated risk for all nonreciprocal preference-receiving members listed in table 8.A.5 is a positive value of US$266.6 million, of which the LDCs account for US$10.4 million. These positive numbers should be interpreted to mean that, overall, developing countries do not face any preference erosion risk. On the contrary, they would benefit in preference erosion terms from an MFN cut. Underlying these net positive numbers, however, are total losses of US$208.8 million (US$3.8 million for LDCs) and total gains of US$475.4 million (US$10.4 million for LDCs).
- Unlike in nonagricultural market access, the risk of preference erosion in agriculture is far more concentrated in terms of particular products and countries. The most affected products include bananas (Belize, Cameroon, Dominica, St. Lucia, St. Vincent and the Grenadines, and Swaziland); sugar (Barbados, Belize, Fiji, Guyana, Jamaica, Mauritius, St. Kitts and Nevis, Swaziland); and beverages and spirits (Barbados, Belize, Jamaica). Much of the impact occurs in the EU market.
- On the basis of assumptions made about the composition of products regarded as sensitive, the sensitive product exclusions have almost no effect on preference erosion, except for sugar in the United States. This result would continue to be the case to a large degree if the share of sensitive products were allowed to increase, but only if the same assumption was made as to the criterion for the choice of products. If the composition of products chosen as sensitive moved in the direction of including those for which preference erosion was a significant risk, the picture could change significantly. Moreover, no attempt has been made here to consider how far quotas may be expanded under current tariff rate quota arrangements by way of compensation for formula cut exclusions.

Annex 8.A: Country-Specific Illustrations on Preference Erosion Risk

To illustrate the very diverse risks at the country level from preference erosion, this annex describes the situation of two ACP members (Cameroon and St. Lucia) and two other countries (Ecuador and Thailand) that benefit less from preferences in the Quad markets. Tables 8.A.1 through 8.A.8 show the relevant data.

The two ACP members rely heavily on the EU market, which takes in more than 95 percent of their exports to the Quad economies (table 8.A.1). Both enjoy considerable preference margins, but only in the EU market, for their export products (table 8.A.4). The trade-weighted preference margins are 29 percent for St. Lucia, linked to its preferential treatment for bananas, and 12 percent for Cameroon, related to a slightly larger basket of goods dominated by cocoa and bananas. In fact, at less than 1 percent, the preference margin for cocoa is negligible (table 8.A.7). The adjusted weighted preference margins are not much lower (22 percent and 9 percent, respectively), which indicates that their export markets are fairly well shielded from other important suppliers. In the case of Cameroon, however, preferential access covers less than half of total exports (table 8.A.2 and 8.A.3), because the larger part of its exports enter the Quad markets—essentially the EU—MFN duty free.

Ecuador and Thailand trade in all Quad markets (table 8.A.1). However, they hardly benefit from any preference margin in any of their markets (table 8.A.4). Thailand faces nonzero MFN duties for two-thirds of its exports. For Ecuador, the share is over one-third (table 8.A.2). In the case of the EU market, the MFN dutiable export shares increase to 80 percent and 61 percent, respectively (table 8.A.3). The weighted preference margins in the Quad markets are just 3 percent and 1 percent for Ecuador and Thailand, respectively. When the competition from other preferential suppliers is taken into account, the adjusted weighted preference margins become negative (-2 percent) in both countries. This finding implies that on average, for their respective products, other exporters with sizable market shares have better preferences than the GSP schemes enjoyed by Ecuador and Thailand. In the case of Ecuador, this result is clearly the effect of the EU banana preferences. In the case of Thailand, it covers a broader spectrum of products. GSP preferences do not seem to give these countries effective preferential access when the preferential arrangements enjoyed by competitors supplying those markets are taken into account.

A lack of product diversification is a key factor that increases the preference erosion effect (table 8.A.8). In the case of St. Lucia, bananas alone account for 94 percent of agricultural exports. Cameroon's two major export products—cocoa and bananas—are fairly evenly split, with a combined share of 84 percent. Such high product concentration renders these economies very vulnerable to external

(*Text continues on p. 342.*)

TABLE 8.A.1   Share of Exports in Quad Markets: Agricultural Products, 2003

Exporter	Share of total exports to Quad economies (%)			
	Canada	Japan	United States	EU
Developing economies				
Albania	0.7	1.8	14.4	83.1
Antigua and Barbuda	1.0	1.6	0.6	96.9
Argentina	1.7	3.1	11.0	84.2
Armenia	1.3	0.9	85.2	12.5
Bahrain	0.2	—	—	99.8
Barbados	8.8	0.1	21.2	69.9
Belize	1.6	3.1	24.4	71.0
Bolivia	3.5	6.8	30.7	59.0
Botswana	0.0	—	0.1	99.9
Brazil	2.9	8.8	13.7	74.5
Brunei Darussalam	0.0	4.8	18.2	76.9
Cameroon	0.7	0.9	3.2	95.3
China	2.9	55.7	16.9	24.6
Colombia	7.2	6.6	44.2	42.0
Congo, Rep. of	0.1	1.3	25.6	73.0
Côte d'Ivoire	2.5	0.7	15.5	81.3
Cuba	4.5	4.5	—	90.9
Dominica	0.3	0.6	5.2	94.0
Dominican Republic	2.5	0.4	71.6	25.4
Ecuador	5.0	6.6	34.4	54.0
Egypt, Arab Rep. of	0.8	4.0	11.9	83.4
El Salvador	4.0	5.1	58.2	32.6
Fiji	0.3	6.5	20.9	72.2
Gabon	14.1	—	31.0	54.9
Georgia	0.7	0.4	12.5	86.3
Ghana	2.3	14.4	1.6	81.7
Grenada	4.8	1.3	18.0	75.9
Guatemala	7.2	5.4	66.9	20.5
Guyana	3.3	0.1	3.7	92.8
Honduras	4.6	3.0	54.5	37.9
Hong Kong, China	11.5	11.2	46.2	31.1
India	3.7	9.9	34.1	52.2
Indonesia	2.1	8.8	29.8	59.2
Jamaica	6.3	10.0	37.4	46.4
Kenya	0.8	2.2	4.8	92.2
Korea, Rep. of	2.9	72.6	19.6	4.9

TABLE 8.A.1 (*Continued*)

Exporter	Share of total exports to Quad economies (%)			
	Canada	Japan	United States	EU
Kuwait	0.0	—	13.4	86.6
Kyrgyz Republic	0.0	0.3	0.1	99.6
Macao, China	37.2	3.9	28.6	30.3
Malaysia	1.4	21.2	22.2	55.2
Mauritius	0.2	1.1	2.2	96.5
Moldova	1.3	0.9	2.1	95.7
Mongolia	0.0	17.5	2.5	80.1
Namibia	0.1	0.1	0.3	99.5
Nicaragua	4.6	2.1	63.5	29.7
Nigeria	2.2	2.1	8.5	87.2
Oman	4.6	59.9	30.1	5.4
Pakistan	3.6	3.9	11.2	81.3
Panama	0.6	1.0	13.7	84.7
Papua New Guinea	0.3	3.5	10.1	86.1
Paraguay	0.3	8.9	7.2	83.5
Peru	4.2	2.2	37.4	56.2
Philippines	2.7	41.9	33.4	22.0
Qatar	—	—	2.7	97.3
Sri Lanka	3.5	22.6	13.0	60.9
St. Kitts and Nevis	0.0	0.2	4.6	95.2
St. Lucia	0.1	—	0.8	99.0
St. Vincent and the Grenadines	0.5	—	2.0	97.5
Suriname	0.1	0.6	2.1	97.1
Swaziland	0.2	3.1	6.1	90.6
Taiwan, China	4.5	54.8	31.0	9.7
Thailand	2.9	44.3	19.2	33.5
Trinidad and Tobago	5.2	1.7	29.0	64.2
United Arab Emirates	0.7	1.4	4.6	93.2
Uruguay	14.5	0.6	22.2	62.8
Venezuela, R.B. de	0.6	5.4	22.5	71.4
Zimbabwe	0.5	6.0	4.5	89.0
Total for developing economies	**3.1**	**18.6**	**21.2**	**57.2**
LDCs				
Angola	—	—	0.3	99.7
Bangladesh	1.4	2.0	9.5	87.1
Benin	0.0	1.1	1.2	97.7

(Table continues on the following page.)

TABLE 8.A.1   Share of Exports in Quad Markets: Agricultural Products, 2003 (*Continued*)

Exporter	Share of total exports to Quad economies (%)			
	Canada	Japan	United States	EU
Burkina Faso	0.1	23.2	1.1	75.6
Burundi	0.9	0.7	21.1	77.2
Cambodia	9.5	—	7.3	83.2
Central African Republic	0.1	—	1.0	98.9
Chad	—	0.1	8.9	91.1
Congo, Dem. Rep. of	0.0	0.2	10.1	89.7
Djibouti	—	3.4	9.8	86.8
Gambia, The	0.0	4.2	—	95.7
Guinea	23.1	0.2	1.1	75.7
Guinea-Bissau	—	—	2.7	97.3
Haiti	2.7	1.3	46.8	49.3
Lesotho	—	—	—	100.0
Madagascar	2.7	3.8	48.1	45.3
Malawi	0.2	9.2	19.5	71.1
Maldives	0.3	—	0.4	99.3
Mali	0.6	0.0	0.4	99.0
Mauritania	2.5	1.7	0.9	94.9
Mozambique	0.1	6.8	10.1	83.0
Myanmar	1.8	63.4	18.8	16.0
Nepal	0.2	4.8	4.1	90.9
Niger	9.8	0.6	40.0	49.7
Rwanda	0.0	0.1	12.2	87.6
Senegal	0.0	0.4	0.8	98.7
Sierra Leone	6.8	0.1	2.2	90.9
Solomon Islands	0.5	4.1	20.8	74.6
Tanzania	1.1	18.3	4.8	75.8
Togo	1.5	1.5	1.8	95.1
Uganda	1.2	2.7	13.3	82.9
Zambia	0.0	12.0	1.2	86.8
Total for LDCs	**1.7**	**7.1**	**19.0**	**72.3**
Total for all exporters	**3.0**	**18.3**	**21.1**	**57.6**

Source: Authors' calculations.

Note: — = not available.

TABLE 8.A.2 Imports of Agricultural Products from Preference Beneficiaries by Type of Market Access to Quad Economies, 2003

Beneficiary	Bilateral imports (US$ million) (1)	Quad markets							
		Share of total bilateral imports (%)				Share of agricultural subheadings with at least one national tariff line with trade on a Quad market (%)			
		MFN duty-free access (2)	MFN dutiable access (3)	Preferential access (4)	Non–ad valorem duties (5)	MFN duty-free access (6)	MFN dutiable access (7)	Preferential access (8)	Non–ad valorem duties (9)
Developing economies									
Albania	23	75	1	25	0	0.9	5.4	5.9	0.0
Antigua and Barbuda	12	88	0	12	0	0.4	3.0	2.9	0.0
Argentina	5,183	57	23	14	6	23.6	30.8	28.9	1.3
Armenia	3	26	31	43	0	2.6	1.5	3.8	0.0
Bahrain	1	88	1	11	0	0.1	1.2	0.6	0.0
Barbados	45	27	0	73	0	0.9	3.2	4.2	0.1
Belize	117	3	5	92	0	0.6	3.6	3.9	0.0
Bolivia	70	75	3	22	0	1.0	6.7	7.4	0.0
Botswana	37	1	0	99	0	0.1	0.9	0.6	0.0
Brazil	11,472	61	31	6	2	32.1	41.2	32.1	1.3
Brunei Darussalam	0	98	0	2	0	0.0	0.4	0.3	0.0
Cameroon	612	57	0	43	0	1.9	7.8	8.0	0.1
China	7,820	35	49	16	0	52.1	55.7	42.8	1.7
Colombia	2,453	49	21	30	0	7.1	22.3	27.6	0.4
Congo, Rep. of	18	61	0	39	0	0.0	2.2	1.3	0.0

(Table continues on the following page.)

TABLE 8.A.2 Imports of Agricultural Products from Preference Beneficiaries by Type of Market Access to Quad Economies, 2003 (*Continued*)

Beneficiary	Bilateral imports (US$ million) (1)	Share of total bilateral imports (%)				Share of agricultural subheadings with at least one national tariff line with trade on a Quad market (%)			
		MFN duty-free access (2)	MFN dutiable access (3)	Preferential access (4)	Non-ad valorem duties (5)	MFN duty-free access (6)	MFN dutiable access (7)	Preferential access (8)	Non-ad valorem duties (9)
Côte d'Ivoire	2,655	68	0	32	0	2.0	10.0	11.4	0.1
Cuba	230	4	35	61	0	3.5	7.5	7.0	0.1
Dominica	11	10	1	89	0	0.4	2.3	3.9	0.1
Dominican Republic	670	22	0	76	2	3.8	18.1	20.7	0.7
Ecuador	1,610	33	35	32	0	4.6	24.8	22.0	0.7
Egypt, Arab Rep. of	411	38	12	49	2	13.3	23.3	26.6	0.9
El Salvador	195	63	1	36	0	3.8	10.1	12.0	0.1
Fiji	157	4	7	90	0	4.2	6.8	7.1	0.1
Gabon	0	89	1	11	0	0.1	2.3	0.7	0.0
Georgia	32	9	9	83	0	1.3	3.0	3.6	0.0
Ghana	755	80	0	20	0	4.1	14.3	19.0	0.7
Grenada	15	95	0	5	0	0.0	2.3	2.0	0.0
Guatemala	1,140	65	1	34	0	2.9	16.9	18.1	0.3
Guyana	162	2	3	79	16	0.6	7.5	5.1	0.3
Honduras	517	62	2	36	0	1.2	10.7	12.6	0.0
Hong Kong, China	169	23	72	5	0	29.1	32.7	10.6	0.6
India	2,040	61	10	23	6	26.2	43.7	37.9	1.3

Indonesia	2,265	51	33	16	0	18.1	27.1	22.7	0.7
Jamaica	327	27	1	73	0	1.3	13.9	15.3	0.1
Kenya	846	32	1	67	0	2.2	10.7	13.3	0.3
Korea, Rep. of	982	16	83	1	1	36.6	27.9	11.1	1.2
Kuwait	2	81	4	15	0	0.6	2.0	1.7	0.0
Kyrgyz Republic	4	74	0	26	0	0.3	2.3	1.9	0.0
Macao, China	1	78	14	9	0	1.3	3.3	1.6	0.0
Malaysia	1,895	28	38	34	0	17.2	24.5	21.3	0.3
Mauritius	336	7	3	90	0	1.3	4.8	6.7	0.0
Moldova	63	43	9	48	0	4.8	6.8	8.1	0.3
Mongolia	17	97	2	1	0	0.4	2.2	0.9	0.0
Namibia	69	10	0	90	0	0.6	4.1	3.0	0.1
Nicaragua	213	56	17	27	0	2.5	6.2	6.7	0.0
Nigeria	545	93	0	7	0	4.2	12.0	14.3	0.1
Oman	7	12	81	8	0	2.2	2.0	2.3	0.0
Pakistan	329	31	5	45	19	8.0	20.6	20.6	0.9
Panama	283	7	77	16	0	1.5	6.2	8.0	0.1
Papua New Guinea	357	34	0	66	0	0.0	3.2	2.2	0.0
Paraguay	316	89	6	3	3	3.5	8.3	6.2	0.1
Peru	759	39	2	59	0	7.2	23.7	27.2	n.a.
Philippines	1,486	22	33	46	0	17.7	24.9	22.7	n.a.
Qatar	0	32	2	67	0	0.1	0.9	1.2	n.a.
Sri Lanka	202	58	16	27	0	9.0	20.3	18.4	0.4
St. Kitts and Nevis	10	4	0	94	2	0.0	1.0	1.0	n.a.
St. Lucia	25	1	0	99	0	0.3	2.6	2.6	0.0
St. Vincent and the Grenadines	16	2	0	98	1	0.1	1.7	1.7	0.1

(Table continues on the following page.)

TABLE 8.A.2 Imports of Agricultural Products from Preference Beneficiaries by Type of Market Access to Quad Economies, 2003 (Continued)

Beneficiary	Bilateral imports (US$ million) (1)	Quad markets							
		Share of total bilateral imports (%)				Share of agricultural subheadings with at least one national tariff line with trade on a Quad market (%)			
		MFN duty-free access (2)	MFN dutiable access (3)	Preferential access (4)	Non–ad valorem duties (5)	MFN duty-free access (6)	MFN dutiable access (7)	Preferential access (8)	Non–ad valorem duties (9)
Suriname	13	12	5	38	45	1.5	4.8	9.7	0.4
Swaziland	130	1	4	96	0	1.5	1.6	5.6	0.0
Taiwan, China	550	40	60	0	0	38.5	32.1	0.0	0.3
Thailand	3,574	16	65	17	2	30.3	36.6	33.9	0.9
Trinidad and Tobago	59	25	0	74	0	1.0	10.0	10.4	0.1
United Arab Emirates	189	91	4	5	0	7.5	13.3	11.6	0.7
Uruguay	507	29	63	7	0	8.7	14.6	10.3	0.7
Venezuela, R.B. de	161	68	9	22	1	—	—	—	—
Zimbabwe	441	19	5	76	0	1.2	6.4	10.1	0.3
Total for developing economies	**55,617**	**46**	**29**	**23**	**2**	—	—	—	—
LDCs									
Angola	1	90	0	10	0	0.0	1.6	1.6	0.0
Bangladesh	18	12	2	80	6	0.4	6.8	11.4	0.6
Benin	27	93	0	7	0	0.0	2.5	1.6	0.0
Burkina Faso	39	79	11	11	0	0.1	2.8	3.2	0.0
Burundi	28	99	0	2	0	0.0	1.3	0.6	0.0
Cambodia	3	16	0	18	66	0.0	1.5	1.3	0.3

Central African Republic	0.0	0.1	1.0	0.0	0	0	0	100	8
Chad	0.0	0.0	1.0	0.0	0	0	0	100	45
Congo, Dem. Rep. of	0.0	2.5	2.8	0.0	0	25	0	75	19
Djibouti	0.0	1.5	1.7	0.0	0	24	0	77	1
Gambia, The	0.0	1.6	1.7	0.0	0	63	0	37	6
Guinea	0.0	4.1	3.6	0.0	0	4	0	96	38
Guinea-Bissau	0.0	2.3	1.3	0.0	0	3	0	97	2
Haiti	0.0	5.1	6.8	0.4	0	30	0	70	26
Lesotho	0.0	0.1	0.1	0.0	0	8	0	92	0
Madagascar	0.6	9.7	10.1	0.1	0	23	1	76	378
Malawi	0.1	2.5	3.2	0.4	0	69	8	23	291
Maldives	0.0	0.1	0.6	0.1	0	1	0	99	1
Mali	0.1	2.8	3.5	0.0	0	2	0	98	41
Mauritania	0.0	1.5	1.6	0.0	0	38	0	63	1
Mozambique	0.0	2.2	2.9	0.1	0	56	11	33	55
Myanmar	0.1	1.7	7.2	4.8	1	0	16	83	28
Nepal	0.0	2.6	4.3	0.1	0	11	73	17	7
Niger	0.0	1.3	1.6	0.3	0	58	0	42	5
Rwanda	0.0	0.9	1.5	0.0	0	2	0	99	15
Senegal	0.1	7.5	4.8	0.1	0	76	0	24	97
Sierra Leone	0.0	3.2	5.1	0.0	0	2	0	98	11
Solomon Islands	0.0	0.1	1.5	0.0	0	10	0	90	2
Tanzania	0.1	7.5	8.3	0.1	0	42	0	58	158
Togo	0.0	5.2	5.5	0.1	0	20	0	80	42
Uganda	0.1	7.4	7.1	0.1	0	30	0	70	217
Zambia	0.4	2.8	2.9	0.3	0	50	28	23	81
Total for LDCs	—	—	—	—	**0**	**37**	**4**	**59**	**1,691**
Total for all beneficiaries	—	—	—	—	**1**	**24**	**29**	**46**	**57,308**

Source: Authors' calculations.

Note: — = not available; n.a. = not applicable.

TABLE 8.A.3 Imports of Agricultural Products from Beneficiaries by Type of Market Access: European Union, 2003

Beneficiary	Bilateral imports (US$ million) (1)	EU							
		Imports (% of total bilateral imports)				Percentage of agricultural subheadings with at least one national tariff line with trade			
		MFN duty-free access (2)	MFN dutiable access (3)	Preferential access (4)	Non-ad valorem duties (5)	MFN duty-free access (6)	MFN dutiable access (7)	Preferential access (8)	Non-ad valorem duties (9)
Developing economies									
Albania	19	71	0	29	0	0.1	4.5	5.6	0.0
Antigua and Barbuda	12	88	0	12	0	0.3	1.6	2.3	0.0
Argentina	4,363	60	20	13	7	10.4	15.5	20.0	1.3
Armenia	0	56	4	40	0	0.7	0.9	2.0	0.0
Bahrain	1	88	1	11	0	0.1	0.9	0.6	0.0
Barbados	31	18	0	81	0	0.4	1.6	2.3	0.1
Belize	83	1	4	95	0	0.1	1.5	1.7	0.0
Bolivia	41	72	0	28	0	0.3	3.8	4.8	0.0
Botswana	37	1	0	99	0	0.1	0.4	0.4	0.0
Brazil	8,551	66	28	4	2	23.3	19.3	14.2	1.3
Brunei Darussalam	0	97	0	3	0	0.0	0.1	0.1	0.0
Cameroon	583	55	0	45	0	1.2	5.6	7.7	0.1
China	1,923	51	10	39	1	15.2	25.9	30.0	1.6
Colombia	1,031	34	45	21	0	1.0	7.0	18.2	0.3
Congo, Rep. of	13	68	0	32	0	0.0	1.6	1.3	0.0
Cuba	209	2	36	62	0	1.9	3.6	6.2	0.1

Côte d'Ivoire	2,158	62	0	38	0	1.3	6.2	9.6	0.1
Dominica	10	9	0	91	0	0.3	1.5	3.3	0.1
Dominican Republic	170	17	0	80	3	0.9	4.3	11.9	0.6
Ecuador	870	10	61	30	0	0.9	7.4	15.5	0.6
Egypt, Arab Rep. of	343	39	5	55	2	5.1	13.8	22.4	0.9
El Salvador	64	85	2	13	0	0.1	1.9	1.6	0.0
Fiji	114	2	0	98	0	0.0	1.2	1.5	0.0
Gabon	0	80	1	19	0	0.1	0.9	0.7	0.0
Georgia	27	6	1	93	0	0.4	1.7	2.5	0.0
Ghana	617	77	0	23	0	1.7	8.1	16.2	0.7
Grenada	12	94	0	6	0	0.0	0.9	1.0	0.0
Guatemala	234	54	1	46	0	0.1	4.8	8.4	0.0
Guyana	150	1	3	78	17	0.3	2.0	1.0	0.3
Honduras	196	70	6	24	0	0.1	3.0	5.4	0.0
Hong Kong, China	53	10	90	0	0	21.1	12.7	0.0	0.6
India	1,065	55	5	28	12	7.1	22.3	27.1	1.3
Indonesia	1,341	34	46	20	0	4.5	12.2	17.2	0.7
Jamaica	152	8	0	92	0	0.1	3.0	8.1	0.1
Kenya	780	29	1	70	0	1.2	6.5	12.3	0.3
Korea, Rep. of	48	39	59	0	3	19.0	8.4	0.0	1.0
Kuwait	1	83	0	17	0	0.3	1.6	1.7	0.0
Kyrgyz Republic	4	74	0	26	0	0.0	2.3	1.9	0.0
Macao, China	0	96	0	4	0	0.1	0.9	0.4	0.0
Malaysia	1,046	19	52	30	0	3.9	11.1	15.2	0.3
Mauritius	324	5	3	93	0	0.6	3.9	6.5	0.0
Moldova	60	43	7	49	0	2.0	4.1	7.2	0.3
Mongolia	14	100	0	0	0	0.0	1.6	0.3	0.0

(Table continues on the following page.)

TABLE 8.A.3 Imports of Agricultural Products from Beneficiaries by Type of Market Access: European Union, 2003 (Continued)

Beneficiary	Bilateral imports (US$ million) (1)	Imports (% of total bilateral imports)				Percentage of agricultural subheadings with at least one national tariff line with trade			
		MFN duty-free access (2)	MFN dutiable access (3)	Preferential access (4)	Non–ad valorem duties (5)	MFN duty-free access (6)	MFN dutiable access (7)	Preferential access (8)	Non–ad valorem duties (9)
Namibia	68	10	0	90	0	0.4	3.3	2.9	0.1
Nicaragua	63	81	0	19	0	0.3	2.3	3.0	0.0
Nigeria	475	93	0	7	0	2.5	7.4	12.0	0.1
Oman	0	41	0	60	0	0.0	0.7	1.9	0.0
Pakistan	268	26	0	50	24	0.9	10.9	16.5	0.9
Panama	240	2	90	8	0	0.6	2.5	4.2	0.1
Papua New Guinea	307	24	0	76	0	0.0	2.8	1.6	0.0
Paraguay	264	93	2	1	3	1.6	5.1	3.8	0.1
Peru	427	41	1	57	1	0.6	10.9	17.7	0.6
Philippines	327	26	54	20	0	3.9	7.0	14.5	0.4
Qatar	0	30	2	68	0	0.1	0.7	1.2	0.0
Sri Lanka	123	59	18	22	0	3.2	10.3	13.9	0.4
St. Kitts and Nevis	9	2	0	99	0	0.0	0.3	1.0	0.0
St. Lucia	25	0	0	100	0	0.3	0.4	1.7	0.0
St. Vincent and the Grenadines	16	1	0	98	1	0.1	0.4	1.2	0.1
Suriname	12	10	5	38	46	1.0	3.6	9.3	0.4
Swaziland	118	0	1	99	0	0.4	0.7	4.9	0.0

EU

Taiwan, China	53	30	70	0	0	18.1	9.4	0.0	0.3
Thailand	1,199	6	80	9	5	21.0	14.2	17.7	0.9
Trinidad and Tobago	38	22	0	78	0	0.3	2.5	3.8	0.1
United Arab Emirates	176	95	48	5	0	2.0	9.7	11.0	0.7
Uruguay	318	43	12	9	1	4.3	9.3	4.9	0.7
Venezuela, R.B. de	115	68	12	21	0	—	—	—	—
Zimbabwe	392	15	1	85	0	0.6	4.1	9.6	0.3
Total developing economies	**31,787**	**49**	**24**	**25**	**3**	—	—	—	—
LDCs									
Angola	1	90	0	10	0	0.0	1.5	1.6	0.0
Bangladesh	16	7	0	87	6	0.1	3.8	8.5	0.6
Benin	26	93	0	8	0	0.0	2.3	1.5	0.0
Burkina Faso	30	72	14	14	0	0.1	2.2	2.5	0.0
Burundi	21	98	0	2	0	0.0	1.3	0.4	0.0
Cambodia	2	0	0	21	79	0.0	0.6	0.7	0.3
Central African Republic	8	100	0	0	0	0.0	0.7	0.0	0.0
Chad	41	100	0	0	0	0.0	1.0	0.0	0.0
Congo, Dem. Rep. of	17	72	0	28	0	0.0	2.5	2.3	0.0
Djibouti	1	76	0	25	0	0.0	1.6	1.2	0.0
Gambia, The	6	34	0	66	0	0.0	1.6	1.6	0.0
Guinea	29	96	0	4	0	0.0	2.6	3.2	0.0
Guinea-Bissau	2	97	0	4	0	0.0	1.2	2.3	0.0
Haiti	13	78	0	22	0	0.1	1.6	1.9	0.0
Lesotho	0	92	0	8	0	0.0	0.1	0.1	0.0
Madagascar	171	47	2	51	0	0.1	8.1	8.5	0.6
Malawi	207	16	1	83	0	0.1	2.5	2.0	0.1

(Table continues on the following page.)

TABLE 8.A.3 Imports of Agricultural Products from Beneficiaries by Type of Market Access: European Union, 2003 (*Continued*)

Beneficiary	Bilateral imports (US$ million) (1)	Imports (% of total bilateral imports)				Percentage of agricultural subheadings with at least one national tariff line with trade			
		MFN duty-free access (2)	MFN dutiable access (3)	Preferential access (4)	Non–ad valorem duties (5)	MFN duty-free access (6)	MFN dutiable access (7)	Preferential access (8)	Non–ad valorem duties (9)
Maldives	1	99	0	1	0	0.0	0.4	0.1	0.0
Mali	41	98	0	2	0	0.0	3.0	2.6	0.1
Mauritania	1	64	0	36	0	0.0	1.0	1.0	0.0
Mozambique	46	31	13	56	0	0.1	2.0	1.9	0.0
Myanmar	4	72	23	1	5	0.1	1.7	1.2	0.1
Nepal	7	12	80	8	0	0.1	2.2	1.7	0.0
Niger	2	63	0	37	0	0.0	1.0	0.9	0.0
Rwanda	13	98	0	2	0	0.0	1.3	0.7	0.0
Senegal	96	23	0	77	0	0.0	4.3	7.0	0.1
Sierra Leone	10	99	0	1	0	0.1	3.6	1.6	0.0
Solomon Islands	2	87	0	13	0	0.0	1.5	0.1	0.0
Tanzania	120	45	0	55	0	0.0	7.1	6.7	0.1
Togo	40	79	0	21	0	0.0	3.9	5.1	0.0
Uganda	180	64	0	36	0	0.0	4.5	7.1	0.1
Zambia	70	11	32	57	0	0.3	2.0	2.6	0.3
Total LDCs	**1,223**	**49**	**4**	**47**	**0**	—	—	—	—
Total	**33,010**	**49**	**23**	**25**	**3**	—	—	—	—

Source: Authors' calculations.
Note: — = not available.

TABLE 8.A.4 Weighted Duty Margins: Agricultural Products, 2003

Beneficiary	Weighted preference margins					Adjusted weighted preference margins				
	Quad economies (1)	Canada (2)	EU (3)	Japan (4)	United States (5)	Quad economies (6)	Canada (7)	EU (8)	Japan (9)	United States (10)
Developing economies										
Albania	2	0	3	1	0	0	−1	1	0	0
Antigua and Barbuda	1	1	1	0	2	0	0	0	0	−1
Argentina	0	0	0	2	1	−1	0	−1	1	−4
Armenia	2	0	3	0	2	0	−1	−1	0	0
Bahrain	0	0	0	—	—	0	0	0	—	—
Barbados	34	4	45	0	8	4	0	6	0	1
Belize	35	0	38	0	31	14	0	15	0	16
Bolivia	8	0	8	0	9	2	0	2	0	2
Botswana	17	2	17	—	0	16	−2	16	—	0
Brazil	1	11	0	0	0	−3	0	−1	0	−17
Brunei Darussalam	0	3	0	0	0	0	0	0	0	0
Cameroon	11	0	12	0	0	9	0	9	0	0
China	1	1	2	1	0	−1	−2	−5	0	−1
Colombia	3	12	2	0	4	−1	−1	−3	0	1
Congo, Rep. of	21	0	16	0	37	4	0	2	0	10
Cuba	7	7	8	0	—	−12	2	−13	0	—
Côte d'Ivoire	4	0	5	0	0	2	0	2	0	0
Dominica	22	0	23	0	4	17	0	18	0	1
Dominican Republic	14	1	19	4	13	6	0	12	0	4
Ecuador	3	0	3	5	3	−2	0	−5	0	0

(Table continues on the following page.)

315

TABLE 8.A.4 Weighted Duty Margins: Agricultural Products, 2003 (Continued)

Beneficiary	Weighted preference margins					Adjusted weighted preference margins				
	Quad economies (1)	Canada (2)	EU (3)	Japan (4)	United States (5)	Quad economies (6)	Canada (7)	EU (8)	Japan (9)	United States (10)
Egypt, Arab Rep. of	2	1	3	0	1	0	−2	0	0	0
El Salvador	12	79	2	0	14	2	0	0	0	4
Fiji	48	0	64	0	8	7	−1	9	0	2
Gabon	1	0	3	—	0	1	0	1	—	0
Georgia	3	0	3	0	0	−1	0	−1	0	0
Ghana	2	0	2	0	2	0	0	0	0	0
Grenada	1	0	1	0	0	1	0	1	0	0
Guatemala	6	19	5	0	5	1	0	1	0	0
Guyana	58	78	59	0	29	8	0	8	0	7
Honduras	4	0	2	0	5	0	0	0	0	0
Hong Kong, China	0	2	0	0	0	−2	−2	−5	0	−2
India	1	1	1	1	1	0	0	−1	0	0
Indonesia	1	1	1	3	0	−1	0	−1	0	0
Jamaica	20	2	41	0	3	5	0	9	0	1
Kenya	7	0	8	2	0	2	0	3	1	0
Korea, Rep. of	0	1	0	0	0	−1	−2	−3	0	−3
Kuwait	1	0	1	—	0	0	−2	0	—	−1
Kyrgyz Republic	1	0	1	0	0	0	0	0	0	0
Macao, China	0	1	0	0	0	0	−1	0	0	0
Malaysia	1	2	1	4	0	0	−1	−1	2	0

Country										
Mauritius	58	4	60	0	12	11	0	11	0	3
Moldova	2	0	2	0	1	-1	-1	-1	0	0
Mongolia	0	0	0	0	0	0	0	0	0	0
Namibia	11	0	11	0	0	10	0	10	0	0
Nicaragua	5	0	5	0	6	1	0	1	0	1
Nigeria	0	0	1	0	0	0	0	0	0	0
Oman	6	0	2	2	0	0	-2	-1	0	0
Pakistan	4	0	7	0	1	2	0	3	0	-1
Panama	4	0	1	2	21	-5	0	-7	1	5
Papua New Guinea	1	3	4	0	5	3	0	3	0	1
Paraguay	8	0	0	1	8	0	-2	-1	0	1
Peru	6	2	7	7	11	3	0	4	0	2
Philippines	2	.	1	1	8	1	0	-1	2	2
Qatar	1	0	2	-1	0	-1	-1	-1	-1	0
Sri Lanka	64	3	1	1	0	0	0	0	0	0
St. Kitts and Nevis	29	0	65	0	0	7	0	8	0	0
St. Lucia	29	3	29	0	4	22	0	22	0	1
St. Vincent and the Grenadines	29	0	29	0	1	22	0	22	0	1
Suriname	7	0	8	0	0	2	0	2	0	0
Swaziland	47	0	48	0	53	7	0	7	0	14
Taiwan, China	0	1	0	-2	0	-2	-2	-4	-1	-2
Thailand	1	1	1	-1	2	-2	-1	-7	1	-1
Trinidad and Tobago	35	4	48	5	15	5	1	6	0	4
United Arab Emirates	0	2	0	-1	2	0	-1	0	-1	-1
Uruguay	0	0	0	-4	2	-2	-4	-1	0	0

(Table continues on the following page.)

TABLE 8.A.4 Weighted Duty Margins: Agricultural Products, 2003 (*Continued*)

Beneficiary	Weighted preference margins					Adjusted weighted preference margins				
	Quad economies (1)	Canada (2)	EU (3)	Japan (4)	United States (5)	Quad economies (6)	Canada (7)	EU (8)	Japan (9)	United States (10)
Venezuela, R.B. de	2	1	3	0	1	1	0	1	0	0
Zimbabwe	10	7	11	0	0	2	2	4	0	−24
Total developing economies	**1.3**	**1.6**	**1.5**	**0.4**	**1.7**	**−0.4**	**−0.4**	**−0.3**	**0.1**	**−1.4**
LDCs										
Angola	4	—	4	—	0	4	—	4	—	0
Bangladesh	10	0	11	2	5	2	0	3	2	−3
Benin	1	0	1	0	0	0	0	0	0	0
Burkina Faso	1	0	2	0	0	−6	0	−8	0	0
Burundi	0	0	0	1	0	0	0	0	1	0
Cambodia	8	0	15	—	1	2	0	4	—	0
Central African Republic	0	1	0	—	0	0	0	0	—	0
Chad	0	—	0	0	0	0	—	0	0	0
Congo, Dem. Rep. of	6	0	7	0	0	1	0	1	0	0
Djibouti	2	—	2	0	—	0	—	1	0	—
Gambia, The	6	0	6	0	1	2	0	2	0	0
Guinea	0	0	0	0	0	0	0	0	0	0
Guinea-Bissau	0	—	0	—	1	0	—	0	—	0
Haiti	1	0	1	0	0	1	0	1	0	0
Lesotho	1	—	1	—	—	1	—	1	—	—
Madagascar	2	0.1	3.8	0.0	0.0	0.1	0.0	0.2	0.0	0.0

	1	2	3	4	5	6	7	8	9	10
Malawi	14	0	17	1	10	2	0	3	1	-4
Maldives	0	0	0	—	0	0	0	0	—	-4
Mali	0	0	0	0	0	0	0	0	0	0
Mauritania	4	7	4	2	0	1	1	1	1	0
Mozambique	11	1	6	0	59	-3	0	-6	0	16
Myanmar	0	0	0	0	0	-1	0	-8	0	0
Nepal	1	0	1	2	2	-43	0	-48	1	2
Niger	2	0	2	0	3	2	0	1	0	3
Rwanda	0	0	0	3	0	0	0	0	3	0
Senegal	6	7	6	0	1	3	1	3	0	0
Sierra Leone	0	0	0	7	1	0	0	0	7	0
Solomon Islands	1	0	1	0	0	2	0	1	0	0
Tanzania	8	0	11	0	0	1	0	2	0	0
Togo	2	0	2	0	0	0	0	1	0	0
Uganda	2	0	3	0	0	1	0	1	0	0
Zambia	5	0	6	0	1	-16	0	-18	0	0
Total LDC	**2.5**	**0.0**	**2.9**	**0.1**	**1.8**	**0.1**	**0.0**	**0.2**	**0.1**	**-0.3**
Total	**1.4**	**1.6**	**1.5**	**0.3**	**1.7**	**-0.4**	**-0.4**	**-0.2**	**0.1**	**-1.4**

Source: Authors' calculations.
Note: Weighted by bilateral imports. — = not available.

TABLE 8.A.5 Effect of MFN Tariff Reduction in Quad Markets on Preference Value and Scope for Future Preferences: Agricultural Products, 2003

	Quad economies									
	Without flexibilities					With flexibilities (2% highest tariff)				
	Change in the preference value for unadjusted and adjusted preference margins				Scope for additional preference (US$ million) (5)	Change in the preference value for unadjusted and adjusted preference margins				Scope for additional preference (US$ million) (10)
	No adjustment		With adjustment			No adjustment		With adjustment		
Beneficiary	Value (US$ million) (1)	Share of imports (%) (2)	Value (US$ million) (3)	Share of imports (%) (4)		Value (US$ million) (6)	Share of imports (%) (7)	Value (US$ million) (8)	Share of imports (%) (9)	
Developing economies										
Albania	−0.2	−1.0	0.0	−0.2	0.0	−0.2	−1.0	0.0	−0.2	0.0
Antigua and Barbuda	0.0	−0.4	0.0	−0.2	0.0	0.0	−0.4	0.0	−0.2	0.1
Argentina	−16.5	−0.3	34.9	0.7	190.2	−16.5	−0.3	31.0	0.6	248.0
Armenia	0.0	−1.1	0.0	−0.1	0.1	0.0	−1.1	0.0	−0.1	0.1
Bahrain	0.0	−0.4	0.0	−0.1	0.0	0.0	−0.4	0.0	−0.1	0.0
Barbados	−9.5	−21.3	−1.2	−2.8	0.0	−9.5	−21.3	−1.2	−2.8	0.0
Belize	−24.3	−20.8	−9.5	−8.1	0.6	−24.3	−20.8	−9.5	−8.1	0.6
Bolivia	−3.2	−4.5	−0.7	−0.9	0.2	−3.2	−4.5	−0.7	−0.9	0.2
Botswana	−6.5	−17.3	−5.8	−15.5	8.6	−6.5	−17.3	−5.8	−15.5	10.8
Brazil	−39.5	−0.3	242.5	2.1	607.6	−39.5	−0.3	178.9	1.6	1,039.6
Brunei Darussalam	0.0	−0.1	0.0	0.0	0.0	0.0	−0.1	0.0	0.0	0.0
Cameroon	−37.4	−6.1	−29.8	−4.9	0.1	−37.3	−6.1	−29.8	−4.9	0.1

China	-49.6	-0.6	44.3	0.6	282.1	-49.6	-0.6	24.9	0.3	304.5
Colombia	-43.7	-1.8	15.0	0.6	68.1	-43.7	-1.8	14.7	0.6	70.9
Congo, Rep. of	-2.5	-13.7	-0.5	-2.5	0.0	-2.5	-13.7	-0.5	-2.5	0.0
Côte d'Ivoire	-54.9	-2.1	-22.1	-0.8	1.5	-54.9	-2.1	-22.1	-0.8	1.5
Cuba	-13.9	-6.0	12.7	5.5	20.5	-13.9	-6.0	12.7	5.5	20.5
Dominica	-1.3	-12.1	-1.0	-8.9	0.0	-1.3	-12.1	-1.0	-8.9	0.0
Dominican Republic	-54.0	-8.1	-21.0	-3.1	0.4	-54.0	-8.1	-21.0	-3.1	0.4
Ecuador	-24.4	-1.5	22.2	1.4	81.6	-24.4	-1.5	22.2	1.4	81.6
Egypt, Arab Rep. of	-8.2	-2.0	-1.4	-0.4	15.0	-8.2	-2.0	-1.4	-0.4	15.0
El Salvador	-15.1	-7.7	-2.5	-1.3	0.3	-15.1	-7.7	-2.5	-1.3	0.3
Fiji	-49.2	-31.2	-6.7	-4.3	7.7	-49.2	-31.2	-6.7	-4.3	19.1
Gabon	0.0	-0.6	0.0	-0.1	0.0	0.0	-0.6	0.0	-0.1	0.0
Georgia	-0.7	-2.2	-0.1	-0.4	0.9	-0.7	-2.2	-0.1	-0.4	0.9
Ghana	-5.3	-0.7	-0.6	-0.1	0.1	-5.3	-0.7	-0.6	-0.1	0.2
Grenada	-0.1	-0.5	0.0	-0.3	0.0	-0.1	-0.5	0.0	-0.3	0.0
Guatemala	-39.7	-3.5	-1.9	-0.2	8.7	-39.7	-3.5	-2.9	-0.3	21.3
Guyana	-51.5	-31.9	-6.6	-4.1	0.9	-51.5	-31.9	-6.6	-4.1	0.9
Honduras	-9.9	-1.9	0.9	0.2	2.1	-9.9	-1.9	0.1	0.0	2.9
Hong Kong, China	-0.3	-0.2	2.1	1.2	5.1	-0.3	-0.2	2.1	1.2	5.1
India	-13.6	-0.7	2.1	0.1	24.1	-13.6	-0.7	1.9	0.1	25.1
Indonesia	-11.9	-0.5	3.0	0.1	37.1	-11.9	-0.5	2.9	0.1	37.1
Jamaica	-40.8	-12.5	-8.5	-2.6	0.7	-40.8	-12.5	-8.5	-2.6	0.7
Kenya	-27.3	-3.2	-5.8	-0.7	2.0	-27.3	-3.2	-5.8	-0.7	2.0
Korea, Rep. of	-0.2	0.0	5.5	0.6	52.4	-0.2	0.0	5.5	0.6	52.4
Kuwait	0.0	-0.6	0.0	-0.1	0.0	0.0	-0.6	0.0	-0.1	0.0

(Table continues on the following page.)

TABLE 8.A.5 Effect of MFN Tariff Reduction in Quad Markets on Preference Value and Scope for Future Preferences: Agricultural Products, 2003 (Continued)

	Quad economies									
	Without flexibilities					With flexibilities (2% highest tariff)				
	Change in the preference value for unadjusted and adjusted preference margins					Change in the preference value for unadjusted and adjusted preference margins				
	No adjustment		With adjustment			No adjustment		With adjustment		
Beneficiary	Value (US$ million) (1)	Share of imports (%) (2)	Value (US$ million) (3)	Share of imports (%) (4)	Scope for additional preference (US$ million) (5)	Value (US$ million) (6)	Share of imports (%) (7)	Value (US$ million) (8)	Share of imports (%) (9)	Scope for additional preference (US$ million) (10)
Kyrgyz Republic	0.0	−0.7	0.0	0.0	0.0	0.0	−0.7	0.0	0.0	0.0
Macao, China	0.0	−0.2	0.0	0.1	0.0	0.0	−0.2	0.0	0.1	0.0
Malaysia	−14.5	−0.8	0.2	0.0	28.4	−14.5	−0.8	0.2	0.0	28.4
Mauritius	−127.6	−38.0	−23.4	−7.0	0.5	−127.6	−38.0	−23.4	−7.0	0.5
Moldova	−0.8	−1.3	0.2	0.3	1.5	−0.8	−1.3	0.2	0.3	1.5
Mongolia	0.0	−0.1	0.0	0.0	0.0	0.0	−0.1	0.0	0.0	0.0
Namibia	−7.5	−11.0	−6.5	−9.5	11.7	−7.5	−11.0	−6.5	−9.5	12.4
Nicaragua	−6.3	−3.0	−1.2	−0.6	4.4	−6.3	−3.0	−1.2	−0.6	4.5
Nigeria	−1.2	−0.2	−0.1	0.0	0.1	−1.2	−0.2	−0.1	0.0	0.1
Oman	0.0	−0.1	0.0	0.2	0.2	0.0	−0.1	0.0	0.2	0.2
Pakistan	−8.0	−2.4	−2.7	−0.8	0.6	−8.0	−2.4	−2.7	−0.8	0.6
Panama	−6.2	−2.2	7.6	2.7	29.4	−6.2	−2.2	7.6	2.7	29.4
Papua New Guinea	−6.4	−1.8	−4.9	−1.4	0.0	−6.4	−1.8	−4.9	−1.4	0.0
Paraguay	−1.3	−0.4	0.8	0.2	2.3	−1.3	−0.4	0.8	0.2	2.7

Peru	−32.1	−4.2	−8.4	−1.1	4.1	−32.1	−4.2	−8.4	−1.1	4.1
Philippines	−65.1	−4.4	−15.6	−1.1	70.1	−65.1	−4.4	−15.5	−1.0	68.4
Qatar	0.0	−1.9	0.0	−0.2	0.0	0.0	−1.9	0.0	−0.2	0.0
Sri Lanka	−1.3	−0.7	−0.1	0.0	2.6	−1.3	−0.7	−0.1	0.0	2.6
St. Kitts and Nevis	−3.9	−40.5	−0.5	−4.7	0.0	−3.9	−40.5	−0.5	−4.7	0.0
St. Lucia	−4.0	−15.8	−3.1	−12.1	0.0	−4.0	−15.8	−3.1	−12.1	0.0
St. Vincent and the Grenadines	−2.5	−15.5	−1.9	−11.9	0.0	−2.5	−15.5	−1.9	−11.9	0.0
Suriname	−0.2	−1.9	0.0	−0.4	0.2	−0.2	−1.9	0.0	−0.4	0.2
Swaziland	−39.1	−30.1	−5.6	−4.3	1.9	−39.1	−30.1	−5.6	−4.3	1.9
Taiwan, China	0.0	0.0	7.0	1.3	17.5	0.0	0.0	7.0	1.3	17.5
Thailand	−29.0	−0.8	35.7	1.0	550.5	−29.0	−0.8	55.7	1.6	312.4
Trinidad and Tobago	−13.3	−22.5	−1.8	−3.1	0.0	−13.3	−22.5	−1.8	−3.1	0.0
United Arab Emirates	−0.5	−0.3	−0.1	0.0	1.1	−0.5	−0.3	−0.1	0.0	1.1
Uruguay	−1.5	−0.3	4.8	0.9	57.3	−1.5	−0.3	4.8	0.9	46.3
Venezuela, R.B. de	−1.8	−1.1	−0.5	−0.3	2.0	−1.8	−1.1	−0.5	−0.3	1.9
Zimbabwe	−24.4	−5.5	−4.7	−1.1	39.1	−24.4	−5.5	−3.0	−0.7	16.7
Developing economies										
Positive	*0.0*		*353.3*			*0.0*		*461.3*		
Negative	*−1,054.1*		*−208.0*			*−1,054.1*		*−205.1*		
Total developing economies	**−1,054.1**	**−1.9**	**145.3**	**0.3**	**2,788.8**	**−1,054.1**	**−1.9**	**256.2**	**0.5**	**1,971.1**

(Table continues on the following page.)

TABLE 8.A.5 Effect of MFN Tariff Reduction in Quad Markets on Preference Value and Scope for Future Preferences: Agricultural Products, 2003 (*Continued*)

	Quad economies									
	Without flexibilities					With flexibilities (2% highest tariff)				
	Change in the preference value for unadjusted and adjusted preference margins					Change in the preference value for unadjusted and adjusted preference margins				
	No adjustment		With adjustment		Scope for additional preference (US$ million) (5)	No adjustment		With adjustment		Scope for additional preference (US$ million) (10)
Beneficiary	Value (US$ million) (1)	Share of imports (%) (2)	Value (US$ million) (3)	Share of imports (%) (4)		Value (US$ million) (6)	Share of imports (%) (7)	Value (US$ million) (8)	Share of imports (%) (9)	
LDCs										
Angola	0.0	−2.6	0.0	−2.3	0.0	0.0	−2.5	0.0	−2.2	0.0
Bangladesh	−0.8	−4.3	−0.1	−0.5	0.3	−0.8	−4.3	−0.1	−0.6	0.8
Benin	−0.1	−0.3	0.0	−0.1	0.0	−0.1	−0.3	0.0	−0.1	0.0
Burkina Faso	−0.2	−0.5	1.6	4.1	1.0	−0.2	−0.5	1.6	4.1	1.0
Burundi	0.0	−0.1	0.0	0.0	0.0	0.0	−0.1	0.0	0.0	0.0
Cambodia	0.0	−1.2	0.0	−0.3	0.0	0.0	−1.2	0.0	−0.3	0.0
Central African Republic	0.0	0.0	0.0	0.0	0.0	0.0	0.0	0.0	0.0	0.0
Chad	0.0	0.0	0.0	0.0	0.0	0.0	0.0	0.0	0.0	0.0
Congo, Dem. Rep. of	−0.6	−3.4	−0.1	−0.6	0.0	−0.6	−3.4	−0.1	−0.6	0.0
Djibouti	0.0	−0.8	0.0	−0.1	0.0	0.0	−0.8	0.0	−0.1	0.0
Gambia, The	−0.2	−2.8	0.0	−0.4	0.0	−0.2	−2.8	0.0	−0.4	0.0
Guinea	0.0	−0.1	0.0	0.0	0.0	0.0	−0.1	0.0	0.0	0.0

	1	2	3	4	5	6	7	8	9	10
Guinea-Bissau	0.0	0.0	0.0	−0.1	0.0	0.0	0.0	0.0	−0.1	0.0
Haiti	0.0	0.0	0.0	−0.5	−0.1	0.0	0.0	0.0	−0.5	−0.1
Lesotho	−0.6	−0.6	0.0	−0.7	0.0	0.0	−0.6	0.0	−0.7	0.0
Madagascar	0.7	0.1	0.3	−0.8	−3.0	0.7	0.1	0.3	−0.8	−3.0
Malawi	48.1	−1.1	−3.1	−8.4	−24.5	19.5	−0.3	−0.8	−8.4	−24.5
Maldives	0.0	0.0	0.0	0.0	0.0	0.0	0.0	0.0	0.0	0.0
Mali	0.0	0.0	0.0	−0.1	−0.1	0.0	0.0	0.0	−0.1	−0.1
Mauritania	0.0	−0.2	0.0	−1.6	0.0	0.0	−0.2	0.0	−1.6	0.0
Mozambique	1.4	2.5	1.4	−6.2	−3.4	1.4	2.5	1.4	−6.2	−3.4
Myanmar	0.5	0.8	0.2	0.0	0.0	0.5	0.8	0.2	0.0	0.0
Nepal	1.2	28.1	2.0	−0.4	0.0	1.2	28.1	2.0	−0.4	0.0
Niger	0.0	−0.7	0.0	−1.1	−0.1	0.0	−0.7	0.0	−1.1	−0.1
Rwanda	0.0	−0.1	0.0	−0.1	0.0	0.0	−0.1	0.0	−0.1	0.0
Senegal	0.0	−0.6	−0.5	−2.8	−2.7	0.0	−0.6	−0.5	−2.8	−2.7
Sierra Leone	0.0	0.0	0.0	−0.1	0.0	0.0	0.0	0.0	−0.1	0.0
Solomon Islands	0.0	−0.2	0.0	−0.3	0.0	0.0	−0.2	0.0	−0.3	0.0
Tanzania	0.0	−0.9	−1.4	−4.8	−7.6	0.0	−0.9	−1.4	−4.8	−7.6
Togo	0.0	−0.3	−0.1	−0.9	−0.4	0.0	−0.3	−0.1	−1.0	−0.4
Uganda	0.0	−0.2	−0.5	−1.1	−2.3	0.0	−0.2	−0.5	−1.1	−2.3
Zambia	5.3	10.6	8.6	−2.4	−1.9	5.3	10.6	8.6	−2.4	−1.9
LDCs										
Positive			*14.1*		*0.0*			*14.1*		*0.0*
Negative			*−6.0*		*−48.2*			*−3.8*		*−48.2*
Total LDCs	**59.0**	**0.5**	**8.1**	**−2.8**	**−48.2**	**30.0**	**0.6**	**10.4**	**−2.9**	**−48.2**
All										
Positive			*367.4*		*0.0*			*475.4*		*0.0*
Negative			*−214.0*		*−1,102.2*			*−208.8*		*−1,102.3*
Total	**2,847.8**	**0.3**	**153.4**	**−1.9**	**−1,102.2**	**2,001.1**	**0.5**	**266.6**	**−1.9**	**−1,102.3**

(*Table continues on the following page.*)

TABLE 8.A.5 Effect of MFN Tariff Reduction in Quad Markets on Preference Value and Scope for Future Preferences: Agricultural Products, 2003 (Continued)

	Quad economies									
	Without flexibilities					With flexibilities (4% highest tariff)				
	Change in the preference value for unadjusted and adjusted preference margins					Change in the preference value for unadjusted and adjusted preference margins				
	No adjustment		With adjustment		Scope for additional preference (US$ million) (5)	No adjustment		With adjustment		Scope for additional preference (US$ million) (10)
Beneficiary	Value (US$ million) (1)	Share of imports (%) (2)	Value (US$ million) (3)	Share of imports (%) (4)		Value (US$ million) (6)	Share of imports (%) (7)	Value (US$ million) (8)	Share of imports (%) (9)	
Developing economies										
Positive	0.0		461.3			0.0		325.0		
Negative	−1,054.1		−205.1			−993.8		−192.7		
Total developing economies	**−1,054.1**	**−1.9**	**256.2**	**0.5**	**1,971.1**	**−993.8**	**−1.8**	**132.3**	**0.2**	**3,050.4**
LDC										
Positive	0.0		14.1			0.0		14.5		
Negative	−48.2		−3.8			−46.3		−5.8		
Total LDCs	**−48.2**	**−2.9**	**10.4**	**0.6**	**30.0**	**−46.3**	**−2.7**	**8.7**	**0.5**	**59.2**
All										
Positive	0.0		475.4			0.0		339.4		
Negative	−1,102.3		−208.8			−1,040.1		−198.5		
Total	**−1,102.3**	**−1.9**	**266.6**	**0.5**	**2,001.1**	**−1,040.1**	**−1.8**	**141.0**	**0.2**	**3,109.5**

Source: Authors' calculations.

Note: Group of 20 proposal applied on 2003 MFN applied rates.

TABLE 8.A.6 Effect of MFN Tariff Reduction in Europe and the United States on Preference Value and Scope for Future Preferences: Agricultural Products, 2003

	Without flexibilities									
	EU					United States				
	Change in the preference value for unadjusted and adjusted preference margins					Change in the preference value for unadjusted and adjusted preference margins				
	No adjustment		With adjustment		Scope for additional preferences (US$ million) (5)	No adjustment		With adjustment		Scope for additional preferences (US$ million) (10)
Beneficiary	Value (US$ million) (1)	Share of imports (%) (2)	Value (US$ million) (3)	Share of imports (%) (4)		Value (US$ million) (6)	Share of imports (%) (7)	Value (US$ million) (8)	Share of imports (%) (9)	
Developing economies										
Albania	−0.2	−1.2	0.0	−0.2	0.0	0.0	0.0	0.0	0.0	0.0
Antigua and Barbuda	0.0	−0.4	0.0	−0.2	0.0	0.0	−1.2	0.0	−0.1	0.0
Argentina	−11.8	−0.3	19.7	0.5	143.3	−2.2	−0.4	15.8	2.8	41.7
Armenia	0.0	−2.6	0.0	−0.3	0.0	0.0	−0.9	0.0	−0.1	0.1
Bahrain	0.0	−0.4	0.0	−0.1	0.0	—	—	—	—	—
Barbados	−9.0	−28.9	−1.2	−3.8	0.0	−0.4	−4.4	−0.1	−0.6	0.0
Belize	−19.3	−23.3	−6.9	−8.3	0.3	−5.0	−17.6	−2.5	−8.9	0.0
Bolivia	−1.9	−4.5	−0.3	−0.8	0.0	−1.3	−6.0	−0.3	−1.6	0.0
Botswana	−6.5	−17.3	−5.8	−15.5	8.6	0.0	0.0	0.0	0.0	0.0
Brazil	−9.0	−0.1	60.6	0.7	299.3	−3.3	−0.2	182.8	11.6	258.9

(Table continues on the following page.)

327

TABLE 8.A.6 Effect of MFN Tariff Reduction in Europe and the United States on Preference Value and Scope for Future Preferences: Agricultural Products, 2003 (Continued)

	Without flexibilities									
	EU					United States				
	Change in the preference value for unadjusted and adjusted preference margins					Change in the preference value for unadjusted and adjusted preference margins				
	No adjustment		With adjustment		Scope for additional preferences (US$ million) (5)	No adjustment		With adjustment		Scope for additional preferences (US$ million) (10)
Beneficiary	Value (US$ million) (1)	Share of imports (%) (2)	Value (US$ million) (3)	Share of imports (%) (4)		Value (US$ million) (6)	Share of imports (%) (7)	Value (US$ million) (8)	Share of imports (%) (9)	
Brunei Darussalam	0.0	−0.1	0.0	0.0	0.0	0.0	0.0	0.0	0.0	0.0
Cameroon	−37.3	−6.4	−29.8	−5.1	0.1	0.0	0.0	0.0	0.0	0.0
China	−28.6	−1.5	47.1	2.4	70.5	0.0	0.0	6.9	0.5	17.9
Colombia	−8.5	−0.8	19.8	1.9	63.6	−19.2	−1.8	−5.1	−0.5	2.0
Congo, Rep. of	−1.4	−10.5	−0.2	−1.2	0.0	−1.1	−23.78	−0.3	−6.30	0.0
Cuba	−13.5	−6.5	12.8	6.1	20.0	—	—	—	—	—
Côte d'Ivoire	−54.8	−2.5	−22.1	−1.0	1.4	−0.1	0.0	0.0	0.0	0.0
Dominica	−1.3	−12.7	−1.0	−9.5	0.0	0.0	−1.9	0.0	−0.6	0.0
Dominican Republic	−17.3	−10.2	−9.6	−5.7	0.1	−36.5	−7.6	−11.3	−2.4	0.0
Ecuador	−11.8	−1.4	23.7	2.7	72.7	−7.0	−1.3	−1.2	−0.2	0.0
Egypt, Arab Rep. of	−8.0	−2.3	−1.5	−0.4	12.5	−0.1	−0.3	0.0	0.0	2.0

Country										
El Salvador	−0.5	−0.7	0.2	0.3	0.3	−9.9	−8.7	−2.7	−2.3	0.0
Fiji	−47.5	−41.8	−6.3	−5.5	0.0	−1.6	−5.0	−0.4	−1.3	0.0
Gabon	0.0	−1.1	0.0	−0.2	0.0	0.0	0.0	0.0	0.0	0.0
Georgia	−0.7	−2.6	−0.1	−0.4	0.8	0.0	−0.1	0.0	0.0	0.0
Ghana	−5.2	−0.8	−0.6	−0.1	0.1	−0.1	−0.7	0.0	−0.1	0.0
Grenada	−0.1	−0.6	0.0	−0.4	0.0	0.0	0.0	0.0	0.0	0.0
Guatemala	−5.6	−2.4	−1.2	−0.5	0.2	−22.3	−2.92	−0.7	−0.10	8.4
Guyana	−47.3	−31.5	−6.4	−4.2	1.0	−1.1	−18.28	−0.3	−4.70	0.0
Honduras	−1.8	−0.9	0.2	0.1	1.5	−8.1	−2.9	0.7	0.2	0.6
Hong Kong, China	0.0	0.0	1.4	2.6	2.5	0.0	0.0	0.6	0.8	1.4
India	−9.5	−0.9	1.8	0.2	18.1	−2.7	−0.4	0.5	0.1	4.6
Indonesia	−8.1	−0.6	3.6	0.3	29.7	−0.5	−0.1	0.0	0.0	2.2
Jamaica	−39.2	−25.9	−7.9	−5.2	0.3	−1.4	−1.1	−0.6	−0.5	0.3
Kenya	−26.9	−3.5	−5.6	−0.7	1.6	−0.1	−0.2	0.0	0.0	0.0
Korea, Rep. of	0.0	0.0	0.9	1.8	1.7	0.0	0.0	2.5	1.3	5.3
Kuwait	0.0	−0.7	0.0	−0.1	0.0	0.0	0.0	0.0	0.3	0.0
Kyrgyz Republic	0.0	−0.7	0.0	0.0	0.0	0.0	0.0	0.0	0.0	0.0
Macao, China	0.0	−0.1	0.0	0.0	0.0	0.0	0.0	0.0	0.1	0.0
Malaysia	−6.3	−0.6	3.7	0.4	24.0	0.0	0.0	0.5	0.1	1.9
Mauritius	−127.1	−39.2	−23.2	−7.2	0.5	−0.6	−7.6	−0.2	−2.1	0.0
Moldova	−0.8	−1.3	0.2	0.3	1.5	0.0	−0.3	0.0	−0.1	0.0
Mongolia	0.0	0.0	0.0	0.0	0.0	0.0	0.0	0.0	0.0	0.0
Namibia	−7.5	−11.0	−6.5	−9.5	11.7	0.0	0.0	0.0	0.0	0.0
Nicaragua	−1.7	−2.6	−0.2	−0.3	0.0	−4.7	−3.5	−1.0	−0.7	4.4
Nigeria	−1.2	−0.2	−0.1	0.0	0.1	0.0	0.0	0.0	0.0	0.0

(Table continues on the following page.)

TABLE 8.A.6 Effect of MFN Tariff Reduction in Europe and the United States on Preference Value and Scope for Future Preferences: Agricultural Products, 2003 (Continued)

	Without flexibilities									
	EU					United States				
	Change in the preference value for unadjusted and adjusted preference margins				Scope for additional preferences (US$ million) (5)	Change in the preference value for unadjusted and adjusted preference margins				Scope for additional preferences (US$ million) (10)
	No adjustment		With adjustment			No adjustment		With adjustment		
Beneficiary	Value (US$ million) (1)	Share of imports (%) (2)	Value (US$ million) (3)	Share of imports (%) (4)		Value (US$ million) (6)	Share of imports (%) (7)	Value (US$ million) (8)	Share of imports (%) (9)	
Oman	0.0	−1.3	0.0	0.0	0.0	0.0	−0.1	0.0	0.4	0.1
Pakistan	−7.8	−2.9	−2.6	−1.0	0.1	−0.1	−0.4	−0.1	−0.1	0.2
Panama	−1.0	−0.4	8.9	3.7	29.3	−5.2	−13.3	−1.3	−3.3	0.1
Papua New Guinea	−5.3	−1.7	−4.5	−1.5	0.0	−1.2	−3.2	−0.3	−0.8	0.0
Paraguay	−0.1	0.0	0.9	0.4	1.3	−1.1	−5.0	−0.2	−0.7	0.9
Peru	−14.1	−3.3	−5.3	−1.3	3.6	−18.0	−6.4	−3.1	−1.1	0.0
Philippines	−2.8	−0.9	0.9	0.3	8.9	−24.7	−5.0	−6.4	−1.3	5.0
Qatar	0.0	−2.0	0.0	−0.2	0.0	0.0	0.0	0.0	0.0	0.0
Sri Lanka	−0.9	−0.7	0.0	0.0	1.3	0.0	−0.2	0.0	−0.1	0.0
St. Kitts and Nevis	−3.9	−42.5	−0.5	−5.0	0.0	0.0	0.0	0.0	0.0	0.0
St. Lucia	−4.0	−15.9	−3.1	−12.2	0.0	0.0	−1.6	0.0	−0.6	0.0

St. Vincent and the Grenadines	-2.5	-15.9	-1.9	-12.2	0.0	0.0	-0.7	0.0	-0.3	0.0
Suriname	-0.2	-1.9	0.0	-0.4	0.2	0.0	0.0	0.0	0.0	0.0
Swaziland	-36.3	-30.9	-4.9	-4.2	1.7	-2.7	-34.3	-0.7	-9.3	0.0
Taiwan, China	0.0	0.0	1.3	2.4	2.2	0.0	0.0	2.3	1.4	3.5
Thailand	-3.8	-0.3	58.2	4.9	125.8	-6.8	-1.0	4.7	0.7	33.0
Trinidad and Tobago	-11.8	-30.8	-1.4	-3.7	0.0	-1.5	-8.9	-0.4	-2.3	0.0
United Arab Emirates	-0.5	-0.3	-0.1	-0.1	0.7	0.0	0.0	0.1	0.6	0.1
Uruguay	-0.3	-0.1	3.1	1.0	29.2	-1.2	-1.0	0.0	0.0	8.6
Venezuela, R.B. de	-1.7	-1.5	-0.5	-0.4	1.8	-0.1	-0.2	0.0	0.0	0.1
Zimbabwe	-24.4	-6.2	-6.5	-1.7	1.7	0.0	-0.1	3.5	17.8	15.0
Positive	*0.0*	*268.8*	*268.8*			*0.0*		*220.9*		
Negative	*-698.9*	*-168.0*	*-168.0*			*-191.9*		*-39.2*		
Total developing economies	**-698.9**	**-2.2**	**100.9**	**0.3**	**995.7**	**-191.9**	**-1.6**	**181.7**	**1.5**	**418.1**
LDCs										
Angola	0.0	-2.6	0.0	-2.4	0.0	0.0	0.0	0.0	0.0	0.0
Bangladesh	-0.8	-4.7	-0.1	-0.8	0.0	0.0	-2.0	0.0	2.8	0.3
Benin	-0.1	-0.3	0.0	-0.1	0.0	0.0	0.0	0.0	0.0	0.0
Burkina Faso	-0.2	-0.7	1.6	5.4	1.0	0.0	-0.2	0.0	-0.1	0.0
Burundi	0.0	-0.1	0.0	0.0	0.0	0.0	0.0	0.0	0.0	0.0
Cambodia	0.0	-1.4	0.0	-0.3	0.0	0.0	-0.4	0.0	-0.2	0.0

(Table continues on the following page.)

TABLE 8.A.6 Effect of MFN Tariff Reduction in Europe and the United States on Preference Value and Scope for Future Preferences: Agricultural Products, 2003 (Continued)

	Without flexibilities									
	EU					United States				
	Change in the preference value for unadjusted and adjusted preference margins					Change in the preference value for unadjusted and adjusted preference margins				
	No adjustment		With adjustment			No adjustment		With adjustment		
Beneficiary	Value (US$ million) (1)	Share of imports (%) (2)	Value (US$ million) (3)	Share of imports (%) (4)	Scope for additional preferences (US$ million) (5)	Value (US$ million) (6)	Share of imports (%) (7)	Value (US$ million) (8)	Share of imports (%) (9)	Scope for additional preferences (US$ million) (10)
Central African Republic	0.0	0.0	0.0	0.0	0.0	0.0	0.0	0.0	0.0	0.0
Chad	0.0	0.0	0.0	0.0	0.0	0.0	0.0	0.0	0.0	0.0
Congo, Dem. Rep. of	−0.6	−3.8	−0.1	−0.6	0.0	0.0	0.0	0.0	0.0	0.0
Djibouti	0.0	−0.9	0.0	−0.1	0.0	0.0	−0.2	0.0	0.0	0.0
Gambia, The	−0.2	−2.9	0.0	−0.4	0.0	—	—	—	−0.1	—
Guinea	0.0	−0.1	0.0	0.0	0.0	0.0	−0.4	0.0	0.0	0.0
Guinea-Bissau	0.0	−0.1	0.0	0.0	0.0	0.0	0.0	0.0	0.0	0.0
Haiti	−0.1	−0.5	0.0	−0.1	0.0	−0.1	−0.6	0.0	0.0	0.0
Lesotho	0.0	−0.7	0.0	−0.6	0.0	—	—	—	—	—
Madagascar	−3.0	−1.8	0.3	0.2	0.7	0.0	0.0	0.0	0.0	0.0
Malawi	−21.5	−10.4	−3.5	−1.7	0.5	−3.0	−5.2	2.8	4.9	19.0
Maldives	0.0	0.0	0.0	0.0	0.0	0.0	0.0	0.0	1.7	0.0
Mali	−0.1	−0.1	0.0	0.0	0.0	0.0	0.0	0.0	0.0	0.0

Mauritania	0.0	−1.6	0.0	−0.2	0.0	0.0	0.0	0.0	0.0	0.0
Mozambique	−1.3	−2.7	2.0	4.3	1.4	−2.1	−38.7	−0.6	−10.3	0.0
Myanmar	0.0	0.0	0.2	5.2	0.2	0.0	0.0	0.0	0.0	0.0
Nepal	0.0	−0.3	2.0	31.0	1.2	0.0	−0.8	0.0	−0.7	0.0
Niger	0.0	−1.0	0.0	−0.4	0.0	0.0	−1.4	0.0	−1.2	0.0
Rwanda	0.0	−0.1	0.0	−0.1	0.0	0.0	0.0	0.0	0.0	0.0
Senegal	−2.7	−2.8	−0.5	−0.6	0.0	0.0	−0.3	0.0	−0.2	0.0
Sierra Leone	0.0	0.0	0.0	0.0	0.0	0.0	−0.6	0.0	−0.2	0.0
Solomon Islands	0.0	−0.4	0.0	−0.3	0.0	0.0	0.00	0.0	0.00	0.0
Tanzania	−7.5	−6.3	−1.4	−1.1	0.0	0.0	−0.13	0.0	−0.01	0.0
Togo	−0.4	−1.0	−0.1	−0.3	0.0	0.0	0.0	0.0	0.0	0.0
Uganda	−2.3	−1.3	−0.5	−0.3	0.0	0.0	0.0	0.0	0.0	0.0
Zambia	−1.9	−2.7	8.6	12.3	5.3	0.0	−0.3	0.0	−0.2	0.0
Positive	*0.0*		*14.7*			*0.0*		*2.8*		
Negative	*−42.8*		*−6.5*			*−5.3*		*−0.6*		
Total LDCs	**−42.8**	**−3.5**	**8.2**	**0.7**	**10.3**	**−5.3**	**−1.6**	**2.2**	**0.7**	**19.4**
Positive	*0.0*		*283.6*			*0.0*		*223.7*		
Negative	*−741.7*		*−174.5*			*−197.2*		*−39.8*		
Total	**−741.7**	**−2.2**	**109.1**	**0.3**	**1,006.0**	**−197.2**	**−1.63**	**183.9**	**1.52**	**437.5**

Source: Authors' calculations.

Note: Group of 20 proposal applied on 2003 MFN applied rates. — = not available.

TABLE 8.A.7   Effect of G-20 Cut on Preference Margins, by Selected Countries and MFN Categories: Quad Markets, 2003

Imports (US$ million)		Barbados	Belize	Cameroon	Dominica	Fiji	Guyana	Jamaica	Mauritius	Namibia	St. Kitts and Nevis	St. Lucia	St. Vincent and the Grenadines	Swaziland
Agricultural and non-agricultural		83	201	2,146	29	329	456	1,067	1,458	679	60	38	64	303
Agricultural products		45	117	612	11	157	162	327	336	69	10	25	16	130
Import share (% of agricultural products)	12 Fruit and vegetables	0.0	46.7	36.4	74.4	2.8	2.3	18.9	0.6	19.5	0.2	98.2	97.3	27.7
Preference margin		3.9	23.8	29.2	28.3	1.3	8.9	15.6	3.9	2.0	17.1	29.1	29.0	8.4
Preference margin adjustment		0.9	17.8	24.3	21.5	−0.1	0.8	10.1	0.7	−0.5	10.2	22.3	22.3	2.6
Preference margin adjustment after cut		0.6	8.1	11.0	9.8	−0.1	0.5	4.7	0.5	0.1	6.3	10.1	10.0	1.9
Preference margin adjustment after cut + flexibilities		0.6	8.1	11.0	9.8	−0.1	0.5	4.7	0.5	0.1	6.3	10.1	10.0	1.9

Change in preference value adjustment, after cut (US$ million)	0.0	−5.3	−29.7	−1.0	0.0	0.0	−3.3	0.0	0.1	0.0	−3.0	−1.9	−0.2
Import share (% of agricultural products) — 13 Coffee, tea, mate, and cocoa		0.0	56.8	7.8	0.0	0.2	11.4	0.1		1.4	0.1		
Preference margin		0.0	1.0	2.0	0.4	0.0	0.1	0.4		0.0	0.0		
Preference margin adjustment		0.0	0.0	0.1	−0.2	0.0	0.0	0.1		0.0	0.0		
Preference margin adjustment after cut		0.0	0.0	0.1	−0.3	0.0	0.0	0.0		0.0	0.0		
Preference margin adjustment after cut + flexibilities		0.0	0.0	0.1	−0.3	0.0	0.0	0.0		0.0	0.0		
Change in preference value adjustment, after cut (US$ million)		0.0	0.0	0.0	0.0	0.0	0.0	0.0		0.0	0.0		

(Table continues on the following page.)

TABLE 8.A.7 Effect of G-20 Cut on Preference Margins, by Selected Countries and MFN Categories: Quad Markets, 2003 (*Continued*)

Imports (US$ million)	Barbados	Belize	Cameroon	Dominica	Fiji	Guyana	Jamaica	Mauritius	Namibia	St. Kitts and Nevis	St. Lucia	St. Vincent and the Grenadines	Swaziland
Agricultural and non-agricultural products	83	201	2,146	29	329	456	1,067	1,458	679	60	38	64	303
Agricultural products	45	117	612	11	157	162	327	336	69	10	25	16	130
14 Sugars													
Import share (% of agricultural products)	43.8	33.5	0.0		78.8	70.5	23.0	90.5		94.9			65.2
Preference margin	66.8	55.4	3.5		61.0	67.4	66.9	64.4		67.1			65.9
Preference margin adjustment	8.0	7.4	–2.2		8.3	8.5	8.4	11.7		7.8			8.7
Preference margin adjustment after cut	2.8	2.6	–2.4		2.9	3.0	2.9	4.1		2.7			3.0
Preference margin adjustment after cut + flexibilities	2.8	2.6	–2.4		2.9	3.0	2.9	4.1		2.7			3.0

Product	Metric													
17 Animals and products thereof	Change in preference value adjustment, after cut (US$ million)	−1.0	−1.9	0.0		−6.7	−6.3	−4.1	−23.3		−0.5			−4.8
	Import share (% of agricultural products)	1.3	0.1	0.2			0.8		5.3	71.4	2.0			2.9
	Preference margin	0.0	0.0	0.0			0.0		0.0	14.9	0.0			11.7
	Preference margin adjustment	0.0	0.0	0.0			0.0		0.0	13.4	0.0			10.4
	Preference margin adjustment after cut	0.0	0.0	0.0			0.0		0.0	0.0	0.0			0.0
	Preference margin adjustment after cut + flexibilities	0.0	0.0	0.0			0.0		0.0	0.0	0.0			0.0
20 Beverages and spirits	Change in preference value adjustment, after cut (US$ million)	0.0	0.0	0.0			0.0		0.0	−6.6	0.0			−0.4
	Import share (% of agricultural products)	51.7	18.1	0.1	3.2	15.3	7.2	37.3	0.8	0.2	0.3	1.1	0.5	3.8

(Table continues on the following page.)

TABLE 8.A.7 Effect of G-20 Cut on Preference Margins, by Selected Countries and MFN Categories: Quad Markets, 2003 (Continued)

Imports (US$ million)		Barbados	Belize	Cameroon	Dominica	Fiji	Guyana	Jamaica	Mauritius	Namibia	St. Kitts and Nevis	St. Lucia	St. Vincent and the Grenadines	Swaziland
	Agricultural and non-agricultural	83	201	2,146	29	329	456	1,067	1,458	679	60	38	64	303
	Agricultural products	45	117	612	11	157	162	327	336	69	10	25	16	130
Preference margin		8.2	27.7	3.0	6.8	0.7	15.9	4.4	7.7	0.0	4.4	18.3	5.3	33.6
Preference margin adjustment		1.8	19.8	0.8	2.9	0.3	4.9	1.6	2.4	0.0	1.6	6.9	0.7	8.3
Preference margin adjustment after cut		0.8	9.4	0.5	1.8	0.2	2.2	0.8	1.4	0.0	0.9	3.1	0.4	4.4
Preference margin adjustment after cut + flexibilities		0.8	9.4	0.5	1.8	0.2	2.2	0.8	1.4	0.0	0.9	3.1	0.4	4.4
Change in preference value adjustment, after cut (US$ million)		−0.2	−2.2	0.0	0.0	0.0	−0.3	−1.0	0.0	0.0	0.0	0.0	0.0	−0.2

Source: Authors' calculations.

TABLE 8.A.8 Share of Exports of Agricultural Products to the Quad Markets for the First Three Subheadings: Selected Countries, 2003

Country	Subheadings	Description	Cumulative share of exports (agricultural products)	Average preference margin
Barbados	220840	Rum and tafia	46	6.6
	170111	Raw cane sugar (excluding added flavoring or coloring)	89	66.9
	220710	Undenatured ethyl alcohol, of actual alcoholic strength of greater than or equal to 80%	94	24.8
Belize	080300	Bananas, including plantains, fresh or dried	36	30.0
	170111	Raw cane sugar (excluding added flavoring or coloring)	67	60.1
	200911	Frozen orange juice, unfermented, whether or not containing added sugar or other sweetening matter (excluding that containing spirit)	79	35.6
Cameroon	180100	Cocoa beans, whole or broken, raw or roasted	42	0.0
	080300	Bananas, including plantains, fresh or dried	76	30.0
	180310	Cocoa paste (excluding defatted)	84	5.8
Dominica	080300	Bananas, including plantains, fresh or dried	70	29.6
	210390	Preparations for sauces and prepared sauces; mixed condiments and seasonings (excluding soya sauce, tomato ketchup and other tomato sauces, mustard, and mustard flour and meal)	77	7.7
	090111	Coffee (excluding roasted and decaffeinated)	81	0.0
Fiji	170111	Raw cane sugar (excluding added flavoring or coloring)	78	61.6
	220110	Mineral waters and aerated waters, not containing added sugar, other sweetening matter or flavored	93	0.6
	151311	Crude coconut oil	94	5.6

(Table continues on the following page.)

TABLE 8.A.8 Share of Exports of Agricultural Products to the Quad Markets for the First Three Subheadings: Selected Countries, 2003 (Continued)

Country	Subheadings	Description	Cumulative share of exports (agricultural products)	Average preference margin
Guyana	170111	Raw cane sugar (excluding added flavoring or coloring)	70	68.0
	100620	Husked or brown rice	86	0.0
	220840	Rum and tafia	92	15.6
Jamaica	170111	Raw cane sugar (excluding added flavoring or coloring)	23	67.1
	220840	Rum and tafia	37	8.2
	220710	Undenatured ethyl alcohol, of actual alcoholic strength of greater than or equal to 80%	52	2.5
Mauritius	170111	Raw cane sugar (excluding added flavoring or coloring)	88	66.3
	010611	Live primates	93	0.0
	170310	Cane molasses resulting from the extraction or refining of sugar	95	0.0
Namibia	020130	Fresh or chilled bovine meat, boneless	61	12.8
	080610	Fresh grapes	78	1.4
	020230	Frozen, boneless meat of bovine animals	88	29.3
St. Kitts and Nevis	170111	Raw cane sugar (excluding added flavoring or coloring)	93	67.1
	170390	Beet molasses resulting from the extraction or refining of sugar	95	0.0
	010611	Live primates	97	0.0

Country	Code	Description		
St. Lucia	080300	Bananas, including plantains, fresh or dried	94	30.0
	070990	Fresh or chilled vegetables (excluding potatoes, tomatoes, vegetables of the *Allium spp.*, cabbages of the genus *Brassica*, lettuces of the species *Lactuca sativa* and *Cichorium*, carrots, turnips, salad beetroot, salsify, celeriac, radishes and similar edible roots, cucumbers and gherkins, leguminous vegetables, artichokes, asparagus, aubergines, mushrooms, truffles, fruits of the genus Capsicum or of the genus Pimenta, spinach, New Zealand spinach, and orache spinach)	97	12.8
St. Vincent and the Grenadines	220840	Rum and tafia	98	23.9
	080300	Bananas, including plantains, fresh or dried	93	30.0
	071490	Roots and tubers of arrowroot, salep, Jerusalem artichokes and similar roots and tubers with high starch or inulin content, fresh, chilled, frozen or dried, whether or not sliced or in the form of pellets and sago pith (excluding manioc "cassava" and sweet potatoes)	96	8.7
	100630	Semimilled or wholly milled rice, whether or not polished or glazed	96	0.0
Swaziland	170111	Raw cane sugar (excluding added flavoring or coloring)	65	66.6
	200830	Citrus fruit, prepared or preserved, whether or not containing added sugar or other sweetening matter or spirit, not elsewhere specified	72	15.8
	080540	Fresh or dried grapefruit	79	1.0

Source: Authors' calculations.

shocks, such as those resulting from preference erosion. Ecuador has a slightly more diversified export structure, and Thailand is a very diversified exporter.

Differences in the impact of preference erosion among countries are, of course, reflected in the tariff-cutting simulation. The reductions in preference margins resulting from the cuts in the MFN duties are quite significant for the two ACP members (table 8.A.5). Adjusted preference margins in the fruit and vegetables category, which includes bananas, are reduced by some 12 to 13 percentage points. This reduction results in a change of the adjusted preference value of about 5 percent and 12 percent of 2003 export values for Cameroon and St. Lucia, respectively. The EU market plays the key role in this scenario (table 8.A.6).

The reduction in exports resulting from increased competition in export markets is likely to be much larger. Estimates of such medium-term developments can be predicted only with more sophisticated dynamic models, and even those models will heavily rely on various assumptions. The figures for the change in the preference value should be thought of more as a cross-country comparative index than as a monetary value that would reflect associated adjustment costs.

Looking at other countries in a similar situation, one can identify bananas and sugar as accounting for a large share of the loss of preference value in several of the small island economies. High export concentration also precludes the option of opening additional product lines for additional preferences.

Bigger and often more efficient agricultural producers such as Ecuador and Thailand, by contrast, appear to gain from MFN liberalization in terms of preference erosion margins. In adjusted terms, both countries gain better market access and improve their adjusted preference value by a significant amount—an amount that is larger in absolute terms than the negative figures shown for most of the smaller economies. Furthermore, there is considerable scope in both countries to benefit from additional preferences or from further MFN cuts, although only in the EU market (table 8.A.6). The latter implied gains would significantly exceed the gain in the adjusted preference value as a result of the simulated MFN reductions. As previously mentioned, such medium-term dynamic effects are likely to outweigh the static calculations presented here.

Annex 8.B: Calculating Adjusted Preference Margins—A Numerical Example

The purpose of calculating adjusted preference margins is to establish the real conditions of competition among suppliers to a given import market. The calculations here involve three steps. First, the adjusted value of the preference is calculated. Then the tariff reduction formula is applied to the MFN rates and the new adjusted value of the preference is recalculated. Finally, the erosion of the preference is computed as the change in the adjusted values of the preference (table 8.B.1).

TABLE 8.B.1 Calculation of Adjusted Preference Margins

Step	MFN duty rate (%) (1)	Actual applied rate (%) (2)	Imports value (US$) (3)	Duty collected[a] (US$) (4)	Preference margin[b] (%) (5)	Preference value[c] (US$) (6)	Adjusted MFN rate[d] (%) (7)	Adjusted preference margin[e] (%) (8)	Adjusted preference value[f] (US$) (9)
1. Situation before tariff cut									
Country A	20	20	5,000	1,000	0	0	8.3	−11.7	−583
Country B	20	5	2,000	100	15	300	15.6	10.6	211
Country C	20	10	4,000	400	10	400	15.7	5.7	229
2. Situation after tariff cut of 25%									
Country A	15	15	5,000	750	0	0	8.3	−6.7	−333
Country B	15	5	2,000	100	10	200	12.8	7.8	156
Country C	15	10	4,000	400	5	200	12.1	2.1	86
3. Change in preference values and margins following tariff reduction									
Country A	−5	−5	0	−250	0	0	0.0	5.0	250
Country B	−5	0	0	0	−5	−100	−2.8	−2.8	−56
Country C	−5	0	0	0	−5	−200	−3.6	−3.6	−143

Source: Authors.

a. Duty collected is calculated as follows: (column 3 × column 2)/100.
b. The preference margin is calculated as follows: column 1 − column 2.
c. The preference value is calculated as follows: column 5 × column 3.
d. The adjusted MFN rate for country A is calculated as follows: (country B column 4 + country C column 4)/((country B column 3 + country C column 3). Rates for countries B and C are calculated in a similar manner.
e. The adjusted preference margin is calculated as follows: column 7 − column 2.
f. The adjusted preference value is calculated as follows: (column 8 ∗ column 3)/100.

The computation of the adjusted measures of the value of the preference requires information about MFN and preferential rates and the volume of trade by type of market access. Step 1 in the table describes the initial situation. It is assumed, for example, that a preference-giving country, country Q, levies an MFN tariff of 20 percent on imports from country A, but provides preferential access to country B and country C at the rates of 5 percent and 10 percent, respectively (column 2). Country Q's imports from A, B, and C equal US$5,000, US$2,000, and US$4,000 respectively. Traditionally, the preference margin for each country (column 5) is calculated as the difference between the MFN tariff rate and the actual applied rate (that is, the preferential rate or the MFN rate depending on whether a country receives a preference), and the value of the preference (column 6) will simply be the product of the preference margin and the value of the imports.

For each country, the adjusted preference margin is calculated as the difference between the average rate applied to the country's competitors (which in the table is the adjusted MFN rate shown in column 7) and the actual rate applied to that country (column 2), where, for example, the adjusted MFN rate for country A is the trade-weighted average between 5 percent and 10 percent, and the tariff rates are applied to countries B and C. The adjusted preference value is simply the adjusted preference margin times the value of imports. It is interesting to note that the adjusted preference margin is negative for country A, because its exports suffer worse than average treatment in country Q's market.

Assume now that country Q decides to reduce MFN import tariffs. Step 2 of the table describes the situation after an MFN tariff cut of 25 percent. The MFN rate falls from 20 percent to 15 percent. By assumption, import values do not change. Following the same methodology described in step 1, both the unadjusted and the adjusted preference margin and the value of the preference are calculated. It is interesting to note that this approach makes it possible to capture the benefit that a country facing the MFN tariff—country A in this example—enjoys in terms of the reduction of its disadvantage relative to B and C, the preferred countries.

Changes before and after the application of the MFN tariff cut are reported in step 3. The figures for the adjusted values of preference erosion are shown in column 9. That is, they are the difference between the adjusted preference value before (column 9, step 1) and after (column 9, step 2) the tariff cut.

Annex 8.C: The Effect of Using Out-of-Quota Rates to Estimate Preference Erosion

To clarify the implications of using out-of-quota rates to estimate preference erosion, one needs to distinguish two cases: when the MFN regime is quota free and when there is an MFN quota.

MFN Quota-Free Scenario

Suppose that country A's imports of good j from country B are subject to a preferential tariff rate quota. That is, imports up to a quota limit are permitted at an in-quota tariff of 10 percent, while the out-of-quota preferential tariff is 20 percent. In addition, assume that the MFN tariff is 50 percent. In this situation, the value of the preference will be given by the total value of the revenue forgone (that is, the difference between the MFN rate and the relevant preferential rate times the import value). Graphically, the value of the preference can be represented by the total shaded area in figure 8.C.1.

Because of data limitations, out-of-quota rates are used in this chapter to estimate the value of preferences. Under the circumstances described previously, the working assumption provides an estimated value of the preference that is lower than the actual value by the value of the dotted area.

This underestimation does not in general undermine the validity of the estimates of preference erosion. The risk of preference erosion is the change in the value of the preference following an MFN tariff cut. Suppose that country A reduces the MFN tariff on good j to 40 percent. The risk of preference erosion is represented by the vertical-line shaded area in figure 8.C.2, which constitutes the difference between the old and the new MFN rate. In general, as long as the new MFN tariff stays above the preferential out-of-quota rate, the estimate of the risk of preference erosion is correct. But if the new MFN rate falls below the out-of-quota preferential rate (to 15 percent, say), the risk of preference erosion will be underestimated by the value of the dotted area.

FIGURE 8.C.1 The Value of Preferences under Preferential Quotas

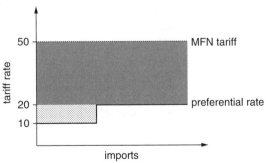

Source: Authors.

FIGURE 8.C.2 Preference Erosion under Preferential Quotas

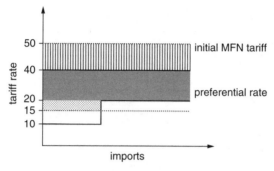

Source: Authors.

FIGURE 8.C.3 Preference Erosion under MFN Quota

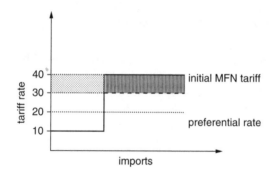

Source: Authors.

MFN Quota Scenario

To analyze the consequences of using out-of-quota rates to estimate the risk of preference erosion in the case MFN tariff-rate quotas, one needs to distinguish between the case when the preferential regime is quota free and the case when it is subject to a quota. Suppose, first, that country A imposes an MFN tariff rate quota on imports of good i with an in-quota rate of 10 percent and an out-of-quota rate of 40 percent. In addition, country A provides preferential treatment to imports of country B on good i at a preferential rate of 20 percent. Suppose that following liberalization, the out-of-quota MFN rate is reduced to 30 percent. Because there is no change in the treatment of in-quota imports, the value of the preference actually eroded will be that of the vertical-line shaded area in figure 8.C.3. However, since this analysis does not distinguish between in- and out-of-quota trade, it will overestimate the risk of preference erosion by the amount of the dotted area.

The implications of using out-of-quota rates to estimate the risk of preference erosion when there are both preferential and MFN tariff rate quotas are more complex. A number of possible situations can emerge, depending on whether the in-quota preference margin is equal, smaller, or greater than the out-of-quota preference margin.

In general, the use of out-of-quota rates may result in an underestimation of preference erosion risk when two conditions are satisfied: (a) the out-of-quota preference margin is smaller than the in-quota preference margin, and (b) the MFN tariff rate after liberalization falls below the preferential out-of-quota rate. Data for Canada and the United States show that the use of out-of-quota rates does not have any significant effect on the estimates for preference erosion developed here. Unfortunately, in the case of the EU, it is not possible to quantify the probability that the simulations underestimate the risk of preference erosion. However, data in table 8.C.1 provide some indication for the case of MFN quotas. The table shows that only 16 developing countries and one LDC have more than 20 percent of exports to the EU under bound tariff rate quotas. Of these, only seven countries (Belize, Botswana, Cameroon, Jamaica, Mauritius, Namibia, and Swaziland) have weighted-average applied preferential rates greater than zero and therefore present a risk of underestimation of preference erosion. In the case of Japan, it was not possible to distinguish between in-quota and out-of-quota rates.

TABLE 8.C.1 Imports of Agricultural Products into the European Union from Preference Beneficiaries, by Type of Market Access and Tariff Lines Subject to Bound Quota, 2003

| | Imports (%) | | | | Weighted MFN duty | | | | Weighted duty applied | |
| | No quota | | Tariff lines with quota | | No quota | | Tariff lines with quota | | No quota | Tariff lines with quota |
Beneficiary	No preference (1)	Preference (2)	No preference (3)	Preference (4)	No preference (5)	Preference (6)	No preference (7)	Preference (8)	Preference (9)	Preference (10)
Developing economies										
Albania	70.9	29.0	—	0.1	0.0	9.1	—	10.9	0.1	0.0
Antigua and Barbuda	88.0	11.0	0.1	0.8	0.0	3.7	12.0	84.2	0.0	61.2
Argentina	69.2	11.0	16.2	3.7	1.9	7.2	65.7	13.9	4.2	13.4
Armenia	59.9	40.1	—	—	0.7	21.6	—	—	15.0	—
Bahrain	88.0	10.6	1.4	—	0.0	13.7	91.1	—	9.9	—
Barbados	18.6	18.7	0.1	62.6	0.0	17.4	23.7	66.9	0.1	0.0
Belize	4.7	8.0	—	87.3	3.4	11.7	—	43.4	0.0	0.5
Bolivia	72.4	27.5	0.1	0.1	0.0	30.3	61.4	3.8	0.1	0.0
Botswana	0.9	1.4	—	97.8	0.0	16.6	—	93.8	0.0	76.2
Brazil	72.3	14.9	12.0	0.8	1.3	10.0	75.1	13.3	9.1	12.0
Brunei Darussalam	97.1	2.9	—	—	0.0	9.8	—	—	6.3	—
Cameroon	54.8	8.7	0.0	36.5	0.0	9.8	5.6	30.0	0.0	0.1
China	55.6	38.9	3.1	2.4	1.4	13.0	13.2	110.8	8.8	108.0
Colombia	34.1	20.8	45.0	0.1	0.0	9.0	30.0	13.8	0.5	0.0
Congo, Rep. of	68.1	8.9	—	22.9	0.0	11.1	—	67.1	0.0	0.0
Cuba	17.8	61.7	18.8	1.7	16.6	20.2	52.0	15.2	7.8	11.7

Côte d'Ivoire	62.1	29.9	0.3	7.7	0.0	8.3	65.3	32.7	0.0	0.0
Dominica	9.4	17.4	—	73.2	0.1	9.7	—	29.8	0.5	0.0
Dominican Republic	16.9	41.6	2.7	38.8	0.1	17.4	—	30.0	0.1	0.0
Ecuador	9.5	29.4	61.0	0.0	0.1	10.5	30.0	14.2	0.6	0.0
Egypt, Arab Rep. of	41.9	41.0	3.3	13.7	0.4	12.1	43.0	13.4	7.1	8.4
El Salvador	84.8	13.3	1.8	—	0.0	11.9	67.1	—	0.0	—
Gabon	80.9	19.1	—	—	0.1	13.3	—	—	0.0	—
Georgia	6.8	93.2	—	1.1	0.4	7.2	—	15.5	3.8	2.2
Ghana	76.8	22.1	0.0	2.8	0.0	7.7	5.6	30.0	0.0	0.0
Grenada	93.8	3.4	—	—	0.0	10.6	—	—	0.1	—
Guatemala	53.9	45.6	0.5	70.8	0.0	10.5	30.0	67.1	0.0	0.0
Guyana	1.8	7.6	19.7	0.1	1.6	16.8	43.8	6.8	0.0	0.0
Honduras	70.3	24.0	5.6	—	0.0	7.9	30.0	—	0.0	—
Hong Kong, China	98.2	—	1.8	—	9.2	—	4.8	—	—	—
India	57.1	25.1	13.4	4.4	0.4	7.8	56.0	13.7	3.4	10.7
Indonesia	34.2	65.8	0.0	0.0	0.0	6.6	45.3	143.0	5.5	139.5
Jamaica	7.6	24.5	0.0	67.8	0.0	13.7	28.1	56.5	0.5	0.2
Kenya	29.0	70.1	0.9	0.0	0.0	10.9	67.1	13.5	0.0	4.4
Korea, Rep. of	93.2	—	6.8	—	6.5	—	19.6	—	—	—
Kuwait	83.0	16.7	0.3	2.5	0.0	11.5	117.0	—	7.4	—
Kyrgyz Republic	74.2	23.3	—	—	0.0	7.8	—	5.7	4.1	2.2
Macao, China	95.9	4.1	—	0.0	0.0	7.8	—	—	2.7	—
Malaysia	18.7	81.3	0.0	90.8	0.0	6.2	18.9	12.5	4.9	9.0
Mauritius	6.8	2.1	0.3	0.1	1.5	9.8	65.3	66.3	0.9	0.1
Moldova	50.5	49.4	0.1	—	2.1	8.9	—	14.8	5.3	14.4
Mongolia	99.9	0.1	—	—	0.0	2.1	—	—	0.1	—

(Table continues on the following page.)

TABLE 8.C.1 Imports of Agricultural Products into the European Union from Preference Beneficiaries, by Type of Market Access and Tariff Lines Subject to Bound Quota, 2003 (Continued)

| Beneficiary | Imports (%) | | | | Weighted MFN duty | | | | Weighted duty applied | |
| | No quota | | Tariff lines with quota | | No quota | | Tariff lines with quota | | No quota | Tariff lines with quota |
	No preference (1)	Preference (2)	No preference (3)	Preference (4)	No preference (5)	Preference (6)	No preference (7)	Preference (8)	Preference (9)	Preference (10)
Namibia	9.7	1.6	0.1	88.5	0.0	9.6	66.7	74.3	0.7	61.9
Nicaragua	80.8	18.9	0.0	0.2	0.0	25.4	30.0	10.7	0.0	0.0
Nigeria	92.9	7.0	0.0	0.0	0.0	7.6	36.9	44.5	0.0	37.1
Oman	40.5	59.5	—	—	0.0	5.7	—	—	2.3	—
Pakistan	26.0	50.4	23.6	0.1	0.0	11.3	44.7	10.0	0.0	0.8
Panama	1.5	8.0	90.6	—	0.0	10.9	30.0	—	0.0	—
Paraguay	93.2	1.6	5.1	0.0	0.0	7.9	77.5	15.2	5.2	11.7
Peru	41.2	54.7	1.4	2.7	0.0	13.0	30.3	14.7	1.4	3.5
Philippines	26.3	73.6	0.2	—	0.1	7.2	60.0	—	5.7	—
Qatar	31.7	68.3	—	—	2.6	8.0	—	—	4.7	—
Sri Lanka	59.6	40.0	0.5	0.0	0.1	6.5	61.2	7.4	3.7	5.1
St. Kitts and Nevis	1.5	1.0	—	97.5	0.0	7.6	—	67.1	0.0	0.0
St. Lucia	0.5	4.9	—	94.6	0.3	14.2	—	30.0	0.1	0.0
St. Vincent and the Grenadines	0.9	0.8	0.9	97.4	0.0	8.5	—	29.7	1.8	0.0
Suriname	10.3	33.2	51.3	5.2	0.1	11.1	43.8	11.3	0.1	0.2
Swaziland	0.0	23.3	0.7	75.9	4.7	16.9	65.1	62.7	0.2	4.2
Taiwan, China	97.6	—	2.4	—	8.1	—	4.4	—	—	—
Thailand	34.6	39.6	25.8	0.1	10.2	13.6	86.7	13.0	12.4	9.5

Trinidad and Tobago	22.2	8.0	—	69.8	0.3	10.2	—	67.1	0.2	0.0
United Arab Emirates	94.6	5.2	0.2	0.0	0.0	17.6	43.8	6.4	11.7	2.9
Uruguay	50.0	9.5	38.5	2.0	2.3	14.4	70.9	18.4	13.5	17.7
Venezuela, R.B. de	68.0	20.2	11.5	0.3	0.0	15.4	30.0	14.2	0.0	0.2
Zimbabwe	14.9	73.8	0.2	11.1	0.2	9.1	65.3	47.6	0.1	5.3
Total developing economies	**54.9**	**27.4**	**12.1**	**5.6**	**1.3**	**9.7**	**54.2**	**45.7**	**4.8**	**9.3**
LDCs										
Angola	89.8	4.3	—	5.9	0.0	20.2	—	54.9	0.0	0.0
Bangladesh	6.9	86.7	1.2	5.2	1.4	12.0	—	16.4	0.0	0.0
Benin	92.5	6.9	—	0.6	0.0	5.9	—	36.2	0.0	0.0
Burkina Faso	71.9	13.8	14.3	—	0.0	11.2	67.1	—	0.0	—
Burundi	98.3	1.7	—	—	0.0	9.4	—	—	0.0	0.0
Cambodia	0.2	20.8	53.2	25.7	0.0	15.1	—	—	0.0	—
Central African Republic	100.0	—	—	—	0.0	—	—	—	—	—
Chad	100.0	—	—	—	0.0	—	—	30.0	0.0	—
Congo, Dem. Rep. of	72.4	27.5	—	0.0	0.0	25.8	—	—	0.0	0.0
Djibouti	75.5	24.2	—	0.2	0.0	7.7	—	13.0	0.0	0.0
Gambia, The	34.2	65.6	—	0.2	0.0	9.8	—	1.5	0.0	0.0
Guinea	95.6	4.3	—	0.1	0.0	6.4	—	12.9	0.0	0.0
Guinea-Bissau	96.5	3.5	—	—	0.0	8.6	—	—	0.0	—
Haiti	78.2	21.7	0.0	—	0.0	5.2	43.8	—	0.0	—
Lesotho	92.4	7.6	—	—	0.0	19.2	—	—	0.0	—
Madagascar	47.1	50.3	2.0	0.6	0.0	6.8	65.3	61.2	0.0	0.0
Malawi	16.1	63.2	1.0	19.7	0.0	7.2	65.3	64.9	0.0	0.0

(Table continues on the following page.)

TABLE 8.C.1 Imports of Agricultural Products into the European Union from Preference Beneficiaries, by Type of Market Access and Tariff Lines Subject to Bound Quota, 2003 (*Continued*)

| | Imports (%) | | | | Weighted MFN duty | | | | Weighted duty applied | |
| | No quota | | Tariff lines with quota | | No quota | | Tariff lines with quota | | No quota | Tariff lines with quota |
Beneficiary	No preference (1)	Preference (2)	No preference (3)	Preference (4)	No preference (5)	Preference (6)	No preference (7)	Preference (8)	Preference (9)	Preference (10)
Maldives	99.1	0.9	—	—	0.0	5.1	—	—	0.0	—
Mali	97.6	2.3	—	0.0	0.0	11.7	—	33.8	0.0	0.0
Mauritania	63.8	36.2	—	—	0.0	9.9	—	—	0.0	0.0
Mozambique	30.9	55.0	13.0	1.1	0.0	8.9	67.1	69.5	0.0	0.0
Myanmar	71.9	0.7	22.5	5.0	0.0	7.0	65.3	—	0.0	0.0
Nepal	12.4	7.5	80.1	—	0.0	10.0	67.1	—	0.0	—
Niger	62.6	35.6	—	1.8	0.0	4.2	—	36.3	0.0	0.0
Rwanda	98.4	0.9	—	0.7	0.0	6.5	—	30.0	0.0	0.0
Senegal	23.4	76.6	0.0	0.0	0.0	8.1	43.8	26.4	0.0	0.0
Sierra Leone	98.6	1.4	—	0.1	0.0	4.6	—	32.4	0.0	0.0
Solomon Islands	86.8	13.2	—	—	0.0	6.4	—	—	0.0	—
Tanzania	45.4	43.8	—	10.8	0.0	7.8	—	67.1	0.0	0.0
Togo	79.4	20.4	—	0.1	0.0	9.6	—	104.7	0.0	0.0
Uganda	63.8	35.9	—	0.3	0.0	7.9	—	8.8	0.0	0.0
Zambia	10.8	56.9	32.0	0.2	0.0	10.5	67.1	13.1	0.0	0.0
Total LDCs	**49.2**	**42.3**	**3.8**	**4.8**	**0.0**	**8.1**	**66.8**	**64.5**	**0.0**	**0.0**
Total	**54.7**	**27.9**	**11.8**	**5.6**	**1.2**	**9.6**	**54.4**	**46.3**	**4.5**	**9.0**

Source: Authors' calculation.

Note: — = not available.

Notes

1. Strictly speaking, the issue has been raised before the Doha Round. Brazil, for example, argued for the preservation of preferential margins in the context of the Tokyo Round (see Document MTN/W/2 of October 26, 1973).

2. Several studies over the years have assessed the role of preferences. See, for example, Borrmann, Borrmann, and Stegger (1981); Brown (1987, 1989); Grossman and Sykes (2005); Karsenty and Laird (1986); Murray (1977); OECD (1983, 2003); Özden and Reinhardt (2003); Sapir and Lundberg (1984); UNCTAD (1999); WTO (2004).

3. The countries thus excluded from the reported estimates are Bulgaria, Chile, Costa Rica, Croatia, Israel, Jordan, the former Yugoslav Republic of Macedonia, Mexico, Morocco, South Africa, Romania, Singapore, Tunisia, and Turkey.

4. See Alexandraki and Lankes (2004); François, Hoekman, and Manchin (2005); and Hoekman, Martin, and Braga (2006) for different analytical approaches.

5. Basing their analysis on the AGOA preference scheme, Olarreaga and Özden (2005) find that on average exporters receive about one-third of the tariff rent.

6. Canada, Japan, and the United States use different tariff codes to differentiate between in- and out-of-quota tariffs. For Japan, it has not been possible to make a correlation table because of the complexity of the tariff schedule. Regarding the EU, the same tariff-line numbers are used for both in- and out-of-quota tariffs; furthermore, only the out-of-quota tariff is available. The methodology that has been adopted is to use out-of-quota duties for Canada, the EU, and the United States (except for sugar); Japan has both in- and out-of-quota duties.

7. To facilitate the interpretation of the series of tables in the annex, annex 8.A describes country cases for Cameroon, Ecuador, St. Lucia, and Thailand.

8. Annex 8.B provides a numerical example of how adjusted preference margins are calculated in this chapter.

9. Recall that the adjustment for competition is made considering all competitors in the same markets, thus including countries that benefit from reciprocal preferences as well as countries that benefit from nonreciprocal preferences.

10. AVE data submissions were not used for Canada, the EU, and Japan because they record final bound rates, whereas the data used here are 2003 applied rates. In addition, AVEs for preferences are needed to make the calculations, and these were not part of the submissions.

11. Table 8.A.2 in the annexes reports data on the percentage of exports to the Quad markets that benefit from preferential access or MFN treatment by each exporting developing country and LDC (beneficiary of exclusively nonreciprocal preferences). In addition, table 8.A.2 reports for the same set of country data on how diversified the exports are (measured by the percentage of tariff lines on which they export). The figures for the value of the preferences, including the adjustment for competition, are reported for each country in table 8.A.4. Note that the overall figures for developing countries refer to those that are members of the WTO, excluding those with reciprocal preferential agreements as listed in note 3.

12. Data for preference margins, adjusted and unadjusted, are reported in table 8.A.4 in the annexes.

13. The percentages do not reflect the G-20 proposal. The G-20 proposed that no more than 1 percent of tariff lines could be declared sensitive. However, there are other proposals for about 8 percent (the EU) and 15 percent (Group of 10). The 2 percent and 4 percent assumptions made in this study were chosen for illustrative purposes only.

14. An exception had to be made for Japan because the complexity of its tariff schedule does not permit a distinction between in- and out-of-quota rates.

15. The 30 percent rate assumed here is the estimated tariff equivalent of the MFN tariff rate of €176 per ton formally adopted by the Council of the European Union on November 29, 2005.

16. A request for consultation under article 21.5 of the Understanding on Rules and Procedures Governing the Settlement of Disputes has been submitted by Honduras to the WTO against the

European Communities concerning the measures the latter recently adopted with regard to the banana import regime. The assumption in no way implies a judgment as to the final outcome in this matter.

17. Recall that the gain from MFN liberalization in this chapter arises from a country's improved market access to the Quad economies relative to the other countries. The figures for the gains from MFN liberalization do not account for the gains arising simply from lower barriers to trade.

18. Note once again that the simulation exercise has excluded developing countries that have reciprocal preference agreements (free trade areas or customs unions) with any Quad market, notwithstanding the fact that these excluded countries may also benefit from nonreciprocal preferences.

19. As discussed previously, the choice between bound rates and applied rates does not, for the most part, make a large difference in the analysis.

20. There are two criteria for the inclusion of countries in table 8.A.7: the adjusted preference value in terms of agricultural exports to the Quad economies declines by more than 2 percent, and the share of agricultural exports to the Quad markets represents more than 10 percent of total exports. Angola, Botswana, Democratic Republic of Congo, and Trinidad and Tobago, which suffer relatively high agricultural preference erosion risk, have been excluded on the basis of the negligible share of agricultural exports in these countries' total exports.

References

Alexandraki, Katerina, and Hans Peter Lankes. 2004. "The Impact of Preference Erosion on Middle-Income Developing Countries." IMF Working Paper 04/169, International Monetary Fund, Washington, DC.

Borrmann, Axel, Christine Borrmann, and Manfred Stegger. 1981. *The EC's Generalized System of Preferences*. The Hague: Martinus Nijhof.

Brown, Drusilla K. 1987. "General Equilibrium Effects of the U.S. Generalized System of Preferences." *Southern Economic Journal* 54 (1): 27–47.

———. 1989. "Trade and Welfare Effects of the European Schemes of the Generalized System of Preferences." *Economic Development and Cultural Change* 37 (4): 757–76.

François, Joseph, Bernard Hoekman, and Miriam Manchin. 2005. "Preference Erosion and Multilateral Trade Liberalization." CEPR Discussion Paper 5153, Centre for Economic Policy and Research, London.

Grossman, Gene M., and Alan O. Sykes. 2005. "A Preference for Development: The Law and Economics of GSP." *World Trade Review* 4 (1): 41–67.

Hoekman Bernard, Will Martin, and Carlos A. Prima Braga. 2006. "Preference Erosion: The Terms of the Debate." In *Trade, Doha, and Development: A Window into the Issues*, ed. Richard Newfarmer, 329–40. Washington, DC: World Bank.

Jean, Sébastien, David Laborde, and Will Martin. 2006. "Consequences of Alternative Formulas for Agricultural Tariff Cuts." In *Agricultural Trade Reform and the Doha Development Agenda*, ed. Kym Anderson and Will Martin, 81–116. Basingstoke, U.K.: Palgrave Macmillan; Washington, DC: World Bank.

Karsenty, Guy, and Sam Laird. 1986. "The Generalized System of Preferences: A Quantitative Assessment of the Direct Trade Effects and of Policy Options." UNCTAD Discussion Paper 18, United Nations Conference on Trade and Development, Geneva.

Murray, Tracy. 1977. *Trade Preferences for Developing Countries*. New York: John Wiley & Sons.

OECD (Organisation for Economic Co-operation and Development). 1983. *The Generalized System of Preferences: Review of the First Decade*. Paris: OECD.

———. 2003. "The Economic Impact of the Generalised System of Preferences." OECD Trade Committee, Room Document 1, OECD, Paris.

Olarreaga, Marcelo, and Çağlar Özden. 2005. "AGOA and Apparel: Who Captures the Tariff Rent in the Presence of Preferential Market Access." *World Economy* 28 (1): 63–77.

Özden, Çağlar, and Eric Reinhardt. 2003. "The Perversity of Preferences: GSP and Developing Country Trade Policies, 1976–2000." Policy Research Working Paper 2955, World Bank, Washington, DC.

Sapir, André, and Lars Lundberg. 1984. "The U.S. Generalized System of Preferences and Its Impacts." In *The Structure and Evolution of Recent U.S. Trade Policy,* ed. Robert E. Baldwin and Anne O. Krueger, 195–231. Chicago: University of Chicago Press.

UNCTAD (United Nations Conference on Trade and Development). 1999. "Quantifying the Benefits Obtained by Developing Countries from the Generalized System of Preferences." UNCTAD, Geneva.

WTO (World Trade Organization). 2004. *World Trade Report 2004: Exploring the Linkages between the Domestic Policy Environment and International Trade.* Geneva: WTO.

9

THE DOHA DEVELOPMENT AGENDA AND PREFERENCE EROSION: MODELING THE IMPACTS

Dominique van der Mensbrugghe

Trade preferences and their erosion may play an important role in the evolving Doha Development Agenda Round of multilateral trade negotiations. Clearly, agricultural interests in rich countries would be happy to hide behind the curtain of trade preferences granted to the lowest-income countries. They could thus avoid any significant movement toward agricultural trade liberalization that could especially benefit such middle-income agricultural exporters as Brazil and Thailand, but also many low-income countries.

Preferences have long been viewed as a core development tool. But recent analyses have questioned—or at least severely circumscribed (Hoekman 2005a, 2005b) the validity of—the conventional wisdom about the positive effects of preferences on growth and development.

Although preferences have been around for decades, it has been difficult to quantify their actual effect on the intended beneficiaries because of the lack of a comprehensive and extensive database on trade preferences. Most previous analyses of multilateral trade reform have been criticized for overstating the gains to developing countries—particularly the poorest—because of the failure to take into account preferences. Some analysts have tried to overcome this criticism, but their efforts are based only on partial data.[1]

Views expressed in this chapter are those of the author and should not be attributed to the World Bank. This chapter has benefited from discussions with Kym Anderson, Carlos Primo Braga, Paul Brenton, Yvan Decreux, Will Martin, Richard Newfarmer, and Hans Timmer.

The latest release of the database of the Global Trade Analysis Project (GTAP), version 6, overcomes some of the difficulties of dealing with preferences.[2] Based on the Market Access Map (MAcMap) database, the new GTAP release incorporates all major preferential agreements—both reciprocal and nonreciprocal—thereby making it easier to quantify the role of preferences in multilateral efforts to reduce trade barriers.[3] The GTAP 6 contains a default set of trade barriers that incorporates preferences, as well as an alternative set that estimates the trade barriers in the absence of preferences (that is, the estimated most-favored-nation, or MFN, rates). The estimate of the preference margin using this new database for the lowest-income countries is 3.8 percent on average for merchandise imports into the European Union (EU) and 0.5 to 0.7 percent for imports into other rich countries.[4]

The preferences are highest in agriculture and food but not particularly high in clothing and textiles (except for European imports). The variation across exporting countries is considerable, mostly reflecting compositional effects.[5] The relatively low preference margins in the aggregate should not be so surprising. Rich countries could easily remove preferences should imports start creating major market disruptions in local markets. Moreover, except for clothing and textiles, rich countries' import tariffs on manufactured goods are low. Rather than constituting an impenetrable barrier, they are more of a nuisance factor that increases the overall cost of trading only slightly.

This chapter answers three questions:

1. What is the current value of preferences for low-income countries; that is, what would be their loss if their imports were taxed at MFN rates rather than at preferential rates?
2. How much would low-income countries potentially gain or lose from preference erosion were all high-income countries to completely liberalize merchandise trade?
3. What is the upper bound of gains and losses to low-income countries from full global merchandise trade reform, assuming MFN rates obtain versus preferential rates? In other words, to what extent does the uncertainty regarding preference utilization rates affect the outcomes for low-income countries from global merchandise trade reform?

The key findings are as follows:

- For developing countries combined, preferences may be worth about US$8 billion in added income, or some 0.1 percent of their income. Nonetheless, the estimates here suggest that they may be worth about 0.3 percent of the income of the lowest-income countries. The preferences are estimated to boost export revenue by US$4 billion for the lowest-income countries, or 2.3 percent. These estimates derive from a scenario in which preferential tariffs on exports of developing countries into rich countries are replaced by MFN tariffs. In the context of the MAcMap database, these estimates provide the upper bound on the value of preferences to developing countries because they assume that the preferences are fully used and that the cost of regulatory requirements is zero or insignificant.[6]

- If only the nonreciprocal preferences granted to low-income countries by the high-income countries are considered, the aggregate value of preferences may not be that large. If high-income countries were to set all tariffs to zero (thus setting the preference margin to zero), low-income countries would gain, because the overall benefits from greater market access would outweigh the loss in preferences, including the gains from products exempted by many preferential trade arrangements.

- In terms of global merchandise trade reform, ignoring preferences would lead to overestimating the income gains to developing countries from reform by about US$16 billion out of a total gain of US$51 billion. Preferences thus reduce the gains from global trade reform for developing countries from 1.0 percent of initial income to 0.7 percent. For the lowest-income countries, the gains fall from 0.8 percent to 0.4 percent. The analysis does ignore additional complexities. As noted, it does not factor in the underutilization of preferences or the costs of complying with entry requirements (such as rules of origin). Nor does it include any perverse effects from rent-seeking behavior or the dynamic effects associated with a more competitive environment.

- With or without preferences, export revenue for developing countries would rise by 24 to 26 percent in a global reform scenario; this figure translates to an increase of between US$390 billion and US$425 billion. For the lowest-income exporters, the increase in export revenue ranges from US$42 billion to US$47 billion. Thus, the increase in export revenue in a global reform scenario is large in either case, which means that preferences are not a major factor.

- Reforms already under way—notably the removal of the textile and clothing quotas and China's accession to the World Trade Organization (WTO)—are playing a significant role in eroding preferences. Those two factors alone account for a US$1 billion loss in real income for the lowest-income countries.

This chapter provides a simple framework for assessing the role of preferences in determining trade outcomes. It shows that the change in export revenues can be derived from a simple formula that depends on existing market shares and the degree of substitutability of goods from different regions of origin. It provides a brief overview of the preference database, focusing on the EU and the United States. It then elaborates on the quantitative effects of preferences using the World Bank's global trade model.

The Economics of Preferences

The value of preferences to exporters is typically assessed by one of three measures: (a) the preference margin on exports, (b) the effect of preferences on exports, and (c) the effect of preferences on incomes. The preference margin depends only on the gap between the duty paid by the preference-receiving country and that paid by other suppliers. The trade and income gains depend also on the effect of the preferences on the volume of exports, which, in turn, depend on the elasticity of demand for preferential imports with respect to the price of nonpreferential goods.

Equation 9.1 describes the MFN-price elasticity for preferential imports—that is, the effect on the demand for preferential imports relative to a change in the price of MFN imports (for example, a decline in the MFN tariff).[7] The expression is a combination of two share parameters, s_m and s_D, and two substitution elasticities. The first share parameter (s_m) is the share of MFN imports relative to total imports, and the second share parameter (s_D) is the share of domestic goods in total demand. The substitution elasticity σ^m determines the degree of substitutability between domestic goods and imports (taken as a whole). The substitution elasticity σ^w determines the degree of substitutability of imports by region of origin.

$$\varepsilon_{p,m} = s_m(\sigma^w - s_D\sigma^m) \tag{9.1}$$

The following discussion assumes more substitution across imports by region of origin than between the domestic goods and imports. This assumption guarantees that the elasticity of demand for preferential imports relative to the price of MFN imports is positive (that is, if the tariff on MFN imports goes up, the demand for preferential imports increases). The higher the substitution is across imports (that is, σ^w), the greater the increase is. Similarly, the higher the share of MFN imports is, the greater the increase is. The other factor plays a moderating role; it partly reduces the full effect of the change in the price of MFN imports by increasing the size of the market as a whole when the price of nonpreferential imports falls. The tariff rise increases the average price of imports and thus lowers the overall demand for imports. Therefore, a lower level of import penetration (that is, a higher domestic share) reduces the elasticity, as does a higher degree of substitution between domestic goods and imports.

Table 9.1 illustrates this elasticity using the base data and parameters from the modeling exercise that is developed in subsequent sections.[8] The first two columns of the table show, respectively, the level of imports from low-income countries,

TABLE 9.1 Impact on Trade of Removing Preference Margin for Imports from Low-Income Countries (Excluding India) Using a Partial Equilibrium Framework

Product	Imports from LIX (US$ billion) (1)	Total importsᵃ (US$ billion) (2)	Elasticity (3)	Preference margin (%) (4)	Change in imports from LIX (US$ billion) (5)	Change (%) (6)	Contribution (%) (7)
EU-25ᵇ							
Rice	97	708	5.0	6.7	22	−23.0	0.3
Wheat	5	999	6.4	1.4	0	−8.7	0.0
Other grains	31	677	5.0	4.0	5	−17.7	0.1
Oilseeds	77	4,230	6.6	0.2	1	−1.4	0.0
Sugar	436	1,149	2.7	0.5	3	−0.8	0.1
Vegetables and fruits	946	9,583	4.4	15.8	516	−54.5	7.8
Plant-based fibers	379	1,385	4.7	0.0	0	0.0	0.0
Other crops	4,175	10,605	2.9	3.6	417	−10.0	6.3
Livestock	181	3,599	3.9	7.8	49	−27.2	0.7
Fossil fuels	6,174	87,710	6.1	0.0	4	−0.1	0.1
Other natural resources	2,152	10,881	2.8	0.0	1	0.0	0.0
Processed meats	183	4,391	3.9	28.2	117	−63.7	1.8
Dairy products	9	853	4.0	18.1	5	−56.6	0.1
Beverages and tobacco	78	4,090	4.0	10.0	27	−34.8	0.4
Other foods	3,108	18,764	3.5	10.4	1,007	−32.4	15.3
Textile	4,788	26,515	3.9	7.7	1,310	−27.3	19.8

(Table continues on the following page.)

TABLE 9.1 Impact on Trade of Removing Preference Margin for Imports from Low-Income Countries (Excluding India) Using a Partial Equilibrium Framework (Continued)

Product	Imports from LIX (US$ billion) (1)	Total imports[a] (US$ billion) (2)	Elasticity (3)	Preference margin (%) (4)	Change in imports from LIX (US$ billion) (5)	Change (%) (6)	Contribution (%) (7)
Wearing apparel	5,794	35,294	4.2	6.7	1,467	−25.3	22.2
Leather	3,729	15,806	4.8	2.9	475	−12.8	7.2
Intermediate goods	7,532	138,496	4.1	1.9	575	−7.6	8.7
Equipment	9,075	337,562	4.6	1.5	597	−6.6	9.0
All merchandise trade	48,948	713,298	4.3	3.8	6,599	−13.5	100.0
United States							
Rice	24	288	4.6	2.1	2	−9.4	0.3
Wheat	0	325	6.5	0.0	0	0.0	0.0
Other grains	7	492	5.0	0.4	0	−2.2	0.0
Oilseeds	7	265	4.8	1.3	0	−6.0	0.1
Sugar	48	813	3.9	10.1	15	−31.1	2.1
Vegetables and fruits	84	6,546	4.9	0.3	1	−1.2	0.1

Plant-based fibers	3	90	3.9	0.3	0	−1.2	0.0
Other crops	1,154	5,957	3.8	4.9	200	−17.4	28.3
Livestock	37	3,327	4.1	0.6	1	−2.3	0.1
Fossil fuels	11,984	87,066	5.5	0.0	17	−0.1	2.4
Other natural resources	177	2,651	2.8	0.1	0	−0.2	0.1
Processed meats	10	4,919	4.1	1.8	1	−6.9	0.1
Dairy products	1	1,142	4.0	11.9	0	−38.0	0.1
Beverages and tobacco	38	8,936	4.1	2.2	3	−8.7	0.5
Other foods	1,167	18,080	3.9	0.6	29	−2.5	4.1
Textile	2,838	29,561	4.3	0.0	5	−0.2	0.7
Wearing apparel	7,003	48,839	4.5	0.1	17	−0.2	2.5
Leather	1,768	20,973	7.4	0.2	27	−1.5	3.8
Intermediate goods	3,045	212,945	4.4	1.1	138	−4.5	19.5
Equipment	3,777	631,546	5.2	1.3	250	−6.6	35.3
All merchandise trade	33,173	1,084,760	5.0	0.5	708	−2.1	

Sources: GTAP release 6.05 and LINKAGE model elasticities.

Note: LIX = low-income countries excluding India.

a. Excludes intra-EU trade.

b. *EU-25* is defined as members of the European Union prior to January 1, 2007.

excluding India (LIX), and the level of total imports.[9] The EU imports more from the LIX—about 7 percent of total imports—than does the United States, whose imports from these countries amount to just 3 percent of total imports.

The third column represents the so-called elasticity: how much the demand for imports from the LIX would change with respect to a change in the price of imports from other countries (which are assumed to face the MFN tariff). This figure is derived from equation 9.1. The fourth column shows the preference margin.[10] In the case of the EU, the highest preference margins occur in five product lines: vegetables and fruits, processed meats, dairy products, beverages and tobacco, and other food. Textiles and wearing apparel also benefit from significant margins. According to the MAcMap database, the preference margins in the case of the United States are significantly less, exceeding 5 percent in only three product lines (sugar, other crops, and dairy products). They are virtually insignificant in all other product lines.

Columns 5 to 7 indicate the partial equilibrium effects of assuming that the preference margin is eliminated for exporters from countries other than the LIX. For low-income countries, excluding India, making exports to the EU, total imports would decline by about US$6.6 billion, or 14 percent, whereas the decline in the United States—as befits the low preference margin—would be less than US$1 billion, or 2 percent. In volume terms, the greatest effect for such exporters to the EU would be in other foods, textiles, and wearing apparel—lines with a combination of relatively high preferential access as well as relatively high export volumes. Processed meats, with the highest preference margin, represent only a small share of total exports from the LIX to the EU. Somewhat surprisingly in the U.S. case, the losses to other manufacturing—both intermediate and capital goods—are more important than the losses in the textile and wearing apparel sectors because the preference margins, though low, are still many times the level in the latter two sectors.[11]

In conclusion, low-income countries, excluding India, making exports to the EU are poised to lose significant market share as their preference margins are eroded, but the impact on such exporters to the United States could be relatively limited. Subsequent sections turn to the general equilibrium effects—where both producers and consumers react to the changes in incentives—and assess both trade and welfare effects.

Preferences from a Global Point of View

How important are preference margins at the global level? From the point of view of global trade models, this question was particularly difficult to answer until recently. Virtually all previous work using global computable general equilibrium models— essentially based on version 5 and earlier releases of the GTAP dataset—relied on imperfect estimates of preferential trade margins (see, for example, Dimaranan, Hertel, and Martin 2003). The GTAP 5 dataset included only the best-known preferential agreements, notably the North American Free Trade Agreement (NAFTA) and the EU arrangement, leaving out many others—both reciprocal, such as the Southern Cone Common Market (Mercosur), and nonreciprocal. By and large, most trade in the GTAP 5 dataset occurred under MFN tariff rates.

The work of the Centre d'Études Prospectives et d'Informations Internationales (CEPII)[12] and the International Trade Centre in creating the MAcMap database on bilateral tariffs has greatly expanded the scope for assessing the role of preferences (see Bouët, Decreux, and others 2004). The database incorporates virtually all preferential arrangements (at the detailed bilateral and HS six-digit level)—including a quantification of both the ad valorem and the specific tariffs. The database has been aggregated to the 87-region, 57-sector level of GTAP using trade weights.[13] The database comes in two variations. The first, the default used for the GTAP database itself, uses the actual tariffs including the preferential arrangements. The second gives the level of tariffs, assuming that imports are taxed at MFN rates. The difference between the two provides the preference margin (the "own" preference margin, as opposed to the margin with respect to competing imports).

This chapter looks only at the preferential margins on trade flows from developing countries to developed countries—excluding Mexico and the countries in Europe and Central Asia. Virtually all the preferences considered are measures such as the Generalized System of Preferences (GSP)—nonreciprocal preferences constituting assistance for development. In other words, the nonpreferential database uses the same level of tariffs (that is, the actual tariffs, including any preferences) for all North-North and South-South trade, for all North-South trade, and for trade between Mexico and Europe and Central Asia and the North.[14]

Table 9.2 provides the relevant summary data for imports into the EU and the United States, with the caveat that these data are aggregate trade-weighted numbers. The columns on the left show the actual applied tariffs for the modeled developing regions for broad sectoral aggregates—agriculture; processed foods; textile, wearing apparel, and footwear; intermediate manufactured goods; and capital goods or equipment. The final column shows the weighted average for all merchandise trade. The columns on the right show the "own" preference margin—that is, the additional amount the relevant country or region imports would pay if the MFN tariff rate applied.

As the table shows, imports into the EU benefit significantly more from preferential access than do imports into the United States. The average preference margin is 3.8 percent on imports from the LIX, with significant margins on imports of agriculture, food, and textiles and wearing apparel. The average for imports from the LIX into the United States is only 0.5 percent—some seven times lower—with only agricultural imports benefiting from any significant preferential

(*Text continues on p. 372.*)

TABLE 9.2 Average Tariff and Preference Margin in the EU and the United States

Country or country group	Average applied tariff (%)						Preference margin (%)					
	Agriculture	Processed foods	Textiles, wearing apparel, and footwear	Intermediate manufactured goods	Capital goods or equipment	All merchandise trade	Agriculture	Processed foods	Textiles, wearing apparel, and footwear	Intermediate manufactured goods	Capital goods or equipment	All merchandise trade
European Union												
Rest of Oceania	104.1	0.1	2.2	0.0	0.9	24.0	0.3	4.3	9.2	0.3	0.9	1.2
Rest of Free Trade Area of the Americas	67.3	3.2	0.4	0.0	1.0	7.2	14.7	7.4	10.4	3.4	4.5	5.7
Botswana	0.0	84.2	0.1	0.0	0.0	2.0	0.0	63.1	9.3	0.0	0.2	1.8
South Africa	9.2	11.6	2.0	0.6	1.6	2.2	2.7	4.3	4.5	1.2	1.8	1.4
Rest of Southern Africa Customs Union	143.8	19.8	0.1	0.0	0.0	21.7	0.6	19.4	5.7	1.3	0.5	5.0
Malawi	17.1		0.3	0.0	0.0	16.3	9.4		11.1		8.0	9.2
Mozambique	0.2	0.0	0.0	0.0	0.2	0.0	5.8	12.6	6.0	6.0	0.8	6.7
Tanzania	5.1		0.0	0.0	0.0	1.4	8.9	11.7	6.0	0.1	0.3	5.8
Zambia	11.7		0.1	0.0	0.0	1.1	9.2		4.6	0.2	4.4	1.4

Zimbabwe	8.9	72.1	0.1	0.0	0.1	7.8	9.9	11.5	7.3	1.7	9.4	7.5
Rest of Southern African Development Community	85.1	0.3	0.2	0.0	0.0	7.6	0.6	19.6	11.7	1.4	0.8	3.9
Madagascar	2.5	0.0	0.0	0.0	0.0	0.3	3.2	14.7	11.6	2.1	2.4	9.9
Uganda	0.9	0.0	0.0	0.0	0.1	0.5	5.8	12.4	0.4	0.1	10.5	6.5
Rest of Sub-Saharan Africa	3.8	0.5	0.1	0.2	0.5	1.0	5.4	12.5	3.6	1.9	1.5	2.9
Brazil	6.1	34.2	4.3	1.5	1.0	9.3	0.9	7.6	0.5	1.6	3.9	2.9
Mexico	17.0	24.2	1.7	1.4	0.6	2.6	4.6	13.0	8.7	2.5	4.3	5.2
Central America	27.8	4.4	0.4	0.2	0.7	16.2	4.9	19.3	7.0	1.1	5.1	3.9
Andean countries	28.1	7.1	0.2	0.2	0.1	6.7	5.2	6.5	1.6	0.9	5.0	3.7
Rest of Latin America and the Caribbean	21.0	11.4	2.8	0.5	0.8	7.1						
Bangladesh	2.1	0.0	0.1	0.6	0.0	0.1	10.0	12.8	11.6	9.3	6.7	11.5
China	23.1	15.2	9.3	2.2	1.7	4.0	1.1	11.9	0.6	2.0	1.3	1.4
India	14.8	7.7	7.1	0.7	0.4	4.6	1.5	4.8	1.6	3.4	5.3	2.9
Indonesia	3.8	8.1	8.8	1.5	2.0	4.3	4.4	3.7	1.8	1.6	2.3	1.9

(Table continues on the following page.)

TABLE 9.2 Average Tariff and Preference Margin in the EU and the United States (*Continued*)

Country or country group	Average applied tariff (%)						Preference margin (%)					
	Agriculture	Processed foods	Textiles, wearing apparel, and footwear	Intermediate manufactured goods	Capital goods or equipment	All merchandise trade	Agriculture	Processed foods	Textiles, wearing apparel, and footwear	Intermediate manufactured goods	Capital goods or equipment	All merchandise trade
Vietnam	2.1	7.7	8.5	0.7	1.9	6.3	2.9	5.6	3.4	2.3	2.8	3.2
Rest of Europe and Central Asia	5.2	16.3	1.2	2.2	1.8	1.8						5.4
Rest of South Asia	10.6	3.8	3.2	0.7	0.4	3.3	2.1	7.6	6.6	3.0	2.3	1.9
Rest of East Asia	22.5	14.4	8.8	1.6	1.1	3.9	4.1	2.3	2.2	1.4	1.9	1.9
North Africa	10.2	13.8	0.1	1.2	0.1	1.0	6.1	9.3	10.8	3.8	2.8	3.5
Middle East	6.4	11.6	3.8	1.2	1.1	1.0	2.0	9.7	4.8	3.3	14.4	4.1
Developing countries	14.9	14.9	4.9	1.5	1.3	3.4	3.3	7.3	3.1	1.3	2.5	2.1
Low-income countries	9.6	5.0	5.4	0.7	0.6	3.4	4.9	10.6	4.8	2.3	2.5	3.6
LIX	8.9	4.6	4.7	0.7	0.7	3.1	5.3	11.4	6.0	1.9	1.5	3.8

United States	4.1	4.3	13.1	0.1	0.1	7.1	2.1	0.6	0.0	0.2	0.4	0.5
Rest of Oceania	15.8	1.0	10.7	0.4	0.1	5.1	13.2	1.6	2.0	1.4	1.6	1.9
Rest of Free Trade Area of the Americas												
Botswana	7.5		11.1	0.1	2.4	3.4	6.8	3.0	0.3	0.9	0.0	0.0
South Africa	46.1	1.1	10.0		0.0	0.8	20.6	0.4	0.0	0.9	1.4	1.1
Rest of Southern Africa Customs Union			12.6			10.8					3.3	0.6
Malawi	14.8		11.2			14.0	38.2					32.6
Mozambique	19.8					19.8	8.9					8.9
Tanzania	3.7		2.8		0.0	1.5	11.6	0.0	1.8	1.0	4.6	5.3
Zambia					0.0	0.0				1.3	0.1	1.1
Zimbabwe	17.8		8.6	0.1	0.0	6.2	37.6	0.0	0.1	2.3	4.2	10.5
Rest of Southern African Development Community	9.6		11.2	0.1	0.0	1.0	5.7		0.0	1.6	0.8	0.1
Madagascar	0.0		12.0			10.3	9.5	0.4	0.0	1.8	2.0	0.5
Uganda	0.0				0.1	0.0	0.4			1.0	0.3	0.4

(Table continues on the following page.)

TABLE 9.2 Average Tariff and Preference Margin in the EU and the United States (*Continued*)

Country or country group	Average applied tariff (%)						Preference margin (%)					
	Agri-culture	Processed foods	Textiles, wearing apparel, and footwear	Interme-diate manufac-tured goods	Capital goods or equip-ment	All merchan-dise trade	Agri-culture	Processed foods	Textiles, wearing apparel, and footwear	Interme-diate manufac-tured goods	Capital goods or equip-ment	All merchan-dise trade
Rest of Sub-Saharan Africa	0.2	0.6	9.7	0.0	0.1	0.1	0.4	3.8	0.2	1.2	0.7	0.1
Brazil	8.9	4.6	8.2	1.8	1.0	2.5	15.1	1.1	0.0			0.7
Mexico	0.2	0.4	0.1	0.2	0.0	0.0						
Central America	3.4	0.7	11.8	0.0	0.0	7.6	3.9	2.1	1.6	2.2	1.0	1.9
Andean countries	1.7	1.3	13.0	0.7	0.2	0.9	3.5	1.9	0.3	1.3	2.2	0.9
Rest of Latin America and the Caribbean	3.1	3.3	4.3	1.5	0.7	2.0	2.6	0.9	0.6	0.1	0.4	0.7
Bangladesh	2.1	0.0	11.6	1.7	3.7	10.3		0.0	0.0	0.4	0.3	0.0
China	1.0	2.8	12.3	2.2	1.6	3.8	1.0	0.6	0.0			0.0
India	1.0	1.2	9.2	1.5	0.1	3.2	1.2	1.2	0.3	1.1	1.5	1.0
Indonesia	1.0	1.8	13.3	0.9	0.1	5.1	2.2	0.9	0.1	1.2	1.3	0.8

Vietnam	0.2	0.8	15.9	1.4	1.3	3.5		0.0				0.0
Rest of Europe and Central Asia	6.0	2.3	11.4	0.7	0.5	3.0						
Rest of South Asia	1.3	1.5	11.2	3.3	1.3	10.1	1.1	1.3	0.1	0.3	1.4	0.2
Rest of East Asia	6.5	2.0	12.9	1.4	0.4	3.0	13.4	1.0	0.1	1.0	0.4	0.6
North Africa	1.9	3.2	10.5	0.3	0.1	3.0	2.0	3.1	0.0	0.4	0.5	0.2
Middle East	1.7	1.7	6.4	1.7	0.0	0.6	7.8	4.0	3.7	1.1	0.5	0.5
Developing countries	2.7	1.7	10.1	1.2	0.6	2.3	3.7	0.9	0.4	0.4	0.2	0.3
Low-income countries	1.8	1.2	11.4	1.2	0.1	4.2	3.6	0.8	0.1	1.1	1.4	0.6
LIX	2.1	1.1	12.1	1.0	0.2	4.4	4.6	0.7	0.1	1.1	1.3	0.5

Sources: GTAP 6.05, MAcMap, and author's calculations.

margin. Any significant variations over regions of origin can be attributed to the different nature of certain nonreciprocal agreements but are most likely the result of composition effects. The averages can nonetheless obscure the importance of preferences for certain countries, particularly those with exports concentrated in a handful of sectors (for example, bananas, sugar, or certain apparel lines).

The table also shows that the preferences are not exclusively enjoyed by low-income countries. In the case of Europe, exporters from Latin America enjoy a margin ranging from 3.3 percent to 5.2 percent on average (excluding Mexico). Even the middle-income countries of East Asia (including China) have an average preference margin of 1.6 percent. The United States tends to proffer larger preferences to its immediate neighbors in Central and South America. Preferences there are higher than average for low-income countries—including 1.9 percent on exports from Central America. Otherwise, U.S. preferences tend to be concentrated in Sub-Saharan Africa.

This chapter focuses on the EU and the United States. Although the other high-income markets provide some preferential access, the preference margins and the associated trade volumes are both small. The preference margins for the LIX proffered by Canada and high-income countries in Asia are 0.7 percent and 0.6 percent, respectively—about the same as from the United States.[15] Canada's preferences show almost no sectoral bias. But in high-income Asia, the preference in agriculture is nearly 6 percent, compared with less than 1 percent in all other broad categories.

Assessing the Impacts of Preferences from a General Equilibrium Perspective

This section provides a quantitative assessment of the effects of preferences using the World Bank's global trade model, LINKAGE. The version of the model used here has been geared to the low-income countries that presumably benefit the most from preferential access. The GTAP 6 database has been aggregated into 33 countries and regions (focusing on low-income countries) and 21 sectors, emphasizing agriculture, food, and textiles and clothing.[16] These sectors were chosen because they encounter the highest trade barriers in the rich countries and because they are the sectors in which developing countries have a presumed comparative advantage.

This chapter uses the comparative static version of the model. Although the dynamic version of the model is able to track future changes in the global economy, it also complicates the analysis. The comparative static version of the model keeps the focus on the role of preferences.[17] In what follows, the baseline of analysis is the situation in 2001.[18] The role of the removal of the textile and clothing quotas and China's accession to the WTO are discussed toward the end of the section.

The analysis is based on two scenarios for evaluating the effects of preferences, neither of which reflects the ongoing Doha Round discussions. The first simply looks at moving from the initial situation with preferences to a situation in which preferential tariffs are replaced by MFN tariffs for imports into rich countries from developing countries (except Mexico and the European and Central Asian countries). The second looks at the effects of full global trade reform. Two simulations are done. The first, the default, has the preferential tariffs in place. The second assumes that the MFN tariffs hold. The difference between the two provides a range of the possible outcomes from global trade reform with and without preferences.

The first simulation simply assesses the effect of moving from the actual preferential tariffs to MFN tariffs (that is, removing the own preference margins). Table 9.3 presents the key results. For developing countries as a whole, the value of the preferences is estimated at about US$8 billion in income terms. Several important caveats apply. First, the estimate may overstate the potential gains from preferences because it assumes that the utilization rate of the preferential access is 100 percent. The analysis also ignores the potentially high cost of meeting entry requirements, such as restrictive rules of origins (see, for example, Brenton 2003). Given the low average level of preferential margins, many exporters may prefer to export at the MFN rate rather than to bother with the added burden of exporting at the preferential rate. One factor—the potential income accruing from quota rents—may lead to underestimation of the benefits of the preferences. The extent to which these rents are captured by agents in the exporting country is still an open question that requires further empirical analysis (see, for example, Olarreaga and Özden 2005).

On a percentage basis, the LIX are the biggest losers from the elimination of preferential access; they lose up to 0.3 percent of income, whereas developing countries as a whole lose only 0.1 percent. At the country level, rather large losses are possible: Bangladesh (0.8 percent), Madagascar (0.8 percent), Malawi (1.8 percent), Mozambique (1.2 percent), Vietnam (0.7 percent), and Zimbabwe (0.7 percent). A good portion of the losses stem from a negative terms-of-trade shock. Removal of preferences reduces the demand for exports from preference-receiving countries and thus leads directly to deterioration in their terms of trade. The restrictions imposed by the general equilibrium nature of the model typically cause a further deterioration, assuming a fixed trade balance. Provided that imports into preference-giving countries from the LIX are relatively unchanged in this shock (so as to maintain market share or make up for lost export revenue), countries that face higher tariff barriers undergo a real exchange rate depreciation that expands exports and leads to an additional, negative terms-of-trade shock. For the LIX, the burden through the terms of trade is some US$1.2 billion,

TABLE 9.3 Impact of Moving from Preferential Tariffs to MFN Tariffs on Real Income, Imports, and Terms of Trade

Country or country group	Amount (US$ billion)			Deviation from baseline (%)		
	Real income	Imports	Terms of trade	Real income	Imports	Terms of trade
High-income Asia	0.8	−3.0	1.5	0.0	−0.3	0.1
EU-25ᵃ with European Free Trade Association	3.4	−6.1	4.4	0.0	−0.2	0.1
Canada	0.0	−0.6	0.0	0.0	−0.2	0.0
United States	1.9	−1.6	2.4	0.0	−0.1	0.2
Rest of Oceania	0.0	−0.1	0.0	−0.2	−0.7	−0.3
Rest of Free Trade Area of the Americas	−0.4	−0.9	−0.3	−0.4	−2.9	−1.0
Botswana	0.0	0.0	0.0	0.1	0.1	0.2
South Africa	−0.2	−0.5	−0.2	−0.2	−1.6	−0.5
Rest of Southern Africa Customs Union	0.0	−0.1	0.0	−0.4	−1.5	−0.5
Malawi	0.0	0.0	0.0	−1.8	−8.1	−3.1
Mozambique	0.0	−0.1	0.0	−1.2	−5.0	−2.6
Tanzania	0.0	−0.1	0.0	−0.4	−2.6	−1.4
Zambia	0.0	0.0	0.0	−0.1	−0.6	−0.1
Zimbabwe	0.0	−0.1	0.0	−0.7	−4.8	−1.7
Rest of Southern African Development Community	−0.1	−0.2	−0.1	−0.3	−2.5	−0.8
Madagascar	0.0	−0.1	0.0	−0.8	−7.8	−2.5
Uganda	0.0	0.0	0.0	−0.4	−2.4	−1.6
Rest of Sub-Saharan Africa	−0.3	−0.8	−0.3	−0.2	−1.6	−0.6
Brazil	−0.5	−1.2	−0.3	−0.1	−1.6	−0.5
Mexico	0.0	−0.2	0.0	0.0	−0.1	0.0
Central America	−0.4	−0.7	−0.2	−0.6	−1.8	−0.8

Andean countries	−0.4	−0.9	−0.3	−0.1	−1.8	−0.5
Rest of Latin America and the Caribbean	−0.5	−1.0	−0.3	−0.1	−1.4	−0.5
Bangladesh	−0.3	−0.8	−0.2	−0.8	−8.2	−2.5
China	−0.8	−3.1	−1.4	−0.1	−1.1	−0.3
India	−0.5	−1.2	−0.3	−0.1	−2.0	−0.5
Indonesia	−0.2	−0.7	−0.4	−0.2	−1.4	−0.4
Vietnam	−0.2	−0.5	−0.1	−0.7	−2.0	−0.6
Rest of Europe and Central Asia	−0.3	0.0	0.0	−0.1	0.0	0.0
Rest of South Asia	−0.3	−0.5	−0.1	−0.3	−2.5	−0.7
Rest of East Asia	−0.8	−2.2	−1.1	−0.2	−1.1	−0.4
North Africa	−1.0	−2.5	−0.7	−0.5	−3.9	−1.1
Middle East	−0.8	−3.6	−1.3	−0.2	−1.7	−0.6
World	−2.1	−33.5	0.6	0.0	−0.5	0.0
High-income countries	6.2	−11.3	8.4	0.0	−0.2	0.1
Developing countries	−8.3	−22.2	−7.7	−0.2	−1.3	−0.4
Middle-income countries	−5.7	−16.0	−5.9	−0.1	−1.2	−0.4
Low-income countries	−2.1	−5.2	−1.5	−0.2	−2.2	−0.6
LIX	−1.6	−4.0	−1.2	−0.3	−2.3	−0.7
East Asia and the Pacific	−2.1	−6.5	−2.9	−0.1	−1.2	−0.4
South Asia	−1.2	−2.6	−0.6	−0.2	−2.8	−0.7
Middle East and North Africa	−1.8	−6.1	−2.0	−0.3	−2.3	−0.7
Sub-Saharan Africa	−0.7	−2.0	−0.7	−0.3	−1.9	−0.7
Latin America and the Caribbean	−1.7	−4.0	−1.2	−0.1	−1.0	−0.3

Source: World Bank LINKAGE simulations.

a. *EU-25* is defined as members of the European Union prior to January 1, 2007.

compared with a total income loss of US$1.6 billion. The overall loss in export revenue for the LIX is US$4 billion—smaller than the partial equilibrium result of US$7.3 billion (table 9.1). General equilibrium factors moderate the overall loss in export revenue. As noted, countries adapt their real exchange rate to make up for some of the lost market share to maintain their given trade balance. World trade (imports) declines by about US$34 billion, or some 0.5 percent of its baseline level.

The next two simulations assess the importance of preferences through a different lens—global merchandise trade reform. In these scenarios, preferences will eventually be completely eroded. In the first global merchandise trade reform scenario, all tariffs are reduced to zero from the 2001 baseline that assumes preferences are fully utilized (this is a global reform scenario from the standard GTAP 6 database). The reform scenario also includes the removal of domestic agricultural protection and the elimination of the textile and clothing quotas. The second global reform scenario is the result of an adjusted database. Instead of using the default preferential import tariffs, the database is adjusted so that the MFN tariffs are binding.[19] Again, this adjustment affects only tariffs on imports from developing countries to rich countries, except for Mexico and European and Central Asian countries, whose imports enter under reciprocal preferential tariffs. The global gains from reform would be expected to be higher in this second scenario, because import barriers would be higher on average.

Tables 9.4 and 9.5 summarize the results. Table 9.4 provides the effects in terms of changes in billions of dollars relative to the baseline. Table 9.5 shows the deviation in percentage terms. Each table has two sides. The columns on the left show the effect from the default tariff rates (that is, those incorporating preferences). Those on the right show the effect when all developing country imports are taxed at MFN rates, with the aforementioned exceptions.

Globally, the real income gains are US$165 billion with preferences and US$190 billion without preferences—equivalent to an increase of 0.6 percent and 0.7 percent, respectively, of global income.[20] The difference for the LIX is particularly sharp. With preferences incorporated, their gains amount to only US$1.8 billion, or 0.4 percent of initial income. Without preferences, their gain would more than double to US$3.8 billion. With the same caveats as already described—that is, if one assumes preferences are fully utilized and ignores any cost of compliance by ignoring preferences—gains to the low-income countries would be overestimated by some 100 percent.

For developing countries as a whole, the income gains from global merchandise trade reform in the absence of preferences would be about US$50 billion, as opposed to US$35 billion if preferences are taken into account (that is, an overestimation of some 31 percent). The effects on the rich countries are much less, with only a US$8 billion differential from a US$130 billion baseline gain.

TABLE 9.4 Global Merchandise Trade Reform and Preferences: Change from Baseline in US$ Billion

Country or country group	With preferences (US$ billion)			Without preferences (US$ billion)		
	Real income	Imports	Terms of trade	Real income	Imports	Terms of trade
High-income Asia	58.7	135.1	6.0	59.7	135.0	4.8
EU-25[a] with European Free Trade Association	53.8	89.7	1.5	63.4	133.1	−2.5
Canada	2.5	7.7	−0.4	2.8	9.1	−0.4
United States	15.3	66.4	3.6	12.1	84.9	1.3
Rest of Oceania	2.6	3.5	0.2	2.7	3.9	0.2
Rest of Free Trade Area of the Americas	0.6	6.7	−0.3	1.4	8.0	−0.1
Botswana	0.2	0.1	0.1	0.3	0.1	0.1
South Africa	0.8	4.6	0.1	1.4	5.6	0.3
Rest of Southern Africa Customs Union	0.5	1.2	0.2	0.5	1.2	0.2
Malawi	0.0	0.2	0.0	0.1	0.4	0.0
Mozambique	0.0	0.1	0.0	0.0	0.2	0.0
Tanzania	0.0	0.4	0.0	0.0	0.5	0.0
Zambia	0.0	0.2	0.0	0.0	0.1	0.0
Zimbabwe	0.2	0.8	0.0	0.2	0.8	0.0
Rest of Southern African Development Community	0.2	1.9	−0.2	0.4	2.2	−0.1
Madagascar	0.0	0.0	0.0	0.0	0.1	0.0
Uganda	0.0	0.0	0.0	0.0	0.1	0.0
Rest of Sub-Saharan Africa	0.4	11.5	−0.9	1.0	12.9	−0.6
Brazil	4.2	23.1	1.1	3.4	22.4	0.8
Mexico	−0.6	17.9	−1.8	−0.4	17.5	−1.7
Central America	0.5	3.8	−0.1	1.0	4.5	0.0
Andean countries	1.5	10.9	−0.3	7.0	24.5	1.5
Rest of Latin America and the Caribbean	3.0	13.9	0.5	4.2	16.0	1.0

(Table continues on the following page.)

TABLE 9.4 Global Merchandise Trade Reform and Preferences: Change from Baseline in US$ Billion (Continued)

Country or country group	With preferences (US$ billion)			Without preferences (US$ billion)		
	Real income	Imports	Terms of trade	Real income	Imports	Terms of trade
Bangladesh	−0.5	2.5	−0.4	−0.2	3.6	−0.3
China	8.0	127.9	−2.2	9.0	128.0	−1.4
India	0.8	40.8	−1.9	1.0	41.9	−1.9
Indonesia	0.1	7.2	0.2	0.5	7.7	0.4
Vietnam	1.2	10.3	0.0	1.5	10.9	0.1
Rest of Europe and Central Asia	1.9	26.7	−1.5	2.8	27.7	−1.4
Rest of South Asia	0.1	7.0	−0.4	0.1	7.6	−0.3
Rest of East Asia	4.6	33.9	−0.4	5.6	34.9	0.2
North Africa	1.3	14.9	−1.3	2.5	18.7	−0.8
Middle East	3.5	17.6	−1.1	5.3	24.8	0.3
World	165.5	688.4	0.2	189.2	788.8	−0.3
High-income countries	130.3	298.8	10.6	138.0	362.2	3.2
Developing countries	35.1	389.5	−10.4	51.2	426.6	−3.5
Middle-income countries	29.2	296.4	−6.8	42.4	325.7	−1.1
Low-income countries	2.7	83.0	−3.4	4.8	89.0	−2.5
LIX	1.8	42.2	−1.5	3.8	47.2	−0.6
East Asia and the Pacific	14.0	179.3	−2.4	16.5	181.4	−0.7
South Asia	0.4	50.3	−2.7	0.9	53.0	−2.4
Middle East and North Africa	4.9	32.5	−2.4	7.7	43.5	−0.5
Sub-Saharan Africa	2.2	21.0	−0.8	3.9	24.2	−0.1
Latin America and the Caribbean	8.6	69.6	−0.5	15.2	84.9	1.6

Source: World Bank LINKAGE simulations.

TABLE 9.5 Global Merchandise Trade Reform and Preferences: Percentage Change from Baseline

Country or country group	With preferences (%)			Without preferences (%)		
	Real income	Imports	Terms of trade	Real income	Imports	Terms of trade
High-income Asia	1.3	13.1	1.1	1.3	13.3	0.9
EU-25[a] with European Free Trade Association	0.8	4.1	0.5	0.9	4.6	0.0
Canada	0.4	3.6	0.1	0.5	3.7	0.0
United States	0.2	6.8	1.7	0.1	6.5	1.4
Rest of Oceania	24.4	51.7	7.9	24.8	53.4	8.3
Rest of Free Trade Area of the Americas	0.6	20.6	−1.8	1.3	24.7	−0.2
Botswana	5.2	3.9	6.2	8.2	5.8	11.2
South Africa	0.8	15.8	0.6	1.5	19.1	1.9
Rest of Southern Africa Customs Union	13.1	33.4	9.0	14.0	35.1	10.0
Malawi	3.0	30.4	3.7	10.3	65.8	15.5
Mozambique	−0.1	7.0	−2.0	1.2	12.3	0.9
Tanzania	−0.8	18.3	−2.4	−0.3	21.5	−0.6
Zambia	−0.4	11.2	−1.3	−0.4	10.8	−1.3
Zimbabwe	2.9	40.5	3.7	3.2	43.5	4.8
Rest of Southern African Development Community	1.3	19.4	−3.8	2.0	23.3	−2.4
Madagascar	−0.8	0.9	−3.4	0.1	8.7	−0.4
Uganda	−0.5	3.5	−1.5	−0.1	5.9	0.3
Rest of Sub-Saharan Africa	0.3	22.8	−3.4	0.8	25.2	−2.4
Brazil	1.1	31.5	4.1	0.9	30.6	3.4
Mexico	−0.1	11.7	−1.9	−0.1	11.7	−1.8
Central America	0.8	9.6	0.3	1.6	11.7	1.5
Andean countries	0.6	20.6	−0.4	2.8	47.2	10.0

(Table continues on the following page.)

TABLE 9.5 Global Merchandise Trade Reform and Preferences: Percentage Change from Baseline (*Continued*)

Country or country group	With preferences (%) Real income	Imports	Terms of trade	Without preferences (%) Real income	Imports	Terms of trade
Rest of Latin America and the Caribbean	0.8	20.0	2.1	1.2	23.2	3.6
Bangladesh	−1.2	25.0	−9.0	−0.4	36.2	−6.7
China	0.8	44.7	−5.6	0.9	46.0	−5.1
India	0.2	65.8	−6.5	0.2	68.1	−6.1
Indonesia	0.1	15.6	0.3	0.3	17.1	0.8
Vietnam	4.0	40.9	−5.3	4.9	43.9	−4.9
Rest of Europe and Central Asia	0.3	13.5	−1.1	0.5	13.5	−1.0
Rest of South Asia	0.1	32.9	−2.9	0.1	35.2	−3.3
Rest of East Asia	1.3	16.7	−0.3	1.7	17.7	0.1
North Africa	0.7	23.9	−4.1	1.2	30.2	−3.1
Middle East	0.7	8.7	−0.6	1.1	12.0	0.7
World	0.6	10.3	0.0	0.7	11.1	0.0
High-income countries	0.6	6.4	0.9	0.7	6.6	0.5
Developing countries	0.7	23.5	−2.1	1.0	26.0	−1.2
Middle-income countries	0.7	21.5	−1.9	1.0	23.9	−1.0
Low-income countries	0.3	35.0	−3.7	0.6	37.8	−3.0
LIX	0.4	24.1	−2.3	0.8	27.1	−1.5
East Asia and the Pacific	0.9	32.0	−3.4	1.1	33.3	−2.9
South Asia	0.1	53.7	−6.0	0.2	57.1	−5.6
Middle East and North Africa	0.7	12.3	−1.5	1.1	16.2	−0.3
Sub-Saharan Africa	0.8	19.9	−1.2	1.5	22.9	0.1
Latin America and the Caribbean	0.5	18.0	0.4	1.0	22.2	2.2

Source: World Bank LINKAGE simulations.

a. *EU-25* is defined as members of the European Union prior to January 1, 2007.

The differential effects on trade are less dramatic than the effects on real income. Global imports increase by 10 percent in the standard case, including preferences, and by 11 percent when preferences are excluded. The relevant numbers for exports from developing countries are 23.5 percent (with preferences) and 26.0 percent (without preferences). Thus, preferences do not play a major role in the growth in trade. One of the key reasons is that a significant contribution to the rise in trade will be generated by freeing South-South and North-South trade where barriers are highest and where preferences (at least as defined here) play no role. Focusing on the LIX, imports increase by 24 percent when preferences are considered and rise to 27 percent when preferences are ignored—not a significant difference. Part of the difference in the welfare effect can be seen in the changes in the net trade revenue implications (that is, the terms of trade). The LIX suffer a greater terms-of-trade shock when preferences are incorporated. Maintaining market share in the countries where preferences are given will require greater effort as preferences are completely eroded: if they face tariffs of 10 percent and their competitors face tariffs of 20 percent, when tariffs drop to zero, the competitors (if fixed costs are assumed) will get a much larger price boost than countries with preferential tariffs. If both face a tariff of 20 percent, the price boost will be identical. Thus, for countries with preferences, the negative terms-of-trade shock is some US$1.5 billion. Without preferences, this negative shock drops to US$0.6 billion. Nonetheless, export revenues for the LIX would increase by more than US$40 billion in either scenario—and by US$21 billion for Sub-Saharan Africa.

For individual countries, the effects of preferences vary significantly—if not dramatically. Malawi is one extreme. It gains 3 percent in real income when preferences are considered but 10 percent when preferences are ignored. Preferences seem to matter little for the rest of Oceania and the rest of the Southern Africa Customs Union, and for both of these regions, the gains from global reform would be substantial.[21] Madagascar and Mozambique are examples of countries that would gain if preferences were ignored but would lose under other scenarios.

The analysis then decomposed the effect of reforms on the trading system into its components. The intention was to isolate the potential consequences of ongoing reforms—such as the removal of the quotas on textiles and clothing and China's WTO accession commitments—from global free trade. The purpose was twofold: (a) to show the relative importance of these two significant changes to the world trading system and (b) to allow for easier comparability with other studies.[22]

The basic idea is to run a presimulation in which reforms that will occur whether or not a Doha agreement is reached are imposed on the model to obtain a baseline against which the results of the Doha experiments can be compared. Anderson, Martin, and van der Mensbrugghe (2006b) impose four reforms in this presimulation: (a) full removal of the quotas on textiles and clothing,[23] (b) final commitments under the Uruguay Round agreement, (c) China's WTO accession commitments, and (d) EU expansion. Only two of these reforms are implemented here: full removal of the quotas and China's WTO accession commitments.[24]

Table 9.6 summarizes the key welfare results. The left side shows the scenarios with the default tariffs (that is, the preferential tariffs). The right side shows the scenarios where MFN tariffs are imposed. Each side has three columns. The first column shows the real income gains from full merchandise trade reform from the baseline data (it replicates the same real income gains from tables 9.4 and 9.5). The second column shows the real income gains from global merchandise trade reform after implementing the two presimulation reforms. In other words, it shows the gains from global reform after the removal of the textile and clothing quotas and China's accession agreement have been implemented. The third column shows the difference between the two and represents the real income gain of the presimulation itself.

Several observations emerge from these results:

- The presimulation is positive on a global basis, although most of the gains accrue to the high-income countries—US$29 billion out of US$32 billion. The lowest-income countries lose about US$1 billion. Thus, any gains they may achieve from the lowering of China's tariffs are clearly outweighed by the removal of the clothing and textile quotas.
- The existence or not of preferential tariffs has only a marginal effect on the gains or losses from the presimulation reforms (that is, the "differences" columns for both sides of table 9.6 are close to zero).
- The relative error in assuming MFN tariffs is lower once the presimulation reform is taken into account for the lowest-income countries. Without the presimulation, the relative error in using MFN tariffs is 108 percent (US$3.8 billion versus US$1.8 billion). With the presimulation, the relative error is 69 percent (US$4.8 billion versus US$2.8 billion).
- The global gain of US$134 billion using the base tariffs with the presimulation reforms is broadly the same as the equivalent figure of US$127 billion cited in Anderson, Martin, and van der Mensbrugghe (2006b). The distribution between developing and high-income countries is also largely the same. This finding accords largely with the conclusion from Anderson, Martin, and van der Mensbrugghe (2006b) that most of the presimulation gains were attributable to the removal of the textile and clothing quotas and to China's WTO accession. The other reforms were of relatively minor importance quantitatively. Other differences may arise from a different level of regional and sectoral aggregation—with more (small) countries and smaller shares of manufactured goods.

TABLE 9.6 Effect of Removal of Textile and Clothing Quotas and China's WTO Accession on Global Merchandise Trade Reform

Country or country group	With preferences (US$ billion)			Without preferences (US$ billion)		
	No presimulation	With presimulation	Difference	No presimulation	With presimulation	Difference
High-income Asia	58.7	55.3	3.5	59.7	56.2	3.4
EU-25[a] with European Free Trade Association	53.8	39.1	14.7	63.4	48.6	14.7
Canada	2.5	1.8	0.7	2.8	2.1	0.7
United States	15.3	5.0	10.3	12.1	1.9	10.2
Rest of Oceania	2.6	2.7	0.0	2.7	2.7	0.0
Rest of Free Trade Area of the Americas	0.6	0.8	−0.2	1.4	1.5	−0.2
Botswana	0.2	0.2	0.0	0.3	0.3	0.0
South Africa	0.8	0.8	0.0	1.4	1.4	0.0
Rest of Southern Africa Customs Union	0.5	0.5	0.0	0.5	0.6	0.0
Malawi	0.0	0.0	0.0	0.1	0.1	0.0
Mozambique	0.0	0.0	0.0	0.0	0.0	0.0
Tanzania	−0.1	−0.1	0.0	0.0	0.0	0.0
Zambia	0.0	0.0	0.0	0.0	0.0	0.0
Zimbabwe	0.2	0.2	0.0	0.2	0.2	0.0
Rest of Southern African Development Community	0.2	0.3	0.0	0.4	0.4	0.0
Madagascar	0.0	0.0	0.0	0.0	0.0	0.0
Uganda	0.0	0.0	0.0	0.0	0.0	0.0
Rest of Sub-Saharan Africa	0.4	0.4	0.0	1.0	1.0	0.0
Brazil	4.2	4.1	0.2	3.4	3.3	0.2
Mexico	−0.6	−0.2	−0.4	−0.4	0.0	−0.4
Central America	0.5	0.9	−0.4	1.0	1.4	−0.4
Andean countries	1.5	1.5	0.0	7.0	7.1	0.0
Rest of Latin America and the Caribbean	3.0	2.5	0.5	4.2	3.7	0.5

(Table continues on the following page.)

TABLE 9.6 Effect of Removal of Textile and Clothing Quotas and China's WTO Accession on Global Merchandise Trade Reform (*Continued*)

Country or country group	With preferences (US$ billion)			Without preferences (US$ billion)		
	No presimulation	With presimulation	Difference	No presimulation	With presimulation	Difference
Bangladesh	−0.5	−0.1	−0.4	−0.2	0.2	−0.4
China	8.0	2.9	5.1	9.0	4.0	5.0
India	0.8	1.3	−0.5	1.0	1.5	−0.5
Indonesia	0.1	0.4	−0.3	0.5	0.8	−0.3
Vietnam	1.2	1.0	0.2	1.5	1.3	0.2
Rest of Europe and Central Asia	1.9	2.1	−0.2	2.8	3.1	−0.2
Rest of South Asia	0.1	0.5	−0.4	0.1	0.5	−0.4
Rest of East Asia	4.6	4.6	0.0	5.6	5.6	0.0
North Africa	1.3	1.8	−0.5	2.5	2.9	−0.4
Middle East	3.5	3.5	0.1	5.3	5.2	0.1
World	165.5	133.8	31.7	189.2	157.5	31.7
High-income countries	130.3	101.2	29.2	138.0	108.9	29.1
Developing countries	35.1	32.6	2.5	51.2	48.6	2.6
Middle-income countries	29.2	25.0	4.2	42.4	38.1	4.2
Low-income countries	2.7	4.1	−1.5	4.8	6.3	−1.4
LIX	1.8	2.8	−1.0	3.8	4.8	−0.9
East Asia and the Pacific	14.0	9.0	5.0	16.5	11.6	4.9
South Asia	0.4	1.7	−1.3	0.9	2.2	−1.3
Middle East and North Africa	4.9	5.3	−0.4	7.7	8.1	−0.4
Sub-Saharan Africa	2.2	2.3	−0.1	3.9	4.0	−0.1
Latin America and the Caribbean	8.6	8.8	−0.2	15.2	15.5	−0.2

Source: World Bank LINKAGE simulations.

a. *EU-25* is defined as members of the European Union prior to January 1, 2007.

The simulations described so far compare the effects of full merchandise trade reform by using two estimates of applied tariffs: one that assumes that all imports are taxed at applied MFN rates, and one that assumes that imports enter with full use of applied preferential rates. One potential drawback in comparing these two simulations is that the definition of *preferences* is rather broad and includes all preferential and nonpreferential trade regimes—both reciprocal (as in the case of Mercosur) and nonreciprocal—and also contains the feedback from liberalizing all merchandise trade including South-South and South-North trade.

Alternatively, one could take the preferential-based database and ask what happens to low-income countries if the rich countries reform unilaterally vis-à-vis all countries (that is, if the preference margin for low-income imports drops to zero in rich countries with no other changes to tariffs). This narrower definition of the value of preferences may more accurately describe the effects of preferential access for low-income countries. Table 9.7 shows the results from three simulations. The left side shows the effects in millions of dollars, and the right side shows the effects as a percentage of baseline income. The three columns in each panel reflect the respective effects of the EU imposing unilateral trade reform, other high-income countries imposing unilateral trade reform, and all high-income countries simultaneously cutting their merchandise trade barriers to zero. For the low-income countries—those supposedly benefiting from preference margins in high-income countries—the overall gains are positive in all three scenarios, with or without India. The gains are small—0.2 to 0.3 percent of initial income—and lower than the gains for the middle-income countries. Some countries could lose by the greater opening of European markets—for example, Bangladesh, Madagascar, Tanzania, and Uganda—but they can recoup some of the losses by the opening of markets in other high-income countries. Some countries—such as Mozambique and Zambia—would lose in both markets.

One can conclude from these results that preference erosion for low-income countries in high-income markets appears to be limited—although obviously not without consequences for specific countries and for sectors within those countries. These estimates should also be considered upper-bound estimates to the extent that they assume that preferences are fully utilized. Although trade constitutes a potentially valuable development vehicle for many low-income countries, such countries should be urging high-income countries to remove remaining high barriers in products for which they have a comparative advantage (for example, sugar and rice). Low-income countries should also be accelerating investment in high-yield supply-side projects, such as roads and ports infrastructure, which will better enable them to exploit existing and future trade opportunities.

TABLE 9.7 Impact of Unilateral Merchandise Trade Reform by High-Income Countries

Country or country group	Amount (US$ million)			Share of baseline income (%)		
	EU-only	Other high-income	All high-income	EU-only	Other high-income	All high-income
High-income Asia	3,491	38,145	41,622	0.1	0.8	0.9
EU-25[a] with European Free Trade Association	13,309	3,134	16,905	0.2	0.0	0.2
Canada	194	1,603	1,712	0.0	0.3	0.3
United States	3,242	−5,974	−2,582	0.0	−0.1	0.0
Rest of Oceania	531	179	720	4.9	1.6	6.6
Rest of Free Trade Area of the Americas	387	161	560	0.4	0.2	0.5
Botswana	145	−2	147	3.8	−0.1	3.9
South Africa	94	120	224	0.1	0.1	0.2
Rest of Southern Africa Customs Union	453	20	473	11.7	0.5	12.2
Malawi	12	22	34	0.9	1.6	2.4
Mozambique	−17	−2	−19	−0.5	−0.1	−0.6
Tanzania	−21	3	−19	−0.2	0.0	−0.2
Zambia	−11	−2	−13	−0.4	0.0	−0.4
Zimbabwe	116	14	129	1.6	0.2	1.8
Rest of Southern African Development Community	−2	8	8	0.0	0.0	0.0
Madagascar	−11	3	−9	−0.3	0.1	−0.2
Uganda	−11	2	−10	−0.2	0.0	−0.2
Rest of Sub-Saharan Africa	−82	8	−66	−0.1	0.0	−0.1
Brazil	4,308	608	5,032	1.1	0.2	1.3
Mexico	84	−1,296	−1,191	0.0	−0.2	−0.2
Central America	1,205	455	1,617	2.0	0.7	2.7

Andean countries	1,604	62	1,705	0.6	0.0	0.7
Rest of Latin America and the Caribbean	1,324	1,040	2,557	0.4	0.3	0.7
Bangladesh	−174	102	−70	−0.4	0.2	−0.2
India	189	178	376	0.0	0.0	0.1
Indonesia	173	106	280	0.1	0.1	0.2
China	1,520	2,620	3,982	0.1	0.3	0.4
Vietnam	319	310	624	1.1	1.0	2.1
Rest of Europe and Central Asia	788	59	882	0.1	0.0	0.2
Rest of South Asia	−91	659	579	−0.1	0.7	0.6
Rest of East Asia	327	552	900	0.1	0.2	0.3
North Africa	−173	11	−148	−0.1	0.0	−0.1
Middle East	73	669	729	0.0	0.1	0.1
World	33,294	43,577	77,668	0.1	0.2	0.3
High-income countries	20,236	36,908	57,656	0.1	0.2	0.3
Developing countries	13,058	6,668	20,012	0.2	0.1	0.4
Middle-income countries	11,606	4,920	16,761	0.3	0.1	0.4
Low-income countries	534	1,409	1,971	0.1	0.2	0.2
LIX	344	1,231	1,595	0.1	0.3	0.3
East Asia and the Pacific	2,338	3,587	5,786	0.2	0.2	0.4
South Asia	−76	939	885	0.0	0.2	0.2
Middle East and North Africa	−101	680	580	0.0	0.1	0.1
Sub-Saharan Africa	665	194	878	0.2	0.1	0.3
Latin America and the Caribbean	8,525	869	9,720	0.5	0.1	0.6

Source: World Bank LINKAGE simulations.

a. *EU-25 is defined as members of the European Union prior to January 1, 2007.*

Conclusions

Preferences will likely remain a sensitive topic in multilateral trade negotiations. Even though tariffs on most manufactured products have declined dramatically over the past two to three decades in rich countries, trade barriers remain stubbornly high in many sectors of particular importance to developing countries—especially agriculture, food, and textiles and clothing. Developing countries thus have a strong incentive to get and keep preferential access in these sectors. Some countries—or at least some sectors or agents within these countries—have undoubtedly benefited from preferences. More doubtful, however, is how beneficial preferences have been as development policy tools and whether policies should continue to be oriented toward maintaining the complex preferences system—particularly because preference erosion is inevitable as progress is made to reduce barriers through bilateral, regional, or multilateral accords.

This chapter uses access to a new global database to assess quantitatively the broad role of preferences in international trade. The default version of the database incorporates most preferential agreements—both (a) reciprocal and nonreciprocal and (b) North-North, North-South, and South-South. The alternative database also provides an estimate of the trade barriers exporters would be subject to in the absence of preferences (that is, by paying the MFN tariff rate). From these two different databases, a mixed scenario was constructed in which the preferences accorded by the North to the South were eliminated (except for Mexico and the European and Central Asian countries), thus permitting the effects of trade preferences to be isolated. A comparison of the two scenarios—the default with preferences and the alternative without preferences—suggests that preferences as currently configured are worth about US$8 billion to developing countries in the aggregate. This finding equates to just 0.2 percent of developing countries' income but to a more significant 0.3 percent of the income of the LIX. Moreover, preferences raise export revenues of these same countries by some US$4 billion.

Most previous analyses of global trade reform largely ignored the role of preferences owing to the paucity of reliable and comprehensive data. The results in this chapter suggest that the global effect of ignoring preferences amounts to about 0.1 percent of global income (that is, the global gains from full trade reform are 0.6 percent of initial income compared with gains of 0.7 percent when preferences are ignored). But for developing countries, the overestimation would be about 0.3 percentage point of initial income, or gains of just 0.7 percent instead of 1.0 percent when preferences are ignored, with a somewhat larger overestimation for the lowest-income countries. Nonetheless, the effects of global reform on export revenue are only modestly altered by the inclusion or exclusion of preferences.

The chapter also evaluated a more narrowly based definition of the value of preferences. It looked at the effects on low-income and developing countries from unilateral merchandise trade reform by high-income countries (that is, setting the preference margin for all countries to zero). Low-income countries on average would nonetheless benefit from removal of all tariffs in high-income markets, even if full preference utilization is assumed—although some countries could lose.

The analysis portrays only part of the picture. It ignores, for example, the costs of meeting entry requirements, such as rules of origin, and the effects of possible rents arising from quotas. It is also a static picture. It ignores, for example, the potential negative externalities from rent seeking and other distortions arising from a skewed system of incentives. As development policies go, the evidence suggests that preferential access has had only minor success. It may well be time to reorient trade policies toward sharpening the competitiveness of low-income countries' exports and improving the whole supply-side chain from farm- and factory-gate to the markets of rich and middle-income countries.

Annex 9.A: Model Details

The model used for this analysis is the World Bank's global computable general equilibrium (CGE) model, known as *LINKAGE* (van der Mensbrugghe 2004). It is a relatively straightforward CGE model. The version used here is comparative static, though most often the model is used in recursive dynamic mode.

The standard version of the model has perfect competition and constant returns to scale. Producers minimize costs subject to constant returns to scale production technology, consumers maximize utility, and all markets—including for labor—are cleared with flexible prices. There are three types of production structures. Crop sectors reflect the substitution possibility between extensive farming and intensive farming. Livestock sectors reflect the substitution possibility between ranch feeding and range feeding. And all other sectors reflect the standard capital versus labor substitution (with two types of labor: skilled and unskilled). There is a single representative household per modeled region, allocating income to consumption using the extended linear expenditure system. The model allows for the fact that the products produced by different countries tend to be imperfect substitutes. To capture this factor, it models trade using a nested Armington structure in which aggregate import demand is the outcome of allocating domestic absorption between domestic goods and aggregate imports. Then aggregate import demand is allocated across source countries to determine the bilateral trade flows.

The model includes six sources of protection. The most important involves bilateral tariffs. There are also bilateral export subsidies. Domestically, there are subsidies only in agriculture, where they apply to intermediate goods, outputs, and payments to capital and land.

Three closure rules are used. First, government fiscal balances are fixed in any given year. The fiscal objective is met by changing the level of lump-sum taxes on households. This approach implies that losses of tariff revenues are replaced by higher direct taxes on households. Second, the current account balance is fixed. Given that other external financial flows are fixed, this rule implies that ex ante changes to the trade balance are reflected in ex post changes to the real exchange rate. For example, if import tariffs are reduced, the propensity to import increases. Additional imports are financed by increasing export revenues, which is typically achieved by a real exchange rate depreciation. Finally, investment is savings driven. With fixed public and foreign saving, investment will be driven by two factors: (a) changes in the savings behavior of households and (b) changes in the unit cost of investment. The latter can play an important role in a dynamic model if imported capital goods are taxed. Because the capital account is exogenous, rates of return across countries can differ over time and across simulations. The model solves only for relative prices. The numéraire, or price anchor, in the model is given by the export price index of manufactured exports from high-income countries. This price is fixed at unity in the base year and throughout time.

The newest version of the LINKAGE model, version 6.0, is based on the latest release of the GTAP dataset, release 6.0. Compared with version 5.0 of the GTAP dataset, version 6.0 has a base year of 2001 instead of 1997, updated national and trade data, and—importantly—a new source for the protection data. The new protection data come from a joint CEPII (Paris) and International Trade Centre (Geneva) project. The product of this joint effort, known as *MAcMap*, is a tariff-level detailed database on bilateral protection that integrates trade preferences, specific tariffs, and a partial evaluation of nontariff barriers such as tariff rate quotas.

The version of the LINKAGE model used for this study comprises a 33-region, 21-sector aggregation of the GTAP dataset (see annex table 9.A.1). It places heavy emphasis on agriculture and food, which comprise 13 of the 21 sectors, and focuses on the countries assumed to benefit the most from preferential access.

Annex 9.B: Derivation of Key Elasticities

The purpose of this annex is to derive the relationship between the demand for imports benefiting from preferences and the price of imports under an MFN regime. It uses a simple model with only three goods: a domestic good, a preferential import, and an MFN import. Trade is modeled using a simple nested constant elasticity of substitution trade structure. The key idea is that goods are differentiated by region of origin; thus, domestic goods are different from imported goods, and imported goods are also differentiated according to the region of origin. The nested structure attempts to capture that the degree of differentiation (or substitutability) differs by pair of goods. In the simple two-nested structure, domestic goods are assumed to be imperfect substitutes with the aggregate imported good. At the next nest, the aggregate imported good is assumed to be composed of imperfectly substitutable imports from different countries. For example, goods from rich countries tend to be identified with well-known brands (for example, Levi's jeans or Coca-Cola) and thus are differentiated from less well-known or unbranded goods from developing countries.[25] Thus, there is typically less substitution between the domestic good and imports, but a higher degree of substitution across imports by region of origin.

The first node decomposes aggregate demand, XA, into a domestic component, XD, and an aggregate import component, XMT. The top-level substitution elasticity is given by σ^m. Equations 9.2 and 9.3 express the relevant demand equations, where the component prices are, respectively, PD and PMT, and PA represents the

TABLE 9.A.1   Regional and Sectoral Concordance between the LINKAGE Model and the GTAP Database

Modeled regions[a]

1	HYA	High-income Asia (anz, nzl, jpn, hkg, kor, sgp, twn)
2	EUR	EU-25[b] with European Free Trade Association (aut, bel, dnk, fin, fra, deu, gbr, grc, irl, ita, lux, nld, prt, esp, swe, cyp, cze, hun, mlt, pol, svk, svn, est, lva, ltu, che, xef, xer, xna)
3	CAN	Canada (can)
4	USA	United States (usa)
5	XOC	Rest of Oceania (xoc)
6	XFA	Rest of Free Trade Area of the Americas (xfa)
7	BWA	Botswana (bwa)
8	ZAF	South Africa (zaf)
9	XSC	Rest of Southern African Customs Union (xsc)
10	MWI	Malawi (mwi)
11	MOZ	Mozambique (moz)
12	TZA	Tanzania (tza)
13	ZMB	Zambia (zmb)
14	ZWE	Zimbabwe (zwe)
15	XSD	Rest of Southern Africa Development Community (xsd)
16	MDG	Madagascar (mdg)
17	UGA	Uganda (uga)
18	XSS	Rest of Sub-Saharan Africa (xss)
19	BRA	Brazil (bra)
20	MEX	Mexico (mex)
21	APC	Andean Pact (col, per, ven, xap)
22	CAM	Central America (xca)
23	XLC	Rest of Latin America and the Caribbean (arg, chl, ury, xsm, xcb)
24	BGD	Bangladesh (bgd)
25	IND	India (ind)
26	XSA	Rest of South Asia (lka, xsa)
27	IDN	Indonesia (idn)
28	VNM	Vietnam (vnm)
29	CHN	China (chn)
30	XEA	Rest of East Asia and the Pacific (mys, phl, tha, xea, xse)
31	XEC	Rest of Europe and Central Asia (alb, bgr, hrv, rom, rus, tur, xsu)
32	MDE	Middle East (xme)
33	NAF	North Africa (mar, tun, xnf)

Postsimulation aggregate regions, by income classification

1	HIY	High-income (usa, can, hya, e25)
2	EPA	Economic Partnership Agreement countries and regions (xoc, xfa, bwa, zaf, xsc, mwi, moz, tza, zmb, zwe, xsd, mdg, uga, xss)

TABLE 9.A.1   (*Continued*)

3	EPX	Non–Economic Partnership Agreement developing countries (bra, mex, cam, apc, xlc, bgd, ind, idn, vnm, chn, xec, xsa, xea, naf, mde)
4	LMY	Developing countries (xoc, xfa, bwa, zaf, xsc, mwi, moz, tza, zmb, zwe, xsd, mdg, uga, xss, bra, mex, cam, apc, xlc, bgd, ind, idn, vnm, chn, xec, xsa, xea, naf, mde)
5	MIC	Middle-income countries (zaf, bra, mex, cam, apc, xlc, xec, chn, xea, naf, mde)
6	LIC	Low-income countries (xoc, xfa, bwa, xsc, mwi, moz, tza, zmb, zwe, xsd, mdg, uga, xss, bgd, ind, idn, vnm, xsa)
7	LIX	Low-income countries, excluding India (xoc, xfa, bwa, xsc, mwi, moz, tza, zmb, zwe, xsd, mdg, uga, xss, bgd, idn, vnm, xsa)
8	WLD	World total (all regions)

Postsimulation aggregate regions, by regional classification

1	EAP	East Asia and the Pacific (idn, vnm, chn, xea)
2	SAS	South Asia (bgd, ind, xsa)
3	MNA	Middle East and North Africa (mde, naf)
4	SSA	Sub-Saharan Africa (bwa, zaf, xsc, mwi, moz, tza, zmb, zwe, xsd, mdg, uga, xss)
5	LAC	Latin America and the Caribbean (bra, mex, apc, xfa, xlc)

Modeled sectors

1	RIC	Rice (pdr, pcr)
2	WHT	Wheat (wht)
3	GRO	Other cereals (gro)
4	OSD	Oilseeds (osd)
5	SUG	Sugar (c_b, sgr)
6	V_F	Vegetables and fruits (v_f)
7	PFB	Plant-based fibers (pfb)
8	OCR	Other crops (ocr)
9	LVS	Livestock (ctl, oap, rmk, wol)
10	FFL	Fossil fuels (coa, oil, gas, p_c)
11	ONR	Other natural resources (frs, omn)
12	PMT	Processed meats (cmt, omt)
13	MIL	Dairy products (mil)
14	OFD	Other food (fsh, vol, ofd)
15	B_T	Beverages and tobacco (b_t)
16	TEX	Textiles (tex)
17	WAP	Wearing apparel (wap)
18	LEA	Leather (lea)
19	NTM	Intermediate goods (lum, ppp, crp, nmm, i_s, nfm)
20	EQP	Capital goods (fmp, mvh, otn, ele, ome, omf)
21	NTR	Nontraded goods (ely, gdt, wtr, cns, trd, otp, wtp, atp, cmn, ofi, isr, obs, ros, osg, dwe)

(*Table continues on the following page.*)

TABLE 9.A.1 Regional and Sectoral Concordance between the LINKAGE Model and the GTAP Database (*Continued*)

Postsimulation aggregate sectors

1	AGR	Agriculture (ric, wht, gro, osd, sug, v_f, pfb, ocr, lvs)
2	PFD	Processed food (pmt, mil, b_t, ofd)
3	TWP	Textile and wearing apparel (tex, wap, lea)
4	OMN	Other manufacturing (ntm, eqp)
5	MRT	Merchandise trade (all sectors except nontradables)
6	TOT	All goods and nonfactor services (all sectors)

Sources: van der Mensbrugghe 2004; http://www.gtap.org.

a. The modeled regions are an aggregate of the 87 GTAP regions. The GTAP abbreviations are in parentheses. For details on the countries included in the GTAP aggregate regions, see either the GTAP Web site or van der Mensbrugghe (2004).

b. *EU-25* is defined as members of the European Union prior to January 1, 2007.

price of aggregate demand. This price can be expressed as a nonlinear aggregation of the two component prices, as in equation 9.4.

$$XD = \alpha^D \left(\frac{PA}{PD} \right)^{\sigma^m} XA \qquad (9.2)$$

$$XMT = \alpha^M \left(\frac{PA}{PMT} \right)^{\sigma^m} XA \qquad (9.3)$$

$$PA = \left[\alpha^D PD^{1-\sigma^m} + \alpha^M PMT^{1-\sigma^m} \right]^{1/(1-\sigma^m)} \qquad (9.4)$$

In the second nest, aggregate imports are decomposed by region of origin. In this small model, two exporting regions are represented by p and m, the former representing the region benefiting from preferences, and the latter representing the region paying the MFN tariff. Equations 9.5 and 9.6 represent the demand equations for imports from p and m, respectively, where the substitution elasticity is given by σ^w. The import prices are given by PM_p and PM_m, where, without loss of generality, one may assume that PM_p represents the cost, insurance, and freight (CIF) price with no additional tariff and that PM_m represents the CIF price with an ad valorem tariff of τ^m. The aggregate price of imports is given by equation 9.7.

$$XM_p = \alpha^p \left(\frac{PMT}{PM_p} \right)^{\sigma^w} XMT \qquad (9.5)$$

$$XM_m = \alpha^m \left(\frac{PMT}{PM_m} \right)^{\sigma^w} XMT \qquad (9.6)$$

$$PMT = \left[\alpha^p PM_p^{1-\sigma^w} + \alpha^m PM_m^{1-\sigma^w} \right]^{1/(1-\sigma^w)} \qquad (9.7)$$

Next, the partial equilibrium elasticities can be derived. Most interesting here is the elasticity of demand for domestic goods and the preferential imports with respect to the MFN tariff rate. Starting with equation 9.2, one can derive the following:

$$\varepsilon_{d,m} = \frac{\partial XD}{\partial PM_m} \frac{PM_m}{XD}$$

$$= \frac{PM_m}{XD} \left[\alpha^D \left(\frac{PA}{PD} \right)^{\sigma m} \frac{XA}{PA} \frac{\partial PA}{\partial PM_m} \sigma^m \right]$$

$$= \frac{PM_m}{XD} \left[\sigma^m \frac{XD}{PA} \frac{\partial PA}{\partial PMT} \frac{\partial PMT}{\partial PM_m} \right] \qquad (9.8)$$

$$\frac{PM_m}{XD} \left[\sigma^m \frac{XD}{PA} s_M \frac{PA}{PMT} s_m \frac{PMT}{PM_m} \right]$$

$$\varepsilon_{d,m} = \sigma^m s_M s_m = \sigma^m s_{m,T}$$

The elasticity of demand for domestic goods with respect to MFN imports is equal to the top-level Armington elasticity times the share of MFN imports relative to aggregate consumption. This formula holds irrespective of the value of the second-level substitution elasticity (as a point elasticity). The elasticity is higher the greater the degree of substitutability is between domestic goods and imported goods and the higher the share of MFN imports is in total demand. If the top-level Armington elasticity is 4 and the MFN import share is 10 percent, then the instantaneous elasticity is 0.4. The elasticity is unambiguously positive—an increase (decline) in the MFN import price leads to an increase (decrease) in the demand for the domestic good.

The share variables are defined by equations 9.9 through 9.12 and represent, respectively, the share of total absorption spent on domestic goods, s_D; the share of total absorption spent on imported goods, s_M; the share of MFN imports relative to aggregate imports, s_m; and the share of MFN imports relative to aggregate absorption, $s_{m,T}$.

$$s_D = \frac{PD.XD}{PA.\,XA} \qquad (9.9)$$

$$s_M = \frac{PMT.XMT}{PA.XA} \qquad (9.10)$$

$$s_m = \frac{PM_m.XM_m}{PMT.XMT} \qquad (9.11)$$

$$s_{m,T} = \frac{PM_m.XM_m}{PA.XA} \qquad (9.12)$$

The derivations also make use of the expression in equation 9.13—that is the partial derivative of the aggregate price (for example, PA) with respect to a component price (such as P_i). The derivative is equal to the component's share in the aggregate times the ratio of the price. For example, if the prices are equal to 1 in some initial period and the component's share is 10 percent, an increase in the price of the component by 10 percent would lead to (more or less) an increase of only 1 percent in the price of the aggregate.

$$\frac{\partial PA}{\partial P_i} = s_i \frac{PA}{P_i} \tag{9.13}$$

Equation 9.14 shows the derivation of the demand elasticity of aggregate imports with respect to the price of MFN imports. This elasticity is unambiguously negative. It increases (in absolute terms) as the top-level substitution elasticity becomes higher, the domestic share of consumption grows higher, and the share of the MFN import relative to total imports grows higher. If the price of MFN imports declines, the demand for aggregate imports will increase, and the increase will be higher as the substitution elasticity, the share of the MFN good relative to aggregate imports, and the share of the domestic good in total demand become greater.

$$
\begin{aligned}
\varepsilon_{MT,m} &= \frac{\partial XMT}{\partial PM_m} \frac{PM_m}{XMT} \\[2ex]
&= \frac{PM_m}{XMT} \left[\alpha^M \left(\frac{PA}{PMT} \right)^{\sigma^m} \frac{XA}{PA} \frac{\partial PA}{\partial PM_m} \sigma^m - \alpha^M \left(\frac{PA}{PMT} \right)^{\sigma^m} \frac{XA}{PMT} \frac{\partial PMT}{\partial PM_m} \sigma^m \right] \\[2ex]
&= \frac{PM_m}{XMT} \left[\sigma^m \frac{XMT}{PA} \frac{\partial PA}{\partial PMT} \frac{\partial PMT}{\partial PM_m} - \sigma^m \frac{XMT}{PMT} s_m \frac{PMT}{PM_m} \right] \\[2ex]
&\quad \frac{PM_m}{XMT} \left[\sigma^m \frac{XMT}{PA} s_M \frac{PA}{PMT} s_m \frac{PMT}{PM_m} - \sigma^m \frac{XMT}{PM_m} s_m \right]
\end{aligned}
\tag{9.14}
$$

$$\varepsilon_{MT,m} = \sigma^m s_M s_m - \sigma^m s_m = \sigma^m s_{m,t} - \sigma^m s_m = -\sigma^m (s_m - s_{m,T}) = -\sigma^m s_D s_m$$

Equation 9.15 determines the demand for imports from the preferential supplier with respect to the import price of the MFN supplier. The elasticity has an ambiguous sign, though in most cases it will be positive. In other words, a decrease in the MFN tariff will be associated with a decrease in the demand for preferential imports. If the ratio of the two substitution elasticities is less than the domestic share of absorption, then the income effect dominates the substitution effect (that is, the overall increase in import demand is sufficient to increase the demand for imports from both regions). However, typically the second-level elasticity is greater than the top-level elasticity.

Consider some typical values. For example, set σ^m to 4 and σ^w to 8, assume the domestic share is 75 percent, and assume the MFN share of imports is 25 percent. The elasticity will then be 1.25. Therefore, a 1 percent decline in the price of MFN imports would generate an approximate decline of 1.25 percent in the demand for preferential imports. A doubling of the MFN share to 50 percent of total imports leads to a doubling of the elasticity; therefore, a 1 percent decrease in the price of imports would lead to a 2.5 percent decline in the demand for MFN imports. An increase in the share of domestic consumption—that is, a decline in the aggregate import share—would lead to a decline in the elasticity, but the decline would be of a relatively small magnitude because the domestic share parameter is multiplied by the MFN share parameter.

$$
\begin{aligned}
\varepsilon_{p,m} &= \frac{\partial XM_p}{\partial PM_m} \frac{PM_m}{XM_p} \\[2ex]
&= \frac{PM_m}{XM_p}\left[\alpha^p\left(\frac{PMT}{PM_p}\right)^{\sigma^w}\frac{XMT}{PMT}\frac{\partial PMT}{\partial PM_m}\sigma^w + \alpha^p\left(\frac{PMT}{PM_p}\right)^{\sigma^w}\frac{XMT}{XMT}\frac{\partial XMT}{\partial PM_m}\right] \\[2ex]
&= \sigma^w \frac{XM_p}{PMT}s_m\frac{PMT}{PM_m}\frac{PM_m}{XM_p} - \frac{XM_p}{XMT}\frac{\partial XMT}{\partial PM_m}\frac{PM_m}{XM_p} \\[2ex]
&= s_m\sigma^w - s_m s_D\sigma^m \\[2ex]
\varepsilon_{p,m} &= s_m(\sigma^w - \sigma^m s_D)
\end{aligned}
\tag{9.15}
$$

The final expression, equation 9.16, shows the own-price elasticity for MFN imports. It is unambiguously negative.

$$
\begin{aligned}
\varepsilon_{m,m} &= \frac{\partial XM_m}{\partial PM_m}\frac{PM_m}{XM_m} \\[2ex]
&= \left[s_m\sigma^w - s_m s_D\sigma^m - \sigma^w\frac{PM_m}{XM_m}\alpha^m\left(\frac{PMT}{PM_m}\right)^{\sigma^w}\frac{XMT}{PM_m}\right] \\[2ex]
&= s_m\sigma^w - s_m s_D\sigma^m - \sigma^w \\[2ex]
&= -\sigma^w(1 - s_m) - \sigma^m s_m s_D \\[2ex]
\varepsilon_{m,m} &= -\sigma^w + s_m(\sigma^w - \sigma^m s_D)
\end{aligned}
\tag{9.16}
$$

Notes

1. See, for example, Dimaranan, Hertel, and Martin (2003). Bouët, Bureau, and others (2004) is the first paper that attempts to integrate more comprehensive estimates of preferential tariffs in a standard trade model.

2. The GTAP database is the global database representing the world economy for a given reference year—2001 for the GTAP version 6.

3. MAcMap is a database developed jointly by the International Trade Centre (a joint agency of the United Nations Conference on Trade and Development and the World Trade Organization) in Geneva and the Centre d'Études Prospectives et d'Informations Internationales in Paris. It provides a disaggregated, exhaustive, and bilateral measurement of applied tariff duties, taking regional agreements and trade preferences exhaustively into account. See Bouët, Decreux, and others (2004).

4. The term *lowest-income countries*, as used here, is equated to the World Bank's definition of low-income countries, excluding India.

5. Partial equilibrium estimates of the impacts of preferences come up with similar results; that is, preference margins are relatively low in the aggregate, with occasional exceptions for some countries with highly concentrated exports. See, for example, Alexandraki and Lankes (2004) and Subramanian (2003).

6. However, they ignore possible interactions with quota rents.

7. Annex 9.B develops this formula and other elasticities.

8. The elasticity reflects the partial equilibrium point elasticity. The actual elasticity from a shock will differ for two reasons. First, there will be general equilibrium effects. For example, the change in tariffs will affect consumer prices and therefore demand, and the balance of payments closure rule plus intersectoral factor mobility will affect export prices. Second, a large shock, beyond having general equilibrium effects, will also affect movement along agents' demand curves; thus, the actual percentage change in demand is likely to deviate significantly from the estimate given by the point elasticity.

9. The EU total import column excludes intra-EU trade.

10. It is only an approximation of the true preference margin, which must be measured at the tariff-line level, and it is not the margin with respect to the exporters from countries other than the LIX. Instead, it measures what the tariff would be on the LIX should they face MFN tariff levels.

11. This partial equilibrium analysis ignores the role of the removal of the Multifiber Arrangement quota system.

12. CEPII is the French research center on international economics.

13. Trade weights are not always ideal, although such alternatives as regional trade weights are also problematic.

14. This implies that reciprocal agreements between the North and South (excluding Mexico and Europe and Central Asia) are treated asymmetrically.

15. Further details are available from the author.

16. Annex 9.A provides a brief model description and details on model aggregation.

17. Anderson, Martin, and van der Mensbrugghe (2006a, 2006b) provide a more detailed analysis of global trade policy scenarios.

18. The standard presimulation exercise includes completion of the Uruguay Round commitments (including abolition of the quotas on textile and clothing), EU expansion, and China's WTO accession.

19. The adjustment procedure uses a variation of the "Altertax" procedure described in Malcolm (1998).

20. The final part of this section discusses how these results compare with other estimates of global merchandise trade reform using the same model and methodology.

21. These gains may be overestimated to the extent that the model allows for a relatively significant supply response, particularly in terms of land use.

22. Such studies include Anderson, Martin, and van der Mensbrugghe (2006b). See also Grynberg and Silva (2004), who include losses attributable to the abolition of textile quotas as part of the potential losses from multilateral reform.

23. The trade-restricting effects of these quotas are modeled using export tax equivalents; that is, the embodied rents are captured entirely by the exporting country. Preferences will be reflected in the export tax rate. Countries benefiting from preferential access will tend to have a lower export tax rate than do countries with highly binding quotas.

24. The others are more difficult to implement in a scenario where MFN tariffs are assumed to hold, because the reforms are based on the existing system of tariffs—not the fictitious system in which MFN tariffs are assumed to obtain. The other two reforms are largely the same in either tariff system.

25. More sophisticated nests are, of course, possible. For example, consumers may differentiate between European imports and Asian imports and then allocate across different exporters. Models with varieties will push the level of differentiation even further by allocating demand to individual firms, not just countries.

References

Alexandraki, Katerina, and Hans Peter Lankes. 2004. "The Impact of Preference Erosion on Middle-Income Developing Countries." IMF Working Paper 04/169, International Monetary Fund, Washington, DC.

Anderson, Kym, Will Martin, and Dominique van der Mensbrugghe. 2006a. "Global Impacts of the Doha Scenarios on Poverty." In *Poverty and the WTO: Impacts of the Doha Development Agenda*, ed. Thomas W. Hertel and L. Alan Winters, 497–528. New York: Palgrave Macmillan.

———. 2006b. "Market and Welfare Implications of Doha Reform Scenarios." In *Agricultural Trade Reform and the Doha Development Agenda*, ed. Will Martin and Kym Anderson, 333–400. Washington, DC: World Bank.

Bouët, Antoine, Jean-Christophe Bureau, Yvan Decreux, and Sébastien Jean. 2004. "Multilateral Agricultural Trade Liberalization: The Contrasting Fortunes of Developing Countries in the Doha Round." CEPII Working Paper 2004-18, Centre d'Études Prospectives et d'Informations Internationales, Paris.

Bouët, Antoine, Yvan Decreux, Lionel Fontagné, Sébastien Jean, and David Laborde. 2004. "A Consistent, Ad Valorem Equivalent Measure of Applied Protection across the World: The MAcMap-HS6 Database." CEPII Working Paper 2004-22, Centre d'Études Prospectives et d'Informations Internationales, Paris.

Brenton, Paul. 2003. "Integrating the Least Developed Countries into the World Trading System: The Current Impact of EU Preferences under Everything but Arms." Policy Research Working Paper 3018, World Bank, Washington, DC.

Dimaranan, Betina, Thomas Hertel, and Will Martin. 2003. "Effects of Incorporating Tariff Preferences in Global Modeling." Purdue University, West Lafayette, IN.

Grynberg, Roman, and Sacha Silva. 2004. "Preference-Dependent Economies and Multilateral Liberalisation: Impacts and Options." Commonwealth Secretariat, London.

Hoekman, Bernard. 2005a. "Making the WTO More Supportive of Development." *Finance and Development* 42 (1): 14–18.

———. 2005b. "Operationalizing the Concept of Policy Space in the WTO: Beyond Special and Differential Treatment." *Journal of International Economic Law* 8 (2): 405–24.

Malcolm, Gerard. 1998. "Adjusting Tax Rates in the GTAP Data Base." GTAP Technical Paper 12, Center for Global Trade Analysis, Purdue University, West Lafayette, IN.

Olarreaga, Marcelo, and Çağlar Özden. 2005. "AGOA and Apparel: Who Captures the Tariff Rent in the Presence of Preferential Market Access?" *World Economy* 28 (1): 63–77.

Subramanian, Arvind. 2003. "Financing of Losses from Preference Erosion: Note on Issues Raised by Developing Countries in the Doha Round." WT/TF/COH/14, International Monetary Fund, Washington, DC.

van der Mensbrugghe, Dominique. 2004. "Linkage Technical Reference Document: Version 6.0." World Bank, Washington, DC.

10

TRADE PREFERENCES FOR APPAREL AND THE ROLE OF RULES OF ORIGIN: THE CASE OF AFRICA

Paul Brenton and Çağlar Özden

Many developing countries receive unilateral or reciprocal preferential access to the markets of developed countries. These preferences are most pronounced for least developed countries (LDCs) and Sub-Saharan African countries. The broad support of these countries for multilateral trade liberalization appears to have been tempered by their fear that lower most-favored-nation (MFN) tariffs in developed countries will erode their advantages and undermine their export performance. On the face of it, such a common fear of preference erosion is difficult to interpret when the total share of the preference-receiving developing countries in global trade has fallen over the years. A careful analysis reveals that the majority of preference-receiving countries obtain very little benefit from existing preference schemes and, as a result, would not appear to lose much from the liberalization of global trade through lower MFN tariffs.

Most developing countries do not benefit from existing preferential market access programs for a number of reasons. First, in many cases, exports are dominated by primary products and raw materials that are already subject to very low—often zero—MFN tariffs. Second, even in the case of products for which MFN tariffs are considerable (such as agricultural products and textiles and apparel), the main unilateral preference programs, such as the Generalized System of Preferences (GSP), may completely exclude such products. Finally, many

---

The views expressed here are those of the authors and should not be attributed to the World Bank.

reciprocal programs (customs unions and free trade areas) cover almost all products as a matter of rule and incorporate unilateral programs that are more comprehensive in their coverage.[1] However, such programs tend to impose rather strict requirements for rules of origin. Compliance with these "generous" preference programs requires significant burdens in terms of additional input costs and bureaucratic paperwork that decrease the use and the benefits of such programs considerably. The rules of origin vary considerably across preference schemes. For example, the available evidence in the apparel sector suggests that there has been a substantial supply response to preferences in a number of developing countries when rules of origin have been nonrestrictive.

The aim of this chapter is to address preference utilization and erosion and the importance of rules of origin in the context of the apparel sector. Apparel provides a unique case because both the European Union (EU) and the United States imposed rather strict protectionist measures on their apparel imports in recent decades within the framework of the Multifiber Arrangement (MFA). Even though the MFA quotas were completely removed as of January 1, 2005, MFN tariffs of about 12 percent in the EU and 20 percent in the United States are still in place. As a result of these trade barriers, the preferences granted by the EU and the United States to apparel exports of many developing countries are potentially among the most valuable. These preferences have been implemented through either reciprocal arrangements, such as the EU-Turkey customs union or the North American Free Trade Agreement (NAFTA), or unilateral programs, such as the EU's Cotonou Agreement and Everything but Arms (EBA) initiative or the Caribbean, Andean, or African Preferences of the United States. A number of developing countries have managed to substantially increase their exports of apparel, a development that would have been rather unlikely if those countries had faced the same barriers as most South and East Asian exporters, such as China. Thus, the effects of preferential access and the rules of origin on exporters from developing countries would be most transparent in the apparel sector.

The desire to extend preferential market access or at least avoid preference erosion caused by multilateral liberalization may reflect a perception that trade preferences can stimulate diversification into a broad range of export categories that have higher value added than traditional agricultural exports. As a matter of fact, when the GSP was implemented more than three decades ago as part of infant-industry promotion policies, its goals were to increase export earnings, promote industrialization, and accelerate economic growth in developing countries by expanding their exports into industrial products. However, evidence of such export portfolio upgrading as a result of preferences is scant. For example, Özden and Reinhardt (2005) find no positive effect of GSP preferences on various export performance measures of the beneficiaries.

Apparel seems to be the main—and possibly the only—product for which developing countries have been able to increase their exports significantly. Stevens and Kennan (2005) note that within the manufacturing sector, effective preferences for Africa are concentrated on a single category of exports: apparel. Indeed, apparel is a key sector for many developing countries because they can exploit their comparative advantage in low labor costs while many apparel products remain subject to relatively high tariff barriers in the EU and the United States. In addition, the technology involved is relatively simple, start-up costs are comparatively small, and scale economies are not as important as for other industries. All of these factors favor production in locations with low labor costs.

From a development perspective, the next critical issue is whether this export performance is a temporary phenomenon responding purely to the preference margin or whether underlying the preferences are sustainable sources of comparative advantage that can be exploited when the preference margin eventually contracts. Nevertheless, a large number of developing countries—particularly in Africa—have not yet been able to exploit the opportunities created by preferences in the main industrial markets because they lack the necessary infrastructure and the business climate. However, they might be able to take advantage of preferences at a future point when these constraints have been removed. Thus, preference erosion would limit such prospects and limit future diversification for these countries. If countries that currently receive preferences are to be compensated for their erosion, should not countries that might benefit from preferences in the future also be compensated?

This chapter focuses first on the situation with regard to apparel preferences in the United States, where a range of preference schemes affect imports of apparel. Recently there has been a substantial impact on the exports of a small group of Sub-Saharan African countries under the African Growth and Opportunity Act (AGOA). The U.S. case is particularly interesting because the different preference schemes have different rules of origin. Next the chapter looks specifically at Sub-Saharan African countries, which have been targeted in recent preference initiatives by the EU and the United States (through the EBA initiative and AGOA). The importance of apparel preferences under the different country schemes in relation to the overall value of preferences is highlighted and then differences in the rules of origin across the schemes are discussed, along with how they might explain the different supply responses that have been observed.

Apparel Preferences of the United States

The United States offers three main categories of apparel preferences: Caribbean and Andean preferences, preferences available under NAFTA, and preferences available under AGOA.

Caribbean and Andean Preferences

The Caribbean and Central American countries were among the first group to receive preferences from the United States. The overall program is generally referred to as the Caribbean Basin Initiative (CBI). The goal has been to promote economic development by expanding foreign and domestic investment, diversifying CBI economies, and expanding those countries' exports. The CBI refers collectively to the Caribbean Basin Economic Recovery Act of 1983 (CBERA), the Caribbean Basin Economic Recovery Expansion Act of 1990 (CBERA Expansion Act), and the U.S.-Caribbean Basin Trade Partnership Act of 2000 (CBTPA).

Articles covered by the MFA were initially excluded from CBERA, but CBERA beneficiaries could receive certain preferences for their apparel exports under the Special Access Program, which was implemented in 1986. First, countries could receive quotas in excess of their MFA quotas, which meant that the MFA quotas ceased to be binding, in most cases. More important, the U.S.-made components of articles assembled in beneficiary countries were exempt from duties. As a result, fabric and textiles formed and cut in the United States were exported to CBI countries for assembly and then shipped back to the United States. In other words, tariffs were imposed only on the fabrics and inputs that came from third countries. This regime, as Krishna and Krueger (1995) argue, is identical to taxation of third-party inputs. Among the main beneficiaries of apparel preferences are Costa Rica, the Dominican Republic, El Salvador, Guatemala, Haiti, Honduras, and Nicaragua.

The CBTPA was signed into law on May 18, 2000, as part of the Trade and Development Act of 2000. It considerably expanded the preferences received by the CBI countries for their apparel exports. This expansion was mainly a result of the intense lobbying by CBI countries that had lost a considerable portion of their preference margin with the implementation of NAFTA in 1994. The main modification was the extension of preferential market access to the following apparel products:

- Products assembled from U.S.-made and U.S.-cut fabric manufactured from U.S. yarn that enter under Harmonized Tariff Schedule (HTS) chapters 61 and 62.
- Products cut and assembled from U.S. fabric made with U.S. yarn, sewn in CBTPA countries with U.S.-formed thread.
- Products knit to shape (other than certain socks) from U.S. yarns, and knit apparel cut and wholly assembled from fabric formed in one or more beneficiaries or in the United States from U.S. yarns.

In short, the rules of origin for apparel require that articles need to be made from U.S. fabric, which in turn must be produced from U.S. yarn, to receive preferential treatment.

NAFTA Preferences

Special rules for trade in textiles and apparel goods between NAFTA countries are set out in annex 300-B and in the rules of origin applying to those products in annex 401 to the agreement. Other elements regarding trade in textiles and apparel goods are also found in the general provisions of the agreement, such as those on tariff elimination and technical standards. To qualify for preferential tariffs, most textiles and apparel must be produced (cut and sewn) in a NAFTA country from yarn made in a NAFTA country. In the case of yarn spun from cotton and manmade fiber, the fiber must originate in the NAFTA area. NAFTA and CBTPA rules of origin are similar in spirit and implementation. Naturally, the effect of these rules on Mexico is likely to be less restrictive, because Mexico can produce more of the input domestically than can much smaller CBI beneficiaries.

AGOA Preferences

On May 18, 2000, President Bill Clinton signed into law the Trade and Development Act of 2000. AGOA is title I of that law. On October 2, 2000, 34 Sub-Saharan African countries were designated as eligible to participate, subject to their ability to implement U.S. customs procedures, effective visa systems to prevent illegal transshipment and use of counterfeit documentation, and effective enforcement and verification procedures. The current number of beneficiaries is 37.[2] AGOA provides duty-free and quota-free treatment for eligible apparel articles made in qualifying Sub-Saharan African countries through 2015. Qualifying articles include apparel made from U.S. or Sub-Saharan (regional) fabric or yarn. However, unlike all other preference programs, AGOA grants special rules of origin for countries that are designated as "lesser developed countries." These countries may use third-country fabric and yarn and still qualify for AGOA preferences. Twenty-six countries are currently qualified for apparel preferences, and all were designated "lesser developed countries," with the exception of Mauritius and South Africa.[3] The special rules have been extended until 2013 but can be renewed by Congress, as has happened in the past. Also, AGOA limits imports of apparel made with regional or third-country fabric to a fixed percentage of the aggregate apparel imported into the United States. The cap was about 3.5 percent for 2006, and it has never been binding.

Apparel Imports of the United States under Preferences

The U.S. preference programs for apparel imports from developing countries, as mentioned earlier, started with the CBI. The next big step was the extension of duty-free access to Mexico under NAFTA, which significantly eroded the preference margins of the CBI countries. After heavy lobbying by the CBI countries, the U.S.

government implemented the CBTPA, which granted more generous preferences. Unlike CBERA, which granted duty-free treatment only on the portion of the value added that is due to U.S. inputs, the CBTPA grants complete duty-free treatment as long as the rules of origin are satisfied. The next step was the establishment of the Andean Trade Preference Act (ATPA) and the AGOA, which granted preferences to Andean countries (as part of the war on drugs) and Sub-Saharan African countries, respectively. Preferences for Andean countries are very similar to CBI preferences in terms of rules of origin. However, AGOA is markedly different: it allows the use of third-party fabric and other inputs as long as the countries are considered less developed (and subject to the aforementioned 2.5 percent cap).

Apparel products are divided into two main categories: knitted (HTS 61) and not knitted (HTS 62). The rules of origin have different implications for these categories, as will be made clear shortly.

Figure 10.1 presents the share of apparel imports of the United States under preference programs for 2001 through 2004. It includes the first four months of 2005 for which data were available. For knitted items, close to 30 percent of total imports were entering under preference programs. The combined share of CBTPA countries and Mexico is stable at about 22 percent. The increase after 2001 is mainly due to expansion of imports from ATPA and AGOA countries and under the terms of the U.S.-Israel free trade agreement (which allows goods wholly produced in the Gaza Strip or West Bank to enter the United States duty free). The key observation is that the relaxation and eventual removal of MFA quotas (on January 1, 2005) did not seem to have any immediate effect on knitted apparel imports under the preference programs. For nonknitted items (mainly made from fabric—for example, shirts), the imports under preference programs peaked at 25 percent in 2002 and gradually declined afterward. The longer-term effect of MFA removal is complicated by the reimposition of certain restrictions as well as by concurrent changes in market access rules for some of the other eligible countries. For example, the Central American countries all signed free trade area agreements with the United States.

The important point is the decline in the shares of the CBI countries and Mexico in nonknitted items. Their combined market share drops from 23 percent in 2002 to 15 percent in 2005. First, the rules of origin are more costly for nonknitted items; they imply that both the fabric and the yarn that the fabric is made from must come from either the United States or the beneficiary. For knitted items, this rule is less costly to satisfy, because typically no fabric is involved. Especially for CBI countries, which do not have a textiles industry (and so cannot produce the relevant inputs), the impact has been rather severe. Their market share declined from 15 percent to 10 percent in the three years from 2002 to 2005 as the MFA quotas were removed.

The main effect of the removal of global trade barriers for the recipients of apparel preferences seems to be the decline in market share in the nonknitted categories. It should be noted that the AGOA and Andean countries enjoyed increasing market

FIGURE 10.1 The Evolution of U.S. Imports under Different Preferential Programs

a. HTS 61: Knitted apparel imports of the United States

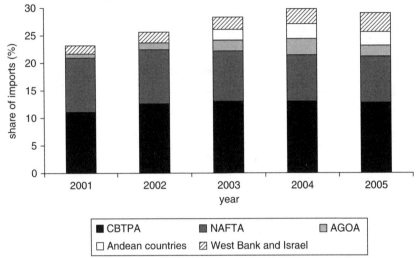

b. HTS 62: Nonknitted apparel imports of the United States

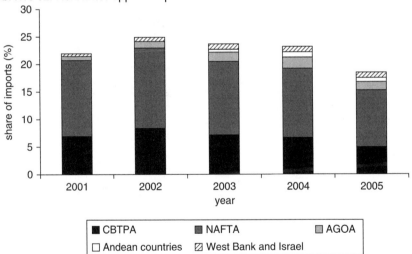

Source: Authors' calculations based on U.S. International Trade Commission data.

share during the same period. There are several reasons for this performance. First of all, they obtained the preferences in 2000. The increased market share is the entry effect—especially as the firms mastered the market dynamics and preference rules. Furthermore, AGOA countries face less restrictive rules of origin than those faced by CBI countries and Mexico. The next section presents the export performance under each preference program—CBTPA, NAFTA, ATPA, and AGOA.

Figure 10.2 shows the export performance of the CBI countries since 1996. It presents total exports to the United States in each category and exports entering under preferences. Because the CBTPA went into effect in 2001, the level is zero before that date. Although CBI exports enjoyed partial preferences before 2001, the data were not recorded separately by the U.S. customs. As both panels of

FIGURE 10.2 Exports of Apparel to the United States by CBI Countries

a. HTS 61: Knitted apparel exports to the United States

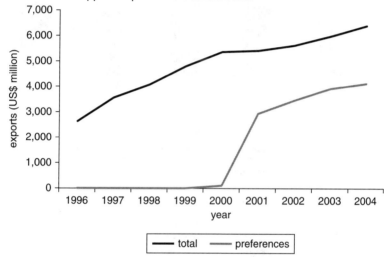

b. HTS 62: Nonknitted apparel exports to the United States

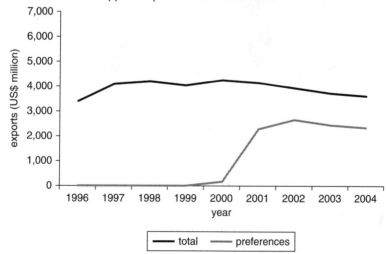

Source: Authors' calculations based on U.S. International Trade Commission data.

figure 10.2 indicate, a significant portion of exports from CBI countries (about 30 percent) still enter the United States without preferences and under full tariffs. This fact indicates the difficulty of satisfying the rules of origin. The figure also indicates that the exports of knitted items continued to increase rapidly. By contrast, exports of nonknitted items are flat. Actually, the data indicate that the CBTPA had no effect on this category, because exports not only failed to increase but actually declined after 2001. However, this finding does not imply that the CBTPA is not valuable; rather, the beneficiaries' exporters now capture a portion of the tariff that was previously collected.

Mexican apparel exports show a different pattern than exports from CBI countries (figure 10.3). First, the exports of both categories start to decline after 2000. The implementation of the CBTPA, AGOA, and Andean preferences naturally had an adverse effect on Mexican exports, as did the gradual relaxation of MFA quotas. Second, a considerable portion of Mexican exports also enter the United States without preferences. One interesting pattern is that over the past few years, the utilization ratio has been increasing. This increase results from Mexican apparel manufacturers redesigning their supply chains over the years to use U.S. inputs so as to satisfy rules of origin. The utilization ratio is actually higher for nonknitted items for Mexico for the more recent years. This finding results from Mexico's larger textiles industry and proximity to the United States; production processes can be better integrated with the suppliers in Mexico than in CBI countries.

The importance of restrictions in rules of origin is most obvious for the Andean countries (figure 10.4). Knitted categories form the largest segment of exports and are rapidly increasing. The effect of ATPA on exports of knitted apparel from the beneficiary countries is clear from panel a of the figure. By contrast, exports of nonknitted apparel have increased at a slower pace (panel b). Furthermore, almost all knitted exports enter under preferences, whereas close to 30 percent of nonknitted exports fail to qualify.

Apparel exports from AGOA countries have been touted as an impressive success story, and the lead role belongs to the liberal rules of origin for the countries that were designated as lesser developed (all beneficiaries except Mauritius and South Africa). Before AGOA, the only exporters were Mauritius and South Africa. Today, several exporters—including Kenya, Lesotho, and Madagascar—have managed to increase their exports rapidly, and apparel forms the largest portion of their total exports to the United States. The rapid increase is clear in both panels of figure 10.5. The most important points are that exports in both categories increase rapidly and that almost all of the exports enter the United States under preferences. The role of the relaxed rules of origin is especially clear for the nonknitted categories.

FIGURE 10.3 Exports of Apparel to the United States by Mexico

a. HTS 61: Knitted apparel exports to the United States

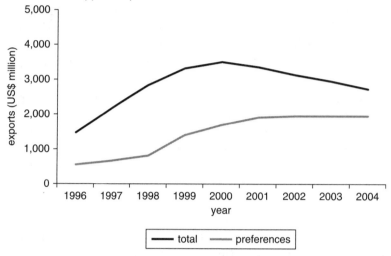

b. HTS 62: Nonknitted apparel exports to the United States

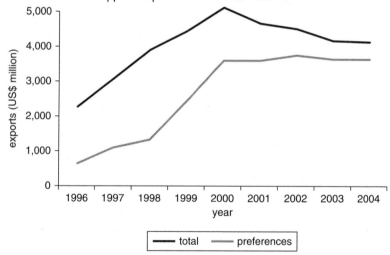

Source: Authors' calculations based on U.S. International Trade Commission data.

MFA Quota Removal and Preference Erosion

Just as the CBI countries lobbied the U.S. government for the CBTPA after NAFTA, similar concerns can be seen about the removal of the MFA quotas. All apparel exporters were extremely concerned about Chinese exports.

FIGURE 10.4 Exports of Apparel to the United States by Andean Countries

a. HTS 61: Knitted apparel exports to the United States

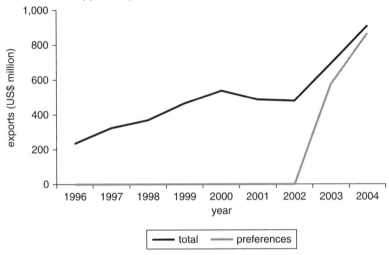

b. HTS 62: Nonknitted apparel exports to the United States

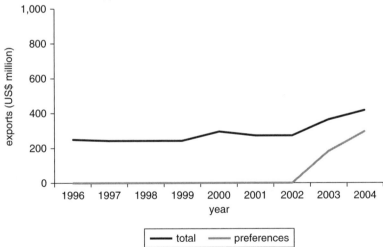

Source: Authors' calculations based on U.S. International Trade Commission data.

Figure 10.6 presents the portion of U.S. imports subject to MFA quotas since 1997. A gradual decline has occurred over the years in the total volume subject to quotas—partially because of the removal of certain quotas and partially because of the rapid increase of imports from preference recipients. Right before the quotas were removed, about 26 percent of knitted imports and 33 percent of

FIGURE 10.5 Exports of Apparel to the United States by AGOA Countries

a. HTS 61: Knitted apparel exports to the United States

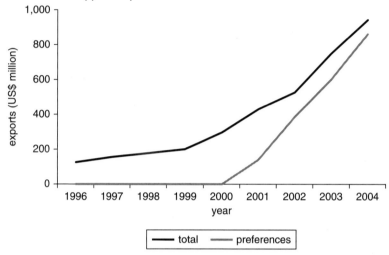

b. HTS 62: Nonknitted apparel exports to the United States

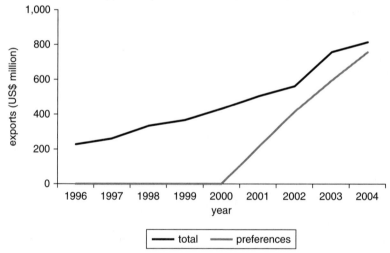

Source: Authors' calculations based on U.S. International Trade Commission data.

nonknitted imports were subject to quotas. The key point of these graphs is demonstrated by the line representing the imports entering under binding quotas (quotas for which the fill rate was above 90 percent). It is very important to note that, although a significant portion of U.S. imports were entering under quotas, only 10 percent were subject to binding quotas as of their removal date. Gradual

FIGURE 10.6 Imports of the United States Entering under Quotas

a. HTS 61: Knitted imports of the United States

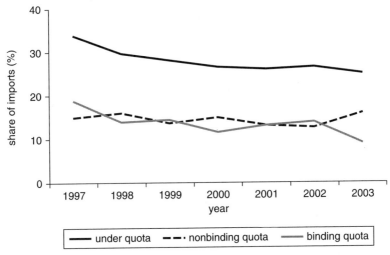

b. HTS 62: Nonknitted imports of the United States

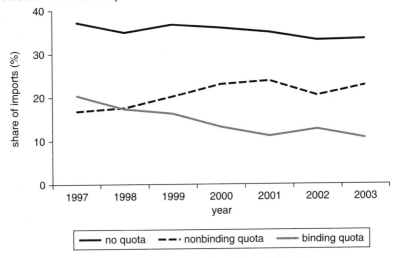

Source: Authors' calculations based on U.S. International Trade Commission data.

quota relaxation caused most quotas to be nonbinding, especially for nonknitted items.

Figure 10.7 presents the average import prices, which are another proxy for the value of preferences and their potential erosion.[4] Panel a shows the average prices of imports from quota-facing countries (mostly in South and East Asia) and from

FIGURE 10.7 Average Import Prices to the United States

a. By type of recipient

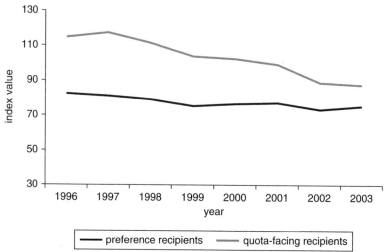

b. By country or region

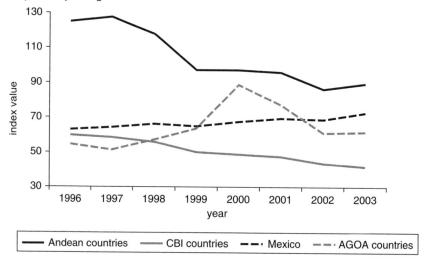

Source: Authors' calculations based on U.S. International Trade Commission data.
Note: Average U.S. import prices for 1996 = 100.

preference recipients. The prices for quota-facing countries are slightly higher; that situation can be due to differences in quality and product mix. The changes in prices are more instructive. The prices from quota-facing countries have declined much more rapidly over the years—by about 25 percent since 1996. These prices are nominal, so the real decline is steeper. The price decline for preference recipients as a whole is less than 10 percent. Looking at the different country groups of preference recipients, the patterns are more divergent. Andean and CBI exporters actually face rapid decline. For AGOA countries, the relative comparison is shown after 2000 because exports were rather limited beforehand. The main message from the era during which quotas were gradually relaxed (before being completely removed on January 1, 2005) is that no large effect on market shares or prices of the preference recipients is seen.

This analysis has shown the important role that preferences have played in explaining the growth of exports of apparel to the United States from key preference-receiving regions. The next section looks at how this role translates into effects on individual countries. It concentrates on Sub-Saharan African countries, the group of countries that remain the most marginalized from the global economy. Assisting the integration of these countries is a development priority, so preference schemes should be designed to benefit them. In this context, the section also looks at the effect of the preferences granted by the EU and the United States to Africa and especially the preferences on apparel, a key sector in establishing a manufacturing base. It begins by briefly explaining the main factors that determine what preferences are worth.

Apparel and Trade Preferences for Africa

Despite the intense discussion of preferences, surprisingly little information is available on what these preferences are actually worth to developing countries. Sub-Saharan African countries are eligible for significantly enhanced benefits, beyond those of the standard GSP preference programs, in the EU (under the Cotonou Agreement and the EBA initiative), in Japan (which provides deeper preferences for LDCs), and in the United States (under AGOA). The effect of a particular set of trade preferences on an individual beneficiary at a particular time is determined by

- the importance of eligible products for preferences in the export and production structure of the beneficiary;
- the margin of preference, which is determined by the size of the MFN tariff and other restrictions faced by excluded countries and by the size of the preference; and
- the utilization of preferences.

The utilization of preferences refers to the extent to which exports that are eligible for preferences actually receive preferential access. For the most part, utilization reflects the costs of satisfying the rules—mainly the rules of origin—that govern preferences.[5] If the costs of compliance exceed the margin of preference, the preference will not be used. There are two elements to the costs of rules of origin. The first consists of the additional costs that are incurred in sourcing inputs and designing production structures to ensure compatibility with the requirements stipulated by the rules of origin.[6] Second is the cost of proving conformity with the rules in terms of documentation, maintenance of complex accounting systems, and expenses incurred in obtaining relevant certificates.[7]

It should be noted that appropriate rules of origin are critical in any preferential trade arrangement, to ensure that the actual products of trading partners receive preferential market access and that exporters from third countries do not use transshipment and "light" processing to circumvent external tariffs. However, rules of origin are often designed to discourage imports of certain products and especially the use of inputs from the rest of the world. In other words, rules of origin become another trade policy tool that supports protectionist political and policy goals. In 1987, the U.S. International Trade Commission suggested that rules of origin should be uniform, simple, transparent, administrable, and economically nondistortionary (Morici 1993). The subsequent practices implemented within numerous preferential access programs of the United States show that this suggestion was mostly ignored. Morici (1993) argues that the trend has been toward more restrictive rules and the textiles and apparel provisions exemplify some of the most abused rules of origin.

Over time, the effect of preferences will reflect the extent to which they facilitate expansion into a broader range of products. That extent is determined by the coverage of the scheme, the margins of preference on products not currently exported, and the rules of origin relating to those products. Whether such preference opportunities are actually exploited depends on the domestic investment environment in the beneficiary country and the extent to which the legal characteristics of the preference scheme constrain investment decisions. The impermanence of preference schemes has often been cited as a factor that limits the supply response to trade preferences. An additional factor, to an extent related to supply capacities, is the ability of exporters from developing countries to satisfy other regulatory requirements for placing their products in markets of developed countries. Probably of most importance are product health and safety standards.

Brenton and Ikezuki (2004) show that the overall value of preferences for African countries in the EU, Japan, and the United States are rather small.[8] In 2002, EU preferences to Sub-Saharan African countries amounted to 4 percent of the value of those countries' exports to the EU. U.S. preferences for these countries amounted to 1.3 percent of the value of exports to the United States, while Japanese preferences amounted to 0.1 percent of the value of exports.

However, these preferences are not evenly distributed across beneficiaries. Under the EU schemes, 60 percent of the benefits accrue to five countries. For the United States, the top five beneficiaries account for almost three-quarters of the value of preferences, and for Japan, nearly 90 percent of the preferences go to the top five countries. For the LDCs, the top 10 beneficiaries account for 100 percent of the benefits under the Japanese and U.S. schemes and more than 90 percent of the benefits offered by the EU schemes. Thus, the value of preferences for the remaining 37 countries (although they are not the same countries in each case) is very small.

Figures 10.8 and 10.9 plot the calculated value of EU and U.S. preferences for each African beneficiary against the contribution of apparel to the value of those preferences. In both figures, most of the beneficiaries are clustered around the origin, so the names are not displayed, reflecting that the preferences are of little value to these countries. In the EU market, there are substantial preferences for Malawi, Mauritius, the Seychelles, and Swaziland, for which the value of preferences exceeds 10 percent of the value of exports (figure 10.8). For Malawi, Mauritius, and Swaziland, these preferences apply mainly to sugar, although the figure shows that about one-quarter of the value of preferences requested by Malawi is for apparel products (see Brenton and Ikezuki 2005). For the Seychelles, the main product receiving preferences is prepared fish. There are then 11 countries for which the value of preferences lies between 5 and 10 percent of the value of exports to the EU. For 14 countries, the value of preferences is between 1 and 5 percent of the value of exports to the EU, and for 16 countries, preferences account for less than 1 percent of the value of exports. Where apparel preferences are important, the

FIGURE 10.8 The Value of Cotonou-GSP Preferences and the Contribution of Apparel, 2002

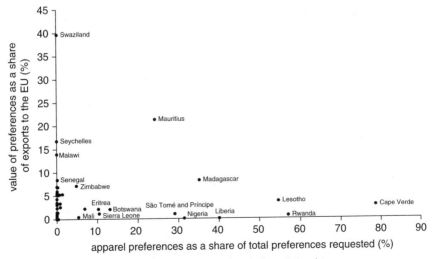

Source: Authors' calculations based on U.S. International Trade Commission data.

FIGURE 10.9 The Value of AGOA-GSP Preferences and the Contribution of Clothing, 2002

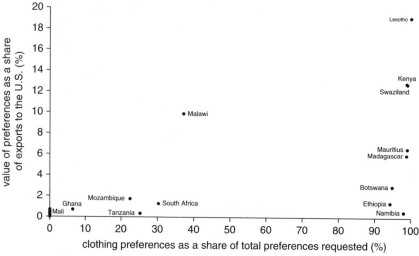

Source: Authors' calculations based on U.S. International Trade Commission data.

overall value of preferences is small. Hence, apparel preferences do not appear to have been a driver of diversification and expansion of African exports to the EU.

U.S. preferences under AGOA and the GSP lead to substantial transfers, equivalent to more than 10 percent of exports to the United States, for three countries: Kenya, Lesotho, and Swaziland (figure 10.9). These preferences are almost entirely for exports of apparel. Apparel accounted for 99 percent, 100 percent, and 99 percent, respectively, of the preferences for these three countries. There are three countries for which the value of preferences amounts to 5 to 10 percent of the value of exports, and for another three countries, preferences account for 1 to 5 percent of exports. For 37 countries, the value of preferences amounts to less than 1 percent of the value of exports to the United States.

Hence, for many countries in Africa, the preferences that are requested in the EU and the United States amount to a very small proportion of the value of exports. As such, the impact of preferences on these countries is likely to be very muted. Only a small number of countries receive substantial transfers under current preference schemes. These schemes mainly provide preferences for sugar in the EU and for clothing in the United States.

On the face of it, for the majority of countries, preferences have done little to stimulate diversification of exports. If preferences were encouraging greater exports of new products, there should be a shift in beneficiaries' exports to products that have positive MFN duties, which should then be reflected by more significant magnitudes for the value of preferences. The fact that the value of preferences is very small for most countries suggests that preferences have not led to a more diversified export structure in most cases. Nevertheless, as is clear from the discussion of U.S. preferences for apparel, preferences can play a key role in stimulating exports of new products if they are consistent with underlying comparative advantages. Where significant, the preferences of Sub-Saharan African countries have been driven by new export activities in the apparel sector. The question is, could preferences play a role in the future in diversifying other developing countries' exports away from agricultural products?

The Apparel Sector and Rules of Origin

This section looks in more detail at exports of clothing under the EU scheme and compares them with that of the United States. It discusses how the nature of the preferences—and especially the rules of origin—can be crucial in determining the extent to which small developing countries are able to respond to the often substantial preferences that are on offer. Figures 10.10 and 10.11 show that there have

FIGURE 10.10 Exports of Knitted Clothing from Sub-Saharan Africa to the EU and United States

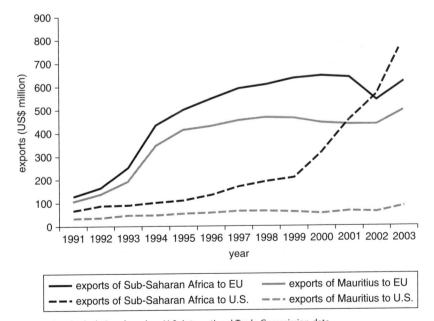

Source: Authors' calculations based on U.S. International Trade Commission data.

FIGURE 10.11 Exports of Nonknitted Clothing by Sub-Saharan Africa to the EU and United States

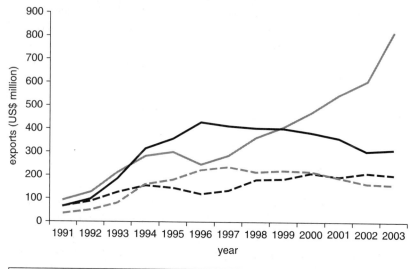

Source: Authors' calculations based on U.S. International Trade Commission data.

been large increases in exports of knitted and nonknitted clothing products from Sub-Saharan African countries to both the EU and the United States. The growth in exports to the EU is concentrated in the early 1990s. Duties had already been removed under the Lomé convention in the 1980s. It is interesting that the supply response for knitted products was stronger than that for nonknitted products. This finding may reflect that the rules of origin for the nonknitted products are more restrictive. The figures show that African exports of apparel to the EU are dominated by the exports of Mauritius.

The figures also show the very strong increase in exports to the United States in the late 1990s and early 2000s, partially because they start from a lower base. Unlike the case of the EU, this increase in exports was not driven by Mauritius. Exports to the EU over the past eight years, however, have remained static for knitted products and have declined by a quarter for nonknitted products. Exports of nonknitted clothing products to the United States now exceed those to the EU by a factor of more than 2.6.

A brief discussion of the nature of the preferences offered by the EU is instructive. EU rules of origin for clothing require production from yarn. This requirement entails that a double transformation process take place in the beneficiary country: the yarn must first be woven into fabric, and then the fabric must be cut and made into clothing. Countries cannot import fabric and make it into clothing and receive preferential access, which constrains the value of the scheme for countries that do not have an efficient textile industry. These restrictive rules of origin are often supported by the argument that they are necessary to encourage substantial value added activities in developing countries and to provide a mechanism for encouraging the development of integrated production structures within individual developing countries—or within regional groups of countries through cumulation mechanisms[9]—that will maximize the effect on employment and ensure that developing countries undertake activities that are not only low in value added.

However, important problems arise from this view. First, such rules discriminate against small countries, where the possibilities for local sourcing are limited or nonexistent. Because most developing countries are small, they are particularly disadvantaged by restrictive rules of origin relative to larger countries. Second, there is no evidence that strict rules of origin over the past 30 years have done anything to stimulate the development of integrated production structures in developing countries. In fact, such arguments have become redundant in light of technological changes and global trade liberalization, both of which have led to the fragmentation of production processes and the development of global networks of sourcing. Strict rules of origin constrain the ability of firms to integrate into these global and regional production networks and dampen the location of any new value added activities in the clothing sector. Finally, it should not be forgotten that these strict rules of origin are the result of a process involving import-competing firms in the EU. Strict rules of origin protect EU clothing firms from competition from preference-receiving countries.

Japan offers an interesting contrast. The rules of origin for knitted products are more restrictive there than those for nonknitted products. The rule for most knitted products requires manufacture from fibers, so imported yarn cannot be used. The rule for many, but not all, nonknitted products allows for manufacture from imported textile fabrics. This difference in the restrictiveness of the rules of origin across the different types for apparel products is reflected in the utilization rates of these preferences (see WTO 2005). More important is the flexibility to source inputs globally that African exporters are permitted under AGOA. This flexibility has allowed a substantial increase in exports from African countries. Clearly, overly restrictive rules of origin can remove the possibility of developing countries—especially LDCs—benefiting from trade preferences.

Conclusions

Apparel offers an opportunity for developing countries to diversify into manufactured products. The analysis of U.S. schemes in this chapter suggests that preferences can play a role in helping countries diversify into these activities. The recent evolution of exports of clothing from Africa to the United States suggests the scope for substantial short-run supply responses in a number of Sub-Saharan African countries. Preferences appear to have played a fundamental role in stimulating this response. However, these preferences will be of long-term development value only if they support activities in which the beneficiaries have a sustainable comparative advantage.

At present, the preferences offered by the main industrial countries differ in terms of duration and certainty and in terms of the rules of origin that govern market access. This chapter highlighted the importance of the specification of rules of origin in governing the effects of preferences for developing countries. A specific apparel product produced in Africa using third-country fabrics can gain preferential access to the United States but not to the EU. The multiplicity of requirements constrains global export strategies and capacities.

Although the erosion of clothing preferences will directly affect only a relatively small number of preference-receiving countries in Africa, it may undermine the prospects for diversification into clothing of a broader group of countries. In other words, current preference erosion might hinder the emergence of a future Lesotho. Within the context of discussions concerning compensation for preference erosion, this possibility raises the question of how to compensate for the erosion of potential future preferences and the removal of an incentive to diversification. In many countries, the principal constraints on diversification include inadequate infrastructure (especially transport, telecommunications, energy, and water); lack of access to credit; and inefficient and costly customs procedures. Obtaining a consensus estimate of the present value of future preferences that have yet to be exploited is likely to be impossible. The priority should be to alleviate the constraints on diversification, which preferences currently help mitigate, while the beneficiaries act to improve the environment for business and investment.

Notes

1. Examples are the Caribbean Basin Initiative, the African Growth and Opportunity Act, the Everything but Arms initiative, and the Cotonou Agreement. See Hoekman and Özden (2005) for an extensive review.

2. According to the AGOA summary on the U.S. government's AGOA Web site (http://www .agoa.gov), countries are deemed to be eligible for AGOA preferences if "they are determined to have established, or are making continual progress toward establishing, the following: market-based economies; the rule of law and political pluralism; elimination of barriers to U.S. trade and investment; protection of intellectual property; efforts to combat corruption; policies to reduce poverty, increasing availability of health care and educational opportunities; protection of human rights and worker rights; and elimination of certain child labor practices." A number of countries have been added and others have been removed over the years. For example, the United States removed Eritrea

and the Central African Republic in 2004, Côte d'Ivoire in 2005, and Mauritania in 2006. Mauritania was reinstated in 2007.

3. Mauritius was temporarily declared eligible (until 2006) for this third-country fabric rule after an amendment to the AGOA Acceleration Act of 2004 and following intense efforts by its government.

4. Note that the average weighted price for all U.S. imports in 1996 is set to 100.

5. Note that utilization rates do not capture situations where the rules of origin are so prohibitive that they prevent any preferential exports and there are no exports at the full duty. In other words, there may be cases in which the beneficiaries can export only with preferences but the rules of origin constrain any uptake of those preferences. In that sense, the utilization rates understate the constraining impact of the rules of origin. Olarreaga and Özden (2005) show that even when preferences are used, beneficiaries do not capture the full preference margin.

6. Krishna and Krueger (1995) show that the effects of rules of origin can be represented as a tax on certain inputs for which the beneficiary (or the donor) country does not have comparative advantage.

7. Empirical evidence suggests that the tariff equivalents of these costs may be quite high. See, for example, Cadot and others (2005) and Carrère and de Melo (2004).

8. Previous studies of the effects of trade preferences have tended to be based on analysis of overall trade volumes using cross-country regression analysis to compare observed preference inclusive trade flows across a wide range of beneficiaries with a counterfactual situation without preferences. The utility of these approaches depends on the extent to which the effects of trade preferences can be isolated from other explanatory variables of trade performance. Brenton and Ikezuki (2004) adopt a more direct approach and calculate (using detailed tariff-line data on trade for which preferences were requested and the relevant tariff) the rents that preferences deliver at observed post-preference trade volumes. Who gets these rents matters; nevertheless, if the calculated rents are very small, there is unlikely to have been a significant impact on trade, employment, or growth.

9. The Cotonou Agreement, but not the EBA initiative, allows for cumulation among African countries, so that regional fabrics can be used without losing originating status. However, the difficulty is in finding regional fabrics that are economically efficient to use.

References

Brenton, Paul, and Takako Ikezuki. 2004. "The Initial and Potential Impact of Preferential Access to the U.S. Market under the African Growth and Opportunity Act." Policy Research Working Paper 3262, World Bank, Washington, DC.

———. 2005. "The Impact of Agricultural Trade Preferences, with Particular Attention to the Least Developed Countries." In *Global Agricultural Trade and Developing Countries*, ed. M. Ataman Aksoy and John C. Beghin, 55–73. Washington, DC: World Bank.

Cadot, Olivier, Céline Carrère, Jaime de Melo, and Bolormaa Tumurchudur. 2005. "Product-Specific Rules of Origin in EU and U.S. Preferential Trading Agreements: An Assessment." CEPR Discussion Paper 4998, Centre for Economic Policy Research, London.

Carrère, Céline, and Jaime de Melo. 2004. "Are Different Rules of Origin Equally Costly? Estimates from NAFTA." CEPR Discussion Paper 4437, Centre for Economic Policy Research, London.

Hoekman, Bernard, and Çağlar Özden. 2005. "Trade Preferences and Differential Treatment of Developing Countries: A Selective Survey." Policy Research Working Paper 3566, World Bank, Washington, DC.

Krishna, Kala, and Anne O. Krueger. 1995. "Implementing Free Trade Areas: Rules of Origin and Hidden Protection." NBER Working Paper 4983, National Bureau of Economic Research, Cambridge, MA.

Morici, Peter. 1993. "NAFTA Rules of Origin and Automotive Content Requirements." In *Assessing NAFTA: A Trinational Analysis*, ed. Steven Globerman and Michael Walker, 226–50. Vancouver: Fraser Institute.

Olarreaga, Marcelo, and Çağlar Özden. 2005. "AGOA and Apparel: Who Captures the Tariff Rent in the Presence of Preferential Market Access?" *World Economy* 28 (1): 63–77.

Özden, Çağlar, and Eric Reinhardt. 2005. "The Perversity of Preferences: GSP and Developing Country Trade Policies: 1976–2000." *Journal of Development Economics* 78 (1): 1–21.

Stevens, Christopher, and Jane Kennan. 2005. "Making Trade Preferences More Effective." Trade Note, Institute of Development Studies, Brighton, U.K. http://www.ids.ac.uk/UserFiles/File/globalisation _team/tradepapers/CSJKTradePreferences.pdf.

WTO (World Trade Organization). 2005. "Options for Least-Developed Countries to Improve Their Competitiveness in the Textiles and Clothing Business." WT/COMTD/LDC/W/37, WTO, Geneva.

11

ECONOMIC POLICY RESPONSES TO PREFERENCE EROSION: FROM TRADE AS AID TO AID FOR TRADE

Bernard Hoekman and Susan Prowse

Developed countries have long granted nonreciprocal (unilateral) trade preferences to various developing countries. Historically, the pattern of these preferences reflected past colonial trade ties. In 1968, the United Nations Conference on Trade and Development (UNCTAD) proposed a Generalized System of Preferences (GSP) under which industrial countries would grant nonreciprocal trade preferences to all developing countries, not just former colonies. Since then, the member countries of the Organisation for Economic Co-operation and Development (OECD) have adopted a range of nonreciprocal preferential access schemes, in addition to an ever-expanding set of bilateral and regional (nonreciprocal) trade liberalization arrangements. Such schemes include

- national GSP programs,
- GSP-plus programs for the least developed countries (LDCs)—such as the Everything but Arms (EBA) initiative of the European Union (EU), and
- special arrangements for subsets of developing countries such as the U.S. African Growth and Opportunity Act (AGOA).

The authors are very grateful to Sheila Page for detailed suggestions that improved the chapter and to Werner Corrales, Joe Francois, Nuno Limão, Patrick Messerlin, Dominique Njinkeu, and Marcelo Olarreaga for helpful comments and suggestions. This chapter draws on a number of background papers prepared for the U.K. Department for International Development project, Global Trade Architecture and Development. The views expressed are personal and should not be attributed to the World Bank or the U.K. Department for International Development.

Trade preferences are a central issue in ongoing efforts to negotiate further multilateral trade liberalization under the Doha Round of negotiations of the World Trade Organization (WTO). Middle-income countries are increasingly concerned about the discrimination they confront in OECD markets as a result of the better access granted in these markets, both to other industrial countries— because of free trade agreements—and to poorer, or "more preferred," developing countries. LDCs and non-LDC African, Caribbean, and Pacific countries worry that liberalization of trade based on general, most-favored-nation (MFN) tariffs and the removal of trade-distorting policies in agriculture by OECD countries will erode the value of their current preferential access.

Such erosion has in fact been going on for decades as a result of unilateral and multilateral reforms in preference-granting countries and the spread of regional trade agreements. As a result, the attention given to the preference erosion has waxed and waned, depending on the impacts of and changes to specific programs. The most recent preference erosion shock was the implementation, under the auspices of the Uruguay Round, of the Agreement on Textiles and Clothing (ATC) on January 1, 2005. This agreement, which removed quantitative restrictions on exports, confronted all countries with the prospect of far greater competition from the lowest-cost suppliers of textiles and apparel—especially in China.[1] Although the shock was not attributable to the removal of a program explicitly aimed at granting preferential access—rather, the aim was to restrain the most competitive suppliers—the effect was to give less competitive producers an advantage in a highly restricted market.

Determining the economic relevance of trade preferences in the context of WTO-based multilateral liberalization—the ongoing Doha Round of trade negotiations—requires both econometric assessments of the extent to which preference schemes are actually used and assessments of the monetary value of potential preference erosion associated with further WTO-based, nondiscriminatory tariff reductions. Preferences are designed to help promote trade and, more important, export diversification. By encouraging trade in sectors where rents are earned, preferences induce specialization in those sectors. And by raising returns, they imply a financial transfer—an improvement in beneficiaries' terms of trade. Although both dimensions are important, induced specialization dominates from an economic development perspective. After all, if the objective had been to transfer resources, it would have been more efficient to do so directly through aid.[2]

This chapter underscores the need to distinguish the likely effects of erosion from the net overall effects after policy responses by recipient countries and actions by the rest of the world are taken into account. Trade reforms by recipient countries and emerging market economies that do not grant preferential access have the potential to substantially attenuate the negative effects of erosion. When the magnitude of the effects of erosion is assessed, much will depend not only on the depth of OECD liberalization—for example, the extent to which such sectors as sugar, beef, or rice are opened up—but also on what other countries do. Much also depends on whether developing countries benefiting from preferential access take actions to improve the competitiveness and productivity of their firms and farmers. Here, development assistance can play an important role.

As economists often point out, many kinds of negative shocks impose adjustment costs on countries, both trade-related costs and costs that are not trade related. Focusing on just one of these while ignoring others is difficult to justify in principle. Although it is true that adverse shocks occur all the time, there are three main arguments for addressing preference erosion losses. First, given that the stated objective of preference-granting countries is to encourage exports from beneficiaries, another instrument needs to be put in place to offset the removal or reduced effectiveness of the initial instrument that was used (that is, preferences). Second, insofar as preference programs have induced investments in activities in which countries do not have a comparative advantage, and to the extent that adjustment to a situation in which they do not have guaranteed preferential access to markets is costly, there is a strong equity argument for donors to assist these countries in the required restructuring. Third, a nondiscriminatory trade regime and MFN-based liberalization by WTO members is a global public good. Multilateral, MFN-based trade liberalization will benefit the world as a whole, and assisting the countries that stand to lose will help achieve this global public benefit. It may help do so by reducing incentives for preference-receiving countries to try to block a Doha deal.

Much more important, an explicit focus on addressing erosion concerns will help remove an instrument that is costly to the trading system as a whole. Preferences distort trade and have been a factor generating the spread of regional trade agreements as excluded (less preferred) countries are motivated to negotiate equivalent access on a reciprocal basis with major preference-granting countries. For the future, lack of progress on the Doha Round and continued deepening of preferential trade arrangements in the interim—notably the EU's Economic Partnership Agreements—are potentially deepening the status quo bias even further, suggesting that erosion concerns may become even more of a constraint in concluding a multilateral trade round.

This chapter begins by reviewing briefly the effects of preference programs and summarizing some of the recent estimates of the value of current programs. It then turns to potential policy responses, arguing that from a mercantilist perspective of quantifying the magnitude of potential preference erosion what matters is to assess the loss of benefits stemming from the removal of a specific policy put in place by OECD countries. From this perspective, it is irrelevant that developing countries may benefit as well from their own liberalization or that of other developing countries—or that such potential benefits may be substantial. But from a development perspective, identifying actions that would generate such benefits is critical, as is determining what the rest of the world—especially richer countries—can do to help poor countries implement such measures. The chapter goes on to argue that assistance for preference erosion should be part of a broader effort by OECD countries to make the trading system more supportive of economic development. This effort is needed in part because erosion is—and will continue to be—an ongoing process, with or without a Doha Round. More important, many developing countries have benefited little from preferences. Hence, the focus should be on identifying actions and policy measures to improve the ability of developing countries to use trade for development.

The Mechanics of Preferences

As discussed in the introduction to this volume, trade preferences involve a mix of benefits for preferential exporters, costs imposed on third-country exporters, and potential losses for the importing country. Only if the (more) preferred country is small, in the sense of not at all affecting the internal price in the importing nation, will there be no detrimental effect on third-country competitors. If so, the preference only creates trade (expands imports), to the detriment of local suppliers in the preference-granting country but not other foreign suppliers, which continue to confront the same price.[3]

Preference erosion involves a redistribution of benefits from those with the best preferences to those that were confronting higher tariffs. Those who faced higher tariffs will gain in exporter surplus, whereas the preferential suppliers will experience a fall in demand for their exports that results in a partial, though generally not complete, loss of the benefits from the original preference scheme. The loss is not complete because preferences include, in part, the benefits from the original tariff-ridden equilibrium produced by a nondiscriminatory tariff reduction by the importer. Preference erosion therefore generally yields a partial, not full, loss of the original benefits of the preference scheme.

Preferences can only have an effect if there is a nonzero tariff in the importing market. Two-thirds of the major items that African countries export to Canada, for example, faced zero MFN tariffs even before the 2003 initiative favoring LDCs. Similarly, 69 percent of EU imports from Africa (by value) in 2000 were in items facing zero MFN duties (Stevens and Kennan 2005)—again, before the EBA was introduced in 2001.

General equilibrium effects must be considered, especially the effects of changes in policies in other countries—both those that do and those that do not grant preferences. Such changes may affect demand and supply and, thus, world prices of the product concerned. Changes in overall (global) trade policies may also affect the relative returns of trading different products or create opportunities for exports that did not exist before.

Compliance costs (for example, paperwork, red tape, and documenting origin) can be significant. The empirical literature estimates, on average, that the documentary requirements impose costs of some 3 to 5 percent of the value of goods (Ansón and others 2005; Brenton and Ikezuki 2005; Brenton and Manchin 2003). Such costs substantially reduce the actual benefits of trade preferences for developing countries, because they require MFN tariffs to exceed an average of 4 percent for preferential access to be meaningful. Given that the average MFN tariff in the OECD is only about 4 percent, preferences can matter only where there are tariff peaks.

To the extent that either importers and distributors (Francois and Wooton 2008) or the transport and logistics sector (Francois and Wooton 2001) have market power, the terms-of-trade benefits of preferential tariff reductions will be captured at least in part by those intermediaries rather than by the exporters (although any diversification benefits will remain). If preferences apply to highly protected sectors in donor countries, they will yield high rents for those able to export free of trade barriers. But buyers will be aware of the existence of these rents, and if they are able to set prices (that is, if they have market power), the rents may be captured mainly by distributors or other intermediaries (Tangermann 2002). The AGOA preference scheme provides evidence that the passthrough of preference margins is indeed partial at best. Olarreaga and Özden (2005) find that the average export price increase for products benefiting from preferences under AGOA was about 6 percent, whereas the average MFN tariff for these products was some 20 percent. Thus, on average, exporters received about one-third of the tariff rent. Moreover, poorer and smaller countries tended to obtain lower shares—with estimates of the share of the loss ranging from 13 percent in Malawi to 53 percent in Mauritius.[4] In terms of market power, the result is a simple redistribution of the benefits of preferences, with rents transferred to importers. In terms of administrative costs, however, the result is not redistribution but a deadweight loss (waste).

Finally, for preferences to have value, beneficiaries need to have the capacity to export the products enjoying preferential access. In practice, GSP programs may exclude products in which developing countries have a strong comparative advantage. Many low-income countries simply do not have the capacity to exploit preferences, lacking either productive facilities or the ability to compete even with the price advantage conferred by the preference, owing to internal transactions and operating costs. Preferences were conceived as instruments to help countries that have the requisite supply capacity to diversify and expand their exports. They have little value for countries without such capacity.

Estimates of the Impact of Erosion

Research suggests that the erosion of all preferences—both the GSP and such deeper, more recent preferences as the EBA initiative and AGOA—would have a substantial impact on some countries, especially those with a high concentration of exports in heavily protected commodities. Relatively larger impacts are concentrated in small island economies and in a number of LDCs that are dependent on sugar, bananas, and, to a lesser extent, garment exports (Stevens and Kennan 2005; Subramanian 2003). These are the commodities subject to high preference margins. Among the LDCs, Cape Verde, Haiti, Malawi, Mauritania, and São Tomé and Príncipe are the most vulnerable to preference erosion. Alexandraki and Lankes (2006) conclude that six middle-income countries—Belize, Fiji, Guyana, Mauritius, St. Kitts and Nevis, and St. Lucia—would also be significantly affected, with predicted export losses ranging from 7.8 percent for Fiji to 11.5 percent for Mauritius. Amiti and Romalis (2007) come to similar conclusions. The limited number and small size of most of the economies concerned argue for closely targeting measures to help mitigate the impact of preference erosion in these countries.[5]

The costs of preference erosion need to be set against gains from MFN liberalization—both for the recipient country and for other developing countries and LDCs. Although LDCs do stand to lose from tariff reductions in sectors or products where preferences matter, they also stand to benefit from improved access to global markets. This benefit offsets—at least partially and often substantially—the more direct losses from the erosion of bilateral preference margins. Thus, preference erosion will be offset by the compensatory effect of broad-based multilateral liberalization, including by emerging-market economies and by beneficiary countries themselves. But research suggests that what matters most in terms of own reform by LDCs is the pursuit of complementary reforms and public investments that enhance the productivity of firms and farmers. Additional trade reforms on their own will not generate significant benefits in terms of poverty reduction (World Bank and IMF 2005).

Finally, implementation and transition periods also matter, as do the depth and scope of the reforms. Total erosion is unlikely to occur quickly, and any MFN reforms will be implemented gradually over several years. Some recent studies quantify the potential income effects of preference erosion.[6] Francois, Hoekman, and Manchin (2006) conclude that complete preference erosion owing to MFN reforms in the EU—including in agriculture—would impose a welfare (real income) loss of some US$460 million on African LDCs and US$100 million on Bangladesh.[7] This conclusion assumes away compliance costs. Limão and Olarreaga (2006) also assess the welfare effects on LDCs of complete preference erosion. They calculate what the income transfer to LDCs would need to be to correspond to the transfer implied by existing preference programs. They conclude that the figure is US$266 million. This is a one-year, short-run effect; all else being equal, the net present value will be several times higher. Hence, Limão and Olarreaga's (2006) results are in line with those of Francois, Hoekman, and Manchin (2006), although the results are not strictly comparable given that Limão and Olarreaga use partial equilibrium methods.

Using a variety of techniques, Grynberg and Silva (2004) estimate the losses in income transfers to producers in economies that depend on trade preferences at US$1.7 billion annually. They argue that producers will require 14 to 20 years to adjust, implying a total net present value of losses ranging from US$6 billion to US$13.8 billion. An important feature of this analysis is that it includes the impacts of abolishing quotas on exports of textiles and clothing. These impacts account for US$1.1 billion of the total loss estimate of US$1.7 billion. Van der Mensbrugghe (in chapter 9 of this volume) concludes that existing preferences generate an additional US$1.6 billion in income for low-income developing countries, as compared with a counterfactual MFN-only regime. Here also the inclusion of ATC quota rents accounts for much of the benefits. In contrast, Francois, Hoekman, and Manchin (2006) include the erosion of ATC quota rents in the baseline scenario. They note that the ATC abolition imposes erosion costs on negatively affected developing countries that are some 10 times larger than the potential overall erosion of remaining preferences under a Doha Round. The estimated losses reflect a combination of greater competition from China and a loss of quota rents. To a significant extent, this erosion has already been incurred, because liberalization of quotas started at the end of the Uruguay Round and was completed in 2005.[8]

If the analysis centers on preference erosion in the broader context of potential tariff reduction by all OECD member countries—or all WTO members, including developing countries—the magnitude of the total erosion loss is generally reduced. This is because the EU has been the most aggressive in using preferences as a tool for development assistance and also has the most extensive trade-distorting policies in a key sector for poor countries: agriculture. Preference programs in other OECD countries have tended to be subject to greater exceptions (for example, the U.S. GSP programs do not include apparel). Thus, the gains associated with MFN tariff reductions by non-EU OECD countries will partially offset the losses attributable to EU liberalization. In the case of Sub-Saharan Africa, Francois, Hoekman, and Manchin (2006) conclude that overall losses will be reduced by a factor of four—to US$110 million—whereas low-income countries in Asia stand to gain.

If compliance costs are also considered, the incidence and magnitude of preference erosion change further, because such costs vary across commodities. Bangladesh, for example, specializes in high-tariff categories, such as clothing, that are subject to restrictive rules of origin. Including compliance costs thus substantially reduces the magnitude of potential erosion. In Madagascar, potential losses become potential gains. For countries specialized in agriculture—such as Malawi and Zambia—the effects of accounting for compliance costs are much smaller, given that such costs are not as big for agricultural exports (Stevens and Kennan 2005).

If one ignores compliance costs and the distribution of rents, estimates of total preference erosion losses for low-income countries range between US$500 million and US$1.7 billion, with much depending on whether the ATC is included.[9] The magnitude of the estimates of preference erosion from even an ambitious Doha Round tends to be less than the erosion associated with the elimination of textile and clothing quotas on exports from developing countries. For example, Francois, Spinanger, and Wörtz (2005) find that the removal of textile restrictions hurts Sub-Saharan Africa, although the impact is smaller than for such Asian countries as India and Vietnam. The ATC-induced negative impact on Africa, however, is smaller than the estimated potential degree of Doha Round preference erosion found by Francois, Hoekman, and Manchin (2006) if no account is taken of compliance costs. If such costs—which they estimate to average 4 percent—are considered, the potential Doha trade preference losses are smaller than those associated with lifting ATC textile and clothing quotas. One reason is that the rents associated with ATC quotas were equivalent to tariffs well above any realistic threshold value of compliance costs.

The importance of the quantitative impacts of the ATC illustrates that a range of policy-induced and non-policy-induced shocks will affect countries almost continuously—reflecting, for example, the global business cycle, changes in consumer tastes, the development of new technologies, and natural disasters. These shocks call for social safety nets and government policies to help firms and households adjust and benefit from new opportunities. The types of shocks and adjustment pressures generated by changes in global trade policies will often be smaller than those generated by other forces. They will also be realized gradually, because trade reforms are generally implemented over a number of years. These considerations have implications for the design of a policy response to erosion.

Possible Policy Responses

According to the literature to date, the aggregate magnitude of erosion will be limited. This conclusion takes into account supply capacity constraints, the costs of satisfying documentary requirements, the fact that rents will be shared with intermediaries in the importing country, and the potential offsetting effects of own reforms and those of other developing countries. But the stand-alone impact of the lost preferential access to the most distorted markets (those in the EU) will be significant for a relatively small number of countries for which a small number of tariff lines are important. This result then raises the policy question of whether to focus on the overall economic net effects, taking into account feasible policy responses, or on the losses incurred in those markets where preferences matter, ignoring any possible offsetting effects.

Both perspectives are relevant. The overall economic effect is clearly the appropriate focal point from a development perspective. It is critical to identify what governments can do to attenuate any negative effects of global MFN liberalization. Indeed, part of the policy response by preference-granting donors should be to help beneficiary governments to adopt measures to better enable firms and farmers in poor countries to exploit trade opportunities and compete with imports. Economic effects are also the focal point of the WTO process, because negotiations involve give and take, with each member trying to maximize net economic gains.

The second focal point, the losses incurred in markets where preferences matter, corresponds to the erosion of benefits stemming from the removal of a specific policy put in place by OECD countries. From this perspective, the existence of other sources of offsetting market access or terms-of-trade gains—whether from liberalization by other developing countries or own liberalization—is irrelevant. What matters is the impact of removing the nonreciprocal access to specific protected markets. The value of total erosion is then the sum over all the products for which the country has been granted preferential access. (If MFN reforms are partial, the loss will be smaller.) This measure assumes away any positive externalities from expanded export production—that is, the focus is only on the terms-of-trade effect. Insofar as countries could or did not benefit (have exports), this measure will show no loss. This important dimension of the preference-erosion question is discussed later.

This analysis does not argue that offsetting actions should not be encouraged, because such actions are in the interest of the developing countries directly affected by MFN liberalization in the OECD. Indirectly, they are in the interest of all WTO member countries. Global liberalization and a shift away from discriminatory trade policies will bolster the trading system and help generate welfare improvements for the world as a whole. These considerations suggest a two-pronged approach involving additional financial assistance (determined by a quantification of the direct bilateral erosion losses that current recipients of preferences will incur) and allocation of funding toward measures that will reduce the negative economic effects of this erosion.[10]

Various approaches can be used to respond to preference erosion losses. One is to seek compensation within the trade negotiating agenda—that is, take actions to improve market access and the terms of trade of the targeted countries. This approach can involve not liberalizing products that are of the greatest value from a preference point of view. It could even entail raising tariffs on products to the degree that they are not bound under the WTO, although raising trade barriers to increase the value of preferential access would reduce global welfare. More common is the argument used by vested interests in the OECD that preferred developing countries should not lose any more preferential access to their (highly distorted) markets and that further MFN reform should be avoided. The result is the potential for status quo bias reflecting a "bootlegger-Baptist" coalition between these protectionist interests and governments of developing countries. Such a coalition would impose a substantial opportunity cost from a global efficiency perspective.

It is difficult to identify trade-based solutions that are consistent with the MFN principle while appropriately targeting those countries that are most affected by the erosion of preferences. A recent proposal to address the erosion issue by converting bilateral preferences into equivalent bilateral import subsidies comes close. As Limão and Olarreaga (2006) argue, this proposal would preserve both the trade-based nature of the assistance and its bilateral (discriminatory) nature, while still implying a multilateral solution. They show that an import subsidy scheme would be superior in welfare terms to trade preferences. Indeed, it would constitute a Pareto improvement, making all WTO members better off by allowing deeper MFN liberalization to occur. This solution assumes, however, continued acceptance by WTO members of exceptions to the MFN principle (that is, it implies continued discrimination across trading partners).

Other options "within" the trading system are to expand preferential access to major emerging markets, to reduce the costs of rules of origin through harmonization toward the most liberal common denominator (Commission for Africa 2005), and to provide discriminatory access in other areas (for example, increased opportunities for the temporary movement of service suppliers under the General Agreement on Trade in Services). Discriminatory access is already occurring on a bilateral basis outside the WTO, as reflected in special arrangements or relationships between OECD members and specific developing countries. Efforts to move down such discriminatory paths in the WTO are not desirable. Indeed, a major rationale for seeking to shift away from using preferential trade as a form of aid is that it undermines the fundamental principle of nondiscrimination and creates incentives to impede MFN liberalization (Karacaovali and Limão 2008; Limão 2006).

Of course, nondiscriminatory solutions could also be pursued within the trading system. An example would be to target MFN liberalization on goods and services in which developing countries have a comparative advantage. Another is to ensure that MFN liberalization proceeds gradually, to allow adjustment to occur over a number of years. Yet another would be to rewrite the rules so as to increase the benefits for poor countries, even at the expense of rich countries' interests. Much of what is discussed in the WTO under the heading "special and differential treatment" and implementation of negotiated commitments is based on perceptions that the existing rules do not fully support development prospects. A willingness to address these concerns could help offset preference erosion losses. Indeed, proactive policies can help address market failures that result in weak trade capacity. Trade policies are unlikely to be effective or appropriate, but some may be subject to WTO rules or the subject of proposed disciplines (for example, subsidies of various kinds). These policies may provide a rationale for greater flexibility in applying disciplines—in particular, greater acceptance of a process that relies on monitoring and transparency of policy more than on rigid enforcement of common rules.[11]

The second broad approach for responding to preference erosion losses by developing countries is development assistance. This option is discussed in what follows because the research summarized above and elsewhere in this volume finds that the main negative monetary impact of erosion flows from the removal of specific trade barriers in specific OECD countries. That is, erosion is primarily a bilateral issue that should be resolved bilaterally, in that those imposing the costs should bear the burden of offsetting them. Preferences are a WTO concern because the system of bilateral preferences has multilateral consequences. In practice, however, feasible WTO-based solutions that are not distortionary do not exist. Because the pursuit of bilateralism in allocating assistance would be inefficient, a multilateral approach that builds on existing instruments is preferable. Moreover, given the objective of preferences—that is, export development—arguably the focus should also be on attaining that goal.

Existing Mechanisms for International Adjustment Financing

In recent years, a number of initiatives have sought to help countries better exploit trade opportunities and deal with adjustment pressures. These efforts include the multiagency, multidonor Integrated Framework for Trade-Related Assistance (IF) and the Trade Integration Mechanism (TIM) developed by the International Monetary Fund (IMF). In addition to these trade-specific initiatives, multilateral development banks support trade-related investments and provide technical assistance when requested by client governments. Although such assistance has been expanding in both absolute and relative terms, the institutions sponsoring these programs do not provide earmarked funding for trade adjustment purposes.

The IMF's TIM illustrates one possible approach to addressing preference erosion costs. It was developed to help countries expecting short-term balance-of-payments difficulties to cope with the effects of multilateral liberalization (IMF 2004). The TIM is intended to address not only preference erosion but also such situations as balance-of-payments shortfalls resulting from ATC quota integration and the possible impact of higher food import prices on net-food-importing developing countries. The TIM is not a new facility but operates through existing IMF instruments. Thus, the impact of possible adjustment costs resulting from such specific shocks as preference erosion is considered in the context of a country's overall macroeconomic policy framework. The usual IMF policy conditionality and terms and costs of lending apply. Therefore, the impact of assistance on a country's external debt burden must be taken into account.

The IF focuses much more on the structural agenda, as opposed to dealing with short-term macroeconomic impacts of external shocks. It brings together the key six multilateral agencies working on trade development issues—the IMF, the International Trade Centre, UNCTAD, the United Nations Development Programme, the WTO, and the World Bank—and 17 bilateral donors (including Canada, the EU, Japan, and the United States). The basic purpose is to embed a trade agenda into a country's overall development strategy, usually the national Poverty Reduction Strategy Paper. The process starts with a diagnostic analysis. This assessment looks at a number of issues, including the complementary policy agenda necessary to support successful trade reform, and generates a proposed action matrix of prioritized, trade-related capacity-building and assistance needs that are linked to the country's overall development strategy.

The philosophy behind the IF mechanism largely mirrors what is now known as the "new aid framework." The goal of this framework is to improve harmonization between the providers of trade assistance (both bilateral and multilateral) and to place trade in the context of a country's overall development strategy (Prowse 2002). Most LDCs (more than 40) have applied for assistance under the scheme. A small trust fund finances the trade assessments and small-scale technical assistance arising from the action matrices. The larger identified and prioritized trade capacity-building plans are presented within the context of consultative group meetings and roundtables in which donors (both multilateral and bilateral) are asked to make pledges. This framework allows bilateral and multilateral donors to respond to each country's identified needs systematically and coherently, according to comparative advantage and preference. Bilateral donors can also continue to contribute bilaterally or to provide resources through multilateral organizations. Either way reduces the duplication and proliferation of vertical initiatives. However, given an aid resource–constrained environment, prioritized trade action plans have had to compete, justifiably, with other priority sectors (namely, health and education). To date, implementation on the ground in prioritized trade areas has been limited. In 2008 the IF was enhanced with significant additional resources (several hundred million U.S. dollars) and a dedicated secretariat.

A Stand-Alone Compensation Fund?

Neither the TIM nor the Enhanced IF (EIF) directly addresses the concerns of developing countries about preference erosion. The TIM involves loans and thus implies that the costs of adjustment to erosion will be borne by the countries that lose preferential access to markets. Moreover, the focus is on the short-term, macroeconomic effects—that is, the net effects taking into account all policy changes and responses, not just the removal of preferential access. Thus, the TIM does not "offset" the losses incurred; rather, it ignores the bilateral nature of the problem. The IF focuses purely on the national trade-related agenda of LDCs. Although funding of priorities will have a large grant component—in contrast to the TIM—there is no guarantee that trade projects will be financed, because the EIF does not earmark funds or specific allocations for countries.

The most direct and simplest solution would be for donor countries to agree to compensate developing countries directly for preference erosion that is attributable to MFN trade reforms (Page 2004; Page and Kleen 2004). This approach would both help realize the potential global efficiency and welfare gains associated with an ambitious Doha Round outcome and help directly offset losses from associated impacts for developing countries. Page and Kleen (2004) argue that because global liberalization is a public good, the associated compensation should not be seen as aid. They therefore propose that a compensation fund be housed at the WTO. How donor countries would provide resources would be a matter of choice, although the level of contributions would be determined by various criteria (for example, share of trade, income, past commitments, and use of preferences). Given that the funds would be regarded as compensation for the removal of a prior benefit, funding would be allocated to beneficiary countries without conditions, according to the estimated preference losses. The fund would need to be secure, leading Page and Kleen to argue that voluntary commitments should be made legally irrevocable.

Grynberg and Silva (2004) offer a similar proposal. They suggest establishing a Special Fund for Diversification to mitigate the impact of preference erosion owing to MFN liberalization. This proposal would have financing (from pooled donor funds) "commensurate with preference losses" provided for export diversification investments led by the private sector. A share of the funds would be set aside for a private sector window to facilitate expanded investment start-ups by small- and medium-size enterprises for restructuring or rehabilitation in nontraditional sectors. The remaining funds would be provided for a public sector window to enable infrastructure investments, as well as for optional windows for technical assistance and a social safety net. The emphasis on the private sector as a recipient of funds to compensate for preference loss would go some way toward addressing a specific aspect of preference programs—that they directly benefit exporters. Under Grynberg and Silva's proposal, this constituency would have the prospect of some direct compensation.

The United Nations Millennium Project's Task Force on Trade (2004) has suggested another option, in which one element of a solution could involve income-support programs for farmers and producers of goods that have enjoyed high rates of protection. Although such programs are targeted at the domestic producers of preference-granting countries and are intended to facilitate a shift away from production support, negatively affected producers in developing countries that benefited from preferential access could also be assisted by being included in the support program. Elements of this approach have been adopted in the new EU sugar regime. It could be extended to other highly distorted markets where preferences matter and where producers will confront adjustment costs as market price supports are lowered. Such programs have an obvious political economy rationale. Moreover, extending support to affected producers in developing countries would also acknowledge the arguments made by groups in OECD countries that continued preferences (and, thus, market price supports) are needed to help producers in developing countries. However, support for affected firms may not benefit the country, insofar as the firms are foreign or do not diversify or invest in the country concerned.

All of these types of programs and mechanisms raise equity concerns, in that those who have benefited the most from preferences are not necessarily the poorest or most vulnerable. Indeed, by definition the assistance will be granted to those who have been most able to benefit from preferences. Within recipient countries, some of these beneficiaries will be among the higher-income groups, raising equity considerations. Moreover the suggestions for a preference erosion fund of some kind go against the emerging wisdom on improving aid effectiveness and enhancing international policy coherence (IMF and World Bank 2004). Aside from the issue of quantification of losses, the adjustment costs arising from preference erosion clearly must be addressed. But establishing a separate fund targeted at one specific structural adjustment need and at a specific set of countries runs counter to a more harmonized approach to development assistance. Adjustment to MFN liberalization will also affect many that have not benefited from preferences but that are, for example, located in highly protected domestic industries and sectors. They will also require assistance to adjust. In general, the shocks that regularly confront countries can be expected to exceed those associated with preference erosion for most countries. The need to diversify is not unique to economies that have benefited from preferences but is common to many countries, especially those with narrow export bases.

Imbs and Wacziarg (2003) suggest that countries at early stages of development experience a positive relationship between export (production) diversification and growth. But the experience with schemes aimed at promoting export diversification is mixed, with many programs that do no more than entrench already inefficient industrial and production patterns. Although there is certainly a case for government intervention to address market failures and for policy flexibility (see, for example, Hoekman 2005; Pack and Saggi 2006; Rodríguez-Clare 2004; Rodrik 2004), funding must be provided in the context of an overall country development program and a broad macroeconomic policy framework for countries to realize the dynamic gains associated with MFN liberalization.[12] As a development tool, stand-alone specific funds and associated mechanisms are unlikely to find widespread support among donors and recipient countries insofar as they are not integrated into national poverty reduction and development strategies. This concern applies more convincingly to suggestions to place a compensation fund in the WTO, which is neither a development nor a financial agency. Placing a funding mechanism for trade adjustment associated with preference erosion in the WTO would change the role of that organization.

Addressing Erosion Costs as Part of the Case for Aid for Trade

As noted earlier, export diversification and development were the main rationales for preferences. Many countries have benefited from preferential access and have graduated from bilateral programs, and others continue to benefit. But many of the poorest countries have been unable to use preferences to diversify and expand their exports. Given the systemic downsides, limited benefits, and historical inability of many poor countries in Africa and elsewhere to use preferences, a decision to shift from preferential "trade as aid" toward more efficient and effective instruments to support poor countries could both improve development outcomes and help strengthen the multilateral trading system (Hoekman 2007).

Tariffs are just one of several variables that constrain exports of developing countries. Other variables include transport and transactions costs, which are often much higher per unit of output than those in more developed countries. With or without preferences, more effective integration of the poorest countries into the trading system requires instruments that are aimed at improving the productivity and competitiveness of firms and farmers in those countries. Supply constraints have been the primary limitation on the ability of many African countries to benefit from preferences (see, for example, Commission for Africa 2005; Page 2004; Stevens and Kennan 2005). This problem underscores the need to improve trade capacity and facilitate diversification. This goal can be pursued partly by shifting to more (and more effective) development assistance that targets domestic supply constraints, as well as to measures that reduce the costs of entering foreign markets.

The Case for Trade Support Extends beyond Preference Erosion

A Doha reform package can be expected to generate sizable gains for both developed and developing countries. The size of these gains is difficult to assess accurately. Much depends on what is agreed, how it is implemented, and how much of the gains are transferred to compensate domestic losers—for example, through expanded income support. But even under the most conservative estimates, the aggregate global gains will be substantial. In absolute terms, developed countries will gain more than developing countries, providing them the means to step up support and development assistance. Such support is needed because the consequent trade liberalization will require adjustment and the pursuit of policy reforms and public investments to bolster trade capacity. What is important is that developed countries recognize the need for additional resources for trade adjustment and integration as the cost of the potential global benefits arising from further multilateral liberalization—which has the characteristics of a global public good.

In undertaking trade reform and in attempting to participate effectively in the global trading system, poorer countries must confront many economic and political concerns. On the economic side, adjustment costs will arise before offsetting investments are realized in other (new) sectors. Preference erosion is just one element of those costs. Some countries (for example, some net food importers) may experience deterioration in their terms of trade. Countries where tariff revenues constitute a significant proportion of total fiscal resources will need to undertake tax reform. Adjustment costs are a function of policy changes; as noted earlier, those associated with preference erosion will be gradual, and tariffs are just one element of the cost function facing exports. A fundamental problem is that many of the poorest developing countries are ill equipped to take full advantage of (new) trade opportunities because of supply-side, administrative capacity and institutional constraints. Improved market access without the ability to supply export markets competitively is of little use. Gains from trade liberalization require an environment that has mobile labor and capital and that facilitates investment in new sectors of activity—requiring, for example, an efficient financial system and good transportation and logistics services. Inevitably, for most poor countries, attaining those gains will require complementary reforms undertaken prior to, and in conjunction with, the trade reforms.

Even if one accepts that trade is likely to generate global gains, the distributive and redistributive dimensions of trade integration must be taken into account to ensure the political viability of the process. Providing sizable assistance has historically been critical in persuading countries of the benefits of integration. It played a key role in building support for the liberalization measures adopted as part of the creation of the European Economic Community and common market. The post–World War II Marshall Plan was conceived in large measure to neutralize the forces that were moving Western Europe away from multilateral trade and to thereby facilitate global economic recovery.

Recognizing the importance of complementary policy actions and the need for support for adjustment and integration to achieve successful trade reform in low-income economies does not imply that the Doha Round should be any less ambitious or deliberately slowed. The reverse is true. Moving ahead multilaterally on a nondiscriminatory basis will do the most to promote development. Trade reform undertaken together with "behind-the-border" policy measures and investments has significant potential to generate additional trade opportunities that would help lift a large number of people out of poverty (United Nations Millennium Project 2004; World Bank and IMF 2005). But it should be complemented by actions to redirect some of the global gains toward helping advance trade and growth in the poorest countries and to give this goal greater priority in aid programs. Such an approach, in turn, would help achieve the original objective that motivated preferential access regimes.

Integrating Preference Erosion into a Broader "Aid for Trade" Initiative

Supporting trade adjustment and integration requires a shift toward more efficient transfer and assistance mechanisms that target priority areas defined in national development plans and strategies. When developing countries opt to incorporate trade into their development strategies, donors should help enable those countries to respond to the opportunities offered by trade liberalization and integration. As Prowse (2006) discusses at greater length, options for trade support should be considered within the emerging "new aid framework," under which aid management and implementation practices are aligned with country policies and programs and bilateral and multilateral efforts are coordinated and harmonized.

Two issues are particularly pertinent with respect to trade support. First, no one multilateral agency has the effective authority to respond to all of a country's needs for trade adjustment and integration; therefore, a system must be designed to better harmonize existing processes with a country's development plans. Second, providing resources for adjustment and integration to benefit from a multilateral trade round requires greater coherence between the development needs of countries and the requirements of the WTO rules-based system.

The EIF has become an established mechanism that provides a programmatic approach to assistance for trade adjustment and integration within the context of a country's development program. To date it has relied on the consultative group and roundtable pledging sessions to finance adjustment needs and capacity building. As already noted, given that consideration of trade and investment activities within the Poverty Reduction Strategy Papers must compete with other sectors, the trade dimension has been relatively limited. Without additional assistance, the program's ability to better integrate a country into the global trading system is questionable. Thus, more resources are needed to identify, prepare, and implement a coherent trade, investment, and growth strategy within a country, in the context of the country's development process, and to address trade adjustment costs and capacity-building needs.

This need has been recognized. Progress has been made, with greater attention now being given to trade policy and trade-related capacity building by developing countries and international agencies. The IF has been strengthened through the creation of a dedicated trust fund and secretariat, with pledges on the order of US$200 million at the time of writing. Numerous operational questions about how additional funding and technical support are best managed and delivered will need to be resolved. Although the increased attention to trade capacity building and assistance is an important positive development, the focus is very much on trade competitiveness. This focus is, of course, very important, because it is necessary to enable firms and workers to benefit more from trade opportunities.

However, to date the prospect of preference erosion has not been a significant factor underpinning increased trade assistance. This may be short-sighted. The overall magnitude of potential erosion is limited, and the absence of a credible mechanism to offset losses may impede progress in multilateral negotiations once the major market access agenda items have been resolved. Thus, there is a case for seeking a binding commitment through which preference-giving countries and trading blocs agree to transfer the assessed value of current preference programs in the form of financial aid. Such an approach implies that assistance would be specific for each beneficiary country.[13] If it is pursued, a separate fund and a parallel institutional structure would not need to be established. Instead, the commitments for each beneficiary would ideally be disbursed through the existing processes and mechanisms through which aid is allocated, on the basis of the framework already described that places trade needs within a country's overall development program. In terms of quantifying the value of preferences, in principle, as previously argued, there is a (political economy) case that the transfer be equal to the bilateral "partial equilibrium" value of preferences received. That is, the quantification exercise—which should be performed through an independent arbitration-type exercise—would ignore the general equilibrium effects of changes in other countries' policies or the country's own policy stance.

Although this approach toward preference erosion is apparently attractive, one must recognize that in practice it is both narrow and potentially difficult to implement. Recall the earlier discussion of the studies that attempted to estimate the value of preferences and potential losses. Much depended on whether the ATC was included or not. Should the effects of the ATC be ignored? Some might argue they should be—that the ATC is water under the bridge because it was negotiated as part of an overall Uruguay Round agreement. Moreover, in the case of the ATC, the policy was not intended to benefit some countries but instead to restrict some exporters (that is, to protect import-competing firms).

Trying to agree on a methodology for quantifying potential erosion losses clearly risks the prospect of lengthy negotiations and disagreements concerning the scope of the analysis. In addition to the ATC, one can consider, for example, the conclusion of free trade agreements or the effects of unilateral liberalization. Should they also be covered? Whatever one's views on whether the Uruguay Round was a balanced package and on the desirability of free trade agreements, the fact is that industries and households around the developing world currently confront adjustment costs stemming from past policy decisions and will continue to do so. Moreover, as noted earlier, countries must regularly deal with many other shocks that are more substantial than preference erosion.

If the focus is on preference erosion, it should be restricted to future losses caused by MFN liberalization as a result of the Doha Round.[14] Although any outcome will be negotiated, and countries will have other ways to improve the overall outcome, the political economy rationale for this restriction is that it will help support a more ambitious outcome in terms of MFN liberalization. MFN liberalization would benefit all WTO members and is an important systemic reason for addressing preference erosion concerns. There is also a case for earmarking funds on a country basis. Although earmarking is generally not regarded as good aid policy, such a constraint should be imposed in the case of preference erosion, because the magnitudes of the associated losses vary substantially across countries. However, if earmarking is done, funding must be disbursed in the context of an overall development program of policy and support.

Of course, this approach will do little for those countries that have been unable to benefit from preferences. The trade assistance needs of these countries clearly are much greater than any estimate of the value of current preferences. Although the proposed methodology for quantifying the required transfers from donors will result in upper-bound estimates of the value of preference programs—which is arguably appropriate from a political economy standpoint—the overall numbers involved will be relatively small in comparison with the trade-related capacity needs of low-income countries. The available research suggests that the transfers needed to offset lost preferences are not large relative to either the overall gains of an ambitious Doha Round or current official development assistance (totaling about US$100 billion). Account should also be taken of the commitment by OECD countries in the Monterrey Consensus to double official development assistance spending and attain the target of 0.7 percent of gross domestic product.

Concluding Remarks

Far-reaching multilateral liberalization will give rise to preference erosion. Erosion will also be a consequence of reciprocal trade liberalization (free trade agreements) by major trading nations. The analyses included in this volume and the extant literature conclude that preference erosion is a major economic issue for a number of countries, although clearly much depends on the extent of multilateral liberalization commitments to emerge from the Doha Round.

There are three main arguments for addressing preference erosion losses. First, given that the stated objective of preference-granting countries is to encourage exports from beneficiary countries, another instrument needs to be in place to offset the removal or reduced effectiveness of the initial instrument that was used (that is, preferences). Second, global trade liberalization will benefit the world as a whole. Assisting the countries that stand to lose will help achieve this global public benefit by reducing the incentives of preference-dependent countries to attempt to block global liberalization. Lack of progress on the Doha Development Agenda and continued deepening of reciprocal preferential trade agreements—notably the EU's Economic Partnership Agreements—are potentially deepening the status quo bias for preferences, suggesting for the future that erosion concerns may become more of a constraint in concluding a multilateral round than they were during 2001 to 2008. Third, insofar as preference programs have induced investments in activities in which countries do not have a comparative advantage and to the extent that adjustment to a situation where they do not have guaranteed preferential access to markets is costly, there is a strong equity argument for donors to assist these countries in the required restructuring.

Given that preferences are bilateral in nature, the countries and trading blocs that reduce the value of past preferential access commitments should address the problem by offering other transfers to former beneficiaries. This chapter has argued that compensation for losses should take place outside the WTO, to minimize distortions to the world trading system. Avoiding additional new preferences and distortions in the trading system is a key reason to address preference erosion explicitly. Doing so will not imply the end of discrimination—many low-income countries will require continued assistance to achieve their export development and diversification goals. Accordingly, this chapter has focused on reducing the use of distorting trade policy instruments and emphasizing other mechanisms, including financial assistance targeted at the variables that limit trade capacity. The associated resources should be allocated through the multilateral channels that have been established to provide funds for trade-related priorities identified by developing countries.

Specifically, there is a political economy case for quantifying prospective losses generated by MFN liberalization on a bilateral basis, estimating what the associated transfer should have been, and ignoring the potential impact of offsetting measures. A bilateral analysis generates the best measure of the value that should be attached to preference programs for compensation purposes. That is, even though compliance costs and the incidence of rents are important determinants of the value of preferences, they should be ignored because they substantially reduce the real value of the programs and thus run counter to the purported objectives that motivate them.

Binding commitments could be sought—as part of a Doha Round agreement—to undertake such assessments and to transfer equivalent financial resources to the affected countries. If so, these funds should be earmarked for the relevant recipient developing countries and delivered through existing aid channels. The ultimate uses of the funds should be determined by the governments concerned on the basis of a policy agenda for trade and growth consistent with their countries' development strategies. Domestic trade reforms and complementary investments and measures to reduce transactions costs, improve the investment climate, and enhance the productivity and competitiveness of farmers and firms are all needed to deal with the adjustment costs associated with erosion losses. But such costs go far beyond the erosion of preferences. More assistance is needed to help countries bolster their capacity to exploit trade opportunities. In the process, the negative effects of preference erosion will be attenuated, and those countries unable to benefit from existing or past programs could be helped to achieve the original goal of trade preference programs: export development and diversification.

Solutions to preference erosion should be multilateral in the sense that the required financial transfers are best allocated through existing multilateral aid mechanisms as opposed to bilateral ones. A number of arguments support this view, including aid effectiveness and the fact that preference erosion is just one of many potential shocks and opportunities that will confront developing countries. Rather than seek to create a stand-alone fund to compensate for preference erosion—whether inside or outside the WTO—it is more efficient and effective to integrate funding to offset preference erosion into the broader "aid for trade" effort—arguably the more important need.

A broader effort would also allow the objectives of preferences to be pursued more effectively and across a broader group of countries—by recognizing that market access is not the most important variable constraining export growth in many developing economies. Dealing with the supply-side constraints will require funds (investments) but also the adoption of policies to address specific government and market failures that prevent a supply response from emerging. As argued in the recent literature, although the case for trade policies in this context is weak, those domestic policies that may be most appropriate and effective may not be obvious, thus suggesting the need for further experimentation and learning (Rodrik 2004). This argument suggests a link between the aid for trade agenda and the issues of policy flexibility and special and differential treatment in the WTO (and regional) trade agreements. Given the presumption that trade policy cannot do much to address the sources of market and government failure that impede supply responses, international cooperation (trade agreements) can help in two ways: (a) by creating institutional mechanisms to help identify those policies that would be most effective and efficient in helping attain specific government-set goals and (b) by increasing the transparency of policies and their outcomes through multilateral monitoring (Hoekman 2005).

Notes

1. Preference-receiving countries are also concerned about the potential negative terms-of-trade effects of multilateral liberalization insofar as it raises the price of their imports—especially of goods that currently benefit from subsidies and protection in OECD markets—by more than the price or quantity of their exports.

2. Hoekman and Özden (2006). However, aid may not be—or have been—politically feasible. Political considerations do affect policy choices, including the use of preferences. This chapter focuses on the economics of the issue.

3. See Baldwin and Murray (1977) for an early discussion. Most empirical studies conclude, however, that preference programs are associated with negative terms-of-trade effects for excluded (less preferred) countries; that is, that there is trade diversion as well as trade creation. Much depends on having good estimates of the elasticities of substitution between foreign and domestic goods and between foreign products of different origin. Early studies assumed that these elasticities were identical. General equilibrium studies, by contrast, tend to use Armington elasticities. For more discussion, see Brown (1987), Langhammer and Sapir (1987), and the references cited there.

4. See Özden and Sharma (2006) for a similar analysis of the U.S. Compliance and Business Integrity program. François and Wooton (2008) obtain similar, size-dependent results in an analysis of the incidence of markups along the distribution chain.

5. The only large country expected to suffer from preference erosion is Bangladesh, which has benefited significantly from the textile quota restrictions imposed on other large competitive developing countries (such as China), which were removed at the end of 2004 under the ATC. However, as discussed later, these costs are already sunk, in that the shock has already occurred.

6. Much of the literature focuses on trade effects. See, for example, Alexandraki and Lankes (2006), Subramanian (2003), and chapters 7 and 8 in this volume. The interest here is in the magnitude of the implied financial transfers, because they provide the most straightforward measure of the value of preferences. This approach does not imply that such transfers were the primary objective of preference programs. The implications of this objective for policy responses to erosion are discussed later.

7. Their conclusion derives from focusing on the LDCs and using a global general equilibrium model and the latest version of the Global Trade Analysis Project database that incorporates data on the major OECD preference programs (Bouët and others 2004).

8. ATC restrictions implicitly favored smaller, higher-cost suppliers in developing countries at the expense of those from China. Although implementation of the ATC was staged, the major importing countries heavily backloaded the implementation, resulting in a much greater than necessary adjustment shock at the end of the 10-year transition period.

9. Figures are higher if the focus extends to middle-income countries, some of which—such as Mexico—stand to suffer potentially substantial losses as preferential access to Canada and the United States is eroded. This chapter focuses mainly on low-income, weak, and vulnerable economies.

10. Another question is whether any assistance should be temporary or longer term. From an adjustment viewpoint, temporary assistance is appropriate. From a development perspective, a case can be made that the duration of assistance should be conditional on development of competitive export capacity.

11. See Hoekman (2005) for some suggestions in this regard.

12. This view provides an aid policy perspective. As noted below, trade negotiators are likely to have a different view, suggesting a case for temporary earmarking of funding.

13. A tariff-line level analysis of the type undertaken in the other chapters of this volume would be necessary.

14. This is not to deny that ongoing erosion-related adjustment pressures can be significant. Such costs need to be addressed through the existing framework for trade-related assistance.

References

Alexandraki, Katerina, and Hans Peter Lankes. 2006. "Estimating the Impact of Preference Erosion on Middle-Income Countries." In *Trade Preferences and Differential Treatment of Developing Countries*, ed. Bernard Hoekman and Çağlar Özden, 397–431. Cheltenham, U.K.: Edward Elgar.

Amiti, Mary, and John Romalis. 2007. "Will the Doha Round Lead to Preference Erosion?" *IMF Staff Papers* 54 (2): 338–84.

Ansón, José, Olivier Cadot, Antoni Estevadeordal, Jaime de Melo, Akiko Suwa-Eisenmann, and Bolormaa Tumurchudur. 2005. "Rules of Origin in North-South Preferential Trading Arrangements with an Application to NAFTA." *Review of International Economics* 13 (3): 501–17.

Baldwin, Robert E., and Tracy Murray. 1977. "MFN Tariff Reductions and LDC Benefits under the GSP." *Economic Journal* 87 (345): 30–46.

Bouët, Antoine, Yvan Decreux, Lionel Fontagné, Sébastien Jean, and David Laborde. 2004. "A Consistent, Ad Valorem Equivalent Measure of Applied Protection across the World: The MAcMap-HS6 Database." CEPII Discussion Paper 2004-22, Centre d'Études Prospectives et d'Informations Internationales, Paris.

Brenton, Paul, and Takako Ikezuki. 2005. "The Impact of Agricultural Trade Preferences, with Particular Attention to the Least Developed Countries." In *Global Agricultural Trade and Developing Countries*, ed. M. Ataman Aksoy and John C. Beghin, 55–73. Washington, DC: World Bank.

Brenton, Paul, and Miriam Manchin. 2003. "Making EU Trade Agreements Work: The Role of Rules of Origin." *World Economy* 26 (5): 755–69.

Brown, Drusilla K. 1987. "General Equilibrium Effects of the U.S. Generalized System of Preferences." *Southern Economic Journal* 54 (1): 27–47.

Commission for Africa. 2005. *Our Common Interest: Report of the Commission for Africa*. London: Commission for Africa.

Francois, Joseph, Bernard Hoekman, and Miriam Manchin. 2006. "Preference Erosion and Multilateral Trade Liberalization." *World Bank Economic Review* 20 (2): 197–216.

Francois, Joseph, Dean Spinanger, and Julia Wörtz. 2005. "The Impact of ATC Quota Elimination on LDC Exports." Background paper for the DFID Global Trade Architecture Project, U.K Department for International Development, London.

Francois, Joseph, and Ian Wooton. 2001. "Trade in International Transport Services: The Role of Competition." *Review of International Economics* 9 (2): 249–61.

———. 2008. "Market Structure and Market Access." Policy Research Working Paper 4151, World Bank, Washington, DC.

Grynberg, Roman, and Sacha Silva. 2004. "Preference-Dependent Economies and Multilateral Liberalisation: Impacts and Options." Commonwealth Secretariat, London.

Hoekman, Bernard. 2005. "Operationalizing the Concept of Policy Space in the WTO: Beyond Special and Differential Treatment." *Journal of International Economic Law* 8 (2): 405–24.

———. 2007. "Doha, Development, and Discrimination." *Pacific Economic Review* 12 (3): 267–92.

Hoekman, Bernard, and Çağlar Özden. 2006. "Introduction." In *Trade Preferences and Differential Treatment of Developing Countries*, ed. Bernard Hoekman and Çağlar Özden, xi–xli. Cheltenham, U.K.: Edward Elgar.

Imbs, Jean, and Romain Wacziarg. 2003. "Stages of Diversification." *American Economic Review* 93 (1): 63–86.

IMF (International Monetary Fund). 2004. "Fund Support for Trade-Related Balance of Payments Adjustments." IMF, Washington, DC. http://www.imf.org/external/np/pdr/tim/2004/eng/022704.pdf.

IMF (International Monetary Fund) and World Bank. 2004. "Aid Effectiveness and Financing Modalities." Development Committee Report and Background Paper, DC2004-0012/Add.1, Washington, DC.

Karacaovali, Baybars, and Nuno Limão. 2008. "The Clash of Liberalizations: Preferential vs. Multilateral Trade Liberalization in the European Union." *Journal of International Economics* 74 (2): 299–327.

Langhammer, Rolf J., and André Sapir. 1987. *Economic Impact of Generalized Tariff Preferences*. London: Trade Policy Research Centre.

Limão, Nuno 2006. "Preferential Trade Agreements as Stumbling Blocks for Multilateral Trade Liberalization: Evidence for the U.S." *American Economic Review* 96 (3): 896–914.

Limão, Nuno. and Marcelo Olarreaga. 2006. "Trade Preferences to Small Countries and the Welfare Costs of Lost Multilateral Liberalization." *World Bank Economic Review* 20 (2): 217–40.

Olarreaga, Marcelo, and Çağlar Özden. 2005. "AGOA and Apparel: Who Captures the Tariff Rent in the Presence of Preferential Market Access?" *World Economy* 28 (1): 63–77.

Özden, Çağlar, and Gunjan Sharma. 2006. "Price Effects of Preferential Market Access: The Caribbean Basin Initiative and the Apparel Sector." *World Bank Economic Review* 20 (2): 241–60.

Pack, Howard, and Kamal Saggi. 2006. "The Case for Industrial Policy: A Critical Survey." *World Bank Research Observer* 21 (2): 267–97.

Page, Sheila. 2004. "Preference Erosion: Helping Countries to Adjust." ODI Briefing Paper, Overseas Development Institute, London.

Page, Sheila, and Peter Kleen. 2004. "Special and Differential Treatment of Developing Countries in the World Trade Organization." Report for the Ministry of Foreign Affairs, Stockholm.

Prowse, Susan. 2002. "Mechanisms for Trade-Related Capacity Building and Technical Assistance after Doha." *World Economy* 25 (9): 1205–33.

———. 2006. "'Aid for Trade': A Proposal for Increasing Support for Trade Adjustment and Integration." In *Economic Development and Multilateral Trade Cooperation*, ed. Simon Evenett and Bernard Hoekman, 229–67. Basingstoke, U.K.: Palgrave Macmillan.

Rodríguez-Clare, Andrés. 2004. "Clusters and Comparative Advantage: Implications for Industrial Policy." Working Paper 523, Inter-American Development Bank, Washington, DC.

Rodrik, Dani. 2004. "Industrial Policy for the Twenty-First Century." CEPR Discussion Paper 4767, Centre for Economic Policy Research, London.

Stevens, Christopher, and Jane Kennan. 2005. "Making Trade Preferences More Effective." Trade Note, Institute of Development Studies, Brighton, U.K. http://www.ids.ac.uk/UserFiles/File/globalisation_team/tradepapers/CSJKTradePreferences.pdf.

Subramanian, Arvind. 2003. "Financing of Losses from Preference Erosion: Note on Issues Raised by Developing Countries in the Doha Round." WT/TF/COH/14, International Monetary Fund, Washington, DC.

Tangermann, Stefan. 2002. *The Future of Preferential Trade Arrangements for Developing Countries and the Current Round of WTO Negotiations on Agriculture*. Rome: Food and Agriculture Organization.

United Nations Millennium Project, Task Force on Trade. 2004. *Trade Development and the WTO: An Action Agenda beyond the Cancún Ministerial*. New York: United Nations.

World Bank and IMF (International Monetary Fund). 2005. *Global Monitoring Report, 2005*. Washington, DC: World Bank.

INDEX

Boxes, figures, notes, and tables are indicated by *b, f, n,* and *t,* respectively.

449